To Nancy Allen —

You are a special
[per]son and a talented
and dedicated with
history. Enjoy this
history. Enjoy.

Roberta Wright
June 21, 2007

Roberta V. Hughes Wright (nee Greenidge) was born in Detroit, Michigan and has lived in the area all her life. She holds a Bachelor of Science degree, a Masters degree and a Juris Doctor degree from Wayne State University and a Doctor of Philosophy degree in behavioral sciences in education from the University of Michigan. She is a member of Alpha Kappa Alpha Sorority; a life member of the NAACP; a member of the Great Lakes Chapter of the Links, Inc.; and a founder and ten year member of the Board of Directors of the First Independence National Bank of Detroit. She is a member of the Board of Directors of Detroit Memorial Park Association and of the Finance Committee for the three cemeteries.

Dr. Hughes Wright, now retired, had a legal practice in Michigan, was a member of the Bar of the District of Columbia and was admitted to practice before the Supreme Court of the United States.

She is the widow of Wilbur B. Hughes and their two children are Barbara K. Hughes Smith, Ph.D. and Wilbur B. Hughes, III, J.D.

Dr. Wright has six grandchildren. She is also the widow of Charles H. Wright, M.D., founder of the Charles H. Wright Museum of African American History and is a member of three Museum Advisory Committees. As a member of the Michigan Support Group for Penn Center-St. Helena, South Carolina she persuaded the South Carolina Historic Department and the United States Historical Commission to award and erect a plaque at the site of the reading of the Emancipation Proclamation on January 1, 1863.

Dr. Hughes Wright is the author or co-author of twelve books and has received several awards and recognitions. She is a member of Plymouth United Church of Christ.

Wilbur Brandon Hughes, III was born in Detroit, Michigan and has lived both in the Detroit area and in Washington, D.C. He holds a Bachelors of Science degree in political science from Tennessee State University in Nashville, Tennessee, and a Juris Doctor degree from Howard University School of Law in Washington, D.C.

Hughes was the owner of W.B. Hughes Enterprises in Arlington, Virginia and worked for the Veterans Administration in Washington, D.C. He worked as a staff assistant on the professional staff of the United States House of Representatives, the House Committee in the District of Columbia. Hughes was the owner of Hello International, Inc., a business support services enterprise on Massachusetts Avenue in Washington, D.C.

Hughes moved back to Michigan in the 1980s and was appointed General Manager of the Detroit Memorial Park Association, Inc. and was elected to the Board of Directors. The corporation owns three cemeteries, a Detroit office building, and Courier & Fax, Inc. Hughes is the founder and president of the courier company which provides same day package pickup and delivery, filings and other services helpful to local businesses.

Hughes is a freelance writer and was co-author of the first edition of *Lay Down Body*, *Living History in African American Cemeteries* as well as co-author of the second edition. He is a member of state and national cemetery and funeral organizations, a member of Alpha Phi Alpha fraternity, Life Member and Heritage Member of the NAACP, and a member of the Charles H. Wright Museum of African American History. Hughes was appointed by the Speaker of the Michigan House of Representatives to the Freedom Trail Commission, which documents Underground Railroad activity in the state.

Hughes is married to Adawork Tsadik. Their children are Christian Wright Hughes and Alexandria Brooke Hughes. His other children are Brent Hughes and Christina Barbara Hughes.

Editor and Contributor:

Barbara K. Hughes Smith, a native Detroiter, attended the Detroit Public Schools. She holds a Bachelor of Science degree from Michigan State, a Master of Arts degree from Wayne State University and a Ph.D. from University of Michigan. Dr. Smith is presently a licensed professional counselor serving as guidance supervisor for the Detroit Public Schools.

A few of Dr. Smith's present and past professional memberships include the American Counseling Association; the Michigan and Wayne County Counseling Associations; National Board of Governors; Executive Board and negotiation team and Member of the Organization of School Administrators and Supervisors.

Dr. Smith is a member of the Alpha Kappa Alpha Sorority Inc, the Great Lakes Chapter of the Links, the FORE Players Golf Group and the Executive Board of the Women's Committee of the Charles H. Wright Museum of African American History.

Three of Dr. Smith's favorite interests are genealogy, including the Underground Railroad, aerobic exercise and golf. She is most proud of her Canadian heritage on both her maternal and paternal lines and is proficient in her genealogical research; she has given presentations on related topics. In 2000-2001, Dr. Smith served on Detroit 300 Committees in both Wayne County, Michigan and Essex County, Ontario and chaired a reception at Second Baptist Church for the descendants of Underground Railroad fugitives and operatives. As a board member of the Fred Hart Williams Genealogical society, she has formed partnerships with related organizations. At the invitation of the State of Michigan Freedom Trail Commission, she made a presentation on one of her ancestors.

Dr. Smith is married to Joseph W. Smith, principal of A. Phillip Randolph Career and Technical Center, a Detroit Public School. Her daughter, son-in-law and grandchild are Blythe Allen Dickerson M.D., Shawn A. Dickerson and Canon; her son, Brett W. Allen, is an attorney in New York. Dr. Smith, who cherishes close family ties, is blessed to have had two fathers who enriched her life: Wilbur B. Hughes, Jr. and Charles H. Wright, M.D.

With love and appreciation to our family
for their timeless and unfaltering support,
and to those in repose,
whose memories surfaced so realistically during our research

THE DEATH CARE INDUSTRY

AFRICAN AMERICAN CEMETERIES & FUNERAL HOMES

The cover photograph depicts the Reverend J.E. Churchman, Sr. in Orange, New Jersey, with his horsedrawn hearse, circa 1899.

Graphic design and layout by Phil Lewis

Published by Hughes Wright Enterprises

This second edition of Lay Down Body includes material on long established, family-owned funeral homes, on many more cemeteries and also new information on the death care industry.

Library of Congress Cataloging-in-Publication Data

Hughes Wright, Roberta

The Death Care Industry African American cemeteries/ Roberta Hughes Wright and Wilbur B. Hughes III; foreword by Michael L. Blakey;

Includes bibliographical references and index.

ISBN 10: 0-9629-4683-4   ISBN 13: 978-0-9629-4683-7

4. African Americans—Funeral customs and rites—History. 2. Cemeteries—United States—History.

CIP

CONTENTS

Foreword xv

Overview-First Edition xviii

Acknowledgements xxii

Introduction xxviii

Lay Down Body, The Song xxxii

CHAPTER ONE

SITES, SUPERSTITIONS AND STORIES 1

    First Burials 3

    Slave Cemeteries in the Americas 4

    Africanisms and Burial Customs 4

    Slave Burial Stories 5

    African Burial Ground - Update 10

    Stories and Folktales through the Years 29

    Small Town Stories 40

    The Unusual 47

        Beneath the Floorboards of the House 47

        Remains Classified as African American 48

        The Bishop's Empty Tomb 49

        On-Line Cemeteries 51

        Whimsical Coffins 53

        Green Graveyards 55

            California 56

            Texas 57

            South Carolina 58

        New Orleans Cemeteries in October 60

        Baby Snookems 63

        Cream of Wheat Man 65

CHAPTER TWO

THE CRADLE: THE SEA ISLANDS AND THE SOUTHEAST 72

Daufuskie Island, South Carolina **75**
  Bloody Point Cemetery 79
  Cooper River Cemetery 80
  Fripp Cemetery 86
  Haig's Point Cemetery. 87
  Maryfield Cemetery 89
  Webb Track Cemetery 90
Hilton Head Island, South Carolina **90**
  Amelia White Cemetery 93
  Braddock Point (Harbortown) Cemetery. 95
  Pinefield Cemetery 98
  Talbot Cemetery 100
  Spanish Wells Cemetery 101
  Simmons Memorial Gardens 101
  Jenkins Island Cemetery 103
  Union Cemetery 104
  Joe Pope Cemetery 105
  Elliot Cemetery 105
  Lawton Cemetery 106
Beaufort, South Carolina **107**
  Beaufort National Cemetery 110
  Sixteen Gate Cemetery. 114
  New Hope Christian Church Cemetery 116
  Pilgrim Cemetery 116
  Red House Cemetery 117
  Three Neglected Cemeteries 118
  Gerhard Spieler of Beaufort 119
St. Helena Island, South Carolina **121**
  Brick Baptist Church Cemetery 128
  Orange Grove Baptist Church Cemetery 131
  Ebenezer Baptist Church Cemetery 132
  St. Joseph Baptist Church Cemetery 133
  Faith Memorial Baptist Church Cemetery 134
  Comer (Major) Cemetery. 134
  Cuffy Cemetery. 134
  Adams Street Baptist Church Cemetery 135
  Coffin Point Cemetery 136
Low Bottom, South Carolina **140**
  Low Bottom Cemetery. 140
Charleston, South Carolina **140**
  Brown Fellowship Society Cemetery 142
  Brotherly Cemetery 143
  Old Bethel United Methodist Church Cemetery 141
  Friendly Union Cemetery 143
  Unity and Friendship Cemetery 143

Columbia, South Carolina 144
   Randolph Cemetery 144
Winnsboro, South Carolina 147
   Camp Welfare Cemetery 147
Savannah, Georgia 149
   Laurel Grove Cemetery 151
   Lincoln Memorial Cemetery 155
   Evergreen Cemetery 156
   Woodville Cemetery 156
   Oak Grove Cemetery 156
   Cherokee Hill Cemetery 156
   Wood Grove Cemetery 157
   Sandfly Cemetery 158
   Lake Mayers Cemetery 158
   East Savannah Cemetery 158
   Zion White Bluff Cemetery 158
   Laurel Grove South Cemetery 158
Thomaston, Georgia and other Vanishing Sites 158

CHAPTER THREE

BURIAL SITES COAST TO COAST 162

GEORGIA 164

Atlanta 164
   Southview Cemetery 165
   Historic Oakland Cemetery 167
Augusta 170
   Summerville Cemetery 171
   Cedar Grove 171
   Walker Memorial Park 171
   Southview Cemetery 173
   Mt. Olive Memorial Park 173
Southeastern 172
   Cairo Cemetery 172
   Springfield Cemetery 172
   St. Paul Primitive (Florida) 173
   St. Paul Primitive (Georgia) 175
   Jonas Lobe Cemetery 175
   Pine View Cemetery 176
   Mt. Pingah Cemetery 177
   Bethel A.M.E. Church Cemetery 176
   Mt. Olive Cemetery 173
   Mt. Zion Cemetery 174
   Munneryln Cemetery 174
   Fleatown Cemetery 174
Northeastern 174
   Paradise A.M.E. Church Cemetery 177

Gospel Pilgrim Cemetery...............................177
DURHAM, NORTH CAROLINA **179**
  Geer Cemetery 179
NASHVILLE, TENNESSEE, AND NEIGHBORING KENTUCKY 183
  Nashville City Cemetery 186
  Greenwood Cemetery and Mount Ararat 186
  (Greenwood Cemetery- West) 186
  Riverside Cemetery 190
  The Alex Haley State Historic Site and Museum 191
  Bethlehem Cemetery 193
  Canfield Cemetery 193
  Zion Cemetery 194
  Greenwood (Co-Haven) Cemetery 194
  The African Cemetery #2 195
FORT LAUDERDALE, FLORIDA, AND AREA **195**
  Woodlawn Cemetery....................................196
  Lincoln Memorial Cemetery 197
  Evergreen Memorial Park Cemetery 198
  Public Cemetery 199
  Springfield A.M.E. Church Cemetery 199
  St. Paul Primitive Baptist Cemetery 199
ALABAMA **199**
  New Grace Hill Cemetery and Zion Memorial Garden 200
  Tuskegee Cemetery 201
  Mobile, Alabama 202
HATTIESBURG, MISSISSIPPI.................................**204**
  Pineridge Cemetery-Hattiesburg 204
  Scott Street Cemetery 205
  Riverview Cemetery 205
  Shady Grove Missionary Baptist Church Cemetery 205
ST. FRANCISVILLE, LOUISIANA, AND AREA **206**
  Rosedown Baptist Church Cemetery 206
  Mt. Olivet Cemetery 207
ST. LOUIS, MISSOURI **209**
  Moses Dickson Cemetery 210
  Bellefontaine Cemetery 211
  Jefferson Barracks and National Cemetery 211
  New Cold Water Burying Ground 211
  T. Charles Borromeo Church Cemetery 212
  Washington Park Cemetery 212

INDIANAPOLIS, INDIANA **212**
  Sutherland Park Cemetery 212

NICODEMUS, KANSAS 213
    Nicodemus Cemetery 213
    Mount Olivet Cemetery 214
    Samuels Cemetery 215

PORT WILLIAM, KANSAS 215
    Mount Gillin Cemetery 215

CHICAGO, ILLINOIS, AND AREA 216
    Burr Oak Cemetery 216
    Miller Grove Cemetery 217
    Free Frank McWorter Burial Site 218

DETROIT, MICHIGAN, AND AREA 219
    Detroit Memorial Park Cemetery, East and West 219
    Gracelawn - Flint (Detroit Memorial Park) 219
    United Memorial Gardens 226
    Metropolitan Memorial Gardens 226
    Elmwood Cemetery 227

PHILADELPHIA. PENNSYLVANIA, AND AREA 230
    Morris Cemetery 231
    Eden Cemetery 231
    Merion Memorial Park 232

NEWPORT, RHODE ISLAND 233
    "God's Little Acre" Common Burial Ground 234

PORTSMOUTH (TRUXTON), VIRGINIA, AND AREA 234
    Lincoln Cemetery 235
    Cedar Grove, Oak Grove, and Mount Olive Cemeteries 235
    Elmwood Cemetery 235
    Woodlawn and Evergreen Cemeteries 235
    Lynchburg, Virginia Cemeteries 236

PETERSBURG, VIRGINIA 237
    African American Cemeteries, eighteenth century 237
    Four Cemeteries Remaining 238
        Peoples Cemetery 238
        Blandford Cemetery 238
        Little Church Cemetery 238
        East View (Witherson Memorial) 239

NEW YORK, NEW YORK, AND AREA 240
    Hudson-Mohawk River Cemeteries 240
    John Brown Cemetery 240
    Fort Hill Cemetery 240

LOS ANGELES, CALIFORNIA 241
    Angeles Abbey Memorial Park 241

Evergreen Cemetery 242
Angelus Rosedale Cemetery 243
Paradise Memorial Park 243

WASHINGTON, DC **244**
Female Union Band Cemetery 244
Old Methodist Burying Ground 244
Mt. Zion Cemetery 244
Woodlawn Cemetery 245

HELENA, ARKANSAS, AND AREA **249**
Bean Cemetery 250
Hampton Springs Cemetery 250
Scott Bond Family Plot 250
Saxon Cemetery 253
Springlake Memorial Cemetery 253
Dixon Cemetery 252
Odd Fellows Cemetery 254
The Beginning 254
The Confrontation 254
Gone, But Not Forgotten 255

TEXAS **255**
College Park Cemetery - Houston 255
Blanco Cemetery - San Marcos 256

BALTIMORE, MARYLAND AND AREA **258**
Arbutus Memorial Park 258
Mount Auburn Cemetery 259

CHAPTER FOUR

AFRICAN CANADIAN CEMETERIES **264**
Ontario and Other Provinces 265
Township of Sandwich East Cemetery 265
North Buxton Cemetery 265
Morris-Hatter Cemetery 267
North American Black Historical Museum and Cultural Centre 268
Fugitive Slave Cemetery 270
Historic St. John's Anglican Cemetery 271
Jackson Cemetery 272
Harrow Cemetery 273
Escaped Slaves Unmarked Graves 282
Endangered, Abandoned, Closed Cemeteries 281
Nova Scotia Cemeteries 275

CHAPTER FIVE

CELEBRITY BURIALS **285**

Louis Armstrong 285
Arthur Ashe 286
Florence Ballard 288
Cab Calloway 289
Johnnie Cochran 289
Nat King Cole. 292
Medgar Evers 293
Ella Fitzgerald 293
Marvin Gaye. 294
Alex Haley 295
Aaliyah Haughton 297
Billie Holiday 297
Prophet Jones. 298
Florence Joyner 301
Martin Luther King, Jr. 302
Joe Louis 303
Jesse Owens 303
Rosa Parks 304
Richard Pryor. 305
Jackie Robinson 307
Luther (Bojangles) Robinson 308
Wilma Rudolph 309
Sarah Vaughn 309
Muddy Waters 310
Flip Wilson 310
Malcolm X and Betty Shabazz 311

CHAPTER SIX

GENEALOGY FOR THE BEGINNER 313
Charting and Record Keeping 314
Vital Records 336
Cemetery Records 345
Creating A Family Tree 366

CHAPTER SEVEN

CEMETERY PRESERVATION AND RESTORATION 374
Common Myths 374
Repairing Graveyard Monuments 387
Chicora Foundation, Inc. 393

CHAPTER EIGHT

BENEVOLENT SOCIETIES, LODGES AND CLUBS 394
The Brown Fellowship Society 398
Humane Brotherhood 401
The Bury League 402
The Knights of the Wise Men Lodge 410
Ladies Union 415

Rome of Victory Society 416
Social Clubs, New Orleans 417

CHAPTER NINE

FUNERAL AND BURIAL CUSTOMS 421
History of Embalming 430
National (Veterans) Cemeteries 441

CHAPTER TEN

WHAT'S NEW, WHAT'S DIFFERENT - FUNERAL AND BURIAL CUSTOMS . . **448**
Above Ground Burials 455
Mausoleums Get Livelier 455
Cremations... 454
Taking Cremations to the Mall 456
Some Find Eternal Rest at Costco 458
Funeral Help is a Click Away.......................... 460
Tri-State Cemetery Fraud 462
Insurance Firms Pay in Bias Suits 463
Funeral Traffic - Menace or Not?..................... 465
Bill Would Cut Funeral Airfares...................... 466
Cremated Remains Pose Airport Problem 467

CHAPTER ELEVEN

FUNERAL HOMES AND DIRECTORS 471
An Overview 471
National Funeral Homes and Morticians Association........ 473
Selected Funeral Homes, Long Time Family-Owned 475
Scarborough and Hargett Memorial Chapel - North Carolina 477
Manigault - Hurley Funeral Home - Columbia, South Carolina ... 481
N.J. Ford and Sons - Memphis, Tennessee 485
Fritz Funeral Home - Detroit, Michigan. 488
Funeral Homes/Indianapolis - Indianapolis, Indiana 491
Churchman - Newark, New Jersey. 499
A.A. Rayner & Sons - Chicago, Illinois 501
Smith and Smith - Lexington, Kentucky. 504
Bynes-Royall - Savannah, Georgia. 505
Angelus Funeral Home - Los Angeles, California 508
March Funeral Homes - Baltimore, Maryland 510
New Bedford Funeral Homes - New Bedford, Massachuetts 513
Santos and Burgo Funeral Home 513
Burgo Funeral Home 513
Onley Funeral Home 513

CHAPTER TWELVE

NEW ORLEANS, LOUISIANA 515

New Orleans Cemeteries 515
   St. Louis #1 516
   Holt Cemetery 523
New Orleans Funeral Homes 530
   Rhodes Funeral Home. 534
   Boissiere-Labat Funeral Home. 530
Katrina Reports 537

CHAPTER THIRTEEN

FEDERAL TRADE COMMISSION RULES **554**

APPENDIX 566

BIBLIOGRAPHY 601

INDEX 611

Presented here for the readers is a timely, thoughtful, and broad-ranging discussion of the African American cemetery. Without proclamation, but simply by virtue of the connections these authors choose to make, cemeteries are shown to resonate with a people's sense of self. African American identities are entombed, marked, fought for, preserved, celebrated, symbolized, mourned, and incorporated in the cemeteries they describe. These memorialized identities are sometimes neglected, lost, or later restored to memory. Once the corporal remains of a human life have been planted under earth, chances are good that they will not be encountered again.

Of course many of the world's greatest monuments represent elaborate burials, such as the great pyramids of the Nile Valley or the mausoleums of the Ashanti nobility. Yet the simplest of societies have also engaged that fundamental act of humanity that cemeteries represent. Indeed, like the making of stone tools and fire, the uniquely human practice of burying the dead sets people apart from the rest of the natural universe. Our species has carefully buried the dead—has made family cemeteries—since paleolithic times. Each time that anthropologists rediscover these ancestors of deep time, our knowledge of who we were and how we have come to be is enriched. Neanderthals having the most rudimentary culture have left these simple monuments to themselves. Enslaved Africans in the Americas had even less control over the course of their lives than those most ancient people. Their very membership in the human family was denied, and even today that humanity is questioned in the societies that slavery built. Yet even those who owned plantations succumbed to a certain level of negotiation with those who were enslaved. Basics of food, shelter, social, and cultural life would be required if this unalterably human labor were to be made useful to Europeans. The cemetery was one such necessary concession. Here in the solemn dignity of funerary ritual, the community would come together to remember, pay respect, and hope for another life.

The book tells of the great variety of African American cemeteries in all parts of the continent. The descriptive documentation of the whereabouts of

African American cemeteries is important enough, and that is only the framework of this compelling book. We learn, furthermore, about the landscape and modest monumental structures that are apparent in a rich accompaniment of beautiful photographs. The authors explain how these cemeteries were founded, along with the symbolism entailed in burial practices and monuments. Yet these historic properties are no more nor less than the centerpiece of the story told.

This is a book about the living. Through the use of diverse sources, including oral history, historical text, news articles, and archaeological insights, the authors weave together the lives of communities of ancestors and communities of living descendants—lives of hardship, despair, courage, triumph, discrimination, disregard, respect, reverence, neglect, revitalization, war, love, tranquility, and political struggle. The story of cemeteries is not unlike that of the people who create them, indeed the authors tell us that "struggle and conflict" often surround African American efforts to preserve their cemeteries at the end of the twentieth century.

The themes of this book resonate deeply with my own personal, professional, and cultural experiences. For several years, I have directed the African Burial Ground Project, which the book describes. As the earliest large African cemetery yet uncovered in North America, the African Burial Ground and the study of its ancestral remains is special for many people throughout the African Diaspora. The work in which my staff and I are involved concerning the African Burial Ground is principally that of biological anthropologists who seek to learn about ancestral lives. Using scientific methods, we reconstruct the health, population structure, traumas, and cultures of the people by examining their skeletons and burial artifacts.

Yet the personal and cultural experiences I share with the rest of the African American community have always been important to my appreciation of what we are doing here. The pitched struggle waged by the descendant African American community to preserve the African Burial Ground was phenomenal. As an insensitive Federal Government agency and their anthropologist contractors persisted in disrespecting the living and the dead, we saw the ire of our community come to bear with extraordinary unity and commitment. The African Burial Ground was saved, though only in part, by dedicated community activism. These events showed clearly that respect (and disrespect) for the dead could not be readily distinguished from respect (and disrespect) for the living. The book tells of the pervasive and ongoing struggles of African Americans to define themselves as who they know themselves to be, despite the challenging conditions all along the road home. To the extent that we lose our cemeteries, we lose recognition of much of who we are in the larger sense of the family, community, and nation. And oh, how the authors convey who and what we are!

Finally, I am impressed by how practical the information of this book is. Anyone wanting to preserve a threatened cemetery will obtain a wealth of practical knowledge about how to lay out a preservation plan, utilizing the successful experiences of others who have met that challenge. Cemeteries are as important to the binding together of a people as any of the other cultural values with which they are associated. How we take care of our ancestral monuments reflects how we care for and think of ourselves. The admonition of the book is clear. If we do not protect our cemeteries, no one else will.

Michael L. Blakey, Ph.D.
Professor of Anthropology,
College of William and Mary, Williamsburg, Virginia,
and the Scientific Director of
the New York African Burial Ground Project

CHASING GHOSTS THROUGH THE FUTURE AND INTO THE PAST

Lara Taubman writes an Overview of Lay Down Body for the American Cemetery Magazine. She gives a critical look at the first edition published as Lay Down Body and now called The Death Care Industry: African American Cemeteries and Funeral Homes. Taubman uses the title, "Chasing Ghosts Through The Future and Into The Past."

Taubman states that Roberta Hughes Wright and Wilbur B. Hughes, III, show that graveyards intricately describe the past as they reveal the future. The authors say the fundamental premise of the book is the "struggle" and the "conflict" – more bluntly known as the oppression of Black Americans. This experience takes the reader on a journey through the Americas, from the deepest South in the Sea Islands, into Canada and as far west as Los Angeles.

The authors' untiring search to document Black American graveyards is impressive. The urgent need to maintain these sites as historical records of the life and heritage of Black Americans is made apparent with the inclusion of traditional stories of death and burial rituals. The graves remind us that, although people inevitably die, their burial spots do not have to die with them.

Wright and Hughes emphasize that not only is it important that the dead be commemorated, but that African rituals and their corresponding black American traditions demand a proper burial and resting place. The need for these places to exist in a formal recorded fashion, such as a book, is understandably a central concern.

Wright and Hughes frame the book in terms of Black American rituals and oral traditions handed down through generations. These stories permeate the book and are perhaps its most enjoyable aspect.

For example, the authors detail a list of rituals on the ways the dead must be treated. One belief claims knowledge of the presence of a ghost because ghosts "...feel hot and smell faintish." Another says, "Dirt from sinners' graves is supposed to be very powerful." Another offers, "It is not good to answer the first time your name is called. It may be a spirit and if you answer you will die shortly."

The authors also include many other forms of lore. Popular old tales such as *Brer Rabbit*, and other tales about the dead relay messages of strength, faith, and heritage. These stories provide readers a better understanding and appreciation of Black American culture, especially regarding death and burial customs. The book gives a bird's eye view of culture and burial rituals and also stands as a defense for the respect and maintenance of Black American graveyards.

The authors apologize for not mentioning many other similar Black American folklore anecdotes, and their chief source is Langston Hughes' and Anna Bontemps' *the Book of Negro Folklore*, an interesting but dated work (published in 1959). A wealth of information on African and Black American culture, far more advanced than this volume, is available from today's Black American scholars. Though not a devastating oversight, the book would have been that much more engrossing with up-to-date information.

The Beginning

Wright and Hughes begin by taking us on a journey around America and Canada, following the areas where blacks have historically been concentrated. They start in the Sea Islands and the Carolinas, leading us through burial grounds they consider historically unique and beautiful.

In many cases, graveyards are chosen because they are in danger of being overrun by developers, particularly in places like Hilton Head and Daufuskie Islands, South Carolina. However, the authors also mention success stories where graveyards have been rescued from the developer's bulldozer.

After a trip through southern burial grounds and cemeteries (where the authors find the graves of the Martin Luther King, Sr. family and other historically significant graves), we are taken northward to Tennessee. The Bethlehem Cemetery in Henning is the birthplace of Alex Haley and the entire Haley family. "Chicken George," the great-great-grandfather of Alex Haley and the character in Haley's novel/family autobiography *Roots* is also buried there.

Wright and Hughes continue the journey in Alabama, where George Washington Carver is buried next to Booker T. Washington on the Tuskegee University grounds. In Chicago, they find the grave of legendary jazz singer, Dinah Washington. Harriet Tubman is buried in Auburn, N.Y., and Madame C.J. Walker, the cosmetics queen for black women at the turn of the century, as well as America's first self-made black female millionaire, is buried in Indianapolis.

These are fascinating historical facts. But what makes them come to life are circumstances surrounding the burial grounds – circumstances that in many cases forced blacks to create their own graveyards because whites would not allow them to be buried in theirs. This typical and painful exclusion is what all the historical figures mentioned above have in common.

The hardship suffered by these people to advance their lives and the lives of other blacks should not be forgotten and makes us turn to burial grounds holding the remains of those accorded less historical significance.

One realizes while touring these burial grounds, that it is these cemeteries that are in danger of vanishing. The authors' documentation of these more obscure burial sites is helpful to the simply curious or perhaps those compiling a family tree. However, they also lend value to these sites by mentioning those buried there who were important individuals in their town or city. Perhaps they were involved in smaller historical events, but certainly they should not be consigned to oblivion.

In this way, the authors begin to safeguard these spots as they remind local and state governments that these precious places exist.

A Technical Discussion
The last section of the book is primarily a technical discussion for those compiling a family tree ("Genealogy for the Beginner") – how to restore an old graveyard for blacks, physically and culturally, as well as how to care for family graves. Although this section might seem only for those with a vested interest, it proves an excellent conclusion in its overtly technical way.

The book describes indigenous aspects of Black America through the study of graveyards, but is also intended to promote preservation of these spaces. Wright and Hughes remind us that Black American burial grounds, whether 10 or 200 years old, require special attention. This is not to say that blacks could or should not be buried with people of various races and beliefs, but that, in many cases, the Black American cultural rituals performed in these graveyards are unique. These rituals leave behind a residue that tells a story that begins to fill the blanks of a history never recorded in writing.

Wright and Hughes began to look for their past and also to plan their future (not surprising for those writing a book on graveyards). The chapter, "Burial Societies and Lodges" is particularly interesting because it recalls old burial societies and lodges that became social centers for the black community. These groups became popular in the mid-19th century and were meant to insure black Americans a proper funeral. Insurance companies of the day often preyed on impoverished blacks. Burial societies and lodges provided the dignity and respect denied/withheld by the larger white community. These organizations facilitated funerals and provided meetinghouses outside of the church. The lodges became places for social and/or religious gatherings, but most of all they helped those who were ill or dying. The authors lament that few of these places still exist. The need for them petered out slowly throughout the twentieth century, probably because insurance became accessible to more people.

At first glance, it seems that this chapter would have been more pertinent in another part of the book. However, it becomes clear that the authors see these lodges as important bastions of hope and healing for the black community, even today. It is understood that there is a smaller black religious community today than perhaps 50 or even 20 years ago, but the authors envision these lodges as potential secular gathering places. They would be run by black community members, not local government. This is Wright and Hughes hope for a future, ironically built around death. I remember hearing it once said that a society that copes with death as a part of life is a healthy society.

This book is recommended not only as a pleasurable and informative historic read, but also as a valuable guide for blacks trying to trace their American family lineage; restore a slave burial ground; or take care of their deceased.

The book also appeals to professionals in the field with a discussion of the hazards of embalming. The authors map out these discussions while providing insights about hazards that embalming poses, particularly to the environment.

The book shows convincingly that the dead cannot be laid to rest and forever forgotten. If we do forget them, we lose a piece of history. Remembering this, Americans must learn how to live with their deceased.

American Cemetery Magazine
Volume 68, November 1996

Lara Taubman's review of the first edition applies, also, to the second edition. However, the new material, by including funeral homes, provides a more expansive glimpse of the many facets of the death care industry.

The authors had hoped they could effectively add many more than the fourteen funeral establishments that were selected. It was plainly and simply a matter of space. Three hundred thirty nine pages had stretched to more than six hundred pages. These additional pages included not only funeral homes, but more burial sites, many lacking perpetual care but strikingly beautiful. Moreover, there are some remarkable stories both unusual and strange.

The selected family-owned funeral homes primarily date back to the 1800s. Cities represented are Durham, North Carolina; Columbia, South Carolina; New Orleans, Louisiana; Memphis, Tennessee; Detroit, Michigan; Indianapolis, Indiana; Newark, New Jersey; Lexington, Kentucky; Savannah, Georgia; Chicago, Illinois; Los Angeles, California; Baltimore, Maryland; and New Bedford, Massachusetts.

African Canadian cemeteries have their own chapter in this edition and so do celebrity burials. The final chapter is a consumers' guide that provides information for anyone, with easily understandable advice on planning a funeral.

ACKNOWLEDGMENTS

We are profoundly indebted to the many people who have assisted us with this book. Thanks go to each and every one of them. Unfortunately, we may have inadvertently missed listing a few persons; they are also thanked.

Gratitude of the highest order goes to those who provided special assistance by contributing to the text. Their contributions made a big difference in the scope and quality of the book. Appreciation goes to:

American Cemetery magazine, for use of excerpts from Melissa Johnson Williams and John L. Konefes's article about the environmental aspects of embalming, and from John E. Sterling's June 1995 article about headstone databases.

The American Genealogical Research Institute staff for information reprinted from their publication *How to Trace Your Family Tree.*

Bantam, for use of Maya Angelou's poem "Elegy: For Harriet Tubman and Frederick Douglass," reprinted by permission from *Maya Angelou Poems,* Bantam, 1981, 1986.

Michael L. Blakey, project director of the New York African Burial Ground Project at Howard University, for contributing the foreword for this book.

The Boston Parks & Recreation Department for *The Boston Experience: A Manual for Historic Burying Grounds Preservation,* second edition, 1989, which comprised much of our chapter on burial ground preservation.

Billie Burn, for the use of information from her comprehensive study *An Island Named Daufuskie,* and for our interview at the Daufuskie Island dock.

Citadel Press, for the use of excerpts from William Wells Brown's *The Negro in the American Rebellion: His Heroism and His Fidelity,* Citadel Press, 1971.

Hennig Cohen for use of his "Burial of the Drowned among the Gullah Negroes," reprinted by permission from *Southern Folklore Quarterly,* Vol. XXII (1958), pages 93, 95-96.)

Vennie Deas-Moore for "Treading on Sacred Grounds," reprinted with the permission of the National Trust for Historic Preservation, copyright 1993 by Lynette Strangstad. Deas-Moore has served as assistant folklorist for the Smithsonian Institute's office of Folklore Program and Howard University's Institute for Urban Affairs and Research. She is consultant for both the South Carolina ETV Network and the McKissick Museum at the University of South Carolina.

Dodd, Mead & Co., for use of "Big Sixteen," "The Bury League," "Concerning the Dead," "Go Down Death," and "Voices in the Graveyard," from *The Book of Negro Folklore,* copyright 1958 by Langston Hughes and Arna Bontemps.

Durham Service Corps, for use of Lacretia Wilkerson and Isaac Johnson's interview with Mr. Willis G. Carpenter, first published in the Corps' pamphlet, *Reclaiming Yesterday—The Geer Cemetery Project.*

Harold Ober Associates, Inc., for use of "The Negro Mother," by Langston Hughes, reprinted from *Selected Poems of Langston Hughes,* published by Alfred A. Knopf, copyright 1959 by Langston Hughes.

"If Winter Comes," by Edna Gullins, reprinted by permission from *Negro Voices,* edited by Beatrice M. Murphy, 1938.

Wesley W. Law, Savannah, Georgia's famed griot, for his assistance with the Savannah story.

"My Epitaph," by Lewis Grandison Alexander, reprinted by permission from *Negro Voices,* edited by Beatrice M. Murphy, 1938.

The National Trust for Historic Preservation, for use of "Cleaning Burial Markers" and "Maintaining and Preserving Burial Sites," reprinted by permission from *Information* (newsletter), information series No. 76, 1993.

Elaine Nichols for "Rediscovering Our Roots Through Jumping the Broom," from *The Last Miles of the Way: African-American Homegoing Traditions, 1890—Present,* copyright 1989 by Commissioners of the South Carolina State Museum. This directory features a wealth of data about the cultural heritage of African Americans in South Carolina and accompanied an exhibition on display at the South Carolina State Museum from June 4, 1989, to December 1, 1989.

Chris Nordmann for the chapter "Genealogy for the Beginner," adapted from "Basic Genealogical Research Methods and Their Application to African Americans," *African American Genealogical Sourcebook,* edited by Paula K. Byers, copyright 1995 by Gale Research.

Sandlapper Publishing, Inc. for use of "Early One Morning" from *Reminiscenses of Sea Island Heritage,* by Ronald Daise, copyright 1986 by Sandlapper Publishing, Inc.

Harriet Jackson Scarupa for information from the excellent article in *American Visions,* June 1994, "Learning from Ancestral Bones: New York's Exhumed African Past."

The *Tennessee Tribune,* for use of its "Tribute to Tennessee's Black Civil War Soldiers," first published in vol. 2, no. 2, February 1993.

Sharyn Thompson, for use of "Tallahassee's Old City Cemetery," reprinted by permission from her pamphlet "Florida's Historic Cemeteries: A Preservation Handbook," published by the Historic Tallahassee Preservation Board of the Florida Department of State.

Mrs. Bertha Smith and the Moving Star Hall congregation for their arrangement of the song "Lay Down Body," Ethel Raim for her lovely transcription, and Guy and Candie Carawan for bringing the song to our attention through their book *Ain't You Got a Right to the Tree of Life? The People of Johns Island, South Carolina—Their Faces, Their Words, and Their Songs,* University of Georgia Press, copyright 1989 by Guy and Candie Carawan.

Dr. John A. Wright for information from *St. Louis Black Heritage Trail,* edited by Diane Scollay, Shirley Wittner, and Carol Shoults.

We are so very grateful for assistance from Charles Alexander of Detroit, Michigan, for initial keying of the manuscript; Edward J. Allen of Beaufort, South Carolina; Link Fannie Allen of Boston, Massachusetts; George Alston of St. Helena, South Carolina; the American Cemetery Association; Link Cheryl Anderson of Denver, Colorado; Link Lucille Barbour of Atlantic City, New Jersey; Richard Barnett of Hattiesburg, Mississippi; Harriet Barnwell of Beaufort, South Carolina; Angela Bates of Nicodemus, Kansas; Robin Benedict of Fort Lauderdale, Florida; Evelyn and John Bingham of Detroit; Charles Blockson of Temple University, Philadelphia, Pennsylvania; Charles Boland of Lexington, Kentucky; Letitia and Carl Bolden of Detroit, Michigan; Catherine Bowser of Truxtun (Portsmouth), Virginia; Alphonso Brown of Charleston, South Carolina; Dr. Margaret Burroughs of Chicago, Illinois; Juan Byars of Hilton Head Island, South Carolina; and Frank Bynes, historian and funeral director in Savannah, Georgia.

We also have abiding gratitude to Charletta J. Campbell of Henning, Tennessee; Emma Campbell and Emory Campbell of Hilton Head Island, South Carolina; James Cato of Beaufort; Michael Cohen of Hilton Head Island; Montrose Cunningham of Dallas, Texas; Century Funeral Home of Hattiesburg; Link Mary Chapman of Des Moines, Iowa; Richard F. Dabbs of Mayesville, South Carolina; Natalie and Ron Daise of Beaufort; Alvin Dahmer and Ellie Dahmer of Hattiesburg; Deborah Dandridge of Chicago; Link Helen Davis of Boston; Emily and Herbert DeCosta of Charleston; the Reverend Kenneth Doe of St. Helena Island, South Carolina; Kathryn Rainbow-Earhart, M.D., of Topeka, Kansas; John M. Estes Jr., Connecting Link of Des Moines; the Fairfield County Museum of Winnsboro, South Carolina; and Carolyn Fisher of Hilton Head (formerly of Dayton, Ohio).

We also owe thanks to Marie Gadson of Coffin Point, St. Helena Island; Helen Galloway of St. Helena; Doris Grant of Hilton Head Island; attorney Fred Gray of Montgomery and Tuskegee, Alabama; Sharony Andrews Green of

Detroit; Dr. Patricia Guthrie of San Leandro, California; Juanita Halfacre of Canfield, Tennessee; Axel Hansen, M.D., of Nashville, Tennessee; Laura Hansen of New York City; Dr. Necia Harkless of Lexington; Jerry Henderson of Austin, Texas; Valentine Hill of Bloomfield Hills, Michigan; Mrs. Lula Holmes of St. Helena Island; Dorothy Houston of Memphis, Tennessee; and Venida Smith Hudley of Coppell, Texas; and Dr. Harris Huntley of Birmingham, Alabama.

We also appreciate the assistance of Mildred Jefferson of Charleston; Lois Jenkins of Beaufort; Angelyne Johnson of Savannah; Audrey Johnson of Atlanta, Georgia; Delores Johnson of Chicago; Matthew Jones of Savannah; Hazel Lee of Detroit; Bertram Lippincott III of Newport, Rhode Island; John Luke of Detroit; Edna K. Luten of Savannah; Malcolm Macdonald of Tuscaloosa, Alabama; Marshel's Wright-Donaldson Funeral Home of Beaufort, South Carolina; Gwen and Robert Mason of Washington, D.C.; Joan Maynard of Brooklyn; Mae Mendoza of Beaufort; Robert L. Moseley Jr. of Nashville; Dr. Henry Moses of Nashville; and the North American Black Historical Museum and Cultural Center of Canada.

We are indebted, also, to Penn Center, St. Helena Island; John L. Poston Jr. of Memphis; Kathy Ramsey of Detroit; Winona Rawls of Detroit; Ed Robinson of Birmingham; Link Dr. Nellie Roulhac of Philadelphia; Dr. Lawrence Rowland of Beaufort; Denise Rowson of Durham, North Carolina; Jean Sanders of Compton, California; Beth Shepard of Boston; Mrs. Agnes Sherman of St. Helena Island; Helen Sheumaker of Lawrence, Kansas; Rosa and Charles Simmons of Hilton Head Island; Brenda Simon of Burton, South Carolina; Josie Skanes of Birmingham, Alabama; Gerhard Spieler, county historian of Beaufort; Dr. Rowena Stewart of Florida; Denise Stinson of Detroit; Lynette Strangstad of Charleston; and Julia Thompson of Hattiesburg.

Many thanks, also, to John E. Walker of Phoenixville, Pennsylvania; David Wallace, M.D., of Cleveland Heights, Ohio; I. E. Washington of Augusta, Georgia; Dennis Watson of Dallas; Roy O. West of Richmond, Virginia; Barbara and Perry White of Hilton Head Island; Charles White of New Jersey and Hilton Head Island, South Carolina; Frances White of Detroit; Nathaniel White of Hilton Head; Rita White of Bala Cynwood, Pennsylvania; the Reverend Horace Williams of St. Helena Island and Beaufort; Cynthia Wilson of Tuskegee; Vernon Wimbrough of Portsmouth, Virginia; Byrd E. Wood of Washington, D.C.; Jack Wood of Jackson, Tennessee; Yvonne at Wright-Donaldson Funeral Home in Beaufort; Myrtle Yancey-Mitchell of Lexington; and Elizabeth Yates of Indianapolis, Indiana.

Edition One of this book could not have been completed without the guidance of managing editor Gina Renée Misiroglu—ever creative, professional, and thorough. Amy Inouye and Charles Mitchell lent invaluable researching skills. Many thanks to the Visible Ink Press team, including developmental editor Christa Brelin, publishers Martin Connors and Diane Dupuis, and editors Dean Dauphinais and Leslie Norback. For permissions research, thank you Margaret Chamberlain and Maria Franklin. Art director

Tracey Rowens created a beautifully designed book.

Author Wright's daughter and author Hughes' sister, Dr. Barbara Hughes Smith, deserves a big thanks for her editing and for monitoring the chapter on genealogy. Other family members who were always there to help and give suggestions were Blythe Allen Dickerson, M.D.; Brett William Allen, Esq. and Christina Barbara Hughes.

Many thanks for assisting with the **Second Edition**, to Dawn Langford, senior staff at the Charles H. Wright Museum of African American History and for the information on College Park Cemetery in Houston, Texas; to Camille Killens for much help including information on cemeteries in southwest and northeast Georgia and for the listing of cemeteries throughout the United States for the Appendix; to Ollie Giles for the story of a San Marcus, Texas Cemetery; to Cassandra Whitfield for her generous assistance with e-mail problems and for typing; to Malcolm Dade, who now lives in South Carolina for information on Columbia funeral homes.

Thanks also to R. Wayne Brown, president of Mount Auburn Cemetery Corporation in Baltimore, Maryland; to the many persons who contributed to the story of Darrell Banks, buried at Detroit Memorial Park, East and to dear Andrea Moore of Windsor, Ontario for all of her contributions including the list of African Canadian Cemeteries; to Cheryl Mosby for computer work and to Ophelia Ford of Memphis, Tennessee for information about N. J. Ford Funeral Home and for "introducing" me to Sharon Seay, director of the National Funeral Directors and Morticians Association and for Vera Ford of Detroit who met with us, with more material on their Funeral Home and her father, N.J. Ford.

We appreciate the assistance of George Dines, president of the Woodlawn Cemetery Association and of Larry M. Smith and Moses J. Manijan, officials representing the Woodlawn Cemetery in Washington, D.C. and the Perpetual Care Association of the Cemetery and for P. Sluby, Sr.

Thanks to Debra Hill, GRS (c) Black Loyalist Heritage Society, Nova Scotia, Canada cemeteries; to Marty Conners for his efforts and success in finding material from Visible Ink Press; to Karl Williams for the history of United Memorial Gardens in Plymouth, Michigan; and for the many great publications and associations of Dr. Michael Trinkley, director of Chicora Research Foundation in Columbia, South Carolina. What an impact he has made with his research and writing about South Carolina cemeteries and the archeological work and preservation information as well as pertinent laws and violations.

Thanks also to Eleanor Robertson Smith, certified genealogist, for material in Nova Scotia's Shelbourne County, Nova Scotia; to Suzanne Smith of George Washington University in Virginia; and to Ivan Ware of Silver Spring, Maryland. Thanks to Lee Blake for the material on New Bedford,

Massachuetts Historical Society and to Randall B. Pollard of New Bedford, Massachuetts. The material sent from Robert C. Hayden's book was very much apppreciated (see Bibliography), and thanks to Robert C. Hayden of Oak Bluffs, Massachuetts. Thanks also to Dr. C. Robert Bass for information on Oberlin, Ohio cemeteries.

Close to the publisher's deadline in June 2006, six friends provided much needed assistance: thanks to Valentine Hill, Cassandra Whitfield, Wonner Lawson, Erma Greene, Patricia Smith and Vera Weiss.

Photographs appearing in **Lay Down Body** were received from the following sources:

Augusta, Georgia cemetery photos, from the Reverend A. C. Redd.

Beaufort National Cemetery plaque from Joseph W. Smith.

Charleston, South Carolina photos, from Julius Watson.

Cover photograph of "Farewell to Eugene" by Romare Bearden courtesy Estate of Romare Bearden.

Daufuskie Island Center, from Joseph W. Smith.

Map of African Burial Ground (New York City) location, copyright 1994 by Steve Harper, Office of Public Education and Interpretation of the African Burial Ground.

Pedigree chart and family tree, copyright 1982 by Rosemary A. Chorzempa, *The Family Tree Workbook: Genealogy for Beginners,* Dover Publications.

Portrait of George Washington Carver, from AP/Wide World Photos.

Portrait of Alex Haley, from AP/Wide World Photos.

Portrait of Benjamin E. Mays, from AP/Wide World Photos.

Portrait of Elijah McCoy, from The Granger Collection, New York.

Portrait of Gen. Robert Smalls, from The Granger Collection, New York.

Portrait of Emmett Till, from AP/Wide World Photos.

Portrait of Maggie L. Walker, from The Granger Collection, New York.

Portrait of Dinah Washington, from AP/Wide World Photos.

Portrait of Whitney Young Jr., from Gerald Davis/Archive Photos.

All other photographs were taken by the authors on their various trips.

The authors send a special thanks to Julius Bennett of Houston, Texas. He is director of Corporate Development for the Houston based Wilson Financial Group, Inc. that operates funeral homes, cemeteries, a monument company and flower shops in nine states. The company has grown from five properties to owning over forty cemeteries and funeral homes. Bennett has been most helpful in recommending to us various businesses and contact persons for assistant with our research.

INTRODUCTION

"The trouble with us," lamented Booker T. Washington, "is that we are always preparing to die. You meet a white man early in the morning and ask him what he is preparing to do . . . he is going to start a business. You ask a colored man . . . he is preparing to die."

Whether you agree with this or not, and we see it as a gross overstatement, there is no doubt that, "when de Lord calls us home to walk de golden streets," it's important to go in style. But going "in style" isn't always easy.

The authors begin writing about cemeteries by looking at the circumstances surrounding the capture and enslavement of Africans and the when, where and how they were buried. The cemetery, too often, was the sea. Africans frequently turned to death, either by forced starvation, by starving themselves, or by leaping into the ocean. Some believed that if they were killed they would return again to their own country. In other words, many of the slaves may have taken solace in the thought that after death, they would return to Africa.

So mixed is the record of funeral procedures during slavery, it is impossible to extract the truth. It is known that some "masters" permitted funeral rites while others objected strongly. Some objected to the use of African drums to announce funerals, some banned singing at slave wakes, and others outlawed Black preachers at slave funerals. Often funerals were only allowed at night.

At the cemetery, the open grave waited, frequently dug along an east-west axis by slaves who knew not to violate the West African strictures against burying a person "crossing in the world." As a rule, each plantation had its own burial ground, but sometimes towns or churches provided a small cemetery in which the slaves of various owners were laid to rest.

Natural weathering, vandalism, neglect, abandonment, agricultural practices, encroachment by development, and industrial pollution all pose threats to these and other African American cemeteries. Why is this important? Because many cemeteries represent the culture of Black America. The sites are significant because burial practices tend to be among the most conservative, or least changed, factors of a group's material culture. The oldest and most persistent values are sometimes preserved only in cemeteries.

The book, *Lay Down Body*, has been expanded and given a new name to reflect the authors' determination to broaden their vision and to address the status of the entire death care industry, particularly as it relates to African Americans. The trend continues, by African Americans, to recognize the importance of maintaining and even strenghtening their ties with Africa. One way to raise the level of knowledge is by studying the history of one's ancestors.

Even the most modern of the twentieth-century Black cemeteries reflect traditions of Africa, we glimpse the similarity in the rites, including the ceremony, the music, the mourning habits, and the family outings at the cemetery. The effort to maintain pride and tradition has been affected also, in some areas, by the intrusion of developers usurping the hallowed grounds for new construction.

The book is not an attempt to list or categorize all the African American cemeteries in the United States, nor is it a book about African American cemetery decorations or grave artistry. Other books have beautifully illustrated many of the unique and elaborate decorative settings found in cemeteries, particularly throughout the South.

Instead, the book concentrates on "you" and "yours". The authors have selected representative cemeteries throughout the United States and Canada and recounted recent stories about the "digging up" of cemeteries where slaves were buried. In the chapter called "The Cradle," focus is on the first, often trouble-plagued cemeteries of the southeastern Sea Islands and nearby areas. Cemeteries both large and small in other parts of the United States and Canada relate to the conflict as well. In "Cemeteries Coast to Coast," we begin with the earliest cemeteries, located in the Southeast, and continue northward and westward to examine burial grounds throughout the continent. In "Genealogy for the Beginner," we provide examples of family trees and discuss how cemeteries themselves, along with cemetery, church, and other records, can help the family historian track down "lost" ancestors. Burial societies and lodges, stories and tales, preservation of historical burial grounds, environmental and business concerns, and an overview of funeral customs and trends complete the story.

Readers will notice that we have varied our use of such terms as African, Negro, Colored, Black, and African American. Our intent has been to use the terms as they were accepted during various periods in our history; that is, using *African* to describe those born in Africa, then *Negro* and *Colored* when describing African Americans during the period up through the 1960s, when *Black* became popular and, indeed, powerful. We employ the term *African American* throughout the book, believing that it best describes our past heritage and our present legacy.

Another concern of ours is the use of the word *slave*. Because the word is used so much throughout history, we have repeated it many times. We strongly believe, however, that people are not born slaves; rather, they are *enslaved,* and we prefer to use the latter term whenever possible.

Our hope is that, in reading this book, you will find enjoyment in the stories of preceding as well as prevailing burial customs and traditions. This might spark your interest for exploring deeper into how our cultural and artistic expressions survived, arising often from unbelievably difficult obstacles and barriers. What thoughts do you envision when looking at a solitary, weather-worn stone marker standing deep amidst nature's foliated debris? Let your imagination soar.

We, Roberta V. Greenidge (Hughes Wright), and Wilbur Brandon Hughes, III were pleased with the overwhelmingly positive response to the 1996 book. Many of our readers not only have told us that they enjoyed the book, but have pleaded with us to write more and to include "their cemeteries and their stories." We have tried to save and include the articles and materials sent to us, as well as to do additional research in this second edition.

Dr. Barbara K. Hughes Smith has joined us as Editor. She brings an expansive knowledge of genealogy. The subject of genealogy was introduced in Lay Down Body by her but needed to be extended. Dr. Smith is a venturous genealogist through her reading and computer research; her recorded forays include manual explorations to Canada, the Caribbean, and other places as well as the United States in search of family histories. She has also contributed additional information on African Canadian cemeteries as did the late E. Andrea Moore of Windsor, Ontario.

The authors were pleased with the cooperation of the funeral directors when we began writing on this new topic. We listened and looked, especially at those who had their beginnings in the 1800s and are still family-owned. They sent us stories of their businesses and all included personal family experiences. Involvement in the community is top priority with these establishments and several have more than one business location.

For those who want answers to questions or specific details about the funeral process, we suggest *Caretakers of the Dead, the American Funeral Director* by Vanderlyn R. Pine. It is an excellent resource describing public and non-public behavior in the funeral home and the role of the funeral director. Pine's analysis of funeral service directories reveals that over ninety percent of the funeral homes in the United States bear the name of an individual funeral director or his family rather than the name of the community served or some local landmark.

The High Cost of Dying, A Guide to Funeral Planning by Gregory W. Young, provides answers to questions expected by the bereaved family. We have included some of his thoughts in chapter thirteen with the following topics: Pre-need; At-need, In-ground Burials, Above-ground Burials (Mausoleums), and Cremations and much more has been added. It includes Federal Commission laws and rulings.

For more detailed information on the role of the funeral director and the training and experience necessary to provide skillful and efficient care and attention, the book *Grave Undertakings* by Alexandra K. Mosca, is a must read as is the book, *Stiff* by Mary Roach.

We hope you enjoy this book. While reading don't hold back your laughter, even though you are reading about "those gone." Some of the stories will leave you no choice. However, some will leave you in tears.

LAY DOWN BODY

ARRANGEMENT BY
MRS. BERTHA SMITH
AND THE
MOVING STAR HALL
CONGREGATION

LEADER: *Lay down body,*
GROUP: *Lay down a little while.*
LEADER: *Lay down body,*
GROUP: *Lay down a little while.*

LEADER: *Oh, my body now,*
GROUP: *Lay down a little while.*
LEADER: *Oh, my body now,*
GROUP: *Lay down a little while.*

LEADER: *Down in the graveyard,*
GROUP: *Lay down a little while.*
LEADER: *Down in the graveyard,*
GROUP: *Lay down a little while.*

LEADER: *I know you tired,*
GROUP: *Lay down a little while.*
LEADER: *I know you tired,*
GROUP: *Lay down a little while.*

LEADER: *Come from a distance,*
GROUP: *Lay down a little while.*
LEADER: *Come from a distance,*
GROUP: *Lay down a little while.*

LEADER: *Ain't you had a hard time?*
GROUP: *Lay down a little while.*
LEADER: *Ain't you had a hard time?*
GROUP: *Lay down a little while.*

LEADER: *Last December,*
GROUP: *Lay down a little while.*
LEADER: *Last December,*
GROUP: *Lay down a little while.*

LEADER: *Tedious was my journey,*
GROUP: *Lay down a little while.*
LEADER: *Tedious was my journey,*
GROUP: *Lay down a little while.*

LEADER: *Rocky was my road, Lord,*
GROUP: *Lay down a little while.*
LEADER: *Rocky was my road, Lord,*
GROUP: *Lay down a little while.*

LEADER: *Ain't you got somebody gone?*
GROUP: *Lay down a little while.*
LEADER: *Ain't you got somebody gone?*
GROUP: *Lay down a little while.*

LEADER: *I got somebody gone,*
GROUP: *Lay down a little while.*
LEADER: *I got somebody gone,*
GROUP: *Lay down a little while.*

LEADER: *Just keep a-rollin',*
GROUP: *Lay down a little while.*
LEADER: *Just keep a-rollin',*
GROUP: *Lay down a little while.*

LEADER: *Body, ain't you tired?*
GROUP: *Lay down a little while.*
LEADER: *Body, ain't you tired?*
GROUP: *Lay down a little while.*

LEADER: *Body, ain't you lonesome?*
GROUP: *Lay down a little while.*
LEADER: *Body, ain't you lonesome?*
GROUP: *Lay down a little while.*

LEADER: *Body, ain't you weary?*
GROUP: *Lay down a little while.*
LEADER: *Body, ain't you weary?*
GROUP: *Lay down a little while.*

LEADER: *Lay down body,*
GROUP: *Lay down a little while.*
LEADER: *Lay down body,*
GROUP: *Lay down a little while.*

NOW IN THE QUIETNESS OF THE GRAVE
I BEGAN TO UNDERSTAND WHAT HAPPENED.
IT ALL OCCURRED BECAUSE I DID NOT KNOW
THE MEANING OF A WORD.
WHEN I WENT TO WORK ON JUDGE SNYDER'S PLANTATION,
HE CLASPED HIS HANDS OVER HIS FAT BELLY AND SAID,
"I ALWAYS BELIEVE IN GIVING A NIGGER A **SQUARE** DEAL".
WHEN SETTLING TIME CAME THAT FALL
AND I DISCOVERED THAT I OWED THE JUDGE A HUNDRED
DOLLARS MORE
THAN THE PROCEEDS FROM MY TWENTY BALES OF COTTON,
I ACCUSED HIM OF CHEATING ME.
HE STRUCK ME AND I SLEW HIM.
I WAS LYNCHED.
NOW I REALIZE THIS OCCURRED BECAUSE I DID NOT KNOW
THE MEANING OF THE WORD **SQUARE**.

—HARVEY M. WILLIAMSON

CHAPTER ONE

On the numerous plantations dotting the fertile land of the Old South, there was one thing that even the most hard-hearted master was never quite willing to deny his slaves. Contemporary accounts dating from the 1700s reflect the Negroes' insistence that proper

1

attention be paid to their dead. They could not bear that their loved ones be interred without ceremony. A funeral was, to these early generations of African Americans, a pageant, marked by the gathering of kindred and friends from far and near. A funeral usually became an all-day meeting—often in a grove—and it drew white and black alike. A related demand—for the slaves knew how to make their demands—was that the Negro preacher "should preach the funeral." In matters of death, at least, the wishes of the slaves usually prevailed.

Along with their burial customs, those enslaved and transported from Africa brought with them to the Americas their ancient storytelling traditions. While slaveholders went to some length to eradicate tribal languages and customs, present-day literature abounds with a wealth of songs and stories that have survived in a continuation of the strong African oral tradition. Such folktales—usually animal stories involving the spider, the jackal, the hare, the fox, or the tortoise—reflect the tribal roots of these African people.

Among the many traditional stories and tales carried over from the homeland are "preacher tales." Such Negro religious tales were primarily told to entertain the listeners. These included both stories told by the preacher from his place in the pulpit and the stories told about the preacher when he had stepped down among his congregation. In addition, the singing of Negro spirituals added to the spirit of the occasion—be it a funeral, a wedding, or a Sunday service.

James Weldon Johnson, a prominent writer of prose and poetry, recognized in the sermons of the old-time Negro preacher an important form of folk expression. He reproduced a number of these in verse, including "Go Down Death," a poem taken from a funeral sermon. The old-time Negro preacher who created such sermons belonged to a unique breed. Inspiring, entertaining, comic—when comedy was needed—he was in every sense the shepherd of his flock. It was he who eased the hard journey of the congregation with the comforting sentiment, "You may have all dis world, but give me Jesus."

When reading these stories and poems, or listening to renditions of the old songs, in addition to being entertained one can hear the messages that once spoke to the very hearts and souls of both the enslaved and the newly freed. Later generations of blacks, although not enslaved themselves, still have a deep and abiding sense of the hurt and humility endured by their brothers and sisters. Little has changed . . . yet much has changed. There is no way to measure the *progress* of the African American. Some believe that the oppression and degradation experienced by so many under the yoke of slavery was so effective that their effects will echo for generations to come. Others feel that their nation's chronicle of slavery can be revisited and embraced as just that—a history from which to learn and grow and change.

The horror stories describing enslavement, death, and "first burials" are beyond interpretation or present-day understanding. It seems appropriate to begin our story with the early burials of native Africans who were captured and removed from their homeland. The history of the slave ship *Henrietta Marie*—brought to light through the underwater exploration of members of the National Association of Black Scuba Divers—provides an illustration of this early era. The *Henrietta Marie* was a 120-ton merchant vessel of seventy feet or so that set sail for the United States in September 1699. Her story is typical of the horribly devastating plight endured by enslaved Africans during what was termed "the middle passage."

The *Henrietta Marie* participated in the seventeenth and eighteenth-century "triangular slave trade," in which merchants navigated the lucrative loop from West Africa through the Caribbean to New England and back. Ships sailed this infamous slave-trading triangle for more than three hundred years, with their cargo of tens of millions of abducted Africans.

On average, the sea voyage ended in death for one out of every eight black passengers; the mortality rate for the transatlantic voyage sometimes climbed as high as 50 to 60 percent. Not surprisingly, a "slave ship" was invariably trailed by a school of sharks. A few captains operated as so-called "loose packers," but the majority were "tight packers," believing that an excessive loss of life would be more than offset by a larger cargo. Disease took its toll, especially when the ship was struck with an epidemic of scurvy or the flux. Suicides, loss of the will to live, and slave mutinies provided greater risks and additional increases in the number of lives lost. But in spite of it all, the slave trade flourished.

The remains of the *Henrietta Marie,* which sank in the early 1700s, were discovered in 1972, about thirty-five miles west of Key West, Florida, across the open waters where the Atlantic Ocean and the Gulf of Mexico merge. Artifacts recovered from the ship—now on display at Key West's Mel Fisher Maritime Heritage Society—reflect her grisly purpose. Shackles of all sizes, glass beads, decayed elephant tusks, and other such items were found. Exploration of the wreck determined that the ship's human cargo was wedged beneath the deck and manacled firmly in place for the grueling three-and-a-half-month voyage across the Atlantic to the Americas. Each person was restricted to a space of only about five-and-a-half feet by eighteen inches. The hold—about ten feet deep and twenty feet wide—was "home" to 250 or more Africans who, along with hungry rodents, were forced to remain there, sweating, relieving themselves, and getting sick, for the duration of the voyage. Death and disease were rampant; the callous, imperious enslavers simply tossed the bodies of those who perished into a "watery grave."

The watery grave of the "middle passage" would give way to land-bound slave cemeteries, many of which have been dismantled or destroyed over the intervening years. As is shown in the following narratives that focus on areas such as New York City and Dallas, shovels and bulldozers preparing

First Burials

land for new construction have come to a halt after the discovery of old slave cemeteries full of skeletal remains. These cities have worked around these "forbidden" areas and have many times provided plaques, parks, and tourist walks for spectators to read about and view the sites.

In 1992, the National Association of Black Scuba Divers sank a one-ton concrete and bronze monument at the site of the wreckage of the *Henrietta Marie*. It read:

> **Henrietta Marie**
> In memory and recognition of the courage,
> pain and suffering of enslaved African people.
> Speak her name and gently touch
> the souls of our ancestors.

Slave Cemeteries in the Americas

Slave cemeteries are not confined to any one section of the country. In most areas where bodies have been found, the discoverers are initially amused and surprised to uncover clumps of bones and artifacts. In some instances, these unknowing amateur archaeologists have not been particularly concerned about the significance of their findings. However, public reaction upon learning what has been unearthed—particularly by the African American and Native American communities—has been intense. The excavators have been forced to stop, assess, and redirect their efforts before proceeding. In most cases, as with the Old Quarters Cemetery in Virginia, homage has been paid in some manner to the dead.

TRIBUTE PAID AT THE OLD QUARTERS CEMETERY

In a pasture next to an old slaves' cemetery in Montross, Virginia, about five hundred people gathered one hot July day in 1991 to pay homage to a forgotten Virginia aristocrat and an enduring ideal—freedom. According to a story in the *New York Times,* the setting was apt. The northern neck of Virginia, wedged between the Potomac and Pappahannock Rivers, was the birthplace of a number of Americans inextricably linked with the concept of Liberty. George Washington was born a few miles from here, as were James Madison and James Monroe. But unlike Robert Carter III, the wealthy planter who was honored that day, none of those familiar figures felt compelled to extend freedom to the dark-skinned people who served as their slaves.

"He was a man ahead of his time," said Nancy Carter Crump, a distant relative of Carter. Two hundred years before, Carter, who owned sixty thousand acres across eighteen plantations and was considered one of the wealthiest men in Virginia, stunned his family, friends, and neighbors by filing a deed of emancipation, or manumission, thereby setting free more than five hundred "Negroes and mulatto slaves" who were his "absolute property."

"I have, for some time past, been convinced that to retain them in slavery is contrary to the true principles of Religion and Justice and, therefore, it is my duty to manumit them," Carter wrote in the document filed on August 1, 1791—more than seventy years before Abraham Lincoln issued the Emancipation Proclamation. Historians believe Carter's action to have been perhaps the largest individual act of emancipation to occur in American history.

Knowledge of Carter and his deed has been lost to all but a few historians and local admirers. He lies buried in an unmarked grave near the site of his mansion, Nomini Hall, which burned in 1850. In 1988, parishioners of the New Jerusalem Baptist Church erected a small monument on the site of the Old Quarters Cemetery, a burial ground for slaves from surrounding plantations that lies on a now-wooded hillside that tumbles down to a rushing creek.

THE AFRICAN BURIAL GROUND UNEARTHED

In 1741, what would become known as the "Great Negro Plot" took place in New York City. Meeting in upper Broadway's Hughson's Tavern, a slave cabal planned to burn down the entire city. A mysterious series of fires followed, prompting a citywide investigation and the roundup of scores of black slave suspects. During the trial that followed, the prosecutor accused the tavern owner, a white man named John Hughson, of allowing the defendants to use his tavern as a meeting place, arguing that plans to take over the city were initiated with Hughson's knowledge.

A sixteen-year-old barmaid and indentured servant named Mary Burton sealed the fate of many of the suspects by giving incriminating testimony. Of the thirty-five people eventually convicted in the plot, thirteen black men were burned at the stake; the rest were hanged, along with Hughson, two white women, and another white man. It is believed that all those executed may have been buried in the Negroes Burying Ground.

The Negroes Burying Ground was a cemetery used by the African population of New York during the British colonial era. Among those interred there were both free and enslaved peoples, most of whom had been uprooted from their homelands and forcibly transported to North America. Until recently, the existence of the burial ground was known to only a few scholars immersed in the fields of colonial New York history and African American studies.

It is still unknown exactly when the burial ground was first used. The earliest historical reference found to date is a letter written by chaplain John

The following image shows a sign that reads:

This enclosed area is a preserved part of the original

African Burial Ground

Closed in 1794, the African Burial Ground once covered more than five acres—about five city blocks. It is estimated that as many as 20,000 or more African men, women and children were buried in the original cemetery. Unearthed during building construction in 1991, the site is now a National Historic Landmark and within the New York City African Burial Ground and Commons Historic District. This remnant of the burial ground is dedicated to the people who are buried here and to those enslaved in the city's early history from 1626 until July 4, 1827, Emancipation Day in New York.

A tribute to the African Burial Ground, located on the corners of Elk and Duane Streets, "is dedicated to the people who are buried here and to all who were enslaved in the city's early history from 1626 until July 4, 1827, Emancipation Day in New York."

Sharpe in 1712, wherein he made note of Africans burying their countrymen in the "town common," a block of land that today encompasses City Hall Park and an area several blocks north. For the remainder of the eighteenth century, the Negroes Burying Ground was pictured on maps and referred to in land surveys. While the beginning date remains uncertain, more than two hundred years have passed since the closure of the cemetery in 1794.

The Negroes Burying Ground was rediscovered in 1991, when construction began on a new, $276-million office tower. The graveyard had been the site of one of New York City's earliest landfill projects, and workmen and experts alike were surprised to discover graves anywhere from sixteen to twenty-eight feet below street level. After the first examples of colonial cultural materials—objects made, used, or modified by people—were discovered, archaeologists were called in and began unearthing skeletal remains from what they believed at the time to be an eighteenth-century cemetery.

Further investigation determined that the area was one of the oldest vestiges of the black community in New York City. After considerable fanfare, federal officials decided that archaeology would take precedence over construction. The site was described by the government as "the only colonial-period African American cemetery to be excavated in the United States." Unfortunately, this decision spawned considerable political bickering when it was determined that excavation would result in a four-month, $6-million delay in construction.

The government wanted to end the painstaking excavation by dental pick and spoon in favor of a faster approach employing wide shovels. Using what he called the "coroner's method," John Rossi, project manager for the pending thirty-four-story federal office tower, argued that only one day would be needed to clean a skeleton, remove it, and place it in a box still surrounded by soil, rather than the three to five days predicted by archaeologists. Several prominent black New Yorkers petitioned the government to allow the excavation to continue at a more deliberate pace, citing the site's historical importance and cultural significance.

"It's bad enough that some of the bodies that may be in those tombs were discriminated against in life," commented New York State Senator David A. Patterson. "But now, they're being discriminated against in death." Rossi's method was put on hold pending a ruling from Washington, D.C., and the archaeological method of excavation continued. During the early days of the excavation, ninety-three skeletons were unearthed in the city block bounded by Broadway, Duane, Reade, and Elk Streets. Historians and archaeologists now believe that the locale once served as a cemetery for black New Yorkers, as well as a potter's field and a Revolutionary War burial ground, before it was closed in 1794. Experts associated with the project believe that as many as twenty thousand African men, women, and children were buried in the original cemetery, which once covered more than five acres, or about five city blocks.

About 40 percent of the remains discovered at this Manhattan site were those of children below the age of twelve. This suggests that the death rate for African American children in colonial New York City was relatively high, especially when compared with the estimated rate of death for similar children in other northern port towns during the same period. Small pox, measles, diphtheria, whooping cough, chicken pox, and scarlet fever were often fatal to children during the colonial era—a time when there were no known cures for such illnesses.

Records show the frequency of death among young, enslaved Africans in the eighteenth century to be more than twice that of their free, European-born counterparts. Often black children—particularly infants—were not wanted by New York slave owners because they required care, food, and living space, and distracted their parents from their other duties.

All of the bodies found that dated from that period were buried in coffins, heads pointing west. Most were clad in shrouds that had long since disintegrated. Experts puzzled over one mystery: the skeleton of a black man whose grave contained four buttons of a type found on a British marine officer's coat of the late 1700s. Who was he? And why would he have a garment of that kind? Such questions have yet to be answered.

In the early part of 1992, New York City archaeologist Daniel N. Pagano stated that on February 14, during the process of pouring a concrete footing on the east side of the site—where it had already been determined that graves were most probably located—jawbones, leg bones, and arms bones were scooped up by the backhoe.

Upon discovering that they were bringing up bones, all work in the area stopped. Plans were made to test the entire area under an archaeologist's supervision. Alan Greenberg, project executive for the General Services Administration (GSA), said that construction crews had relied on an out-of-date drawing to gauge which part of the site was deemed "culturally sterile"— that is, unlikely to yield remains or artifacts to archaeologists working on the excavation. An amended drawing, made after a more recent investigation, had shown the limits of the "sterile" area more precisely, but it never arrived at the field office. Mr. Greenberg attributed this to a "simple human error or miscommunication." Then-Mayor David N. Dinkins was described as "exceedingly distressed that, despite a memorandum of agreement that protected the area, twenty burials were destroyed."

The existence of the African Burial Ground (as the site was renamed after its rediscovery) is strong evidence that enslaved Africans in colonial New York City built a lively communal and spiritual life despite their legal and social disenfranchisement. It would appear that, contrary to the assumptions of many historians, slavery in northern cities did not isolate enslaved Africans from one another, but instead provided the impetus for the growth of a uniquely African American society and culture.

In addition, the rediscovery of the African Burial Ground has changed the way future urban archaeology will be conducted. Standard archaeological testing procedures, particularly in this area of Manhattan, will now need to consider the possibility of deeper deposits due to the shifting land gradations caused by continued urban development.

In November 1993, after the site at Elk and Duane Streets had been declared a National Historic Landmark, local African Americans paid tribute to the African Burial Grounds during a candlelight ceremony in lower Manhattan. Howard Dodson, director of the Schomburg Center for Research in Black Culture, observed: "The African Burial Ground offers proof of what has indeed been our role in New York and America. Our role and social influence was a well-kept secret. Now we have the kind of evidence that establishes Africans as having a private claim—a real investment in America."

A number of West African chiefs and delegates paid a visit to Howard University on August 2, 1995, where anthropologists are studying the bones found in the African Burial Ground project. According to Patrice Gaines of the *Washington Post*, Nana Oduro Numapau II, president of the Ghana National House of Chiefs, reflected, "This is clear evidence, indeed, [that] these are our brothers and sisters who were enslaved. Normally when we go to a cemetery, we go home to have a day of mourning. I want to declare this a day of mourning for African people."

In a September 1992 article in the *Detroit News,* reporter Bruce Frankel recorded anthropologist Sherrill Wilson's thoughts on the burial ground, thoughts that mirror the sentiments of historians and citizens familiar with this special site: "It's a rare window into the past, where we can learn from those people what they can never tell us."

...lives lost, what they can never tell us!

Our story continues with the great destruction of September eleventh, 2001 of the World Trade Center. Because the Office of Public Education and Interpretatiion (OPEI) was located in an adjacent building that had considerable damage, it was a traumatic experience that remains in the minds of the employees. Fortunately, no members of the staff were killed.

The office was relocated to 201 Varick Street and in April 2002, the African Burial Ground site work was resumed.

A Sankofa III Conference, hosted by the College of William and Mary in Williamsburg, Virginia and started May 15, 2002 was organized by Dr. Michael Blakey. Dr. Blakey moved from Howard University in Washington, D. C. to become a professor of anthropology at the college of William and Mary and he also is the Scientific Director of the New York African Burial Ground Project.

Analysis of the discovered artifacts was continued. Many of the grave goods and artifacts buried within individual coffins had been previously removed from the World Trade Center office and shipped to Washington, D.C. for preparation of burial with the ancestral remains back in New York.

After the disaster, removal of hundreds of boxes including thousands of photos was done with the assistance of several local and federal organizations.

Beginning in 2003, the OPEI also opened an information desk at the historic site at 290 Broadway. This allows tourists, individual and groups access to the education service and informational expertise without visiting the Varick Street Office.

The reinterment ceremonies were highly successful and attended by thousands, in 2003. Howard Chaka Ferguson of the Associated Press wrote in September 2004 about the dissatisfaction of some activists regarding the Burial Ground.

When more than 400 slaves were reburied last year at a site unearthed by construction workers in lower Manhattan, the occasion was marked by singing, dancing—and promises for an elaborate memorial.

Today, the site is marked by only one small sign, continues Ferguson.

Although a large-scale memorial is in the works, those involved with the burial ground say the government needs to do more to make it a prominent landmark among New York's myriad cultural and historical attractions.

"Everybody needs to know this is not just part of African-American history, it is a part of New York history and American history," said Howard Dodson, director of the Schomburg Center for Research in Black Culture.

Closed in 1794 and long forgotten as construction landfill eventually buried it 20 feet underground, the five-acre spot was the final resting place for tens of thousands of slaves and free blacks. It was unearthed during construction of a federal office tower in 1991.

The site — today surrounded by City Hall and other municipal buildings — had as its first deadline a 12 million dollar memorial by fall 2005. Plans for a 12 million dollar interpretive center were under consideration as well.

But community activists have complained about the slow pace and selection process.

The Federal General Services Administration, which manages the site with the assistance of the National Park Service, were to choose a winning design from five finalists — called from more than 60 submissions — after public hearings.

Many blacks did not want a memorial that covered too much of the burial site or required digging because that "would further disturb our ancestors," said Ayo Harrington, chairwoman of Friends of the African Burial Ground, an informal advocacy group.

She also is disappointed that the public will not select the winning design for the memorial.

Eileen Long-Chelales, a regional administrator for the GSA, said the agency will consider public comment along with recommendations from a board that included architects and historians. The finalists already have incorporated ideas into their designs from community feedback, she said.

When the burial ground was discovered, it was community pressure that prompted the government to abandon work on the federal office tower and begin examining the remains when the burial ground was discovered. A final scientific report on the remains is expected to provide insight into the little-known lives and deaths of blacks in the northern United States.

Volunteer training sessions, film festivals and prayers and tributes continue. An African Burial Ground Kwanza Celebration at the Broadway and Duane streets site was held on Saturday December 18, 2004.

See Appendix for updated information on the memorial design, and the designer Rodney Leon who was finally selected.

OTHER ANCIENT GROUNDS BENEATH THE NEW YORK METROPOLIS

In a 1993 article for the *New York Times,* Steven Lee Myers addressed the political issues surrounding the unearthing of citywide cemeteries. Equating such activities to opening a Pandora's box, Myers wrote that efforts to study the remains of Manhattan's Negroes Burying Ground helped focus attention on the scores of other cemeteries throughout New York City, including those beneath such established sites as Washington Square, the Waldorf-Astoria Hotel, and LaGuardia Airport. Attempts to save other cemeteries have had mixed results and have incited considerable controversy.

"In Queens," reported Myers, "Mandingo Osceola Tshaka, the retired [Broadway] singer, has succeeded in forcing the Department of Parks to delay a $1.2 million renovation of a playground, Everett P. Martins Field in Flushing, after he came forward with evidence that the tiny park served as the Colored Cemetery of Flushing for much of the 1800s. Mr. Tshaka began his campaign [in the summer of 1992] after he found a 1919 survey showing four marble tombstones and newspaper clippings suggesting that hundreds of people may have been buried there until after the Civil War.

"The cemetery, on 46th Avenue at 165th Street, had gradually deteriorated into a weedy lot until the city acquired it in 1913 and later turned it into a park. [A newspaper article] in 1936 told of how workers digging the park's wading pool unearthed 'bones galore and rare pennies . . . that had covered the eyes of the dead.'" The article noted that there was no way to identify the graves, Myers explained, "so the digging was continued. . . . [In 1993] the Department of Parks . . . agreed to delay the renovation until archaeologists could study the graves." Plans to renovate the park have been canceled; the site is presently maintained by the Queens Department of Parks and Recreation.

Other slave cemeteries dot the countryside stretching to the north of New York City, including one on the south side of Phillips Road, just west of Fishkill Creek, in Hopewell Junction, Dutchess County. The site was once the property of the Storms, a family of Dutch descent. The slaves buried in the cemetery were the property of different branches of the Storm family, who shared this common burial ground for their human chattel during the eighteenth and nineteenth centuries. Restoration of the site has been undertaken by the black community of nearby Poughkeepsie.

Another cemetery for "colored inhabitants" of the nineteenth century is located in Westchester County, adjacent to Rye's Greenwood Union Cemetery. The land for the cemetery was donated by Elizabeth and Underhill Halstead in 1860 for use as a cemetery for black residents of "Rye

Town" and for black Civil War veterans. It was donated to the Rye trustees "and their successors in office forever" for use as a "cemetery or burial ground for the colored inhabitants." The Town of Rye and the City of Rye began a dispute over the cemetery and its maintenance; eventually the cemetery was forgotten. In 1981 the local newspaper took up its cause once again and the neglected cemetery was cleaned up to some degree by volunteers. But the dispute rekindled as to which government was responsible for its maintenance. In 1986, the burial site received a historic marker from the Westchester Tricentennial Commission.

Mount Moor Cemetery, considered to be the oldest African American cemetery in Rockland County, is located in the town of Clarkston, West Nyack. It contains grave sites dating back to the pre–Civil War period. The original burial grounds were purchased by a small group of black residents in 1849; the cemetery was expanded by an additional land purchase in 1855. Many black veterans of the Civil War, Spanish-American War, and other wars are buried here.

Weeksville, a nineteenth-century African American community located in the ninth ward of Brooklyn, was named for James Weeks, a black man who purchased land from the Lefferts family estate in 1838. A civic organization, the Society for the Preservation of Weeksville and Bedford-Stuyvesant History, has been established to restore the site's historic structures. Joan Maynard, in her 1983 booklet "Weeksville: Then and Now," traces the area's history from its inception as the Dutch colony of New Amsterdam in 1638. In 1646, she notes, eleven Africans were captured at sea and brought to port by the Dutch West India Company, a gigantic slave-trading operation. Some of the men remained under slavery, while others—as free blacks—purchased land that was eventually confiscated. By 1790, one-third of the county's population were slaves, making Kings County the largest slave-owning region in New York State. Maynard writes of New York's free black population:

> In the late 1700s and the early 1800s, most free blacks lived in Manhattan. They had formed many religious, social, educational, and economic organizations before the abolition of slavery in New York State in 1827. The influence of free blacks in Manhattan was enormous on their brothers and sisters in Brooklyn. The role of the black church was especially important in the lives of the people.

> In Brooklyn, churches like the Bridge Street Church, incorporated in 1818, became a station or terminal on the Underground Railroad. Siloam Presbyterian, 1847; Concord Baptist, 1848; and others formed the core of the earliest black settlement in Brooklyn. They were located near the present day downtown area of the Borough. The opening of the Brooklyn Bridge in 1883 brought new waves of settlers to Kings County and changed much of the character and identity of the early black enclaves.

The village of Brooklyn received a charter as a city in 1834; by 1896 it

had greatly increased in size. The city of Brooklyn, Kings County, was incorporated as a borough of the city of New York in 1898. Under the ward system of government, the hamlet of Bedford was a part of the original town of Brooklyn. Weeksville, a part of the ninth ward, became a Bedford neighborhood.

Near this small African American community, also within the ninth ward of Brooklyn, once stood the Citizens Union–Mount Pleasant Cemetery. Its history illustrates an all too familiar struggle. On September 1, 1851, Alexander Duncan, Robert Williams, and Charles Lewis purchased twenty-nine and a half acres of land from white landowner Johnson Leake for use as the Citizens Union Cemetery. Two months later, they formed the Citizens Union Cemetery Corporation, sold the land to the corporation, and invited others to purchase stock.

Duncan, Williams, and Lewis represented families who had been banned from burial privileges in the area's "white" cemeteries. Theirs would be a burial ground open to the colored members of the community: Fees charged for opening and closing graves were low, and other minor fees and charges were sometimes waived altogether in cases of extreme poverty.

When the corporation began to suffer losses in May 1853, the three founders and other stockholders reorganized, changed the name to Mount Pleasant Cemetery Association, and began operating as Mount Pleasant Cemetery in June of the following year. This did not solve their growing problems—financial and otherwise—which included an award by the court in favor of original landowner Leake, who regained title to the property. Leake had no use for the cemetery, so he sold it back to Duncan, then acting as association agent.

In 1869 an event occurred that at the time appeared to be a problem, but may actually have been a blessing. The city purchased a section of the land, prompting the Mount Pleasant Cemetery Association to request to sell the rest of the land for noncemetery purposes (the Eastern Parkway now covers the location). The cemetery organization was, behind the scenes, thick with conflict, misrepresentation, and personal squabbling. And the surrounding neighborhood considered the cemetery a "nuisance." In order to sell the land, according to Maynard, the cemetery had to "remove from said burial grounds, the remains of all bodies buried and now remaining therein and all monuments and headstones and reinter them to some suitable burial ground, purchased by the association for that purpose."

The cemetery association purchased a one-acre plot at neighboring Cypress Hills Cemetery and hired two men to move all of the bodies. During the process, the association discovered, to its dismay, several bodies that had been interred surreptitiously in unmarked graves, apparently by Duncan. These were removed by steam shovel and dumped along the roadside; in 1872 the board of trustees sold the Citizens Union–Mount Pleasant Cemetery land.

EXCAVATING THE FREEDMAN'S CEMETERY

In July 1990, Rod Richardson of the *Detroit News* reported on a Dallas, Texas, freeway-widening project that had been placed on hold after initial excavation had uncovered a layer of Dallas history; namely, the bodies of hundreds of former slaves and black settlers who lay buried in forgotten graves just north of the downtown area. Richardson reported that archaeologists had been called in to relocate some of the remains before work could resume on the expressway expansion through the city's center.

Road work on Dallas's North Central Expressway came to a halt after a backhoe scraped across what turned out to be portions of caskets, wooden markers, and gravestones. As more and more graves were uncovered in the path of the freeway—some containing historic relics—the official calculation for the length of time needed to complete the archaeological dig was revised from a few weeks to two years.

"It is an emotional, archeological, and historical issue," commented archaeologist (Ms.) Jerry Henderson, who oversaw the job for the State Highway and Transportation Department. "Let's face it: The people who were buried here were wronged. And it's up to us to see that their final resting place is restored and their memories preserved." More than one thousand graves were eventually identified; of those, about five hundred were moved to accommodate the freeway expansion project.

In August 1990, Lisa Belkin reported in the *New York Times* that the aptly named Freedman's Cemetery had been the burial site of as many as two thousand freed slaves and their descendants. Although few written records remain, Henderson speculated that most of the black Dallas residents buried there were interred between 1861 and 1925. More than a century ago, the area was dubbed North Dallas Freedmen Town, after the emancipated slaves who lived there. It was virtually wiped out in the 1940s, its cemetery partially desecrated, when construction began on the North Central Expressway.

A point of pride among local black residents between the Civil War and the Depression, the cemetery is not much to look at today. Over the years, its few stones have been flattened by vandals and its grounds either littered with decades of accumulated trash, partially capped by concrete, or transformed into a rarely used children's park.

The plot, which once extended over two acres, would still be a park today had it not gotten in the way of the state's plans to widen the expressway. Beginning in early 1991, residents and officials began paying attention to the cemetery. The widening was delayed for several years while workers restored parts of the original grounds and sorted through neglected decades of black history in Dallas.

Residents of Dallas who had relatives buried in the cemetery were overwhelmed by the restoration effort after years of neglect. "In my lifetime, it's a wonderful thing to see," said Dr. Robert Prince, a local physician whose family Bible documents at least four great-aunts and great-uncles at rest somewhere amid the jumble of graves.

Shortly after the plans to widen the highway were announced, Henderson took a walk around the area to study the possible effects of the proposed construction on both the environment and the historical integrity of the area. She found a sign for "Freedman's Memorial Park" that claimed the park as the site of a former cemetery. It is illegal in Texas to cover a burial plot without moving the bodies.

Henderson began to research the size of the original grounds and her best sources turned out to be the memories of Dallas citizens, particularly Prince, who had written records dating from the 1860s and a colorful oral history from earlier still. Prince, who was born in 1930, believes that the land was originally a slave cemetery; the reason that no one has discovered written records dating prior to the Civil War is because slaves were not allowed to read or write.

After the war ended, he speculated, many of the two hundred thousand newly freed slaves in Texas headed toward the cities to be closer to the Freedmen's Bureaus that were established during Reconstruction. They settled in places that were familiar; in Dallas it was the area around the slave cemetery where they pitched tents and eventually built a community.

The land that would one day house part of the cemetery was owned by William and Elizabeth Boales, former slaveholders who agreed to sell the one-acre parcel to a group of freedmen in 1869 for $25, a substantial price for the time. A decade later, an adjacent acre was bought by a larger group of freedmen for $425, payable over two years. Prince's great-grandfather, Dock Rownen, was the last surviving member of that group.

Prince recalls walking through the grounds with his great-uncles, who would point to plots marked only with wooden crosses and tell him which relative was buried in each. He remembers them telling of the 1870s, when a railroad was built through the two acres, covering many of the graves.

And he himself recalls when the original North Central Expressway was dug along the path hewn by that railroad—and still more graves were lost. Prince claims that his family was offered $10 by the state for each relative whose grave could be proved to have been moved or destroyed during the construction.

Prince watched for nearly fifty years, as the few remaining granite headstones were vandalized and the abandoned land became the property of the city. He was saddened when the land was made into a playground in 1965. As recently as five years ago, Prince asked the Parks Department to turn the park into a memorial containing a plaque or monument commemorating the site. His suggestion was not approved.

Soon after Henderson learned of the cemetery, she contacted Prince. She explained that Texas law simply required that the graves be moved. But before that was done, she wanted to excavate the entire area. "We need to know how it was laid out originally, so we can maintain its integrity," she told him. "Families were buried together. We need to keep them together."

The excavation proceeded slowly. The gray clay at the site, which stuck to the tops of the coffins when wet, cracked along the edges of the lids when it dried in the sun. During such dry periods, each of these revealed coffin outlines was traced with a piece of string and nailed to the ground for future reference. Hundreds of string outlines eventually filled the lot.

Along the way, Henderson and a half-dozen assistants discovered trinkets that had been left in the graves as gifts: a casing that once held a pocket watch, a palm-size doll carved in stone, a tiny glass vase. Only two headstones were found. One, marked only with the initials *A. T.,* was planted firmly at the foot of a grave. The other belongs to Emma, daughter of one Mary McCune, born June 29, 1855, who died May 5, 1903. Her stone was discovered lying on its side, away from any grave site. Descendants of Emma McCune contacted the highway department after reading about the stone's discovery. Archaeologists will use what they learned about McCune's life and death, along with other such information, to help piece together the Freedman's Cemetery's past.

The reinterment of the bodies posed several problems. With insufficient space to allow for reinterment in the portion of the original cemetery remaining, the archaeology crew searched for space within the limits of Calvary Street. Once called Lemmin Avenue, Calvary Street had been thought to serve as the southern boundary for Freedman's Cemetery. Once the street was donated by the city of Dallas and the pavement removed, however, 133 more burials were identified. Another option, involving acreage to the south of Freedman's Cemetery, proved more fruitful. The property had been foreclosed on and was owned by the Federal Deposit Insurance Corporation (FDIC), who cooperated with the city of Dallas to provide the land needed to relocate all the graves. A December 2, 1994, ceremony marked the closing of the eight-year project, as the last of the remains were buried in the reconfigured Freedman's Cemetery. According to Montrose Cunningham of the Texas Department of Transportation's Public Information Office, the city of Dallas plans to erect a $2 million memorial over the site.

EXCAVATING THE NEW GUINEA CEMETERY

Edna K. Luten is secretary and one of several hard-working members of Savannah, Georgia's Eugenia Cemetery Historical Society, which has undertaken the task of rejuvenating the New Guinea Cemetery. Luten reports that during the period when Negroes were held in bondage, an area located on Savannah's Old Montgomery Cross Road was set aside for slave burials. A former plantation, the property was sold to the Chatham County Commissioners for use as a prison where inmates would live self-sufficiently, raising all that they ate. The deed stipulated that the Negro cemetery must remain as a burial ground.

Down through the years, the fact that the county owned the New Guinea Cemetery was forgotten, although area residents continued to bury ex-slaves and descendants there. In 1953, realizing the importance of keeping the graveyard clean, a group of people from community churches began to hold monthly meetings on cemetery grounds. They established a five-dollar cleaning fee per burial and ten cent contributions per member per meeting. They also sold fish and chicken dinners in order to pay attorney Harry Ginsburg to do research on the cemetery land.

Ginsburg's research revealed that the property was indeed owned by the county; the deed was recorded in the Chatham County Courthouse. In 1980 the Department of Transportation decide to widen Old Montgomery Cross Road, planning to move the dead and relocate them elsewhere. After months of meeting, wrangling, and arguing with county commissioners, the Eugenia Cemetery Historical Society was offered the deed to a portion of the cemetery, set off by a brick fence. The county's roadwork ended up encroaching only fifteen feet into the north side and fifteen feet onto the south side.

The society was asked to provide a list of officers, trustees, and meeting dates for county review. On May 6, 1992, after four weeks of legal advertisement, the society was notified of the date for the planned sale. Their president, trustees, and members met with county officials on June 1, 1992, and bid one dollar for the land. The deed to the cemetery property was presented and accepted, officially giving members of the Eugenia Cemetery Historical Society title to the land where their descendants lie buried and which they continue to maintain today. For more information about the purchase of Eugenia Cemetery, please see next chapter.

WESTWOOD CEMETERY

Wellington-Oberlin, in Lorain County, Ohio, became the site of a slave rescue that was said to have raised nationwide consciousness of the antislavery movement. In 1858, John Price, a fugitive slave living in Oberlin, fell into the hands of four slave catchers using the ruse of offering him a job picking tomatoes at a local farm. However, halfway to Wellington, a small town south of Oberlin where the slave catchers intended to put Price on a train bound for Kentucky, they were spotted. A crowd gathered and freed Price.

Up to the Civil War Lorain County served as a passage for many fugitive slaves heeding the instructions of abolitionist Frederick Douglass, who counselled following the North Star to freedom in Canada. Oberlin's Westwood Cemetery is now the final resting place for many of these fugitive slaves, as well as area activists. In fact, Westwood lays claim to being one of the first cemeteries in the United States to bury all races together, with no distinction made between blacks and whites. The cemetery now provides many visitors with a reflective, meditative setting in which to explore the histories of those who effected vital changes in U.S. civil rights.

Many famous African Americans have called Lorain County home for varying amounts of time. **John Mercer Langston** was perhaps Oberlin's most famous African American. The son of an enslaved mother and white father, he was born into slavery on a Virginia plantation. Langston moved to Oberlin for an education and became the first black attorney in Ohio, the first black to practice law before the U.S. Supreme Court, and the first black to be elected to any office in the nation. He was also the first black homeowner on Oberlin's East College Street, a prestigious address then shared by only the city's most prominent and wealthy citizens. Langston served on the board of education in Oberlin for eleven years and was responsible for the formation of the 127th Colored Ohio Volunteer Infantry. He was a president of the Equal Rights League—the forerunner of the National Association for the Advancement of Colored People (NAACP)—and fought hard against slavery and for the enfranchisement of blacks; became inspector general of the postwar Freedmen's Bureau; established the law department; and eventually became president of Howard University. Langston served as minister to Haiti in 1877 and later became the first and, as yet, only black congressman from Virginia.

Other activists from Oberlin, Ohio who are buried at Westwood Cemetery include:

Lewis Clarke—Known for being the "real George Harris," Clarke's life formed the basis for that character in Harriet Beecher Stowe's *Uncle Tom's Cabin*. He made a daring escape from slavery and risked recapture by appearing as a speaker at abolitionist meetings in the free states. When Clarke died, the governor of Kentucky ordered that his body lie in state so that people could pay homage to the ex-slave who made an impact on pre–Civil War history.

John Copeland—Copeland was an Oberlin carpenter and freeborn black who was the son of a slave. He was very active in the Oberlin Anti-Slavery Society and was well known for his fiery activism. Copeland played a role in the Wellington-Oberlin slave rescue, and it was rumored that he escorted fugitive slave John Price to freedom in Canada. Copeland was in the rifle works at Harpers Ferry when it was assaulted by Lee's troops. As a result, he was wounded, captured, and almost lynched on the spot. After a local minister saved him, he was charged with treason, convicted, and sentenced to be hanged. He said before his execution, "If I am dying for freedom, I could not die for a better cause—I'd rather die than be a slave!" He was hanged, after John Brown, on December 16, 1859. Like others, his body was stolen by medical students from Winchester Medical College. At the request of

the deceased's family, James Monroe traveled to Virginia to retrieve Copeland's body but was unable to do so. A memorial service was held for Copeland and fellow-activist Shields Green on Christmas Day, 1859, at the First Church in Oberlin.

Marie DeFrance—DeFrance was the only single black woman who owned her own business in Oberlin during the period. Called Millinery M. DeFrance, her shop was located at 24 South Main Street. She operated it for thirty-five years while living with her mother at 103 East College Street.

Lee Howard Dobbins—Dobbins was a four-year-old slave child who, in 1853, died in Oberlin on his way to freedom in Canada. His mother had died in slavery; his adoptive mother was forced to leave the boy behind in Oberlin because he was too ill with consumption to travel. Dobbins died several days later in the care of an Oberlin family. A funeral was held in Oberlin's First Church, where over one thousand attended. A granite plaque was installed in honor of Lee Howard Dobbins. The above marker reads:

> In Memory of The Fugitive Slaves Whose Journey To Freedom Brought Them To Oberlin

> Shielded By An Almighty Arm Thy Griefs And Sufferings Now Are O'er Beyond The Reach Of Tyranant's Harm Freed Spirit, Rest Forever More!

> Lone Little Wanderer, Now No More Mid Stranger Hearts To Seek For Love Thou'st Gained Thy Home, Thy Native Shore And Boundless Love Thy Bliss Will Prove

> Thy Father Called Thee Suffering One He Knew And Felt Thy Untold Grief To Him Complexions All Are One He Died Alike For Their Relief

> Lee Howard Dobbins, Age 4 yrs, died in Oberlin

> A Fugitive Slave Orphan March 26, 1853

Shields Green—Green was a runaway slave from South Carolina and a newcomer to Oberlin when he left to help John Brown. His real name was Esau Brown; he used Shields Green for the sake of anonymity. He escaped to Canada but later moved to Rochester, New York, and became a servant to Frederick Douglass. Green decided to join John Brown's army against the wishes of Douglass, who knew the raid meant certain death. Green was hanged for his participation on December 16, 1859, alongside John Copeland.

Mary Kellogg—A Louisiana slave who was willed by her father to the wife of Oberlin College president James Fairchild, Kellogg was the mulatto daughter of a wealthy plantation owner. Arriving at Fairchild's home at the age of forty-three, Kellogg was immediately emancipated but remained with Fairchild and his family as their servant.

Sarah "Margu" Kinson (Green)—Green was the youngest passenger on the slave ship *Amistad* when the slaves aboard successfully mutinied. The ship floated into Long Island Sound in 1839, where, fortunately for those on board, the slave trade was illegal. After a long court battle, the slaves were freed by the Supreme Court in 1841. "Margu," as she was called, was from Kaw Mendi, West Africa. She was the first female foreign student and first African to study at an American college—Oberlin College. After spending time at Oberlin, Margu returned to Africa as a missionary.

Lewis Sheridan Leary—Leary, along with fellow-Oberlinite John Copeland, was in the rifle works at Harpers Ferry when it was assaulted. He died the next day after being shot and wounded. Leary was twenty-four years old at the time of his death. His body, along with two others, was stolen by local medical students; he was eventually buried at John Brown's farm in North Elba, New York, along with others killed during the raid. Previous to the raid, Leary played a role in the Wellington-Oberlin slave rescue but was not indicted. He is also known for his address to a meeting of the anti-slavery society, where he said, "Man must suffer for a good cause."

John H. Scott—Scott was a freed slave who became a harness and trunkmaker in Oberlin. He joined the Fifth Ohio Cavalry in 1865. Scott also gained a reputation as a fervent temperance man. In one instance, he became incensed when an Elyria beer company sent a wagon to Oberlin to sell its product, believing that black residents were being targeted as the wagon's best patrons.

Orindatus S. B. Wall—This emancipated slave was the son of a slave woman and a wealthy planter. Active with John Mercer Langston (his brother-in-law) in recruiting black troops to serve in the U.S. Army, Wall became the first regularly commissioned black captain in the army early in 1865. He was a member of the first graduating class of Howard University and went on to become a lawyer in Washington, D.C.

Africanisms and Burial Customs

Africanisms involve a body of knowledge that is often passed down from the oldest living members of the community. The encompassing expressions, sayings, and superstitions relate to music, dance, religious beliefs and practices, and the arts. Many of the stories and superstitions relating to death and burials are still told and believed today, especially in the southern United States. Since the Sea Islands, particularly, have strongly rooted Africanisms, their culture is assured of a continued relationship with the African homeland. The countries of Angola and Sierra Leone are most commonly thought of as having the closest identification to their African heritage.

The psychic atmosphere that encompassed African village life was—and in some instances, still is—rooted in a belief in mystic powers. Many manifestations of this belief remain with us today. There exists, however, a distinction between those that have become integrated into the African American belief system and those that are "lighthearted" mental challenges. The dividing line is hazy; each must make the determination for himself:

- Every effort must be made to carry out the wishes of the dead, carefully. For if this is not done, the dead person will haunt the family or the individual responsible for going against his wishes.

- The dead look out for their loved ones.

- If a dog howls or a rooster crows in the doorway, it is a sign that someone will die.

- When an individual is asleep, his spirit leaves his body. Therefore, if you harass him and he wakes up before his spirit has returned, he will die.

- Don't kill a bluebird—this means bad luck—and if a spider descends on a string of his web, don't let him rise again. This means death.

- If anyone is lying down, don't step over him or you'll catch all of his sickness and possibly die.

Reverend A. C. Redd of Augusta, Georgia, a former trustee of Penn Center in St. Helena, South Carolina, provides a list of Africanisms in *African American Funerary Practices* that helps illustrate some of the superstitions and words of advice that prevailed in times past. Others are definitions of much-used terms:

- Animism: The belief that natural phenomena and animate and inanimate things have an innate soul or spirit.

- Breaking dishes: This act releases the spirit.

- Secondary burials/presermons: Final ceremonies that also mark the end of mourning.

- Decoration of graves with household items or personal possessions: This reflects the belief that items are there for the spirit.

- The soul leaves the body via the mouth.

- Importance of being buried feet facing east: To allow rising at Judgment Day; otherwise the person is in the crossways of the world.

- Singing style: Rhythm is emphasized more than melody or harmony during grave-side hymns.

- If it rains while a man is dying, or if the lightning strikes near his house, the devil has come for his soul.

- It is thought to be bad for anyone to work around a dead person when he is tired, that is, in a weakened condition where spiritual harm might result.

- Among the West Africans, an old saying existed about the need to dig a grave over several days, because of the danger that a fatigued worker might perspire and allow a drop of sweat to fall in the excavation. The ghost could then utilize this to take with him the soul of the one who had labored too hard.

- Always cover the body; never place it directly on the ground.

- A dead person's spirit remains on earth and can do good or evil.

- Coins were placed on the eyes of the dead to keep them closed. However, coins were also sometimes placed in the hands as the deceased person's contribution to the community of the ancestors— or perhaps, as a token for admittance to the spirit world.

- Ceremoniously broken possessions of the deceased should be placed on top of the grave to prevent the spirit from returning to this world in search of them. Breaking objects also breaks the chain of death, or saves other family members from immediately following the deceased in death. Lamps found on the graves symbolically provided light for the spirit searching for home. Bed frames were also placed on graves so that the spirits could rest while journeying home.

The Book of Negro Folklore provides a startling and exciting look at the many superstitions concerning the dead. According to this source, all over the South—as well as in the Bahamas—the spirits of the dead have great power, which they use chiefly to harm.

- Frequently, graveyard dust—often called "goofer dust"—is required in the practice of hoodoo (a black version of the familiar word "voodoo").

- The Ewe-speaking peoples of the west coast of Africa all make offerings of food and drink— particularly libations of palm wine and banana beer—upon the graves of the ancestor. In America the spirit is always given a pint of good whisky.

- It is well known that church members are buried with their feet to the east so that they will arise on that last day facing the rising sun. Sinners are buried facing the opposite direction. The theory is that sunlight will do them harm rather than good, as they will no doubt wish to hide their faces from an angry God.

- Ghosts cannot cross water—so if a hoodoo doctor wishes to sic a dead spirit upon a man who lives across water, he must first hold the mirror ceremony to fetch his victim from across the water.

- People who die from the sick bed may walk any night, but Friday night is the night of the people who died in the dark— those who were executed. These people have never been in the light. They died with a black cap over the face. Thus, they are blind. On Friday nights they visit the folks who died from sick beds and they lead the blind ones wherever they wish to visit.

- Ghosts feel hot and smell faintish. According to testimony, all except those who died in the dark may visit their former homes every night at twelve o'clock. But they must be back in the cemetery at two o'clock sharp or they will be shut out by the watchman and must wander about for the rest of the night. That is why the living are

GO DOWN DEATH

DAY BEFORE YESTERDAY MORNING

GOD WAS LOOKING DOWN FROM HIS GREAT,

    HIGH HEAVEN

LOOKING DOWN ON ALL HIS CHILDREN

AND HIS EYE FELL ON MY SISTER CAROLINE

TOSSING ON HER BED OF PAIN

AND DEATH HEARD THE SUMMONS,

AND HE LEAPED ON HIS FASTEST HORSE,

PALE AS A SHEET IN THE MOONLIGHT.

UP THE GOLDEN STREET DEATH GALLOPED,

AND THE HOOF OF HIS HORSE STRUCK FIRE FROM

    THE GOLD,

BUT THEY DIDN'T MAKE NO SOUND.

UP DEATH RODE TO THE GREAT WHITE THRONE,

AND WAITED FOR GOD'S COMMAND.

AND GOD SAID: GO DOWN DEATH, GO DOWN,

GO DOWN TO SAVANNAH, GEORGIA,

DOWN IN THE YAMACRAW,

AND FIND SISTER CAROLINE.

SHE'S BORNE THE BURDEN AND HEAT OF THE DAY,

SHE LABORED LONG IN MY VINEYARD,

AND SHE'S TIRED—

SHE'S WEARY—

GO DOWN, DEATH, AND BRING HER TO ME.

—JAMES WELDON JOHNSON

frightened by seeing ghosts at times. Some spirit has lingered too long with the living person it still loves and has been shut out of its resting place.

- Dirt from sinners' graves is supposed to be very powerful, but some hoodoo doctors will use only dirt from the graves of infants. They say that dirt from a sinner's grave is powerful enough to kill, but the spirit is likely to get unruly and kill others for the pleasure of killing. It becomes too dangerous to commission.

- The spirit newly released from the body is likely to be destructive. This is why a cloth is thrown over the face of a clock in the death chamber and the looking glass is covered over. The clock will never run again, nor will the mirror ever cast any more reflections, if they are not covered so that the spirit cannot see them.

- When it rains at a funeral it is said that God wishes to wash the tracks of the deceased off the face of the earth, they were so displeasing to him.

- If a murder victim is buried in a sitting position, the murderer will be speedily brought to justice. The victim sitting before the throne is able to demand that justice be done. If he is lying prone he cannot do this.

- A fresh egg in the hand of a murder victim will prevent the murderer from going far from the scene. The egg represents life; the dead victim is holding the life of the murderer in his hand.

- Sometimes the dead are offended by acts of the living and slap the faces of the living. When this happens, the head is slapped one-sided and the victim can never straighten his neck. Speak gently to ghosts, and do not abuse the children of the dead.

- At any time, anywhere, it is not good to answer the first time your name is called. It may be a spirit and if you answer it, you will die shortly. They never call more than once at a time, so by waiting you will miss probable death.

This list by no means exhausts the monumental collection of sayings, beliefs, and superstitions that exist around burial traditions, but these are among the most lively and thought-provoking.

Africa is a large continent with many different cultural groups. Many are poorly understood. The 10 to 20 million Africans forcefully transported as slaves to the shores of the United States came from a number of different cultures. Further complicating this approach is the interaction of different religious beliefs once the slaves arrived on the plantations - most planters were Christians, while some blacks were Moslems and many others held other religious beliefs.

One anthropologist, Margaret Washington Creel, has examined a range of African beliefs and religious practices in an effort to better understand slave religion. In her study, *"A Peculiar People": Slave Religion and Community-Culture Among the Gullahs*, she explores the beliefs of the BaKongo, Ovimbundu, and other groups on the Windward and Gold Coasts.

African American slaves died by the thousands. One study, for example, found that the mortality rate of black children on the South Carolina and Georgia coastal rice plantations was astonishingly high - nearly 90% of all children died before they reached the age of 16 years. Even on more interior cotton plantations it is likely that nearly one out of every three slave children died before adulthood. Death was certainly a way of life for African American slaves and they had ample opportunities to make the trip from slave settlement to cemetery for their friends and family.

Thomas Chaplin, a Sea Island cotton planter on St. Helena Island in Beaufort County, South Carolina, mentions the making or purchasing of coffins for black slaves on two occasions. He describes only one African American burial, on May 6, 1850:

Got Uncle Ben's [slave] Paul to make coffin for poor old Anthony. The body begins to smell very bad already, had it put in the coffin as soon as it came. Buried the body alongside of his son about 11 o'clock at night.... There were a large number of Negroes from all directions present, I suppose over two hundred.

At another nineteenth century South Carolina slave burial reported by Creel:

Calling Upon the Spirits

Perhaps the simplest way for an ordinary person to see ghosts is to look back over his or her own left shoulder, though the same result may be accomplished by looking through a mule's ear; by punching a small hole in your ear; by looking into a mirror with another person; by breaking a raincrow's egg into some water and washing your face in it; or by breaking a stick in two.

Some say that if you go to the graveyard at twelve o'clock noon and call the name of anyone you know who has died, his or her spirit will answer you, though generally the procedure is more complicated. Some suggest that you go to a graveyard at twelve o'clock noon or midnight and take with you a piece of mirror and a pair of new steel scissors. At exactly twelve o'clock, hold up the mirror before your eyes and drop the scissors on the ground. Call upon that person with whom you desire to talk. You'll see his or her reflection in the mirror and can ask of that person what you please. The blades of the scissors will begin to work of their own accord, metaphorically cutting away any doubt or fear that might arise in your mind.

Another method involves putting half a dozen pure white dinner plates around the table at home, and then proceeding into the graveyard at twelve noon. Call the name of a dead acquaintance. His or her spirit will answer you at once.

The coffin, a rough home-made affair, was placed upon a cart, which was drawn by an old Gray, and the multitudes formed in a line in the rear, marching two deep. The procession was something like a quarter of a mile long. Perhaps every fifteenth person down the line carried an uplifted torch. As the procession moved slowly toward "the lonesome graveyard" down by the side of the swamp, they sung the well-known hymn:

"When I can read my title clear

To mansions in the skies,

I bid farewell to every fear

and wipe my weeping eyes."

.... the corpse was lowered into the grave and covered, each person throwing a handful of dirt into the grave as a last farewell act of kindness to the dead.... A prayer was offered.... This concluded the services at the grave.

Yet another slave burial, on Georgia's Butler Island, was described by Frances Anne Kemble in early 1839:

Yesterday evening the burial of the poor man Shadrack took place.... just as the twilight was thickening into darkness I went with Mr. [Butler] to the cottage of one of the slaves ... who was to perform the burial service. The coffin was laid on trestles in front of the cooper's cottage, and a large assemblage of the people had gathered round, many of the men carrying pine-wood torches .... the coffin being taken up, proceeded to the people's burial ground.... When the coffin was lowered the grave was found to be partially filled with water - naturally enough, for the whole island is a mere swamp, off which the Altamaha is only kept from sweeping by the high dikes all round it. This seemed to shock and distress the people ....

All of these slave burials are similar. They seem to have invariably taken place at night, possibly to allow slaves from neighboring plantations to attend, but just as likely because no other time was available. This may help explain why so many African American burials continued to be held on Sundays even into the early twentieth century. All of the accounts suggest that the burials were rather significant affairs, with prayers, singing, and sometimes even an air of a pageant. Sometimes the service was reported to continue until the morning. Many accounts from the mid- and late-nineteenth century reveal that African Americans were uniformly buried east-west, with the head to the west. One freed slave explained that the dead should not have to turn around when Gabriel blows his trumpet in the eastern sunrise. Others have suggested they were buried facing Africa.

Even where the slaves were buried seems similar. All seem to represent marginal property - land which the planter wasn't likely to use for other purposes. The burial spots have been described as "ragged patches of live-oak and palmetto and brier tangle which throughout the Islands are a sign of graves within, - graves scattered without symmetry, and often without head-stones or head-boards, or sticks ...." A more recent researcher, Elsie Clews Parsons, observes that the African American cemeteries were:

> hidden away in remote spots among trees and underbrush In the mid-dle of some fields are islands of large trees the owners preferred not to make arable, because of the exhaustive work of clearing it. Old graves are now in among these trees and surrounding underbrush.

Frances Anne Kemble reported that while an enclosure was erected around the graves of several white laborers buried on Butler Island, the graves of the African American slaves were trampled on by the plantation cattle.

A black cemetery in the South Carolina up country was described by John William DeForest shortly after the Civil War. He commented that while a few marble and brick headstones were present, most were "wooden slabs, all grimed and mouldering with the dampness of the forest...." At the time, some of the wooden slabs had painted names and dates. The paint likely flaked off only shortly before the wood itself rotted away.

Graves were marked in a variety of ways besides wood or stone slabs. Sometimes unusual carved wooden staffs, thought perhaps to represent reli-gious motifs or effigies, were used. Some graves were marked using plants, such as cedars or yuccas, and anthropologists have suggested this tradition may reflect an African belief in the living spirit. This tradition can be traced at least to Haiti, where blacks, probably mixing Christian religion with African beliefs, explain that, "trees live after, death is not the end." Yuccas and other "prickly" plants may also have been used "to keep the spirits" in the cemetery. Other graves were marked with pieces of iron pipe, railroad iron, or any other convenient object.

At times shells were used to mark the grave. One anthropologist in the early 1890s remarked that "nearly every grave has bordering or thrown upon it a few bleached sea-shells of a dozen different kinds." This practice has been traced back to at least the BaKongo belief that the sea shell encloses the soul's immortal presence. There was a prayer to the mbamba sea shell:

> As strong as your house you shall keep my life for me. When you leave for the sea, take me along, that I may live forever with you.

Even into the twentieth century some Gullah explained the use of shells on graves as representing the sea:

> The sea brought us, the sea shall take us back. So the shells upon our graves stand for water, the means of glory and the land of demise.

Probably the most commonly known African American grave marking practice was the use of "offerings" on top of the grave. One of most detailed discussions of this practice is provided by John Michael Vlach, in *The Afro-American Tradition in Decorative Arts*. He notes that the objects found on graves included not only pottery, but also "cups, saucers, bowls, clocks, salt and pepper shakers, medicine bottles, spoons, pitchers, oyster shells, conch shells, white pebbles, toys, dolls' heads, bric-a-brac statues, light bulbs, tureens, flashlights, soap dishes, false teeth, syrup jugs, spectacles, cigar boxes, piggy banks, gun locks, razors, knives, tomato cans, flower pots, marbles, bits of plaster, [and] toilet tanks."

This practice may be traced back to Africa, where a wide variety of items used by the dead individual were placed on the grave. Some believe that the symbolism is that of the body destroyed by death. Others trace the practice to a belief that the practice guards the grave, preventing the dead from returning to direct the lives of those still living. Some suggest the symbolism of the various items is particularly important - with reflective items, like glass and mirrors, used to show the "mirror image" of this life compared to the next. Other items focus on water as symbolism, both as representing how African Americans were transported as slaves and also as representing how they will be transported into the next world. A number of the grave goods are also "killed," or deliberately damaged. This is to perhaps help the item to stay in the afterlife with its owner.

Writing in the first quarter of the twentieth century, Elsie Clews Parsons commented that African American cemeteries did not typically preserve family groupings. Although generations of related kin would be buried at the same graveyard, the tie was to the location, not to a particular three by six foot piece of ground. The Bennett Papers, in the South Carolina Historical Society, reveal several stories of African Americans wanting to be buried in very specific graveyards, although specific plots are never of concern. In one case a black was reported to have specifically warned his friends, "don't bury me in strange ground; I won't stay buried if you do. Bury me where I say." A somewhat similar account is provided in an article from the *Journal of American Folklore*. An article recounts the legend of a slave who begged not to be buried in the graveyard of his mean-spirited master. When his dying request was ignored, he found retribution by haunting the plantation.

Creel offers one of the more detailed explorations of African American beliefs toward death during slavery, noting that many of the spirituals provide rare glimpses of the slaves' belief systems. One, in particular, was especially telling:

I wonder where my mudder gone;

Sing, O graveyard!

Graveyard ought to know me;

Ring, Jerusalem!

Grass grow in de graveyard;

Sing, O Graveyard!

Graveyard ought to know me;

Ring, Jerusalem!

Creel observes that while the anguish is clearly conveyed by this song, so too is a sense of hope - most clearly revealed in the line, "Grass grow in de graveyard." She relates this to the BaKongo tradition that although there is certainly death, there is also life and rebirth. She wonders if the line, "Graveyard ought to know me" is a reference to the many trips slaves took there burying their friends or family, or whether it might have a deeper meaning, perhaps referring to the slaves' previous journeys to the world of the dead as "seekers."

A map of Palmetto Grove Cemetery on the marsh of Boone Hall Creek in Charleston County shows the location of graves identified during an archaeological survey of the tract. This cemetery also helped us better understand burial practices among slaves and freedmen shortly after the Civil War. For example, the burials were typically fairly shallow, with none being deeper than perhaps four feet. There was evidence of both coffins and bodies wrapped in shrouds. A large number of coffin hardware items were recovered, including handles, thumbscrews, escutcheons, studs, coffin screws and tacks, and several coffin plates. In fact, at least seven silvered coffin plates were found. Curiously, there is one account of African American folklore in the Bennett Papers which explains that a "silver coffin-plate with the name of the deceased is believed to confine the spirit of the dead to its proper resting-place to constrain it to remain within the coffin."

Stories and Folktales Through the Years

There are many stories and folktales that have been carried down through the years. During the days of enslavement, the historical presence of Africa helped to insure the survival of families in the culture. Language usage, folktales, and religious practices from the homeland were the source of an almost limitless number of songs, spirituals, and stories passed on from generation to generation. With their imagination and ingenuity, the enslaved would, untiringly, try to amuse themselves. Sometimes, sittting in the sultry summertime with its accompanying humiliations—mosquitoes, sand flies, and plagues of small-pox—the repetition of stories was inevitable. The beauty of the spoken word shone brightly; lending meaning to the past and nurturing the strength and hope needed for times to come. A few of the favorite stories are included here.

"VOICES IN THE GRAVEYARD"

As with many of the stories and folktales included in this section, little is known about the origin of "Voices in the Graveyard." However, the story, beloved by most who hear it, maintains a cadence and flow that reflect both the fun and sense of mischief of the narrative.

One night two slaves on the Byars plantation entered the potato house of the master and stole a sack of sweet potatoes. They decided that the best place to divide them would be down in the graveyard, where they would not be disturbed. So they went down there and started dividing the potatoes.

Another slave, Isom, who had been visiting a neighboring plantation, happened to be passing that way on the road home, and, hearing voices in the graveyard, he decided to stop and overhear what was being said. It was too dark for him to see, but when he stopped he heard one of the thieves saying, in a singsong voice, "Ah'll take dis un, an' yuh take dat un. Ah'll take dis un, an' yuh take dat un."

"Lawd, ha' mercy," said Isom to himself, "Ah b'lieve dat Gawd an' de debbil am down hyeah dividin' up souls. Ah's gwine an' tell ol' Massa."

Isom ran as fast as he could up to the master's house and said, "Massa, Ah's passin' th'oo de graveya'd jes' now, an' what yuh reckon Ah heerd? Gawd an' de debbil's down dar dividin' up souls. Ah sho' b'lieves de Day ob Jedgment am come."

"You don't know what you are talking about," said the master. "That's foolish talk. You know you are not telling the truth."

"Yas, sah, Massa, Yas, sah, Ah is. Ef yuh don' b'lieve hit, cum go down dar yo'se'f."

"All right," said the master, "and if you are lying to me I am going to whip you good tomorrow."

"Aw right, Massa," said Isom, "case Gawd an' de debbil sho' am down dere."

Sure enough when Isom and the master got near the graveyard they heard the singsong voice saying, "Yuh take dis un, an' Ah'll take dat un."

"See dar, didn' Ah tell yuh, Massa?" said Isom.

In the meantime the two slaves had almost finished the division of the potatoes, but remembered they had dropped two over by the fence, where Isom and the master were standing out of sight. Finally when they had only two potatoes left, the one who was counting said, "Ah take dese two an' yuh take dem two over dere by de fence."

Upon hearing this, Isom and the master ran home as fast as they could go. After this the master never doubted Isom's word about what he saw or heard.

"EARLY ONE MORNING" AND OTHER SEA ISLAND TALES

"Early one mornin', Death come creepin' in m'room!"

Martha Jenkins of Coffin's Point Plantation in St. Helena Island, South Carolina, tells an eerie tale set forth in *Reminiscences of Sea Island Heritage:*

> My cousin an' some other boys went huntin' one day, an' they hunt all through the graveyard. An' while they was in there, he pick up this clock off of one of the graves an' brought it home an' clean it up. After cleanin' it, it start to run. So he put it on his dresser in his room.
>
> That night after he went to bed, ev'rytime he doze off, that thing tell him: "Bring my clock back!"
>
> That went on all night. An' early the nex' mornin,' he got his brother with him, an' he took that clock back! An' that person did not bother him anymore!

The Sea Islands are noted as a haven of lingering spirits. Tales of haints and hags abound, as well as belief in root doctors, hoodoo, or black magic. A dying custom, most probably of African origin, called for placing a dead person's personal effects—pipes, pots, pans, jewelry, and clocks—upon his or her grave. Accordingly, a person's "spirit," when freed from the grave, would "go after" whoever disturbed its grave site. Jenkins continues:

> My grandaunt died an' they give us [Jenkins, her sisters, and brother] all her things: broom, bucket, dipper an' a rockin' chair. So that night [after the burial], she came in the house an' she played with everything that they give us. An' she did that all night! The rocking chair creaked, the water dipper clanged against the metal bucket, and the broom's sweeping sounds spooked the listeners' ears until morning.

Another custom witnessed on St. Helena Island was the placing of a dollar bill in the first grave of a cemetery before the casket was lowered. The action was to "pay the ground" for receiving the dead. And a deceased person's family members younger than age six were passed once back and forth

Rediscovering Our Roots Through Jumping the Broom

During the antebellum period, black Americans customarily gathered for burial ceremonies to perform a traditional dance which had great religious and cultural significance. Known as the Circle Dance in West and Central Africa, it was and is called "ring shouts" or "plantation walk-around" in black American culture. Although styles of shouts vary greatly from community to community, they share basic similarities. All ring shouts combine music and dancing in a counterclockwise circle. In some cases, the feet are never lifted from the floor, but are shuffled one in front of the other.

These words are spoken with complete wonder and respect by Elaine Nichols, curator of the South Carolina State Museum in Columbia, who recorded her knowledge of early African customs in her pamphlet "The Last Miles of the Way."

A growing number of African Americans have begun to reexamine slavery, remembering it through ritual and ceremony, in an attempt to celebrate the spirit of ingenuity and survival that existed in the face of suffering. It is not unusual to find African Americans celebrating history by incorporating the customs of their forefathers, especially burial customs, such as the ring shouts.

continued on next page

over the opened casket to keep the dead person's spirit from bothering them.

Because it was believed that the spirits of the dead roamed about, particularly in graveyards, cemeteries were shunned as much as possible. Jenkins begins another tale:

One day we went in the graveyard to get some hick'ry nuts. An' while we was there getting those nuts, we heard these footsteps! We listen for awhile . . . but after we didn't hear them again, we didn't think anything about it.

When we hear it again, it was right up on us! We then turn and run, but we remember what our dad use to say: "If anything scare you an' you run, make sure you don't fall. Because if you do an' that thing stop over you, you will die!" So I don't think any one of us fall—because every one of us is still here today!

Another traditional bogey, the hag, still haunts the minds of those who believe in it. Whenever a person is unable to sleep soundly or awaken completely, and has a frightening feeling of being smothered and weighted on their face and chest, and "hearing" screams that are inaudible—it is said that they are being "ridden" by a hag.

A hag, supposedly, straddles an individual's face and "rides" them, causing disorientation and panic. Unbelievers say that the state of being hag-ridden arises from poor blood circulation, nervousness, or excessive worrying.

Tale bearers, though, declare that hags are ordinary community members who are empowered to shed their human skins, change their forms to become invisible, and torment others by "riding" them. One could rid himself of a hag by throwing salt at it (in which case it could not return to its human skin and, consequently, would die) or by cursing at it vehemently. Others would pray. Babies were protected by placing matchsticks in their hair. Embellishments of the belief include:

- A hag sucked the blood out of an individual and sold it for profit; hence, if a supposedly poor neighbor spoke frequently about visits to distant places, he or she was labeled a "hag."

- A hag was any elderly family member who wanted to get back at someone who had wronged or annoyed him or her.

- If a broom was placed near the doorway, a hag, even in its human form, would not enter someone's house.

TALES OF BROTHER RABBIT

Storytelling was one of the slaves' most successful methods of maintaining their native language and remembering their customs. In order to placate eavesdropping slaveholders, the slaves used Brother Rabbit—sometimes "Bra Rabbit" or "Brer Rabbit"—as their hero, often representing him as a helpless creature. They wittingly, however, gave their hero characteristics that allowed him to "outdo" bigger and stronger animals. Brother Rabbit was cunning, amusing, and even sometimes naive.

A group of St. Helena Island residents and students under the direction of Penn Center's executive director, Emory Campbell, and project director, Walter R. Mack, compiled a compelling booklet called *Five Gullah Folktales*. These tales exemplify those that were derived from African folklore and have existed in the Sea Island culture (South Carolina, Georgia, and Florida) for more than two hundred years. What follows are the Gullah versions—a language that combines West African dialects with English—and the English version of a story recorded by Matthew Polite.

continued from previous page

Although such introspection is not new, some recent scholars say that this celebration, recently inspired by the Afrocentric movement, represents a transition from shame and denial about slavery to an embrace of that painful past. The unsealing of memory has taken place in many ways. Across America, black couples jump over a broom to seal the bond of matrimony, a ritual created by slaves, who were often forbidden to marry.

Harriette Cole, an editor at *Essence* magazine and the author of *Jumping the Broom*, says that the flourishing of such rituals shows that many blacks are beginning to understand that they do not have to reach back to Africa for tradition. "We can go to our grandparents, our great-grandparents. We have family we can trace back to slavery," Cole says.

And the customs continue. According to Nichols, many years ago—to protect children from spirits and to alleviate any fears of the dead—children were sometimes passed over a deceased person's coffin. Babies and young children were passed over the coffin of their relatives, especially deceased parents and grandparents. The preservation of this custom, occasionally still practiced in the Carolina low country, is one example of cultural continuity in both form and function. It keeps the child from fretting or being afraid of the dead, and it keeps the spirit from claiming the life of the child. Any attempts by the spirit to haunt or harm the child are thwarted.

continued on next page

continued from previous page

Although some might perceive the adherence to such a custom as strange, others see within the act a respectful observance of tradition. Ms. Thomas, manager of the Shrine of the Black Madonna bookstore in Atlanta and creator of its exhibit, "The Black Holocaust," which has drawn more than fifty thousand visitors, explains the resurgence of interest in the slave trade and black rituals quite succinctly: "Every group of people is allowed to remember the past and pay homage to those who have come before them. Why shouldn't we? It's that whole ritual of memory and honor. That's part of being human."

Bra Rabbit an Bra Shaak: Gullah Version

Dere was a island, an Bra Rabbit he had ta go oba dere ta marry dis couple. So, wen he got down dere, ebrybody don leabe Bra Rabbit.

So, Rabbit play a trick. Call Bra Shaak ta take him oba on dis island. So, Bra Shaak come, you kno, an Rabbit got on de shaak back an went on cross, come ta de islant. Come back down again. De people done leabe him again. He hadn't pay Bra Shaak nottin, now.

So, he call Bra Shaak again. Bra Shaak come back. Come sho, an Rabbit got on Shaak back an e take him back oba.

So, Bra Rabbit ta keep from pain Bra Shaak, he said, "Hmmm, Bra Shaak, A smell you back fin stink."

Bra Shaak say, "Wa you say Bra Rabbit?"

"Man, we mos git ta sho!"

Wen dey git ta sho dat he could jomp off, he say de same ting again. An Bra Shaak look aroun. Bra Rabbit jomp op an gone.

Now Bra Shaak he gone study way how ta ketch Bra Rabbit. He went on de sho an play ded. De people come by an carry de nyews ta Bra Rabbit. Bra Rabbit comin back now ta preach his funeral. An Bra Shaak gon habe de chance ta ketch Bra Rabbit.

So, Bra Rabbit said, "Why, Shaak can't be ded! Man, bot Shaak can't be ded! Him just bring me oba yestaday."

Day tell um, "Well, bot Shaak's ded now."

So, Rabbit went down dere wid his Bible, you kno. He didn't get close ta de shaak. Bra Rabbit suppose be smaat. He wouldn't git close ta de shaak.

So, Rabbit went aroun an say, "You kno, wen somebody ded, dey habe a different scent."

He git op close nough ta smell de scent. "Oh no, Bra Shaak ent ded!"

An you kno one ting, dey could neba git Bra Rabbit ta go close ta de shaak. Cause ef anybody ded, dey gone smell. Bot dey ent neba git Bra Rabbit. Bra Rabbit stay faa nough dat dey couldn't ketch um.

Brother Rabbit and Brother Shark: English Version

There was an island, and Brother Rabbit had to go over there to marry a couple. So, when he got down there everybody had left Brother Rabbit.

So, Brother Rabbit played a trick. He called Brother Shark to take him over to the island. So, Brother Shark came, you know, and Brother Rabbit got on the Shark's back and went on across to the island. He came back down again. The people had left him again. Now, he hadn't paid Brother Shark anything.

So, he called Brother Shark again. Brother Shark came back. He came ashore, and Brother Rabbit got on the Brother Shark's back and Brother Shark took him back over.

So, Brother Rabbit, to keep from paying the Shark, said, "Hmmm, Brother Shark, I smell your stinking back fin."

Brother Shark said, "What did you say, Brother Rabbit?"

"Man, we almost have gotten to shore!"

When they got to shore so he could jump off, he said the same thing again. And Brother Shark looked around. Brother Rabbit jumped up and left.

Now Brother Shark thought of a way to catch Brother Rabbit. He went on the shore and played dead. The people came by and carried the news to Brother Rabbit. Brother Rabbit was coming back now to preach Brother Shark's funeral. Now Brother Shark's going to have a chance to catch Brother Rabbit.

So, Brother Rabbit said, "Why, Brother Shark can't be dead! Man, but Brother Shark can't be dead! He just brought me over yesterday."

They told him, "Well, Brother Shark is dead now."

So, Brother Rabbit went down there with his Bible, you know. He didn't get close to the shark. Brother Rabbit is supposed to be smart. He wouldn't get close to the shark.

So, Brother Rabbit went around and said, "You know, when some-body's dead, they have a different scent."

He got up close enough to smell the scent. "Oh no, Brother Shark isn't dead!"

THE NEGRO MOTHER

CHILDREN, I COME BACK TODAY
TO TELL YOU A STORY OF THE LONG DARK WAY
THAT I HAD TO CLIMB THAT I HAD TO KNOW
IN ORDER THAT THE RACE MIGHT LIVE AND GROW,
LOOK AT MY FACE—DARK AS THE NIGHT—
YET SHINING LIKE THE SUN WITH LOVE'S TRUE LIGHT.
I AM THE CHILD THEY STOLE FROM THE SAND
THREE HUNDRED YEARS AGO IN AFRICA'S LAND.
I AM THE DARK GIRL WHO CROSSED THE WIDE SEA
CARRYING IN MY BODY THE SEED OF THE FREE
I AM THE WOMAN WHO WORKED IN THE FIELD
BRINGING THE COTTON AND THE CORN TO YIELD.
I AM THE ONE WHO LABORED AS A SLAVE
BEATEN AND MISTREATED FOR THE WORK THAT I
     GAVE—
CHILDREN SOLD AWAY FROM ME, HUSBAND SOLD, TOO.
NO SAFETY, NO LOVE, NO RESPECT WAS I DUE.
THREE HUNDRED YEARS IN THE DEEPEST SOUTH
BUT GOD PUT A SONG AND A PRAYER IN MY MOUTH
GOD PUT A DREAM LIKE STEEL IN MY SOUL.

continued on next page

And you know one thing, they could never get Brother Rabbit to go close to the shark. Because if anybody's dead, they're going to smell, But they never got Brother Rabbit. Brother Rabbit stayed far enough away so they couldn't catch him.

THE WRONG MAN IN THE COFFIN

This is another delightful story that is amusing and fun. One wonders, here, if maybe this story doesn't hit a little too close to home. Perhaps the character Sadie was as serious as she was witty.

You know de chu'ch folks in de Bottoms hab a love for big funerals. 'Reckly attuh freedom, dey hab de funerals on Sunday, 'caze de boss-mens don' low' no funerals in de week-a-days. Nowadays, dey hab al funerals on a Sunday jes' for de sake of de love of big funerals.

In dem days comin' up, womens ain't gonna talk 'bout dey men folks while dey's livin'. Dey wanna keep folks thinkin' dey hab a good man for a husband, but dese days an' times hit's a lot diffunt. De gals what ma'ied nowadays talk 'bout dey husbands to any an' evuh-body. You can heah 'em all de time talkin' 'bout "dat ole scoun'al ain't no 'count." Dey say, "If'n you been ma'ied a yeah an' yo' husband ain't nevuh paid a light bill, ain't never paid on de insu'ances, what you think 'bout a scou'al lack dat?"

One time dere was a han' what died on de old McPherson fawm by de name of Ken Parker. De membuhship of de Salem Baptis' Chu'ch think Ken's a good man, 'caze he hab a fine big family an' he 'ten' chu'ch regluh as de Sundays come. De pastuh think he a Good Christun, too. So when he git up to preach Ken's funeral, he tell 'bout what a good man Brothuh Ken was, 'bout how true he was to his wife, an' what a good providuh he done been for his family an' all lack dat. He keep on an' keep on in dis wise, but Ken's wife Sadie know de pastuh done errored; son she turn to de ol'es' boy, Jim, an' say, "Jim, go up dere an' look in dat coffin an' see if'n dat's yo pappy in dere."

BIG SIXTEEN

A complex story, "Big Sixteen" carries a message of strength. Langston Hughes and Arna Bontemps immortalized it in their 1958 collection, The Book of Negro Folklore.

It was back in slavery time when Big Sixteen was a man and they called 'im Sixteen 'cause dat was de number of de show he wore. He was big and strong and Ole Massa looked to him to do everything.

One day Ole Massa said, "Big Sixteen, Ah b'lieve Ah want you to move dem sills Ah had hewed out down in de swamp."

"I yassuh, Massa."

Big Sixteen went down in de swamp and picked up dem 12 x 12's and brought 'em on up to de house and stack 'em. No one man ain't never toted a 12 x 12 befo' nor since.

So Ole Massa said one day, "Go fetch in de mules. Ah want to look 'em over."

Big Sixteen went on down to de pasture and caught dem mules by de bridle but they was contrary and balky and he tore de bridles to pieces pullin' on 'em, so he picked one of 'em up under each arm and brought 'em up to Ole Massa.

He says, "Big Sixteen, if you kin, ketch de Devil."

"Yassuh, Ah kin, if you git me a nine pound hammer and a pick and shovel!"

Ole Massa got Sixteen de things he ast for and tole 'im to go ahead and

continued from previous page

NOW, THROUGH MY CHILDREN, I'M REACHING THE GOAL

NOW, THROUGH MY CHILDREN, YOUNG AND FREE,

I REALIZE THE BLESSINGS DENIED TO ME.

I COULDN'T READ THEN. I COULDN'T WRITE.

I HAD NOTHING, BACK THERE IN THE NIGHT.

SOMETIMES, THE VALLEY WAS FILLED WITH TEARS.

BUT I KEPT TRUDGING ON THROUGH THE LONELY YEARS.

SOMETIMES, THE ROAD WAS HOT WITH SUN,

BUT I HAD TO KEEP ON TILL MY WORK WAS DONE.

I HAD TO KEEP ON! NO STOPPING FOR ME—

I WAS THE SEED OF THE COMING FREE.

I NOURISHED THE DREAM THAT NOTHING COULD SMOTHER

DEEP IN MY BREAST—THE NEGRO MOTHER.

I HAD ONLY HOPE THEN, BUT NOW THROUGH YOU,

DARK ONES OF TODAY, MY DREAMS MUST COME TRUE.

ALL YOU DARK CHILDREN IN THE WORLD OUT THERE,

REMEMBER MY SWEAT, MY PAIN, MY DESPAIR,

REMEMBER MY YEARS, HEAVY WITH SORROW—

AND MAKE OF THOSE YEARS A TORCH FOR TOMORROW.

continued on next page

continued from previous page

MAKE OF MY PAST A ROAD TO THE LIGHT

OUT OF THE DARKNESS, THE IGNORANCE, THE NIGHT.

LIFT HIGH MY BANNER OUT OF THE DUST,

STAND LIKE FREE MEN SUPPORTING MY TRUST.

BELIEVE IN THE RIGHT, LET NONE PUSH YOU BACK,

REMEMBER THE WHIP AND THE SLAVE'S TRACK.

REMEMBER HOW THE STRONG IN STRUGGLE AND
    STRIFE

STILL BAR YOU THE WAY, AND DENY YOU LIFE—

BUT MARCH EVER FORWARD, BREAKING DOWN BARS.

LOOK EVER UPWARD AT THE SUN AND THE STARS—

OH, MY DARK CHILDREN, MAY MY DREAMS AND MY
    PRAYERS

IMPEL YOU FOREVER UP THE GREAT STAIRS—

FOR I WILL BE WITH YOU TILL NO WHITE BROTHER

DARES KEEP DOWN THE CHILDREN OF THE NEGRO
    MOTHER.

—LANGSTON HUGHES

bring him de Devil.

Big Sixteen went out in front of de house and went to diggin'. He was diggin' nearly a month befo' he got where he wanted. Then he took his hammer and went and knocked on de Devil's door. Devil answered de door hisself.

"Who dat out dere?"

"It's Big Sixteen."

"What you want?"

"Wanta have a word wid you for a minute."

Soon as de Devil poked his head out de door, Sixteen lammed 'im over de head wid dat hammer and picked 'im up and carried 'im back to Ole Massa.

Ole Massa looked at de dead Devil and hollered, "Take dat ugly thing 'way from here, quick! Ah didn't think you'd ketch de Devil sho 'nuff."

So Sixteen picked up de Devil and throwed 'im back down de hole.

Way after while, Big Sixteen died and went up to Heben. But Peter looked at him and tole 'im to g'wan 'way from dere. He was too powerful. He might git outa order and there wouldn't be nobody to handle 'im. But he had to go somewhere so he went on to hell.

Soon as he got to de gate de Devil's children was playin' in de yard and they seen 'im and run to de house, says "Mama, Mama! Dat man's out dere dat kilt papa!"

So she called 'im in de house and shet de door. When Sixteen got dere she handed 'im a li'l piece of fire and said, "You ain't comin' in here. Here, take dis hot coal and g'wan off and start you a hell uh yo'own."

So when you see a Jack O'Lantern in de woods at night you know it's Big Sixteen wid his piece of fire lookin' for a place to go.

"DIXIE"

Oh, I wish I was in the land of cotton,
Old times there are not forgotten,
Look away,
Look away,
Look away, Dixie land.
In Dixie land where I was born
Early on a frosty mornin'
Look away,
Look away,
Look away, Dixie land.
Hurray, Hurray,
In Dixie land, I'll take my stand
To live and die in Dixie.
Away, away, away down South in Dixie.
Away, away, away down South in Dixie.

Ben and **Lee Snowden's** gravestone in a small cemetery north of Mt. Vernon, Ohio, reads: "They taught 'Dixie' to Dan Emmett."

"'Dixie,' the anthem that has been a fixture at rallies 'away down South' for more than one hundred years, may have been written by this black family—and Yankees, no less," asserts *Detroit Free Press* reporter Phillip Rawls.

The popular notion was that white minstrel performer Daniel Decatur Emmett wrote the song; his performance of it on Broadway in 1859 is the earliest on record. Now, authors Howard L. and Judith R. Sacks speculate that Emmett learned the song from the Snowdens, a family of black musicians who also lived in Emmett's hometown of Mt. Vernon, Ohio. Apparently, the Snowdens lived across the street from a tavern and stagecoach stop. They started entertaining travelers in 1850 with a style that later became parodied in minstrel shows.

"They were performers primarily for white audiences," Sacks says of the Snowdens. "White folks wrote to them constantly asking for songs they had heard them perform." The matriarch of the Snowden family, Ellen Cooper Snowden, was born a slave in Maryland in 1817. When she was ten, her owner freed her and sent her to Mount Vernon, on the Ohio frontier, to work for his cousins. So why would the descendants of a freed slave "wish I was in the land of cotton"?

Speculation is that there were no other blacks in Mt. Vernon. They were not lamenting slavery, but there was a strong sense of loss of family, tradition, and culture. To be in the North and be free was not always an entirely positive experience for an African American, especially one without family.

Over the years, the words to "Dixie" have changed many times. Some versions have up to ten stanzas, but the two stanzas printed here are generally in use today.

The narratives related to burial customs and cemeteries most pointedly pay tribute to African American heritage. From stories of death are reflected stories of life. African Americans recall how they shed their identity during slavery; even in the postbellum years there remained an uneasiness about oneself. The telling of tales, the belief in voodoo or hoodoo, the singing of spirituals: all were important ways of finding a comfort spot and assessing one's self-worth.

In time, as blacks became increasingly educated and socialized within their new homeland, there still remained a common bond and a common experience in being black and encumbered by continued social and political indignities.

As one reads of the black cemeteries and black towns that arose between the 1800s and the early 1900s, one can't help but sense an attempt to deal with an increasing frustration over adverse conditions. The separation of black towns from the established "white" communities developed from a social and political environment that excluded blacks from the "larger world." This, too, caused the proliferation of black cemeteries, the chance to create havens of peace and freedom through the legal means of possession and ownership.

Small Town Stories

ONE SMALL TOWN IN MISSISSIPPI

Many people are familiar with Fannie Lou Hamer, the legendary civil rights leader who began picking cotton and ended up exciting an entire nation with her impassioned plea for racial justice at the 1964 Democratic National Convention. A close friend of hers relates the following story, which took her by surprise as the phone rang one day in 1972:

> Mrs. Hamer described how, on the previous night, a carload of white boys in a small town in Mississippi had shot and killed a black girl who had just graduated from the formerly all-white high school. As Mrs. Hamer shouted her anger over the phone, I could hear the dead girl's mother wailing in the background.
>
> The senseless slaying set off days of protest marches and drew reporters from around the world. After the funeral, I rushed along back streets to get a good place at the town cemetery. But when I got there, there were

no gravediggers. And no grave site. Then it hit me. They were burying the slain girl in "the colored cemetery."

I found the funeral—at a poorer, leaner, almost grassless version of the first cemetery. Later, when I told Mrs. Hamer, she shook with bitter laughter. "You," she said, "should know better."

Mrs. Hamer went on to explain that while segregation was officially dead, blacks seldom asked to be buried in the white cemeteries. They wanted to be buried with their friends and relatives in the "colored cemeteries." But in the rare cases when a black person did want to be buried in the "white cemetery," something—money, lack of space, lack of "reservations"—almost always seemed to deter them.

There was something particularly painful about the thought that—even in death—blacks were segregated.

STORIES FROM FLORIDA

In 1970, a cemetery in Fort Pierce, Florida, refused to bury a twenty-year-old black man slain in the Vietnam War because of a "Caucasian only" deed restriction. The burial proceeded only after a federal judge ruled that such clauses were unconstitutional. His mother apologized for all the trouble. "I just wanted him there because it was better kept than the other cemetery," she says.

In 1986, as fifty people watched, Dania, Florida, officials unveiled a granite monument designed to lay to rest a sign from the town's past. The monument publicly recognized a sad event from 1940, when the remains of blacks were dug up from the city's cemetery to make room for more white graves. The black remains were then reburied in a new "colored cemetery"— literally on the other side of the railroad tracks. Thereafter, many black families were never able to locate the graves of their loved ones.

But on that day the city commission discarded the unofficial names Westside Cemetery and Dania Colored Cemetery and officially combined the two under the name Westlawn Memorial Cemetery.

At the dedication, a black man, Marvin Merritt, put aside his past bitterness and reminded those assembled of the common resting place that awaits the faithful of all races. "When the trumpets of the Lord shall sound and all these days are past, all these bones are going to rise up and God is going to take them all in His hand," Merritt said.

And all the people said, "Amen."

In 1988, as part of an out-of-court settlement, Deerfield Beach, Florida, dug up the body of **Mayo Howard**, a twenty-eight-year police veteran, from a public cemetery historically used for blacks and buried him in another public cemetery historically used for whites. Howard's wife Evelyn claimed that the city had refused her original request to bury her husband, an African American, in the historically white cemetery. Mrs. Howard's lawyers called segregated cemeteries one of the last entrenched vestiges of American segregation, and alleged that across the South, there were still countless cemeteries with old "Caucasian only" restrictions.

In July 1991, the *Washington Post* printed the story of a 104-year-old black Florida woman, Ada Dupree, who was denied her wish to be buried in the all-white cemetery in Esto, the town she helped settle. She was interred in an all-black burial ground seven miles away.

Dupree's family took her silver coffin across Florida's panhandle, from Esto to Graceville, and buried her as some Esto residents made public apologies for anonymous racist threats directed at the Dupree family.

Several dozen relatives were joined by a dozen white friends as they prayed, sang and paid respects to the oldest citizen of Esto, a town of 250 near the Alabama border.

Dupree wanted to be buried in Esto, where she moved in 1902 and cared for many white families who settled there. "If anybody deserved to be buried there, it was she. She was there before any white person was," said a white mourner. Relatives had changed their plans to bury Dupree at the Esto Farm Cemetery after callers threatened to "shoot up the hearse and any black mourners."

The Duprees were the only black people in Esto for many years. Ada's husband, Gilbert, died in the 1940s.

FREEDMAN'S VILLAGE

The January 1985 issue of *Crisis* magazine includes an interesting story written by Major General Jerry R. Curry, Deputy Commanding General of the U.S. Army. He writes:

> One summer day last year, I was riding one of my favorite mounts along the north wall of Arlington National Cemetery. Just inside the wall was a marker stone with the chiseled words, "Jubal Diggs, A citizen," . . . I wondered why the phrase, "A citizen?" Most of those resting beneath the greening sod of Arlington National Cemetery were citizens, but "citizen" wasn't written on their marker stones.
>
> A few weeks and much research later, an intriguing bit of history yield-

ed its secrets. Between 1864 and 1866, approximately 3,800 Civil War "Contrabands," which was the name at that time for Negro refugees or escaped slaves, were buried in Section 27.

Section 27, just inside the north wall of the cemetery, is near the Netherlands Carillon, where three or four times a day its chimes melodiously drench the air with sweet sound.

In 1863, a Contraband Camp was established at the Arlington Estate of Robert E. Lee. It sprawled north from what are now the Amphitheater and Tomb of the Unknown Soldier to Section 27. Diseases, such as smallpox and typhoid fever, remained rampant in the camp, and many now buried in Section 27 died of these and other diseases.

In 1865, the camp was renamed "Freedman's Village." Over 1,000 people lived there in approximately 100 one-and-a-half story frame houses. Each family was given a plot of land to farm and was paid $10 a month by the federal government, which charged $3 a month to rent. Families worked in various trades and skills. . . .

About 1890, the Government bought the land back from them and helped them relocate to other areas, so the area of the now active cemetery could be expanded. This was accomplished with a minimum of discomfiture to the families scattered throughout the area and neighboring states. One of those who relocated was Mr. James Parks. He was "born a slave" in 1845 and was owned by the Curtis-Lee Estate.

Even though Mr. James Parks was a free man, he decided to stay on at the Arlington Estate and work for wages. He continued to work there for many years. . . . When the Curtis-Lee Estate became Arlington Cemetery, Mr. Parks again elected to stay on to work as an employee of the cemetery . . . . Mr. Parks was so well respected and loved that, upon his death in 1929, the Secretary of the Army made an exception to policy and directed that he be buried in Arlington National Cemetery.

Back along the north wall, also buried in Section 27, are Union soldiers with the notation on their marker stones of "USCT," which stands for United States Colored Troops. The casualties of the Freeman's Camp combine with the USCT war casualties and all are interred in a beautiful and peaceful location in Arlington National Cemetery. Together they total more than 5,000.

Most of the slaves buried at the Slave Burial Grounds at Mount Vernon did not know freedom in their lifetimes. Yet, they rest in peace and honor no less than their American citizen brothers and sisters of Freedman's Village who lie buried in Section 27 of Arlington National Cemetery.

In October 1992, a *Cleveland Plain Dealer* article highlighted the 130th anniversary memorial service held in the Freedman's Village section of Arlington National Cemetery in Arlington, Virginia; the address was by Ohio representative Louis Stokes. The site has gained increasing notice recently among the four million tourists who visit the cemetery each year. On this October day, veterans, historians, and government officials gathered to honor forgotten heroes whose graves are marked simply, "civilian" or "citizen."

Efforts by the Committee to Memorialize African Americans of the Civil War, as well as by Representative Stokes, recently led to the graves being refurbished and information about the site being added to tourist brochures. Dismayed by the lack of maintenance and recognition of the site, Stokes, in 1992, won approval for spending $250,000 in federal funds to upgrade and designate the area.

Cemetery administrators unveiled a handwritten burial registry restored by staff at the Library of Congress that will enable visitors to locate ancestors' graves or research village history. Mobile tours of the cemetery now note Freedman's Village and Section 27. There are approximately ten thousand burials in Section 27. Burials are mixed, but include nearly four thousand former residents of Freedman's Village and thousands of combat troops.

SERGEANT BRENT WOODS RECEIVES HIS RITES WITH HONOR

Sergeant Brent Woods, a former slave who was buried in obscurity in 1906, was finally awarded the Congressional Medal of Honor—the nation's highest decoration—for bravery during the Indian Wars. In 1984 he was honored with full military rites at Mill Spring National Cemetery near Somerset, Kentucky.

Lorraine Smith of Somerset learned of Woods's heroism through records in the National Archives in Washington, D.C. Woods joined the army in 1873 at the age of eighteen and became a sergeant, but was demoted to private five times. Smith believes that the demotions came because of his race, "but each time," she said, "he did something outstanding, so they'd raise him back to sergeant."

In an 1881 incident, Sergeant Woods's cavalry company was trapped by a group of Apaches in a New Mexico canyon. After the commanding officer was killed and the second in command deserted the company, Woods took charge, helped a group of civilians to safety, and led his company in a successful attack.

Woods retired from the army in 1902 and returned to Pulaski County, his birthplace in south central Kentucky, where he spent the last four years of his life in relative obscurity. He was buried beneath an unmarked headstone in a cemetery in downtown Somerset, Kentucky, that has since been abandoned. Lorraine Smith's research efforts into Woods's heroism eventually led to the 1984 ceremony at the Mill Spring National Cemetery, where Woods's remains were moved.

COFFINS WASHED AWAY

The tiny farm town of Hardin, Missouri, was turned topsy-turvy during the summer of 1993 when the Missouri River barreled through its streets like white water rapids. The flood destroyed the Assembly of God Church, the city hall, grain bins, houses, and barns, and cut off electricity, running water, and phone service. Residents were already devastated by the catastrophe when the unthinkable happened: The river washed away the town cemetery where most of the area's deceased were interred. Close to nine hundred coffins and burial vaults floated downstream toward St. Louis, Missouri, and the Mississippi River. At one point, the nine-acre cemetery was under about thirty feet of water.

The river carved out the cemetery's oldest section, where inadequate records and memories have yielded few clues as to who occupied the graves. The section, for example, included a segregated acre where blacks were buried decades ago, many in unmarked graves. After the flood, the county coroner and others marked newly dug graves for identified bodies, but placed others in huge mass graves.

The American Cemetery Association (ACA), which was founded in 1887 and comprises cemeteries and funeral homes in more than twenty countries, contributed more than $20,000 to the Missouri Funeral Directors Association. The ACA thus demonstrated a spirit of helping one's neighbors in a time of distress and bereavement and brought different segments of the funeral and remembrance industry together to accomplish a common goal. The organization later contributed additional money directly to the fund for the Hardin town cemetery.

THE BLACK MINERS CEMETERY

Some of the most frequently visited cemetery grounds on the West Coast lie quietly nestled in a valley just outside the small city of Roslyn, Washington. Surrounded by the thick pines of the Cascade Range, this quaint setting has, surprisingly, become a bustling, but still folksy, town. Made popular as the filming location for the recent television series *Northern Exposure*, the town attracts as many as twenty-four thousand tourists a year, most of whom are surprised when they are encouraged to visit one of Roslyn's twenty-five cemeteries.

Roslyn prides itself on its cemeteries, most which are adjacent to one another. Some have the original moving turnstiles, and fences are maintained to provide an orderly procession of visitors and to keep away herding animals and foraging wildlife. Each cemetery has its own character.

Roslyn was founded in 1886, when the Northwestern Mining Company discovered millions of tons of coal waiting to be tapped in huge veins under the town, which in its heyday had a population of six thousand. A small city bustling with a melting pot from all different racial and ethnic backgrounds, the miners were quick to organize and establish fraternal lodges of social orders and ethnicities.

Some miners and their families belonged to more than one lodge at a time, and could choose between a variety of cemeteries that offered some form of perpetual care, but not all those in the community could afford such a fitting tribute. Many burials remain unmarked, while some graves are outlined by rocks, large and small, as well as markers without names.

The lack of marked graves is most apparent at Mount Olivet, the black miners cemetery established in 1888. The miners and their families buried in these grounds were among the first blacks to settle in Washington and buy cemetery property in the valley. Mount Olivet is now a barren hill said to be filled to capacity with more than two hundred burials, although at first glance it is hard to believe judging by the dozen or so remaining markers.

Many of the unmarked graves are those of Roslyn's young children and victims of infant mortality. Sickness, epidemics, plagues, and outbreaks of fatal diseases took their toll in the city around the turn of the century, often taking the lives of the young and the weak.

Often parents were not able to afford a fitting burial or monument. Instead they would get boxes from local grocers—designed to hold long, oversized macaroni—to serve as makeshift coffins. These macaroni box burials were common throughout several of the city's cemeteries.

Roslyn's coal mining days came to an end in 1964, when Northwest Mining pulled out of town. Over the years since then, the cemeteries fell into disrepair from lack of maintenance, but a sense of camaraderie and pride eventually filled the local community and prompted its residents to ensure that the town's cemeteries be well maintained. A common sight in recent years—whenever the weather allows—are groups of townspeople working in the town's cemeteries, cleaning them up and working together to revitalize a piece of their town's heritage.

The next ten stories will provide some surprises for you; they are indeed unusual.

BENEATH THE FLOORBOARDS
OF THE HOUSE

Desiree Cooper, in the *Detroit Free Press*, writes that a mother's pain is the same through time. In 1725, in a slave cabin near Annapolis, Maryland, a family laid a six-year-old child to rest. According to African tradition, the child was buried beneath the floorboards of the house so its soul could sleep in the bosom of the family for eternity.

Cooper contrasts this to the many thousands of remains uncovered in the country of Iraq from years ago. The Iraqis could never visit the graves until Saddam Hussein was toppled. Now, of course, only parts of bodies, unknown, can be found.

In 2003, the slave child who had been at rest for 278 years was unearthed by archaeologists excavating the site of a vanished building in the colonial tobacco port of London Town, Maryland. They had been preparing the site for the reconstruction of a wooden building that likely housed the

The Unusual

slaves of tavern owner Stephen West. Dusting back layers of dirt in a small grave shaft, they found rusted nails and 11 small, human teeth.

There was no family left to claim the remains of the child, so the community did. This month, they placed the remains in a tiny cypress casket and mourners gathered for the reinterment of the child.

Joyce Hayes-Williams of Legacy Productions staged an interpretation of an 18th-Century slave burial. She poured libations – an African tradition of pouring water to invoke the ancestors' spirits – and she wept. A local author who attended observed that the child was "symbolic of thousands of people of color who came to the Chesapeake."

So, too, the bones in the mass grave at Mahaweel are symbolic of the throngs who died at the hands of Saddam Hussein. Amnesty International maintains a list of 17,000 Iraqis who have disappeared since 1979, presumably victims of unspeakable torture. While the international community is demanding that the graves be protected for evidence of war crimes, the mothers want to be reunited with their children, even after death.

At the slave child's funeral, the county executive and other elected officials attended the ceremony, a level of respect no slave child could have garnered nearly three centuries ago. Suddenly, "the skies opened up and she was received into heaven," said Hayes-Williams. The rain helped erase the horrors of the past, freeing everyone to embrace a future free of violence and oppression. From above, a mother's spirit must have smiled.

REMAINS CLASSIFIED AS
AFRICAN AMERICANS

Boyce Rensburger, writing for the *Washington Post*, tells the story of Smithsonian Institution scientists' new discovery that four skeletons dug up decades ago at colonial Jamestown are among the oldest known remains of African Americans. The bones, thought to date between 1650 and 1700, were originally classified as American Indian.

Indians were present at Jamestown, the first successful English settlement in the New World, from its founding in 1607. Africans may have arrived as early as 1619. Until now scientists knew of only one other black person's skeleton of comparable antiquity in the United States, a man whose remains were found years ago at Patuxent Point, Maryland.

One of the Jamestown skeletons, that of a man in his mid-twenties, is riddled with pits and deformations typical of end-stage syphilis. Researchers say the man must have been in great pain and probably suffered severe dementia. The skull also shows that he died of a gunshot wound to the head, possibly the result of a mercy killing.

It may be possible to determine what parts of Africa the men came from, Owsley, one of the scientists said. Africans are the most physically diverse people of any continent and individual tribes often have characteristic differences in head and face shape.

Owsley said the African origin of the Jamestown skeletons came to light as he was reexamining ancient human remains in a collection at Jamestown. The National Park Service, which administers the site, had contracted for the study to comply with a federal law that requires reburial of American Indian remains if a Native American group can show they are related to the deceased and if scientific analysis is completed.

"I think this shows that when we use modern forensic techniques, we can go way beyond what we used to do," Owsley said. He noted that if skeletons had been reburied, as has happened with other skeletons, the new knowledge would have been lost.

Owsley and other anthropologists are waging a major effort to keep very ancient skeletons from being reburied on the grounds that they are too old to be related to any modern tribe and that as science advances, new analytic methods will be available to reveal new facts about how ancient Americans lived. The Jamestown misidentification occurred in 1940 and 1955, when anthropologists noticed that the bodies had been buried in a way not typical of English settlers. And their "shovel-shaped" incisor teeth were a form once thought to exist only among people resembling modern Asians. It was believed then that American Indians descended solely from such people. So, the early researchers concluded that the skeletons were of Native Americans.

Owsley said he recognized immediately that the skulls were narrower than those of modern Asiatic peoples. A detailed, computer-assisted analysis of scores of measurements of the skulls showed a pattern typical of African men.

It is well established that Africans, some slave and some free, accompanied many exploring and colonizing groups of Europeans in the New World from the earliest days. Historical records show that blacks were living in Jamestown by 1624, just 17 years after the colony's founding. There is some evidence African Americans had been brought to the area as early as 1619. They are thought to have been servants but it is not clear whether they were slaves.

THE BISHOP'S EMPTY TOMB

Cindy Loose, a *Washington Post* writer, tells us about a woman calling herself Adetta George expressed great excitement at the prospect of buying a grave site near that of the late Bishop Walter "Sweet Daddy" McCullough.

"I want to be buried near him, because that's the only way I'll get the glory," she explained to a salesman at Lincoln Memorial Cemetery in Suitland. When the salesman assured her that the Bishop's head lay pointed in the direction of the six plots that she was contemplating buying, the woman nearly shouted with joy: "I can almost smell the tonic off his hair."

Problem is, the former bishop of the United House of Prayer is not buried in Lincoln Cemetery. And Adetta George was not a serious buyer, but part of a videotaped sting operated by Carolyn Jacobi, whose self-proclaimed mission is to clean up the cemetery industry.

"The sales pitch was corrupt, fraudulent, deceitful and devious," said Jacobi, of Silver Spring, who arranged for friends to pose as devoted House of Prayer members from South Carolina. Jacobi, a former cemetery director, is the founder of an unincorporated organization called Eternal Justice. Her probing into irregularities in the cemetery industry led earlier this month to the exhumation of three bodies at Maryland National Cemetery in Laurel. She said separate complaints led her to investigate practices involving the bishop's empty tomb at Lincoln.

Her November videotape, viewed Wednesday by a *Washington Post* reporter, shows a salesman at Lincoln taking Jacobi's three sting partners on a tour of land near the bishop's empty mausoleum and sarcophagus. He apologizes that he couldn't get six grave sites any closer to the bishop's tomb, saying, "I'm trying to get you something real, real close, but many members of your congregation have bought up real close."

The comment, said Jacobi, "makes you wonder how many people were buying under false pretenses. . . . My hurt is that people with spirituality are being fooled."

Lincoln salesman Walter George, who was videotaped showing grave sites to the sting operators, complained he was the one who was deceived because the so-called buyers weren't interested in purchasing plots.

The revelation that at least one salesman used the empty mausoleum at Lincoln as a selling point also opened old wounds for the McCullough family, which has fought for years for burial rights for the charismatic bishop.

The story of that battle, and how there came to be an empty tomb, includes lawsuits and continuing hurt. It is the story of how a prominent family lost its position in 1991, when McCullough disproved, by dying, some followers' belief that he might be immortal.

Understanding why anyone would care about being buried near his body requires understanding his role while he was alive.

When he sat on "the mount," a throne in the United House of Prayer's mother church at Seventh and M streets NW, young girls in white dresses would encircle and fan him. After donating 10 percent of their income in tithes, church members would jostle for the chance to thrust extra "love gifts" into his hands, which were laden with diamond rings.

He built a multimillion-dollar empire, with churches, apartment buildings and stores in 23 states and the District — all part of his vision for black self-sufficiency. Among other properties, the House of Prayer owns the Harlem building where arson killed eight people last month. The fire was set by a man protesting rent increases on a record store owner who subleased part of the building.

After "Sweet Daddy" died March 21, 1991, people in six cities waited for hours to glimpse his open casket. His 4½-hour funeral in the District was so intense that paramedics stood by to treat those overcome with emotion.

"Sweet Daddy" was temporarily entombed while the church made plans for a mausoleum at Lincoln Memorial. But in May 1992, the church's new bishop, S.C. Madison, told McCullough's widow that she would not be allowed to be buried with her husband. Some time later, Madison stripped the widow's son, C.L. McCullough, of his D.C. church and preaching credentials in the United House of Prayer, whose full name is the United House of Prayer for All People on the Rock of the Apostolic Faith.

Clara McCullough – who had been revered as "Saint Madame McCullough" while her husband was alive – launched a battle to gain custody of her husband's body in May 1992. One day after she held a tearful press conference, the Prince George's County state's attorney granted her custody.

By December 1992, McCullough, now 80, laid her husband to rest in a marble crypt where she, too, can be buried one day. The family mausoleum at Fort Lincoln Cemetery in Brentwood is 12 miles from the empty tomb at Lincoln Cemetery.

Despite the family's wishes, however, the church under Madison proceeded with its own plans, erecting a $700,000 memorial with a statue, a mausoleum and a sarcophagus with the bishop's dates of birth and death. The church runs bus tours to the empty tomb; flowers are laid around it. Sometimes, people literally crawl to it, according to the deceased bishop's son.

The family sought in Prince George's County Circuit Court to have the empty tomb at Lincoln moved, or at least have the McCullough name removed. The church responded that the mausoleum was a merely a memorial and that the widow's claimed mental anguish was "ambiguous and peculiar to her." The case was thrown out of court twice, the second time on appeal.

According to McCullough, Lincoln salesman Raydell Dukes offered to sell for $1 million half of a historic chapel on the grounds of Lincoln. "He said the family and the cemetery could then sell different spaces in the chapel. I would make back my investment and a profit besides," he said.

ON-LINE CEMETERIES

Reid Kanoley of Knight-Ridder newspapers wrote about Cynthia Edwards, a Dallas freelance writer, saying she wept for most of the week in September as she uploaded her grief onto the Internet's World Wide Web.

"I had bottled up a tremendous amount of sorrow," said Edwards, 42, about the death of her brother last year. "When I started putting up his memorial page, it was the first time I had started getting those feelings out."

On-line memorials to the dead are taking on a life of their own on the Internet. In recent months, the World Wide Web has flowered with such sites as the World Wide Cemetery, the Virtual Memorial Garden, the Garden of Remembrance and the Cemetery Gate. There's even a Virtual Pet Cemetery.

At these sites in cyberspace, visitors can view pictures, stories or poems about the deceased, and others who are grieving may leave similar remembrances about their own loved ones.

Memorials to departed celebrities (recent notables include guitarist Jerry Garcia, baseball's Mickey Mantle and assassinated Israeli Prime Minister Yitzhak Rabin) have also sprung up to document public comment and sorrow.

In the Garden of Remembrance, there is a poem honoring Baylee Almon, the 1-year-old who became famous in death when her battered body was pictured in the arms of a firefighter after the April 19 Oklahoma City bombing. Called "A Message from Baylee," it includes the lines: "From

Policeman to Fireman, gently she was passed. Held in their arms, each man hoping, 'Lord let this one last.'"

Dale Larson, 26, a Philadelphia computer programmer and Grateful Dead fan, said his web page, "A Tribute to the Dead in Philly," evolved from an exchange of E-mail that followed his attendance of a Jerry Garcia memorial at the Liberty Bell.

"It made a lot of sense to me that, for a public figure who represented something to us as a society or as a community, we would have some kind of public mourning. It always used to be that the media was a one-way thing. TV preached to you, or you read a novel or whatever. The Internet really provides an interactive medium, to speak back."

The World Wide Cemetery greets visitors with a picture of a stone and wrought-iron graveyard gate under the spreading boughs of a leafless tree, and the words "Welcome to a place where Internet users, their family and friends, can erect permanent monuments to our dead."

So far, the price of a global remembrance is quite low. The 10-month-old Virtual Memorial Garden, which lists 530 dead people and 242 pets, charges nothing for entries.

"Perhaps I am old-fashioned or just naïve in these matters, but I do feel this service should be free," computer science lecturer Lindsay Marshall writes on the introductory screen. Marshall, who created the service, lectures at the University of Newcastle in Tyne, England.

At the World Wide Cemetery, a basic plot with enough room to write an obituary or reminiscence costs $5. Leaving pictures, sound bites or video clips costs extra because of the disk space they take up, said Michael Kibbee, a Toronto structural engineer who got the idea for the World Wide Cemetery last spring when he was going through a bone-marrow transplant and dealing with his own mortality.

The charges may account for the fact that there are only about 20 people in the cemetery, but Kibbee said he hopes to maintain the tributes indefinitely for the onetime fees.

A cyber cemetery offers a number of advantages over the real thing, Kibbee said. For example, he said, "a person's able to include multimedia with the monument. With a physical monument, you can't do such a thing, and a physical monument can't be visited by people around the world."

Everyone is invited to leave "flowers"–electronic messages with comments, or just the name and E-mail address of the visitor. "Rest in Peace, Greetings from Iceland," reads one. There are others from Italy, Switzerland and Australia.

The monuments and flowers show the tremendous power of the Internet to allow people to communicate globally about the "significant things in their lives," Kibbee said.

Edwards said she decided to create a separate site to reminisce about her brother and to display his drawings and photographs when she came across a reference to a virtual cemetery while she was surfing the Internet for something else – information about France.

So on September 6, she began preparing "Jon's Page," a display of her own writing about her brother, Jonathan Tuttle, an artist with schizophrenia who committed suicide at age 43. He was "the kindest, noblest, gentlest person I have ever known," she typed.

Then there are Tuttle's photographs, his drawings, paintings and cartoons. Edwards also promises to make her brother's original music recordings available on-line as soon as she can master the technology that allows it.

To Edwards' surprise, hundreds of people have logged on to Jon's Page, and many have left E-mail. A university professor in Virginia said she intended to make the page a reading assignment in a course on schizophrenia.

WHIMSICAL COFFINS

Laryea Okai of Teshi, Ghana as reported by Howard W. French, was seated in his roadside workshop, where he put the finishing touches on a coffin in the form of a bush taxi that was realistic down to the curves of the front bumper. He is surrounded by coffins in the form of gigantic crabs and lobsters, pods of cocoa and ears of corn. There is a boom in designer coffins along the two-mile stretch of beach-hugging road, where the carpenters of his Ga ethnic group have long hammered together exotic burial vessels. The coffins are used in everything from traditional burials of African chiefs, in which local religions figure prominently, to virtually all manner of Christian burials.

When death strikes in West Africa, even the poorest have long dug out hard-earned savings from their mattresses to organize feasts and hire the orchestras whose music helps see off their loved ones in style. For the wealthier classes, special cloth is printed, often bearing the likeness of the deceased, to be worn by all who take part in the funeral.

But for many Ghanaians nowadays, burial in an ordinary coffin is becoming déclassé. Among those who can afford it, more and more people are choosing a carved and painted coffin as the ultimate status symbol for the burial of their relatives.

A loaf of bread might be a family's choice for a baker, a fish for fisherman, a huge hen for the mother of a large family–whatever best serves as a statement about the deceased's life or livelihood.

"Most of what I do is still for chiefs," Mr. Okai said, pointing to the dozen or so coffins, none of them the rectangular boxes commonly associated with burial, that crowded his dusty workplace.

"Some people will come in and order a Mercedes-Benz or a Bedford lorry, and I will have to turn them down. I am an artist, and I save my art for those who can most appreciate it."

Mr. Okai can afford to turn his nose up by deciding on his own what is an appropriate coffin for a particular customer. Although he feigns to service only the noble, like other Ga coffin builders in the area, he runs a handsome side business selling his wares to collectors in the United States and Europe. In a country where annual per capita income is about $400, his works often fetch $2,000 or more.

Down the road, Paa Joe, 50, will have none of his colleague's snobbery. He has been building designer coffins for 18 years, and he remembers well the days when tradition more than popular tastes governed his coffin business.

He says he now has trouble keeping enough apprentices on hand, because as soon as they feel they have reached basic competency, each one wants to strike on his own in what has become a lucrative business.

"There was a time when we too only sold to chiefs and the like," Mr. Joe said. "Nowadays we average 10 or so a month, and the only thing we don't do is make coffins for children. There again, the reason is that children don't have a trade yet, not because of any taboo."

Modesty prevents him from saying so himself, but Mr. Joe, who was an apprentice under some of the trade's past masters, is considered by many of his peers to be the coffin world's ultimate craftsman. Among his wealthy clientele, some customers are known to buy their coffins long before death, placing them on display as decoration in a family room for all to see.

As he flips through his voluminous catalogue of creations with a visitor, Mr. Joe seems proudest of the requests that have posed the most unusual technical challenges.

"I once had to make a coffin for a very popular lorry driver," he said. "The man's colleagues insisted that I build a lorry complete with all the wiring: a horn, the headlights, a radio and cassette player, even a light on top. I told them there was nothing I could do about the battery once it had run down."

In a region where poverty stunts peoples' lives and clips their dreams, Mr. Joe likened being a coffin builder to being a sort of Santa Claus of the afterlife.

"Someone may have wanted to travel overseas all of their life, but never made it beyond their village," he said, pointing to a scale model of an Air Canada jet, seemingly ready for takeoff. "It makes people very happy when their relatives offer them something like this for burial. It makes me happy too."

Over the hills and across the ocean, a museum in Houston, Texas exhibits coffins made in Ghana. The National Museum of Funeral History on Barren Springs Drive offers a wide survey of funeral articles in 20,000 square feet. A central current display is that of colorful and playfully ornate coffins designed by Ghanaian sculptor, Kane Quaye. The fanciful coffins are built in the form of everything from a crab to a Mercedes-Benz.

In addition, the museum displays a hearse with carved-wood window coverings, a Victorian-era mourning tableau complete with kneeler and foldable organ set to play. Robert M. Boetticher is vice chairman and president of the museum. He states that aside from the physical trappings of funerals, one of his biggest fascinations is the interplay between the consistency of religious funeral rites over the years and the comparatively faddish nature of the more secular customs surrounding death.

BACK TO NATURE BURIALS –
"GREEN GRAVEYARDS"
TEXAS, CALIFORNIA, SOUTH CAROLINA

The year 2000 brought to light a few old and new cemeteries that have followed the concept of "green cemeteries" in previous years. Increased interest is noted recently, particularly in Texas, California, and South Carolina. Lee Austin, writing for Associated Press, tells about Texan George Russell, who believes in ashes to ashes and dust to dust. No embalming fluid. No airtight caskets. No steel vaults.

That's why he offers a different kind of funeral at his Ethician Family Cemetery – Texas' first "green cemetery." There, bodies are wrapped in cloth for burial under towering pine and oak trees near Lake Livingston.

"Isn't it wonderful if my body nurtures this huge oak tree and in its branches are the nests of beautiful songbirds," said Russell, 58, who plans to be buried the same way at his family's private plot near the cemetery. "In that way, you really never die, because you become a part of that songbird, you become a part of that tree, you become a part of that beauty."

The cemetery on 81 acres of dense forest about 90 miles north of Houston marks a growing trend in burial options that don't harm the environment and allow the body to decompose naturally.

Green cemeteries are common in the United Kingdom, but the first one labeled as such in the United States opened in South Carolina in 1996. Another followed in Florida, and Russell opened his in November. No national statistics track the number of green cemeteries, but Billy Campbell, president of Memorial Ecosystems in South Carolina, said a handful of others are planned around the country.

Bob Fells, external chief operating officer for the International Cemetery and Funeral Association, said it's hard to predict whether green cemeteries will become more commonplace.

"I don't think anyone really knows what things are really going to click with the public ... and what kind of things just have a novelty value," he said.

Terri Reed, an investigations assistant with the U.S. Department of Homeland Security who lives near Russell, was the first person to buy a plot in his cemetery.

Reed said traditional funerals have become too materialistic.

"I'm the kind of person who just doesn't like the way modern America commercializes everything," said Reed, 52. "I've always been interested in the idea of just being passed into the earth, you know, without all the rigmarole that the funerals go through nowadays."

Russell had those same concerns. He said he wanted to give families an affordable alternative to funerals, which industry experts say average around $5,000. That excludes a burial plot, which can average thousands.

Environmental reasons, not cost, motivated David Cocke to buy a plot. The chemistry and civil engineering professor at Lamar and Texas A&M universities says he disapproves of the huge amounts of water, pesticides and herbicides used to keep cemetery grounds immaculate. And cremation, he says, wastes energy and pollutes the air.

"You're left with not much of an alternative, if you want to be environmentally conscious about what you're going to contribute to the future pollution load, said Cocke, 59.

Russell, who owns an educational video production company in Huntsville, got the idea for the cemetery in 1968, when he and his wife lived in Central America. After seeing natives bury their dead in the rain forest, he said he knew he wanted to avoid a traditional cemetery.

"It was just as if you had returned to the Garden of Eden," he said.

The plan germinated in Russell's mind for decades before he discovered Lake Livingston and the surrounding undeveloped land and realized it was the perfect spot for his 248-plot cemetery.

The land was mapped out in the 1970s as a resort and retirement community called Waterwood. But largely because of the global oil slump in the 1960s, it never was developed.

Russell's family wanted to preserve Waterwood, so he and his parents bought 2,500 acres near the lake. Besides the cemetery, they have used the land to establish sanctuaries for alligators and eagles, a 131-acre kingleaf pine preserve, and a 110-acre research forest.

People who buy a plot, each of which can accommodate up to 12 graves, cannot plant flowers or cut down or damage trees. They are encouraged to install markers with short biographies of the deceased and must submit a record of the exact location of each grave using global positioning equipment.

Anyone can buy a one-quarter to one-third acre plot by making whatever donation they can afford to the Universal Ethician Church, an interfaith, ecumenical congregation that Russell founded a few years ago. The funeral can cost next to nothing if that's what the family wants, he said.

"I've seen so many families who spent money, sometimes tens of thousands of dollars, to pickle grandmother or their mother or their father or their child," he said. "The sad thing is that we tend to be so caught up in our material selves and our material world and what other people think."

The green cemetery in California is even more strict. Markers are not allowed. Global positioning system devices and native boulders are used as markers. Lisa Leff of Associated Press writes in June 2004 about the Mill Valley property calling it the ultimate expression of back-to-nature. Three entrepreneurs are creating what they say is California's first organic cemetery, hoping their ban on floral arrangements and formaldehyde will serve as a national model.

Embalming fluid, metal caskets and marble headstones won't be permitted at Fernwood forever. Instead, the dead will be placed in biodegradable boxes or shrouds and interred in nondescript graves that mourners can dig themselves.

To ensure visitors pay their respects at the right spot, the cemetery will provide global positioning system devices and native boulders as markers.

The partners think their business model can be easily replicated in other crowded areas where space is at a premium. Co-owner Tyler Cassity said they are scouting potential sites in Oregon, near Seattle and outside Chicago.

Besides offering environmentally conscious San Francisco Bay area residents a green alternative to identical plots on heavily landscaped grounds, the cemetery will preserve 32 acres of open space between San Francisco Bay and Stinson Beach, Cassity said.

Some proceeds from each funeral will be used for restoring and maintaining the meadows, oak forests and scrub hills that make up the property, a portion of which has been in use as a conventional cemetery since the 19th century.

"The idea is returning to the land what we have taken from it," said Cassity, 34, a second-generation veteran of the mortuary business whose family renovated the celebrity-rich Hollywood Memorial Park Cemetery in 1998. "If you talk to someone about this concept, they will often say, 'I always wanted to be buried naturally under a tree.' It just rings true to them."

Fernwood Forever must clear state and local regulatory approval, but its owners expect it to open later this year. It would be the nation's second eco-cemetery, according to project partner Joe Sehee, a Los Angeles writer. The first was opened in South Carolina by physician Billy Campbell, who has joined Cassity and Sehee for what they are calling their "memorial nature preserve" in this Marin County town.

About 50 people have chosen to spend eternity at Campbell's 35-acre Ramsey Creek Preserve in Westminster, S.C., since it opened in 1996. Cassity and Sehee see a bigger market in the Bay Area, where they estimate that 80 percent of the deceased are cremated. They say they have a waiting list of about 100 interested customers.

The owners aren't sure how much room they'll have – they're doing an ecological survey that will determine how many people can be curried on site. Prices haven't been set yet either, but Sehee said he expects the cemetery to cost less than a traditional venue.

In attacking the expense, trappings and "obsolescence" of the funeral industry, Cassity said he also hopes to provide survivors with more meaningful bereavement rituals. Relatives will be encouraged, for example, to accompany the bodies of their loved ones to the crematorium or to participate in candlelit memorial services sitting in circles with an urn in the center.

Along with a GPS device, visitors will be given hand-held audio-video units that display mini-documentaries about a dead person's life. Staff members will be called "stewards" instead of funeral directors and – when they aren't helping grieving families – will build trails and remove nonnative plants.

The partners say they will also want Fernwood Forever to be a place for celebrating the living as well as the deceased. Accordingly, they plan to encourage the public to use the cemetery for weddings, baptisms and other meaningful occasions.

"The whole idea is to provide a space where people can get in touch with the cycles of life, where death and decay can exist alongside rebirth and renewal," Sehee said. "That's what you see in nature."

Barbara Basles writes an article "Green Graveyards A Natural Way to Go" and emphasizes back-to-nature burials in biodegradable caskets to conserve land.

In lovely woods just outside the tiny town of Westminster, South Carolina, discreetly scattered among the tall pines and poplars, are 20 graves, many hand-dug by Billy Campbell.

The graves, mounds of earth dotted with wildflowers and bathed in dappled sunlight, are marked with flat stones engraved with the names of the dead – from a rock-ribbed Southern Baptist to a gentle New Age hippie.

Campbell, the town's only doctor, is an ardent environmentalist. He buries patients, friends and strangers – without embalming them – in biodegradable caskets, or in no caskets at all, in the nature preserve he created along Ramsey Creek.

The burials are legal and meet all state regulations and health requirements. But in the beginning, many in this conservative town of 2,700 people were skeptical, even angry, about the Ramsey Creek Preserve, where the dead protect the land of the living.

'We weren't doing anything weird or outlandish," Campbell says, "but people accused us of throwing bodies in the creek or laying them out for buzzards to eat." He recalls one irate woman, apparently convinced of the bodies-in-the-creek rumor, who "told me I was a rich doctor who could buy bottled water, but she would have to drink my dead men's soup."

In the six years since the burial ground opened, Westminster has come, slowly but surely, to accept it. And now, Campbell's idea – nurtured in the backwoods of South Carolina – is spreading to rich, trendy Marin County, California.

Campbell, 49, and his new partner Tyler Cassity – a 34-year old entrepreneur who owns cemeteries in three states – are scheduled to open the new burial preserve this summer on a hillside in the shadow of the Golden Gate Bridge.

Campbell says he and Cassity hope to work with conservation groups to open similar natural burial grounds across the country, each crisscrossed – like Ramsey Creek – with hiking trails. "What we are doing is basically land conservation," Campbell says. "By setting aside a woods for natural burials, we preserve it from development. At the same time, I think we put death in its rightful place, as part of the cycle of life. Our burials honor the idea of dust to dust."

At Ramsey Creek, burial in a simple casket costs about $2,300. The National Funeral Directors Association says the average conventional funeral costs about $6,500. That includes mortuary services, embalming, a casket and a cement vault or box for the casket, which is often required for a cemetery burial. A cemetery plot adds even more to the cost.

"The mortuary-cemetery business is a $20-billion-a-year industry, and if we could get just 10 percent of that," Campbell says, "we'd have $2 billion a year going toward land conservation on memorial preserves where people could picnic, hike or take nature classes."

A native of Westminster – his family's roots here go back to the Revolutionary War – Campbell concedes he's a bit of an eccentric, but then "small Southern towns are good places for eccentrics," he says. Westminster, after all, was home to the Guns, Cabinets and Nightcrawlers store, "and I think that's a whole lot stranger than Ramsey Creek," he laughs.

The folksy, erudite doctor and the hip young businessman who owns Hollywood Forever, a celebrity cemetery where Rudolph Valentino and Cecil B. DeMille are buried, believe they have the potential to revolutionize the funeral industry and conserve a million acres of land over the next 30 years.

Campbell and Cassity, who has been a consultant to HBO's television series *Six Feet Under*, think the idea of burials that protect, rather than consume, green space will appeal to boomers, including those who want their cremated ashes scattered or buried. In Marin County, they plan to designate three of the site's 32 acres for interments and conserve the rest.

In place of the perpetual care fund of the conventional cemetery, "where money is set aside to mow the grass and battle back any natural growth," Campbell says, funds in memorial preserves will be used to restore the land.

Campbell's Ramsey Creek – the first "green" burial site in America – has inspired another in Florida, and a third has recently opened in Texas.

Campbell remembers that when his father died, he wanted to bury him in a simple, dignified biodegradable wood box. But his father was buried in the only wood box the funeral home offered – an eye-popping, ornate oak casket the funeral director assured him was the same model that held actor Dan Blocker, who played Hoss Cartwright on the TV hit *Bonanza*.

"You know, I didn't take any real comfort in that," Campbell says.

CEMETERIES GET EERIE IN BIG EASY, LAND OF VOODOO, GHOSTS AND JAZZ

Craig Guillot *Free Press* Special Writer writes about New Orleans
On a quick October night, the back streets of the French Quarter can be an unnerving place. Never mind the thieves or shady characters, the dark under-belly of what is often known as America's most haunted city bears the scars of a brutal history.

Cool breezes blow through the walkways of 18th-Century buildings, the clacking of horse carriages echo off the brick walls and the white facade of the St. Louis Cathedral rises above it all. Throw in paranormal activities, voodoo practitioners, and it's enough to send shivers down anyone's spine.

Every October, thousands of travelers descend upon the Cresent City in search of horror and hauntings. Costumed guides lead visitors through crum-bling cemeteries, the drumming voodoo ritual thump through the walls of homes and reported sightings of ghost come from every crack and crevice in the French Quarter. This is a city that takes no shame in its macabre attrac-tions. Marie Laveau, voodoo queen, is buried here.

Cemeteries convey haunted history
In a place where the dead are honored, it's natural they are sent to their resting places with a celebration. Since the city was first established, promi-nent musicians and politicians have been sent off to the cemeteries in jazz funerals, joyous occasions in which beers and trombones outnumber tears and flowers.

The roots of these burial rituals are traced back to Africa. It all ends in the cities of the dead where histories of mystery, danger, disease and horror lie encased in massive crypts. Behind the rusty iron gates, the ghost-white tombs lie adorned with crosses and angelic statues that exude both beauty and mystery.

Since the city was founded in 1718, the dead in New Orleans have never been content staying in the ground. Corpses buried on the banks of the muddy Mississippi river once washed into city streets, and those buried with-in the city often broke from their coffins and rose to the surface during floods and heavy rains.

Even today, heavy flooding can bring up bones in some of the older cemeteries. It wasn't until Mayor Esteban Miro in the 1780s adopted Spanish-style wall vaults that New Orleans finally kept its rotting corpses and skele-tons off the streets.

There are more than 40 cemeteries in the New Orleans area, each with its own legends and histories. Nestled in the historic neighborhood of Treme, St. Louis No. I (there are two other St: Louis cemeteries) was founded in 1789 and is the city's oldest.

Many historical figures are buried here including Ernest Morial, the city's first black mayor, and Laveau. To this day, many still leave offerings and mark an X on her tomb, evidence of those who have asked for her wishes.

Built in 1872 on what was once the Metairie Race Course, Metairie Cemetery is the first cemetery to be patterned after the park-like cemeteries of the East. There are more than 150 acres of mystifying tombs and statues, many of which take influence ftom around the world. There's a tomb designed with Egyptian influences, another modeled after a Greek temple and even a memorial to the Louisiana division of the Army of Northern Virginia, which fought in the Civil War.

Set as the filming location for a number of movies, including "Double Jeopardy," "Interview with the Vampire" and "Dracula 2000," Lafayette No.1 is another of one other the city's best-known cemeteries.

Built on the Livaudais plantation in 1833 and originally established as a cemetery for the City of Lafayette, this was the city's first planned cemetery and is on the Register of Historic Places. It is a setting in many Anne Rice novels, and a number of German and Irish yellow fever victims are buried here.

Paranormal power abound

Doing away with the fear of death altogether, there are some in the city who believe immortality can be achieved through vampirism. Even before Rice brought her vampires to the Big Easy, gothic types had sought New Orleans as a dark sanctuary.

While those aspects of vampirism – etemal life, creation of vampires through biting on the neck- portrayed in movies is no more than fiction, Rice's "Interview with the Vampire" efforts have resulted in dozens of dark landmarks, which can be visited on vampire tours.

There is also a group called the Louisiana Area Vampire Association. (It is said some people who are into vampirism go so far as to engage in consensual blood drinking.) Les Temps de Vampires, a vampire ball spawned by Anne Rice fans, draws a wide mix of tourist, fans and "real" vampires.

Even without the children of the night, the French Quarter can be plenty scary, a Halloween natural. With a history of disease, death, war and murder, it's no surprise the place is a paranormal playground littered with horrific tales. One such legend is that of the "Axeman of New Orleans," a serial killer who was reputed to have butchered 13 people with an axe between 1911 and 1919. To this day, it is often disputed whether the killer was found; some believe it was the work of a ghost.

Such stories can be found in every comer of the city from the oak-shaded streets of Uptown to the cobblestone alleys of the French Quarter. The Beauregard-Keyes House, one of the most famous, was the former home of Confederate Gen. Pierre Gustave Toutant de Beauregard, who took over a commanding officer of the Southern troops at the battle of Shiloh. It is said that at 2 a.m. on moonlit nights, he and his troops materialize in the hallway near the ballroom.

The LaLaurie House, considered one of the most haunted places in the French quarter, often had trouble keeping residents throughout the 1800s and 1900s due to reported ghostly activities.

It was said Madame LaLaurie, a socialite who lived there in the 1830s, tortured and abused her slaves, but in 1834 when fire broke out at the residence, firefighters discovered one of the most brutal scenes in the city's history. Slaves had been chained to the wall, tortured, mutilated, disemboweled and decapitated. Madame LaLaurie, reports say, got away.

Ghosts might love the city but they seem to haunt the countryside in even greater numbers.

Few places in the world have received such haunted press as the Myrtles Plantation in the small town of St. Francisville.

Legend says there have been at least 10 suicides and homicides on the property since it was settled in 1796. Paranormal events have been documents there, and the house remains on the Smithsonian Institution's list of most haunted places in the world.

Those who make the two-hour trip upriver and opt to spend the night at the plantation during Halloween might be in for one of the most haunted experiences of their lives. (See Chapter 12 for New Orleans, Louisiana.)

AT LAST, AFTER 85 YEARS, BABY "SNOOKEMS" HAS A STONE

Ralph Blumenthal writes from Corpus Christi, Texas
The graves do not take up much room in the Baby Rest section of Rose Hill cemetery, where the ages on the markers are measured in months and the sentiments are achingly simple: "Our Doll Baby," "Our Little Man;" "Our Girl."

Among them, a small new stone was laid Thursday. It bore only a nickname and imprecise details: "Unknown Baby Girl, Victim of 1919 Storm."

Finally, 85 years after a stealthy September hurricane obliterated much of this coastal city, claiming as many as 1,000 lives, the infant of about 11 months and known as "Snookems" was getting her long overdue memorial, a last testament to one of the nation's worst disasters.

The delay was strange, but her little-known story is far stranger.

Her body, along with hundreds of others, had been left at a funeral home, where her mother supposedly promised to return to claim it but never did. Whether out of hope that the mother would someday return or carelessness or callousness, the child, who was black, remained unburied for 70 years, her preserved body laid out in a yellow pinafore in a crepe-lined casket at the Maxwell P. Dunne funeral home in Corpus Christi. It was seen by only a handful of people who learned the secret.

One was James A. Skrobarcek, a local lawyer, who had been allowed a viewing of the mummified body with his Cub Scout troop in the 1950's and was instrumental in finally getting the headstone. Another was a girl at the time whose father had worked at the funeral home. But over the years even they and funeral home seemed to forget about it.

In 1982 Ronald J. Alonzo was working at Maxwell P. Dunne, founded in 1908 and the only undertaker in town at the time of the hurricane. "I was in the preparation room cleaning on top of the cabinets and found a baby casket." Mr. Alonzo recalled this week. "I moved it to clean and then opened it and there was the baby."

Astonished, he said, he reported his find to the office. "They told me the baby had been lost in the storm, her name was Snookems," he said. "I said 'O.K.' and put it back."

"I don't know why they decided to keep the baby," said Mr. Alonzo, who now owns the business. He said the condition of the body left him unsure of the baby's race. But by 1990, he said, "we all agreed it was pretty much a good idea to bury it; there was no need for it to be here."

Rose Hill Memorial Park - where hundreds of victims of the storm were buried in a mass grave under a boulder placed by the American Red Cross "in memory of the unidentified dead who lost their lives in the storm of Sept. 14, 1919" - donated a plot in the children's section, and the baby was laid to rest on March 26,1990. But there was no marker.

Mr. Skrobarcek, now 55, said that for decades he had lost the memory of his 1957 or 1958 Cub Scout trip. But last year's anniversary of the hurricane, he said, suddenly brought the baby to mind.

The coffin, he now remembered, had been brought out from the back and set down on a maroon velvet settee past which the riveted young scouts filed by respectfully. The child was in a yellow pinafore, he said, "her skin like hard leather." He remembered realizing she was black "and I came away with a greater sense of humanity."

Mr. Skrobarcek said he went to Mr. Alonzo to check his recollections and found other confirmation in a cemetery burial record.

Another longtime resident, Rita Gunter, 72, a retired kindergarten teacher, recalled seeing the baby - and even being given it to hold by her father, a funeral home employee - as a 12 year old in 1944. Ms. Gunter recalled the baby's being kept for a time in a drawer and said the nickname came from a popular 1930's Fanny Brice character, "Baby Snooks," that the funeral home later condensed to "Snookems." Yellowing index cards at the funeral home show that it handled hundreds of storm victims of various races, so this child appears to not have been left unburied on account of race, but whether a white child would have been kept so long is arguable. A descendant of Maxwell Dunne, who spoke on the condition of anonymity because, he said, "it sounds like a creepy Southern story to me," said that Mr. Dunne fought to keep the Ku Klux Klan out of Nueces County in the 1920's.

Mr. Alonzo, after talking to Mr. Skrobarcek, donated the stone that was laid Thursday (with a date initially inscribed incorrectly).

Mr. Skrobarcek's findings have drawn high interest at the Corpus Christi library, where a vast archive on the storms contains no reference to the baby. The original typed death list testify to the democracy of the carnage: "male unknown, stiff black hair can't tell if white or colored; body of child about 2 years old, red sack, white undershirt, diaper pinned with extra large safety pin."

The storm struck 19 years after the nation's worst hurricane leveled Galveston, killing up to 12,000. Although the authorities played down the toll of the 1919 storm, as many as 1,000 may have perished, according to a 2001 dissertation for a master's degree at Texas A&M Kingsville by Mary Jo O'Rear, adjunct history professor at Del Mar College.

There are still some people alive who remember the storm, if not the baby. Alclair Mays Pleasant, 98, a former teacher now living in Tulsa, Okla., said she was 13 and living with her grandmother - a former slave - when the hurricane hit. The house, high above the 15- foot storm surge" withstood the 110-mile-an-hour winds. But the next morning, Ms. Pleasant said, "the debris was floating around and the bodies were floating." A tanker had broken apart in the gulf, she said, "and the oil was all over the bodies of the dead."

CREAM OF WHEAT MAN
WOODLAWN CEMETERY, LESLIE, MICHIGAN

A short walk into the cemetery in Leslie lies a flat, grayish stone no bigger than a paper dinner napkin.

There are no markings on the stone's surface other than scars left by a lawn mower and grime that has collected since 1938.

The stone - flush with the ground - is the type a man would have if he had neither kin nor money.

Yet the man buried there, 79-year-old Frank L. White, had kin. He also was a bit of a celebrity. He had a memorable, well-known, if anonymous, face, according to the yellowed record book in the office at Woodlawn Cemetery. For scribbled under White's name are the words "Cream of Wheat man."

Mr. White might be pleased by the mystery he's stirred up in this town of about 2,000 people. In the 15 years White lived in Leslie, he had told folks he was the man on the Cream of Wheat box - the friendly chef, holding the piping-hot bowl of enriched farina.

But was he really? And if he was, is it right in today's politically correct America to dredge up his connection to ads that feel very Jim Crow?

The mystery has spurred interest in Leslie history and in buying a proper grave marker for one of the community's own.

"Here's a person of color who dies in 1938 and his story is not really told," said Jesse Lasorda, who is leading the movement to give White a marker.

Lasorda, a historian, has raised about $100 and hopes to collect $1,000 to buy a gray granite stone that would stand 6 to 8 inches at its highest point. On the front face, engravers would carve White's name, date of birth and date of death. On the back, Lasorda is thinking of having the image of the Cream of Wheat chef engraved.

"It's a can't-win situation," said Clinton Canady, a Lansing lawyer and leader within one of the area's prominent black families. "Somebody is going to claim they are offended."

Why would talk of White and Cream of Wheat bother anyone?

Well, unlike today's image of a handsome black chef looking pleasant and confident, the old ads clearly show a black man in a subservient role to whites.

Print ads in the Boston Cooking-School Magazine in 1913 and 1914 show an amiable black cook, working as a household servant to white children.

It's part of American history, whether anyone wants to admit it or not.

The man behind the face

There's no doubt that Frank White could have been the inspiration for the Cream of Wheat icon.

By all accounts, White was an affable character in town and the head of what was likely the only black family living in Leslie at the time.

Norman Lantz, now 75, delivered newspapers and fire kindling to White and his wife, Mary. He was about 8 years old at the time.

"I can almost visualize him," Lantz said. "He was more striking."

White was a thin man, about 5 feet, 7 inches tall, with white hair in tight curls.

"As I recall, they both would come to the door," Lantz said. "I don't know if they ever invited me in. They were the type of people who would."

It's a bit of a mystery why the Whites would have come to Leslie about 1923. Lantz recalled that they were the only black family in town, but Lasorda said his research has turned up information that a vibrant black community once centered on Rice Street, where White and his wife lived.

Today, only the oldest generations of Leslie know of Frank White, who married twice but had no children. He has no living relatives to pass on his legacy, only a few written records to explain the mystery kicked up by the man in cemetery plot No. 310.

Fame or claim?

It was Woodlawn grounds- keeper Art Raymond who penned "Cream of Wheat" into the Woodlawn record book. He did so 10 or 12 years ago, after reading about White's connection in a Leslie history book.

Recordkeeping in the cemetery book wasn't all that detailed decades ago.

"Some just say 'burial,' which is bloody helpful," Raymond said.

So he was happy to find a mention of a Frank White on page 348 of "Leslie: A Place in Time."

The book, published in 1986, attributed the "Cream of Wheat" fact to White's obituary, but a close look at two obituaries for White - one in the Ingham County News and the other in the Local-Republican - don't mention Cream of Wheat by name. They say only that White said he posed for a breakfast- cereal company. The Ingham obituary noted White told folks he was paid $1,000 for his image.

Why did local historians assume White posed for Cream of Wheat?

"Everybody said that," said Jennett Wood, a co-author of the history book. "It was just well known."

People knew White as the Cream of Wheat man, so Wood figured the omission in the obituaries was just a mistake.

As any historian or historical anthropologist knows, history can be inexact. The cemetery records unequivocally declare White to be the Cream of Wheat man because the groundskeeper wrote it to be so.

Some pieces of White's story, though, don't add up.

The case against:

In 1938, $1,000 would have been more like $18,000 - an awful lot of money to pose for a single photo.

Kraft, which now owns the Cream of Wheat label, doesn't know who the model was. There is an indication that a waiter posed for a photo some time between 1900 and 1910 and that the image inspired a number of ads. But that waiter was paid only $5, according to a clipping of a 1938 issue of Fortune magazine in the corporate archives.

It's possible White was that model, but unlikely, according to the Smithsonian in Washington, D.C.

Blacks were a significant part of American advertising by the 1890s, said Faith Davis Ruffins, curator of African-American history and culture at Smithsonian's National Museum of American History. The three North Dakota men who started the Cream of Wheat company wouldn't have needed a model.

"One of them remembered an image of a black man holding a skillet:" Davis Ruffins said.

That image was the inspiration for the advertising campaign. She said that it wasn't until the 1940s - after White's death - that a man posed as a model. That's when the icon was tweaked, giving us today's familiar Cream of Wheat face.

Even Lasorda has questioned whether White was really paid $1,000, but he decided to believe White's story.

"Why would he say that?" Lasorda said. "What's to be gained by that?"

Lasorda, a historian of black history, believes that boasting would have drawn attention, and that blacks in Jim Crow America likely weren't interested in drawing attention to themselves.

Leslie residents today are intrigued by news that there may be an advertising celebrity buried in their community cemetery. The fact that the details of the story are a bit of a mystery, makes it even more fascinating.

"It's the proverbial human- interest story," Lasorda said.

There is already interest in Leslie to look at other unmarked graves in Woodlawn and to look at black history within the community.

Canady isn't offended by the dredging up of White and the old Cream of Wheat ads.

"If he was the person on the Cream of Wheat box, then why not remember him?"

A DEATH THAT WASN'T

The New York Times reported this strange story that to a "lay person" seems to be extreme negligence. It appears that Larry Green stepped out of the darkness so suddenly that the car that hit him did not have skid marks. He ended up beside a trash-strewn ditch, where he was examined by paramedics and declared dead.

Over the next two and a half hours, Mr. Green's bloody body with a gaping head wound was zipped into a black vinyl bag, taken to the morgue and slid into a refrigerated drawer.

There was one problem: Mr. Green was alive.

Two weeks after that shocking discovery, Mr. Green is in a hospital intensive care unit, paralyzed. Family members have listened in horror as officials described the miscues that led to the error. They and others in this rural tobacco community northeast of Raleigh are left to wonder how something like this could have happened – and whether it has happened before.

On the chilly night of Jan. 24, Mr. Green and two friends went to a grocery store about 8:45 p.m. to pick up a few tall-boy cans of Natural Ice beer to take back to his trailer down the road.

According to reports from state troopers and the Franklin county attorney's office, the driver that hit him, Tamuel Jackson, did not have time to stop her car before it slammed into Mr. Green as he tried to cross the highway in front of his trailer.

Randy Kearney, an off-duty paramedic, was on the scene at 8:54 p.m. and found no pulse or sign of breathing.

When two county paramedics, Paul Kilmer and Katherine Lamell, arrived moments later, Mr. Kearney told them Mr. Green was dead but asked Mr. Kilmer to double-check. Mr. Kilmer replied that his determination was "good enough for me." According to Mr. Kearney and two fire fighters, Mr. Kilmer told officials he could not remember saying that, but he does not deny it.

Although the law does not require the medical examiner to go to accident scenes, Dr. J. B. Perdue showed up half an hour later and began examining the body, lifting and twisting Mr. Green's broken right leg, rolling him over and inserting a gloved finger into the gash in Mr. Green's head.

When Dr. Perdue opened Mr. Green's jacket, several firefighters noticed what appeared to be an in-and-out movement in Mr. Green's chest and abdomen.

"Doc, is he breathing?" the firefighter's heard Mr. Kearny ask. Dr. Perdue told Mr. Kearney that it was just air escaping or moving around inside the body.

Paramedics put Mr. Green in a body bag and drove him to the morgue in nearby Louisburg. There, Dr. Perdue examined the body a second time. He took a blood sample, lifted Mr. Green's eyelids and sniffed around the man's mouth for alcohol.

Pamela Hayes, a paramedic who had accompanied the body, thought she noticed twitching in Mr. Green's right eyelid. She asked Dr. Perdue if he was sure Mr. Green was really dead. Dr. Perdue responded that the twitching was a spasm, "like a frog leg jumping in a frying pan." Ms. Hayes told colleagues, "I don't feel good about this," according to the county attorney's report.

The body bag was zipped back up, and Mr. Green was placed in the portable morgue unit, where the temperature is kept a few degrees above freezing.

Mr. Green would probably have remained there had Trooper Tyrone Hunt of the state police not arrived around 11:20 p.m. and asked Dr. Perdue to help him determine the direction from which Mr. Green had been struck.

This time, Dr. Perdue observed slight movement. He could not find a pulse in Mr. Green's neck, thigh or wrist, even with a stethoscope. Dr. Perdue summoned paramedics and an electrocardiogram, which was able to pick up a faint heart rhythm.

Family members who have kept vigil at Mr. Green's bedside say that his eyes shutter at times and that he shows signs he recognizes those around him. It Is unclear whether his paralysis is from the accident or from the handling of his body.

Within days, Mr. Kearney, Mr. Kilmer, Ms. Hayes and Ms. Lamell, the paramedics, were suspended with pay. Mr. Kearney and Mr. Kilmer have been fired; Ms. Hayes and Ms. Lamell were ordered to undergo remedial training before coming back to work. Mr. Kearney declined a request for comment, and the others did not respond to messages.

Dr. John Butts, the state's chief medical examiner, said that Dr. Perdue did everything the law required of him and that there were no plans to censure him.

"He went because he was informed that a man was dead as a result of violence or trauma," Dr. Butts said. "He did not come with a doctor's bag and a stethoscope."

Dr. Perdue said, "I am not in any shape form or fashion responsible for pronouncement of death."

THE CRADLE: THE SEA ISLANDS AND SOUTHEAST

I KNOW MOON-RISE, I KNOW STAR-RISE,

LAY DIS BODY DOWN.

I WALK IN DE MOONLIGHT, I WALK IN DE STARLIGHT,

TO LAY DIS BODY DOWN.

I'LL WALK IN DE GRAVEYARD, I'LL WALK THROUGH

DE GRAVEYARD,

TO LAY DIS BODY DOWN.

I'LL LIE IN DE GRAVE AND STRETCH OUT MY ARMS,

LAY DIS BODY DOWN.

I GO TO DE JUDGEMENT IN DE EVENIN' OF DE DAY

WHEN I LAY DIS BODY DOWN,

AND MY SOUL AND YOUR SOUL WILL MEET IN DE DAY,

WHEN I LAY DIS BODY DOWN.

—AUTHOR UNKNOWN

CHAPTER TWO

There are hundreds, if not thousands, of sea islands along the Georgia, South Carolina, and Florida coasts—settings for some of the most unique burial sites imaginable. Much of the area, particularly in South Carolina, is also known as the Low Country. Burial grounds of the Sea Islands and the Low Country are predominantly family- or church-related. Most exist without a state mandate for perpetual care.

The lush magnificence surrounding many of these cemeteries is unexcelled. Tropic-like landscapes reveal nature at its finest. Live oak trees laden with Spanish moss and green- to brown-leafed palmetto trees tower over scrub bushes and wildflowers that display their blooms amid clumps of fallen leaves, some so old they appear petrified.

Set within this scene are granite memorials to forgotten loved ones: upright, tilted, or ground level, some with legible inscriptions and others on which the message has faded with time. Often the markers have been homemade, constructed of material of traditional significance.

Most of the cemeteries in this region are located beside a river or marsh and are less than ten acres in size. Walking through the grounds requires stepping high to avoid stumbling over tree roots and scattered, matted brush. There is no symmetry, no order or plan, to the location of the markers. A family member visits the burial ground prior to the funeral, selects a spot for the grave, and informs the funeral home so that digging can commence. Care is taken to try to avoid disturbing areas where there are burials without markers.

Because these cemeteries are often "just across the way" or "down by the church," they are as familiar as the local school, the church, or the general store. Children here do not view the cemeteries as scary or haunted as they do in other areas of the country. And for both residents and visitors of these special areas the fascination and quest for knowledge about death and burial rituals remains fervent and real.

Daufuskie Island, South Carolina; Hilton Head Island, South Carolina; Beaufort, South Carolina; St. Helena Island, South Carolina; Low Bottom, South Carolina; Charleston, South Carolina; Columbia, South Carolina, Winnsboro, South Carolina and Savannah, Georgia, introduce the Sea Islands and the Low Country cemeteries. The mossy fringe of the Sea Islands edges a 250-mile stretch of southern coastline reaching from northern Florida up to Charleston. The islands—marshy, low land veined by numerous tidal streams—appear everywhere.

Because the deep waterways offer good harbors, captive Africans were put ashore off ships hailing from West Africa or the Caribbean. The slave population—by 1860 more than four hundred thousand in South Carolina alone—provided the muscle for plantations of rice, indigo, and cotton. During the Civil War, General Sherman issued Special Field Order Fifteen, reserving land for former slaves. Unfortunately, the order was widely ignored within a year, and many whites held onto their land and bequeathed it to their heirs.

Several fairly large parcels of land, however, were purchased and kept by the freedmen—those blacks emancipated at the end of the war—who now began to receive wages for their labor. They planted crops and built houses, churches, and, of course, cemeteries. On St. Helena Island, in particular, much of the area is divided into communities that maintain the same names as the plantations before the war. In fact, it is still common for residents to ask each other, "What community do you live in?" rather than, "What street do you live on?"

Further north, in South Carolina, are Columbia's Randolph Cemetery and, a little farther north, Winnsboro's Camp Welfare Cemetery. The quaint town of McClellanville lies further east, in a wildlife and National Forest area just a sandspit from the Atlantic Ocean. McClellanville is the hometown of Vennie Deas-Moore, previously assistant folklorist at the Smithsonian Institute's Office of Folklore Program and Howard University's Institute of Urban Affairs and Research. Woven within her sensitive recollections are the traditions that still remain and shadows of the history lost in many similar coastal towns.

Over a small graveyard alongside my family's church, Old Bethel A.M.E., hover the spirits of my ancestors. African American burial traditions in McClellanville . . . still reflect the belief that at death, the physical body is lowered into the soil, but the soul/spirit remains among the living. This spirit must be satisfied and not disturbed. The belief [holds] that these spirits have an invisible circle of spiritual bonding with their family and loved ones. My mother often talks about how I was passed across the coffin of my grandfather. The belief was that since I was still a tiny, weak soul—only a baby and the youngest of my family—my grandfather could come back and take me with him, causing my death at this young age. Passing me across broke that spiritual bond.

In earlier times a broken wooden wagon wheel was placed on the grave, breaking the spiritual links, so that the spirit would not tantalize the living. Today floral designs are arranged in the shape of a broken wheel. The yucca plant is frequently planted among the graves. This thorny bush makes it difficult for the spirit to roam about the graveyard. Sweet-smelling plants are also found among the foliage. The dead are attracted to the sweet smell of the gardenia bush. One lady chuckles as she tells me, "I not too long ago dug up a large gardenia bush out of my yard because it was drawing too many spirits to my house."

Immediately after death, open vessels of water are emptied, so the roving spirit will not remain in the home. Broken plates, drinking containers, and utensils, items last used by the deceased, are placed on the grave site. One may also find medicine bottles, furniture, cigar boxes, doll heads, and other personal items.

Deas-Moore also offers these words of advice to those who visit a cemetery: "Do not cross over the grave, walk around. . . . Do not stand on top of the grave. . . . Do not point at the grave or your finger may drop off. . . . Do not remove grave goods or you will carry the discontented spirit with you." She further explains the importance of family traditions within burial services and cemetery maintenance:

The family plot is an important part of African American family structure. As death comes, each member must be placed within the family plot, so that the family will remain together. This may mean bringing the body from miles away. Some family plots are likened to gardens. The care of these plots is restricted to the family. It is the responsibility of the family to maintain the spiritual, as well as physical, continuity of the grave site. There is usually a grave keeper, but his responsibility is to maintain the overgrowth of the cemetery, taking care not to disturb the grave sites. Another important role of the grave keeper is to watch the cemetery against intruders.

Conservation of African American cemeteries means "let it be." It is not unusual to find an African American grave completely overgrown, especially when burials are no longer taking place. This does not necessarily signify neglect, but is done so that the dead will not be disturbed.

Whether intentional or not, the coming of resort developers to the South Carolina coastline has erased many remote African American burial grounds. The grave sites of slaves, remnants of the southern plantations, have vanished forever without any records of their existence. Someone once told me that what was once her family's burial site is now a golf course. The opportunity for preservation is past, except for a few elders with memories of where their ancestors' physical bodies were once buried. As for the souls or spirits, who knows?

Deas-Moore's story reflects the kind of generational, hand-me-down history that exists among many African Americans. The history of Deas-Moore's parents and her parents' parents is preserved through word-of-mouth, a tradition that is commonplace throughout the South and other regions. When researching the various cemeteries, it was found that often very sketchy information exists, precisely because word-of-mouth acts in place of conventional recordkeeping in many small towns. For this reason, interviews with local residents must supplement death certificates and other facts found in city and county records offices, if any documents of this type existed. In the descriptions that follow, information is sometimes missing, but even what is missing speaks to the flavor of the particular burial site.

Daufuskie Island, South Carolina

Daufuskie Island lies between Hilton Head and the Tybee Islands along the Atlantic Coast. It was the first inhabited Carolina sea island and is part of the southernmost tip of South Carolina territory. Without a bridge, the island—two-and-one-half miles wide by five miles long—is bordered on the north by the Cooper River, on the east by Calibogue Sound and the Atlantic Ocean, on the south by Mongin Creek, and on the west by New River.

In recent years, when property, especially beach property, had been nearly depleted on other islands in Beaufort County, all eyes focused on Daufuskie. By 1990 developers were on the scene with bulldozers and earth-movers. Trees were cut and burned and roads changed drastically. Residents, who once walked the seven-mile stretch of beach to gather clams, oysters, conch, arrowheads, and shells, found they could no longer do so.

Much of the island, however, has remained undeveloped, and visitors arrive daily to take in its natural splendor. It takes twenty to thirty minutes by ferry to reach the island; ferries make the run several times each day from docks in neighboring Hilton Head Island and Savannah, Georgia, both less than twenty miles away. In addition, private boats frequent the waterways with country club members and golfers headed for the island's new and expensive "play areas." Buses wait at Daufuskie's dock for tourists; their guide-bus drivers constantly circle the island, providing visitors with a running narrative of what is and what was.

For some who knew the island in years past, there is sadness. Some of the blacks who remain have fought the system, winning in a losing kind of way. Native islanders who had to sell their land because of high taxes and those who now look out their windows and see guard towers and gates have a feeling of hopelessness. The gates barricade the entrances to the costly private clubs built on the land that they and their neighbors once owned. However, some of the native islanders are not as concerned about the changes. Jobs are guaranteed to all residents who apply, and this has been particularly helpful to the young islanders who rely on after-school jobs.

An interesting account of traditional rites of burial on the island is included in the book *An Island Named Daufuskie*, by Billie Burn. The story of the struggle as it relates to the island's cemeteries touches one's heart; it prompted a special trip to Daufuskie to meet Ms. Burn, who has been a resident of the island since 1935. Serving both as island postmaster and school bus driver from 1963 until the early 1980s, Burn has accumulated a limitless cache of wonderful stories.

A trip to Daufuskie in the 1990s is a far cry from the homey aura of the "tugboat" trip that was taken in the 1960s, although regular tourists can still travel by slow boat from Hilton Head and Savannah. In the 1960s, Daufuskie was called a black island. Although large portions of land remained in the hands of whites, blacks were visually and importantly dominant. Tourists visited the island regularly, some expressly to sample the delicious seafood and mouth-watering crab cakes sold at the dock by the native islanders. But now only a handful of African Americans remain on the island, left behind by those who left by choice and those who sold their property because of the inability to pay the increasingly high property taxes.

But even in this smaller black community, some oral traditions still remain. Here is what Burn relates about burial practices on the island:

Seeing that the dead have a decent burial is a very important segment of Daufuskie life. Black undertakers, in years past, were Joseph Haynes, Mose Ficklin, Joseph Grant, and Sarah Grant. Each of them kept a supply of $100 caskets on hand at all times.

Joe Grant was Sarah's husband; and when he passed away in 1962, Sarah took his place and was the last undertaker on the island. She was already the midwife, which caused a person on the island to remark, "Granny bring 'em 'n she take 'em away." When Sarah ceased from her work, an undertaker had to be summoned from the mainland.

He would come over and prepare the body right in the home. Sometimes a family could not afford to buy a casket. In this case, a local carpenter was called upon to make a pine box coffin, which cost, if anything, very little.

At a person's death, the one officiating laid the body out in the home on a "cooling board" which was usually an ironing board. The body was bathed (the men shaved) and then dressed in the Sunday-best clothes. Coffee grounds and turpentine were placed in the body cavities to prevent seepage and odors. If it was in the summer, the burial was usually the same day. But if the body was held over and the weather warm, the casket was placed on the front porch, where there was plenty of air and a person stood guard all night. Or, if the body stayed inside, fans kept the body cool. "Wakes" were held each night prior to the burial. Relatives and friends would be present to mourn the passing of a loved one. Food and drinks would be available to sustain them.

Persons digging the grave were usually friends of the family or in later years the county road workers, among whom were Joseph Bryan, Daniel (Fastman) Mitchell, Clarence and Willis Simmons, Frankie Smith, and Thomas Stafford.

Customarily, the preacher conducted the funeral at the home, but if the body came from Savannah, it was sometimes moved from the boat to the church, or in most cases, from the dock to the cemetery with a grave-side service.

Following the service, in the early years, the casket was then placed in a wagon pulled by oxen or a horse. A procession of mourners walked behind the wagon and sang all the way to the cemetery. The casket was opened so that everyone could file past and see the loved one for the last time. Black and white people attended all funerals.

According to the black tradition, before the body was placed in the ground, if there was a surviving child or grandchild, this child would be lifted over the casket so that the child would not fret for his parent or grandparent, and so that the spirit of the dead person wouldn't take the child to the grave with him or her. Facing the east, the casket was lowered into the ground and the dirt was rounded over the grave. A piece of oak limb was shoved into the ground as a head marker. All of the things that the person used during his/her illness were placed on the grave. Everything the dead needed would be right there, and they would have no reason to return for anything.

Contents of the bottles of medicine were spilled and the bottles inverted; cups, saucers, toothbrushes, drinking or reading glasses, spoons, knives, forks, clocks, razors, false teeth, combs—all were sticking out and highly visible in this mound of dirt. Unless the funeral came from Savannah, floral arrangements were few.

Established during the plantation days, there were actually eight cemeteries on the island. However, the pyramid-type vault for [the white] Mongin family at Haig's Point, by the eastern gate, was moved circa 1880 to Bonaventure Cemetery in Savannah, Georgia. Now, there are seven cemeteries, one for white people, known as the Mary Dunn Cemetery, and six for the blacks. These six are: Bloody Point, Cooper River, Fripp, Haig's Point, Maryfield, and Webb. The two largest and most active have been the Cooper River and Maryfield cemeteries.

Land for the cemeteries was acquired in various ways. There were eleven plantations on the eve of the Civil War: Benjie's Point, Bloody Point, Cooper River, Eigleberger, Haig's Point, Mary Dunn, Maryfield, Melrose, Oak Ridge, Piney Islands, and Webb Tract. Titles to Daufuskie land changed hands often and most of it was under absentee ownership for sometime. When Union warships headed for South Carolina waters, planters left Daufuskie before the invasion. They forsook everything they possessed, including fields white with cotton, waiting to be picked. The land went into Union hands as abandoned land or for non-payment of taxes.

Some of the land was returned to the planters after the War but often with the provision that the ex-slaves be allowed to remain on the land and to retain crops of the season, harvested or unharvested. On 28 December 1865 an agreement gave land to twenty-two former slave families for one year. Two-and-one-half acres in the corn field and two-and-one-half acres in the cotton field were allotted to each family. The War had changed things. Those whites that regained control of their plantations now had to pay wages to former slaves for their labor. Land was most often set aside by the planters for burial grounds, previously for the enslaved and, later, for the ex-slaves.

An Island Named Daufuskie further reports that several of the native islanders were consulted as to who was buried in which cemetery. Burn herself acknowledges the sketchiness of island history: "It is very difficult to try to remember the names of those who have been dead for so many years. . . .

If anyone is omitted, it is only because that person's name could not be recalled. Some of the cemeteries have very few headstones."

But the lack of history exists only insofar as the recording of actual names. One step onto any of the Daufuskie Island cemeteries and one can't help but notice how each exudes its own special history. Each cemetery is its own treasure, its own private historical landmark. It's the sheer "charm," if that word is appropriate to describe a cemetery, of these tucked-away burial sites that captures the imagination. And they are certainly a contrast to some of the bigger, better known, and more immaculately kept cemeteries of the Southeast.

BLOODY POINT CEMETERY

When the first white men set foot on Carolina soil, they displayed their guns, hoes, axes, knives, and other farm tools. Native Americans, whose ancestors had been on the island for thousands of years, watched patiently as the white settlers shot deer, planted seeds, and cut down trees. After some years of life together, during which the Indians traded corn, beans, squash, furs, and finally acres of land for cheap trinkets from the white men, the first skirmish began. This greed and abuse led to the Indian Uprising of 1715. The beach sand on the "point" was left red with the blood of those slain.

A second skirmish occurred a few years later when the settlers fought Native Americans they had accused of looting. They killed twenty-eight Indians, and for the second time the beach was crimson with blood. The third skirmish took place in 1728. This time a Yamassee war party surprised the settlers, and white men's blood was spilled on the beach. After 1715 the area had become known as Bloody Point, and the later battles helped cement the name forever.

Burials in Bloody Point Cemetery, a black cemetery situated on the west side of Bloody Point by the waters on Mongin Creek, began in the 1800s. As noted in *An Island Named Daufuskie,* many of the markers at this cemetery have been vandalized, and only four remain:

James Jones Jr.
Born April, 6, 1886
Died October 16, 1909
Sweet Be Thy Sleep

William (Dollar Bill) Bryant
Husband of Alice Bryant
Died October 21, 1930
Age 52 years

Grace Ficklin
Was born on Daufuskie
May 15, 1874

Died February 5, 1939
In Her Own Home Age 65
At Rest

In Memory of Silas Bryan
Born January 10, 1884
Died January 24, 1945

Joseph Michael does not have a headstone, but his granddaughter, Frances E. Jones, states that he was born in 1865 and died November 7, 1933. Cleveland Bryan has a record of his little brother being buried at Bloody Point: **Thomas Bryan Jr.**, born Friday, May 12, 1916; died Thursday, November 3, 1916.

Also buried here is **Pender Hamilton,** the cook for Michael Doyle, who was responsible for erecting the Bloody Point light tower; and **Jimmy Lee**, a basket maker on the island.

The names of the following black people could be remembered, but their birth or death dates have passed from knowledge: **Best:** Florence; **Brown:** Isaac (Son); **Bryan:** Martha, Nathanal, Robert Jr., Silas; **Sylvia:** William; **Hamilton:** Morris, Pender; **Heyward:** Flora, Leotha; **Jackson:** George, London, Mary; **Lee:** Henrietta, Jimmy; **Mongin:** "Crab," Hezekiah (Kyah), Lemon (Robinson); **Robinson:** Charles, Edward, Ollie; **Walker:** Hester, Simon.

COOPER RIVER CEMETERY

Cooper River Plantation consists of about seven hundred acres. Its land was confiscated by Union troops during the Civil War, but in 1867 the former owner redeemed the property and divided it into small tracts, which he sold to former slaves. One of them, Cato McIntire, bought a choice piece of land containing the two-story mansion house, which stood until fire destroyed it in 1940.

The cemetery is situated on the west side of the plantation, on the bank of the Cooper River. It was here that the African American communities in Daufuskie, Hilton Head Island, and elsewhere mobilized when construction began on a house and pathway to be built on a portion of cemetery land.

In the fall of 1990, residents of Daufuskie Island filed a suit in county court, charging the Melrose Company and Cooper River Landing Company, Inc., with trespassing and desecrating the graveyard. The two had joined together to lease the home and pathway illegally constructed on cemetery land. The Melrose Group Limited Partnership used the new house as a reception center and transportation office.

The lawsuit sought an end to the "trespass" of cemetery boundaries—first plotted in 1884—unspecified compensatory and punitive damages, and

restitution. Specifically, the lawsuit charged a Daufuskie Island businessman with building a house atop a black cemetery, and held that a dock leading to the property from the Cooper River cut off access to the cemetery from the water. The plaintiffs argued that the dock interfered with a burial tradition of native Sea Islanders, who believe that water is the gate to their spiritual world and that the water serves as a channel for the spirits of the dead to return to their native Africa. The Beaufort County master in equity (a circuit court judge in civil cases) remarked during the hearing, "Now, all that's a bunch of junk insofar as I'm concerned. If the spirit can go to Africa by the water, this 'bridge' ain't going to stop it."

The 1884 Daufuskie plot-map indicates that the cemetery, used primarily by black native islanders, was originally intended to cover one acre. A half-acre portion with headstones was fenced off when the house was built; the remaining half-acre became part of the property leased by the Melrose Company.

On January 25, 1991, islanders scored a victory when Judge Thomas Kemmerlin of Beaufort's Court of Common Pleas ruled that the lawsuit against the developers for desecration of the African American graveyard on Daufuskie Island, South Carolina, could proceed. He rejected the developers' request to have the suit dismissed with a simple statement: "All right-thinking people would sympathize with ones whose loved ones' graves have been disturbed, as perhaps they were here."

Silver Dew Winery Daufuskie Island's Cooper River Cemetery lies on the west side of the plantation, on the bank of the Cooper River.

The Melrose Company agreed to move its Reception Center, built on top of burials at the Cooper River Cemetery, as part of an out-of-court settlement in 1993.

At the hearing on January 15, 1991, the judge's small courtroom was packed to overflowing with plaintiffs and their supporters. The case also attracted a lot of media attention, including NBC-TV and several magazines and newspapers. Lawyers for Melrose Company argued that the developers had clear title to the cemetery land because of a "quiet title" action. "Quiet title" is a legal action that enables a prospective land buyer or owner to insure their ownership of the land by notifying anyone with possible claims to the land and then cutting off their rights to it.

The developers tried to have the case dismissed at the hearing, and attorney Lewis Pitts of the Christic Institute (now the Southern Justice Institute)—a nonprofit group that helps needy people with problems like land questions, property taxes, and questionable losses of land and cemeteries—argued that denying the plaintiffs the right to bring their suit to court would deny them their right to due process under the U.S. Constitution.

The judge's ruling meant that the case could go to the next step of discovery. "We will be taking depositions from the defendants in the case, to show that they knew what they were doing all along," said Pitts. "They saw the cemetery as valuable waterfront and they were determined to make money off it."

Plaintiff Lillian Spencer, a retired mathematics teacher whose grandmother is buried in Cooper River Cemetery, cited a similar case, where developers in Georgia also built on top of a graveyard called Richmond Hill. Her father's relatives are buried there, and the owners went so far as to name their new development after the graveyard.

"Destruction of graveyards is part of the genocidal effect of the so-called 'New Plantations' being developed in the low country area of South Carolina," Pitts continued. "These areas depend on cheap black labor, theft of black land, and destruction of black communities and culture. It used to be indigo, rice, or cotton plantations; now it's golf, tennis, and equestrian plantations. It's all based on economics and racism."

The June 25, 1993, edition of the *Savannah Morning News* reported good news about the outcome of the lawsuit and plans to continue the fight for justice:

> The Melrose Co. Reception Center will be relocated away from its current waterfront site by the end of 1993, according to the terms of the out-of-court settlement reached in June of 1993. [Mr. Pitts stated] "[T]his is a good first step to reclaim African American heritage and culture on Daufuskie. We consider the agreement an important victory, an important first step toward achieving reparations for the people of Daufuskie who've had so much taken from them for so many years."

As part of the cemetery settlement, a nonprofit Cooper River Cemetery Preservation Society was formed, with the six plaintiffs as officers, to preserve and restore the cemetery. Following are the headstones that have been found at Cooper River:

James Givens
Born February 13, 1906
Died November 30, 1943
Age 37

Lizzie McIntire
Born 1865
Died February 27, 1921
Age 56

In Memory of N. Simmons
Born January 31, 1933
Died July 24, 1945

Willie Hudson
Born June 6, 1870
Died October 28, 1942

In Memory of Cato McIntire (II)
Born April 20, 1908
Died May 27, 1936
Age 28

Cato McIntire once owned the mansion house in the Cooper River region, where he is now buried.

"My Beloved Husband"
Cato McIntire
Born April 27, 1847
Died October 27, 1919
"Resting with Jesus"

Lottie Carter
Born September 6, 1906
Died March 3, 1937
Age 31

In Memory of Rebecca Chisolm
Born July 4, 1872
Died March 1, 1960
"At Rest"

Tina Jenkins
Born June 2, 1883
Died January 1, 1941

In Memory of Elizabeth Riley
Born October 27, 1882
Died August 13, 1948

Robert Hamilton
Age 66 (Born 1851)
Died March 31, 1917

Gabrial Washington
South Carolina
Pvt. 1cl
321 Serv. Bn
Died June 11, 1943

Prophet Jenkins
Georgia
803 Co Trans. Corp.
Died August 28, 1957

In Memory of
Benjamin Riley
Born May 26, 1916
Died July 2, 1939

There are also headstones with the inscriptions:

Brown, Derald
July 24, 1964–July 26, 1964

Hamilton, Jane
died 1962
(Hamilton donated land for the school that bore her name.
After the school was abandoned she lived in the school
building until her death.)

The following are among those with names and dates, but no stone
markers:

Michael, Margaret (Peggy)
May 30, 1865–April 17, 1963

Stafford, Charlease Marie (stillborn)
December 31, 1966

Washington, Agnes
February 28, 1894–August 22, 1971
(Agnes Washington was one of the cooks at Melrose
Plantation.)

Washington, Lillie Mae
1954–1963

Wilson, Paul
March 27, 1927–September 6, 1968
(Paul Wilson was a relative of Jane Hamilton. He lost sight in
one of his eyes and one day he slipped and fell into New
River at the public landing. His body was found two weeks
later.)

The following have no dates on markers: **Brisbane:** Charlotte;
Brown: Jackson; **Chisolm:** Reverend; **Grant:** Priscilla; **Hamilton:** Bunkum,
Lexi, Robert Jr.; **Houston:** Jeremiah; **Manuel:** Amelia; **Mitchell:** Victoria;
Riley: Joe, Julia.

FRIPP CEMETERY

This black cemetery on Mary Dunn Plantation is located by the bank of the
New River on property that now belongs to a member of the Ward family.

The plantation is named after Mary Martinangele Dunn, who had owned the last of her family's slaves.

Two of the cemeteries are on land that belonged to the Martinangele family: Mary Dunn Cemetery for the white population, and Fripp Cemetery for the black population. Fripp Cemetery was probably started by Mary Foster Martinangele to bury slaves after she purchased the property in 1762. Mary's daughter, Mary Martinangele Dunn, owned the three hundred acres of the family land that would become known as Mary Dunn Plantation.

In 1874 Dunn sold all her property, with the exception of the four acres she stated as being a burial ground. She sold this property to her brother-in-law, William Fripp Chaplin Sr., who had it surveyed in lots and sold, mostly to blacks, many of whom were Mary Dunn's former slaves.

Richard Fuller Fripp Sr. was left in possession of the land that held the cemetery. He continued to allow blacks to bury their dead there; hence the name Fripp Cemetery. It is unknown whether any tombstones remain, but the following list of some of those buried at Fripp Cemetery were either some of Mary's slaves or descendants of her former slaves: **Bryan:** Abraham, Aleck, Baccus Sr., Baccus Jr., Ben, Biggam Sr., Biggam Jr., Clara, Cynthia, Ella, Ellen, Ernestine, Essie, Flora, Janie, Molly I, Molly II, Patsy, Paul, Richard; **Holmes:** Tom (Rose Brisbane's first husband); **Mack:** Miriah Bryan (cook for Fuller Fripp).

HAIG'S POINT CEMETERY

Haig's Point Plantation, consisting of approximately 358 acres, was sold in 1850 to Squire Pope Jr. It was later combined with the adjacent Freeport Plantation and grew to 958 acres. When northern troops invaded Daufuskie Island in 1861, they took possession of the entire plantation. The mansion was torn down, and the heavy timbers and even the nails were salvaged to use for building roads to more easily move troops during the Civil War. The Haig's Point Cemetery is unique among Sea Island burial grounds as one of only two sites located away from either water or marshlands—the other is the cemetery at Webb Tract. Haig's Point Cemetery is located just east of the Savannah Walk, off Haig's Point Road, and contains graves bearing the following markers:

John Stafford
1888–1944
He Kept the Faith
Kate Holmes
Born Barnwell, S.C.
July 4, 1868
December 19, 1945

Doctor Mills
Born April 18, 1866
Died August 17, 1917

In Memory of
Kattie Byers
1889–1950

May Hamilton
Co. B.
21 U.S.C.I.

In Memory
Elizabeth F. Holmes
Born August 3, 1903
Died 1959

Mrs. Adres
Born 1834 (85 years old)
Died June 25, 1919

In Memory
Samuel Holmes
Died June 8, 1969
(Samuel Holmes was a carpenter who built several houses on Daufuskie. He had a horse named Friendship that carried Samuel and his box of tools to every job.)

The following have small foot-markers provided by the funeral home:

Ida Holmes
Infant
Died, 1921

Ida Holmes
Teenager

Nora Lawrence
Died 1956
(Mother of Johnny Hamilton)

These are the names of people buried with no markers but some dates remembered: **Stafford:** Herbert, 1918–June 26, 1968; **Stafford:** Lula, 1882–July 27, 1964; **Young:** Tara "Missy," August 17, 1893–February 23, 1965; **Frazier:** Fred; **Holmes:** Theresa J., Rubin; **Lawrence:** Frank; **Mills:** Jim, Susie; **Rivers:** Dan, Prince; **Simmons:** Milton, Pink, Rufus; **Smalls:** Ben, Lucie, Maggie; **Wiley:** Jane; **Williams:** Margaret; **Young:** Leroy.

MARYFIELD CEMETERY

This black cemetery borders a marsh on the west side of Maryfield Plantation, located near what is now known as Governor's Point. Haig's Point, the area's main road, leads down to Governor's Point Road. In its heyday, Maryfield Plantation consisted of 530 acres. Confiscated during the Civil War, the land was later redeemed by its former owners, then surveyed and laid off in forty-two lots that were sold to former slaves and their families. A group of spiritual black men got together and, on January 29, 1881, purchased twelve acres for $82. The First Union African Baptist Church was built on this land, but burned in 1884; pleas for funds to help the rebuilding effort appeared in the Savannah newspaper. A new church was constructed just south of where the original church had stood; both it and a black school still remain on the plantation. Maryfield Cemetery is thought to be the most popular and probably, at over ten acres in size, the largest black cemetery in the area. A great number of markers still stand at the site. Following is a list of those with dates:

THE BENTLEY FAMILY:
Charley, December 31, 1875–March 24, 1944
Eddie, February 28, 1909–June 15, 1954
Janie, April 8, 1908–August 8, 1979
Mingo, May 26, 1906–September 26, 1936
Robert, April 10, 1902–February 5, 1953

THE BRYAN FAMILY:
Alfred (Plue) August 1, 1899–December 11, 1941
Anthony William, January 26, 1953–March 7, 1956
Arthur, Died January 6, 1938
Elizabeth, May 4, 1876–April 29, 1963
John Sr., May 1, 1875–November 20, 1962
John Jr., October 16, 1905–April 9, 1946
Lawrence Sr., July 28, 1912–July 22, 1938
Sarah, 1902–August 5, 1982
Thomas, November 3, 1888–July 26, 1980
Vernetta, February 20, 1949–November 24, 1977
William (Hamp), 1901–April 22, 1984

Also buried at Maryfield are **Cornelia Grant**, March 15, 1895–March 10, 1981, a midwife; and **Louvenia (Blossom) Robinson**, June 10, 1897–January 12, 1982. Robinson was one of the main characters in Pat Conroy's book *The Water Is Wide*.

A few names were recalled by a group of Daufuskie residents, who, over the years, were questioned every time they caught a ride on Billie Burn's school bus—not just children were transported; anyone who needed a ride was welcome to climb on. No dates could be remembered: **Bentley:** Sally; **Demery:** Frank; **Grant:** Hester; **Graves:** Sylvia; **Haynes:** Joseph, Maggie (Mongin); **Hudson:** Chloe, William; **Johnson:** July, Lizzie; **Jenkins:** Abe; **Lock:** Betsy; **Loyd:** Sam, Susie; **Miller:** Aaron, Ben, Jesse, Kit, Liz, Marshall,

Mingo, Phoebe; **Mongin:** Bradley, John, Lillie; **Robinson:** Sippio Sr., Sippio Jr.; **Sanders:** Chance, Clara; **Smith:** Susie (Susie Smith was the lady who first began making deviled crab to sell in 1917, then taught others how to make them. She was also a midwife).

WEBB TRACT CEMETERY

The Webb Tract Plantation—also known as Newburgh Plantation—consists of 740 acres and, like many large homes in the area, was claimed by Union soldiers during the Civil War. It remained confiscated for unpaid taxes by the U.S. Direct Tax Commission for the District of South Carolina and was sold in December 1875 for $260. Webb Tract Cemetery seems to be the smallest of the black cemeteries. It is located just north of the present Hargray Telephone Company on Cooper River Road and east of the gate on Webb Tract that leads down to Rabbit Point. Two headstones are known to remain, but only one is inscribed:

> Robert Bryan
> Born July 18, 1892
> Died July 1, 1960

Following are the names of a few of the people known to be buried here, with no dates: **Bacon:** William; **Bentley:** Amelia; **Bryan:** Ben, Katie, Matilda; **Jenkins:** Virginia; **McGraw:** Hagar; **Mordeci:** Robert; **White:** Andrew, Daffney, Katie.

Hilton Head Island, South Carolina

Hilton Head Island, occupied by Native American peoples since 1200 B.C., was visited by the Spanish in the 1520s and explored by William Hilton, its namesake, in 1663. Settlement began by the British, who finally drove the local Yamassee Indians out of South Carolina in 1718. About that time, settler John Bayley began to sell the property claimed by his family and the settlement of Hilton Head Island began. At forty-two miles square—twelve miles long and five miles at its widest—Hilton Head is the largest of the Sea Islands between New Jersey and Florida. By 1766, there were at least twenty-five families on the island; most were engaged in producing indigo, a plant valued for its deep blue color. After the Civil War, the island, largely isolated from the mainland and other sea islands, was occupied by black farmers. By the 1890s, however, there was increasing pressure to sell island property to wealthy northerners looking for hunting and recreational preserves.

By the 1930s Hilton Head Island's black population had dropped from three thousand to a mere three hundred. The island maintains its beauty today, but has undergone an incredible growth in both residential and commercial development. Bordering one of the few remaining unpolluted marine

estuaries on the East Coast, its development as a resort island was begun in the 1950s. The shoe-shaped island's remaining black population includes native islanders, retirees, and part-time residents. Black families from California, Illinois, and Michigan predominate, but many other states are represented.

Charles L. Blockson, a renowned historian, professor at Temple University, and director of the Charles L. Blockson Afro-American Collection–William Penn Foundation, points out that African American island tradition places great importance on burials taking place on "home ground." Native islanders will pay all their lives on insurance policies designed to ensure an island funeral costing many thousands of dollars. Many who once lived on the islands believed that a person is composed of three parts—body, soul, and spirit. When the body dies, the soul departs, but the spirit remains behind and is capable of doing good or mischief to the living. As in West Africa, graves in the sea islands traditionally have been adorned with belongings of the departed and with charms designated to contain or placate the spirit of the person buried there. Real or imagined threats to graveyards are, therefore, a cause of disquiet.

The cemeteries of Hilton Head Island included here are Amelia White, Braddock Point (also known as Harbortown), Pinefield, Talbot, Spanish Wells, Simmons Memorial Gardens, Jenkins Island, Union, Joe Pope, Elliott, and Lawton.

Hilton Head Plantation, a region on Hilton Head Island, contains Talbot and Elliott cemeteries.

Historic Sites on Hilton Head Island

The Museum of Hilton Head Island sponsors walking tours of many of the island's historic sites. Barbara B. Lothrop, executive director of the museum, has "found that many of the visitors to Hilton Head are not golfers or tennis players—they are vitally interested in the history, ecology, and culture of this area. This is why our historical and nature walks and tours have been so successful. . . . The museum was doing ecotourism before the word 'ecotourism' came into use." Among the sites included on museum tours are:

Fort Mitchel (Hilton Head Plantation): An earthwork fortification constructed in 1862 as part of a larger system of defense that stretched from Fort Sherman (Port Royal Plantation) to Skull Creek.

Fort Howell (Beach City Road): A large earthwork built in 1864 to strengthen the defense of Mitchelville. This fort was never manned, and probably never armed.

Fish Haul Plantation (off Beach City Road near the county baseball complex): First established as a plantation in 1717 by Colonel John Barnwell. By the time of the Civil War, Fish Haul was owned by Thomas F. Drayton, who commanded the Confederate forces on Hilton Head Island. Only chimneys remain from the "slave street," but a recent description states that "no plantation on the island had more comfortable or substantial Negro quarters."

continued on next page

While space on the island is limited, in the 1800s many of the black communities had their own churches and cemeteries nearby. Braddock Point and Lawton cemeteries, for example, are located on Sea Pines Plantation, while Talbot and Elliott cemeteries lie on Hilton Head Plantation at the other end of the island. Other cemeteries are in areas where some of the land is still black-owned. Most Hilton Head cemeteries are church-related or family-owned. In some instances, however, an extended family may find its loved ones buried in three or four different locations due to marriages, etc.

All the cemeteries of Hilton Head Island are all on prime waterfront property. Some families feel confident that their land is safe; others keep a watchful eye. Island land is now a scarce but valuable commodity; the city is flexing its muscle and both Pinefield and Jenkins Island cemeteries are in danger of being lost to developers. Indeed, growing numbers of blacks with loved ones interred on the island have experienced a sense of disquiet and frustration in recent years. Often there have been continuous battles to fight off developers seeking rights to as much of this prime property as possible. In areas where the struggle has been particularly fierce, only the diligence of various families has saved the land.

As the community of Hilton Head grows into the year 2006, a cross-island highway designed to relieve the congestion of U.S. Highway 278 has been constructed. This new roadway, while adjacent to both Pinefield and Spanish Wells cemeteries, has not encroached on either burial ground. Even so, Perry White, former owner of the Gullah Market on Highway 278 and an official of the NAACP, has encouraged business owners to become involved with local politics and advocacy. Others native islanders such as Doris Grant, Juan Byars, Moses Grant, and Michael Cohen have also expressed interest and concern; to a certain extent they each feel that the legacy of these cemeteries is in danger of being lost through developers' hands.

Because of the warmth and beauty of the islands of Hilton Head, African American visitors often pose the hypothetical question to native islanders: "And where could I be buried if I so chose?" The silence is often deafening. All of the islands are racially integrated in business ownership, public and private schools, and in recreation activities and country club memberships. However, the churches and cemeteries are primarily limited to *a single race;* and space within these black burial grounds is increasingly threatened with extinction.

Most of the black cemeteries on Hilton Head Island do not display names. If a cemetery sign is missing, however, a query to any native islander will result in directions to any of the cemetery sites.

AMELIA WHITE CEMETERY

Amelia White Cemetery, founded in the 1800s by the family of Amelia White, can be reached from Squire Pope Road, and is located behind the offices of Davis Landscape Company. Doris Grant, a Hilton Head resident and native islander, whose grandmother and other relatives are buried there, spearheads much of the one-family cemetery's maintenance and cleanup.

One family member, Bobbie Green, sold his portion of the property—about three acres—to a white church, the Church of God, in 1989. A survey done during the sale caused a dispute concerning the site's boundary; the surveyor thought that the land contained two different, but adjacent, cemeteries. The circa-1800 grave site of a White family member, Ms. Raleeh, in the center of the property, helped to clarify the situation.

The area purchased by the Church of God was eventually determined to be protected by the state due to the location within the grounds of the

continued from previous page

Mitchelville (east of Fort Howell): The first town developed specifically for freed slaves was laid out here on Fish Haul Plantation in 1862.

Zion Chapel of Ease (on Highway 278 at Matthews Drive): A chapel was built on this site in 1786 for members of the Episcopal Church in Beaufort; hence the name "Chapel of Ease." The church was destroyed in 1868, but the communion silver is still in use today.

Stoney-Baynard Ruins (Sea Pines Plantation): The ruins of a plantation house and outbuildings built circa 1790–1800 by James Stoney, a successful cotton planter. A thriving cotton plantation until the Civil War, the site was occupied by Union forces until 1865.

Fort Sherman (Port Royal Plantation): Fort Sherman, one of the largest earthwork forts ever constructed, was built by the Union during the Civil War as a landside fortification for Fort Walker. This site is now accessible only through the Museum of Hilton Head Island tour.

Fort Walker (Port Royal Plantation): Fort Walker was first built by the Confederate Army, but was captured by Union troops in the Battle of Port Royal on November 7, 1861—the largest amphibious assault on the shores of the continental United States in history. Fort Walker was renamed Fort Welles in honor of Gideon Welles, secretary of the navy to President Abraham Lincoln, but it is commonly referred to as Fort Walker. A large complex and town emerged adjacent to the fort when the Union Army made Hilton Head their Department of the South headquarters. This fort is also accessible only through the Museum of Hilton Head Island tour.

somewhat mysterious "green shells." Too late the church found it was prohibited from building on the land, primarily because the site had been
declared a state landmark after it was discovered that these valuable shells
dated back to the time of slavery. It became a memorial to the Indians and
the enslaved who once inhabited the area.

Church of God pastor Reverend Carr eventually sold the land to the
town of Hilton Head Island and the South Carolina Department of Natural
Resources, and ended up deeding two-tenths of an acre back to the Amelia
White Cemetery Preservation Society. A local museum now sponsors visits to
the Green's Shell Enclosure (named after Bobbie Green), one of only two
known sites of its kind in the Low Country. Not to be confused with the
Indian Shell Ring on another part of Hilton Head, the historical Green's Shell
Enclosure sits off Squire Pope Road, abutting the Amelia White Cemetery.

Amid its lush setting, the cemetery often becomes thick and overgrown,
making it difficult to walk through. Grant sets aside each Mother's Day as the
time to clean up the burial grounds. "As long as I have breath in my body,"
she declares, "this cemetery will be clean." During a visit to the Amelia White
Cemetery, it is easy to see Grant's personal touch. She has provided seating,
"so different members of the family can come here and sit as long as they like.
My father said, 'God's out here,'" she adds. Grant has planned additional projects to enhance her family burial ground. "I'm going to plant one purple and

94

one white lilac bush and when they bloom they will add beauty to the grounds." Other related family members buried in Amelia White Cemetery include Draytons, Owenses, and Greens. There is no charge for burial.

BRADDOCK POINT (HARBORTOWN) CEMETERY

Braddock Point Cemetery, also known as Harbortown Cemetery, was founded in the 1800s by a distant ancestor of island resident Juan Byars. The cemetery is located in the section of Hilton Head Island where Byars's family once lived. Once known as the Harbortown area of the original plantation, it now lies near Harbortown Golf Course. Byars is a sixth-generation islander; among his related family members who, together, own this beautiful site are the Williamses, Campbells, Bryants, Fraziers, and Chisholms.

Byars's ancestors moved from the Harbortown area to another part of Hilton Head during the last century because of the frequency of strong storms. In the 1950s a young Harvard graduate named Charles E. Frazier conceived the idea of a resort in the area and bought the five thousand acres of land known as Sea Pines.

Green's Shell Enclosure

Green's Shell Enclosure is a unique archaeological site on the north end of Hilton Head Island. It consists of a three-acre tract of land between Squire Pope Road and Skull Creek that currently houses a prehistoric "structure" of oyster shells. The site was excavated by archaeologists in 1968, and again in 1994. Archaeological experts maintain that the four-foot-high, twenty- to thirty-foot-wide semicircular ring of oyster shells was originally the substructure of a palisade wall that protected a Native American village dating back to 1335 A.D.

The site is currently preserved and maintained as a nature park by the town of Hilton Head in conjunction with South Carolina's Heritage Trust program, part of the South Carolina Department of Natural Resources. The Museum of Hilton Head Island sponsors walking tours while being careful to tread lightly near an old family burial ground, the Amelia White Cemetery, which is adjacent to the shell enclosure. Although at a distance the enclosure appears to be "just a mound in the woods," closer inspection reveals a boundary constructed in the formation of an irregular circle enclosing almost two acres of land. In contrast to the shell enclosure, the neighboring cemetery is clearly defined, housing a handful of graves that are adorned with fresh flowers by Doris Grant, a local woman dedicated to maintaining the graves of her ancestors.

Now called Sea Pines Plantation, this large tract of island property currently houses some of the island's most luxurious homes. The area has several golf clubs and courses, tennis courts, marina shops, restaurants, a lighthouse, and a dock for the ferries that provide shuttle-service to nearby Daufuskie Island. Around-the-clock security guards stop each car entering the area; unless a sticker of residency is displayed a $3 entry pass is required.

Although family members connected to the Braddock Point Cemetery are allowed entry, it is painful for some, many of whose close relatives are buried at the cemetery, when they try to enter the Sea Pines gates. "I'd like to

Left photo: **Braddock Point Cemetery was founded in the 1800s by a distant ancestor of island resident Juan Byars, shown here speaking with Dr. Charles Wright.**

Right photo: **Braddock Point Cemetery grave marker with the "father's plate".**

put a 'blood cuff' on them," Byars exclaims, "to measure their pressure as they approach this gate." Although Byars and his relatives have a personal connection to this portion of the island, because they are not residents of Sea Pines Plantation they are asked to pay for the visitor pass.

As one approaches the cemetery at the far end of Sea Pines, the reality of it all is shocking and frightening. A luxury condo has been built in a position to block its residents' view of the graves; marked and unmarked burial sites lay right outside its walls. Byars sometimes imagines the affect of a funeral taking place during the time of the resort's Heritage Golf Classic—the course's eighteenth hole is practically on cemetery grounds. "I put in a request to the good Lord," he chuckles, "for good timing on my death."

From within the cemetery itself, villas now block the vista of Calibogue Sound that the original founders had planned as the view "over to Africa"— across the water—as a comfort for lonely souls. Byars explains that African Americans once believed their spirits would more easily make the trip across the water to return to Africa if they were buried near the water. "There is a strong spiritual feeling. . . . Daufuskie Island is directly across the water—and ostensibly, so is Sierra Leone, Africa."

"In order to get a grave," Byers explains, "you mark the spot you want. It's understood as family that you do that. The funeral home handles the

96

digging. The family cleans the cemetery. One sad feature," he adds, "is that we had people who were buried and couldn't afford headstones. I've a grand aunt who is buried here. She's buried outside this area that the developers fenced in and designated as the cemetery." He explains that the developers filled in the cemetery land bordering their property to make room for the eighteenth hole of Plantation golf course. "My great[-great] uncle showed us the real boundaries of the cemetery. They built right over some graves that were not marked."

A tour of the graveyard reveals some interesting local customs. Byars explains the tradition of attaching plates to the headstones of departed loved ones. "When they would bury the head of the household, [they] would show respect by taking his plate and have it pressed into the headstone. The father, the head of the household, had the plate. It was too costly for others to have a plate; they ate out of a pan or whatever."

Byars has been approached by the township regarding the possibility of making Braddock Point Cemetery a historic site, but he questions whether this is an attempt to halt burials. "We plan to keep burying here," he states. The cemetery contains about a hundred clearly marked graves, with many more now lost to view. Some grave sites marked with small artifacts have been lost through time. Others have disappeared due to the construction of Sea Pines Plantations' condos and villas and golf course. Of all the cemeter-

The lovely Braddock Point Cemetery has been beset by modern woes: Villas now block the view across Calibogue Sound. This view was important to African Americans, who believed their spirits would more easily return to Africa if they were buried near the water.

ies on Hilton Head Island, Braddock Point is, perhaps, the saddest to visit. One of the oldest graves here is that of **Susan Brown Williams**, born in 1861. Now surrounded by some of the most expensive and valuable property in South Carolina, one has to wonder how much longer she will be allowed to rest at the edge of the sea.

PINEFIELD CEMETERY

This large expanse of land is beautiful beyond description. But, wildly overgrown with shrubs and the undergrowth born of the varied forest that shelters it, Pinefield Cemetery is difficult to explore. A construction company working nearby adds to the confusion by dumping materials in an area adjacent to the burial ground, which was founded in the late 1700s. Unfortunately, such a situation is all too common in this region, as commercial overindustrialization eats away at many of the historical lands and special properties.

Pinefield Cemetery lies at Broad Creek; it can be reached by turning off Highway 278 onto Matthews Drive, and proceeding to Marshlands Road. While recorded in the records of the state of South Carolina as Otter Hole Cemetery, it is known under the name given to it by Hilton Head residents many years before.

Some graves are marked with homemade concrete tombstones, names and dates scratched carefully onto each surface. Others are discernible only as depressions in the sandy earth. One marker reads:

Sandy Stafford
Died April 14, 1883, at the age of 98.

Residents Joseph Mitchell and Doris Grant and a local boy scout troop have tried to mark off the property and do some minimal cleaning. Recent rumors have indicated that developers are attempting to take over this valuable, marshlands-bordered property. The construction that moves ever closer would tend to confirm these reports.

Beautiful Talbot Cemetery

on water's edge.

TALBOT CEMETERY

Talbot Cemetery, less than ten acres in size, is on Skull Creek Road on Hilton Head Plantation. It is heavily wooded and dates back to the 1800s, when blacks farmed the land and made the island their home. Although today only the cemetery remains amid streets lined with plush homes, a country club, and well-manicured golf courses, one can see that area developers made a clean sweep of only the old houses and churches, and left burial grounds like Talbot Cemetery somewhat intact. Markers at Talbot show such inscriptions as:

> **Edward Landson**
> Born December 1840
> Died December 26, 1904
>
> **Katie Miller**
> Born December 14, 1854
> Died April 15, 1935

Although it would be wonderful to be able to discover all the others who have been laid to rest here over the years, many markers are unreadable. Today, Talbot Cemetery seems but the skeletal remains of what was once a prominent burial ground.

SPANISH WELLS CEMETERY

Some of the extended family of island native Juan Byars are buried in this small cemetery located off Spanish Wells Road; Chisholm and Campbell family members also have ties to this spot. Spanish Wells Cemetery can be reached from the road that bears its name, not far from the bridge at the entrance to the island. The Oak Marsh subdivision is adjacent to the cemetery, which also borders on a large expanse of marsh. Like some of the other island burial grounds, an overgrowth of bushes and grass competes with the burial sites and marshes. Although little is known about when the cemetery was founded, and native islanders can recall little information about its heritage, an off-the-beaten-track cemetery such as Spanish Wells can provide useful information to the African American seeking his or her roots. Spanish Wells is one of a number of cemeteries that has a family lineage attached to it; it is precisely these types of cemeteries that the investigative genealogist or curious family member is sure to appreciate. If nothing else, it's interesting to see how some of these cemeteries become almost transparent amid the natural beauty that surrounds them.

In Spanish Wells Cemetery, as in other island burial grounds, an overgrowth of bushes and grass competes with the burial sites and marshes.

SIMMONS MEMORIAL GARDENS

In 1927, Charlie Simmons Sr. provided a welcome service to island residents when he purchased a boat. He made trips from Hilton Head to nearby

The Simmons Memorial
Gardens was established
in June 1968 by island
resident Charlie Simmons.
His mother, Estella,
was the first to be
buried in the cemetery.

Savannah and Daufuskie Island three times a week, picking up passengers and freight. His cargo included produce, oysters, pecans, chickens, and other staples. Business was so good that Simmons purchased a larger boat, and then another. He traveled the route for many years but halted deliveries to Hilton Head in the 1950s after a motor bridge to the island was built. However, he continued to assist Daufuskie residents crossing to Hilton Head Island until 1986. The Simmons family also ran the first bus transportation service on the island. Charles Jr. had a store and barbershop at the entrance to the island.

The Simmons Memorial Gardens was established in June 1968 by Simmons. His mother, **Estella**, was the first to be buried in the cemetery. The son of Rosa and Charles Simmons Jr., **Charles E. Simmons III**, and their grandson **Charles E. Simmons IV**, are also buried in the garden.

JENKINS ISLAND CEMETERY

This beautiful, wooded cemetery, founded in the 1700s, is just off Highway 278, not far from the Hilton Head bridge. It cannot be seen from the highway, and must be approached by a narrow path that leads through brush and trees to this oasis. Even though hidden, it faces the increasing threat of development. Michael Cohen, a native islander, whose family is buried alongside members of the Gadson family in Jenkins Island Cemetery, explains that the site is being watched carefully. Thus far, developers have staked the property right up to the cemetery line. Local residents report rumors of a possible expansion of the marine base that lies adjacent to the site. "All of the black cemeteries in Hilton Head are 'on water,' except Union Cemetery," Cohen says, discouraged that the desire for resort living increasingly threatens the peaceful repose of the dead.

Union Cemetery, on Union Cemetery Road just off Highway 278, is nestled near one of Hilton Head's popular golf courses.

UNION CEMETERY

Union Cemetery, on Union Cemetery Road just off Highway 278, is nestled near one of Hilton Head's popular golf courses. Among the cemetery owners is the Benjamin White family. Nathanial White explained that the nearby St. James Baptist Church, at the intersection of Dillon and Beach City Roads, helps to maintain the grounds. He is undecided about the rumors that the site once served as a Civil War battleground, a speculation that prompted the name of both the street and the cemetery.

Frank Shelton, a writer for the *Island Packet,* asked sixty-nine-year-old island native Gene Wiley about his love for Union Cemetery: "That's my uncle right there," Wiley pointed out on a walk through the grounds, "and that one over there is my father. Half the people in here are related to me." Wiley, owner of the Golden Rose Restaurant on Beach City Road, has lamented the area's development: Companies purchased tracts of land around the cemetery and turned it into a private, fenced-in community called Port Royal Plantation. Wiley speculates that developers "took advantage of the landowners." According to Shelton, the situation reflects the days when whites "us[ed] their [blacks'] lack of education against them as they purchased land acre by acre for prices that could barely buy a meal on the island today. . . . Wiley said his grandmother, Sarah Polite, once sold twenty-five acres near Union Cemetery Road for $50 in 1939."

Among the families buried here are the Wiley and Hay families.

JOE POPE CEMETERY

The Queen Chapel holds the deed to this valuable property, a practice the cemeteries try to adhere to for safekeeping. Joe Pope is in an unusual location; its surroundings are far different than they were in the 1800s, or even as late as the early 1900s. The front of the cemetery faces Hilton Head's first cross-island road, busy Highway 278. The grounds cover approximately five acres and are heavily blanketed with bushes and trees. The foliage is so thick, in fact, that it allows only the truly inquisitive to see the many tombstones. On one side of the cemetery—from the highway to the rear marsh—is the driveway for the local Piggly Wiggly supermarket. With no fence surrounding it, one can park at the grocery store and walk through this beautiful property, being careful, of course, not to disturb those areas where freshly laid flowers have been placed. Buried in Joe Pope are members of the Christopher, Grant, Day, Bryan, and Mitchell families.

ELLIOTT CEMETERY

Elliott Cemetery, located on the grounds of Hilton Head Plantation, is on the beautiful, expansive Port Royal Sound. Densely wooded, it is frequented by deer who sleep among the graves. Founded in the 1830s, Elliott Cemetery is now bordered on one side by a golf course. That and the water, which forms its other boundary, makes parking most difficult for the regu-

larly used cemetery. It is necessary to circle through and around a surrounding neighborhood of palatial homes and leave one's car in a small park before walking through the woods to the cemetery site. One has to wonder how a funeral procession can manage the trip; the only clear ground is the golf course bordering the wooded area. After parking, the coffin would have to be carried anywhere from twenty-five to one hundred yards. Among the islanders buried in this beautiful isolated cemetery are members of the Barnwell family.

LAWTON CEMETERY

Lawton Cemetery is one of the oldest burial sites on Hilton Head Island. It lies inside Sea Pines Plantation at the corner of Oyster Landing Road and Oyster Landing Lane, on a tiny finger of Broad Creek. The site is heavily wooded; only four markers, all professionally made, are visible through the brush, and some yards away stand elegant condos with showcase lawns and gardens. The headstones stand firmly, singularly, and solemnly, but almost comically in the thick ground cover—comically because it is doubtful that any of the residents of Oyster Landing Road or Oyster Landing Lane have the slightest idea that, as they idle their cars daily at the corner, they stand less than twelve yards from an early 1800s African American burial ground.

The near-forgotten cemetery is no longer used for burials, possibly because there are no heirs living. Buried in Lawton is **Rosetta Frazier**, great-aunt of Walter Green, a Hilton Head native. Her stone bears the inscription, "born December 25, 1847 and died March 21, 1936." Frazier is buried next to **Thomas Frazier**, whose grave is marked with a Civil War–era federal tombstone.

Lawton Cemetery - hidden in the bushes

Beaufort, South Carolina

The delightful town of Beaufort, South Carolina, is, ostensibly, also an island. The Bay Street area is home to quaint shops and restaurants, while the beautiful waterfront is the scene of the city's air and water shows, art and market festivals, and a busy docking area. The drawbridge from Bay Street over Port Royal Sound to Ladys Island responds regularly to boats whose masts are too tall to pass under it. The bridge turns slowly and grace-fully as drivers on both sides idle their cars' engines restively, waiting for the water traffic to glide by.

First discovered by Spanish explorers in 1514–1515, early attempts to settle the area were unsuccessful. The town was almost destroyed by Native Americans in 1715, then captured by the British during the American Revolution. Beaufort flourished as a shipping port for rice and cotton grown on its many plantations, then was captured and evacuated by northern

Civil War hero Robert Smalls is buried at Baptist Tabernacle Church in Beaufort, where a monument now stands in his honor.

troops during the Civil War. Rebuilt slowly after the war, it has become a lovely community whose main businesses are tourism and the military.

Theaters and strip malls and other businesses line Boundary Street at the far end of the city. Also along Boundary Street are located several cemeteries, including Beaufort National and Sixteen Gate. Farther into the city, near where the large plantation houses of yesteryear still stand, are several historic churches and cemeteries. Among them is the Tabernacle Baptist Church, resting place of Civil War hero Robert Smalls.

Other black cemeteries in the Beaufort area are Citizens, Mercy, and Wesley United Methodist. In the surrounding county are Bonny Hall Plantation River Cemetery (Yamassee) and Hope Bunny Cemetery. In the town of Burton, on Highway 21 just outside of Beaufort, is the South Carolina Marine Corps Air Station, built on and around New Hope Christian Church, Pilgrim, and Rose Hill cemeteries.

While all but Beaufort's National Cemetery are similar in appearance, each cemetery in Burton and Beaufort is distinct in some way. Burton's cemeteries tend to be smaller and all are church-owned. Sixteen Gate Cemetery in Beaufort is owned by a group of businessmen. Beaufort National Cemetery is, of course, federally owned.

Traveling to the area from the north on Highway 21, the town of Burton is the first stop. At its traffic light, on the left, three air corps planes stand on display, marking the entrance to the Marine Corps Air Station. Quite near this entrance is New Hope Christian Church Cemetery; just past it is Pilgrim Cemetery.

A busy intersection a few miles down marks Burton's downtown, the theaters, restaurants, a bank, and small shops all bustling with small-town activity. At this point, Highway 21 changes its name to Boundary; a mile further down stands the sign welcoming travelers to Beaufort.

Proceeding down Boundary on the right is Sixteen Gate Cemetery, just before the corner of Ribaut Street, where stands the Beaufort County government complex. Turning onto Ribaut takes travelers to Port Royal and the United States Naval Hospital. It was on the grounds of the naval hospital that the first public reading of the Emancipation Proclamation took place, on January 1, 1863, and where the first black South Carolina volunteers were mustered into the Union army. The Michigan Support Group, in conjunction with Penn Center, held annual reenactments at that site. The January 1, 1996, unveiling of a plaque awarded by the South Carolina Department of Archives and History and the U.S. Department of the Interior represents the pinnacle of the efforts of Roberta Wright. (See her book *Penn Center* and the *Proclamation of Emancipation*.)

A few miles further down Boundary is the pristine and starkly mysterious Veterans Cemetery. Boundary then becomes Cateret and follows the beautiful Beaufort River. The University of South Carolina's Beaufort Campus is located on Cateret.

The Sea Island area has become important to Hollywood: the motion pictures *Conrack* and *Prince of Tides* were filmed in Beaufort, *Forrest Gump* in Beaufort and Savannah, and *Daughters of the Dust* on St. Helena and Hunting islands.

"Pass the *Planter!*"

Robert Smalls was born in Beaufort, South Carolina, of an enslaved family. He moved to Charleston at an early age to work. There, at the age of seventeen, he married fellow slave Hannah Jones. The year was 1856.

Five years later the Civil War began. Smalls was secretly on the side of the North, where black people were free. However, he was drafted into the Confederate navy and forced to work as a wheelsman on the gunboat *Planter.* Captain Relyea of the *Planter* and his two mates were white, the rest of the crew enslaved blacks. Smalls worried about his freedom; buying freedom for himself, his wife, and two kids was expensive. He decided to escape by sea and risk the threat of discovery from three forts that had their guns trained on the harbor, looking for enemy ships venturing north.

Why couldn't he capture the *Planter,* Smalls thought, and sail her right past those guns? The northern fleet was anchored seven miles outside the harbor. Freedom was only seven miles away.

Smalls discussed his plan with the slave crew and all were eager to join him. If anything went wrong, they would blow up the ship and die rather than be captured. On May 16, 1862, Smalls and his followers made their move. Eight family members were hidden aboard a second ship, anchored in the Cooper River, with the cooperation of that ship's steward, a fellow slave. They would be taken aboard the *Planter* after Smalls took command.

continued on next page

continued from previous page

That night, after the captain and his mates went ashore, Smalls took over and readied the ship for action. Firemen Jackson, Alston, and Tarno shoveled fuel into the furnaces. John, the engineer, checked the instruments. Jebel raised the Confederate flag, while Alfred cast off the ship's lines.

At the wheel, Smalls—wearing the captain's broad-brimmed hat—steered the *Planter* away from the dock. The desperate trip had begun. As he neared the second ship, he sent a rowboat for the five women and three children. The steward also came aboard, increasing to sixteen the *Planter*'s total number of enslaved passengers.

Smalls headed the ship upstream. He did everything he had seen Captain Relyea do. As the *Planter* approached Fort Jackson, he pulled the cord on the steam whistle and gave the proper salute. As the *Planter* often steamed upriver before dawn, there was no reason for the sentry on shore to think its passage unusual; he yelled: "Pass the *Planter*."

Passing Fort Moultrie was the next challenge. Smalls repeated the whistle salute and again they passed safely. But the most dangerous part was yet to come. It was now near dawn and Smalls could make out the menacing cannons of Fort Sumter. Would the sentry be able to see that he was not Captain Relyea beneath the broad-brimmed hat, but a slave?

continued on next page

BEAUFORT NATIONAL CEMETERY

A brick wall surrounds the grounds of the Beaufort National Cemetery. Laid out in the shape of a half wheel, the cemetery's oyster-shelled roads form the "spokes," and the large iron gates are set at the "hub." The grounds are serenely landscaped with numerous shrubs and large trees, predominantly magnolia, live oak, and palmetto.

Beaufort was one of the first national cemeteries designated by President Abraham Lincoln, who personally authorized its establishment in a letter dated February 10, 1863. The commanding general of Federal Occupation troops bought the twenty-nine-acre tract known as Jolly's Grove for $75 at a tax sale on March 11, 1863. It became the final resting place for soldiers who gave their lives during the war between the states.

The cemetery is the resting place for veterans from every military conflict involving U.S. troops since the Civil War, including the remains of Union troops that were moved from eastern Florida, Savannah, Charleston, Morris Island, Hilton Head Island, and other islands near Beaufort. About twenty-eight hundred remains were removed from Millen, Georgia, and reinterred in Beaufort National Cemetery.

There are more than seventy-five hundred Civil War veterans interred here, including 4,019 unknown Union soldiers and 117 known Confederates. Many of the troops fell on battlefields in Georgia, Florida, and South Carolina. In addition, there are presently more than five thousand veterans of the Spanish-American War, World War I, World War II, Korean War, and Vietnam War who have joined their comrades in final peace here.

Boundary Street hums with the activity of ships, businesses, and nearby residences. The charming historic churches and refurbished plantation houses bordering the river are in proximity to Bay Street, with its boutiques, restaurants, antique shops, parks, and boat docks. On most days, tourists can enjoy carriage rides around the historic district. The beautiful "swing" bridge, from Bay Street across the river to Cat Island, Ladys Island, and St. Helena, Hunting, Harbour, and Fripp islands, regularly opens to allow tall pleasure boats to pass. The other bridge to the islands starts just below Parris Island in Port Royal.

Beaufort National Cemetery, located on Boundary, occupies many acres of walled-in property. Although its gate is almost flush with the sidewalk, cemetery grounds are almost invisible to motor traffic. But, as with any national cemetery, a clear view of the immensity of the site graphically illustrates the horror of war. The absolute beauty of the grounds stands in clear contradiction to the reality and purpose of its existence. Row upon row of stately white crosses stand in silent testimony to the courage of those who fought and died for their country.

Beaufort's story has not ended with the interment of casualties from the Vietnam War, however. On May 29, 1989, thanks to the efforts of the local community, members of the Civil War's all-black 55th Massachusetts Regiment were buried, with pride, honor, and dignity, within its walls. Organized in Readville, Massachusetts, on June 22, 1863, the regiment was stationed at New Bern, North Carolina, before being transferred to Folly Island, South Carolina. There, about fifteen miles southeast of Charleston, it participated in operations against Charleston and Johns Island, five miles due west of Charleston. It was in this area that many perished, their bodies dumped in the brigade cemetery on Folly Island. It is from this cemetery that archaeologists excavated their remains in 1987.

Members of a Union reenactment unit reinterred the soldiers of the

continued from previous page

Smalls leaned on the windowsill of the pilot house. He folded his arms across his chest as he had seen the captain do. Jebel pulled the signal cord. Smalls waved to the sentry on shore. The sentry did not answer. Smalls prayed silently. "Let us through safely."

Finally he heard the sentry yell: "Pass the *Planter*. Pass the *Planter!*" They were not going to be blown out of the water! They were saved! Smalls piloted the ship past the Fort's huge guns and out to the open sea. By the time the sentry realized something was wrong and fired, the *Planter* was out of range.

The crew and their families crowded to the rail. They had gambled with death and won. Smalls and Hannah looked at each other and at their children. They were free. No longer would they have to call any man "Master." Jebel pulled down the Confederate flag and raised the white flag of truce. When they reached the ships of the Northern Fleet, Robert turned the *Planter* over to the fleet captain.

After the North won the war, Captain Smalls, as he was now called, returned to Beaufort with his family. He was eventually elected to Congress, where he served five terms, championing the cause of equal rights for his people. He was buried at Baptist Tabernacle Church in Beaufort, where a monument now stands in his honor; his home is a National Historic Landmark, though not open to the public. Smalls is remembered today as a true hero. As a boy, he had only dreamed of freedom; as a man, he had risked all he had to win it.

55th Massachusetts in black wooden caskets during a ceremony prescribed by 1863 military codes. Dirt brought from Massachusetts was sprinkled over some of the graves, and the ceremony was led by the then-governor of Massachusetts, Michael S. Dukakis, and his wife. Twin historic monuments now overlook the rows of small marble markers in Section 56 of the cemetery, each bearing only a number to identify each of the unknown soldiers. The all-black 54th Massachusetts Regiment was the "sister" regiment to the 55th. On July 18, 1863, the 54th Regiment attacked Confederate Fort Wayne, at Morris Island in the Charleston, South Carolina, harbor. At day's end, one half of the 54th was either wounded, missing in action, taken prisoner, dead, or dying. The soldiers of the 54th—along with those of the 55th Massachusetts—were buried at the National Cemetery in Beaufort. Their heroism and valor was movingly illustrated in the movie *Glory*, released in 1989.

The following black defenders of the Civil War and late soldiers of the 54th Massachusetts Regiment answered the command of God Almighty during the period 1863–1865 and assumed the position of "at ease" in peaceful rest:

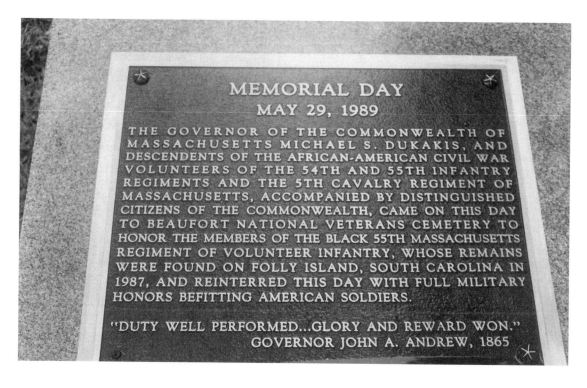

MEMORIAL DAY
MAY 29, 1989

THE GOVERNOR OF THE COMMONWEALTH OF MASSACHUSETTS MICHAEL S. DUKAKIS, AND DESCENDENTS OF THE AFRICAN-AMERICAN CIVIL WAR VOLUNTEERS OF THE 54TH AND 55TH INFANTRY REGIMENTS AND THE 5TH CAVALRY REGIMENT OF MASSACHUSETTS, ACCOMPANIED BY DISTINGUISHED CITIZENS OF THE COMMONWEALTH, CAME ON THIS DAY TO BEAUFORT NATIONAL VETERANS CEMETERY TO HONOR THE MEMBERS OF THE BLACK 55TH MASSACHUSETTS REGIMENT OF VOLUNTEER INFANTRY, WHOSE REMAINS WERE FOUND ON FOLLY ISLAND, SOUTH CAROLINA IN 1987, AND REINTERRED THIS DAY WITH FULL MILITARY HONORS BEFITTING AMERICAN SOLDIERS.

"DUTY WELL PERFORMED...GLORY AND REWARD WON."
GOVERNOR JOHN A. ANDREW, 1865

NAME; COMPANY;
DATE OF BIRTH

Private Anderson Lewis; G; August 7, 1863
Private John Bancroft; A;
  July 29, 1863
1st Lieutenant William Biggs; E; July 21, 1863
Private Charles Cane; A; August 15, 1863
Private Charles Clark II; G; July 21, 1863
Private Thomas F. Cooper; E; March 1, 1864
Private Anthony Davis; G; March 25, 1864
Sergeant William Ellis; G; August 10, 1863
Private Emanuel Williams; F; October 28, 1863
Private Elia Franklin; C;
  July 31, 1863
Private John H. Freeman; I; February 1, 1864
Private Martin Gilmore; D; July 27, 1863
Private Alex Green; D; March 19, 1864
Private Charles Green; C; April 10, 1864
Private Adrastus Hazzard; F; July 7, 1865
Private George Holmes; F; August 14, 1863
Private Franklin Jackson; K; April 11, 1864
Private Sanford Jackson; A; September 13, 1863
Corporal Charles H. Johnson; F; September 18, 1863
Corporal Joseph Johnson; I; July 27, 1863

This is one of two plaques that overlook the Section 56 of Beaufort National Cemetery, commemorating members of the 54th and 55th Massachusetts infantry regiments. These soldiers' heroism during the Civil War was illustrated in the 1989 movie *Glory*.

Corporal Alex Jones; D; July 7, 1864
Private Robert Jones; D; May 10, 1865
Sergeant George F. Merriman; B; August 1, 186
Private John Nettle; A; August 8, 1863
Private James Nelson; F; December 27, 1863
Private George Parker; E; March 2, 1863
Corporal Henry T. Peal; F; January 24, 1864
Private Gallahill Porter; I; June 23, 1863
Private Samuel E. Price; I; August 28, 1863
Private Charles R. Reason; E; July 27, 1863
Private Charles Rideout; I; February 16, 1865
Private Albert Scott; H; February 29, 1864
Private George Streets; D; July 22, 1863
Private Ezra Tobias; K; June 15, 1865
Private George Washington; E; August 3, 1863
Private William Wells; E; May 29, 1864
Private Nathan Young; C; July 19, 1863

SIXTEEN GATE CEMETERY

Sixteen Gate Cemetery is located on the south side of Boundary Street; the cemetery's southern boundary is the marshes of Battery Creek. Although just a few steps from a busy thoroughfare, as one enters the grounds one

is transported from the present. Although the cemetery is very much in use, the aura and solemnity of the past are most intense. Walking through and around, and unfortunately sometimes on, the graves brings to mind questions: "who?," "what?," "when?," "why?" Many of the inscriptions on the tombstones have faded with the passing years and the small stories are not legible.

New Hope and Pilgrim cemeteries both lie near the Marine Corps Air Station.

Lois Jenkins and her son, Edward J. Allen, are Beaufort residents and descendants of former owners of Sixteen Gate. Part of the current corporate ownership, they are understandably proud of the beautiful cemetery. Gerhard Spieler, Beaufort County historian and columnist for the *Beaufort Gazette,* writes of the many stories behind the cemetery's name. One version is that in the 1880s, sixteen black social and fraternal organizations united in establishing a cemetery for their members. However, the most likely story is that Sixteen Gate refers to a military post, or gate, that stood on the Old Shell Road during Civil War times. An old plot shows a proposed black village named Higginsonville and lists XVIII, XIX, and XX streets. It is assumed there may have been a XVI street, giving its name to the cemetery.

The cemetery had its beginning on March 8, 1888, when Annie M. Bartlett and her husband, both from New York City, sold the land to Edward Wallace for $100. A declaration, dated a month later and attached to the deed, stated that Wallace was holding the land for the benefit of the Beaufort Memorial Burial Association. In 1966, Gilbert Walker and William Pegler, trustees of the unincorporated Beaufort Memorial Burial Association, transferred the deed to Sixteen Gate Cemetery, duly incorporated in August 22, 1966.

Among those buried at Sixteen Gate are **George Moody**, and his sons **George Jr.**, **Alvin**, and **Bennie**.

NEW HOPE CHRISTIAN CHURCH CEMETERY

This cemetery, owned by New Hope Christian Church, Disciples of Christ, is approximately seventy-three years old. It faces Highway 21 and extends for more than four acres, bounded on its remaining sides by the Marine Corps Air Station. The cemetery is beautifully maintained.

The church and cemetery were established in 1924, at a time when the entire area was farmland or wooded. The church was separated from the cemetery by five or six miles; while that meant nothing to the original residents, today it seems a longer distance because of busy Highway 21. Buried at New Hope are members of the well-known **Rivers** family: **Bennie**, the eldest, **Josie**, and **Hector Rivers**.

PILGRIM CEMETERY

What remains of the once-vast Pilgrim Cemetery fronts Highway 21, a few hundred yards from the main entrance to the Marine Corps Air Station. The cemetery was once called Donaldson Cemetery after the family that was buried there.

The cemetery was founded in the early 1800s by members of the now defunct Pilgrim Baptist Church. In 1899, three prominent families within the church, the Donaldsons, Grays, and Griffens, split from the congregation to form the Pine Grove Baptist Church. The new church was built a few miles down the road from Pilgrim Baptist Church, next to a tall cedar tree that Pierce Gray, one of the new congregation's leaders, had dreamt about months earlier.

Eventually almost the entire congregation of Pilgrim Church migrated to the new church and Pilgrim Church ceased to exist. The Pine Grove congregation eventually took over caretaking duties of the cemetery.

At present there are less than forty graves in the Pilgrim Cemetery and only a handful of headstones have survived. Most of the cemetery was lost with the construction of Highway 21; those whose graves were disrupted were reburied at other cemeteries in the area. Among the prominent local African American residents buried at Pilgrim Cemetery are descendants of the same three families who once abandoned the church after which it is named.

RED HOUSE CEMETERY

The 1800s-era Red House Cemetery, just over an acre in size, is still in use. The cemetery is located on property that was formerly known as the Edgely Plantation, home to many black families. When the air base property was purchased, these families were forced to move. Although technically on the air base property, the cemetery is owned by Second Jordan Baptist Church of Burton.

Red House Cemetery is accessible only by entering the grounds of the Marine Corps Air Station, which gives immediate consent to all interested parties. However, it is only natural that families are unhappy about having to weave their way around barracks and buildings to reach the grave sides of family members. The cemetery itself has been fenced off and is protected by a gate, but it is difficult to get to for maintenance; the lush foliage seems to reclaim the grounds almost immediately after it is cut back. Buried at Red House are longtime Burton residents **Victoria Frazier**, **Betty Frazier**, **Nell Frazier**, **Rose Bryan**, and **Barney Bryan**.

THREE NEGLECTED CEMETERIES

Much is written about the picturesque cemeteries in this low country area, in *Lay Down Body*, first edition, but the *Beaufort Catalyst* writer focuses on three neglected cemeteries. These properties are adjacent to the beautiful, mystic, heart-wrenching National Cemetery on Boundary street. Two of the small cemeteries cannot be seen by motorists driving by.

These cemeteries typify the small cemeteries scattered throughout the South where there is no routine care other than by family members still living and able to undertake the sometimes difficult task of cleaning and weeding around the graves.

Mercy Cemetery is located beside the National Cemetery and is clearly visible from Boundary but is partially overgrown. Stranger's Cemetery, located beside the National Cemetery also, but is not visible from the street. It is completely overgrown by trees. Citizen's Cemetery is located by a gym and behind the well-kept Evergreen Cemetery which is cleaned and maintained by the city of Beaufort for whites.

Neighbors, asked five questions about these properties, gave the expected responses: (1) Who owns the three cemeteries? (2) Who is paid to clean and maintain Mercy and Citizen's Cemeteries? (3) Who can be buried in them? (4) Why does the city of Beaufort clean the Evergreen Cemetery, but it does not clean the Citizen's Cemetery, which is beside Evergreen? And (5) What happens to a cemetery when it is so neglected that it looks like a wooded area, as Stranger's Cemetery does?

A resident, Carline Robinson, responded that "the land that the three cemeteries are on was given to African Americans to be used only for cemeteries, therefore anyone can be buried there, at no charge. Since no one person owns the cemeteries, no one is paid to clean and maintain them. Many years ago, those people who had relatives buried in the cemeteries cleared them; however, after they and their descendents died, no one cleaned except a few people."

Fred Washington, Jr., while on the Beaufort City Council took an interest in the cemeteries after seeing that they were completely overgrown. He recruited some fraternal groups to adopt the cleaning as a project. He also asked individuals to petition City Council to take on the responsibility. This idea was rejected by African Americans when warned that if the City of Beaufort cleaned the cemeteries it might try to take control of the land.

Another resident, Benjamin Redmond, began cleaning Mercy and Citizen's cemeteries several years after Washington asked for help. He had no relatives at either cemetery and said he cleaned them because they needed to be cleaned.

Sometimes he worked alone with his own mower, other times there were a few helpers such as Carline Robinson, Jake Richardson, and Jerry Mitchell. Redmond complained that there are too many graves and too much land for only a few people to clean. There are, in fact, some graves that are never cleaned because its too difficult to try to clean them with a mower. Mr. Redmond also spoke of the trash that people dump in the cemeteries and wonders why he cares.

Gerhard Spieler of Beaufort

Gerhard Spieler, columnist for the *Beaufort Gazette* and a widely recognized historian and author, quotes information from *Lay Down Body* and shares our continued interest in little-known cemeteries. He writes about the old history of the Marine Corps Air Station (MCAS) in Beaufort, South Carolina:

> Even today little is known about the original plantation cemeteries and the later African American church and family burial places. Antebellum plantations in the area now occupied by the MCAS Beaufort included Mount Pleasant, Red House, Edgerly, Lawrence, Wilkinson, and Talbird. A 1995 study by this writer included the following known cemeteries on MCAS grounds: the deTreville-Lawrence cemetery, on DeLallo Avenue, opposite the Staff NonComissioned Officers' Club; an unnamed black cemetery, south of the intersection of Drayton Street and DeLallo Avenue and still in use; the Givens Family cemetery adjacent to the runway access road in the northern section of the MCAS; an unnamed cemetery southwest of the intersection of Geiger Boulevard and Moore Street; and a black cemetery on the east side of U.S. 21, old Shell Road.

> Since 1995, some of the above unnamed black cemeteries have been identified in the 1996 book, *Lay Down Body: Living History in African American Cemeteries*, by Roberta V. Hughes Wright and Wilbur Hughes III.

> The black cemetery on the east side of U.S. 21 is the New Hope Christian Church Cemetery, "approximately 73-years-old." An unnamed black cemetery south of the intersection of Drayton Street and DeLallo Avenue and still in use, is the Red House Cemetery.

> Another African American burial site to be added to the above list is the Pilgrim Cemetery of which the Wright-Hughes book stated: "What remains of the once vast Pilgrim Cemetery fronts Highway 21, a few hundred yards from the main entrance to the Marine Corps Air Station."

> The deTreville-Lawrence Cemetery, about one-quarter acre, surrounded by a wire fence, is on DeLallo Avenue, near the deTreville great house. It contains the graves of at least five people, not all marked by memorials.

> The Givens Cemetery, adjacent to the runway access road, is surrounded by a tabby wall. Inside the tabby enclosure are two primary burial sites, consisting of brick monuments, covered by marble slabs. Both have been

vandalized, but one marble slab is still legible. It marks the grave of young Thomas Givens, who died in October 1820-, age 4 years and 7 months.

The plantation on MCAS grounds was owned by John Givens (1726-1785). He married Mary Stone in 1751 and a daughter, Jane, married into the Lawrence family. It is evident that familial relations existed between the deTreville, Lawrence and Givens families, all of whom owned neighboring plantations.

An unnamed cemetery southwest of the intersection of Geiger Boulevard and Movre Street is marked on a map of the air station, but no information about it is known.

According to the book by Wright and Hughes, "Red House Cemetery, just over an acre in size, is still in use. The cemetery is located on property that was formerly known as the Edgerly Plantation, home to many black families." When the air base property was acquired for government purposes, those black families were paid for their land, but had to seek new homes.

According to Wright and Hughes, "the cemetery is owned by Second Jordan Baptist Church of Burton. Red House Cemetery is accessible only by entering the grounds of the Marine Corps Air Station, which gives consent to all interested parties... buried at Red House are longtime Burton residents Victoria Frazier, Betty Frazier, Neil Frazier, Rose Bryan and Berney Bryan."

Again, quoted Wright and Hughes, the New Hope Christian Church Cemetery, owned by New Hope Christian Church, Disciples of Christ, is about 73 years. "It faces Highway 21 and extends for more than four acres, bounded on its remaining sides by the Marine Corps Air Station. The cemetery is beautifully maintained."

"What remains of the once vast Pilgrim Cemetery," according to Wright and Hughes, "fronts U.S. 21, a few hundred yards from the main entrance to the Marine Corps Air Station. The cemetery was once called Donaldson Cemetery after the family that was once buried there.

The cemetery was founded in the early 1800s by members of the now defunct Pilgrim Baptist Church. In 1899, three prominent families within the church, the Donaldsons, Grays and Griffins, split from the congregation to form the Pine Grove Baptist Church..."

During the Civil War, plantations of the area were seized by the federal government for non-payment of direct taxes. The Historic Preservation Plan for Marine Corps Air Station Beaufort stated:

"...planters of the area abandoned their property to the thousands of slaves, who were then forced to fend for themselves. The resulting neglect of the fields, coupled with the destruction of processing mills and the loss of lands to taxes, brought ruin to the economic system of the area.

The Reconstruction era was one of economic and social instability. Cotton cultivation continued to support the small farmer and timber harvesting grew in importance. For a brief time, phosphate mining flourished, employing a large number of local workers.

These successes were all rather short lived as the boll weevil, phosphate taxes and competition, and timber depletion all produced severe economic setbacks."

St. Helena Island, South Carolina

St. Helena Island, as described in the historical text *Tombee: Portrait of a Cotton Planter* by Theodore Rosengarten, is situated off the Atlantic coast, about fifty miles southwest of Charleston, South Carolina, and forty miles northeast of Savannah, Georgia. About fifteen miles long and three to five miles wide, St. Helena belongs to a fertile chain of islands separated from each other and from the mainland by rivers and creeks. Many of these streams might better be described as "arms of the sea," because they bring the salt water inland to a pine belt and carry it out again without meeting significant sources of fresh water.

Twice each lunar day, the tide flows toward the land, then ebbs seaward. When the moon is in the first and third quarters, the tides rise six to eight feet around St. Helena. At the new moon and the full moon, the waters rise eight to ten feet. As the tides ebb, the islands appear to draw closer together. The flats exposed at low tide are mud-filled moats, friendly only to oyster catchers and armies of hungry crabs. St. Helena is larger than the neighboring islands of Ladys and Port Royal—located west along Port Royal River.

In the 1800s there were no farms on St. Helena Island worked by free labor, and no cotton that was not produced by slaves. Plantations usually bore the names of their owners, who by 1795 were sowing seeds of a new, long-staple cotton plant in beds where indigo had grown before demand for it collapsed. The planter's family lived in a plain, low house with a sprawl of rooms that had been added over the years. A porchless front facade looked out on an irregular row of Negro houses, stables, and provision grounds, including a piece set aside for a house garden.

Fifteen years later, fattened by the high prices paid for his cotton, the typical planter had moved into a mansion, or "Big House," on the creekside of his plantation. Today these homes line the banks of the island, reminding visitors of the past: the stately mansions standing arrogantly before the windowless cabins and shacks of the enslaved. Tombee House and Coffin Point House, are two of the largest and most popular of the old island mansions.

St. Helena is practically the only sea island that retains vestiges of a style of life commonplace on the islands during the early 1900s. Traveling to Jekyll, Hilton Head, Kiawah, or some of the other islands stretching from

Florida to the Carolinas, one is awed by the trappings of an increasingly more affluent society. St. Helena, on the other hand, counts among her significant landmarks the live oak trees draped with Spanish moss, the beautiful marshes, the small homes and family-owned businesses of her warm and friendly people—though the islanders are cautious of outsiders. There are no traffic lights or supermarkets; the island boasts only a single motel and three restaurants. Luxury homes border the ocean, while at St. Helena Sound, numerous shrimp boats rev up their motors "at day clean" as they set out to cast their nets for the day's catch.

Penn Center dominates life on the island. Emerging from Penn School in the mid-1950s—after Beaufort County took over the responsibility of educating African Americans on St. Helena and the surrounding islands—it sits on fifty acres dotted by groves of towering oak trees heavy with moss. In 1863 Penn School teacher and diarist Charlotte Forten described the trees as breathtakingly beautiful. They still are. The campus consists of approximately sixteen buildings, all recently remodeled and refurbished, but retaining the charm and distinctiveness of the original buildings of a century ago. Along with its campus, the Center's activities and programs have grown through the years, and the extent of its involvement with and effect on the island is immeasurable.

Penn's current mission, under executive director Bernie Wright, who succeeded Hilton Head native Emory Campbell, is to preserve Sea Island history, culture, and environment. The center serves as a local, national, and international educational resource center and acts as a catalyst for the development of programs for self-sufficiency. Penn's three main service programs are History and Cultural Affairs, Land and Environmental Education, and the Program for Academic and Cultural Enrichment.

The difference between church and community cemeteries on St. Helena, as elsewhere, is minimal. Church cemeteries are usually located at the side or rear of the edifice, and they tend to have "older" burials, some dating back to the post–Civil War era. All the church cemeteries are well cared for and do not have the problem of encroaching undergrowth that some of the community cemeteries face. Longtime parishioners and church officials are most often interred in church cemeteries.

Community cemeteries tend to be in more secluded, natural areas. Most are maintained by residents of the community who take pride in maintaining them. Some, however, receive a bit more "tender, loving care" than others. The history and heritage of the island can be "read" in the cemeteries, part of the wonderful charm of St. Helena Island.

Dr. Patricia Guthrie, a professor in the Department of Women's Studies at California State University at Hayward, wrote about St. Helena and has surveyed the island's black churches. Those marked with an asterisk have a

These signs on St. Helena Island indicate main roads such as Lands End—also known as Martin Luther King Drive in acknowledgement of his contributions to island history—and the famous Penn Center.

cemetery at their location: Adams Street Baptist Church; Brick Baptist Church*; Ebenezer Baptist Church*; Faith Memorial Baptist Church*; First African Baptist Church (the church uses Coffin Point and Fripp cemeteries); Grace Truth Bible Chapel; Jehova Holiness; Oaks Holiness; Orange Grove Baptist Church*; Scott Holiness; Scottsville Baptist Church; Seven Day Adventist; St. James Baptist Church; St. Joseph Baptist Church*.

Most of the churches on St. Helena still actively serve the black community. There are also Jehovah's Witness and Black Muslim congregations on the island; most white residents attend St. Helena Baptist Church and Holy Cross Catholic Church, both located off the island in Beaufort.

A close relationship exists between the island's communities and churches and its praise houses. Historically, slaves did not find true pleasure or spiritual expression at church. They depended on the weekly talks and shouts at the praise house that could be found on every plantation. Sometimes the plantation owner erected a little praise house for the express purpose of giving his slaves a place of their own to worship; if not, a family would declare its cabin the plantation praise house.

Praise houses (or "prays houses") were devised by farmers to provide slaves with a spiritual outlet that wouldn't take their servants and field workers off the plantation for religious services. They were often used for mid-

South Carolina
PENN SCHOOL
One of the first schools for blacks in the South, Penn School, opened in 1862, was reorganized as Penn Normal, Industrial and Agricultural School in 1901. As a result of this change, incorporating principles of education found at both Tuskegee and Hampton Institutes, Penn became an international model. Its program was removed to the Beaufort County school system in 1948.

Penn Center, which emerged from Penn School in the mid-1950s, dominates life on the island. The resource and educational center's mission is to preserve Sea Island history, culture, and environment.

week services when distances to established black churches were too great to travel. Praise houses also served as centers for social and political activity. It was at the praise house that blacks found their spiritual release in song, prayer, and dance. Although plantation owners sanctioned praise house meetings, they were often frightened and disturbed by the sounds. Shouts would often last well into the night, and the monotonous thud of feet prevented sleep up to half a mile away.

Members of the praise house would often oversee funerals and assume the role of unofficial keepers of the burial plots scattered throughout the plantations. Funerals would often take place at the praise house or in the yards of the deceased. "One of their key functions was to provide a proper burial service for the dead," says Lula Holmes, a longtime resident and historian for St. Helena Island.

Most praise houses eventually vanished as mainstream black churches expanded into the area following the abolition of slavery. However, there are at least four praise houses still operating on St. Helena Island: Coffin Point Community Praise House, on SC Road 77, one-third mile northeast of US 21; Croft Community Praise House, on SC Road 74, 1.3 miles north of US 21; Eddys Point Community Praise House, on SC Road 183, one-tenth of a mile

Praise houses such as this one, located on St. Helena Island, served as centers for religious, social, and political activity.

north of DC Road 73; and Mary Jenkins Community Praise House, on SC Road 74, 2.1 miles north of US 21. The Moving Star Hall is located on neighboring Johns Island, on SC River Road, about six miles south of Charleston.

In Guthrie's *Catching Sense: The Meaning of Plantation Membership among Blacks on St. Helena Island, S.C.* is an interesting discussion of praise houses on the island:

> After the slave laws discouraged the gathering of slaves away from their own plantation, masters allowed their people to worship in plantation groups, usually at the house of one of the older people, sometimes in a special praise house. The "leaders" of these plantation groups were persons of considerable authority in spiritual matters. They have been referred to as the lineal descendants of the African medicine man, and they were the forerunners of the pre-

The Penn School of St. Helena

In 1861, at the start of the Civil War, some twenty thousand Union troops landed on Hilton Head Island, just across from St. Helena. The Union forces moved onward, seizing control of other nearby islands, including St. Helena, and freeing ten thousand slaves. Defeated, the former plantation owners fled to the mainland.

The Philadelphia Port Royal Commission was formed to send superintendents to St. Helena as quickly as possible to continue operation of the plantations. In addition, it enlisted teachers to go to St. Helena to teach the newly freed blacks. Thus, with the Civil War still in its infancy, President Abraham Lincoln rose to the challenge of equality, believing that former slaves could and would work the fields, attend school, and learn to read and write. He overthrew the fundamental Slave Code of 1790, which had prohibited the teaching of reading and writing to slaves.

Penn School was established at St. Helena's Oak Plantation in April 1862 as one of the first schools for blacks in the South. Its first two teachers, Laura M. Towne and Ellen Murray, traveled to St. Helena from Philadelphia; Towne, who had some limited medical training, was frequently referred to as a physician. Before long, the school outgrew its space at the plantation and classes were moved a short distance away, to the Brick Baptist Church.

continued on next page

sent African American ministers. They presided over meetings, gave spiritual advice, and in some cases officiated at weddings and funerals.

With the breakdown of the antebellum plantation and the shifting of the freed population, praise houses disappeared from most sections, to be supplanted by churches. In the sea islands, churches were organized, but were merely superimposed upon the praise house system.

Holmes recalls stories of a time when islanders congregated at praise houses two or three times a week; the houses also provided accommodation for the infirm and the elderly. "They were close to the plantations and much more accessible than some of the churches. For those who attended, they could also hear the community happenings and announcements that were part of the regular program. Some praise houses even had Sunday school classes for the children." Two praise houses, Mary Jenkins and Eddys Point, still have fairly regular bimonthly meetings. Both are located near Penn Center and are led by Deacon Henderson and Deacon James Smalls.

Today, on St. Helena, praise house leaders no longer officiate at weddings and funerals. They do, however, continue to preside over meetings and give spiritual advice, though any links with "African medicine men" have long since been severed. The twentieth-century praise house, far different from those of earlier centuries, serves as a sanctuary to reflect, "shout," and pray in a wonderful historic setting. Like area cemeteries, praise houses offer a rare glimpse into African American history and provide an opportunity for those walking the area to supplement their historical knowledge and satisfy their curiosity of what once was.

Dr. Guthrie's survey has also included the plantations—now called communities—located on St. Helena Island. Those with an asterisk have cemeteries at their location: Brisbane; Pope; Capers*; Tom Fripp*; Pritchard;

Cedar Grove*; Frogmore*; Saxtonville Memorial Gardens* (Brick Church owns the cemetery); Fuller*; Scott Farm; Cherry Hill; Club Bridge; Hopes*; Coffin Point*; Indian Hill*; Corner (Major)*; Mary Jenkins*; Tombee and Cuffy*; Croft*; Lands End*; Wallace*; McTureous*; Warsaw*; Dataw; Mulberry Hill; Dr. White*; Oakland*; Eddings Point*; Oaks*; Fripp Point*; Orange Grove*; Ann Fripp*; Pollywanna*.

Membership in the community is essential to burial in its cemetery. As Dr. Guthrie writes:

> Members of a plantation, regardless of their residence at the time of their death, have the right to burial in the graveyard of the plantation where they hold membership. It is not at all uncommon for people to ship the bodies of deceased plantation members back to the island for burial. Spouses of plantation members may be buried alongside their mates, if they so desire, even when they hold membership elsewhere. If, however, a person had multiple spouses during his/her lifetime, only one pair of mates will be laid to rest in the same graveyard. This is the only right that accrues to plantation members who are not residents on the plantation where they are members. Plantation members who reside on the plantation where they belong are eligible for the office of leader, may seek land use rights for a dwelling site, and also have the right to burial in their plantation's graveyard.

Individuals who reside on St. Helena but do not hold membership in a plantation lack access to the rights of plantation members. Specifically, non-members of a plantation are not eligible for the office of praise house leader, they are not buried in the plantation graveyard and, except under unusual circumstances, they are not eligible to seek use rights in land for the purpose of establishing a dwelling.

Each of the essential ingredients of personhood accrue to every person

continued from previous page

In October 1862 Towne and Murray were joined by Charlotte Forten, a black teacher who had taught school in Salem, Massachusetts, and in Philadelphia. Forten, like her father and grandfather, had been active in abolitionist movements in Pennsylvania, New York, and Massachusetts.

Towne supervised the instruction and traveled to and fro in her carriage, traversing St. Helena's dirt roads and thick woods on her "doctoring expeditions." Murray and Forten spent most of their time with the children. Even in its new location, the school soon became overcrowded, and the restlessness of the students—especially the very young—made teaching difficult. Forten's beautiful singing voice helped charm and interest the students as she taught them a variety of songs.

In March 1864, little more than a year after President Lincoln issued the Emancipation Proclamation, the Philadelphia Commission began efforts to secure a building for a new school. In 1905, the need for industrial education led to the establishment of trade courses in carpentry, blacksmithing, wheelwrighting, basket weaving, harness making, cobbling, and mechanics. Students and community people also took agricultural courses and teacher training, and the school became known as Penn Normal, Industrial, and Agricultural School.

continued on next page

continued from previous page

Until 1948 the school continued to serve children and adults of the area. It was, in fact, the major source of formal educational training for African Americans on St. Helena Island and the surrounding regions. In the late 1930s, the South Carolina State Board of Education and the General Education Board used Penn School to host an experiment in elementary school teacher training for the South Carolina State College at Orangeburg. Rosa B. Cooley and Grace B. House succeeded Towne and Murray as principal and assistant principal; Forten, because of ill health, had left the school much earlier.

In 1948, the South Carolina public school system was extended to St. Helena. All island schools operated concurrently until the Penn class of 1953 had graduated. The school was then reformed as Penn Community Service; a further name change dubbed it Penn Center, and the center initiated new programs such as Penn Nursery School and the Rosa B. Cooley Health Clinic.

Penn Center was the facility where biracial groups in South Carolina could meet during the 1950s and early 1960s, and it became a major retreat for civil rights groups. From 1961 to 1967, Dr. Martin Luther King Jr., the Hon. Andrew Young, and their staffs met often at the center to formulate strategies for social change in the South and throughout the rest of the country. The historic March on Washington, D.C., was, in part, planned on Penn's campus.

who is a member of a plantation on St. Helena Island regardless of his/her affiliation. In the context of this discussion, bear in mind that the rights of full personhood, that is, access to the office of praise house leader, the right to seek land use rights, and the right to burial in the plantation graveyard, come into existence when persons attain plantation membership.

Although Guthrie's comments were written several years ago, much is still true. However, as with many customs and mores, changes have occurred over time. St. Helena's changes are small but, nevertheless, they would likely shock the elders of previous generations who formulated some of the island's strict burial rules and procedures.

BRICK BAPTIST CHURCH CEMETERY

Brick Baptist Church Cemetery, which extends from the front of the "yard" to the rear, elegantly epitomizes a historic countryside cemetery. The two tall monuments overlooking the road are dedicated to Penn's first two teachers, Laura Towne and Ellen Murray. Popular tourist attractions, they date back to the early 1900s.

A few of the family graves in the cemetery are ringed by tabby walls—sturdy oyster shell constructions that have withstood the passing of time—that represent the kind of structures common during that early period. Scattered among the cemetery's older markers stand headstones conspicuous in their newness. These headstones mark the burial place of those more recently interred.

The Brick Baptist Church was built in 1855, using the labor of the enslaved. After it was completed, whites sat on the first level while blacks were remanded to the balcony or sat outside under a nearby grove of live oaks.

Under the trees on a Sunday morning would be tied every conceivable combination of horse and vehicle: from six-seated carriages with fine northern horses to one-seated sulkies and mules saddled with cotton bags. But horses were a luxury to many, including those of color whose possessions numbered few. Some men would carry their shoes in their hands on the walk to the service, putting them on only when they got to church; many more owned no shoes at all. By mid-century there were still relatively few whites on the island.

A granite memorial honoring Charlotte Forten, the first African American teacher at Penn School, was erected in 1992.

After the start of the Civil War in 1861, the Brick Baptist Church doubled as the local schoolhouse. In December 1992, the Michigan Support Group for Penn Center presented the church with a granite memorial honoring Charlotte Forten, the first African American teacher at Penn School. It now stands at the doorway nearest the walkway leading from the cemetery. Like Forten, the school's first two white teachers, Laura Towne and Ellen Murray, are buried in Pennsylvania.

After the war, Brick Baptist became a black church. Inside its plain white interior, its galleries and central hall filled with black people who stood at the doors, near the windows, and in the aisles. The "elders" were seated under the pulpit and in the front seats. They were all well dressed—a few in gaudy toggery, hoopskirts, and shabby bonnets, but most in simple "head handkerchers." The service has remained essentially unchanged to the present day. Parishioners begin each service with song. There are no hymnals; when it's time to sing, someone leads off with a song and everyone seems to know all the words. It's a wonderful service, led today by the Reverend Ervin Greene, a member of the committee that recently completed the Gullah translation of the Book of Luke.

Among the many Penn School graduates buried at Brick Baptist Church Cemetery are **York W. Bailey**, M.D.; his nephew, **David Chisholm**, M.D.; and **Celia Chisholm**, David's mother and Dr. Bailey's sister. Dr. Bailey became St. Helena Island's only resident doctor in 1906, in a community where islanders regularly utilized nature's medications and there was widespread practice of superstitious beliefs. A graduate of Penn School, Bailey furthered his studies at Hampton Institute in Virginia and Howard University in Washington, D.C. Before retiring in 1956, he served for half a century, providing proper medical care to the island's black community. During his early years of practice, island residents had no money to pay him; he was compensated with corn, peas, chickens, ducks, or turkeys, which he sold in Beaufort.

Also buried at Brick are **George Brown**, father of current resident **Leroy Browne** (who changed the spelling of his surname), and **A. J. Brown**, another Penn student who taught shoemaking at the school. Brown was one of four singers who comprised the renowned St. Helena Quartet.

Today, the live oak trees on both sides of Lands End Road (now called

Martin Luther King Drive in acknowledgment of King's involvement with the local Penn Center), form a breathtakingly beautiful canopy to the approach of the church. With its great history and heritage, the Brick Baptist Church, standing regal and charming atop a slight hill, attracts visitors who enjoy roaming the surrounding grounds and cemetery, hopefully getting the chance to see the church interior. Like a living thing, the church once extended its arms outward to masses of recently freed blacks; today it embraces an equally loyal congregation. The church recently purchased a large tract of land about three to five miles down Lands End Road, in Saxtonville. Destined to be the church's new cemetery, it is called Memorial Gardens.

Oyster shell walls dating back to the 1800s ring some of Brick Baptist Church Cemetery's family graves.

ORANGE GROVE BAPTIST CHURCH CEMETERY

Orange Grove Baptist Church Cemetery is about two acres in size and lies to the side and rear of the church. Both were founded in 1917. The church is a spin-off of Brick Baptist Church. Its first pastor was Reverend Handy Johnson; Reverend William H. Carpenter, the present pastor, has been at the church over twelve years. It is situated in a beautiful grove of trees and, as with other church cemeteries, is maintained by church employees and members. Buried

Kathleen Singleton and many more St. Helena islanders are buried at the two-acre Orange Grove Baptist Church Cemetery.

in the church cemetery are **Rebecca Mitchell Daise** (March 1986), **Gibbs Daise** (December 1994), the Freeman family, the Johnson family, **Kathleen Singleton**, and many more islanders.

EBENEZER BAPTIST CHURCH CEMETERY

Ebenezer Baptist Church Cemetery runs the width of the church grounds and lies to the rear of the edifice. Its markers date back to the 1800s and the cemetery, like the church, is quite large. Walking through the cemetery one cannot help but feel the nostalgia of the past; real and artificial flowers reflect the constant visits and other expressions of caring for departed loved ones.

After the Reverend Kit Green, pastor of the Brick Baptist Church, died in 1881, some members of the congregation left to form a new church, which they organized and named the Ebenezer Baptist Church. The building was constructed in 1883–1884 at a site just half a mile down Lands End Road from Brick Baptist. Through the years, the church has enjoyed a succession of pastors. The longest years of service were given by the Reverend D. C. Washington, who served as pastor from 1895 to 1934. A native St. Helena

islander and Penn School graduate, Washington was descended from a line of ministers and was loved and respected far and near. Ebenezer is the largest church on St. Helena, both in space and membership. The original building burned in 1938; it was rebuilt in 1940.

ST. JOSEPH BAPTIST CHURCH CEMETERY

St. Joseph opened in October 1937 as a spin-off from the nearby Ebenezer Baptist Church. Its quaint, well-cared-for cemetery dates back to the 1950s. St. Joseph's first pastor, Reverend Joseph Heyward, is buried there.

St. Joseph's Baptist Church Cemetery tends to be a smaller and more structured burial ground, with tombstones more patterned and specially placed. Pastor Kenneth C. Doe has been with the church for almost twenty years. The Kiwanis Club of Beaufort named him 1995 Clergyman of the Year due to his contributions to the civic, moral, cultural, and educational welfare and betterment of the community. Particularly cited were his Young Men's Academy at the church and his ministry at the Beaufort Detention Center.

St. Joseph, Ebenezer, and Brick Baptist churches are less than half a mile apart. On any given Sunday, Lands End Road and their parking lots are full to capacity.

FAITH MEMORIAL BAPTIST CHURCH CEMETERY

Founded in 1955, Faith Memorial Baptist Church and Cemetery are located on Lands End Road, just a few miles from Penn Center. The cemetery at the side of the church is approximately one-half acre in size and has about fourteen graves. Faith Memorial Baptist Church was an offspring of Brick Baptist Church, created when some of the members of Brick decided they wanted to form a "less historic" church, in a "less historic" building.

The church's first pastor, **Reverend Johnson**, died after only two years in service. He is buried in the church cemetery, as are longtime island residents **Mazie Greene** and **Florence Parkes.** Reverend Horace Williams, the present pastor, has been at Faith for twelve years. An ambitious and active churchman and educator, he has developed a strong youth ministry, along with other significant programs for the church.

CORNER (MAJOR) CEMETERY

The small private road to Penn Center's Retreat House leads to a right-hand turn and the hidden Corner Cemetery. A visit to the small burial grounds reveals various small objects and artifacts left by loved ones, in memoriam. Although the area is widely overgrown with bushes and ground cover, recent markers confirm the continued use of the cemetery. Situated in a hidden and unexpected location, the site is both lovely and lonely. The Dudley and Major families and other African American families from the community are buried here.

CUFFY CEMETERY

Cuffy Cemetery is located down Seaside Road, just past a large commercial farm, and not far from the marsh and the Atlantic Ocean. It is almost one-half acre in size and is well cared for. Buried in Cuffy are longtime island res-

idents **Liza Johnson** and **Colleen Jefferson.** More recently buried here was **Becker Johnson.** When the 1994 purchase of Tombee Place House denied Tombee community residents access to their cemetery, they joined Cuffy Cemetery, which is located nearby. Resident George Alston said, "The community does an excellent job caring for our cemetery. We are proud of it and enjoy keeping it beautiful."

ADAMS STREET BAPTIST CHURCH CEMETERY

Adams Street Baptist Church is situated far down Lands End Road past a few miles of beautiful trees near large tomato and other agricultural farms. The church is fairly new, and the cemetery at the rear of the church suggests that burials began in the 1980s. The grounds are high and treeless, and the granite markers—some with intimate inscriptions—are rather more elaborate than those of the other small cemeteries. The name **I. H. Middleton,** significantly engraved on the church entrance, tells the story of his prominence as the first pastor. His tombstone toward the front of the cemetery is dated 1987. Others interred are **Nancy Rivers Wrotten** (1980), **Catherine Pearl Mack** (1987), **Ezekiel Paul** (1990), and **Pheobe G. Green** (1987). These, among about twenty others, comprise the small attractive cemetery.

Coffin Point Cemetery
stands on a lovely,
oak-lined street leading
directly from Coffin
Point House.

COFFIN POINT CEMETERY

Founded in the 1800s as a burial ground for the enslaved, Coffin Point Cemetery stands on a lovely, oak-lined street leading directly from Coffin Point House. The cemetery, about eight acres in size, while rustic in appearance, is neither overgrown or unkempt. It is frequently used by residents of the Coffin Point community, as well as native islanders who have lots in the cemetery and who previously lived—or had a family living—in the area. It is open and bright and has its own distinct character as a pleasant, peaceful resting place.

Only a small amount of St. Helena Island history is recorded in books and diaries. In *Letters from Port Royal, 1862–1868*, a letter from Harriet Ware, a white Gideonite from Boston, written June 9, 1862, reveals her negative reaction to the ways of the recently freed blacks and sheds some light on the black burial practices of the time.

Gideonites comprised a sect of professionals, businessmen, and a few ladies from New York and Boston who were sympathetic abolitionists. At the call of Edward Pierce (selected by President Abraham Lincoln to lead the challenge), they banded together in the mold of the fighting prophets of the Old Testament. Although the desire to travel to Port Royal to strike a blow for freedom was compelling, there were underlying inducements—such as adventure, and the semi-tropical climate—that made such philanthropy especially attractive. Ware writes:

> Just after dinner, we saw the people assembling at their burying place. This burying place was an unfenced quarter of an acre of perfectly wild, tangled woodland in the midst of the cotton field, halfway between here (Coffins Point manor) and the quarters. Nothing ever marks the graves, but the place is entirely devoted to them. . . .
>
> Uncle Sam followed us, book in hand and spectacles on nose, reading as he walked. As we drew near to the grave, we heard all the children singing their ABCs through and through again, as they stood waiting round the grave for the rest to assemble and for Uncle Sam to begin. Each child had his schoolbook or picture book that Mr. Gannett [a do-gooder who came from Boston to work with the newly freed slaves] had given him in his hand, another proof that they consider their lessons as some sort of religious exercise.
>
> We were joined at once by Mr. Edward S. Philbrick [who came to the island from Boston when President Lincoln started the Port Royal Experiment] and stood uncovered with the rest about the grave, at the mouth of which rested the coffin, a rough board one, but well shaped and closed. Uncle Sam took off his hat, tied a red handkerchief round his head, and, adjusting his glasses, read the hymn through, and then deaconed out two lines at a time for the people to sing. He repeated the process with a second hymn, when Abel made a prayer; then Uncle Sam read from the Burial Service and began his exordium apologizing for his inability to speak much on account of a sore throat, but holding forth for about half an hour upon the necessity for all to pre-

Burial of the Drowned Among the Gullah Negroes (1958)

The Gullah Coast of South Carolina extends from Murrell's Inlet in Georgetown County southward to the Savannah River, a rural region except for the metropolitan area about Charleston near its midpoint. . . .

Most of the cemeteries at Hilton Head are situated near the water's edge, for if a Negro drowns he must be buried so that the water, at night from the high spring tides, will wash over his grave. If this is not done it is said that another member of his family will drown within the year. This appealing custom is accounted for on the grounds that "you must give back to the sea what belongs to the sea."

There are, however, several island graveyards on Hilton Head. If the body of a drowned man is interred in one of them, members of the family will be spared misfortune provided they "pay the water," a fee which consists of casting a few coins into the sea, pennies or perhaps a silver half dollar. But "paying the water" is not exclusively a mortuary ritual. A coin dropped into the sea before a hazardous voyage will insure a safe return; and sometimes when a fisherman is drowned, his death is attributed to failure to pay the water. This way of propitiation has numerous parallels. An Abenaki Indian informant states that "we used to go down the river in our canoes to burrow for cranberries in the autumn, and . . . we always threw tobacco into the water as an offering, so that we might have a calm time going and returning." The sacrifice of the hapless

Iphigenia at Luis and the espousal of the Doge of Venice to the Adriatic on Ascension Day are examples which immediately come to mind.

Jacob Benjamin Green, a Hilton Head Negro born in 1874, denies any harmful results from failure to bury the drowned in the accustomed manner or to pay the water. He explains that the tradition is maintained because his people like to "follow the same thing" that their ancestors have done. The rite has been performed as long as Green can remember, or in his own words, "ever since I had sense."

—HENNIG COHEN, *Southern Folklore Quarterly, 1958*

pare for "dis bed," filling his discourse with Scripture illustrations and quotations aptly and with force, using the story of "Antoninus and Suffirus" as a proof that God would not have any "half religions"—that if anybody had "hid his Lord's money in de eart' he must grabble for it before 'twas too late."

He read from the service again, one of the men throwing on earth at the usual place. When they came to cover up the grave, the men constantly changed hoes with those who had not handled them before, that each might aid, women and old men stopping to throw in a handful. Abel made another prayer, they sang again and dispersed.

It was of this scene that W. C. Gannett of Boston wrote the following lines, also included in *Letters from Port Royal:*

The Negro Burying-ground

'Mid the sunny flat of the cotton field
Lies an acre of forest-tangle still;
A cloister dim, where the grey moss waves
And the live oaks lock their arms at will.

Here in the shadows the slaves would hide
As they dropped the hoe at death's release,
And leave no sign but a sinking mound
To show when they passed on their way to peace.

This was the gate—there was none but this
To a Happy Land where men were men;
And the dusky fugitives one by one,
Stole in from the bruise of the prison pen.

When lo! in the distance boomed the guns
The bruise was over, and "Massa" had fled!
But Death is the "Massa" that never flees
And still to the oaks they bore the dead.

'Twas at set of sun; a tattered troop
Of children circled a little grave.
Chanting an anthem rich in its peace
As ever pealed in cathedral-nave.

The A, B, C, that the lips below
Had learnt with them in the school to shout.
Over and over they sung it slow
Crooning a mystic meaning out.

A, B, C, D, E, F, G,
Down solemn alphabets they swept;
The oaks leaned close, the moss swung low,
What strange new sound among them crept?

The holiest hymn that the children knew!
'Twas dreams come real, and heaven come near;
'Twas light, and liberty, and joy.
And "white folks" sense—and God right here!

Over and over; they dimly felt
This was the charm could make Black white,
This was the secret of "Massa's pride,"
And this, unknown made the negro's night.

What could they sing of braver cheer
To speed on his unseen way the friend?
The children were facing the mystery Death
With the deepest prayer that their hearts could send.

Children, too, and the mysteries last!
We are but comrades with them there,
Stammering over a meaning vast,
Crooning our guesses of how and where.

But the children were right with their A, B, C;
In our stammering guess so much we say!
The singers were happy, and so are we:
Deep as our wants are the prayers we pray.

The Coffin Point Cemetery, as it exists today, differs from Mrs. Ware's cryptic description. It is well kept and lovely, signs of the work of the elder Leroy Jenkins, who for many years has tended the grounds. Many family members of native islander Marie Gadson are buried here, including **Julia Smalls Holmes, Lula Jenkins,** and **York Smalls.** The land for the cemetery was given to the people of the area by the late Senator Campbell, owner of the plantation during the 1800s.

It is not known if the name Low Bottom was taken from the designation "Low Country," a name that local residents love with a passion that is both fierce and possessive. The area is low and flat and is dotted by numerous wetlands and marshes. Consequently, a drive from "here to there" is always spectacular in beauty. Since the area is unbuildable, there is the assurance of trees and more trees, birds, and wildlife to be enjoyed for generations to come. Low Bottom Cemetery, which is actually on a slight hill, sits alone on a road that would see no traffic were it not for the Callawassie Golf and Country Club, a few hundred yards away.

The area is sparsely populated. No homes line the road leading from the highway to the cemetery, though at one corner and a few yards down stands a small community of houses.

Low Bottom, South Carolina

The road from St. Helena Island to Hilton Head Island directs motorists past a guarded entrance to the Parris Island Marine Corps Recruiting Base, across the wide expanse of beautiful Broad River, over the smaller Chechessee River, to a corner where sits the little, white, country-style St. Luke's Church. Highway signs encourage travelers to turn left, toward the sales office of the residential and golf resort, Callawassie Golf and Country Club.

Following the half-mile drive to view the manicured, flower-lined entrance to the resort, a quarter-mile down, an unexpected sign attracts the eye. "Low Bottom Cemetery—Going Home to Rest," it says. The first surprise is to see the cemetery name posted. A second surprise is to see the cemetery, sitting in still solitude—the tombstones in unstructured patterns throughout its few acres—in this particular location. Interred here are **Wright Young** (buried just after the Civil War), the **Rev. Bolden** and his family, the Austin family, the Jenkins family, and **Deacon Gaston**. Beyond the cemetery are live oaks, flowers, landscaped gardens, and the security gates leading to the beautiful country club.

LOW BOTTOM CEMETERY

Low Bottom Cemetery is two acres in size, and although the ground is covered with fallen leaves it is splendid in appearance and presentation. However, it comes to mind that the cemetery founders encountered a far different setting. No doubt this was once a secluded field, a fitting location for church and cemetery. Perhaps, particularly after the Civil War, scattered cabins graced the landscape and freedmen plowed their crops. Several inquiries to residents in the area reveal that the cemetery is owned by St. Luke Baptist Church, which sits on nearby Highway 802, between Hilton Head Island and Parris Island, in proximity of the beautiful Broad River.

A visit to the church on a Sunday morning reveals a closely knit, upbeat congregation led by the Rev. Luther Jones and Deacon Joseph Young Jr. Recently, the congregation has been approached by developers; as one parishoner said, describing a visitor one hot August day in 1995, "The man has come from one of those big companies to buy our property." The little white church, once on a country corner, now finds itself on land that is extremely valuable.

It is unusual to find signs for such small cemeteries as Low Bottom.

Charleston, South Carolina

Charleston is, beyond a doubt, one of the South's most fascinating cities. It exudes charm and creates in one's mind imagined memories—both good and bad—of life in the Old South. Though African Americans might be mesmer-

ized by the beauty of the place, one cannot help but remember those whose backs were bent and broken while they toiled under the threat of the master's whip to help build the beauty that now surrounds visitors to this grand old city.

Nevertheless, Charleston is truly an elegant city. Stately, white-columned mansions overlook the great park and the ocean. A plethora of carriages, the clump of their horses' hooves sounding through the brick streets, lead tourists to the tall, balconied building where, in the 1700s, former Africans waited to be sold and enslaved. From this building, now part of the Charleston market, a colorful array of goods and products extend like tendrils down several streets. The aisles are saturated with jewelry, sweet grass baskets, dolls, rugs, perfumes, paintings, clothes, books, teas, hot sauces, and other assorted items. Weaving through the market is a not-soon-to-be-forgotten experience.

In Charleston County, at the end of the 1700s, 775 free "colored people" resided. They included skilled artisans and businessmen of considerable intelligence who had accumulated considerable property. The "community-active" St. Phillips Church rector suggested to some of his parishioners that they organize a society for mutual benefit along the lines of similar groups organized by white people. The parishioners proceeded with the undertaking at once and, in 1790, formed the Brown Fellowship Society. One of the first steps taken by the five founding members was the purchase of a burial lot for the dead. Within a few years other societies were formed; the period between

1790 and 1820 seems to have been one of great prosperity for these people, though not for other blacks.

By 1820 there began to be a marked change. The great national struggle over carrying slavery into new states had begun and the abolition movement was making itself felt. South Carolina was alarmed. Then, in the spring of 1822, a planned Negro insurrection orchestrated by Denmark Vesey was discovered. Vesey was a Negro who had purchased his liberty by working after-hours for his master, a sea captain with whom he sailed to many ports. After his emancipation, Vesey settled in Charleston as a carpenter and put his mind to the problem of emancipating all slaves. When his conspiracy was uncovered, he and thirty-four associates were tried, convicted, and hanged.

These events put free colored people in a very delicate position. Formerly able to travel freely, they were now watched closely and with suspicion. Laws were enacted to forbid meetings of more than several blacks. The societies were able to survive, however, with help from some of the more noble-minded and Christian white members of the community. Vesey's home in Charleston is now a National Historic Landmark, though it is not open to the public.

In the 1860s Charleston had an ancient, quaint, and almost foreign appearance. It contained several public buildings and churches of pleasing architecture. About half of the city's forty thousand inhabitants were white. Within close proximity to each other in the city's downtown area were the public buildings, leading churches, law offices, merchants, railroads, steamboats, and telegraph agents. Virtually all of the buying, selling, and hiring of slaves that was transacted was done in this section of the city. From the colonial period through the mid-nineteenth century, hundreds and even thousands of slaves were sold annually to the highest bidder.

Many of the cemeteries and burial sites from the 1700s still exist. Among the cemeteries of beautiful, historic Charleston are Brown Fellowship Society, Brotherly, Old Bethel United Methodist, Friendly Union, and Unity and Friendship Society cemeteries. Brown Fellowship Cemetery was moved to the downtown area from another part of the city.

BROWN FELLOWSHIP SOCIETY CEMETERY

When Brown Fellowship Society was founded in 1790, one of their first steps was to purchase a burial lot for their dead. The society had an interest in maintaining schools for colored children, promoting "social purity," protecting family life, and befriending orphans. The organization proved so successful that it inspired a number of others that were later started on a similar plan. The Humane and Friendly Society was started in 1802 and the Friendly Union in 1813, followed by the Friendly Moralist, Brotherly Association, and the Unity and Friendship group. Each of these had its own burial lot and its system of mutual benefit.

Brown Fellowship Society Cemetery was originally laid out on land bordering Pitt Street, near the College of Charleston. In the 1940s a private Catholic school named Bishop England bought the cemetery. By 1957 the school needed more space for a parking lot and purchased some more land. When the Brown Fellowship Society moved its cemetery to a new location near 88 Smith Street, it left behind several unidentified, broken tombstones in a pile near a historic home called Blacklock House.

Brown Fellowship Society Cemetery is currently maintained by perpetual care funds—funds obtained through the sale of some property. In October 1995, Brown Fellowship celebrated its 205th anniversary. Among those buried at Brown are the Craft and Holloway families.

Septima Clark is among those buried at Old Bethel United Methodist Church Cemetery, an activist in the civil rights movement and a dear friend of Martin Luther King Jr.

BROTHERLY, OLD BETHEL UNITED METHODIST CHURCH, FRIENDLY UNION, AND UNITY AND FRIENDSHIP CEMETERIES

Nearby the Brown Fellowship Society Cemetery, behind and to the left of 88 Smith Street, lie four cemeteries. They all share the same block, running from one street to the next, separated from each other by a fence. Together they create a spectacular picture, with their various sizes and styles of tombstones and markers.

The founder of Brotherly Cemetery, Thomas Smalls, was a wealthy man with over $7,800 in real estate assets, but he was dark-complected and didn't qualify for the Brown Fellowship Society. In 1843, he established the Brotherly Cemetery in an effort to have a society where he would be welcomed.

Brotherly and Friendly Union cemeteries flank Brown Fellowship and are larger in size. The Friendly Union Cemetery was founded in 1813 by the Friendly Union Society, which still meets occasionally. Philip La Roche's family is buried here, as is **Joseph Irvine Hoffman**, father of Michigan resident Norma Davis, who died in August of 1988.

Old Bethel United Methodist Church Cemetery was started in 1807. **Septima Clark**, a dear friend of Martin Luther King Jr., and very active in the civil rights movement, is buried here.

Unity and Friendship Cemetery is also located within the montage of cemeteries just off Meeting Road. As with the others, its grounds are well cared for and the appearance of the cemetery is good. The Unity and Friendship Society meets annually and collects dues to offset the cost of maintaining the grounds. Buried here are well-known Charlestonians **Lelia Hoffman Drayton**

143

(1947); **Hubert Drayton** (1969); and **Eva Dawson Hoffman** (1953). The society was founded in the early 1800s, as was the cemetery.

Columbia, South Carolina

On December 17, 1860, a convention assembled in Columbia's First Baptist Church and drew up the Ordinance of Secession, setting off a chain of events that culminated in General William T. Sherman's troops occupying the city. Scarcely more than five years later, the city was reduced to ashes. A total area of eighty-four blocks, housing 1,386 buildings, was destroyed. From those ashes, the present city has risen.

Columbia, the capital of South Carolina, which lies just north of the Low Country and Sea Islands, similarly possesses unlimited stories of the struggles and the valor of its black residents. Although it is relaxed, beautiful, and historic, as a capital city Columbia is busier and more formal than its sister cities. Besides containing the capitol building and offices for U.S. lawmakers, it has more of everything: more shops, more restaurants, more local museums than any of its neighboring cities. Columbia also houses the State Department of Archives and History, the South Carolina State Museum, and an abundance of schools and colleges in or near its boundaries. Its residential neighborhoods are diverse and beautifully maintained. From its position in the center of the state, Columbia is the city of choice for those who want to reside at the hub of activity.

RANDOLPH CEMETERY

Randolph Cemetery is two blocks west of Elmwood Avenue at Interstate 126. In 1871, nineteen black men founded the cemetery as a memorial to fellow African American **Benjamin F. Randolph**. Randolph Cemetery has been under the spotlight in recent years due to the efforts of a group of Columbians fighting to preserve the wealth of black history that it represents.

Benjamin Randolph was a Methodist minister and Reconstruction-era Republican legislator. Ernest L. Wiggins, staff writer for Columbia newspaper *The State*, writes that in the outlying areas of South Carolina in 1868, resentful whites began gunning for blacks who attempted to campaign for public office. While seeking reelection, Randolph was warned to stay out of Abbeville County; as a former Union Army chaplain he was no stranger to conflict, so he bravely—or recklessly—rode the rails into Abbeville on October 16, 1868. As he emerged from the train in Hodges Depot, he was ambushed by three white men and killed. They were never tried for the assassination; a witness to the shooting was mysteriously murdered a few days after Randolph's death.

Historians say that Randolph fought for the rights of all children to an education. A stone obelisk memorializing his life as both pastor and politician marks his death at the cemetery that now bears his name. In 1992, members of the Columbia chapter of Delta Sigma Theta Sorority and the Committee for the Restoration and Beautification of Randolph Cemetery together honored Randolph by laying a wreath to commemorate his life and the lives of those buried at this three-acre site just west of Elmwood Cemetery.

Elaine Nichols, curator of African American History and Culture for the South Carolina State Museum and member of Delta Sigma Theta, states that Randolph Cemetery is a historical and cultural treasure of national significance because it holds the remains of nine black legislators from the Reconstruction Era. In addition to Randolph, buried here are **Charles M. Wilder**, the first black postmaster in Columbia; **Henry Cardozo; Fabriel Myers; William B. Nash; R. J. Palmer; William H. Simons; Samuel Thompson;** and **Lucius Wimbush.** Also interred here are Columbia's first black physician, several presidents of Allen University, and veterans of America's wars abroad.

Time and vandals have toppled many of the markers. Urban development has obscured the cemetery from view; I-126 runs along and above the road leading to the burial grounds. Though there is no significant count, between three and four hundred burial plots lie in Randolph Cemetery. Families continue to lay their dead in its red clay soil.

The difficult job of preservation and maintenance continues in this beautiful and very popular cemetery. While many of the markers are beautifully inscribed and are surrounded by a wrought iron fence that enhances the beauty of the grounds, time is taking its toll. The cemetery's restoration committee plans the construction of a wrought iron gate to dissuade vandals,

Randolph Cemetery Is Showcased

In 1989 the South Carolina State Museum sponsored an exhibit, "The Last Miles of the Way: African American Homegoing Traditions, 1890–Present," that showcased Columbia's Randolph Cemetery.

Elaine Nichols, then guest curator for the museum, led a research team that included professors, archaeologists, archeology students, museum curators, individuals donating or loaning artifacts, and scholars and researchers from area colleges in a massive effort to make this a one-of-a-kind exhibit. The catalog accompanying the exhibit, edited by Nichols, documents many of the material expressions of traditional West African concepts, as well as information about funerals and burial procedures:

"Today, one of the most visible manifestations of West African religious thought in the New World can be found in the black cemeteries of the South, where many meaningful and seemingly unusual objects adorn individual graves. Ranging from bed frames and bathroom tiles to car parts and Christmas tinsel, these decorations reveal artistic and philosophical roots in the ancient Kongo civilization of central Africa. . . .

"At an A.M. Zion church in Bladen County, North Carolina, an inverted coffee cup marks the site of one woman's grave. Next to it is a grave decorated with a candy jar and an inverted plastic bowl. A black Baptist church in the same county contains graves marked by jugs, pitchers, ceramic figurines, and an upside down bowl.

erection of a sign to aid visitors, and repair of damaged and uprooted grave-stones. Hard at work here, the national office of Delta Sigma Theta is promoting the preservation of black Americans' monuments and sites in other states as well.

The update on Randolph Cemetery as of August 2005, written by John C. Drake, staff writer for "the State" in Columbia, S.C. reflects some of the same problems as the 1996 story. He writes that the concerned community wants to fix Randolph Cemetery, a neglected, active burial ground with a historic past.

Ethel Johnson Berry's son was not pleased when they went to visit her father' tombstone at the historic Randolph Cemetery in Columbia.

"Why did you bury my grandmother under all those weeds?" Berry remembered her son asking.

Berry, who has more relatives buried at Randolph than she can count, has been toiling for years with other descendents of those buried there to fix up the burial ground.

But drug-dealing, prostitution, vagrancy and vandalism have stained the cemetery, and it is not clear whose job it is to fix it.

Historic preservationists, descendents and city officials met regularly at the State Museum to assess what it would take to ensure the site is an appropriate memorial to those buried there and is maintained for future generations.

Named for the late state Sen. B.F. Randolph, the cemetery includes the grave sites of at least nine black Reconstruction era lawmakers and is generally considered a place where middle to upper class African Americans were buried. Berry' father, for example, was local educator C.A. Johnson.

Unlike some old black cemeteries in Columbia that are considered abandoned, like the nearby Douglas Cemetery, Randolph Cemetery is still active, with relatives visiting and burials continuing. Published obituaries indicate people were buried at Randolph as recently as May of 2005.

A small network of Columbia area descendents at one point formed the Committee for the Beautification and Restoration of Randolph Cemetery, near Elmwood Cemetery on Elmwood Avenue. But they were able to muster only about $2,000 a year, which primarily paid for mowing the weeds (there is no turf grass), said Frank Williams, whose parents are buried there.

"We did the best we could," he said. "By and large, we did not get a lot of money."

State law authorizes, but does not require, local governments to maintain cemeteries that are abandoned or in disrepair.

Who owns the cemetery is unclear. Much of it is divided among families—many of whom long moved away from Columbia –who own individual plots.

Williams said he was encouraged by the interest in the cemetery shown at Tuesday's meeting. "I'm anxious to see something finally develop out of this meeting."

Winnsboro, South Carolina

Accessible from Highway 77 on County Road 20, Winnsboro is approximately a half-hour's drive north of Columbia. Now the Fairfield County seat, Winnsboro had one of the highest concentrations of black slaves in South Carolina before the Civil War.

The area was first settled in the 1740s by white English farmers. Blacks first entered the region a decade later, when settlers along the Broad River began importing slaves to grow indigo. However, the first large-scale plantations didn't appear until early in the 1820s.

According to a local census dating back to 1830, black slaves in Winnsboro and the surrounding county already outnumbered the white population. By 1860, black slaves outnumbered whites by two to one. Today, African Americans make up more than sixty percent of Winnsboro's 3,475 residents.

General Sherman and fifty-eight thousand Yankee troops briefly made Winnsboro their headquarters during the general's "Carolinas Campaign" in 1865. However, they later pillaged and burned the prosperous town—a blow from which, many local residents claim, Winnsboro never fully recovered.

Among Winnsboro's most famous residents are Sergeant **Webster Anderson**, South Carolina's second African American son to earn the Congressional Medal of Honor during the Vietnam War, and a former dean of Howard University, Professor **Kelly Miller**, who died in 1939.

To this day there are scores of unmarked African American grave sites scattered throughout Winnsboro's farmland.

CAMP WELFARE CEMETERY

The eleven acres of the campground are owned by the African Methodist Episcopal Church (A.M.E.), although people of all denominations are welcomed. Lying twelve miles from the city of Winnsboro, the camp is nestled

in a grove of oaks and pines, a circle of "tents" surrounding an open arbor containing benches for the worshippers. The original tents—built of boughs and brush—gave way to log cabins, pine board cabins, and small buildings made of cinder-block.

Camp Welfare opened a few years after the Civil War, sometime between 1870 and 1878. Before the war Negroes attended camp meetings with their white "masters." When freedom came, it is said that one Charles Hall, who lived in nearby Mountain Gap, wrote to New York City's Old Zion Church, asking for a minister. Reverend James H. Jackson and three other persons were sent. As they traveled, they stopped for the night at this site. In the morning, when Reverend Jackson was asked how he slept, he answered, "I fared well." Hence the name.

Annually each August, after the "crops are laid by" and before the fall harvest, about four hundred people spend between a day to a full week at the camp; increasing numbers of participants tend to be businesspeople and other professionals, whose secular demands prohibit them from staying the entire week. Most who attend are descendants of persons who camped here in the 1870s. In years past, buggies and carriages lined the rocky, red clay roads, laden with supplies that included tallow candles, kerosene lamps, large iron pots, and live chickens. In more recent times, families bring prepared food, small refrigerators, and mattresses for the built-in beds. Although many of the campers are from the Carolinas, others come from New York, New

Jersey, Pennsylvania—even as far as California—to join family members for this one-week religious celebration.

The Zion Church sits at the entrance to the campground and opening services are often held there. As more people arrive, services are moved to the open arbor. A different pastor is assigned to preach each night; the campers know that the sermons and the prayers will last well into the morning hours. Each preacher knows his Bible and gives it his all. The "choir" and the congregation raise their voices in wild abandonment and the air is filled with joyous singing to the Glory of God.

Camp Welfare Cemetery

On Sunday, the campers move out of their tents and silently steal away. By the next day the quiet in the campground has an eerie quality, as if it were "lying in wait" for the clamorous voices of next year's campers.

The Camp Welfare Cemetery, located at the end of the long row of tents, is where the descendants of slaves and campers are interred. Regular camping families and Fairfield County residents such as the Browns, the Gaithers, the Halls, and the Gladdens, have relatives there. Freeman Gladden, who was first taken to the camp by his parents when he was still a baby, says that his parents and his grandmother "sleep in the cemetery," which has bridged the gap down through the generations.

Savannah, Georgia

The city of Savannah, a stone's throw from both Hilton Head and Daufuskie Islands of South Carolina, is situated at the Georgia-South Carolina border. Much of Savannah's charm starts right at water's edge, where the city has smartly lined the cobblestone walkway with quaint shops and restaurants. A few yards in front, tug boats, freighters, and large, tourist-filled ships glide through the deep waters of the Savannah River. Up the cobblestone road, traversing a steep hill, sit a major hotel, inns, and vintage buildings such as the old courthouse and the famous cotton exchange.

In many ways, Savannah rivals Charleston, South Carolina, which lies approximately ninety miles to the north. Both have histories that reflect the heritage and the struggles of the South. Both cities also manage to retain significant replicas of the past. In days past, Charleston boasted expansive plantations, each with a sizable slave population. Savannah, on the other hand, was a fast-paced riverboat city where slaves busily worked the docks. Both cities, however, possessed a significant cadre of wealthy, mint julep-sipping landowners, and both can lay claim to the fact that many of their buildings were built by the enslaved.

For those who have toured old Savannah and walked the busy, shop-lined Savannah River waterfront, no description of this town is necessary. For those who have not, there is no easy way to do justice to the city. Perhaps a day spent with city expert, the late W. W. Law, former president of the King-Tisdell Cottage Foundation for the study of African American culture, and president of the Savannah branch of the Association for the Study of African American Life and History, was the best solution. A griot in the true sense of the word, he always left his audience spellbound.

In search of information about the city's cemeteries, another source is retired army major Frank Bynes, owner of Bynes-Royall Funeral Home on Hall Street in Savannah. His funeral home is, reportedly, the oldest continually operated Negro business in the state of Georgia. Law and Bynes alternately relate the history of burial practices in Savannah:

> The funeral business originated in 1876 as a result of a yellow fever epidemic that broke out in Savannah and lasted for two years, from 1876–1878. During that period, the dead were piling up all over Savannah. The city's limits ended at Gaston Street, the boundary when the city of Savannah was laid out.

> When General James Oglethorpe, the founder of Georgia, came over, he brought the blueprint and plans with him from London, England. The Savannah River was the north boundary and the very first street south of the Savannah River was called North Broad Street. The eastern boundary was called East Broad Street; it's still East Broad today. The south boundary is called South Broad Street, now known as Oglethorpe Avenue. The west boundary was West Broad Street, which is now known as Martin Luther King Boulevard.

> West Broad Street was the black business and commercial street of Savannah. Following the end of the yellow fever epidemic, there was one white funeral business, a combination of a funeral home, a furniture company, and what they called a hair treatment company. In other words, it was a barber shop combined with casket sales and furniture sales and it was owned by two brothers, the Henderson brothers. They were white Northerners. There was no system of embalming. All of the dead were taken care of by this white funeral home. With the epidemic, with people dying all over the city and county, Henderson needed some help. So he got a man, who happened to be literate and black, by the name of William H. Royall.

> Mr. Royall was literate because he came from a background where training and education were permitted. Those people were trained in order that they might be the tools for training white children; but they were convicted if they were caught teaching black children to read and write. Mr. Royall was a man who could be trained to handle the dead. At the end of the yellow fever epidemic, there was no other way to dispose of contaminated equipment except to burn it. Rather than burn it, Mr. Royall wanted it.

Now, Mr. Royall had something else going for him as well; the burial of the dead involved transportation. Royall was already equipped with a transportation system. His main line of duty was as a drayman [one who used a wagon to carry rocks, etc.]. If you go down the Savannah River, you'll find that those ramps leading up to the street levels are paved with big cobblestones, ranging in diameter from four to fifteen inches. You had to have very strong draft animals, like mules, to pull a 600-pound bale of cotton up those ramps. That's the way he earned his living. Mr. Royall was listed, in 1876, as a drayman and as a caretaker of the Henderson Bros. Coffin & Casket Co., at 22-1/2 Whitker Street.

Royall's high adaptability rendered him quite successful to come in and take over all of this contaminated equipment that they gave to him, without charge. Thus, at the end of the two-year yellow fever epidemic, he was equipped with experience and know-how, and he had the keys to get in and out of the one gate leading into Laurel Grove Cemetery.

The Eugenia Cemetery Settles In

Edna Luten, secretary of the Eugenia Cemetery Society, is a trailblazer in Savannah. For decades, Luten and other relatives of those interred in Eugenia Cemetery cared for the graves and grounds under the assumption that the property was theirs. She tells this story:

"During the period of slavery when Negroes were held in bondage, the area about which I am describing was set aside for the burial of slaves. . . .

"This area was located at a slave plantation, located now on the Old Montgomery Cross Road. The plantation was the home of the slave master and his slaves or field hands. According to history, the owner's name was a Mr. Hugunin but the emancipated slaves spelled it the way they heard and interpreted his name. When it ceased to be a slave plantation, the owner or descendants sold it to the Chatham County commissioners for a prison for inmates, who lived and raised all of the foodstuff they ate. . . . It stipulated in the deed that the Negro cemetery must remain a burial ground.

continued on next page

Spending time with Law and Bynes—not only hearing the stories of the cemeteries but trying to keep them "on track"—is no easy task. Both men are totally consumed with fascinating stories about Savannah. There is constant interplay and chiding over minor historical incidents and dates. Both men have superior knowledge of national as well as local history, and the city is blessed to have them as residents. Through such individuals, African American history is being recorded for posterity. (See chapter eleven)

LAUREL GROVE CEMETERY

Laurel Grove Cemetery, founded in the 1700s, is said to be one of the largest

continued from previous page

"Down through the years, the families did not know that the county owned the cemetery, and we continued to bury ex-slaves and descendants there. In the year 1953, we realized the importance of keeping the graveyard clean for burials. Approximately ten or twelve persons from the community churches began to hold monthly meetings, paying ten cents per meeting to encourage community people to become interested in the graves of their relatives. . . . We raised enough money by selling fish and chicken dinners to pay a lawyer, Harry N. Ginsberg, fifty dollars to research what he could find relative to the plot.

"Mr. Ginsberg found that, sure enough, a deed was recorded in the Chatham County Courthouse, and that the cemetery was owned by the county. In the early years of the 1980s, we learned that the Department of Transportation was widening Montgomery Cross Road and there was a probability of moving the dead and relocating them elsewhere. Since it was county property, we faced the commissioners at several of their meetings. In June 1986, the commissioners agreed to take forty-five feet of the cemetery, which would have reduced the cemetery to nothing. This was done to keep from interfering with white homes on the other side.

continued on next page

cemeteries still in use in the entire area of Savannah. It can be reached by entering on West 37th Street, which actually ends at the cemetery gate. From early times, there was a dividing line between burial sections for blacks and those for whites; the south end of the cemetery was referred to as the "colored section." Mr. Royall was in charge of this operation and he kept records and issued deeds in the city's name for lots sold. Royall became active manager of the black section of Laurel Grove. Law and Bynes relate their knowledge of the history of Laurel Grove Cemetery:

One of Mr. Royall's employees or co-workers was Ernest Johnson. Ernest Johnson was actually the first man that the city put on record as the official caretaker of the colored section of Laurel Grove Cemetery. Johnson started a little funeral business with a man named Fields, called Johnson & Fields. After four years, William Royall bought them out and absorbed it into his business, Royall Funeral Business. He continued until about 1905, when he died.

People did most of what they called "random burying" at Laurel Grove Cemetery. It was close to 1900 when the city actually surveyed it off and began to lay out lots with definable lines. The average burial lot down there is about fourteen feet by twenty-eight feet. They are set up in nine grave lots. You can put almost twice that many graves on a lot. They allowed three-and-a-half feet by nine feet per grave, for grave space. The cemetery has approximately 255 acres.

Because many lots are abandoned or unaccounted for (because deeds cannot be found, families have moved away or descendants have forgotten), ownership to some lots remains confusing. There is no way to account for all those sales at Laurel Grove and even some burials. It is better now, of course. The exact location of every grave is registered, as required by law.

General Oglethorpe called the land Colonial Cemetery when he laid it out and designed it. Records do show that Buttin Gwinett and Lyman Hall, signers of the Declaration of Independence, are buried there.

According to friends, Law has worked tirelessly and diligently to improve the cemetery in every way that a determined individual can. He has been described as a one-person stampede, naming the streets in the cemetery and posting a map in the cemetery office with arrows showing burial locations of many of Savannah's prominent blacks. And, thanks to Law, the grave of Andrew Bryant, one of the founders of the county's first organized black Baptist church, is buried at Laurel Grove. Law took it upon himself—with no help from any organization—to have Bryant's remains moved from a deserted area outside the city and properly marked and memorialized in Laurel Grove Cemetery, where he could be laid to rest with other members of his family. He also had street markers and signs put up in the cemetery to lead visitors to this historical plot.

continued from previous page

"Again, we faced the commissioners and came to an agreement to take fifteen feet from each side. On the fifteen feet taken were graves of slaves unknown and recent graves, so it was finally agreed to relocate these deceased on the back side of the cemetery, with markers. Finally, the county put a brick fence around the cemetery and agreed to deed the cemetery, taken from the 1889 map, to the organized board of directors—and got out of the cemetery business.

"Before we received the deed we had to organize and present to the board a list of officers, trustees, and meeting dates. We received from the county's law office a letter informing us to be present at the courthouse after four weeks of legal advertisement for the sale of the property. I, along with the president, members, and trustees met on June 1, 1992, and bid one dollar for the land.

"The cemetery is still located on Montgomery Cross Road between Sally Mood Street and Kent Drive. The county chairman, Robert McKorkle, gave the deed to us. I think we got a good deal."

Bynes spoke of the Mutual Benevolence Burial Society and his role as chairman of the 100th anniversary celebration. Unlike other lodges and societies, the Mutual Benevolent Society (MBS) was not organized as a burial society. Founded in Savannah in 1876, the blacks who formulated this group were so-called elite Savannahians—most had never been enslaved. In the fall of 1875, after the Civil War ended, a group of men formed a nucleus of leadership in Chatham County, Savannah's Negro community, and strove for political, fraternal, economic, industrial, social, and spiritual progress. Edwin Belcher, who had organized the MBS in Macon, Athens, and Augusta, Georgia, had planted the seed from which this organization soon sprang. (His grand niece, Eursaline Belcher Ingersol Law, now lives in Savannah.)

"The society was, in reality, an answer to the Ku Klux Klan which the civilian white community invented as its own bureau for reconstruction," explains Bynes. "Thousands of illiterate, destitute, unskilled, and socially disoriented ex-slaves poured into the city from the plantations of South Carolina and numerous Georgia counties. The Freedmen's Bureau was in shambles, the northern troops had withdrawn and the local constabulary forces were under white southern command."

A few members of the MBS, all of whom were buried in Laurel Grove Cemetery in the late 1800s or early 1900s, are **James M. Simms, James Porter, John H. DeVeaux, Anthony K. DesVerney,** and **Andrew Monroe.**

James H. Simms was one of the most dynamic of the group. His mother, a mulatto, purchased his freedom when he was nine. Simms was buried in Laurel Grove Cemetery in 1912. The only member of the Mutual Benevolent Society who was born a slave, he was an educator, politician, orator, carpenter, musician, publisher, and fraternal organizer. In 1867, Simms published a newspaper called the *Southern Radical,* the first Savannah newspaper to be published by a black. He served a term in the Georgia House of Representatives, representing Chatham County from 1872 to 1874. Prior to the Civil War, he was repeatedly caught violating the law by teaching blacks to read and write. Upon his second conviction, he was given thirty-nine lashes at the public whipping post and chased out of town.

In the fall of 1862, Simms headed back to Savannah, stopping in Richmond long enough to pick up a pre-release copy of the proclamation that Lincoln was planning to issue on January 1, 1863. Simms brought the advance copy with him and filed a report on behalf of himself and two others for permission to have a New Year's Eve party. The city granted the request and on New Year's Eve, 1862, the first emancipation celebration took place—before the document had been officially signed into law. Simms died on July 9, 1912.

James Porter was laid to rest in Laurel Grove Cemetery in 1895. Born in Charleston, South Carolina in 1826, he was an educator, musician, tailor, politician, fraternal organizer, military officer, preacher, lecturer, linguist (German, French, and Spanish), and a Christian gentleman. Porter went to Savannah in 1854; from 1870 to 1872, he served a term in the Georgia House of Representatives from Chatham County. From 1876 to 1878, he served as U.S. Collector of Customs at the Port of Savannah. In 1868 he became the first person ever hired by the Savannah Chatham Board of Education to teach blacks to read and write. Porter was made principal of Broad Street Church where, in 1879, he was ordained as a minister. His Methodist itinerary took him to many states before he died in New York City on September 26, 1895.

John H. DeVeaux was buried in Laurel Grove Cemetery in 1909. He was born in Savannah on May 10, 1848. In 1866, the governor of Georgia awarded him a life commission as a colonel in the Georgia militia. In 1875, DeVeaux was one of the organizers of the Republican party of Georgia and a founder of the Wage Earners Bank. From 1868 to 1869, and again in 1896, he was U.S. Collector of Customs at the Port of Savannah. In his later appointment as Collector of Customs, he operated the port single-handedly through an epidemic of yellow fever while both the city and the port lay under quarantine. For his efficiency, DeVeaux was cited by the U.S. Department of

Commerce and the Coast Guard for valor beyond the call of duty. He died at his home on June 7, 1909.

Anthony K. DesVerney was buried in Laurel Grove Cemetery in 1892. Born in Charleston, South Carolina, in October 1831, he came to Savannah at the age of twenty-six. In 1864, DesVerney served as captain and commanding officer of an infantry company known as the Colquet Blues; in 1866 he became a cotton shipping agent and buyer, and, later, a bookkeeper and cotton buyer in the firm of C. A. Shearson. He subsequently became an independent cotton buyer, which was comparable to a seat on the Savannah Cotton Exchange. At his death, DesVerney was claimed to have been the wealthiest Negro in Chatham County.

Buried in Laurel Grove Cemetery in 1920, Andrew Monroe had the distinction of being the first black to be entombed in a mausoleum in the city of Savannah. Monroe was a Savannah native and operated an ice cream parlor in the city for many years. Electric refrigeration had not been invented and when closing time arrived each night, fellow society members would bring their children to his parlor to eat up all the ice cream that had not been sold during the day. In 1891 Monroe became a bank porter in the Georgia Railroad Bank and in 1910 he established the Monroe Funeral Home. He was a member of the Second Baptist Church. The church pipe organ was his donated by Monroe prior to his death.

Although Laurel Grove Cemetery is now city-owned, there are numerous other cemeteries throughout Savannah that are black-owned or designated as black cemeteries. These are basically small and owned by individuals or by funeral homes.

LINCOLN MEMORIAL CEMETERY, GEORGIA

Lincoln Memorial is presently owned by Frank Bynes. Both the city of Savannah and the U.S. Army have vied for the land on which the cemetery is located; each has been successful in nipping off some of this valuable property. In 1940, when the country was about to enter World War II and air traffic was becoming increasingly popular, the city made a deal with Walter Scott, the cemetery's former owner, to buy some of the property for landing strips. At the same time, the military negotiated with the city for much-needed air space. Some of the Lincoln cemetery land the city had just purchased was sold, in turn, to the federal government; the army then fenced in the cemetery.

Bynes recalls former President Bush's visit to Savannah in 1991: To thank the 24th Infantry troops for going to Saudi Arabia, the presidential entourage found itself occupying the air base surrounding the cemetery.

Everybody was put on tight security, and only dignitaries and media that were clearly identified could come through the gate. The military extended Bynes the courtesy of calling to inform him that if there were any funerals planned, a conference would be necessary with the provost marshal. Since no funerals were scheduled for that day, the conference was unnecessary.

Lincoln Memorial Cemetery is now down to nineteen and six-tenths acres, with access from White Bluff Road or from Montgomery Street (open 7 a.m.–5 p.m.) through military police gates. The beautiful, well kept burial ground, it is definitely worth a visit.

EVERGREEN CEMETERY, GEORGIA

Evergreen Cemetery is located on the west side of Savannah, on Atlantic Coastline Boulevard. A newer cemetery started in 1936, it is owned and operated by Jones Funeral Home, and was purchased as a result of problems with harassment by both the city of Savannah at Laurel Grove and by the former owners of Lincoln Memorial. Evergreen is one of the few cemeteries with room for expansion.

Evergreen is about twenty acres in size and is well-maintained amid some areas of dense undergrowth. The funeral home handles the cemetery's management and maintenance. Buried here are **Norman Rivers**, a longtime city firefighter, and members of the Rickenbacher family, longtime residents of Savannah.

WOODVILLE CEMETERY, GEORGIA

Most other community or individually owned cemeteries in Savannah date back to Reconstruction or pre-Reconstruction days, and Woodville is no exception. Like Woodville, most were started by plantation owners for burials of their blacks.

Over the years, Woodville's acreage has diminished. At one point, the city's Board of Education needed land on which to build a school and the cemetery's underdeveloped land was purchased, although the dates are sketchy regarding exactly when the transaction took place. Today, the cemetery, which is located on the west side of the city, can be reached from West Bay. The burial ground is operated by the Woodville Community Association, and is used primarily by members of the community. Woodville is a quaint cemetery and a colorful addition to the rich tapestry of African American history.

OAK GROVE CEMETERY, GEORGIA

Originally called Skidaway Island, Oak Grove Cemetery, on the grounds of Wilmington Baptist Church, is located on Skidaway at 52nd Street. The church pastor is Reverend Lewis Stell, and the manager of the cemetery is Joseph Williams. The Bolton family bought the ten-acre plot of land for use as a burial ground for their plantation people. Later it was deeded it to the Oak Grove Community Association as a black cemetery for the burial of black people.

CHEROKEE HILL CEMETERY, GEORGIA

Cherokee Hill Cemetery, owned by Clifton Baptist Church, 100 Big Hill Road, is about five miles northwest of downtown Savannah. The community, in older times referred to as "Five-Mile Bend," is now known as the Garden City community.

Many of the older graves have no headstones. More recently, since the 1950s, more headstones have been erected, and today the cemetery remains very much in use. Cherokee Hill is about two miles from the church. Not plotted well, the grounds have become somewhat overrun with trees and shrubs. Members of the church, along with the Reverend Claud Cobb, are planning an extensive study of the old cemetery. Buried here are members of the Russell, Williams, and Wiley families.

WOOD GROVE, SANDFLY, LAKE MAYERS, EAST SAVANNAH, ZION WHITE BLUFF, AND LAUREL GROVE SOUTH CEMETERIES

These cemeteries are also Reconstruction- and pre-Reconstruction-era burial grounds that were originally part of plantation properties. Wood Grove Cemetery is owned by the Wood Grove Community Association. Sandfly Cemetery, located at the intersection of Ferguson Avenue and Skidaway, is owned by the Stiles family. Only families who have existing lots can use this pre-Reconstruction cemetery. Less than one hundred fifty feet away is Lake Mayers Cemetery, at Montgomery Cross Road and Eisenhower Drive. It is bounded on the east by Skidaway and on the west by Sally Mood Road. East Savannah Cemetery, also closed to new sales, is owned by the East Savannah Community Association. It borders a little creek running off the Savannah River and is at the end of Gwinnet Road. Zion White Bluff Cemetery is located just off newly named Hodge Memorial Drive. The cemetery, now bounded by a newly built subdivision, is named after the Hodge family, philanthropists who constructed the first "old folks home" for blacks in Savannah in the 1920s.

MY EPITAPH

I AM NO BETTER THAN THE BIRDS THAT SING,

SO, WHEN I DIE DO NOT BRING ME FLOWERS,

DIG NO GRAVE, ERECT NO MONUMENT;

BUT LAY ME HIGH UPON A LONELY HILL

CLOSE TO GOD'S WINDOW-SILL CALLED HEAVEN.

LET BIRDS OF PREY COME FEAST UPON MY BODY

AND WHEN MY BONES OF FLESH ARE EMPTY QUITE,

LET THEM REMAIN TILL TIME HAS PLAYED ITS PART.

THE SUN AND WIND AND RAIN AND TIME, ALAS,

SHALL DWINDLE THEM TO NOTHING BUT WHITE DUST.

THEN LET THIS DUST COMMINGLE WITH THE HILL,

AND DRIFT DOWNWARD INTO SOME HUNGRY STREAM,

THERE TO BE LOST FOREVER TO MEN'S SIGHT.

I NEED NO GRAVE, I NEED NO MONUMENT.

LET ME BUT BE REMEMBERED THROUGH MY SONG.

—LEWIS GRANDISON ALEXANDER

In December 1991, Daniel Ellsberry, who as director of cemeteries managed the city's four cemeteries, wrote a brief statement of their histories. Of the four—Laurel Grove North and South, Bonaventure, and Greenwich—Laurel Grove was founded in 1852, and was the city's second public burial grounds. At the time, fifteen acres were set aside for the burial of "free persons of color and slaves." This section of the cemetery was later to become known as Laurel Grove South; Laurel Grove North was reserved for the burial of white citizens.

Laurel Grove South was placed on the National Register of Historic Places in 1978. This cemetery holds a significant record of black history in the Savannah area and documents various aspects of black social history in the nineteenth century. Interred in the cemetery are the bodies of slaves as well as the largest number of free blacks of any cemetery in Georgia. Laurel Grove South is an important landmark in Savannah's black community because its stones and grave markers are in many cases the only visible memorial and record of many of the important blacks in the city's history.

Thomaston, Georgia Cemetery and other Vanishing Sites

Andrew Jacobs of the *New York Times*, writes from Thomaston, Georgia stating that the old dead lie beneath a noxious carpet of brambles and poison ivy, their tombstones mostly shattered and their names long forgotten. The graves of the recent dead, fresh mounds of ocher clay, are equally anonymous, without a single stone or marker among the strewn beer cans and candy wrappers.

Hundreds of people – or perhaps more than a thousand, no one really knows – are buried in this single acre of sloping earth. Former slaves, sharecroppers, teachers and preachers who lived in Thomaston's black section in the 1860s lie beside modern-day indigents brought here by funeral homes. Local records show that impoverished Confederate veterans were buried here, too, but their headstones are nowhere to be found.

Old Mill Cemetery, as it is known, is a no man's land of the dead. Diane Caldwell comes here once in a while to tear out saplings and vines, but she knows nature is winning.

"I go through this cemetery and I can feel people crying out for help," said Ms. Caldwell, 38, a genealogist who lives near this faded mill town of 9,400 people. "They're saying 'Please don't forget us.'"

But there are thousands of graveyards like this in the South. From North Carolina to Arkansas, time, development and neglect are swallowing abandoned cemeteries, historians and preservation groups say.

The Mississippi Heritage Trust, alarmed by the destruction and disintegration of so many historic burial grounds, recently included a handful on its list of the state's most endangered places.

In Montgomery County, Tennessee, a local historian estimates that there are as many as 500 lost or abandoned black cemeteries in the county. And in Palatka, Florida, the Francis Community Black Cemetery was recently paved over for the parking lot of a fast-food restaurant.

Glenn Jones, who runs a cemetery preservation group in Benton County, Arkansas, said he believed that a dozen graveyards in his state were buried beneath asphalt each year When he complained to a local developer, Mr. Jones said he was told, "Life is for the living, not for the dead."

The old cemeteries are under siege on several fronts. Suburban developers are taking advantage of weak laws or lax enforcement to bulldoze them. Vandalism laws provide little protection – in South Carolina, for example, those prosecuted for destroying abandoned cemeteries must be shown to have done so "willfully and intentionally," a difficult burden of proof.

In most states, disused cemeteries are legal orphans, ineligible for public money that might rehabilitate them and strapped state and county governments seldom get involved.

"I get a few calls a day from people who ask for our help, but the most I can do is tell them, "It's your project," said Ken Wilson. a historian with the Historic Preservation Division of the Georgia Department of Natural Resources. "I mean, there are thousands of these cemeteries across the state."

But preservationists say the most imperiled burial grounds are those historically used by African Americans. Part of the problem, they say, is that 18th and 19th century graveyards were often poorly marked, their occupants too poor to afford lasting monuments. In many places, the vast 20th-century migration of blacks to Northern cities depopulated many rural Southern towns, leaving black cemeteries hopelessly neglected.

And throughout the South the traditional days of cemetery tending, family events in the spring and fall, have long since been eclipsed by modern life.

"People have become so busy, no one has time to travel four or five hours just to clean up the family grave." said Christine Van Voorhies, a historic preservationist who wrote a how-to guide for cemetery maintenance called "Grave Intentions."

Not all the neglect, however, is entirely benign. In some cases, local authorities may be less vigilant in maintaining black cemeteries than white ones, said Michael Trinkley, an archaeologist from South Carolina who frequently testifies in cases of grave desecration. Compared with the neatly planned and monument-filled cemeteries established by white communities, black burial grounds were rarely conceived as manicured places, and in most cases, were relegated to the least desirable parts of town.

"Black cemeteries are easier to overlook, whether intentionally or unintentionally," said Mr. Trinkley, the director of the Chicora Foundation, a non-profit organization that advocates the preservation of historic cemeteries. "Still, if we were seeing as many white cemeteries destroyed, people just wouldn't stand for it."

In 1994, when David Paterson decided to compile a history of black Thomaston's transition from slavery to Reconstruction, he was surprised to find that the local historical society had produced three volumes on white cemeteries but nothing on black ones.

"When I asked why the books didn't include black cemeteries, the answer I got was, 'We couldn't find any blacks interested in copying headstones,'" said Mr. Paterson, an amateur historian. "I didn't know it took black people to copy black tombstones."

The steady degradation of Thomaston's Old Mill Cemetery, which sits a few blocks from the city's historic square, began in the 1950s, when the last of the original trustees died. Still, workers from Thomaston Mills, a textile plant that nearly envelops the site, did their best to keep the briars at bay until the company went under four years ago.

"We would cut the grass because it was the courteous thing to do," said George Hightower, 54, whose family founded what, for a century, had been the city's largest employer. Local residents tried to get the city and the county to take over the cemetery but were politely rebuffed.

But communal apathy, it would seem, is colorblind. When one of Thomaston's black undertakers, Johnny Enoch Bentley Jr., tried to raise restoration money through his Sunday radio show, only $150 came in. "Just about everyone in town feels there's no hope for doing anything about that cemetery," said Mr. Bentley, 77, who has buried 4,000 people over the last four decades. "It's just a lost, lonely place in the minds of most people."

That has not stopped Mr. Bentley and his two competitors from using it as a potter's field, with about a dozen interments a year. Mr. Bentley, for one, thinks there is room for as many as 200 more. "The colored people of Thomaston own it," he said. "Who can say anything?"

Ms. Caldwell, the genealogist, has been saying plenty. She accuses Thomaston's funeral directors of casting aside old headstones and graves to make room for new interments. Mr. Bentley and the others deny that accusation.

"This cemetery has long been filled," Ms. Caldwell said on a recent Sunday, whacking at the underbrush. "This is downright disgraceful."

Her goal, she said, is to stop burials, fence in the grounds and form a group to restore the cemetery. She and others also want to solve a mystery of the Old Mill Cemetery: What happened to the graves of the Confederate soldiers? The original deed, filed a year after the end of the Civil War, described the grounds as a final resting place for "soldiers only."

Penny Cliff, the Upson County archivist, said she found it hard to believe that Thomaston's white citizenry would have allowed the intermingling of' soldiers and former slaves. The theory of some local historians is that the soldiers' bodies were moved to another cemetery.

Citing the stories of his father, who died recently at the age of 85, Mr. Hightower, the former mill owner, believes no body has ever been removed from the cemetery. "If they're buried there," he said, "they're still there."

BURIAL SITES COAST TO COAST

WHEN I AM COLD AND BURIED DEEP AWAY,

AND HAVE NO ZEST TO LIVE OR TO RETURN,

COME TO MY GRAVE AND FLOWER-STREW THE CLAY,

AND DANCE AND SING, BUT NEVER WEEP OR MOURN.

—EDYTHE MAE GORDON

CHAPTER THREE

Like the burial grounds of the Sea Islands, cemeteries in other parts of the United States vary in size, structure, and ownership. It is, of course, not possible to include all of the black-owned or predominantly black cemeteries in the United States. Nor is it possible to give a count—or even an estimate—of the number that exist. Besides the large, well-established urban cemeteries, thousands of African American burial grounds lie scattered in churchyards and neighborhoods all across the country. Those in urban areas are more likely to be state-regulated; they are required to maintain a perpetual care fund, which is the setting aside of money for care and maintenance of the cemetery in perpetuity. Although regulation assures at least a minimum level of maintenance, cemeteries vary in their presentation to the public.

Cemeteries in the Civil War regions of the South are especially distinctive for their rich history. Those in larger cities often have facilities for care and maintenance, while most smaller cemeteries are cared for by the families of the deceased. Large facilities in cities like Atlanta, Georgia, as well as select smaller cemeteries, have adequate funding. But, in general, there are very few exceptions to the continual struggle against time and the encroachment of "progress."

Several cemeteries with unique, fascinating, and sometimes quite troubled histories exist. Among them is Geer Cemetery in Durham, North Carolina, where focused, loving effort was expended towards making it a showcase property, a goal that was not achieved. And Mount Ararat, in Nashville, Tennessee, with its great heritage, showed a promising beginning but a sad ending—until its rescue.

There are fewer African American–owned cemeteries in the North than in the South; most burial grounds of the Northeast are integrated. Throughout this historic region stories of struggle and hope abound. Helen Y. Davis, a Boston funeral director, tells of a cemetery in nearby Nantucket that was traditionally a black cemetery, but which is now overseen by the Nantucket County office. Lucille Barbour, a licensed mortician in New Jersey, explains that burials are not permitted in Atlantic City because it is actually an island. The nearest cemetery on the "mainland" is seven miles away in Pleasantville, and it is not black-owned. "Many years ago," she writes, "there was a black-owned cemetery called Lincoln Memorial Park, located in Mays Landing, New Jersey, about fifteen miles from Atlantic City. Mr. Rice, the owner, died, and the cemetery was sold to whites."

Burial grounds located in the less temperate regions like the Northeast and northern Midwest face additional maintenance problems. The ability to keep driveways and paths clear for processions in wintertime, and to open and close graves during freezing weather, takes on added dimensions of difficulty. Even during the warmer months, groundskeeping must also be more aggressive. Unlike the heavily wooded Sea Island cemeteries, which have little or no grass, lawn upkeep becomes a regular chore in other locations. Cemeteries that adhere to the "memorial park plan" forbid upright markers on the graves; maintenance is somewhat easier when markers are flush with the ground.

There are also few exclusively black cemeteries in the Middle and Far West. Most cemeteries are not owned by African Americans and most are reportedly integrated. The cemeteries of the central states have special histories and traditions, as do those of the South. In general, however, they are owned and managed by boards of directors. However, the board of Detroit's Memorial Park Cemetery is still comprised of "family"; most members are related to the founders of 1925. In the West, California has several black-owned cemeteries, including Angeles Abbey Memorial Park, which is owned by active cemeterian Jean Sanders.

KING

THE REV.
MARTIN LUTHER. SR.
'DADDY KING'
DEC. 19. 1899
NOV. 11. 1984
'I LOVE EVERYONE'
STILL IN BUSINESS JUST MOVED UPSTAIRS'

ALBERTA WILLIAMS
SEPT. 13. 1904
JUNE 30. 1974
HER LIFE SHALL BE FILLED WITH MUSIC

Canada, too, has some quaint "family style" burial grounds, a reflection of the major role that she played in the lives and struggles of those escaping bondage prior to the Civil War. Canadian cemeteries like the Fugitive Slave Cemetery in Puce, Ontario, and the North Buxton Cemetery serve primarily family and extended family.

The Reverend Martin Luther King Sr. and Alberta Williams King lie in Atlanta, Georgia's Southview Cemetery.

The beautiful city of Atlanta was, in 1860, one of the newest jewels in Georgia's crown. Its white population numbered 7,615 and its colored, 1,939—nearly all of whom were slaves. In comparison with Augusta and Macon, Atlanta was not a convenient location for the buying and selling of slaves, but it was never without a few dealers regularly engaged in the trade.

Atlanta, Georgia

More than almost any other southern city, Atlanta has begun to break away from the traditional mold of the "Old South." The city has grown by leaps and bounds, and although the hectic pace and noise level is less than in Chicago and New York, a big-city atmosphere predominates. Even before the advent of the 1996 Olympic Games, construction in the "peach tree" city was at an all-time high.

Atlanta history abounds with stories of the enslaved, freedmen, and

Southview Cemetery in Atlanta, Georgia, was established in 1886 when several black, church-related organizations purchased twenty-five acres of land on Jonesboro Road.

the progress of blacks throughout the years. The embodiment of the Old South in its grandest manner, Atlanta was always a busy, bustling community. Today it is a good example of a megalopolis. Expressways and highways intersect its center and extend like spokes to connect with major suburban cities. It is a favorite meeting and conference site: tall hotels flank and overlook restaurants, churches, libraries, government buildings, medical facilities, and the Underground, where a variety of shops cater to thousands of tourists daily. There are several sizable black-owned eating establishments and areas of black residences ranging from "just adequate" to residences that surpass the mansions of many other cities. The famed Martin Luther King Jr. Center for Non-Violent Social Change, the Apex Museum, and other history-related sites welcome their share of tourists as well. However, the pride and joy of Atlanta must most certainly be its black colleges. Spelman, Morehouse, Morris Brown, Clark, and Atlanta University form an educational conglomerate that has achieved national recognition.

Atlanta is home to several cemeteries, including those that follow.

Southview Cemetery

This cemetery was established on April 21, 1886, when several black, church-related organizations purchased twenty-five acres of land on Jonesboro Road. The Friendship Baptist Church, Sister's Union, the Youth Society, the Daughters of Bethel, Brother's Society, and the Mutual Aid Society of Atlanta

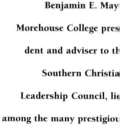

and Thomasville worked together to provide a form of burial insurance for blacks who could not get such support from white insurance companies.

Before 1886, some blacks were buried at Westview Cemetery, located on the west side of the city. Westview, which opened to the public in the late 1880s, required that blacks be buried in the most undeveloped portions of the cemetery and that they use the back gates as an entrance for funerals and visiting. The white caretakers of Westview suggested that area blacks purchase their own cemetery. These caretakers were instrumental in helping blacks locate the Southview property and assisting with initial arrangements for the land purchase. Additional acquisitions of land have brought Southview cemetery grounds to over 125 acres.

The gravestones of this famous, chartered, black cemetery read like a "Who's Who" of city history. Albert Watts, Southview Cemetery's third-generation caretaker, is a source of pertinent information about the over seventy-five thousand persons interred here, many of whom are also memorialized in names of city streets or schools. Among them are **Dr. H. Moss**, one of the first black doctors in the city, and his brother, the first black postmaster of south Atlanta; **Alonzo F. Herndon**, founder of Atlanta Life Insurance Company and namesake of the Herndon Homes public housing project; **Bishop Bowen**, a Methodist minister associated with Gammon Seminary; and Bowen's son. The Bowen Homes Housing project is named for Bishop Bowen.

The **Reverend Martin Luther King Sr.** ("Daddy King"; 1899–1984); his wife, **Alberta Williams King** (1904–1974); and **Benjamin E. Mays** (1894–1984) beautify the grounds with their elegant and elaborate tombs. A mathematics teacher, president of Morehouse College, chairman of the Atlanta Board of Education, a preacher and church historian, and an advisor to the Southern Christian Leadership Council, Mays was dean of Harvard University's School of Religion early in his career. By the time of his death he had earned forty-three honorary degrees.

Historic Oakland Cemetery

Historic Oakland Cemetery, Atlanta's oldest, was established in 1850 as a Victorian-style burial ground at 248 Oakland Avenue, S.E. The layout, as well as the monuments themselves, speak to the history of the period through their symbolic interpretation. Oakland boasts early founders of the city—including seven Georgia governors and five Confederate generals—as well as author Margaret Mitchell are among the Atlanta residents buried here. Some of the city's earliest African Americans were laid to rest in Oakland Cemetery; until Westview opened in 1884, Oakland was the only burial ground available.

By the start of the Civil War, 860 African American people had been buried at Oakland, the oldest believed to be a 125-year old slave. The recorded burial took place in 1853, after a ruling by the Atlanta City Council, that African Americans be allowed burial in the cemetery, but a part from the public grounds. Until then, they were buried in church yard cemeteries or private family lots.

But, after the war ended, more and more prominent black individuals inhabited the city, living and dying in Atlanta and choosing Oakland as their final resting place. They studied their choices and selected Oakland Cemetery because of the significant heritage.

Selena Sloan Butler and her husband, Dr. Henry Rutherford Butler, were two such people. Sloan Butler graduated from Atlanta's Spelman College, becoming a teacher. In 1893, she married Butler, who became one of Atlanta's most prominent black physicians, as well as a partner in the city's first black-owned and operated drug store. As an educator, Sloan Butler began to see the need for an African American parent teacher association. Single-handedly, she founded a grass roots organization which grew to national prominence, merging in 1970 with its white counterpart and becoming what we know today as the PTA.

Although Sloan Butler did not live to see the merger, dying in 1964, at the age of 92, she is one of three women honored each year on February 17, the PTA Founders' Day. Her portrait hangs in Georgia's State Capitol and a park is named in her honor. She is buried along with her husband who preceded her in death.

Another formidable woman buried in this section is Carrie Steele Logan. Born into slavery in 1829 and orphaned as a child, Logan was self-educated. As an adult, she found employment at Atlanta's Union Station, where she noticed the large number of orphaned children. Moved by their plight, Logan founded the first black orphanage in Atlanta in 1888, an institution still in existence. She funded it with the proceeds from the sale of her house, funds solicited from the community, and the profits from her autobiography, which she hawked on the street.

A century later, Logan was honored posthumously by being inducted into the Georgia Women of Achievement. Logan is buried next to her husband, Josehia Logan, who continued the work she began, after her death. Her gravestone is aptly inscribed, "The Mother of Orphans. She Hath Done What She Could."

Yet another former slave who prospered after the war was Antoine Graves. The patriarch of an accomplished family and an uncle to entertainer Lena Horne, he became a teacher and was instrumental in finding much of the land for black schools. In addition, Graves had a flourishing real estate practice, one of the first black-owned firms, which still thrives today. It is fitting that the only mausoleum in the black section of Oakland houses the remains of this prominent realtor who died in 1941.

The following are among the many born during the times of slavery or just after, who became notable citizens:

Dr. Roderick D. Badger was a prominent black dentist. He learned dentistry while enslaved and grew in popularity in Atlanta among both black and white patients.

Mary Combs was the first black to actually own property in Atlanta. Oakland Cemetery shows a Mary Combs buried on April 4, 1877, but indicates her age at death to be thirty years. While this could be an error, Oakland is not entirely sure it is the same woman.

William Finch, a tailor by trade and an ordained minister, served on the city council in 1870, one of two black councilmen that year. George Graham was the other.

Bishop Wesley J. Gaines was the second pastor of Big Bethel and Bishop of the African Methodist Episcopal Church. He founded Morris Brown College and was president of its board.

Antoine Graves was a widely known black real estate broker esteemed throughout his fifty-five-year career for his integrity.

Georgia Harris was one of two documented cases of black interments in the white sections of the cemetery. The Boyd family received permission for this interment from city officials and neighboring lot owners.

Dougherty Hutchins owned a barber shop and in the early 1880s employed **Alonzo Herndon** as a journeyman barber. Within six months Hutchins and Herndon were partners. Herndon became the wealthiest black in Atlanta.

Ransom Montgomery was a former slave whose courage in rescuing passengers from a train caught on a burning Chattahoochee River bridge won him the purchase of his freedom by the State of Georgia. His "freedom," such as it was, thus moved from private ownership to ownership by the state.

Reverend Frank Quarles organized Friendship Baptist Church. He supported the Atlanta Baptist Female Seminary, now Spelman College, which was founded in the basement of the church.

Henry A. Rucker was president of Georgia Real Estate Loan and Trust Co.—one of two black financial institutions of his day—and served as internal revenue collector for Atlanta from 1897–1910.

Dr. Thomas H. Slater, a popular physician, opened the first black-owned and operated drug store with Dr. Henry Butler.

James Tate Sr. began the first black business in Atlanta in 1866—a grocery store—with six dollars' worth of inventory. He also opened and taught in the first school for black children in the city.

Augustus Thompson, a master blacksmith by trade, was active in the politics of the city and ran for a council position in 1880.

Reverend Joseph A. Wood was the first pastor of Big Bethel A.M.E. Church.

One of the most recently prominent Atlantans buried at Oakland was Mayor Maynard Jackson, Atlanta's first black mayor. A three times mayor, he was, at 35, the youngest person ever elected to that office in Atlanta. On June 23, 2003, Jackson, 65, was felled by a heart attack. Mayor Shirley Franklin offered two city owned burial spaces to the Jackson family, which they gratefully accepted.

"They had options and we were honored they chose us," said the landscape manager, Kevin Kuharic.

"We had four days to pull Oakland together visually and esthetically, for this important funeral," he added. In fact, the staff went so far as to clean up the cortege route they would take to the cemetery. And that's not all. Kuharic, himself, helped dig the grave by hand, the way all graves are dug at Oakland. Although he never thought he would be doing the digging, "It was necessary. I jumped right in. Never say never."

Although the funeral services were open to the public, the burial was for family, friends and invited guests only. Atlanta Mayor Shirley Franklin and Rev. Jesse Jackson were just two of the city officials and visiting dignitaries in attendance.

At the end of the service, a lone saxophone player, perched on the hill, played some of Jackson's favorite tunes. Jackson is buried at a 45 degree angle, his grave in clear view of the downtown skyline.

Jackson's burial was of enormous significance for Oakland on many levels: It showed that the cemetery is open and active, embracing all races and religions. Above all, said Kuharic, "It brought up to date the continuing tradition of burying Atlanta's mayors and that is important to us."

Augusta, Georgia

Located on the banks of the Savannah River, Augusta was founded in 1735 and was named after the mother of King George III of England. Augusta was the second city in Georgia, established as a trading post. Tobacco became the dominant agricultural product of the region until cotton took over with the invention of the cotton gin in 1793. Today, Augusta is a thriving industrial and transportation center.

The Reverend A. C. Redd of Augusta, prominent citizen and former member of the board of directors of Penn Center on St. Helena Island, provided a wealth of information on Augusta's black-owned or black-only cemeteries. Hillcrest Memorial Park, a large, well-landscaped cemetery with an impressive mausoleum, is open to all races.

Summerville Cemetery, Augusta

Summerville, located at 2700 Fetten Street, was chartered in 1906, and is owned by twelve men. The city of Augusta helps maintain the grounds. Summerville Cemetery is in a more wooded setting than other Augusta cemeteries; burial plots are divided into square sections and lined with bricks to designate family plots.

Cedar Grove, Augusta

Cedar Grove was organized by Springfield Baptist Church in the early nineteenth century; Morehouse College was started in this same church. The cemetery, now owned and maintained by the city of Augusta, is located at Watkins Street and East Boundary, and occupies forty-five acres. Called the "crown jewel" because so many of Augusta's distinguished citizens are buried here, Cedar Grove was named after the giant cedar trees that grace the ceme-

tery's entrance. **Judson Lyons,** a black registrar for the U.S. Treasurer buried at Cedar Grove, was later exhumed and moved to Arlington National Cemetery. Also buried at Cedar Grove is **Colonel Wimberly,** a customs collector for Savannah, Augusta, and Charleston, South Carolina.

Walker Memorial Park, Augusta

Walker Memorial was developed in the 1960s. Land for the cemetery was purchased and developed by a group of business and professional men to honor the memory of Dr. C. T. Walker. It is located at the lower end of Laney Street at Walker Boulevard.

Southview Cemetery, Augusta

The land for Southview was purchased in the late 1930s. It was developed as a cemetery by the late John H. Strother and is located off 15th Street in the southern section of the city, at 1225 D'Antignac Street. It is a wide open, beautifully landscaped cemetery.

OTHER GEORGIA AND NEARBY FLORIDA CEMETERIES

**Camille Killens of Detroit tells the story of other cemeteries
"back home."**

Cairo Cemetery,
Cairo, Georgia

Julian Evers was born into slavery in Virginia either in 1817 or 1820. As so often families were torn asunder by the ravages of slavery, Evers created a rhyme she taught her children so they would not forget who their family members were. The rhyme began, "Julian, Maryann, Marthaann, Francesann." Evers added Ann to the end of each of the children's name. This rhyme is remembered today by family and friends as one of "Aint Julan's" enduring legacies.

When the Battle Cry for Freedom was rung, Evers was in Cairo (pronounced Kay-row), Georgia. Through hard work, Evers was able to acquire land in the small southwestern Georgia town. In the early 1900s, town leaders approached Evers asking if she would donate land for a cemetery. Evers acquiesced to the request with the proviso that both minority and majority residents be allowed to be buried in the cemetery. Evers was a Civil Rights pioneer. Town leaders agreed and the cemetery was divided down the middle. One half was designated for the sons and daughters of persons of color and the other half containing the remains of Caucasians. Upon her death in 1932, "Aint Julan" was buried in the center of the African American plots under a tree.

Early graves include Ame Morgan who died November 19, 1902 at age 54 and Charles Morgan who died at age 56 in 1908. Although there is no list of souls whose final resting place is the Cairo Cemetery, the list of African Americans who purchased lots is maintained in the Cairo City Hall.

Springfield A.M.E. Church Cemetery,
Gretna, Florida

Springfield A.M.E. Church is located along Highway 90 in the city of Gretna in Gadsden County, Florida. The church was established in 1890. Allen Ganious also spelled Gainer, deeded the land to the church for $15.00 in 1907. A.A. McKinney served as the first pastor of the first church. The first trustees were S .N. Brown, S.D. Desaw, B.W. Laneue, J.H Jones, and Noah House. After the first church burned a new structure was built in 1908.

Souls began being laid to rest at this time. Gretna now has a population of more than two thousand citizens. However, back in the early 1900s the town was so small that church services were the first and third Sundays of each month while St. Paul Primitive Baptist Church down the road held services the second and fourth Sundays.

After the Creator in his infinite wisdom saw fit to call from labor Gretna citizens such as Sanford Killens in 1918, Fanny Mae Harris in 1971 and Mrs. Fanny Lou Gainous were laid to rest in eternity in the Springfield A.M.E. Church Cemetery.

St. Paul Primitive Baptist Church Cemetery
Gretna, Florida

Gretna, Florida is home to St. Paul Primitive Baptist Church. The church is located off Highway 90 between Tallahassee and Marianna in Gadsden County. Gadsden County is one of the state's most economically depressed areas. The county also is predominately African American. In 1860, with a population of almost 10,000 there were only six "free persons of color" in the entire county. After the conflict between the states resulted in emancipation of all persons of color, the African American population in the county was more than 6,000. Former slaves, along with the first pastor Lyndon Allen established St. Paul Primitive Baptist Church and cemetery. Gadsden County residents such as Herbert Killens and Archie House are buried in the cemetery.

St. Paul Primitive Baptist Church Cemetery, Whigham, Georgia

After paying off the mortgage, two brothers donated land for the church to be constructed. Many former slaves buried there saw freedom before making their transition to ancestors. These individuals include Benjamin Pope, Wes' father-in-law who died in 1895, his wife Tempie Pope who died in 1919. Wes was buried there in 1923 and his brother Sim, in the 1930s. All were brought as slaves to Decatur County in the 1850s from Oglethorpe County, Georgia from the plantation of David C. Barrow.

St. Paul Primitive Baptist Church is located off the Hawthorne Trail in what is now Gadsden County

Bethel A.M.E. Church Cemetery
Decatur County, Georgia

A journey south on U.S. 27 from Bainbridge will take you to Bethel A.M.E. Church and cemetery "down yonder" from the city limits of Attapulgus. The cemetery began as a burial spot for majority citizens but over the years is now a final resting spot of many minorities.

Mt. Olive A.M.E. Church Cemetery
Decatur County, Georgia

Founded in 1886, the Mt. Olive A.M.E. Church and cemetery are located near the Fowlstown community in Decatur County, Georgia. Soldiers from WWII who are buried there include Walter Anderson, Douglas Bradley, Thomas Anderson and Leis Scott, a Korean War fatality.

Mt. Zion A.M.E. Church and Cemetery
Decatur County, Georgia

Among the abandoned roads with the names Alligator Stagecoach Road and Chattachochee Turnpike is the Mt. Zion A.M.E. Church and cemetery. Although the roads have been abandoned the church and cemetery have not. Graves of the Cameron, Emanuel, Faison Screen, Tyler and Wimbush families are here.

Munneryln Slave Cemetery
Decatur County, Georgia

In 1861, one of the wealthiest men in the county was Charles James Munneryln. He owned over 3,000 acres of land and over 200 slaves in 1861. Many of those resting for eternity in these graves are known only to the Creator yet contain the spirits of those who found freedom. Among those known is Pashion Moore who at a late age often celebrated with her elders the sweetness of freedom. Moore was buried in the cemetery in 1941.

Although the cemetery name denotes the resting place of those whose time on Earth never knew anything but bondage, there are graves of those who were born in freedom.

Biennially, descendants of the Screen and Emanuel families gather and pay homage to their ancestors.

Fleatown Cemetery
Climax, Georgia

On Georgia 262 north of the town of Climax is the Fleatown Cemetery. According to oral history the original tenants were goats as part of a goat farm. The animals were infested with the interminable pest, hence the name Fleatown. Located on Earl Hester Road, the cemetery with the red clay of Georgia, caresses the remains of many who toiled there under the bondage of slavery, including Henry Philipee and Sabella Matin. Veterans from World War I include Calvin Bobb and Eddie Hines; World War II, Budd Donaldson, Jairus Shoat, Jr. and Norman Philippe; Korean War, Robert Donaldson and James C. Douglas.

Mount Olive A.M.E.

Church Cemetery

St. Paul Church Cemetery
Fowlstown, Georgia

This burial ground is a resting place for many former slaves of the Munnerlyn Plantation in Decatur County, Georgia. George Thomas was 18 years old and Charlotte Thomas was 11 years old when "Seechest*" such as Charles Munnerlyn was forced to call all his slaves up to the big house by bell and tell them of their freedom. Brown and Thomas both died in the 1930s and lived to see not only African American men but also African American women receive the right to vote.

*Seechest was a term used by African Americans to describe those southern citizens who had supported secession from the Union.

Jonas Lobe Cemetery
Bainbridge, Georgia

Jonas Lobe Cemetery is located on the east end of Carter Street in Bainbridge, Georgia. Lobe was the town blacksmith during a time when horsepower truly referred to how many huffs were pulling the load. Although the cemetery bears Lobe's name, his final resting place is in the Pine View Cemetery. Lobe's grave has been lost to time in Pine View Cemetery

Founders of one the first private schools in Decatur County were Harry S. Dixon and his wife. Prof Dixon lived from 1884 until 1965. The emancipator, Abraham Lincoln and many individuals in the Republican party ushered in freedom, the right to vote and liberty for African Americans heretofore unknown. African Americans in return supported the elephant party until Franklin Delano Roosevelt was elected president. Dixon like countless other African Americans proudly waved the Republican Party banner in Decatur County for many a day now gone by.

Men from the Armed Services include Jesse Moore in Word War I, Lonnie Lingy in World War II and Bobby Williams in Korea and Vietnam now rest in the Jonas Lobe Cemetery, after faithfully serving their county in the pursuit of freedom and liberty.

Pine View Cemetery, Georgia

Pine View Cemetery is located on College Street in the southwestern town of Bainbridge, Georgia. The origin of the cemetery was lost along with the memories of our ancestors. A small contingent of African Americans have been entrusted with the care of grounds. Among those buried in the cemetery are Fayette Guyton born in 1851 and died in 1948, and Missouri Pope Guyton who lived from 1880 to 1955.

Prominent citizens who rest there include George Reuben Hutto. He was a native of the sister state of South Carolina, having been born in Barnwell County, March 7, 1871. He grew to manhood in South Carolina. His parents were Richard and Nancy (Daniels) Hutto. His grandparents were George and Alice Daniels. Prof. Hutto was married on July 17, 1892 to Miss Addie Dillard, of Columbia. He and his wife built and taught at the Hutto Middle School. Tending to the sick and ailing was Edward A.R. Lord who died in 1960 at age 63.

The epitaph for Prof. Walter V. Powell who died in 1951 read, "He died as he lived, a Christian."

Among those who served our country are Louis Robert Harper, 1876-1967 who served with the 48th Regiment, U.S. volunteers in the Spanish-American War. Oliver Lee Chambers who died at the age of 85, left an enduring memory by wearing his World War I khaki uniform on Armistice Day.

In the 1980s Bainbridge made national news when a cemetery there was flooded and many caskets were shown floating down cascading waterways. A northern relative had a brother buried in the Pine View Cemetery. After a telephone call to inquire about the possible devastation to the cemetery she learned it was "not our cemetery but the other folks" cemetery that had flooded. African Americans had not been allowed to be buried in the cemetery near the water.

Mt. Pingah AME Church Cemetery, Tallahassee, Florida

This cemetery and church are located on Tram Road in southwest Tallahassee, near the intersection of Tram and Capital Circle. It's a small cemetery and church and is well kept.

And the recent recognition of two of Northeast Georgia's oldest cemeteries have local officials hoping to dig up some of the untold stories of African-American contributions in the Athens area. Georgia lists it as their area cemetery but it is located in Tallahassee, Florida.

Paradise A.M.E. Church Cemetery, Georgia

"It's almost shocking that slaves could be this empowered," the Rev. Sharon Miller said after leading a Bible study at the Paradise African Methodist Episcopal Church in Jefferson last week, remarking on the organization shown by slaves in forming the church.

Paradise's graveyard, founded around the same time as the church in 1854, was recently named to the National Register of Historic Places. Although the earliest recorded burial there took place in 1880, several graves are unmarked, and others are marked simply by stones.

The cemetery, located just east of the Southern railroad site between Lawrenceville Street and Mahaffey Circle, is the only remaining part of a larger complex that once included the first Paradise A.M.E. Church, a parsonage and a school.

John Kissane, a self-employed historic preservation consultant who did the research on the Paradise A.M.E. Church cemetery for the Jefferson Historic Association, said the cemetery's intricately carved markers and pre- Civil War beginnings make it noteworthy.

Miller said the church spends about $1,200 a year on general maintenance for the cemetery. But she's hoping the historic designation will snag some federal grant money for the cemetery's upkeep and spark an interest in tourism.

African-American heritage and civil rights tourism draw many visitors to the South, with some states now shifting their focus from Civil War sites.

Trish Croll, a media relations manager with the state Department of Industry, Trade and Tourism, said Atlanta draws most of Georgia's African-American heritage tourists. The lowland culture of the Savannah area also draws a lot of interest.

Gospel Pilgrim Cemetery, Georgia

In Athens, officials at the East Athens Development Corporation applied with the National Register of Historic Places as part of their current revital-

ization efforts at the Gospel Pilgrim cemetery off Fourth Street in east Athens, according to EADC Executive Director, Winston Heard.

Gospel Pilgrim, founded in the 1880s, sits on a wooded 10-acre lot off West Fourth Street in Athens, and contains the remains of former African-American state legislators and the area's first African-American doctor tucked beneath its trees. EADC has used a $100,000 state Labor Department grant to remove about 30 tons of undergrowth and rubbish from the site and to map out the 3,000-plus grave sites.

"These are places where proper respect and honor can be shown to people who made their way through difficult times," said Al Hester, a retired University of Georgia journalism professor.

Hester recently completed a book about Gospel Pilgrim from the findings of his independent research. The book is titled simply, "Gospel Pilgrim Cemetery: An African-American Historical Site."

Heard said the cemetery's soil has already sprouted some much-needed history.

"The African-American community has been struggling to have our history be American history," Heard said.

Part of that history was a rigidly segregated society that warranted the creation of African-American cemeteries. Many white cemeteries did not allow the burials of African Americans in the 19th century, Hester said.

Heard said hunters still find unmarked graves littering the woods of Northeast Georgia, many times the graves of African Americans who had no other place for burial.

"There weren't many choices for African Americans," Hester said.

In the antebellum South, slaves often only had informal burials on the grounds of the plantations they worked.

In Athens, though, African Americans were also buried in a portion of the old town cemetery, and in Oconee Hill cemetery.

But as a rule, even after the Civil War, there were few graveyards set aside specifically for African Americans.

Charles Davis, 70, a member of Paradise A.M.E. Church, said that now, even with other options open to them, many African Americans seek burial in a place that preserves their past. Paradise and Gospel Pilgrim cemeteries are still used for burials.

Davis, a lifelong Georgia resident, hopes to lay there one day beside his mother, father and both sets of grandparents - near the church that means so much to him.

Miller said church has always been important in the African-American community, providing a place of power and self-determination for an oppressed people.

Heard sees not just spirituality but a chance at education lying in the old graveyards - a place of healing where all Southerners can confront the injustices done and the contributions made by Georgia's African Americans.

George Watson, a volunteer with the Athens Welcome Center, said the center offers an African-American heritage tour which includes Gospel Pilgrim. But Watson said the majority of tourism calls he gets comes from people interested in antebellum homes, the large pre-Civil War mansions owned by whites and paid for through slave labor.

For now Gospel Pilgrim's main tourists are the EADC members and University of Georgia volunteers who have been clearing its wooded paths where conch shells, colored glass and velvet tree adornments tell of a culture's forgotten customs, while the graves and names they cover start to speak of a remembered past.

These stories were published in the Athens Banner-Herald on Monday, March 8, 2004.

Durham, North Carolina

Durham, located outside the Low Country but still in the Southeast, was left with fewer than one hundred residents after the Civil War. Within a few years, however, business began to grow, tobacco farming grew profitable, and Durham became a busy manufacturing town. The city's mild climate and the beauty of the nearby Great Smoky Mountains have made it an increasingly popular city to which northerners choose to migrate.

African Americans have achieved significant financial success in Durham's business community. North Carolina Mutual Life Insurance Company, established in 1898, grosses more than one billion dollars annually. Its home office was declared a National Historic Site in 1975.

GEER CEMETERY

Geer Cemetery is located on Camden Street at Colonial Street in Durham. For years there was talk that the city of Durham was considering renovating this all-black burial ground, which had been closed in 1939 and abandoned to time, overgrowth, and vandals. In 1990, the newly formed Durham Service Corps, a nonprofit organization promoting young adults' employability, approached the city and secured a contract for the Corps' first work project—the clearing of Geer Cemetery. Corps members began working in the cemetery the following April, cutting down trees, hacking back vines, clearing heavy brush, and removing old mattresses and other debris that had been dumped there over the years.

In 1995, Denise Rowson of the Durham Service Corps regretfully reported that the cemetery had reverted back to its original condition. "It's the same as before and it is most disheartening," she said. The money awarded to the service corps, it appears, was a one-time grant. The funds were not sufficient to complete the improvements or build a fence. The Service Corps requested a second grant, noting the very pressing need for additional cleanup and a fence to enclose the property, but the request was denied.

The only available written material about the cemetery is a document written by Kelly Bryant Jr., a well-known historian of black Durham. The Service Corps members learned the area's history from Bryant's writings and from oral histories they conducted. In 1876, they learned, an eleven-year-old black farm hand of Jesse B. Geer was accidentally killed after being dragged by a horse on the Geer plantation. With no cemetery for blacks in the area, Geer entrusted this two-acre piece of land to the other black sharecroppers to be used as a burial ground. On March 28, 1877, Geer sold the land for fifty dollars to three men: Willie Moore, John Daniels, and Nelson Mitchell. The deed they drew, signed by Geer and his wife, Polly, stated that the land was to be used for burials and that the heirs of Moore, Daniels, and Mitchell were to be responsible for the property.

The cemetery was closed in 1939 after the health department inspected the cemetery and found that it was overcrowded. Nothing more was done for the site's upkeep until 1991, when the Durham Service Corps took on the cemetery as a work project.

Two of the Corps members toured the cemetery to read tombstones that came to light after the brush was cleared. They discovered approximately 117 names. After comparing birth and death dates, corps members wondered why so many infants and children were buried at Geer Cemetery. This led them to discover, through oral histories and information from the city health department, that an epidemic of influenza occurred in Durham in the early 1900s and probably caused many of these children's deaths.

The following oral history was given by Mr. Willis G. Carpenter, a seventy-five-year-old gentleman who lived near Geer Cemetery and has distinct memories of it. The following excerpts are from Lacretia Wilkerson and Isaac Johnson's interview as related in Durham Service Corps' pamphlet,

Interviewer: *Mr. Carpenter, where were you born and what is your connection with the Geer Cemetery?*

Carpenter: I was born in Durham in 1917 and my family is originally from Durham County. We lived right adjacent to the cemetery. I lived on the corner of what is now Colonial and McGill. A fellow, Cal Rush in the 1920s, he had some pretty white horses, mainly used for horse and buggy. He worked for my father. I was only about six or seven years old. I would help Cal carry wood around on those two horses.

Do you know anyone buried here?

Cal was buried up there. We went up there to the grave. I can carry you right exactly where it is now. All the young 'uns were crazy about Cal. They got flowers and throwed them on the grave after the funeral was over.

What were some of the practices when they buried people? Were they the same as today?

Most of them were buried in wooden boxes. They since decayed and that's reason why there's all those sunken places. Y'all saw them up there didn't you? They buried so many up there that they filled the graveyard up. And then they started burying where graves was. I saw them digging up out there and they dug up a skeleton.

So they started burying people on top of each other?

That's when the health department come out there and told them they couldn't bury no more if they didn't have no more spaces. That was probably in the early 30s or something like that.

Is that around the time the cemetery started to deteriorate?

Well, after they quit burying them up there, a few people came out there but then all of the people's relatives in there is dead and it just went down to nothing. Until y'all started doing something it just went down to nothing. I talked to a woman at the public library. I went to a session on genealogy. There was a lady trying to find out something about that. I got to talking about it to her and she got real interested about it. I told her that I wish someone would get a hold of it and clean it up. It was a shame to have all those people laying up there and no record of them or nothing. I don't know whether she did anything or not. You all were the next to do something about it.

Were there any black funeral homes in the area?

That one on Dowd Street, not Scarborough.

Fisher?

Edison, that's it.

That one was in business at that time?

Probably some of his ancestors was around. They had some big funerals out there. There was as many people walking as in cars. There are several preachers out there. A Reverend Joyner is out there. He's close to the front.

We found his gravestone.

Those stones were up just like any other cemetery. Some vandals come out there and push those stones over. I don't know what fun they get out of that.

During the time the cemetery was being used, what was the race of most of the residents who lived out there?

It was mostly whites out there but it was just about all of that land, there was only two houses out there, but the rest was farmland. I used to farm back there. All out there where the telephone company is and out near the creek to the railroad, I farmed every bit of that land. And then went behind those two houses near Camden Avenue. Let me tell you something funny. I was plowing right along the side of the cemetery. That street wasn't there then. I stopped about twelve o'clock until it got cool in the evening when I could go back. Well in the meantime, I was eating my dinner and they had a funeral out there. Well I didn't know it. I went back over there to plow where I had left off that morning and all of a sudden that horse jerked that plow out of my hand like that and hit the [inaudible].

This boy was working out on the farm. They bought a new mule. He wasn't but eleven years old. He wanted to plow the new mule. So they let him plow one thing. We told him to ride it but don't get on his back. And when you get ready to come home just leave him. So he went ahead and plowed. And he got ready to eat dinner, he said I'm gonna ride that mule anyhow. He hopped up on his back. That mule started kicking and he didn't take the harness off of him. He left the harness on him and somehow or other it got around his ankle and when it did, the mule just took off to the house like that and started dragging him and when he got to the house his head had hit every rock on the way and the whole back of his head was off.

Old man Geer, he owned the place, said we got to bury him some-

Edian D. Markham

1824 - March 31, 1910

Founder of St. Joseph's
AME Zion Church and
organizer of Durham's
Hayti District, and all-
Black business district in
Durham. Buried in Geer
Cemetery.

where, so he buried him up under that old tree. Someone else came along later and wanted to bury someone. So old man Geer said I'm gonna let y'all have this for a graveyard. I ain't gonna charge nobody nothing to be buried here. And that's why its the Geer graveyard. They didn't have no place in town to bury them so everybody started coming out there. As far as I know, there's all blacks in there—no whites, no Indians, no nothing else in there.

What did it look like?

It looked nice out there. It had a fence going around it. It had a big gate with an arch on it. Back in the '20s it was a nice place out there. Everybody kept it just as clean. Folks would drive buggies out there and work on the graveyard. When the old people died off, it started to go down. Some people said the city should do something, but the city said it was private property, it ain't ours.

Who kept the deed to the place?

I don't know. The church didn't pay no taxes or keep no deeds or nothing else. So nobody could do anything with it. That's the reason it went down.

Do you know anyone who might have pictures of the graveyard?

No, everyone who was around in those days is just about dead; 1920 to 1990. That's seventy years. Most of the people then were fifty or sixty years old or so; 70 and 60 is 130 years old and no one is that old. I don't think they kept records of the city cemetery until way after that.

Rowson remains hopeful that in time, funds will be made available so that they can renew their efforts and complete their plans for maintenance and fencing of this important historic site.

Nashville, Tennessee, and Neighboring Kentucky

Nashville, the capital of Tennessee, is an active and vibrant city that serves as the home of the country music industry and numerous publishing companies. The historic Grand Old Opry, considered the "Mother Church" of country music, makes its home in a part of the city's renovated downtown area. For some time, however, Nashville, like many other U.S. cities, was enmeshed in struggles against blighted housing, poverty, and the destruction of neighborhoods by highway construction. The city's recent revitalization has been encouraging. Among Nashville's jewels are its many colleges and universities, three of which are historic black colleges. Fisk University was founded in 1866, Tennessee State in 1866, and

Meharry Medical College in 1867.

Greenwood Cemetery, founded in 1888, lies a few miles from downtown Nashville.

The two large black-owned cemeteries in Nashville are Greenwood and Mt. Ararat. The latter, now known as Greenwood-West, was founded in the 1860s and served as a showcase property for many years; many of Nashville's most prominent citizens are buried at Mt. Ararat. Tragically, the cemetery suffered years of neglect because lack of money prevented the owners from maintaining the grounds and preventing vandalism. Fortunately, in 1982 neighboring Greenwood Cemetery assumed management of its thirty-nine acres of grounds. Since the beginning of restoration efforts by Greenwood, several acres have been restored and hundreds of new grave spaces created.

Nashville stood in the midst of heavy conflict during the Civil War. The city had been under federal control since February 1862 and had been a haven for freed men and women throughout the war. During the winter of 1865–1866, Nashville's muddy streets were crowded with hundreds of impoverished former slaves who had settled there. To accommodate those who had no means, several small cities bearing the local names of "By-Town," "Hell's Half-Acre," and "Black Center" sprang up within the larger one. Newspaper editorial columns carried stories of assaults, starvation in the open streets, widespread illness, and people freezing to death on a daily basis.

In time, secular benevolent societies and auxiliaries began to send volunteers to aid the freed people of the South. In Tennessee the most active were the American Freedmen's Union Commission, the Western Freedmen's Union Commission, and the Western Sanitary Commission. The Interdenominational American Missionary Association, which also founded Fisk University, and the Freedmen's Aid Society of the Methodist Episcopal Church, which founded many black colleges, were the leading church-sponsored relief agencies.

In May 1865, President Andrew Johnson organized the Freedmen's Bureau and appointed Major General Oliver Otis Howard commissioner. Brigadier General Clinton B. Fisk was appointed assistant commissioner for the district comprising Kentucky and Tennessee, with Nashville as his headquarters. Fisk, through persistent work, persuaded many blacks who had crowded into Nashville to return to the countryside and resume farming. In Howard's view, the most urgent need of the freed people was education; his bureau made a strong commitment to providing instruction to freed blacks and their children. The bureau's educational work was carried on in close cooperation with benevolent societies from the North. Meharry Medical College drew its sustenance from both the Methodist church and the benevolent societies of the time. As Nashville's educational community grew, its business, professional, and religious communities also flourished.

Dr. Robert Fulton Boyd, a pioneering Nashville physician and dentist, was memorialized at Greenwood Cemetery in 1992 during Black History Month.

Nashville remains proud of its strong educational heritage. Among all the cities with black colleges, it attracts the greatest number of former students back to alumni meetings. Meharry Medical College, long recognized as the largest predominantly black medical school in the country, continues to graduate a substantial number of the nation's black physicians and dentists.

Nashville City Cemetery

The Nashville City Cemetery located at 1001 Fourth Avenue South on the corner of Oak Street is the oldest existing public cemetery in Middle Tennessee. It was established south of the city in 1822, just twenty-five years after Tennessee became a state. At that time, the population of the city was over three thousand and growing. As one of the earliest integrated cemeteries in the United States, it was truly a public cemetery where people of different races, religions and economic status could be buried.

Tallahassee's Old City Cemetery, Tallahassee, Florida

Tallahassee's Old City Cemetery was officially established in 1829, five years after the town was founded as the capital of Florida Territory. A cross-section of early Tallahassee's population—slaves, planters, governors, yellow fever victims, soldiers killed in battle, and the many other citizens who were part of "everyday life"—are buried there. Because it is the final resting place of so many of the men and women who contributed to the history of Florida during its territorial and antebellum periods, the cemetery is of statewide significance. All Floridians have a vested interest in its remarkable history and in its preservation.

City commission meetings minutes reveal how Old City Cemetery and other city cemeteries reflected Tallahassee's social and political climate. In 1936 and 1937, efforts began to close the city's public cemeteries to Negro burials.

continued on next page

The cemetery is on the National Register of Historic Places, both because of who is buried there and for artistic carvings on tombstones. In addition to two of the founders of the city, four Confederate generals are two of the original Fisk Jubilee Singers, Mable Imes and Ella Sheppard. Fisk University purchased a plot for the burial of Mable Lewis Imes. She was buried near the Sheppard family plot where Ella Sheppard is buried with her family.

Every year Fisk University honors its original Jubilee Singers and the tradition of singing the spirituals of slavery by laying a wreath on the graves of Imes and Sheppard and singing at a memorial service held in the cemetery.

Greenwood Cemetery, Ohio and
Mount Ararat (Greenwood Cemetery–West), Nashville

In February 1992, Tammy Smith, staff writer for the *Tennessean*, wrote of the memorial service inaugurating Black History Month: "The service was held at the old Mount Ararat Cemetery off Elm Hill Pike in honor of Dr. Robert Fulton Boyd. Ironically, Sam Cameron, who helped plan the service, was memorialized along with Dr. Boyd."

continued from previous page

Tallahassee's earliest burying ground allowed burials of all races, although in segregated areas, as decreed by city ordinance in 1841. The minutes of the January 12, 1937, city commission meeting show that the city sexton recommended to the city commissioners that the Negro section of the old cemetery be closed. The commissioner directed the city attorney to draw up an ordinance "requiring that that part of the old cemetery devoted to the burial of Negros be closed unless they can show title to family lots in the said cemetery."

On January 26, 1937, the ordinance was introduced: "An ordinance closing that part of the city cemetery heretofore designated as the public burying ground for the purpose of the burial of the dead bodies of colored persons and prohibiting the further burial of the dead bodies of colored persons in said cemetery."

On February 9, 1937, the members of the city commission voted upon and passed the ordinance. This action resulted in the establishment of the Greenwood Cemetery Company in 1937, a private corporation that purchased land to be developed as a burying ground for the city's black population.

—SHARON THOMPSON,
Florida's Historic Cemeteries: A Preservation Handbook

Sam Cameron, a Meharry Medical College archivist, was gunned down a month prior to the service by an assailant during an apparent robbery attempt. It was Cameron who had discovered the location of Mount Ararat Cemetery several decades earlier during research on a paper about Dr. Boyd. And with his energy and enthusiasm, efforts to restore the cemetery were undertaken. A Meharry student speaking of Cameron stated, "His enthusiasm and love of history should always encourage us to keep the dream alive." Dr. Richard Garvin, a personal friend of Cameron's, stated, "For Sam, the restoration of Mount Ararat was the implementation of a historic venture. For Sam, each one of the stones represented history."

Greenwood Cemetery, located a few miles from downtown Nashville at 1428 Elm Hill Pike, celebrated its 100th anniversary a few years before Cameron's tragic death. The thirty-seven-acre cemetery, with its impressive entrance, seven monumental sections, and six memorial gardens, appears well groomed and cared for. Greenwood's purchase of the newly discovered Mount Ararat Cemetery, and its scheduled long-range improvements, have made it a point of pride within the community.

Elder Preston Taylor, founder of the cemetery, was one of many Nashville residents who became a distinguished and courageous citizen in the post-Civil War period. Born of slave parents in Shreveport, Louisiana, in 1849, he heard God's word and, even in early childhood, expressed a desire to become a minister. This ambition directed his entire life; Taylor studied with a white preacher and undertaker and learned the ministry as well as the undertaking business. In 1888 he established Greenwood Cemetery and served as its chief executive officer for forty years.

Elder Taylor was a Christian church minister and Nashville's first black funeral director. He sponsored an amusement park for black families and children and in 1903 helped found Citizen's Bank, which continues to be one of the major black-owned and controlled banks in the South. Preston Taylor died in 1931 and is buried near the front entrance of the historic burial ground.

Greenwood Cemetery and Mount Ararat Cemetery are now owned and operated by the National Christian Missionary Convention. Greenwood assumed management of Mt. Ararat in 1982, and four years later renamed it Greenwood Cemetery–West. In February 1992, plans to sell the new acquisition to the neighboring Cummings Sign Company for a parking lot were stalled when archaeologists discovered there may be five to six hundred graves in a part of the cemetery then thought to be unused. Officials were mystified since no records existed on that part of the cemetery. "That area had been abandoned for thirty or forty years," said Robert Moseley Jr., manager of Greenwood Cemeteries. "It looked like it would not be of any use for further burials. We initially thought there were less than a dozen graves there." The 1.17 acre lot bounding the site's northern edge had always been badly overgrown and was prone to flooding.

Billy Earley, a columnist for the *Tennessean,* writes of some of the distinguished black citizens who are buried at Greenwood Cemetery:

Dr. Robert Fulton Boyd (1858–1912), a pioneering Nashville physician and dentist, was memorialized in 1992 during Black History Month. Dr. Boyd ran for Mayor of Nashville in 1893, and later was cofounder and first president of the National Medical Association, which celebrated its 100th anniversary in July 1995. Boyd was a graduate of Meharry Medical College and, like a third of all early Meharry graduates, was trained in both medicine and dentistry because patients at that time did not have that many sources of medical care available to them.

Reverend R. H. Boyd, one of the founders of Citizen's Bank, is buried fairly close to cofounder Preston Taylor. Boyd, who also founded the National Baptist Publishing Board, died in 1922. The Publishing Board continues to publish Sunday School literature and other similar church books and materials for affiliates of the six-million-member National Baptist Convention.

Benjamin F. Cox (1874–1952), a well-known and respected educator is buried at Greenwood Cemetery alongside his wife, Jeannette Keeble Cox (1876–1956), and her father, Sampson W. Keeble (1833–1887). Keeble was the first Negro representative of the Tennessee state legislature.

Z. Alexander Looby (1899–1971) is among many prominent Nashville citizens buried in Greenwood Cemetery. Looby, a West Indian native, arrived in the United States in 1926. Tom Norman of the *Banner* wrote, "The local civil rights climate would never be the same after Looby's arrival. Looby, civil rights advocate, attorney, retired city councilman, was the one black Middle Tennessean who made the greatest contribution to the development and culture of American life." As Looby told a reporter in 1972, "Things have changed from the time I first came here. I feel the major change is in the attitude of the people—there is less hate based solely on color."

J. C. Napier was another of Citizen's Bank's founders. He served as registrar of the United States Treasury under Presidents Taft and Wilson. Napier, an attorney, lived to be almost ninety-five years old.

Dr. Charles Spurgeon Johnson (1893–1956), the sixth president of Fisk University, is buried at Greenwood. He served Fisk from 1946–1956 and wrote several books, including *The Negro in American Civilization* (1930), *The Economic Status of the Negro* (1933), *The Negro College Graduate* (1936), and *Education and the Cultural Crisis* (1951).

William B. Reed. Billy Eisley, writer for the *Tennessean,* stated that "Greenwood Cemetery holds the bodies of some black citizens who left big footprints in Nashville history—and it contains the remains of others not so well known. But all of them, the well known and the little known, were once special to someone—many of them special to a lot of people. A rail car wheel was made into a headstone at the grave of William B. (Uncle Billy) Reed. His marker reads: Born December 26, 1849; joined the church July 2, 1866; went to work for NC and St L on March 3, 1883; honor roll, June 1, 1901; died August 26, 1934; His creed for life: I love my Lord. I love my family. I love my job." A grave close by has the name D. W. B. Reed (1890–1961), probably the son of the railroader.

Dr. Harold D. West Sr. was buried here in 1974. His monument identifies him as the first black president of Meharry Medical College, serving from 1952–1966. From the time of its founding until 1952, Meharry's presidents were white doctors even though nearly all the school's students were black.

Others buried at Greenwood and Mount Ararat include **Cornelia Shepherd** and two fellow members of the original Fisk Jubilee Singers; civil rights leaders **Dr. Kelly Miller Smith** and **Alfred C. Galloway;** former Tennessee State University head football coach **John Merritt**, remembered as one of college football's winningest coaches; Grand Ole Opry legend **DeFord Bailey**, the first black performer to appear at the Ryman Auditorium; and **Dennis Comer Washington**, a former Baptist Sunday School Publishing Board executive director.

The Alex Haley State Historic Site and Museum, where Alex Haley is buried, was the author's boyhood home.

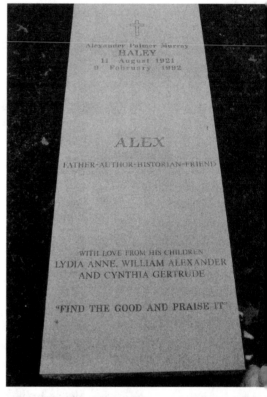

Riverside Cemetery

"Here sleep the founders of Jackson" are the words carved on a plaque at the entrance to this historic and beautiful cemetery in southwest Jackson, Tennessee. Today, not only the founders sleep here; many families have also purchased lots and individual graves.

The site has undergone several name changes. Prior to 1820, the site was known as Pioneer Graveyard. Those buried there were reinterred in the 1820s, after local resident Tom Shannon gave an acre to the city of Jackson for a cemetery. Some records dating to around 1928 call the cemetery Lancaster Graveyard, and in 1878 the name was changed to Jackson Graveyard. Immediately afterwards, a newspaper notice requested readers to help select a new name for the burial ground. The name "Riverside" was submitted by Benjamin Davidson, a cotton buyer from Jackson whose grave, along with his wife's, can now be found in the cemetery.

Research and study by the Mid-West Genealogical Society has shown that through the years slaves and whites were buried side by side in the ten-acre Riverside Cemetery. The first burial, that of Mary Jane Butler, occurred on September 12, 1824. Also interred here is her father, Dr. William Butler, who was called "the father of Jackson." A veteran of the War of 1812, he married a niece of President Andrew Jackson.

The recent research of Jackson resident Jonathan Smith has revealed that many previously believed facts about Riverside Cemetery may need revision. It appears that the bodies moved from Pioneer Graveyard were reinterred without identification, so that it is impossible to compile a complete listing. However, there was an area of the new cemetery where the enslaved and free Negroes were buried. During slavery, some family plots contained the nuclear family and the slaves. Blacks buried at Riverside include **Bishop Isaac Lane** (1937), for whom Jackson's prominent black college, Lane College, is named. Also buried here are members of

Twelve years of research culminated in the publication of *Roots*, for which Alex Haley received the Pulitzer Prize in 1977.

the Lane family: **Francis B. Lane**, a World War I veteran (1899–1956), and **Joshua Lane** (1869–1949).

The cemetery is the final resting place for veterans of all the wars, including Confederate and Union soldiers of the Civil War and servicemen from World Wars I and II. Also buried here are several prominent Jackson citizens, including attorney **Milton Brown**. Brown defended John Morrell, a land pirate accused of murder and of stealing slaves. While Brown successfully argued against the murder conviction, his client, Morrell, went to prison for robbery. Brown subsequently became a judge and railroad executive. As a congressman he submitted the bill for the annexation of the state of Texas. He was buried in Riverside in 1830.

The Alex Haley
State Historic Site and Museum

This site, established in the mid-1980s, contains the grave of author **Alex Haley.** It is the first state-owned historic site in western Tennessee and the first devoted to an African American in Tennessee. The boyhood home of Alex Haley, it was historically known as the Palmer House. The ten-room, bungalow-style home is located at 200 South Church Street and Haley Avenue in the small incorporated town of Henning, Tennessee, about forty-five miles north of Memphis. The museum is open year-round and annually attracts thousands of visitors from all over the world, many of whom follow the museum's tour map to the town's historic homes and churches. One spot on the tour is the Bethlehem Cemetery, where Haley ancestor Chicken George is buried in the Haley family plot.

Henning, a picturesque town of Victorian houses and turn-of-the-century storefronts, was founded in 1873, close to the tracks of the Illinois Central Railroad. The city developed industries based on the sawmill, grist mill, and cotton gin.

Will E. Palmer, grandfather of Haley and a well-known businessman and community leader, had the Palmer House constructed in 1918. Currently the house is being restored to the period of Haley's youth, when he would sit on its front porch listening to his grandmother, Cynthia Palmer, aunts Liz, Plus, Viney, and Till, and cousin Georgia tell stories about the family's history.

They spoke of Africa, and of the Mandingo youth Kunte Kinte, who was seized by four slave catchers near his village of Juffure on the Kamby Balongo in West Africa. Just sixteen years old, he was dragged aboard the slave ship *Lord Ligonier* and carried to Annapolis, Maryland, where he was sold into human bondage. These *griots* traced the lineage of Kunte Kinte, called "Toby" by his owner, John Waller; to Kinte's daughter, Kizzy;

to her son "Chicken George," a game-cock trainer who won his freedom even before the Emancipation Proclamation; to his son, Tom Murray; to Murray's daughter, Cynthia, who married Will Palmer; to Will and Cynthia Palmer's daughter, Bertha, who married Simon Alexander Haley; and finally to Alex Haley.

Haley's relatives related the saga of how their ancestors were led from Alamance, North Carolina, to the western Tennessee settlement of Henning, by Haley's great-great-grandfather, nicknamed Chicken George. The six women conversed about how the families who arrived in "Rockaways" established themselves and became productive citizens in their new-found "Promise Land." After the families built their homes, barns, sheds, and fences, they turned their energies to building a house of worship, the New Hope Colored Methodist Church, in which they placed a stained glass window purchased from Sears and Roebuck. It was in this church that Tom and Irene Murray's daughter, Cynthia, married Will Palmer in 1893.

Palmer was a highly motivated and ambitious young man. For several years he managed the local lumber mill for its owner, Mr. James. James suffered from alcoholism, which caused him to declare bankruptcy in 1893. After he became insolvent, ten white businessmen consigned a note to reopen the mill under Palmer's proprietorship. Palmer continued to operate and manage the mill in a very astute and businesslike manner, becoming esteemed in circles of commerce and a leader in the Negro community.

As Palmer's business acumen bore fruit, he built the ten-room, electric, bungalow-style Palmer House. In 1921, Simon and Bertha returned to Henning and presented Will and Cynthia with a grandson, Alex Haley. Young Alex and his mother remained with the Palmers while Simon returned to New York to continue his graduate studies. Simon later returned to Henning and, after the death of Will Palmer in 1926, operated the family business. In 1929 Simon Haley began a teaching career, and the family moved. Two years after they relocated his wife died in Normal, Alabama.

Alex and his brothers spent every summer in Henning. The stories Alex heard as a youth in the 1920s and 1930s prompted his exploration of his ancestry during the 1960s. Twelve years of research culminated in the publication of *Roots,* for which he received the Pulitzer Prize in 1977. *Roots* was significant not only because it documented the history of a single family, but because it also characterized the trials and tribulations experienced by African Americans in a manner meaningful to readers of all backgrounds. Haley accomplished what was considered an impossible task: tracing his ancestry back over seven generations—more than two hundred years—to a small village in West Africa. *Roots* inspired many to explore their family histories and helped many African Americans realize that they had a heritage of which to be proud.

Bethlehem Cemetery, Tennessee

"Chicken George," great-great-grandfather of *Roots* author Alex Haley, is buried in Henning, Tennessee, in this cemetery that contains the Haley family plot. Bethlehem Cemetery is one mile east of Henning, on Durhamville Road. This gently rolling land was given to the Bethlehem Methodist Church by the Currie family at a time when the area was known as Stonewall, a little settlement of few families. A log building was made from hand-hewn logs cut from the forest that once stood on this land. A few years later, the log building was used as a school, the Stonewall Academy, and a larger frame building was erected for a church.

Church members gradually began to bury their dead at the east end of the property, and their servants on the northern boundary. The Haley family plot, where Chicken George is buried, is in this northern section of the cemetery. After the battle of Fort Pillow, during the Civil War, the doors of the church were opened to the wounded and suffering. Those who died were buried here. Bethlehem Cemetery, one of the oldest in Lauderdale County, continues to serve the community in the present as it did in the past.

Canfield Cemetery, Tennessee

In Ripley, Lauderdale County, Tennessee, a story circulates that dates back to 1893. Realizing the necessity for a common burial ground for black residents, members of four churches—Holly Grove Baptist Church, Miles Chapel Methodist Church, and Morning Star Baptist, all of Ripley, and Nelson Chapel, of the neighboring town of Flippen—met and appointed two members from each to form a committee to find land for a cemetery. On February 18, 1893, Isaac Russell, Elias Clay, Phil Lee, Gilbert Parker, Charles Henning, and Calvin Dupree, acting as trustees of the Canfield Cemetery Association, purchased land from H. H. Glass and his wife.

Canfield is hallowed ground to members of the black community. It was through the hard work and dedication of their forefathers that money was raised to purchase land for the burial of blacks in this common burial ground. Through the years, many have given both their time and money to carefully maintain the ten-acre cemetery. In years past, Memorial Day was considered a special day to gather to pay tribute to the deceased, clean up and beautify the grounds, and collect donations for the maintenance of the cemetery. Through the years, this practice has slowly disappeared.

Located about fifty miles north of Memphis and about six miles from Henning, Canfield is a place of consolation for the friends and families who visit the grave sites of loved ones. While it is heartening to realize they are resting in peaceful surroundings, many improvements are still needed, including year-round maintenance. Among those buried here are **Dennis Holcomb**, a member of Holly Grove Baptist Church, and **Ralph Anderson**, of New Hope C.M.E.

Zion Cemetery, Tennessee

Zion Cemetery is located on Range Road and Hickory Hill Road, about five miles from Memphis, Tennessee. The C.M.E. Church was founded in 1888, and the one-acre cemetery that was started around that same time is still in use. The last owner, a descendent of the Sons and Daughters of Zion who once owned the land, left the burial grounds to the C.M.E. Church.

Several members of the church congregation are concerned about the condition of the cemetery and are hopeful that a massive effort will be launched to make the grounds beautiful again. C.M.E. members buried in the cemetery include **Sam Walker,** superintendent of the Sunday School who died in 1949; **Porter Tuggle,** a former chairman of the board of the church; **Della Walker** (died 1938); **Alice Jones; Cora Calhoun; Betty** and **Polk Brown,** who owned considerable land in the area; and **Roxy Brown,** sister of Polk Brown.

Zion Cemetery, in the heart of the black community, is also the site of the graves of three black men who were lynched in 1892. **Thomas Moss, Calvin McDowell,** and **Henry Will Stewart** had opened People's Grocery Company on a Memphis streetcorner in what was primarily a black neighborhood. Nearby, however, was a grocery store owned and operated by a white man, and he saw People's as unwanted competition.

Constant fighting and harassment soon broke out, eventually resulting in the jailing of the black three men. One night, while they lay in their cells, a group of men were admitted to the jail; they took Moss, McDowell and Stewart to a switch engine behind the jail building and shot them to death. A mob destroyed the store and the murderers were never apprehended.

Whitney Young Jr., buried at Greenwood Cemetery in 1971, was a longtime presi dent of the National Urban League and earned the nation's highest civilian award, the Medal of Freedom, in 1969.

Greenwood (Co-Haven) Cemetery, Kentucky

Kentucky's fifteen-acre Greenwood Cemetery, sometimes also called the African Cemetery #1 and officially named Co-Haven since 1987, is located on Lexington's West End, or Georgetown, neighborhood. Constructed in 1907, it abuts the Lexington Cemetery, which was built in 1849 to serve white Kentuckians. The original owners and board members of this fifteen-acre burial site have all passed away, and with them, much of the cemetery's history.

Whitney Young Jr. was buried at Greenwood on March 11, 1971. Young was prominent nationally; in 1961 he was elected president of the National Urban League, and during the next ten years the League grew from sixty-three to ninety-eight affiliates. Young served on numerous commissions and advisory committees and was selected by President Lyndon Johnson to receive the Medal of Freedom, the nation's highest civilian award, in 1969. Young died two years later, while attending a conference in Africa.

The folklore surrounding Young's burial is muddled. It seems that local residents wanted him to be buried in Kentucky, the state where he was born and raised. They proceeded to plan for this with a good deal of fanfare, arranging for his burial in Lexington, near the graves of his parents. President Richard Nixon and other dignitaries attended the funeral. After the ceremony, however, Young's wife had his body moved to New York so that "he would be near her."

Young's father, **Whitney Young Sr.**, was buried at Greenwood Cemetery on August 21, 1935; his mother **Sally** was buried in November 1951.

The African Cemetery #2, Kentucky

Lexington, Kentucky's oldest cemetery, the African Cemetery #2, is located in the city's East End. Two to three acres in size and bordered on the east by 7th Street, the cemetery was renovated during the mid-1980s with block grant funds. African Cemetery #2 is run by a private, nonprofit group, the members of which are selected by the mayor. Although no burials have taken place here since 1865 and all heirs have apparently moved away or are deceased, the city of Lexington continues to maintain the historic cemetery.

Fort Lauderdale, Florida, and Area

Fort Lauderdale, Florida, is often called "the Venice of America" with its twenty-three miles of Atlantic Ocean beaches and a myriad of rivers, inlets, and man-made canals. The city was named for Major William Lauderdale, who built a fort there in 1838 during the Seminole War. It is in close proximity to the larger, more metropolitan Miami, also in southern Florida.

During the past few years, a growing public awareness has developed concerning the importance of early graveyards and cemeteries. At the same time this appreciation has emerged, however, the sites themselves have been rapidly deteriorating and disappearing from the landscape. This is especially true for the state of Florida. Still, while touring the state's burial sites, the amateur genealogist is sure to uncover some remarkable history about African Americans, many of whom heroically laid down their lives in the name of freedom.

Despite the fact that Florida's Bureau of Historic Preservation, assisted by the Historic Preservation Advisory Council, has provided grant support for preservation planning, surveying, and restoration of many of the state's cemeteries, some sites have—both literally and figuratively—fallen by the wayside.

Legislation that affects both the preservation and protection of Florida's historic cemeteries and graveyards has been passed in recent years, an indication of the concern and seriousness of the state in protecting these properties. The Florida statutes, chapter 872, called "Offenses Concerning Dead Bodies and Graves," were made effective October 1, 1987. The two pertinent amendments concern: (1) Injuring or removing tomb or monument, or disturbing contents of grave or tomb; penalties are either misdemeanor of the first degree or felony of the third degree; and (2) Unmarked human burials; equal treatment and respect must be accorded, and respect common to human dignity.

Woodlawn Cemetery, Florida

Woodlawn Cemetery, on Northwest Ninth Street and 19th Avenue in Fort Lauderdale, was founded in the 1920s to provide blacks a place to bury friends and family members. Segregation followed them even in death; blacks were not accepted in the city's main cemeteries. Until Woodlawn's creation, relatives were forced to bury their dead in the woods. Although burying in the woods was often done, it was a heart-wrenching, unacceptable alternative for African Americans to endure. Knowing the customs, traditions, and care exercised at death, particularly in the early 1900s when life itself was so difficult, it was a gross disservice to blacks to be refused burials at private and city-owned cemeteries.

A story in Fort Lauderdale's *Sun Sentinel* tells of the plight of high school teacher Mary Foster, who went to Woodlawn Cemetery in 1991 to bury her aunt and was shocked to tears. Instead of a peaceful, manicured resting place, the grass was knee-high and weeds had overtaken the tombstones. Buzzing swarms of insects that hovered nearby were drowned out by the rush of traffic on Interstate 95. The graves of Broward County's black pioneers—and all the history resting with them—were lost in a tangle of overgrowth.

"It hurt to leave my aunt there." Foster said, recalling the pain she felt laying her beloved aunt to rest in a field of rubble. On that hot June day in 1991, Foster decided that her aunt—and all those buried in Woodlawn—had the right to rest in dignity, a fitting honor for all they had accomplished in life.

Foster organized the Woodlawn Revitalization Committee, a group committed to transforming Woodlawn into a beautiful burial ground worthy of its historic promise. "Many of the pioneers of Broward and Fort Lauderdale now rest there," notes Roosevelt Walters, president of the Fort Lauderdale branch of the NAACP. "These are people who made or caused dramatic changes for black people in our area."

Buried there are people like **Raleigh P. Moore**, publisher of Fort Lauderdale's *Colored Bulletin*, the city's first black newspaper. Moore ran a candy store, fixed cars, and was deeply involved in church activities. Widowed, he raised three daughters by himself. "He was very concerned about the black community," remembers Ceaniel Ford, Moore's daughter. "He felt the black community should have its own newspaper . . . and the newspaper did really well. He was a great man. Woodlawn is important to me because of him."

Foster is determined that Woodlawn be known for its pioneers—not for its shoddy condition and neglect. Her committee plans to immortalize the cemetery's history by publishing a book about the pioneers buried there. "It won't be easy," she is quick to admit, "because . . . accurate burial records were never kept and the cemetery is filled with unmarked tombstones." Her committee hopes to discover the names of those buried underneath the fallen and crumbling tombstones by interviewing relatives of the fifteen families known to be interred in the cemetery. Such efforts at research, which include plans to comb newspapers and other archives, will be the second project undertaken by Foster and her associates. In August of 1991 the committee encouraged the community to spend several weekends cleaning the cemetery. They cut weeds, washed tombstones, and attempted to reorganize the chaos. "Our dream is to leave a legacy to the children," Foster said.

That legacy includes pioneering school reformer **Reverend O. W. Wells,** buried in Woodlawn in the 1960s, who led the fight to repeal the law shortening the school year to allow students to work longer in the fields. Modern-day activists like Roosevelt Walters see the value in handing down that legacy. "It is important that the children know where they come from, so that they can decide where they should be heading," he says.

The Woodlawn Revitalization Committee also hopes to build a monument inscribed with the names of the interred, pave the roads in the cemetery, and install a sprinkler system. "Everything requires a lot of time, planning, and dedication—from not only the African American community, but from the entire Fort Lauderdale community—to make our dreams a reality," Foster realizes. Walters agrees. "It must be the entire community's goal to bring the cemetery and its history the honor they deserve," he says. "Most people now don't want folks buried there because they feel it's degrading. It should be the reverse. It should be a great honor to rest with such great people."

Lincoln Memorial Cemetery, Florida

One of several historic Florida cemeteries in Dade County is the Lincoln Memorial Cemetery in Brownsville. It, along with so many other of the nation's black historic burial grounds, has suffered from vandalism and maintenance problems through the years. Recently, however, the Metro-Dade Historic Preservation Board approved a historic designation for the site. Says Lincoln's present manager Ellen Johnson, "This is good because it will help perpetuate the history of black people in Dade County."

Also, $50,000 from the U.S. Department of Housing and Urban

Development, administered through Dade's Department of Community Development, has helped the cemetery reverse the toll of time, lack of funds, and vandalism. This grant was the fruit of efforts by residents, the Community Action Agency, Dade's Preservation Office, and Johnson.

Lincoln Memorial Park Cemetery was purchased in 1929 by **Kelsey Pharr**, funeral director, philanthropist, and Liberian consul. Pharr, who died in 1964, is buried in the cemetery.

At the urging of Johnson, Lincoln was designated as a local historic site in 1991. The cemetery, which now operates under the legal name of Lincoln-Evergreen, is twenty acres in size and in good condition. Located on 46th Street in Miami, the cemetery has many above-ground interments; some caskets are even encased in concrete, a holdover from the era when a high water table prevented traditional burials.

Others buried at Lincoln include **Dr. D. A. Dorsey**, Miami's first black millionaire, who donated land to the Miami school board to build the junior high school that bears his name; **Arthur** and **Polly Mays**, residents of nearby Homestead who, in the 1930s, arranged to transport African American children to a Miami high school when that facility did not exist in Brownsville; **Dr. William Sawyer**, founder of Christian Hospital, and, with his wife, **Alberta Sawyer**, the Mary Elizabeth Hotel, the first overnight accommodation in the area for blacks.

Many other prominent blacks are buried there. Among them are **E. S. Reeves**, founder of the *Miami Times;* **Artemus Brown**, Miami's first blacksmith; and **Julia Baylor,** who established the first YMCA for black women.

Evergreen Memorial Park Cemetery, Florida

Evergreen Memorial Park Cemetery has been owned alternately by blacks and whites through the years. The most recent owner, Garth Reeves, is an African American who purchased it from a white family in 1991. That same year, Lincoln Memorial Park manager Ellen Johnson worked to get Evergreen designated as a local historic site. Approximately fifteen acres in size, Evergreen is one of many cemeteries that could benefit with more upkeep.

James E. Scott was buried at Evergreen in May 1995. He was a Tuskegee airman; the area's first government-sponsored low-rent housing development was named after him. Scott's very well attended funeral included an honor guard.

George Washington Carver

George Washington Carver (1864–1943) was a scientist, agronomist, and educator who revolutionized the southern agricultural economy by demonstrating that a single food—like the peanut or sweet potato—could be translated into hundreds of different products. By 1938, the once lowly peanut had grown to become a $200-million industry and one of the chief products of the state of Alabama. For this and other contributions to the economic welfare of the South, Carver was memorialized by a federal monument, the first black scientist to be so honored in the United States. In 1953 the George Washington Carver National Monument was erected on his birth site near Diamond, Missouri; it was dedicated July 17, 1960.

George Washington Carver is buried near his friend Booker T. Washington in the small cemetery on the Tuskegee grounds.

Public Cemetery, Florida

The Union soldiers buried in Tallahassee's Public Cemetery lost their lives in the battle of Natural Bridge. Their graves are situated in the southwest corner of the cemetery. In 1936 and for many years after, efforts were made to close Public, as well as the city's other public cemeteries, to Negro burials.

Birmingham, Alabama

Alabama seems to have always been a battleground. French, British, and Spanish explorers fought here for both land and control of the New World. It served as the site of perhaps the single most bloody battle between European settlers and Native Americans, which occurred in 1540. Many Civil War skirmishes took place here. In the 1860s, Alabama's slave population accounted for nearly half its total, a fact essential to illustrating the thriving agricultural economy of the time. After Reconstruction, the state became more industrialized. Steel became an important industry, inspiring the state's nickname of "the Pittsburgh of the South."

Despite the victories of Union troops, the outcome of the Civil War did little to erase the conflict in Alabama's atmosphere. A century later, Birmingham was targeted by the South Christian Leadership Conference to be the site of demonstrations and rallies for desegregation. The bombing of the Sixteenth Street Baptist Church and the subsequent rioting focused the nation's attention on the issue, and the civil rights movement gained momentum. In his "Letter from Birmingham Jail," Dr. Martin Luther King Jr. wrote, "One day the South will know that when these disinherited children of God sat down at lunch counters, they were in reality standing up for what is best in the American dream."

Today, Birmingham is the largest city in the state of Alabama. A leading financial, industrial, and educational center, this city has much to be admired. Watched over by a statue of Vulcan, blacksmith to the gods, it remains a busy, sophisticated, and now peaceful city that has retained much of its southern charm.

continued from previous page

New Grace Hill Cemetery, Alabama and Zion Memorial Gardens, Alabama

New Grace Hill Cemetery is about 150 acres in size, and is very well maintained. It is located in Mason City, a black community within the city of Birmingham. Informally known as Mason City Cemetery, New Grace Hill is the burial place of many prominent families, such as the Lees and the Montgomerys.

The original directors were Dr. A. G. Gaston, president/treasurer; Louis J. Willie, executive vice-president; and P. L. Butler, secretary. An impressionable youth of eighteen when he read Booker T. Washington's *Up from Slavery,* Gaston heard the legendary Washington speak at a black church in Birmingham. "He held me transfixed," Gaston wrote fifty years later, then enjoying his status as the state's most successful black businessman. He and the other directors of New Grace Hill have now been replaced; the new directors include president/treasurer Louis J. Willie, executive vice-president K. R. Balton, and secretary James Johnson.

New Grace Hill Cemetery purchased the fifty-six-acre Zion Memorial Gardens, located about eighteen miles away, in 1972. One of the busiest black cemeteries in the area, Zion Memorial Gardens handles over four hundred interments a year; construction began on a mausoleum in 1979. Buried at Zion are famous blues harmonica player **Sonny Terry,** who, along with his many performances with fellow musician Brownie McGee, appeared in the film *The Color Purple,* and the Woods family.

All the property encompassing the present New Grace Hill complex was at one time owned by Dr. Gaston. Eventually the property was transferred to the employee ownership stock plan at the Booker T. Washington Insurance Company, which means that employees now own both their company and the two cemeteries, which are both beautifully maintained. Both cemeteries sell pre-need and at-need service. While there are, at present, no perpetual care laws in Alabama, the cemetery association, funeral homes, and suppliers are lobbying for the passage of some legislation.

Carver was born into an enslaved family; his mother was "owned" by Moses Carver. In 1894, he became the first black to graduate from Iowa State College, where he received a master's degree. He joined the faculty of Tuskegee Institute—"on a scientific basis"—in 1896 at the invitation of Booker T. Washington. There, Carver developed a program of research in soil conservation and crop development, among other accomplishments during his forty-seven-year tenure. Originally planning to be an artist—he continued to paint throughout his lifetime—Carver turned his creativity to science; emphasizing materials at hand, he devised hundreds of uses of and products from the most ordinary sources. In 1938, he used his savings to establish the George Washington Carver Foundation to continue his work for the benefit of humankind.

The Orientation Center and Carver Museum on the Tuskegee University campus are dedicated to the work of this incredible man, and to the contributions of both Carver and Booker T. Washington.

The Tuskegee Study

James H. Jones's book *Bad Blood* tells a strange story set in the city of Tuskegee, Alabama. It describes a study—held in the early part of the twentieth century but not revealed until 1972—wherein for forty years the U.S. Public Health Service (PHS) followed the effects of untreated syphilis on black male residents of Macon County, of which Tuskegee is the county seat. The Tuskegee Study involved a substantial number of men: 399 who had syphilis, and an additional 201, free of the disease, who were chosen to serve as controls. All of the syphilitic men were in the later stages of the disease when the study began.

Both Jones and Fred Gray, the attorney for the families of many of the men involved in the experiment, were questioned about the burial sites of these men. Both men indicated that those involved in the study were buried in various churchyard and family cemeteries and that no specific burial site was required for participants.

Bad Blood offers vivid details of the study's need to "bring them to autopsy." The need to perform autopsies on study subjects introduced a significant twist to experiment protocol. The study's nurse director informed the doctors overseeing the study that families were hesitant to allow the autopsies because of the resultant disfigurement. Because the idea of autopsy was distasteful to both the nurse director and to the relatives of those in the study group who died, a compromise had to be made.

continued on next page

Tuskegee Cemetery

A student at Tuskegee University was overheard asking a teacher, "Where is the cemetery where Booker T. Washington is buried?" She was told it was the place she walked by everyday, the unassuming cemetery where markers stuck up out of the ground. Located near the University Chapel and next to a parking lot, Tuskegee Cemetery is not a "formal" cemetery; it is overshadowed by a historic building that once served as the school's creamery.

Booker Taliaferro Washington was laid to rest on the campus of his beloved college, Tuskegee Normal and Industrial Institute, now known as Tuskegee University, after his death on November 14, 1915. A monument to his honor on the campus, attracting students as well as visitors, is stately in its dominance. Washington, born in Virginia in 1856 into an enslaved family, learned the value of both labor and discipline at an early age. He graduated from Hampton Institute after an early life of poverty and struggle. Washington later moved to Alabama, where he dreamed of building a school for black students in Tuskegee. Traveling for four weeks through rural Alabama to observe the people and assess their needs, the poverty and despair he witnessed reinforced his determination to model Tuskegee after Hampton Institute. Washington contacted a coalition of Alabama legislators and several northern philanthropists to gain the funding needed to build his school.

George Washington Carver, who died on January 5, 1943, was buried beside his dear friend, Booker T. Washington, in the small cemetery on the grounds of Tuskegee University. In addition to Washington and Carver, **Frederick Douglas Patterson**, who served as president of the university for twenty-five years and was laid to rest in 1988, and president emeritus **Luther Hilton Foster Jr.**, who died in 1994, are among all former Tuskegee University presidents save one who are buried here.

For many years, historic Tuskegee University was famous for offering vocational opportunities. In the 1950s, however, emphasis began to shift more towards a liberal arts curriculum. Tuskegee University, located at 339 Old Montgomery Road, stands today as the pride and joy of Alabama.

MOBILE, ALABAMA

Ebenezer Baptist Church, Oaklawn Cemetery, Lincoln Cemetery, and Gethsemane Cemetery - cultural symbols on the verge of extinction as related in *Lay Down Body*, first edition. Cheryl Washington, Mobile, Alabama reporter, writes:

If Lee Dinkin's grandfather were alive today, he would probably tell stories of death for black Mobilians, often mirrored life - separate and unequal. A century ago, black burials were restricted to plots on family homesteads, church cemeteries and, in some cases, white-owned cemeteries when there was a relationship between the deceased and a white family. Black servants were sometimes buried in their employer's family plot.

Dinkins has been digging graves at the cemetery for twenty years, having taken over from his father who took over from his father. Grave sites which are adjacent to the church are free to members of the predominately black congregation. Families of the deceased pay Dinkins $50.00 or $150.00 to dig a grave. While many visible barriers restricting integrated burials are gone, cemeteries in Mobile, like most around the country, remain segregated.

Although times have changed and Americans have become more tolerant of cultural differences, the grave remains a powerful symbol of African American culture and tradition, says Roberta Hughes Wright, who has written a definitive history of black cemeteries. The black cemetery is one of the few tangible monuments to African Americans, says Wright, co-author of *Lay Down Body, Living History in African American Cemeteries*. The book which

continued from previous page

Beginning in 1935, the PHS began offering burial stipends in exchange for permission to perform autopsies. The idea seemed to have originated in a request for a cash payment from the widow of the first subject on whom an autopsy was performed. According to the nurse, the woman asked "for a hundred and fifty dollars for her husband's body we performed an autopsy." This request was politely refused, but October 1934, the PHS submitted a formal request to the Rosenwald Fund for $500, with the understanding that the application would be renewed every year for the next ten years in order to provide ten burial stipends annually, each of $50.

The Rosenwald Fund refused, but in May 1935 the Milbank Memorial Fund, a New York medical foundation, awarded $500 to the PHS to pay the burial expenses of the men whose families consented to autopsies. Later, one of the doctors reported that the $50 that had been set aside for each death had been "insufficient to meet both the cost of burial and incidental expenses connected to the autopsy," and asked that the fund "continue to support this study to the extent of providing for a maximum ten autopsies per year." The request was approved. The fund renewed the grant every year for nearly four decades, increasing the amount of its annual appropriations as necessary to keep up with rising costs.

continued on next page

continued from previous page

The nurse director viewed these burial stipends as a godsend for many participants and their immediate families, who could not afford decent funerals. The cash payment also provided protection against losing the opportunity to autopsy subjects who died away from the hospital. "They would not let me know when somebody died," she observed. "[But] in those early days, fifty dollars was a whole heap of money for a funeral." Most of the families accepted the offer without hesitation, considering themselves fortunate to receive aid. The nurse director's interest in the families didn't end after permission for the autopsies had been granted. She attended every funeral service and often sat with the relatives of the deceased.

Wilbur B. Hughes III co-authored, explores the cultural tradition associated with African American cemeteries in North America.

Ms. Wright's father, Robert I. Greenidge, helped create the Detroit Memorial Park Association in 1925, because of the discriminatory treatment of blacks by white-owned cemeteries. Inconvenient hours and special side entrances restricted blacks from being buried in the city's white cemeteries.

Ms. Wright calls black cemeteries 'black history' because they offer an unique glimpse into some of the oldest and most fundamental values of African American culture. 'Much of this is only preserved in our cemeteries,' she said in a telephone interview from her office in Detroit, where she practices law. The history Ms. Wright speaks about is in danger of being destroyed.

Bishop Cornelius Woods of Mobile says he can't predict the future of Oaklawn Cemetery, one of the largest black cemeteries in the city. But the signs don't look good. Founded in 1931, Oaklawn does not offer perpetual care for its grave sites. Woods, who operates Oaklawn and owns Memorial Funeral Home, says it's the family's responsibility to maintain the graves at Oaklawn, and if families can't or won't, the graves to remain unkempt.

Some people never come back to the cemetery, he says. Oaklawn, like many black cemeteries, has no maps of its cemetery plots, Bishop Woods says. It's the family's responsibility. The ones who do come and clean the graves are the older people, but what's going to happen when they are gone?

Dinkins, the grave digger at Ebenezer says that although most of the older church members are familiar with their family plots, he occasionally has to choose a spot for a church member's burial. The cemetery at Ebenezer, which is about 125 years old, was recently enlarged to accommodate more burials and to prevent overlapping graves.

Lincoln Cemetery is located at the edge of the city limits. It dates back to the 1800s. The property was abandoned, but in 1973 was used to make way for Gethsemane Cemetery.

Hattiesburg, Mississippi

Hattiesburg, a city of approximately forty thousand people, is now famous because of its beautiful gambling casinos. It stands today a far cry from its former incarnation, a gritty industrial town on the confluence of the Bowie and Leaf Rivers about seventy-two miles from Biloxi, Mississippi. Before the Civil War, Hattiesburg had one of the smallest black slave populations in the South. Copiah County, of which Hattiesburg is part, was one of the last holdouts against the state of Mississippi joining the Confederacy.

The railroad lines that pulsed through Hattiesburg were a key lifeline for Confederate troops—and thus a frequent target of Union raiders based out of New Orleans. The first black regiment formed by Union forces in New Orleans used the area near Hattiesburg as a base for guerrilla raids against the rail lines.

Once the slaves were freed, many African Americans used the Southern Homestead Act to open small farms. Today, several families remain that still work land obtained through the Homestead Act in the 1860s. As the timber industry boomed and the railroads expanded, land prices quickly rose above the ten-cent-per-acre price blacks paid under the Homestead Act, creating a strong, black middle class in Hattiesburg. It was this middle class that played an active role in politics during the Reconstruction era and beyond.

John Roy Lynch, the first black to represent Mississippi in the U.S. Congress (1873), represented a district that included Hattiesburg. Another of the city's famous African American sons was **Jesse Brown**, winner of the Distinguished Flying Cross and the first black to become a U.S. Navy pilot. Brown was also the first black naval officer to be killed in the Korean War. In another honor, the christening of *USS Jesse L. Brown,* a destroyer escort, in 1973 made him the first black man to have a naval vessel named after him. Hattiesburg now has an African American military museum; a memorial to Brown stands at the corner of Country Club Road and Jesse Brown Drive.

Pineridge Cemetery–Hattiesburg

Pineridge Cemetery, owned by the Mt. Olive Church, is located on church

IF WINTER COMES

THE FROST HAS KISSED THE FLOWERS—
NOT WITH THE CRUEL TOUCH OF UTTER DESOLATION,
BUT WITH THE CALM CARESS OF TENDER LOVE.
HAVE THEY NOT DONE THEIR WORK?
SHOULD THEY NOT SLEEP A SPACE
AND WAKE WITH SPRING TO FULLER LIFE?
DEATH COMES AND TOUCHES ALL—
NOT IN AN ANGRY MOOD THAT BRINGS OBLIVION,
BUT IN A REVERENT HUSH THAT QUIETS PAIN.
FOR AS THE NIGHT DRAWS ON,
SHOULD WE NOT REST A WHILE
UNTIL THE TRIUMPH OF A BRIGHTER DAWN?

—**EDNA GULLINS,** *Negro Voices*

grounds on Country Club Road. It is approximately seven acres in size, and members of the church and the community are buried here. The current pastor is the Reverend Arthur Siggers. Hattiesburg residents **Alice Barnett, Ella Williams,** and **Cozy Hudson** are among those that lie buried here.

Scott Street Cemetery, Hattiesburg

This cemetery, used by the city's African American residents, is approximately ten acres in size. Buried here are **Mack Nunley, Camel Jackson, Mrs. Olivia Allen,** and **Joshua Harris,** who drowned at age ten in the city's Leaf River on June 8, 1995.

Riverview Cemetery, Hattiesburg

Riverview is an African American burial ground that has fallen into extreme neglect over the years. A local newspaper, the *Hattiesburg American,* described it thusly: "The tracks of small animals are visible in the sand and dirt near some of the sunken grave sites at Riverview Cemetery. Jagged holes in the earth reveal vaults at two sites. High mounds of untidy red sand hide some graves from view. Some markers slant at strange angles, following the sunken contour of the ground. The years of neglect are evident." The city of Hattiesburg closed Riverview Cemetery in 1994.

Shady Grove Missionary Baptist Church Cemetery, Hattiesburg

Still in use in Hattiesburg is this cemetery, located on Church Road at the point where Monroe ends. The white Providence Church deacons founded Shady Grove for their African American neighbors. In turn, the members of Shady Grove helped organize the other African American churches in and around Hattiesburg.

Shady Grove, which covers about ten acres, is the burial place of civil rights activist **Vernon Dahmer.** Dahmer was an ardent worker for voting rights for blacks. "If you don't vote . . . you don't count," he repeated just before his violent death at the age of fifty-eight.

One January night in 1966, three carloads of Klansmen in white hoods circled Dahmer's front yard, shooting rifles and tossing gasoline bombs through the windows of his home. Dahmer helped his terrified wife, Ellie, and their three children escape out the back before braving the flames and attempting to fight off the attackers. He died the next day of third degree burns.

Besides the Dahmer family, buried at Shady Grove are members of the Mott, Kelly, Craft, and Eaton families, the **Reverend W. Holloman,** and other church members.

St. Francisville, Louisiana, and Area

Visitors to New Orleans are usually fascinated by the strange, picturesque appearances of its cemeteries, so different from the grass-carpeted, tree-lined vistas and the marble and granite monuments of conventional cemeteries in other parts of the country. In most of the cemeteries in the area, the dead are buried above the ground in tombs resembling small, windowless houses, built close together, row upon row. The tombs are usually made of brick, plastered and whitewashed. Many are protected by iron fences with gates. The reason for constructing cemeteries in this fashion is the city's low, swampy soil and the climate, which boasts a rainfall of about sixty-four inches annually.

St. Francisville, also in northern Louisiana, up the Mississippi River from New Orleans and Baton Rouge, sprang up around a 1720 French fort. The parish encompassing it, Feliciana, is often referred to as English Louisiana due to its history of heavy English settlement.

Rosedown Baptist Church Cemetery, Louisiana

An anonymous donor bought the Rosedown Baptist Church and its cemetery and donated them to the church members, all African American families. The new owners had to negotiate with their neighbors, however, to create access from the main road to the church. It was also necessary to move the baptismal font and rearrange parking. Church members are buried in the cemetery, including the Reverend Lafayette Veal, former pastor of Rosedown Baptist. In a February 10, 1994 *New York Times* article, Peter Applebome wrote:

> On the surface, the majestic Rosedown plantation house, perhaps the most famous antebellum home in Louisiana, and the tiny Rosedown Baptist Church, most of whose 90 members are descended from the slaves who built the house, don't share much more than a name and some common soil.

> But often the surface does not tell very much about life in a place like St. Francisville, which is about as Old South as it gets. Just ask the out-of-town businessman who bought the plantation and is now trying to evict the church, bringing down the wrath of an unlikely alliance whose most visible members are black parishioners and white dowagers.

> "This is heinous, it's dastardly, it's so unkind and reprehensible I don't know what else to say," fumed Elisabeth Dart, president of the West Feliciana Historical Society. "It's morally indefensible to attack a church, and a small church at that. White, black, green, purple, it doesn't matter."

Since Rosedown was built, the plantation had belonged to only two families until last month [January 1994], when it was sold to Gene Slivka, a businessman from Townsend, Ga. He made an immediate impact, telling members of Rosedown Baptist, which sits on a tiny slice of the 2,000-acre plantation well away from the main house, that they would have to move. They had six months to demolish the church building and put a black fence around its adjacent cemetery, which they could no longer use.

"He came and told us the church is the people, not the building, and we would do just as well elsewhere," said the Reverend Lafayette Veal, Jr., pastor of Rosedown Baptist and son of its previous pastor. The current building dates from 1972, but the congregation dates to before the Civil War.

Blacks and whites have now joined in a petition drive, imploring Mr. Slivka to leave the church alone. There has also been much frosty public comment. Mamie Austin Rouzan, an elderly white woman, wrote the St. Francisville newspaper, for example, calling Mr. Slivka's action "a cruel blunder that even the veriest Scrooge would shrink from making."

When the dispute became public last month, Mr. Slivka told the *Morning Advocate* in Baton Rouge that the community should "appreciate that a sensitive owner has bought Rosedown." But he would not say why he wanted the church to go nor what he intended to do with the land. He has since stopped talking to the press.

Unlike many other black churches founded on plantation grounds, Rosedown Baptist was never given title to the land and has no lease. It is considering both legal action against Mr. Slivka and the possibility of trying to buy the land.

Some people here believe that racial amity coexists with white paternalism and that it is only Mr. Slivka's move against the church that has united whites and blacks in the same cause.

Many individuals and events have contributed to the heritage of New Orleans since its founding in the early 1700s. This heritage will be forever perpetuated in the city's cemeteries—lasting monuments to the men and women who, in the words of Henry Wadsworth Longfellow, "have left behind them / footprints on the sands of time."

Mount Olivet Cemetery

Established in March of 1918, Mount Olivet is located at 4000 Norman Mayer Avenue in New Orleans. According to the booklet *Preserving Black Heritage for Future Generations*, it is one New Orleans cemetery where "an afternoon's stroll past a number of picturesque, stately tombs and copings, and through contemporary mausoleum corridors provides insight into the city's black heritage. Throughout the years, many prominent individuals have chosen Mount Olivet Cemetery as their final resting place. Whether in the arts or business, education, medicine, or religion, these individuals have made their mark not only on New Orleans, but in their chosen fields, as well."

Following is a list of individuals that provides a sense of the breadth and scope of the contributions made by the black citizens of New Orleans:

Oscar "Papa" Celestin died December 15, 1954. In a city renowned for its jazz heritage, he was one of the greatest New Orleans jazz musicians ever to rise from the ranks. Affectionately dubbed "Papa" by Louis Armstrong, Celestin's musical talents as a cornetist and trumpeter surfaced around the turn of the twentieth century when he played with the Algiers Brass Band. He went on to establish the Original Tuxedo Orchestra in 1910 and the Tuxedo Brass Band in 1911.

Joseph A. "Cle" Frazier Sr. died January 10, 1985. Since a teenager in the early 1920s, Josiah "Cle" Frazier Sr. enjoyed playing the drums. Having begun when traditional New Orleans jazz was still in its formative years, Frazier's career as a jazz drummer spanned more than six decades. He started playing professionally around 1921 with Lawrence Marrero and, in 1923, was a member of the Young Tuxedo Brass Band. Frazier worked in the ERA and WPA bands during the mid-1930s, and performed, at one time or another, with all the leading brass bands of his day.

Alphonse Picou, a renowned jazz clarinetist, is best remembered as the creator of a celebrated chorus in the musical "High Society." He adapted a written piccolo variation of "High Society" for the clarinet. During the 1930s Picou took up the trade of tinsmithing—working with sheet metal. It was not until the late 1940s that he was seen with the Celestin Band or, more frequently, working in the Paddock on Bourbon Street. He died February 4, 1961, and it is said that Picou's funeral, held during Mardi Gras, was one of the biggest in New Orleans' history.

Herman J. Roth, who died April 8, 1988, was a native New Orleanian whose rise to fame was as a baseball athlete. His career began when he was fourteen years old, playing semipro baseball with the Grand Dukes. Roth made his professional debut as a catcher with the Caulfield Ads, which represented New Orleans in the Negro Southern League. In 1923, he was called up to the Negro Major League, joining the Chicago American Giants through the 1925 season. For the next four years Roth was back with the Caulfield Ads in the Negro Southern League where, as catcher and team captain, he lead the team to its first Southern League championship. In 1979, Roth was elected to the Greater New Orleans Sports Hall of Fame.

Dorothy Doretha Lawless, a lifelong resident of New Orleans and founder of the Dorothy Lawless Mortuary, was active in the Progressive Baptist Church, New Zion Baptist Church, NAACP, and the Ladies Tammany Social Aid and Pleasure Club.

Avery "Kid" Howard, best known for his interpretation of spirituals, was a trumpeter and cornetist who played in both his own and many other bands from the 1920s through the 1960s.

Emmanuel V. Gregoire was a public school teacher, principal, and newspaper columnist.

Octave Lilly Jr., a businessman prominent in the insurance industry, was a recognized writer whose works included the collection *Cathedral in the Ghetto, and Other Poems,* published in 1970.

Archibal E. Perkins, a civic leader and educator, served as principal of the R. T. Danneel School for twenty years. He also authored *A Brief History of the Negro in Louisiana* and regularly contributed articles to the *Journal of Negro History.*

Theodore L. Miller was a pharmacist who eventually used his pharmaceutical background to create face creams and soaps, which he developed into a very successful nationwide business.

Thomas H. Mims, M.D., though not a native of the city, lived almost seventy-five years in New Orleans as a practicing physician and active community leader.

Louis Reimonenq, founder and pastor of New Orleans's Calvary Spiritual Church, was a New Orleans native very active in the community, and a veteran of World War II.

Lillian D. Loeb was a Grand Worthy Matron Emeritus of Martha Chapter O.E.S., and Royal Grand Matron of the Masons. (See chapter twelve - New Orleans, Louisiana.)

St. Louis, Missouri

Black men and women have been a strong part of the St. Louis fabric since the year of the city's founding. St. Louisians prided themselves then, as now, on the efforts of blacks striving to bring about major changes in education, housing, and other facets of life.

A brief glimpse into the city's colorful history shows one such effort: the establishment of Freedom School in 1847. That same year, out of fear of a slave uprising like the Nat Turner Rebellion, the Missouri General Assembly passed one of the harshest laws against blacks: one prohibiting Negroes or mulattos from learning to read or write.

This did not discourage the **Reverend John Berry Meachum.** He defied the laws of Missouri by building a steamboat and anchoring it in the middle of the river—federal territory outside the jurisdiction of the Missouri authorities. Each morning Meachum picked up his students from the riverbank and took them to his "boat school" to learn reading, writing, and arithmetic. At the end of each day he returned them to the bank. Meachum's floating school became famous throughout the nation. During the 1840s and 1850s, hundreds of black children learned their "three Rs" in the middle of the Mississippi River.

The construction of the old courthouse in St. Louis, an interesting architectural example of government structures of its era, began in 1839. Its great historical significance extends back four years to 1847, the same year the Freedom School was established. During that year, a slave named **Dred Scott** appeared in one of the building's courtrooms to bring suit for his freedom. The Dred Scott case was in the state and federal courts for ten years. It became a raging political and social issue throughout the country and made Dred Scott the most famous enslaved person of his time.

The chief issue of the case was whether Scott was, in fact, a slave. His master had taken him into Illinois, where slavery was forbidden by the state constitution, and to the Wisconsin Territory, where it was banned under the Missouri Compromise. Ultimately, the case went to the U.S. Supreme Court. Chief Justice Taney ruled that slaves could not become free by escaping or being taken into free territory, and blacks could not become citizens. The decision started a furor that continued until passage of the Fourteenth Amendment at the close of the Civil War. By that time, it made no difference to Dred Scott; his owner had liberated him as soon as the case was settled and Scott died a year later, in 1858.

St. Louis lives up to its reputation as a city in the "Show Me" state. It is aggressive and innovative in its attack on the status quo. Improvements and beautification programs continue to make a difference. The Gateway Arch stands regally over a city that prides itself on being equally accessible to all parts of the country.

Moses Dickson Cemetery

Moses Dickson Cemetery is named in honor of the founder of the Knights of Liberty. Dickson was born a free black man in 1824, in Cincinnati, Ohio. According to the records of the Knights's exploits, his was "a gigantic, desperate movement. We expected to arrive at Atlanta, Georgia, with at least 150,000 well-armed men. Dickson advised his men to wait when the Civil War began. The Knights of Liberty fought with the Union forces. There were many casualties but Moses Dickson survived. After the war, Dickson became an ordained minister of the African Methodist Episcopal Church. He joined the successful effort to get the Missouri legislature to adopt the `separate but equal' doctrine that made black schools possible in the state. Moses Dickson, along with **James Milton Turner**, the country's first black diplomat, is buried in the cemetery."

Bellefontaine Cemetery, Missouri

Bellefontaine Cemetery is located on the city's northwest side, at 4947 West Florissant. In the old Baptist church lot of the cemetery lie buried the two spiritual advisors of Dred Scott: **John Berry Meachum** and Scott's pastor, **John Richard Anderson** of the Second African Baptist Church.

Jefferson Barracks and National Cemetery

There stands a marker on grave number 15009 in Section 57 of the Jefferson Barracks burial ground that recalls a hazard of nineteenth-century warfare even more costly than bullets. It is dedicated "to the memory of 175 non-commissioned officers and privates of the 56th U.S. Colored Infantry who died of cholera, in August 1866." The remains of these soldiers were brought here from Quarantine Station, Missouri. The probability is that these men were sent there from Helena, Arkansas, where their unit was stationed from March 1864 to September 1866, and where they most likely contracted the epidemic. Much of their service was in garrison duty, although they saw action at other points in Arkansas and Mississippi on several occasions. During two-and-a-half years of service, the 56th Infantry lost 674 men: twenty-five were killed or mortally wounded in action, and 649 died from disease.

New Cold Water Burying Ground, Missouri

New Cold Water Burying Ground is located on Old Halls Ferry Road, adjacent to Paddock Golf Course. The cemetery was created in 1866 by five trustees who purchased the one-half acre for $50. The deed specified that the land was to be used "as a graveyard or burying ground under the name of New Cold Water Burying Ground." The 1878 atlas showing a colored school and church already located across the street from the cemetery is a further reflection of the close-knit community that created these institutions. The 1909 atlas shows "African church and school" still in this location. Subsequently, they disappeared. Not much information can be had regarding who is buried at New Cold Water, but a walk through the grounds reveals old markers juxtaposed with the new.

St. Charles Borromeo Church Cemetery, Missouri

St. Charles Borromeo Church Cemetery is located on West Randolph Street between South Wheaton Drive and Mission Court. It was to this location that the remains of **Jean-Baptiste Point Du Sable** were moved in 1854. Unfortunately, his tombstone was broken and lost during one of the two cemetery relocations as the town grew. The first non–Native American settler in the region and considered the founder of Chicago, Illinois, Du Sable was born to a French mariner father and an African-born "slave mother." His date of birth is unknown; his place of birth has variously been reported as Santo Domingo, Haiti, and French Canada. After his mother's death, Du Sable's father sent him to Paris to be educated. Later, he worked as a seaman on his father's ship. After the ship wrecked, he came to St. Louis by way of New Orleans, with a French companion by the name of Jacques Clamorgan. The two started a trading business in the late 1760s. From St. Louis, Du Sable went on to Peoria and then to Chicago, where he became the first non-Indian to establish a permanent settlement in the area. In 1800, Du Sable sold his real estate holdings and moved in with one of his children in St. Charles, Missouri. He died a pauper; a priest at St. Charles Borromeo Church recorded his death as August 28, 1818.

Washington Park Cemetery, St. Louis

ALEX CHADWICK, Host: The time is 24 minutes past the hour. Digging began this week in a St. Louis cemetery that's in the direct path of the city's new light rail system. A court order is allowing the company that will operate the system, called MetroLink, to exhume about 2500 bodies and move them to other St. Louis cemeteries. Moving bodies out of Washington Park, the last large African-American cemetery in the city, has delayed construction of the $350 million rail line and led to opposition from some of those who have relatives buried there. NPR's Kathy Lohr reports.

Indianapolis, Indiana

Indianapolis prides itself on being a renaissance city. Famous as the home of the Indianapolis Motor Speedway, it is also an industrial and manufacturing center. The largest city in Indiana and a leading agricultural center, its downtown—as well as many of its neighborhoods—has seen extensive rebuilding and beautification. There are numerous African American "treasures" in the city, including the Madame Walker Urban Life Center and Theatre. **Madame C. J. Walker**, the first African American woman millionaire in the United States, moved to Indianapolis in the early 1900s and established numerous beauty shops and an entire line of cosmetics.

Sutherland Park Cemetery, Indiana

Sutherland Park Cemetery, the only black-owned cemetery in Indianapolis, is located at 4141 North Tacoma Avenue. It was founded in the mid-1930s and is just under ten acres in size. The owner of the cemetery is Melvin D. Thompson.

The cemetery management began a refurbishing program in 1993, which thus far has resulted in the addition of a wrought iron fence around its grounds, new columns adorning its entrance, a beautiful sign, and extensive landscaping and cleanup.

Presently, the cemetery is used by families who purchased grave space from previous owners of the cemetery. There are very few new grave purchases, but the present owner has begun to increase sales. Prices of the graves vary, depending upon location within the cemetery. Among the families buried at Sutherland are the Hollins family, longtime Indianapolis residents, and the Southgate family, interred here in the 1950s.

Also buried here are **Charles Horn** (1938), **Susan Horn** (1939), **Alphonse Petition** (1937), **John McGreevy** (1939), and **Ella McGreevy** (1954).

State of Kansas

Nicodemus, Kansas

Nicodemus, a small, Midwestern farming community, lies approximately two hundred miles from Topeka on the dry, arid, light-brown land of the high plains of northern Kansas. The town is a cluster of small and unassuming buildings, just off Kansas Highway 24. It is the welcome sign erected by the Kansas State Historical Society at the highway rest stop that gives visitors an idea of the uniqueness of this little village.

Nicodemus is the earliest Midwestern black settlement associated with the massive westward migration of former slaves out of the South during Reconstruction. Deliberately begun as a commercial venture, Nicodemus capitalized on the anxieties and desires of southern blacks for freedom, land, and opportunity. By segregating themselves on the great expansiveness of the High Plains, black settlers hoped to gain opportunities that the South simply would not allow.

The first residents of Nicodemus were largely Kentucky-born, although a wide mix of home states was present. Despite their origins, the settlers were united in their common experience as slaves.

After years of trials and tribulations that included intense racial problems with neighboring white farmers, Nicodemus today remains committed to preserving its proud history. In July 1994 the town celebrated its 116th annual "Emancipation Day" homecoming.

Although the town has few residents, the celebration drew some five hundred former Nicodemites, including businessmen and philanthropists, farmers and athletes, writers, nurses, and others. Children enjoyed attending the reunions and hearing stories about the black pioneers, four and five generations back, who arrived here in covered wagons.

The Nicodemus town company was formed April 8, 1877, by one white and six black residents of Kansas. By 1878 the town boasted nearly seven hundred residents. Its prominence was short-lived, however, when the railroad bypassed the community ten years later. A majority of the businesses relocated to nearby communities and the town slowly withered. About fifty descendants of the town's original immigrants still reside in the area and some historic structures remain.

Angela Bates, a Nicodemus native and historian, is president of the Nicodemus Historical Society. She is working diligently to have this National Historic Landmark designated as a National Historic Site so it can become part of the National Park Service.

The honor that the first settlers warrant is exhibited in the town's three cemeteries. The grave markers are visual reminders of the community founders. All three cemeteries are small, rural burial grounds, each with its own colorfully lettered sign.

Nicodemus Cemetery

Nicodemus Cemetery, founded in 1877, is the largest of the town's three cemeteries. In 1983, the National Park Service prepared maps and rosters for both Nicodemus and neighboring Mount Olivet cemetery, to help visitors locate areas of the cemetery that might be of interest. Nicodemus has several ornamental cedar trees and decorative plantings. The oldest known marker is that of **Junior** and **Vergie Vaughn**, who died in 1880. Members of the Alexander and Williams families are buried here.

Mount Olivet Cemetery, Kanasas

Also founded in the 1800s, Mount Olivet is one-half mile north and half a mile west of Kansas Highway 24, on County Road 183. The cemetery is on the former site of the Mount Olivet Sanctuary, begun by the Reverend Daniel Hickman. Hickman's first church, the Mount Olivet Church of Stamping Ground, was in Scott County, Kentucky. It was at this church that W. R. Hill visited and gave his most important sales pitch; three hundred families at the area relocated to Nicodemus as a result. When Hickman arrived, he started a church under the same name as his church in Kentucky.

The oldest marker on the site is that of **Norma Thomas**, who died in 1885. The Bates, Jones, and Moore families traditionally have used the Mount Olivet Cemetery to bury their dead.

A Celebration of 134 years

Samuels Cemetery, Kansas

The Samuels Cemetery, a few miles south of Wildhorse Township Cemetery in Bogue, is on land donated by John and Lee Anna Samuels, two early Nicodemus settlers. Historically, the Garland, Napue, Samuels, and Scruggs families of Nicodemus have been buried in this cemetery. The oldest grave marker is that of **William Napue**, who died in 1890. The cemetery is on a rolling, hilly stretch of grazing land, just southwest of the Nicodemus town site. It has few decorative plantings and no trees.

Port William, Kansas
Mt. Gillin Cemetery, Kansas

In 1870, Kentucky natives Walker and James Henry Johnson divided the NE Quarter of Section 9, Township 7S, Range 21E in Atchison County. The west half going to Walker Johnson and the east half going to James Henry Johnson. That same year the Mount Gillin Cemetery was established near the NE corner of the Quarter Section, on land donated by James Henry Johnson. On January 10th, 1896, a General Warranty Deed was executed transferring the land to H.C. Buchanan, Prior Dickey, Henry Dickey, James H. Johnson, Charles Ingram, James Prior, and Joseph Bell. The acre of land in a square was to be used as a cemetery, called and known as Mount Gillin.

The *Weekly Atchison Globe*, dated: June 27, 1907, states - Improvements have lately been made to the Mt. Gilead (Gillin) Cemetery, at Port William. The Cemetery was laid out nearly 40 years ago. The first person buried there is said to have been a son of the late "Uncle Billy Lewis," of Atchison. "Uncle Billy" was one of the patriarchs of the Port William settlement. Several interesting characters are buried in Mt. Gillin Cemetery. Among them, the body servants of two contending generals of the Shenandoah Valley campaign of the Civil War. John Halsey was Gen. Phil Sheridan's servant while John Taylor remained with Gen. Jubal Early throughout the war. Also buried there are Henry C. Buchanan, 5th US Cavalry, inducted in at Camp Wilson, Kentucky in 1864; John Farmer, Buffalo Soldier, killed in army service in the mid-1870's, and "Aunt Liza" Porter, who died at the age of nearly 103 years. This venerable colored woman was born on August 16, 1792, in Logan County, Kentucky and once worked for Gen. Andrew Jackson. She was acquainted with Henry Clay and other noted men of that period. Her 100th birthday was celebrated by the white and black people of Walnut Township in 1892. "Uncle Bob" Richardson, who cleared the timber from the present site of the Soldiers' home at Wadsworth, is buried there. He was also a freighter on the plains and a gold prospector in the West. Washington Marks, another tenant of Mt. Gillin, was for many years doorkeeper of the Kansas State Senate.

The Cemetery was incorporated "not for profit," by the State of Kansas on January 27, 1969, as the Mount Gillin Burial Association. The incorporators were: Adrian Boldridge, Hubert Craddock, Gilbert Campbell, C.J. Ferguson, and Kenneth Wallingford. The corporation was later declared defunct due to failure to file annual Corporation Reports with the state of Kansas.

On March 5, 2002, Articles of Incorporation of Mt. Gillin Cemetery Association were filed with the State of Kansas to reincorporate the cemetery. The incorporators were: Wilbur Ferguson, Amelia Jones, Elaine Tittsworth, Henry Buchanan, and Gorman Wallingford.

Chicago, Illinois, and Area

Chicago, a busy metropolis, was built in and around the Chicago River and along the shore of beautiful Lake Michigan. It is one of the country's most commercially successful cities. Its first permanent non–Native American settler was **Jean-Baptiste Point Du Sable**, an African American who arrived in the 1700s and is commemorated in the city's Du Sable Museum of African American History, established in 1961 by Dr. Margaret Goss Burroughs.

Dr. Burroughs, a writer, educator, historian, organizer, and cultural leader, is a distinguished artist in her own right. She is the author of several books and the recipient of many citations for her poetry. The Du Sable Museum, the oldest African American history museum in the United States, was first opened as the Ebony Museum in her home. In 1973, after a successful community-based campaign, the museum moved to its present location in Washington Park on the city's South Side. A twenty-five-thousand-square-foot wing named for Chicago Mayor Harold Washington allowed the museum to expand its extensive permanent collection of artifacts, books, and photographs. Among the holdings are original slave documents and civil rights memorabilia.

Burr Oak Cemetery, Chicago

Burr Oak Cemetery is located in Alsip, Illinois, approximately twenty minutes by car from downtown Chicago. Because of this, the cemetery services families from all sections and neighborhoods of Chicago. Unlike numerous other cities, Chicago allows funeral processions to drive on Chicago freeways and expressways. Cemetery vice-president Delores Johnson indicated that many funeral directors nevertheless prefer the surface streets because of safety factors. She also explained that five or six years ago the city ordinance was changed, prohibiting funeral cars from driving through red lights. The only exception is when written permission is requested and received from the proper authority.

Burr Oak Cemetery is approximately 120 acres in size. A small back por-

Dinah Washington was acclaimed by blues, jazz, gospel, pop, and R&B audiences alike.

tion of the grounds is designated as a nonperpetual care section. The costs for burial in this section are considerably lower than for other, more attractive, parts of the cemetery.

Burr Oak was purchased by a group of five or six black men in the early 1930s. It was operated as a memorial park with its markers at ground level. Although all of the original members are dead, certain members of the cemetery's current eighteen-person board have served for many years. The board chairman, John H. Johnson, is the publisher of *Jet* and *Ebony* magazines.

Many persons of both little and great renown are buried at Burr Oak. Among the more well known interred here are **Dinah Washington**, **Ezzard Charles**, and **Emmett Till**.

Dinah Washington (née Ruth Jones), whose singing style helped lay the groundwork for numerous rhythm-and-blues and jazz artists, died on December 14, 1963, at the age of thirty-nine, in her home in Detroit. She was buried at Burr Oak after a large funeral in Chicago, where she'd started her career singing gospel at St. Luke's Baptist Church on the South Side. With composer and critic Leonard Feather, Washington later gained legendary status with songs like "What a Difference a Day Makes" and "Unforgettable," and she proved to be such a versatile artist that she was acclaimed by blues, jazz, gospel, pop, and rhythm-and-blues audiences alike.

Emmett Till's murder at the age of fourteen provoked outrage within Chicago and across the country.

Emmett Till was a young resident of Chicago's South Side. In the forty years since World War I began, Chicago's black population had grown from some forty thousand to half a million. Many blacks had moved up from the South, seeking jobs and a better way of life. Fourteen-year-old Emmett Till was part of this immigrant community. On August 20, 1955, he was in the delta town of Money, Mississippi, population fifty-five, to visit relatives still living on his family's home place.

Till was accused of saying, "Bye baby" to a white woman in a candy store; a few nights later he was taken from his uncle's house and killed, his body later found in the Tallahatchie River. His mother, Mamie Till, wanting the world to see her son's mutilated corpse, brought his body back to Chicago. The black press was outraged about the killing. *Jet* magazine ran a photograph of the corpse. The *Chicago Defender*, one of the country's largest national black weeklies, gave the Till case and the open-casket funeral prominent coverage. Till's body was buried in Burr Oak Cemetery.

Miller Grove Cemetery, Illinois

Miller Grove Cemetery, while located near the Macedonia Free Will Baptist

Church in Golconda, is far less accessible than the church. Even in dry weather it is recommended to come by truck or have a good pair of hiking boots. The old Miller Grove Cemetery is the last remaining vestige of what once was an early African American settlement. Some burials date back as far as 1865.

Some claim that this area was the first all-black community in Illinois, established before the Civil War. Free families came to the area as early as the 1830s. All, however, had departed by 1925.

Free Frank McWorter Burial Site

The cemetery of the McWorter family is located less than twenty miles from the Mississippi River across from Hannibal, Missouri. This cemetery is one of only three Illinois sites listed on the National Register of Historic Places.

Dr. Juliet E. K. Walker, great-great-granddaughter of Free Frank and a professor of history at the University of Illinois at Urbana, notes in her biography of Free Frank that he was "an ex-slave who purchased his own freedom and that of fifteen of his family members at a total cost of about $15,000."

Frank McWorter was born in 1777 and came to Illinois from South Carolina, via Kentucky, making the six-hundred-mile journey in a covered wagon. McWorter, a saltpeter manufacturer, small land speculator, commer-

Many persons of renown are buried at Chicago's Burr Oak Cemetery.

cial farmer, and town founder, died in 1854.

Though no longer in existence, New Philadelphia, the town Free Frank founded in 1836, was, until the 1880s, a thriving frontier community that served as a way station for travelers heading west on Illinois roads. The site of the station is commemorated by a marker.

Detroit, Michigan and Area

Founded in 1701, in the name of Louis XIV of France at *le place du détroit* (the place of the strait), this was a quiet city—until the automobile changed it forever.

Falling into decay after the racial tumult of the 1960s dislodged its formerly close neighborhoods, by the mid-1990s Detroit, Michigan, has become a city once again on the move. The beauty of this motor-car capital, bordered on one side by the magnificent Detroit River and neighboring Canada, is slowly being revived. Detroit's cultural center is home to some twenty cultural institutions, including the Charles H. Wright Museum of African American History, the Detroit Institute of Arts, the Science Museum, and Wayne State University. Among its other jewels are the Motown Museum, the New Center area, and some magnificent residential areas such as Rosedale Park, Palmer Woods, Sherwood Forest, and to the east, Indian Village.

The beautiful grounds of Detroit Memorial Park, East and West, and Gracelawn Cemetery in Flint, Michigan are among the jewels of the city. Detroit Memorial Park is the oldest African American–owned corporation in Michigan.

Detroit Memorial Park Cemetery,
East and West and Gracelawn cemetery
Flint, Michigan

Detroit Memorial Park Association owns three cemeteries: The East cemetery is located on eighty-five acres at 4280 East 13 Mile Road in Warren; a sixty-two-acre site at 25200 Plymouth Road in Redford - Detroit Memorial Park West and Gracelawn Cemetery in Flint.

Prior to 1925, blacks in Detroit suffered unspeakable indignities because of the white-operated cemeteries. A few of these cemeteries allowed burials of blacks but only on certain designated days and at inconvenient burial hours, and most often the funeral entourage was directed to a side entrance. Added to this were the exorbitant fees charged for the burial of a black person.

This embarrassment and degradation inspired a small group of business and professional men, under the leadership of funeral director Charles C. Diggs Sr., to purchase land for a cemetery of their own. When Diggs announced the idea of the sale of stock for the purchase of land, many local businessmen responded, recommending investment in the cemetery to their friends and clients and writing newspaper articles of endorsement. The other real "angels" in this venture were the ministers. They advised their congregations to invest in a corporation that would grow and repay them, someday, and a place where they could lay loved ones to rest with full dignity and complete satisfaction. The Detroit Memorial Park Association was incorporated in July 1925, with thirteen persons selected as the first board of directors.

During the spring of 1926, special meetings were held to consider methods of raising the money necessary to pay for the property in full. Since Michigan cemetery laws required that land available for human burial could not be encumbered by a mortgage, the organizers were forced to borrow money, on faith and credit. The only lending institution willing to extend credit to the corporation was the newly organized Michigan Mutual Savings Bank, which insisted that association investors make deposits in its bank. Board members and stockholders faced a monumental task: secure the $25,000 loan they required with an equal amount of cash deposits in the bank. Amazingly, they succeeded. Among the fifty initial investors who purchased shares in 1925 and 1926 were Charles C. Diggs, Sr.; Robert I. Greenidge, M.D.; Reverend Robert L. Bradby; Haley Bell, DDS; Aaron Toodle; Henry S. Dunbar; Walter O. Allen, M.D.; Cornelius L. Henderson and Walton A. Lewis.

The cemetery was designed in accordance with the "Memorial Park Plan," meaning there would be no upright grave markers or monuments. A Perpetual Care Fund was to be set aside from each burial or lot sale, its interest to be used to keep the cemetery beautiful forever.

With the money in hand, the board purchased a total of eight-five acres of farmland in what was then Warren Township. Although the Township community had agreed to sell to black investors, soon after the land was sold, some within the community urged the Township not to sell the land. The board hastily agreed that in order to prevent a legally successful reacquisition, a burial or interment had to be made on the property. On the night of October 30, 1926, two morticians unceremoniously buried a stillborn baby, **Emma L. Brown**, on the grounds, thus evaporating any opposition to their intended use of the land.

The grounds are divided into sections and in some areas, into gardens, each with its distinctive feature or marker, bearing names such as "Garden of the Cross," "Garden of Love," and "Garden of Prayer." There are also sections for burial of children and a veterans' section.

In the 1940s and 1950s the board began studying the process of dou-

Detroit Memorial Park was founded by and for the African American community in the mid-1920s.

DETROIT MEMORIAL PARK CEMETERY

Detroit Memorial Park Cemetery was organized in 1925 to serve the rapidly expanding post-war Detroit black population. Concerned with the indignities and poor quality of service received by the black community, several distinguished Detroiters established the cemetery to provide reasonably priced and dignified burials. This was the first black-owned and operated business of its kind in the state. Its incorporators included Charles Diggs, a mortician and acknowledged founder, and Dr. Aaron Toodle, a druggist and first president. By careful management the cemetery corporation survived the Great Depression and expanded into financial services. Famous inventor, Elijah McCoy, is buried here among doctors, lawyers, ministers, teachers, and business, civic and political leaders.

ble burials and of the construction of a mausoleum; a forty-eight tomb mausoleum was completed in 1971. The need for double burials became acute by the 1970s. After meeting with state officials, it was determined that double interments—using a large container box holding the casket of one family member and reserving space for another—were legal.

The first attempt of Detroit Memorial Park to acquire additional land was by the company's first General Manager, Wilbur B. Hughes, ll. Ten years passed before a suitable location for expansion could be found. At the suggestion of Wilbur B. Hughes, Ill, General Manager, the Detroit Memorial Park board began to give serious consideration to the purchase of National

Memorial Gardens, a sixty- two acre cemetery located at 25200 Plymouth Road, Redford, Michigan. On July 8, 1987, the board met to inspect the grounds, and soon after voted to purchase the property. The closing of the sale to the now-named Detroit Memorial Park West took place on June 25, 1988.

Immediate changes and improvements to buildings, signs, fences, and the grounds were made. The West cemetery had a steady and consistent growth. The company simultaneously beautified the grounds, improved the roads, constructed two mausoleums and late in the year 2000 broke ground for a new office building on the grounds.

In 1996, Detroit Memorial Park directors and stockholders agreed to purchase Gracelawn Cemetery, a 50-acre property in Flint, Michigan. This once beautiful cemetery had met with hard times and many Flint citizens were greatly disturbed by the appearance and neglect. After the purchase, the company made changes and improvements to the office building and

Emma Brown

First Burial, 1926

grounds. The city now views the cemetery with pride.

In 2001, Detroit Memorial Park purchased 2658/60 West Grand Boulevard. It is located in a historic area, surrounded by several long established African American owned businesses. The building was completely remodeled and renovated by the cemetery association and is used for auxiliary businesses.

In 2004, a beautiful new mausoleum and chapel were built at the East cemetery. The additional mausoleum is adjacent to the mausoleum that was completed in 2001 and attached to a beautiful new "chapel of the old rugged cross" that serves as a place to hold services and allows ease of visitation 365 days a year. In the spring of 2006, a mausoleum was completed with the capability to accomodate oversized deceased persons whose families prefer above-ground interments.

As mentioned, Detroit Memorial Park was a child of necessity created by the city's black community in its pursuit of racial pride and human dignity. As a result of the efforts of founders, shareholders, and supporters, the cemetery has been able to provide dignified burials for all. In addition, the cemetery association has returned significant portions of its earnings to the community through wages, donations to numerous organizations, and, during a period of economic depression, extended loans to residents. This attention to the needs of the community has produced one of the oldest and most profitable African American businesses in the state. The book *Detroit Memorial Park: The Evolution of an African American Corporation* by Roberta Wright relates the complete story of the cemetery, from its inception in 1925 to the present time. The story's interest lies not only in its description of the cemetery, but also as a chronicle of an African American corporation in the United States.

In the days, when so many corporations are experiencing difficulties, Detroit Memorial Park has maintained profitability. Throughout the years the company has always paid dividends and has exceeded requirements for perpetual care payments and obligations to the State of Michigan.

The Detroit area has a rich heritage of black-owned funeral homes. They are distinctive in setting, but universal in maintaining high standards and good business practices. On Memorial Day, May 31, 1976, the State of Michigan,

Left to right: Allen Rawls, Wilbur B. Hughes, III, general manager; Robert Bell Bass; Winona Rawls; C. Robert Bass, DDS, board president; Roberta Hughes Wright; William Andrews; George Dunbar

The Detroit Memorial Park

Board of Directors, 2004

designated Detroit Memorial as an official historic site, installed a historic marker on the cemetery ground.

Among those interred at this historic burial ground is Elijah McCoy. Born in Canada, McCoy studied in Scotland and moved to Ypsilanti, Michigan, after the Civil War. Interested in science, McCoy acquired some fifty-seven patents for his inventions, devices primarily connected with the automatic fabricator he designed for moving machinery. One of McCoy's most important and valuable efforts was the "drip cup", a small container filled with oil that flowed to the moving parts of heavy-duty machinery. This device

Elijah McCoy, interred at Detroit Memorial Park, invented the "drip cup" that helped perfect lubrication systems.

perfecting overall lubrication systems continues to be used in large industry today. McCoy was buried in Detroit Memorial Park in 1929.

Detroit Memorial Park Association enterd into a partnership Project with Fred Hart Williams Genealogical Society (FHWGS). The Society was the first genealogical organization in the State of Michigan formed to focus on the study and preservation of African based family history and genealogical research. In 2002, FHWGS donated three bound volumes of burial records from DMP East Cemetery, to the Burton Historical Collection of the Detroit Public Library. They are as follows:

#1   Interment Report 10/30/1926 - 12/31/1930
        (A-Z) Abernathy, Archie - Zooper, Della

#2   Interment Report 1925 - 1938
        Aaron, Isom - Hadley, James H

#3   Interment Report 1925 - 1938
        Hagerbrook, Willaim

In order to preserve the records for longtime use, FHWGS professionally bound the reports with special covers. More reports are in progress guided by Peggy Sawyer Williams, president of FHWGS and Barbara K. Smith, board member of FHWGS and stock holder of Detroit Memorial Park and project chairperson Rosemary Clemmons.

Current Board Members, all related to the 1925 investors are Dr. C. Robert Bass DDS, President; Wilbur B. Hughes, III, General Manager; William Andrews, Jr.; Robert Bell Bass; George Dunbar, Jr.; Allen Rawls; Winona Allen Rawls and Roberta Hughes Wright. The company controller is Tibebu Tsadik.

Dr. Bass is only the fourth company president in the company's eighty years. Previous presidents were Aaron C. Toodle, Dr. Haley Bell, and the Honorable Richard Austin.

Westlawn Cemetery, Michigan
(Wayne and Ypsilanti)

Westlawn Cemetery, located at 31472 Michigan Avenue between Merriman Road and Gloria Street in Wayne, was founded in 1920 by the Clearview Association, a group of prominent local undertakers. The association purchased eighty acres of land from the Merriman family to set up a predominantly Lutheran cemetery. The burial ground has been open to all races since its inception.

Metropolitan Memorial Gardens, Michigan

Metropolitan Memorial Gardens is located at 48300 Willow Road in Belleville, Michigan, a few miles west of Detroit's Metropolitan Airport near Lake Belleville. The cemetery was founded in 1958 by businessman Sid Frunkin and is currently owned by the Reverend J. Herbert Hinkle of Detroit's Cathedral Center of Faith, who purchased the land in 1985.

The cemetery is about seventy acres in size, and is well cared for. An impressive chapel graces the grounds, which include several plots owned by Detroit's Wayne State University Medical School to bury the remains of human anatomy specimens donated for research. The plots' inscriptions read: "These people died so others could live."

Among the prominent African Americans buried at Metropolitan Memorial are the **Reverend J. J. Worth**, founder of Detroit's First Baptist Church; the **Reverend Ray Jackson**, founder of Detroit's Church of God and Christ; Deacon **Henderson Hendricks**, **Zula Hendricks**, and **Donald L. Smith Jr.**

United Memorial Gardens, Michigan

(Booker T. Washington Memorial Park - 1929-1930)
(Mount Vernon Memorial Park - 1930-1955)

Although never owned by African Americans, at one time it was known as a "colored" cemetery. In 1929, a cemetery was established in Superior Township, which, by intent or through circumstances accepted a large number of indigent, welfare, and unclaimed bodies from the City of Detroit and Wayne County. It was a corporation owned cemetery operating for profit and there was no oversight from religious or government institutions, or from relatives or descendants of those buried there. Locally it was known as a "colored" cemetery and eventually it acquired the reputation of being a potter's field. Over the years, because of neglect and mismanagement it became essentially abandoned. In 1953, as a consequence of a change of ownership, United Memorial Gardens was created and promoted as an inter-racial non-denominational cemetery; Through the hard work and dedication of Edwin

Wensley, Jr., United Memorial Gardens rose from an obscure unkempt burying ground to the well tended and beautiful facility that it is today.

The sale was completed in September 1929 when Gastov Lidke, a farmer in Superior Township, Michigan, sold 2.9 acres to Park Estates, Inc., a Michigan Corporation of the City of Detroit. It was part of a 46 acre parcel owned by Lidke. Park Estates selected the name of their cemetery as Booker T. Washington Memorial Cemetery. A map of the layout was drawn on July 1, 1929 and the first burial occurred July 20, 1929 - prior to the completion of the sale in September.

In March 1930, Park Estates sold the 2.9 acres to buyers Arthur Cotzhausen, already the cemetery superintendent and to salesman, W.J. Smafield.

Karl Williams, author of this unfolding and interesting history of United Memorial Gardens informs us that the 75th burial occurred in February 1931 and the name of the business was changed from the Booker T. Washington Memorial Cemetery to Mount Vernon Memorial Park.

"The name change," he states, "was most likely because of the objections from the black community of a white organization using the Booker T. Washington name." There existed, at the time in Detroit, an African American organization known as the Booker T. Washington Trade Association. It also was probably that Cotzhausen and the directors wished to be less identified with the black community.

By all indications the cemetery was successfully operated during the 1930's and the number of burials was considerable. Mount Vernon Memorial Park derived a good deal of its interments from the indigent, welfare agencies, and unclaimed bodies of Detroit and Wayne County, and because of this it became known as a "colored" cemetery and a potters field. By the later half of the 1940's Mount Vernon Memorial Park had become unkempt and overgrown.

The cemetery was sold several times and had good years and bad years. On May 20, 1953, Mount Vernon Memorial Park, Inc. sold its interest to United Memorial Gardens, Inc. and to Ezra H. Frye and eventually to Ed Wensley. Wensley improved and expanded the cemetery and in 1996 sold it to the Loewen Company. It then was sold to the Summerfield Group. As stated, today it is a beautiful and well-operated cemetery.

Elmwood Cemetery, Detroit

In 1846, Elmwood Cemetery opened. The graveyard's 52,000 residents form a who's who of famous Detroiters; Six Michigan governors, 11 U.S. senators, 12 presidential cabinet members, 15 generals and many explorers, teachers, firefighters, police officers and inventors. Big names include Bernhard Stroh, Lewis Cass, Joseph Campau and Coleman Young. The cemetery's ancient trees and rolling hills offer a view of what Detroit was like before the land was leveled for fast food outlets, factories and gas stations.

Elmwood Cemetery stands in Detroit's Lower East Side and was founded in 1846. It is the final resting place for twenty-seven Detroit mayors, six governors, the builder of the first and third cars driven in Detroit, many figures from the American Civil War, and numerous others prominent in Michigan history. This beautiful cemetery sits along the banks of historic Bloody Run Creek, the site of the Pontiac uprising against the British. Like Historic Oakland Cemetery in Atlanta, Georgia, Elmwood is a beautiful historic landmark. Although the cemetery is white-owned, throughout the years many of Detroit's early black families selected Elmwood. A Black Heritage Tour, outlined by the cemetery, highlights black civil rights workers and leaders who are buried there:

Cora Brown, the first black woman in the nation to be elected to state senate in 1953.

Amos Burgess, an early civil rights leader.

Albert Burgess, son of Amos, and the first black child to graduate from Detroit High School.

Reverend Supply Chase, pastor of Second Baptist Church from 1861–1874.

Lomax B. Cook, considered by many to be the best barber in Detroit during the late 1800s and known throughout the Midwest as an unbeatable checkers player.

George DeBaptiste, White House steward and close personal friend of President Harrison prior to his residency in Detroit. He became a successful merchant and used his ships to transport runaway slaves to Canada.

Dr. Joseph Ferguson, a physician, community leader, and abolitionist. One of Michigan's first black doctors, he was a practicing licensed physician as a "freed man" in Richmond, Virginia, before coming to Detroit.

William Ferguson, the first black child admitted to Detroit's public schools in 1871. He became Michigan's first black legislator in 1893 and, in a landmark civil rights case, argued successfully as plaintiff attorney before the Michigan Supreme Court in 1890.

Elizabeth Denison Forth, one of the first black landowners in Detroit and Pontiac. An ex-slave who fled to Canada with the help of Colonel Elijah Brush in 1807, she worked for John Biddle, mayor of Detroit, for over thirty years. Money from her estate was used to build St. James Episcopal Church on Grosse Ile.

William Lambert, a community leader for almost fifty years. An important agent for the Underground Railroad and organizer of the "African Mysteries," Lambert owned a successful tailoring business.

Robert Millender Sr., an attorney and campaign manager for Mayor Coleman Young. Millender died in 1978. Detroit's Millender Center is named after him.

Benjamin and Robert Pelham, brothers who helped found the *Detroit Plaindealer* in 1883, the first successful black newspaper in Detroit. It was located at Shelby and State Streets.

Curtis Randolph, Detroit's first black firefighter to die in action. Randolph was killed in 1977.

Fannie Richards, the first black schoolteacher to teach in the Detroit public school system in 1871. She taught kindergarten and Sunday school and helped found the Phillis Wheatley Home for destitute and aged black women in 1897.

John D. Richards, a businessman and supporter of the Underground Railroad. The brother of Fannie Richards, he was instrumental in organizing the 102nd U.S. Colored Infantry during the Civil War.

James Robinson, who fought in the American Revolution and War of 1812. Robinson was personally awarded the gold medal of valor by General Lafayette. The oldest person buried in Elmwood, he died in 1868 at the age of 115.

D. Augustus Straker, known as the "black Irish lawyer." The brother-in-law of Fannie and John Richards, he was the attorney in *Ferguson v. Gies* (1890) and served as Michigan's first black judge.

Charles Stone, a famous orchestra leader in the early 1900s. His Stone Family Orchestra played on the Put-in-Bay ferries and, later, at Fairlane Manor in Dearborn. He was Henry Ford's favorite musician for social gatherings.

William Webb, an attorney, community leader, and abolitionist.

Charles H. Wright, M.D., a physician, author, civil rights activist and founder of the Charles H. Wright Museum of African American History.

Lorenzo C. Wright, who won the Olympic gold medal in the 480-meter relay in London in 1948.

Members of the 102nd U.S. Colored Infantry, formed entirely of volunteers from 1863–1865. The First Michigan Colored Regiment was organized at Camp Ward, which once stood on the present day Duffield School grounds. The regiment saw service in South Carolina, Georgia, and Florida. More than fourteen hundred men served in the regiment; ten percent gave their lives in battle. The regiment disbanded in October 1865. Among those Michigan soldiers fallen in battle and interred in Elmwood Cemetery are: **William H. Carter, London Floyd, Charles Gilbert, George H. Griggs, Greenbury Hodge, Albert J. Ratliff, George A. Holmes, Frank Robinson, William Riley, Augustus Stewart, Robert K. Russell, Henry Smith, William Shorter, Berry Thomas, Robert Thomas, Henry Williams,** and **Daniel B. Walker.** Although these names are not easily recognizable to most, their prominence in the cemetery forms a vital link to African American heritage.

See Appendix for Detroit Mayors buried in Elmwood Cemetery.

Philadelphia, Pennsylvania, and Area

Although many of the cemeteries in the East, as in the western United States, are integrated, stories of African American burials still need to be told. Northeastern cemeteries, particularly in the Philadelphia area, tend to be on a larger scale than in the South. However, the same struggle exists; the same fight for equality in life and death dominates the stories of those who rest there.

Evidence suggests that Africans arrived here as early as 1639. In 1694, three years after the first Quaker settlers arrived, 154 enslaved Africans were brought to Philadelphia on the ship *Isabella*. Many prominent area merchants, religious people, and political figures were involved in the trade of African men, women, and children, including William Penn and other members of the Society of Friends. A short distance from where the Liberty Bell now stands, enslaved Africans were once sold.

Where were they buried? As in New York City, Dallas, Texas, and other cities, burial grounds exist beneath many of the buildings. During the existence and legal acceptance of slavery in the "City of Brotherly Love," Philadelphia once contained the largest free African American community in the United States. As a result, pioneering black leaders and abolitionists created local institutions for the purpose of collectively challenging slavery and racism and championing the cause for the universal application of "life, liberty, and the pursuit of happiness."

Today, as in the past, Philadelphia boasts a diversity that provides a sources of strength and stability to the African American community. Although there are presently no black-owned cemeteries in use within the city of Philadelphia and the surrounding Philadelphia County, some burial sites in the close environs are black-owned, and most white-owned cemeteries in the city are now burying blacks. One such cemetery is Mount Peace on Lehigh Avenue.

Morris Cemetery, Pennsylvania

Historic Morris Cemetery was established in 1867 at 428 Nutt Road, Phoenixville, Pennsylvania. Located on the property is the chapel, which is also a historical landmark, as well as a Civil War monument erected in 1868. The monument marks the town's highest elevation in Phoenixville. Morris Cemetery is owned by John Walker, an African American who has been in the cemetery business for fifteen years and plays an active role in the community. With a diverse background in speaking, theater, and production, Walker worked at several other cemeteries before purchasing Morris Cemetery.

Morris is one of the first cemeteries in the area that allowed both blacks and whites to be interred together. It is also one of the few cemeteries in the area to offer a choice of markers or a mausoleum. Among those buried in Morris Cemetery are former governor **Penny Packer** and **Samuel Whitaker**, famous for his role with the American Legion.

Eden Cemetery, Pennsylvania

Eden Cemetery was chartered on June 20, 1902, as Eden Cemetery Company. Jerome Bacon, founder and organizer, was a teacher for the Institute of Colored Youth, later named Cheyney State College, as well as an employee of Philadelphia's Millbourne Flour Company. In his determination to establish Eden, Bacon motivated J. C. Asbury, Daniel W. Parvis, Martin Lehman, and Charles W. Jones to join him.

Eden Cemetery Company began with horse and wagon; today it has the latest equipment to perform all of its functions. While continuing to be black-administered, it has never been discriminatory and has all races reposing in the facility.

Remains from the First African Baptist Church Cemetery—also of Delaware County—dating from 1824–1842 were transferred to Eden when that church's cemetery was excavated during the mid-1980s. Also reinterred at Eden are bodies from the Olive, Lebanon, and Home cemeteries, which were moved when those cemeteries were condemned. Eden, comprised of fifty-three beautiful rolling acres, had, as of 1990, more than eighty thousand bodies reposing in its confines.

Some of the outstanding citizens interred in Eden since the cemetery's first burial on August 12, 1902, are **Stephen Smith**, founder and benefactor of Stephen Smith Home; **Col. John McGee**, black millionaire; **Amos Scott**, first magistrate for Philadelphia; **Ed Henry**, magistrate for Philadelphia; **Chris J. Perry**, founder of the *Philadelphia Tribune;* **William and Letitia Still**, authors of *The Underground Railroad;* **Dr. Caroline Anderson**, Philadelphia's first black female physician; **Dr. Rebecca Cole**, another female physician; **William Cole**, an ambitexter; **Caroline Lecount**, principal of O. V. Catto

School; and **Henriette S. Duterte,** first black female undertaker.

The Reverends **John Bunyan Reave, Charles Tindley, J. Campbell Beckett, Wesley Parks, William Creditt, Father McDuffy, Father Bright,** and **Bishop Ida Robinson** are also interred in Eden.

Several organizations acted upon their belief in Eden Cemetery's worth and purchased lots for their members, including the British Great War Veterans, Veterans of Both Wars, House of Refuge, the Association for Colored Orphans of Philadelphia, Home for Destitute Colored Children, the Prince Hall Masons, the IBPOE, Odd Fellows, the Cyrenes, African Presbyterian Church, Lombard Central Presbyterian Church, Wesley A.M.E. Church, Grace Union A.M.E. Church, Church of God and Saints of Christ, St. Thomas P.E. Church, St. Mark P.E. Church, Church of the Crucifixion, St. Mary P.E. Church, St. Simon the Cyrenian Church, and Union Baptist Church.

Merion Memorial Park, Pennsylvania

Historic Merion Memorial Park, in Bala Cynwyd, Pennsylvania, was founded in the late 1880s and is the final resting place of many prominent blacks.

The cemetery is in good condition, and the families whose loved ones are interred here are pleased. The new management has erected a sign, built a new fence, and made road repairs, and it has begun selling memorials.

The Merion Memorial Park was originally owned by James Smart. It was sold to John and Katie Laird in 1894, who immediately sold it to the Merion Cemetery Company. From the start, people of all colors and religions were buried at Merion. In the 1940s, Hobson Reynolds became the cemetery's first black owner; in 1947 he sold it to C. Percy White. Ownership then passed to his son, Donald White, who was succeeded by his wife, Rita White, the present owner.

In 1951, Asian associations began buying sections of the cemetery. Presently, five sections of the cemetery are owned by the Philadelphia Chinese community. They, like the African Americans, have had difficulty finding a cemetery willing to accept their business.

Of eight black sections, most are named for prominent personalities in black history. Among them is the Benjamin Banneker section, which honors the black scientist who served on the commission that planned Washington, D.C., and who, for ten years, edited a popular almanac published in Philadelphia.

The Charles Sumner section is named for the Massachusetts senator who, from 1851 to 1874, fought for desegregated schools and championed equal suffrage for blacks. Thaddeus Stevens, Pennsylvania congressman in 1848 and 1858, is remembered in another section. He was a chief anti-slavery and pro-equal suffrage spokesperson.

There is an Abraham Lincoln section and another named after George H. White, the North Carolina congressman who, in 1900, introduced a bill to make lynching a federal offense.

Among those buried here is **Robert Mara Adger** (1837–1910). Born in Charleston, South Carolina, Adger was one of thirteen children. In 1848, he moved to Philadelphia with his family and developed business skills working with his father. Later becoming director of the Philadelphia Building and Loan Association, one of the first African American mortgage companies, Adger joined the Black Enlistment Committee to help recruit black soldiers for the Union army.

In 1865, Adger served as a delegate to the first state conference in Harrisburg to discuss the creation of a Pennsylvania Equal Rights League. He later organized the Afro-American Historical Society, which contained his personal collection of rare books and pamphlets of black history and the anti-slavery movement. He died of a heart attack on June 10, 1910.

Not far from "Bishops Row"—resting place of six A.M.E. bishops—is the burial site of composer **James A. Bland.** Born on Long Island in 1854, he studied at Howard University and became a prolific songwriter and minstrel, living in London for twenty years. He authored "Oh Dem Golden Slippers" and "Carry Me Back to Old Virginny," which became Virginia's state song thirty years after Bland's death. He traveled widely, but died in obscurity at Philadelphia in 1911. Bland's grave is in the Catto section of the cemetery.

Also buried here are **Nehemiah James**, jazz musician; **Walter P. Hall**, largest wholesaler of meat and game, who employed many and paid them all the same as he paid himself; and **Skip James**, a well-known Mississippi blues man whose popular biography is titled *I'd Rather Be the Devil.* Old and stately monuments give tribute to the Allen family. Two black Philadelphia physicians, **Dr. William Warrick** (1900–1979) and **Orlando B. Taylor** (1904–1986), are also buried at Merion, as is the first black Philadelphia caterer of the Trower family.

Newport, Rhode Island

Founded as a shipbuilding center and port in 1639, Newport rivaled New York and Boston in importance in the seventeenth and eighteenth centuries; during the Civil War the U.S. Naval Academy was located here. The city's African American community was large and diverse and included a large number of professionals and skilled artisans. Newport's clergy was at the center of the abolitionist movement prior to the Civil War. Black clergymen in the city were prominent in the African colonization movement during the early nineteenth century, as well as the counter-reaction espoused by integrationists.

Slavery was abolished in Rhode Island in 1784, and for years following, Quakers and other abolitionists developed stations for the Underground Railroad. Portsmouth, Providence, and Newport have, through the years, built many cultural centers to highlight the accomplishments of these early refugees. The museum in Providence holds periodic displays of local history and also sponsors discovery tours of black roots in Rhode Island.

Today, Newport is a thriving resort town and is home of the Naval Underwater Systems Center. Historic downtown Newport is a bustling tourist attraction. The city lies on a beautiful harbor, the setting for many resort hotels and shopping facilities. Tours to the classic Newport mansions and the numerous museums are not to be missed. More details about the role of African Americans in the community can be found in the book *African Americans in Newport: An Introduction to the Heritage of African Americans in Newport, Rhode Island, 1700-1945,* by Richard C. Youngken.

"God's Little Acre"
Common Burial Ground, Rhode Island

In early times, this was apparently a large section of what was then called the Common Burial Ground in Newport, Rhode Island. Several of the markers in the cemetery include the words Negro, black, and servant. There is some indication that, possibly prior to 1865, some siblings—who had the same parents but different masters—had different surnames. Each adopted the name of the family for which he or she labored.

Portsmouth (Truxton), Virginia, and Area

Portsmouth, part of the Hampton Roads port, is known for its commercial shipping and shipbuilding. It is connected to Norfolk by two bridge tunnels and a pedestrian ferry that crosses the Elizabeth River. Truxton, a planned neighborhood of Portsmouth, Virginia, is unique in that it was built especially for workers in the nearby Norfolk Naval Shipyard, the largest naval shipyard in the world. The forty-three-acre community, designated for black families, was built around 1919 by the U.S. Housing Corporation. The 253 houses were surrounded by a church, school, grocery, and drug store. The Truxton houses were later sold to two black businessmen who, in turn, sold them to some of the original tenants.

In 1995, the Portsmouth mayor declared May as "Truxton Month," and more than three hundred families joined the parade and celebration that followed. Longtime residents, remembering the past, encouraged their children to take pride in the community. Catherine Harris Bowser and Lucy Overton are two of the residents who actively promote the community.

Lincoln Cemetery, Virginia

Black-owned Lincoln Cemetery, on Deep Creek Road, has eleven acres and is currently in use. It is owned by Vernon Wimbrough of Wimbrough & Sons Funeral Home. Lincoln was originally owned by the Smith "box container" family, but in 1925, its ownership reverted to the American National Bank. In 1935, Wimbrough began management and soon purchased the cemetery. Families maintain the cemetery, which displays a good appearance. Several prominent local persons are buried in Lincoln, including the Hall family.

Cedar Grove, Oak Grove, and Mount Olive Cemeteries, Virginia

Cedar Grove, which opened during the Spanish-American War, has only a few acres and is not currently in use. Oak Grove, which opened in 1910, has a section at the front of the cemetery set aside for black soldiers buried during World War I. Before World War I, the cemetery was divided into four parts, each owned by a separate black family. Two of the owners were undertakers. Mount Olive has twenty-five acres and was opened less than thirty years ago.

Elmwood Cemetery, Virginia

It is estimated that there were seventy thousand former slaves in Norfolk, Virginia, at the end of the Civil War. However, in May 1862, the city's fall before Union forces terminated its allegiance to the Confederacy. The city became a focal point for black refugees.

After the U.S. Army agreed to accept blacks into service, many were recruited from Norfolk. Elmwood Cemetery, located on Princess Ann Road in Norfolk, has on its grounds a memorial to the many black soldiers of the Civil War who are buried here. Elmwood also serves as the burial place for black veterans of the Spanish-American War.

Woodland and Evergreen Cemeteries, Virginia

Until about 1970, blacks could not be buried in city-operated cemeteries in Richmond, Virginia, so their only choices were privately owned Woodland, located just outside of Richmond in Henrico County, and Evergreen, a private black cemetery in Richmond. Unfortunately, maintenance of both properties had been neglected, and one citizen of Richmond reports that Evergreen had become so overgrown it had to be closed.

The death of world renowned tennis player Arthur Ashe in 1993 prompted Richmond City Council member Roy O. West to complain to city officials, who, with the help of the state, cleaned up Woodland in preparation for Ashe's burial next to his mother. Also buried at Woodland was Maggie L. Walker, the first woman to organize a U.S. bank. Her remains were later moved to Evergreen Cemetery in Richmond.

'FOOD TO DIE FOR' —AND SO MUCH MORE

Lynchburg, Virginia

"Food to Die For: A Book of Funeral Food, Tips and Tales" is a delicious read in more ways than one. You certainly don't have to be someone whose first thought upon hearing of a death, is "What shall I make to take to the family?" to savor it.

As the subtitle suggests, this book of more than 100 recipes compiled by Jessica Bemis Ward ("experienced cook, hostess, and most importantly, funeral goer") includes practical advice about making funeral food and also "for lending thoughtful, practical, non-edible support to those who are dealing with loss." Her "tips" cover, among other things:

   • Visiting the bereaved, which she assures the reader is "heartening and healing."

   • Writing an obituary. She begins by saying, "Start early. Write your own," then provide a list of the basic ingredients.

   • Writing condolence notes and thank-yous.

Ward's "tales" include explanations of funeral/cemetery jargon such as "cortege" and more colloquial terms such as "funeral Tsar" and "Dying order." (For those definitions, you'll have to buy the book!)

And then there's the food. Ward introduces not only each section (casseroles, soups, vegetables and side dishes, etc.) but each recipe, including cooking advice and other tips ("accommodates a crowd," "fabulously simple").

The cookbook, a project of the Southern Memorial Association to benefit the Old City Cemetery in Lynchburg, Virginia, is described as containing "Central Virginia's favorite comfort foods." No volume that includes a recipe for orange blossoms (which calls for almost as much sugar as flour) is likely to be mistaken for a diet manual, but Ward includes a good variety of dishes (lentil salad, black bean soup and baked eggplant are in there), and after all, this is supposed to be "comfort food."

There's a section called "pick-up food," in which one learns why a funeral repast should resemble a cocktail party—with or without the alcohol—

and, for gatherings that do include alcohol, "George Phelps' Bar List."

This charming cookbook is spiral bound for easy use, and is not only well written but also beautifully printed. Since most recipes are one to a page, there's plenty of room for adding your own notes. Stories and photos about the cemetery are mixed in with the recipes.

ICFM readers will want to know if this is a pro-preneed cookbook. Of course. Would we recommend any other kind? Passing along advice from "a young widow," Ward says, "plan funeral and burial arrangements while [you] have the wits and health, so that those decisions do not have to be made in a hurry by grieving families."

The African American Cemeteries of Petersburg, Virginia

Petersburg has long been recognized as having a special place in African America history. The First (African) Baptist Church, on Harrison Street, and Gillfield Baptist Church, on Perry and Gill streets, were organized during the last quarter of the eighteenth century. By the end of the century the area's free black population represented an anomaly in Southern society, and Petersburg, for reasons still being explored, appears to have been one of the most attractive locations for their settlement.

It is against this backdrop that a study was funded to explore Petersburg's African American graveyards and cemeteries, focusing on four still extant today: People's, Blandford, Little Church, and East View (which includes Wilkerson Memorial). Excluded from consideration are the several graveyards which have been lost to development activities.

The historic research not only focused on issues of ownership and the evolution of the property, but also on the role that African American lodges, societies, and organizations (both secret and fraternal) played in ensuring the proper burial of Petersburg's African American community. This, in turn, led to our exploration of lodge stones as a particular type of funeral marker not previously surveyed in the literature.

Associated with these investigations at People's, this study also explored several of the seemingly vacant areas (one of which was being considered for cemetery access parking by the City), using a penetrometer to determine if graves were present. We formed, as part, the study group that found that a number of graves were present, even in areas with no outward appearance of burials (i.e., lacking markers or even sunken depressions).

Incorporated into the research at People's was the preparation of a preliminary preservation plan for the cemetery. This information focuses on issues of access, routine maintenance, and historic "restoration" efforts appropriate for the property.

Although less detailed, research at Blandford's black section, Little Church Cemetery, and East View Cemetery provided not only historic overviews and sketch maps, but also allowed a much broader range of grave markers and burial practices used by the African American community to be examined. As a result, the study provides new information on the range and styles used by African Americans in the Petersburg area and compares them to other areas of the South.

The study covers a tremendous amount of ground, Petersburg's early burial grounds, the city's African American funeral directors, the historical development of several benevolent organizations, the importance of lodges and benevolent societies in the black community, the interconnections between the funeral directors and the ownership of cemeteries, the variety of mortuary art and styles found at black cemeteries, and more.

While due study has documented tremendous variation among Petersburg's five African American cemeteries, it also reveals broad trends and similarities. What is perhaps most significant is that none of the cemeteries are what you might call overtly African American. That is to say, at a distance, perhaps at the entrance, none of them could immediately be recognized as having some ethnic or cultural affiliation or peculiarities that would set them apart from the dominant white paradigm. From a distance they all appear more white than what some scholars have led us to believe black cemeteries should look like.

They all show evidence of one or more of the broad traditions of cemetery development; they all reveal styles of monuments that form what might be considered the main stream of American mortuary art; and they all have a strong adherence to the family plot as a central theme.

Returning to the issues of status and ethnicity for a moment, we have found that status has been very difficult to determine. We initially thought that the different cemeteries in Petersburg, which seem to overlap in use, might reflect different status. This does not seem, however, to be the case. We have found the same families burying in all five. We also see the same lodges using all of the cemeteries (suggesting that certain lodges were not tied specifically to certain cemeteries). It seems more likely that the choice of which cemetery to use was tied to which burial place was "in vogue" or was being best maintained at that particular time, or perhaps even to which undertaker you used. In other words, each cemetery appears to have had its "ups and down" throughout its period of active use and specific cemeteries seem more closely tied to particular undertaking firms over different periods of time.

With the acquisition of People's Memorial Cemetery, the city assumed a variety of obligations. Two of the most significant involve future use of the cemetery and the cemetery's maintenance. These are clearly important issues to the African American community in Petersburg.

With so much uncertainty, the number of deeds for People's lots and the general failure of families to record their own plots, it is prudent for the city to officially close People's and make plans for alternative burial locations.

Allowing continued burials at People's is courting disaster. Sooner or later an interment will disturb an earlier (probably unknown) burial. Although this is currently happening at adjacent Little Church Cemetery, the city should not allow it to occur at People's Cemetery.

History Lives on at Cemetery

The Old City Cemetery in Lynchburg, Virginia, run by the Southern Memorial Association, has a number of museums and educational displays. One display highlights burial customs brought to America by enslaved Africans.

Most of the customs depicted were practiced by the Bakongo people of west- central Africa during the time of the American slave trade (1550-1850), according to the cemetery sign, which also provides the following information:

• Grave goods were placed to honor the departed spirit and prevent it from wandering or returning to haunt the living.

• Bottle trees outside a home protect the household from evil spirits. Evil spirits are lured inside the bottles, then trapped there. Dirt from the grave was often placed in the bottles.

• Bed frames (under the bottle tree) symbolized "resting in peace" while the spirit journeys to the world of the dead.

• Dishes and jars were often broken to release their spirits and prevent the soul of the deceased from returning in search of them.

• Lamps and bonfires on the grave led the soul of the deceased to glory.

• Sacrificing a white chicken over the grave released the powers of the spirit world.

• Ancestral spirits could be seen in the bright sunlight reflected by shiny objects, including mirrors.

• Seashells, especially white ones, represent the world of the dead, which is white and connected to the world of the living by water or the ocean.

New York, New York, and Area

The African American presence both within New York City and throughout New York state has been most significant. The history of African Americans in New York City dates from the time of the Dutch settlement; the stories highlight the gross injustices, poor education facilities, and extreme prejudices of the period. This, perhaps, is the reason that, even after the Civil War, blacks chose to live on farms or in rural areas of the state and why the countryside is flanked by numerous small cemeteries. (See African Burial Grounds)

HUDSON-MOHAWK RIVER CEMETERIES

Cemeteries along the Hudson-Mohawk rivers and in the Champlain Valley contain the remains of many black soldiers. Some chose to join up with the 54th Massachusetts. Others stayed with the New York troops, becoming part of the 20th, 26th, and 31st U.S. Colored Troops. A small graveyard atop Cedar Hill holds the remains of two blacks, **John W. H. Atkins** of Company B, 20th Regiment, and **William Henry Jefferson** of the 8th Pennsylvania Regiment, who died on July 14, 1864, at Yellow Bluff, Virginia. The remains of two brothers who served with the 31st New York Colored Troops, **Charles** and **George King**, are buried in nearby Beekman Precinct. The remains of the **Freeman** brothers—**Agustus**, **John**, and **Perry**—lie in Union Vale Cemetery, also in Dutchess County. They served in the New York 20th Regiment of Colored Soldiers.

John Brown Cemetery

The John Brown Farm in Lake Placid, New York, is where the famous nineteenth-century radical abolitionist is buried. Fellow abolitionist Gerrit Smith deeded the land to Brown in 1849, and Brown lived there for a short time. Restless, he left in the mid-1850s to fight in "Bleeding Kansas" and in 1856, Brown and his followers won a victory over a large number of Missourians.

Brown was for many years busily engaged in anti-slavery activities and crusades. Famous in the annals of American history is his seizure of Harpers Ferry, Virginia. He was caught and executed on December 2, 1859, for his role as leader of the raid. After his death, Brown's remains were brought back to the Adirondacks. He, his two sons, and the ten followers who also died at Harpers Ferry are buried some two hundred feet east of his farmhouse. The John Brown Farm Historic Site is currently operated as a museum and historic site by the New York State Historic Trust.

Fort Hill Cemetery

Harriet Tubman, one of the most illustrious persons whom historians have ever studied, was buried in Fort Hill Cemetery in Auburn, New York. She died at the age of ninety-three and was buried in March of 1913. The cemetery is just three blocks from Thompson Memorial A.M.E. Zion Church, where she was a member. Born circa 1820–1821 in Maryland, Tubman, sometimes called "the Moses of her people," was enslaved and suffered harsh punishment. In 1848 she escaped to the North, but as a free woman she made plans to assist others. For the next ten years she made nineteen trips back into the South and rescued more than three hundred slaves. A reward of $40,000 was posted for her capture.

Tubman met and aided John Brown in recruiting soldiers for his raid on Harpers Ferry. She spent time in Canada and in South Carolina, where she was valuable to the army as a scout. Tubman's birthplace has been awarded a historical marker. The plantation, near Bucktown, Maryland, is eight miles south of Cambridge. Her home in Auburn, New York, is also on exhibition. It has been restored to its appearance during her lifetime and contains some of her possessions.

Los Angeles, California

Los Angeles and its surrounding area have beckoned African American settlers since the early 1900s. The largest influx of black settlers, however, began just after World War II. Many were families of military men who were assigned to the Army and Air Force bases of the West. Often the entire family became enamored of the semi-tropical beauty and the pleasant, all-year climate—a big change for those used to the hot, humid conditions of the South.

Los Angeles is home to the popular and frequently visited California Afro-American Museum. The museum regularly sponsors exhibits about the history, art, and culture of African Americans.

Angeles Abbey Memorial Park

Angeles Abbey Memorial Park is a beautiful resting place for the families of Compton, California, and other surrounding communities. It is conveniently located in the hub of Los Angeles County, only seventeen minutes outside of Los Angeles. The peaceful grounds are sequestered amidst Moorish, Byzantine mausoleums.

Within a ten-acre area, the owners built their first mausoleum, the famous Abbey of the Angeles, whose name arose from the magnificent stained glass window of the famed Millet painting "The Angelus," which overlooks the Cathedral chapel. The cemetery's mausoleums have won praise from visitors from around the world, who are awed by both their fine art and architecture.

Angeles Abbey Memorial Park is a composite of the finest old-world artistry and the enduring steel-laced construction of today. In 1933, during a most devastating earthquake, not a stone, tile, or panel of glass in the mausoleum was damaged, a testament to its construction. Angeles Abbey Crematory is equipped with modern, automatic "all-industrial" and "American" retorts. The park has an endowment care trust fund for future care of the cemetery.

David Reid, in *Sex, Death and God in Los Angeles,* tells this story: "It wasn't too long ago that finding a plot of soil to bury a black body posed a problem in Los Angeles. In some areas, private charters blocked these interments as late as 1966. African American families, in black veils and ash-gray suits, loaded caskets onto streetcars and rode to Evergreen Cemetery in East L.A. That is where three generations of the family of Jean Sanders are interred."

Ms. Sanders has watched this neighborhood change three times—predominantly white, predominantly black after Watts went up in flames in 1965, and then mainly Latino. Angeles Abbey has adjusted well to the community's changing face, welcoming the Gypsies, for example, who throw noisy feasts and roast pigs in honor of the newly departed, and the Vietnamese, who fill caskets with the loved one's earthy possessions, then decorate the grounds with ripe fruit and flora. The gang funerals, Sanders explained, despite what is reported in the dailies, have been low key and uneventful. "They come in, do their thing, and then they leave."

"These kids are more afraid of the known than the unknown," Sanders states. "They live with the known everyday. Live with a father on crack or a mother on welfare, maybe a brother in the gangs. They take their hostility out on buildings—mark it up with graffiti, break windows. They take their hostility out on people. They take human lives. I had a lot of babies coming in recently. A lot of babies. Young adults with gunshot wounds—victims of violent crimes."

Evergreen Cemetery, Los Angeles

This sixteen-acre cemetery located in the Boyle Heights section of Los Angeles was founded in 1877, and is one of the oldest privately owned cemeteries in the Los Angeles area. Evergreen was unusual at the time because its burial plots were open to all races and grave sites were not segregated by race. Among the most famous African Americans buried at Evergreen are:

> **Biddy Mason,** a freed Mississippi slave, nurse, midwife, and philanthropist who later became one of Los Angeles's more wealthy property owners before her death in 1891. She was the first black woman to own land in Los Angeles after she purchased a home on Spring Street in the heart of downtown Los Angeles in 1866. She parlayed that $250 pur-

chase into a sizable property empire. Her grave remained unmarked for nearly a century before Los Angeles Mayor Tom Bradley and members of the First African Methodist Episcopal Church donated a memorial tombstone.

Reverend William Seymour, a driving force behind the Holiness religious movement at the turn of the twentieth century, led the Azusa Street Revival in Los Angeles and preached that speaking in tongues was evidence that one had received the baptism of the Holy Spirit. Thousands of believers continue to visit his grave annually.

Mathew Beard, an actor who played the role of Stymie in the *Little Rascals (Our Gang)* comedy series.

Angelus Rosedale Cemetery

Angelus Rosedale Cemetery, one of the last cemeteries established in Los Angeles during the end of the nineteenth century, comprises sixty-five acres of land facing Washington Boulevard between Normandie Avenue and Walton and Catalina Streets. The cemetery was incorporated June 9, 1884, by the Rosedale Cemetery Association. The original stockholders included many prominent Los Angelians, like William Vickery and F. C. Howes.

Angelus Rosedale was one of the first cemeteries in the Los Angeles area open to people of all races and the first in Los Angeles to adopt the concept of a "memorial park" where the grounds were landscaped with decorative trees, shrubs, flowers, and works of art. It also housed the second crematory in the United States, built in 1887.

Among the prominent African Americans buried at Angelus Rosedale is **Hattie McDaniels,** known as Hi-Hat Hattie. She was a singer, songwriter, and actress who appeared in more than three hundred films during her career. McDaniels became the first black woman to sing on radio when she made her debut in 1915, singing with Professor George Morrison and his Negro Orchestra in Denver, Colorado. McDaniels, who was best known for her role as Beulah (1947) on the nationally broadcast radio series of the same name, died in 1952.

Paradise Memorial Park, California

In June 1995, the California State Cemetery Board took control of this once black-owned private cemetery, located in Santa Fe Springs about thirty miles east of Los Angeles, and shortly thereafter closed the cemetery. The takeover followed a scandal that involved the reselling of burial plots—a felony punishable by up to eight years in prison and a $5,000 fine per violation—and the alleged destruction of the remains of many of those interred there.

This small cemetery originally held about 2,700 graves, but it is almost impossible to determine just who lies where now. State officials have found dirt mounds scattered throughout the cemetery laden with disinterred remains, according to cemetery employees; one pile was reportedly seven feet high. According to *American Cemetery* magazine in August 1995, one mourner, Betty Campa, related her story to the *Los Angeles Times* in June 1995. Campa learned that the remains of her grandfather, who was buried in the cemetery in 1933, had been disinterred in 1992 and dumped in a pile. Six bodies were later buried in his grave. "Here I think I'm talking to my grandfather and I'm talking to someone else," she told the *Times*. "They said his bones were in that pile. It's too sacrilegious."

Among those buried at Paradise Cemetery is **Latasha Harlins,** a black teenager who was shot dead by a Korean grocer in Los Angeles in 1992, in an incident that triggered a sharp rise in racial tension between the two ethnic communities.

Washington, D.C.
Washington, D.C. Cemeteries
Old Methodist Burying Ground

Mt. Zion Cemetery
Female Union Band Cemetery and
Woodlawn Cemetery
These two neighboring cemeteries, situated behind 2515-2531 Q Street, N.W. in Georgetown recall the blacks who helped to develop a prosperous Georgetown and later the city of Washington. Long before George Washington's commissioners laid out the capital city, Georgetown was a thriving Maryland port on the Potomac River. Its residents included both slaves and free blacks, many of whom attended Georgetown's first Methodist church - Montgomery Street Church (now Dumbarton United Methodist). Deceased parishioners, white and black, were buried in the Old Methodist Burying Ground.

Because of the church's segregationist practices, more than 100 black members withdrew in 1816 to form a separate congregation, Mt. Zion United Methodist (now at 1334 29th Street, NW). The new church flourished despite the loss of some parishioners, noted in the registry as "sold to Georgia traders" or "escaped."

In 1842, a benevolent association of women church members calling themselves the Female Union Band purchased a property adjacent to the Old Methodist Burying Ground for the burial of free blacks. In 1879, Mt. Zion Church leased ($1 for 99 years) the Old Methodist Burying Ground, which whites had abandoned after Oak Hill Cemetery opened in 1849. Some whites even disinterred relatives for reburial at Oak Hill. Mt. Zion Cemetery along with the Female Union Band Cemetery form today the oldest predominantly black burying ground in Washington.

Interred in the adjoining cemeteries are some of the black leaders from the city's past: lawyer Clement Morgan; Joseph Logan, a principal of Shaw Junior High School; businessman Caleb Hawkins; and Charles Turner, sometimes called the black mayor of Georgetown.

As rising costs in Georgetown and opportunities elsewhere prompted many black families to leave the area, the congregation of Mt. Zion Church shrank. Neglected, its cemetery became overgrown with vines and weeds. Most of the hand-lettered wood markers disappeared. The last interments were recorded in the 1950s. The site almost suffered the fate of other burial grounds in Washington, as developers sought the land for apartments and townhouses. But in 1975 U.S. District Court Judge Oliver Gasch saved the two cemeteries, ruling "the violation of their graves involves the destruction of a monument to evolving free Black culture in the District of Columbia." He appointed trustees to oversee restoration and work for perpetual care. To raise money, a community festival is held on 29th Street each October. Surviving gravestones have been plotted and recorded; renovation as a memorial park awaits funding.

Woodlawn Cemetery

Historic Woodlawn Cemetery established in 1895, is the final resting place for thousands of Washingtonians, many of whom were known locally and nationally. However, the once beautiful grounds have deteriorated over the years due to the lack of perpetual care funds. Today, it is a continuing challenge to keep these hallowed grounds free of overgrowth and clear of debris.

Among the thousands of departed loved ones resting at Woodlawn Cemetery are those whose names are recognizable for their extended contributions to local and national history. Following is a listing of several of these individuals, many of whom have schools in Washington, DC, named in their honor:

Blanche K. Bruce was born a slave (sic) in 1841. By 1864, he had organized and taught school in Hannibal, Missouri. He later became Sergeant at Arms in the Mississippi State Legislature, a member of the Mississippi Levee Board, Sheriff and Tax Collector of Bolivar County, and County Superintendent of Education. In 1875, Bruce was elected to the U.S. Senate and served there until 1881. He held several political positions in Washington, DC, and was a trustee of Howard University and of the public schools of the District of Columbia.

James F. Bundy, born during slavery in 1862, was educated at Oberlin College and later at Howard University, In 1890, Bundy was appointed Secretary treasurer of the Howard University Law School in Washington, DC, where he served until his death in 1914.

W. Bruce Evans, born in 1866, graduated from the Howard University Medical School in 1891. He developed Armstrong High School, the District of Columbia's first technical school and was its initial principal in 1901.

John R. Francis was born in 1859, in Washington, DC. He graduated from Howard University and later from the University of Michigan School of Medicine. Francis was the first Assistant Surgeon at Freedmen's Hospital and in 1894, was acting Surgeon-in-Chief. From 1886-1889, he was a trustee of the public schools of the District of Columbia.

John Mercer Langston, born during slavery in 1829, became a lawyer, educator and representative in Congress from Virginia. He was also Inspector General of the Bureau of Freedmen (1868), Dean of the Howard University Law School (1869-1879), Vice-President and Acting President of Howard University (1872) and a delegate to the Republican National Convention (1876).

Winfield Scott Montgomery, born in 1853, in Mississippi, served in several prestigious positions elsewhere before making Washington, DC, his home in 1892. During a long career in the District of Columbia school system, he earned a medical degree from the Howard University School of Medicine in 1890.

Other Prominent Woodlawn Interments

Amanda Bowen: Founder of the Teachers' Benefit and Annuity Association.

Roscoe Bruce: Assistant Superintendent of colored schools, 1907-1921.

Mary Powell Burrill: A teacher of dramatics at Dunbar High School.

Will Marion Cook: Writer intellectual and noted musician and violinist.

John W. Cromwell: Writer, historian, intellectual, and first president of the Bethel Library and Historical Society.

William Andrew Joyner: Writer and scholar.

Frank Langston: Assistant Assessor and son of John M. Langston.

Jesse Lawson: Community organizer and leader, **Whitfield McKinley**, Collector at the Port of Georgetown, **Daniel Murray**, the first Negro Assistant at the Congressional Library.

Major Frederick Revels: A commander of the First Separate

Battalion. DCNG (colored).

James C. Wright: Teacher at Dunbar High School, "Father of the Three Cent Car Fare," and ardent fighter in the 1930s for the preservation of Woodlawn Cemetery.

1800-1895

Designated as the seat of the federal government in 1800, the citizenry of Washington, D.C. was indeed diverse. Free white persons, free colored persons and slaves interacted to develop the city into a thriving metropolis. Among the many social needs to be addressed was the need for cemeteries. In 1802, the city established two public cemeteries: the Western Burial Ground (formerly Holmead's Cemetery) and the Eastern Burial Ground.

Subsequently, several cemeteries dedicated to the interment of the black population were founded. These included Harmoneon (Harmony) Cemetery (1828), the Female Union Band Cemetery (1842), and Mt. Zion Cemetery (1879), all located in the northwest section of the city. Graceland Cemetery was founded in 1872 near the intersection of Benning Road and H Street, NE, and convenient to the section of the city near the Anacostia River. Eventually, disuse and city expansion caused Graceland's management to seek burial ground elsewhere and to establish a new cemetery. Thus, Graceland, a predominately black cemetery, became the forerunner of Woodlawn Cemetery.

1800-1895

Woodlawn Cemetery was established in 1895 at its present site 4611 Benning Rd., S.E. in D.C. The original officers of the association were Jesse E. Ergood, President; Charles C. Van Horn, Secretary/Treasurer; Seymour W. Tullock, Director; William Tindall, Director; and Odell S. Smith, Director. Many of these individuals also were founders of, or associated with Graceland Cemetery. The initial interments at Woodlawn Cemetery consisted primarily of more than 6,000 reinterments from Graceland Cemetery. These were made from May 11, 1895, to October 7, 1898.

No specific information remains regarding the appearance of Woodlawn Cemetery during its early years. However, there is little doubt that it conformed in upkeep to other popular cemeteries of that time and remained a desirable interment area. This becomes evident by reading the list of recognizable names of those interred there and by looking at the large and imposing grave monuments standing in the grounds. However, overwhelming factors caused this status to change. Foremost was that the sales of burial sites diminished while upkeep expenses increased. Thus, any funds once intended for perpetual care purposes were used for continuing maintenance and repair needs. By 1930, Woodlawn's beauty began to fade and numerous complaints arose regarding its untended appearance.

1930-1965

In 1933, civic leader J. C. Wright led one of the first efforts to highlight the need for maintenance at the cemetery. He circulated a petition that was signed by plot owners who complained of Woodlawn's appearance. Noted were miserable roadways, inconvenient briargrown aisles and antiquated vault facilities. In his plight, Wright proclaimed that the cemetery was a sad and humiliating challenge.

In 1936, Wright's action brought about new management of the cemetery. Known as Elmwood Memorial Park, Inc., this group improved the entranceway and added fencing and a small brick office building inside the main gate. The Elmwood efforts apparently failed, however, since Wright again complained that the deplorable conditions had returned by 1938. Woodlawn's care increasingly depended upon individual efforts.

Throughout these trying times burials continued at Woodlawn Cemetery. In 1940, for instance, the remains of 129 bodies removed from the Colored Union Benevolent Association Burial Ground were reinterred there. In 1958, there were 1,271 interments at Woodlawn. Since 1960, however, interments there have diminished significantly.

A second attempt to revitalize Woodlawn took place in 1961 when land speculator Louis Bell acquired a number of lots and became, in effect, majority stockholder in the Woodlawn Cemetery Association. From 1961-1970, Bell attempted to rehabilitate the cemetery through grading, clearing and restoring fences. Operating at a loss, however, Bell dissolved his interest in the cemetery.

1965-Present

From 1967 to 1969, the condition of Woodlawn somewhat improved as the Bell management responded to cleanup notices served by the District of Columbia Health Department. By 1970, however, maintenance of the grounds again reverted to volunteer efforts. On November 15, 1972, Bruce O. Hawkins led a group that incorporated as the Woodlawn Cemetery Perpetual Care Association. Its goal was to accumulate enough funds through donations to restore the area to a level of respectability.

During the 1990s, Woodlawn Cemetery was added to the District of Columbia's Register of Historic Sites and the National Register of Historic Places.

Today, the Woodlawn Cemetery Perpetual Care Association seeks financial and volunteer support to restore and preserve the beauty of this historic treasure.

African American Cemeteries in Arkansas

**(Listed on the National Register
of Historic Places)**

Dr. Frank Latimer gave a presentation about the cemeteries in Arkansas that are listed on the National Register of Historic Places. His information was educational and particularly interesting as he discussed the Bean Cemetery, the Hampton Springs Cemetery and the Scott Bond Family Plot in Arkansas' St. Francis County.

Dr. Latimer writes: The first property to be discussed is the Bean Cemetery near Lincoln in Washington County. Once associated with a Colored Methodist Episcopal Church (now demolished), the Bean Cemetery contains 251 burials of which 202 are historic (over 50 years old). The earliest date to be identified is 1874 and includes at least one man known to have been born into slavery. This may be the only property associated with Antebellum African American occupation in Washington County known to survive.

Following the Civil War, most former slaves remained in the counties where they had lived, often forming settlements of black residents. Lincoln was such a community. The Bean Cemetery was established as a central burial facility for African Americans in several neighboring communities. Because the other properties associated with African American history in the area have been lost, the Bean Cemetery has assumed social and historical significance to local residents.

The Black Section of the Hampton Springs Cemetery near Carthage in Dallas County contains 128 known burials. The earliest observed date is 1916 although local tradition holds that there are burials dating to the 1880s. One problem in locating these early graves is that commercial headstones are rarely encountered here. Markers tend to be homemade facsimiles of commercial headstones. Simple artifacts of stone or wood placed as headstone or footstones are encountered in great numbers. Glass jars, bottles, and urns are also found. Anthropologists have indicated that the burials display a distinctly African tradition.

In 1860 the population of Dallas County was 43% black, all of them slaves. Following the Civil War, most remained, forming African American communities. When the Hampton Springs Cemetery was built, it was divided into two sections. The Black Section remains the only surviving property in Dallas County exhibiting an African influence.

The last property to be covered is the Scott Bond Family Plot at Madison in St. Francis County. Built within what local residents call "The Scott Bond Cemetery" the Bond Family Plot contains the burials of Bond, his wife, Magnolia, and 10 of their eleven children (all sons).

Bond was born a slave in 1852 in Mississippi. His mother was a housekeeper and his father was the nephew of the plantation owner. By 1857, his mother was married to another slave and they were sent to the Bond Farm in Cross County, Arkansas. It is assumed that this is where Bond obtained his last name, it not being uncommon for freed slaves, who often had no legal last names, to take the names of their former owners.

Bond had no formal education beyond being taught how to read and do simple mathematics. But he was a man of strong character who favored hard work and self-reliance over waiting for someone else to take care of him. He started as a farmer, leasing acreage until he was able to buy his own farm. He continued to acquire property and by the late 1920s, he was the largest landowner in the state of Arkansas.

Bond never missed a business opportunity. He would ride his horse from his house to the fields each morning. He would stop along the way and set a trout line in the river. In the evening he would collect the fish he had hooked and sell them to neighbors along the road home.

Being ambitious, Bond opened his own lumber mill. He found that bricks needed to be imported as there were no brick-making facilities in Arkansas. So he built a brick-making plant. To learn how to make bricks, he went to a brick-maker and offered to work for free for a month to learn the business. When Bond arrived home, he found a check in the mail. The man who ran the out-of-state brickworks had paid him for his labor because he had worked so hard while learning how to make bricks.

Bond didn't want to hire architects to do what he could for himself so he designed several buildings that he had constructed to house his various enterprises. Not only was he the first black person to open many specific businesses in Arkansas, he was often the person of any race to do so.

On one occasion the woman from whom Bond had been leasing farmland sent her son to negotiate with him for the purchase of her land. They

Reverend Elijah Camp Morris, D.D. buried in Dixon Cemetery

met at lunchtime, and when the man invited Bond to sit with him and eat together, it was the first time in Bond's 49 years that be had sat at the same table with a white person.

Despite his own lack of formal schooling, Bond was an advocate for educating young people. He described taking children out of the classroom to work in the fields as "false economy." All of his own children who survived to adulthood were sent to college.

Bond did not appear to be a man who held a grudge. As he prospered in his 20s, he made a trip to Mississippi, visiting the plantation where he had been born. He wished to see his birthplace and meet his father, if possible. One of the reasons he gave was that Bond wanted to help him if he needed it. Bond met his former owner, who welcomed him into the house and shared information about the rest of the family. Bond learned that his father had died several years earlier, but he had three half-siblings living in the area. He went and met them, introducing himself simply as "Bond from Arkansas." They would never know that the man they met was, in fact, their brother.

Even with all of his other business ventures Bond was always a farmer. In 1933, at the age of 81 he died as he had lived; on the farm. He was gored to death by one of his bulls. His son, Ulysses, would later describe the incident by saying "he went down swinging."

Despite all of his accomplishments, all of the buildings he built, owned, lived and worked in during his long life, his final resting place is the only surviving property associated with this amazing man. This is why preserving cemeteries is so important. In many cases it is all we have left in the historical record.

Author Wright was invited to Arkansas to the First Cemetery Preservation Conference, "Reclaiming Our Past to Preserve Our Future." In addition to the Preservation of African American Cemeteries (PAAC, Inc.) the Conference was sponsored by a grant from the Arkansas Humanities Council and the National Endowment of the Humanities. We visited three Historic African American Cemeteries in Helena, Arkansas. The vice president and president of PAAC, Inc. - Tamela Tenpenny-Lewis and Phyllis Hammonds, along with other members, contributed to Arkansas' recognition in the United States African American Cemetery study consolidation.

Three historic cemeteries - Saxon Cemetery, Springlake Memorial Cemetery, and Dixon Cemetery reflect the same struggle as do the small African American cemeteries throughout the South, primarily but not exclusively. And as with other cemeteries, there are programs initiated to improve these lands.

In June 1999, the Arkansas Archeological Survey, University of

Arkansas System, conducted a cultural resources survey of the three African American cemeteries in and near Helena, Arkansas. With support from the Department of Arkansas Heritage and the Delta Cultural Center, Survey archeologists located, recorded and mapped over 400 graves in the three cemeteries. Many of the grave markers date to the mid-nineteenth century and have been damaged by exposure and vandalism, and obscured by thick vegetation. Other graves are unmarked, or markers have fallen and broken. There are many such small African American cemeteries in Phillips County.

What can historical archeology tell us that we don't already know? Actually, much that occurred in the past does not appear in historical accounts. Ordinary life was often not considered worth recording. Through archeology, we can discover unrecorded parts of the past. Archeologists have a suite of techniques at their disposal that allow them to find and record older cemeteries and related features, such as fence lines and artifact scatters. Our goal is to collect valuable historic data with as little disturbance to the cemetery as possible. All information collected during this project will be housed at the Delta Cultural Center.

Springlake Memorial

Cemetery

Under the auspices of the non-profit Phillips County African American Cemetery Association, signs have been erected at these cemeteries, and improvements such as clearing, construction of gravel roads, paths, and benches have begun. The brochure is intended to provide basic information on each of the cemeteries. It is hoped that descendents and family members will come forward to tell the stories of those who helped build Helena and Phillips County.

The grave markers reveal much about the lives of Phillips County's African American community in the late nineteenth and early part of the twentieth century. Many individuals belonged to fraternal societies that provided burial services at a reasonable cost. One of these groups, the Royal Circle of Friends of the World, was organized in Helena in 1909. Grave markers indicate that 14 men served in the military during the first and second world wars. There are several ministers and at least one physician among those buried in the cemeteries.

Dixon Cemetery, Arkansas

More is known about a famous man buried in Dixon Cemetery than we know of the cemetery itself. The focal point of the cemetery is a large and imposing obelisk-type monument marking the grave of the Reverend Elijah Camp Morris, D.D. Morris was the second pastor of Centennial Baptist Church in Helena (listed on the National Register of Historic Places), founder of Arkansas Baptist College, founder and publisher of the Baptist Vanguard, and president of the National Baptist Convention for 28 years. Members of his family, as well as those from the Adams, Anderson, Clark. Cooper, and Drew families, among others are buried in Dixon Cemetery. Dixon Cemetery is on

Phillips County Road 239, 1.3 miles north of intersection of Holly and Jackson streets, Helena, Arkansas.

Saxon Cemetery, Arkansas

The Saxon Cemetery may have been associated with one of the two large plantations that once existed in Lexa. One was owned by Judge John T. Jones, and the other by Charles Coolidge. It is a small cemetery, containing fourteen individuals and eighteen monuments. Individuals buried in the cemetery belong to one of four families: Hicks, Sutton, Jackson and Robertson. The earliest legible birth date is 1802, while the latest death date is 1900. Thus, Saxon is probably one of the oldest cemeteries in Phillips County. Saxon Cemetery is on Phillips County Road 218, off Southland Road about 1150 feet north of the county road in cultivated field, Lexa, Arkansas.

Springlake Memorial Cemetery, Arkansas

The Springlake Memorial Church and Cemetery were founded in 1872 by the Reverend Henry Pruitt. The church originally stood at the north end of the cemetery, and a brick-lined cistern still marks its place. The church subsequently moved, but the cemetery continued to serve the community, and is actively in use today. Springlake Memorial Cemetery is on Phillips County Road 222, off Southland Road in Lexa, Arkansas.

Odd Fellows Cemetery, Arkansas

The Beginning

This story is told by Robynne Carlson. The North Little Rock History Commission and the Odd Fellows Cemetery History and Preservation Group sponsored an Odd Fellows Cemetery Project. The birth and death of the project would be shocking were we not acclimated to this kind of action.

On October 20, 1891, the United Order of Odd Fellows purchased land from James & Elizabeth Burton for the sum of one thousand and fifty dollars ($1,050). The land located in Military Heights was used to bury blacks in North Little Rock until the late 1950s. In the space of time, on December 11, 1943 the Argenta Lodge #2197 of the Grand United Order of Odd Fellows sold the cemetery to E.S. Hubble for the sum of five hundred dollars ($500) who continued to operate and maintain the cemetery for seventeen years.

The Military Heights area was a poor black neighborhood in North Little Rock with no paved roads. In the early 1960's urban renewal was coming to Arkansas. Millions of federal dollars would be earmarked to create an intersection for the interstate and build a new library, police station with courts, post office and expand the high school campus. Private businesses such as hotels and restaurants would also be a part of the area now known as Pershing. So on October 14, 1960, Freeway Development, Inc. purchased the land still known as the Odd Fellows Cemetery from H.H. and Mary Hubble for the price of fifty-four hundred dollars ($5,400) for the purpose of building a motel directly on the site.

But there was a little problem for the whites who wanted the project. Not with the more than 2,500 blacks who lived in Military Heights and had to find new places to live, but the Odd Fellows Cemetery and the state statues that protected the integrity of cemeteries.

The Confrontation

Since there is no way of stopping progress, urban renewal is going full speed in North Little Rock. In December 1960, the new Police and Courts building was underway in the Military Heights area and would be the first building to be constructed. But before then in September 1960, the powers that be had gotten around the state statues protecting cemeteries by having it declared abandoned. Abandonment means: (1) No permanent maintenance fund, (2) Not suitably maintained and preserved, and (3) No burials within the last seven years since 1953, even though some have said there was a burial there as late as 1959 (20-17-905 Public Health & Welfare Statues). In April 1961, Freeway Development, Inc. commenced breaking ground to move the 711 bodies buried in the Odd Fellows Cemetery so that they can begin construction on the new Holiday Inn Motel.

On April 5, 1961, a temporary injunction was issued and halted the transfer of graves from the Odd Fellows Cemetery to Haven of Rest Cemetery in Little Rock. Curtis Morman of West 25th St. and Hazel Bright of East Broadway filed the suit which claimed ownership of burial spaces in the cemetery. Judge Williams who issued the injunction would give 30 days for others to come forward and enter the case. Approximately 30 people intervened and declared ownership of grave spaces and or they had relatives buried there.

In October 1961, Judge Guy Williams who issued the injunction halting the removal of the bodies from the Odd Fellows Cemetery, dissolved it and entered a decree sanctioning an agreement that the grave spaces would be made available in Gabriel Heights Cemetery in Marche and Haven of Rest Cemetery in Little Rock.

Gone, But Not Forgotten

In late January of 1963, the new Holiday Inn was open at 27th & Main Streets (formerly 27th & Orange) directly on top of the Odd Fellows Cemetery. In March of the same year the new post office was approved for location in the civic center area and a new health center was being erected in the new Civic Center (formerly known as Military Heights).

On Sunday, May 30, 1999, at the urging of Curtis Sykes, the city recognized the Odd Fellows Cemetery with a monument at the Laman Library (The Laman Library is named after the then mayor of North Little Rock who was instrumental in working toward a legislative bill authorizing North Little Rock to create an Urban Renewal Agency). At the one-hour ceremony speeches and apologies were made by politicians for dishonoring the people who were buried in the Odd Fellows Cemetery.

The Odd Fellows History and Preservation Group is still working towards identifying the names of all the 711 people who were buried in the Odd Fellows Cemetery. Curtis Sykes, a member of the History Commission says "This project is part of a larger effort to preserve African American History," and thanks the many people involved in making this possible.

Texas

College Park Cemetery

Houston, Texas

Don't expect to take a pleasant Saturday afternoon stroll in this graveyard. It's swampy, mosquito infested, often overgrown and dark, and, in the Houston heat, sometimes smells like rotten garbage. Many of the markers are broken or hidden in brush. Sunken graves, like potholes, make walking without looking where you're stepping hazardous. Despite several clean-up and restoration attempts in recent years, College Park's upkeep has never been sustained. Established in 1896, this primarily African American cemetery contains 4,400 graves on 5.2 acres. It was named after the Houston Central College for Negroes that was located across W. Dallas in the early 20th century. The cemetery is at 3500 W. Dallas in Houston.

It is a sad surprise to see the marker of the Jack Yates family in such a dilapidated cemetery. His house is one of the few that have been preserved in downtown's Sam Houston Park. Born in 1828, Yates was brought to Matagorda County as a slave from Gloucester County, Virginia in about 1863. After emancipation, in 1865. Yates and his family came to Houston where he worked as a drayman by day and a Baptist minister at night and on Sundays. Having been taught as a child to read, illegally, by his master's young son, Yates became a prominent Black leader in Houston. He was the first minister of Houston's first Black Baptist church, Antioch Baptist Missionary Church, which is still in use on Clay St. downtown. As one of the first Black Houstonians to own land, Yates urged other Blacks to buy their own homes and supported them in doing so. In 1872, he was instrumental in Antioch and Trinity Methodist Episcopal Church's purchasing of Emancipation Park on Dowling St. "for the Black people of Houston" (*The New Handbook of Texas*). He organized the Houston Academy, a school for Black children, in 1885, and made sure that his own children were all educated. Five of his children eventually taught school. Yates died in 1897 and in 1926, Jack Yates High School was named in his honor.

San Marco-Blanco Cemetery
Hays County, Texas

Ollie Giles sends the interesting stories of the San Marcos-Blanco Cemetery. The cemetery was founded by the San Marcos-Blanco Association in 1893 to serve the needs of African American residents of the surrounding communities. It is situated northeast of San Marcos, approximately halfway between the two communities which it serves, on what was then called the Old Austin Highway or Stage Coach Road, now called Post Road.

A total of 10.62 acres of land was purchased in that year, but the land was used as a graveyard prior to the purchase as records indicate the first burials in the area took place in 1886 and 1891. Emma Hamilton, born 1837, died August 15, 1886, age 49 and Lewis Tucker, born June 19, 1865, died January 1891, age 26.

For some reason the caretakers of the cemetery decided to change the

Arbutus Memorial Park,

Baltimore, Maryland

name of the cemetery to the San Marcos Colored Cemetery and the San Marcos Community Cemetery in 1981, only to revert back to the original name in 1996.

In addition to hosting the graves of African Americans, the cemetery also served as the final resting place for the destitute. At times the parcel was referred to as the Pauper's Plot. The grounds in parts of the cemetery are covered with bluebonnets and other wild flowers. Concrete markers are found throughout the cemetery. However, since the cemetery is over one hundred years old, it is felt that the dearth of stones may in fact be due to the fact that there are many unmarked graves, some of which are discernable only upon close examination of the grounds.

Later efforts were made by a new cemetery association to restore and take care of the beautiful historical burial site. As money was raised, they were able to have a cyclone fence installed and the grounds tended. After the fence was paid for, again funds stopped coming in. The cemetery fell in to disrepair and people disrespectfully began using the burial site as a dumping ground, a junkyard.

Like many other African-American cemeteries in Hays County, Texas, San Marcos-Blanco Cemetery became filled with tangled weeds obscuring the inscriptions on the old tombstones. Many of those buried here are in unmarked graves, with no more than a pile of rocks or a stone marking the site. The records of local undertakers are of very little help in determining some of the names, because in the early days of the cemetery, African Americans were often identified in mortuary records by nothing more than their race, sex, and cost of their funeral.

There are laws governing historic Texas cemeteries. The Civil Statutes of the State of Texas, volume 7A, Article 2351f, Section 1, shows that Commissioners Courts of the counties of this State are hereby authorized to spend moneys in the general fund for the purpose of maintenance and upkeep of public cemeteries in their respective counties. This writer went before the County Judge and the Commissioners and gave each one a copy of the Civil Statutes, reminding them of their obligation to keep that historic cemetery cleaned and looking good at all times. Today the upkeep of that beautiful site is great.

During the 109 years of the cemetery's existence, it has served the San Marcos and Blanco communities well. On 19 June 1997, the cemetery was honored with an Official Texas Historical Maker. The founders signed the deed on 16 June 1893; what a Juneteenth our ancestors celebrated then, buying their own property and paying cash for it. And now, 104 years later, we had another big celebration on the same grounds. An Official Texas Historical Marker for the San Marcos-Blanco Cemetery on Post Road. (Ollie Gates walked and read the cemetery in 1990. For information, write actors_65@hotmail.com).

Baltimore, Maryland

Arbutus Memorial Park

Arbutus Memorial Park has served Baltimore, Maryland community since 1936. Its eighty acres are located at 1101 Sulphur Spring Road near Rolling Road, not far from I-95, Wilkens Avenue and the University of Maryland Baltimore County (UMBC), in the historic African American community of Cowdensville. The entrance to Arbutus Memorial Park features fine stone pillars and wrought iron gates. Arbutus Memorial Park was established for the burial of African Americans and features rolling hills, traditional ground burial, lawn crypts, community mausoleum, cremation options and private estates. Arbutus although not owned by African American is the resting place to some of Baltimore's most distinguished and well known African Americans. Among them is William H. (Chick) Webb, musician; Cambria S. Murray, actress; Reverend Ernest Lyons, U.S. diplomat; Leon Day, 1995 Baseball Hall of Fame inductee and Negro Leaguer; State Senator Troy F. Bailey, civil rights leader; Al Sanders, television news anchor; Colonel William A. (Box) Harris, goodwill ambassador to Japan; Judge Theodore Hayes; Henry Parks, founder of the Parks Sausage Company; Carl Murphy, founder of the African American Newspaper; Dr. Emerson Julian, physician and congressman; Ben Taylor, Baseball Hall of Fame, Negro League; Dr. George Crawley, clergy; Dr. Lawyer Swinson, clergy; Otis Warren, realtor; Henry C. Johnson, principal; Alice Pinderhughes, school superintendent;

Herbert Frisby, first black Artic explorer; Jefferson Davis, labor union leader; Dr. Elmer Henderson, businessman and fraternal leader; Francis M. Wood, school superintendent and first private estate owner; Dr. Phyllis Wallace, labor economist and professor of Massachusetts Institute of Technology (MIT), and first woman to be named full professor. Arbutus Memorial Park also honors the remains of thirty-nine unknown Negro slaves. The cemetery is presently owned by Service Corporation International.

Mount Auburn Cemetery, Baltimore

Sharp Street Methodist Episcopal Church, now Sharp Street United Methodist Church, has owned and operated a cemetery as far back as the early 19th century. It once owned a cemetery next to the Wiessner Brewery on Belle Air Road (now Belair Road). It is reputed to have owned an earlier one, but that cannot be documented by this writer.

In 1872, the Reverend James Peck and the trustees of Sharp Street Church purchased land known as Mt. Winans from the Glenn estate. The Glenns were among the wealthiest whites of their time. The land near Mt Winans was populated by a substantial number of blacks. Mt. Winans had a Methodist Chapel, and there is every reason to believe that there was probably a small cemetery located there already. In fact, Owen Dorsey, Acting Steward for the Methodist Episcopal Church, applied to the Western Precinct Commissioners in 1816 for money to establish a burial ground at Mt. Winans. Under John Henry Smith, agent, the cemetery became one of the church's most profitable ventures.

Among the many people buried in Mount Auburn are doctors, teachers, civil rights activists, the first black ship chandler in Baltimore, judges, lawyers and at least one bishop of the black Methodist Church. Political and social leaders of Baltimore's black community such as the Mitchell family and the Murphy family, founders of the Afro-American newspapers are buried here. Katie Williams (?-1963), an undertaker lies here. Another notable black woman here is Lillie Mae Carroll Jackson (1889-1975) who was president of the Baltimore chapter of the NAACP for 35 years.

On May 21, 1894, a long procession of black dignitaries and citizens ascended the slope of Laurell Hill Cemetery to hear a choir assembled from various black Methodist churches and to hear Frederick Douglass speak. The occasion was to dedicate a monument to Bishop Alexander Payne, the senior bishop of the African Methodist Episcopal Church. At that moment and for many years before and after, the cemetery was a beautiful place and the "premier" cemetery for Baltimore blacks.

The land, bought in 1851 from Thomas Burgan, Jr., had "been for years

used as a burial ground for the black servants of local merchants and land owners". New Laurel, as it was alternatively called, was to become the first "non-sectarian cemetery for the exclusive use of Blacks".

Mount Auburn Cemetery,

Baltimore, Maryland

Some bodies from the Bethel and Sharp Street Church cemeteries, which were less than a mile from Laurel on Belair Road (then called Belle Air Road — now Gay Street), were reinterred in 1886. An act of the Maryland State Legislature had called for the removal of the bodies for road widening.

Further road work in 1911 caused the city, "without the permission of the Federal Government or the owners of the cemetery [to dig] up the remains of the Civil War veterans buried in the sixty-seven lots owned by the Government. The remains were reinterred at Loudon Park Cemetery on Frederick Road. Both the Federal Government and the owners of the cemetery filed suit against the city, a suit that was to remain unresolved for forty-six years". When the cemetery was dissolved in 1958, the suit became moot as the Federal Government reburied all the veterans' remains that could be found and very few private plot owners were left to do battle.

Those relatives and friends who buried 230 "colored soldiers of the

Federal Army" who fought in the Civil War between 1863 and 1865 must have felt they had done their best by them. What they did not count on was the neglect of time and the covetousness of mid- twentieth century man.

By 1937, the cemetery was in ruins. The Depression put the care of the living before the dead. Of serious consequence was the declaration of bankruptcy of the New Laurel Cemetery Company in 1952 followed closely by the creation of the McKamer Realty Company, whose chief aim was to acquire the property. Two directors of the company were Lloyd G. McAllister and Clement R. Mercaldo who worked for the city in condemnation proceedings and in the real estate division of the City Law Department. A third director was Dorothy M. Klipper, a legal stenographer who also worked for the city. McKamer is an amalgam of their names. The president of the New Laurel Cemetery Company was a real estate dealer named John G. Kaufman. Five days after the U.S. District Court declared the cemetery had no further value as such and had no monetary value, McKamer Company offered the cemetery company $100 for the 15.68 acres and took possession.

Then Delegate Marvin Mandel and his colleague in the House of Delegates, Carl Bacharach, introduced a bill in the 1957 Legislative Session pertaining only to Baltimore, stipulating a condemnation and order to sell off a cemetery that fit the description of New Laurel exactly. This bill was duly passed and signed by Governor Theodore McKeldin. In Maryland, cemeteries can only be dissolved by state law.

Using the new law as a basis, the McKamer company filed suit in Circuit Court against the heirs and next of kin "and some unknown" to force removal. After many city officials testified to the "neglected, sunken graves water draining to the street, broken or overturned tombstones, fires, refuse, weeds, tramps, attacks and other difficulties over a period of decades", the referee in bankruptcy authorized the sale of the cemetery to the McKamer Company for $100. Interested parties were to later state that the eviction notice was published only in *The Daily Record*, a paper read mostly by lawyers and businessmen.

Within a few months, in spite of the protests of the dispossessed plot holders, the cemetery's remaining Civil War dead were interred in Loudon Park and all others were reburied in a three-acre tract in Carroll County, specifically Johnsville, Freedom District near Eldersburg. Only 400-500 bodies were recovered from the nearly 3,000 burials made. The remains were put into boxes measuring 13" x 2' x 2 $^1/_2$ '. Witnesses saw stones crushed by bulldozers. The McKamer Company now prepared to take their profits.

Belair Road Enterprises, Inc., created in 1958 and dissolved in 1965, bought the property from McKamer for $15,500. A shopping center now stands on this once sacred ground. A longer article and a list of those who were buried here can be found in *Flower of the Forest; Black Genealogical journal*, 1984, at the Enoch Pratt Free Library.

Mt. Auburn Cemetery was founded in 1872.

On March 10, 1886, Sharp Street Mission Chapel Church was built on a section of Mt. Auburn Cemetery to provide a place for worship for the people of the Mount Winans community. On June 8, 1986, the deed was transferred to Mount Winans United Methodist Church.

Mt. Auburn, a city of the dead, is approximately 32 acres. One acre is 43,560 square feet. So, 32 acres are 1,393,920 sq. ft. Further, divide 1,393,920 sq. ft. by one grave, for example, 4' x 8' that is 32 sq. ft. As a result, you have 43,560 graves.

The cemetery is a model of the "rural" cemetery ideal made famous during the early 20th century revealing the customs of the times for burying the dead.

Baby Land was set aside for burials when families could not afford to pay for a grave.

Public ground was set aside for Baltimore City. Accordingly, Mt. Auburn Cemetery would have racially diverse burials. The cemetery, therefore, is integrated.

Mt. Auburn Cemetery is a primary source for genealogical research (African American families with roots in Maryland).

In Mt. Auburn Cemetery, an administrative office building has an office, work shop, bathrooms and garage. Also, there is a vault house. This has historical significance, but it has lost its use and occupancy.

Joe Gains, the first black light-weight boxing champion is there. So is Lillie May Carroll.

Jackson (noted civil rights activist) and Bishop Edgar Love (1st African-American Bishop of the Methodist Episcopal Church). The first black in Maryland to run for the U.S. Senate, the first black female doctor, scores of noted religious, business and education leaders are there.

But this gathering certainly is not limited to just the famous and celebrated. Mount Auburn Cemetery is the oldest African American cemetery in Baltimore City. Founded in 1872 as "the City of the Dead for Colored People", the burial ground's name was changed to Mount Auburn Cemetery and exists today as a monument to our history and heritage.

When Rev. James Peck and the Trustees of Sharp Street United Methodist Church purchased land in the Westport community of Mt. Winans, plans were made immediately to build, own and operate the first cemetery in Baltimore where African-American people could be buried with dignity.

And for 135 years, the cemetery has existed as a monument to the cultural, historical, religious, social and funerary customs of African-Americans throughout the State of Maryland. One would be hard-pressed to find a family or institution without some tie to Mount Auburn.

Mt. Auburn Cemetery was designated a historical site by the United States Department of the Interior on September 7, 2001.

OAK HILL CEMETERY - PONTIAC, MICHIGAN

Historic site -Elizabeth Denison Forth also known as Lisette

Apart from her final place of rest in Elmwood Cemetery, Detroit, the living memory of Elizabeth Denison Forth is also celebrated in "monumental fashion" in Pontiac. There, upon ground which once constituted her first real estate transaction of 48 acres, the present-day Oak Hill Cemetery includes both a stone and a state historical marker in Lisette's honor.

In April of 1825, Elizabeth Denison acquired a quit-claim deed to four Pontiac lots from Detroit magnate Steven Mack for the selling price of $226. Today the former landowner is remembered not only as the first black female to purchase property in Oakland County, but also to be among the earliest of black women to do so within the nation.

In October of 1987, the City of Pontiac planted a tri-colored birch tree near the stone in Lisette's honor. The stone's inscription proclaims:

"In memory of Elizabeth Denison Forth the owner of this section of the Oak Hill Cemetery. A slave who achieved freedom and was the first black woman landowner in Pontiac"

In the summer of 1988, a State Historical Marker was unveiled and dedicated by the Pontiac Area Historical and Genealogical Society. This marker includes a capsule of Lisette's legacy of slavery, her flight to Canada and her return to Detroit. The marker's text concludes with citation of her death, burial, posthumous endowment of St. James Episcopal Church and the fact that "part of Oak Hill Cemetery now occupies Elizabeth Denison Forth's property."

AFRICAN CANADIAN CEMETERIES

CHAPTER FOUR

Ontario, Canada

Canada was viewed by African Americans as a land of hope and freedom for millions of enslaved people in the United States. With the assistance of Quakers and other abolitionist workers—both black and white—many thousands of slaves were able to make their escape from bondage.

What was termed the "Underground Railroad" was a changing system of "way stations" with "leaders" called conductors. In the ten years preceding the Civil War, this network of "freedom roads" led from every slaveholding state in the South to states such as Michigan, Ohio, Indiana, Pennsylvania, and New York. From these states many chose to secure their freedom by traveling into Canada. The Fugitive Slave Laws of 1793 and 1850 marked the beginning of this massive migration. Although slaves escaped into Canada along its entire border, one of the most highly concentrated areas was southwestern Ontario, particularly the Buxton, Elgin and Oro settlements.

From 1800 to 1861, it is estimated that approximately forty thousand fugitive slaves left the United States for freedom in Canada. Canada's Slavery Abolition Act of 1833 virtually cleared the way for the safety of the fugitives. As early as 1793, however, Ontario had already taken the first steps toward abolishing slavery and many fugitives had already made their way to freedom by following the North Star.

Some of the early families settling in Canada were the Watts, Shadd, Riley, Morris, Binga, Prince, Shreve, Rhue (assisted by Harriet Tubman), Carter, and Hatter families. The Timbers, Smith, and Robbins families were among the thousands of others that settled in places like Amherstburg and Dresden (as in *Uncle Tom's Cabin*) as well as North Buxton.

Township of Sandwich East Cemetery

One of the oldest graveyards in the Windsor, Ontario area lies just outside the city in the Township of Sandwich East, Concession No. 3, west of Banwell Road. Here, in a section of Farm Lot 143, lie some of the oldest settlers of Windsor's colored community. There are many graves here; some are sunken and many have been overgrown by weeds. The stonework on many of these markers borders on art. Some that remain standing are those of **Eliza Bush**, born October 6, 1877 and died December 2. 1930; **Louis Smith**, who died December 10, 1922, at age 51; and **James H. Wray**, who was born in 1855 and died in 1931.

Other headstones are marked 1877, 1865, and 1870, but names are illegible. This was definitely a black graveyard, as Clarence Ouelette, the former clerk of Sandwich East, has verified.

North Buxton Cemetery

Buxton was a settlement of woods and fields through which passed the "unseen" railroad. North Buxton is a unified community located about an hour's drive from Windsor, a few miles from Chatham, and about a two-hour drive from Toronto, Ontario. It prides itself on its Annual Homecoming and Labour Day Celebration; 1994's celebration marked its seventieth anniversary. James Ricci reminds us in a May 24, 1992, *Detroit Free Press* article that no place helps us link the past to the present like a graveyard: "There's no forgiving slavery; there's no forgetting it either." There are two small graveyards at North Buxton, near Chatham, Ontario. The village was once part of the Elgin Settlement, a community of freed and fugitive American slaves established on the tabletop-flat southwest Ontario landscape in 1849.

North Buxton Cemetery, built in the late 1770s, stands flush with North Buxton's main road. The annual homecoming celebration takes place in the school and church grounds that surround the cemetery and the

Buxton Museum and Historic Site. The lovely cemetery seems more like a park; markers indicate the Shadd and Robbins family members. According to James Ricci's article:

> In its graveyards lie bones that are positively radioactive with the base element of the American dilemma. Buried there are men and women who knew racial division as the snap of the lash and the clang of neck irons, not merely the sanitized bigotry of office seekers in modern business suits.

> Stand, for example, at the graves of Dennis Calico Robbins in the North Buxton cemetery. Contemplate his story, the details of which are on file at the nearby Buxton Museum and Historic Site. Given his freedom on condition that he marry his master's slave mistress, who'd borne several of the white man's children, and that he adopt one of the master's ancestral surnames, Robbins. Dennis Calico (Robbins) died in 1871 at age 66.

> The wind vibrating the dandelions around his marker might bring the sound of clanking machinery from a farm on the other side of Centre Road. A stocky black man atop a huge John Deere tractor hitched to a discing machine might wave congenially. The name on the farmhouse mailbox is "Robbins." The 200 black Canadians who make up the pre-

A notable Canadian family, the Shadds, lie interred at Ontario's North Buxton Cemetery.

North Buxton's annual
homecoming celebration
takes place in the school
and church grounds that
surround the cemetery and
the Raleigh Township
Centennial Museum.

sent day North Buxton populace trace their roots to the Elgin settlers. Next, commune for a bit with Eliza Ann Parker (acquitted in the killing of a slavecatcher in Christiana, Pennsylvania, died in 1899 at age 82) and Charles Watts, (allowed to live free after saving his master's life during the Mexican War; died in 1903, age 86.) At the Elgin Settlement, people built and owned their houses, farmed their own land, set up prosperous businesses, forswore alcohol, built churches, and emphasized religion. The school they established was so advanced, white farmers preferred to send their own children to it, rather than to the local public schools. The Buxton National Historic Site and Museum director, Bryan Prince, hosted the 81st Homecoming Weekend and the 8th Annual United States/Canadian History and Genealogy Conference in September 2005.

Morris-Hatter Cemetery

About an acre in size, the Morris-Hatter Cemetery lies within a family farm in South Buxton, Ontario, fifty miles east of Windsor. Frances Belfon White cares for the cemetery, along with her sister, Letitia Belfon Bolden, and other family members who jointly own the property.

The cemetery was established in the late 1800s and named, in part, for **George** and **Mary Hatter** and their descendents, many of whom are buried in the cemetery. George Hatter was nineteen years old when he sought freedom

Frank Morris, the younge[r] of James and Barbara Morris's thirteen children, stands in Morris-Hatter Cemetery in the early 1980s, about ten years before he died in Detroit at the age of 101. He was the uncle and great uncle [of] this book's authors.

in Canada in 1837. He peddled goods along the roadside in Niagara Falls, Ontario, amassing a modest fortune. In 1844 Hatter married Mary Baker, who was born in Liverpool, England. Six years later, they moved with their five children to South Buxton, Ontario. One of their daughters, Barbara Hatter, married James Louis Morris, who lent his name to the Morris-Hatter Cemetery.

THE NORTH AMERICAN BLACK HISTORICAL MUSEUM AND CULTURAL CENTRE

Many slaves came across the Detroit River into Amherstburg because it was the narrowest point at which to cross. This made Amherstburg one of the Underground Railroad's largest terminals for coming into Canada.

he grounds of the Walls

istoric Museum site

clude a covered bridge,

g cabins, a museum,

ooded "escape trails,"

xciting to

oth children and adults.

In the summer many fugitives swam the river with their few belongings tied to their backs. During the winter months, many who saw snow and ice for the first time crossed the frozen river with great difficulty. Most brought with them new energy for developing prosperous farms and businesses, and focused their many skills into meaningful trades, like building churches, schools, and homes.

It was because of his deep concern for the past that Melvin Simpson founded a museum in Amherstburg in 1964. He wanted to uncover and preserve the record of the rich heritage of black people. In 1966 a major effort was undertaken to gather information and to establish appropriate research. The pastor and members of the Nazery A.M.E. Church raised money to build a hall adjacent to the church for the black museum. In 1971 five members of the A.M.E. Church purchased the adjacent property. A log house on the land later became part of the museum complex. The North American Black Historical Museum became incorporated on October 20, 1975. Melvin Simpson died on January 7, 1982.

FUGITIVE SLAVE CEMETERY, PUCE ONTARIO

Located less than twenty-five miles from Windsor, the Fugitive Slave Cemetery in Puce, Ontario, can be reached from Windsor via the QEW Route

401. This fascinating site, which includes log cabins, a museum, wooded "escape trails," and the cemetery, is exciting to both children and adults.

John Freeman Walls and his wife, Jane—the former wife of a declared slaveholder—made their perilous way from Troublesome Creek, North Carolina, through the woodlands of Virginia, Tennessee, Kentucky, Ohio, and Michigan. There were stretches when the only food was raw squirrel. Surviving endless weeks of being tracked by search parties, bounty hunters, and even a pack of wolves that John had to ax to death, their travels ended on the flatlands of Puce, thirteen kilometers east of Windsor, where the Puce River makes it meandering way. The story of their lives, described in *The Road That Led to Somewhere*, by Dr. Bryan E. Walls, epitomizes the contrasting triumphs and tribulations such fugitive slaves experienced.

After some years in Canada, John and Jane purchased land in Puce, Ontario. John, whose father, Hannabal, was from Africa, had never owned land. John told his wife, "I want to leave some land to my heirs and then have a family cemetery on it that is never to be sold. I want as many of your and my descendants as you desire, resting there, in a family cemetery, when Judgment comes."

John lived to be ninety-six; Jane died at age eighty-eight. They were buried in the Walls's cemetery, beside the log cabin he built and which still

John and Jane Freeman Walls, after their own harrowing escape from slavery, established the Fugitive Slave Cemetery in 1846.

stands on the historic site. The Fugitive Slave Cemetery was built in 1846. Among the family persons buried in the cemetery are **John Freeman Walls** and **Jane Walls,** known by all in the area for her active involvement in numerous organizations, groups, and causes. Also buried here is **Stella May Butler,** born August 16, 1884, and died August 13, 1986, at the age of 102.

THE HISTORIC ST. JOHN'S ANGLICAN CEMETERY, WINDSOR

The Historic St. John's Anglican Cemetery is located in the Sandwich area, Windsor, Ontario's west side. In June 2003, the Cemetery was horrifically desecrated. Over 200 tombstones, some weighing over two tons, were either broken or toppled. The Cemetery was vandalized in this terrible manner, causing multiple thousands of dollars damage. This Cemetery, with stones dating as far back as 1793, is the resting place of so many of the area's pioneers from both sides of the international border. The graves are those of the War of 1812 veterans, the United Empire Loyalists and escaping slaves who sought freedom by way of the Underground Railroad, and others. A community generated effort involving engineers, historians, parishioners, teen groups, trade unionists, war veterans, community activists, politicians, and people from every walk of life, continue to help restore this sacred and important site. In addition, groups such as Essex County Black Historical

Research Society, sponsored fundraising programs as did other organizations to help support the restoration.

JACKSON CEMETERY, CANADA

Andrea Moore writes that she attended a meeting in the Town of Belle River at the home of Councillor, Victoria Beaulieu. Victoria (and I) recently have become aware of an abandoned Black cemetery in Lakeshore (vicinity of County Road 42 and the Puce Road). The older folks in the community have known about it for years and refer to it as the "Jackson Cemetery".

It is called that because there is one well-preserved headstone that bears the names of Lewis and Mary Jackson. Lewis Jackson's side of the stone says, "Born a Slave in Kentucky, Died Free in Canada". The cemetery is in ter-

St. John's Cemetery was completely repaired due to the great financial support from the entire community. The re-dedication service was conducted by Bishop Bob Bennett in March 2004.

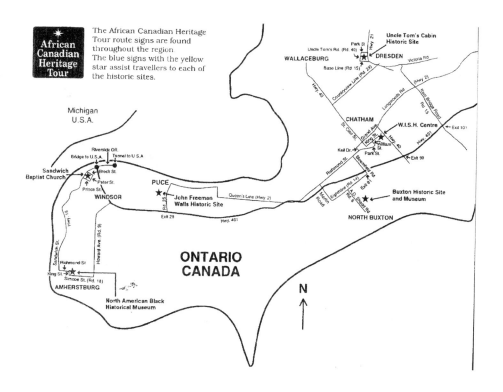

rible condition - a lot of brush and undergrowth and standing water.

A few people are now coming forward and telling that they have an ancestor buried there. A man named Glen Cook says that his great-grandfather is buried there; and Dr. Bryan Walls (John Freeman Walls Historical Underground Railroad Site and Museum) said that his mother told him that her "Great-Uncle Smith" was buried in that cemetery. During the Detroit 300 celebration period, I met a physician who works at Henry Ford Hospital, Dr. Rick Smith, who said that his family once lived in the Puce/Elmstead (now Lakeshore) area. He was attempting some genealogical research at that time regarding his own connection with the Underground Railroad.

Dr. Bryan Walls owns and, with family members, operates the John Freeman Walls Historical Site. He has taken interested persons on a mini-tour to see this historic cemetery.

The Walls Site and this cemetery fall within the boundaries of the original tract of land owned by the Refugee Home Society. This Society (whose members included Reverends William Troy, Madison Lightfoot and George French, as well as Laura Haviland) was administered by Henry and Mary Bibb. Henry Bibb was the editor and publisher of "The Voice of The Fugitive",

Canada's most famous abolitionist newspaper, which was also widely read throughout the United States. The purpose of this Society was to assist refugees (who had been enslaved in the South) in getting started with making a living here by farming. The community was once a substantial one. After Emancipation in the USA, most returned to the States, leaving behind homes, barns and churches.

The community had at least three churches, British Methodist Episcopal, AME Zion and Baptist. The cemetery that I am writing about, Jackson Cemetery, belonged to the BME Church. The church had been vacant for decades, but the cemetery was used until the 1930s. Evidently the BME and AME Zion were directly across the road from each other. About 85 years ago, a new highway - the King's Highway No. 2 was put through the northern part of Essex and Kent Counties to provide a connection between Windsor, Chatham, London and communities further east. Until that time, people travelled via the Talbot Trail (Highway 98) or they hugged the Lake St. Clair shore. Because the existing narrow northern trail was to be widened to create the King's Highway, the road crew arbitrarily and without permission demolished things and buildings that were in their way. Two of the structures that they demolished were the BME and AME Zion (abandoned) Churches. In the book, *the Doctrines and Disciplines of the BME Church* (1913), this property is listed.

HARROW CEMETERY, CANADA

Ken Turner writes: I was contacted by the Town of Essex on short notice, that an archeologist would examine the British Methodist Episcopal (B.M.E) church site in Harrow on August 3, and 4th. I observed the examination to make sure that everything was done properly and that all areas in question would be examined. The back (southwest) corner of the cemetery was found to be all infants and children. The northwest and south boundaries were consistent with the present boundaries. The boundary in question was the east boundary on Walnut Street. A row of graves was found beyond the trees which were thought to mark the east boundary. I insisted that testing be done up to Walnut street to ensure there were no graves in this area. The area up to Walnut was clear of any burials. There were old stone foundations found and a garbage pit. The original east boundary fence line could be seen. The town then gave a 15 foot buffer zone beyond the last row of graves. The purpose of the dig was to locate the cemetery boundaries. In all, over 22 graves were located and mapped. Since the centre of the cemetery and northwestern corner were not examined, it is no doubt there are more graves. The original lane into the cemetery was located as well. There are a great deal of empty plots in the cemetery. I am surprised that burials did not continue, there was plenty of room left. I suppose it could be due to the somewhat haphazard nature of the graves. Some were in rows, but others were scattered. Perhaps there was no map and the families forgot where burials were located.

One tombstone was discovered in the area of examination. It said..

In Memory of Rev. Noah C. Cannon
Died Oct. 1850 Aged 60 yrs
A Native of Maryland
A faithful preacher resteth here

Even the tombstone maker name is visible at the bottom of the stone - J.G. Stanton - Chatham

Oiivia Ellen Moore was found to be buried there also

Footstones were also found for Rachel OBanyon, Theodore Baylis, Charlotte E. Crump, and and one other unmarked.

Nancy Allen, the late E. Andrea Moore and Ken Turner, kept us informed. Allen sends the news that she was recently contacted by a woman named Ann Flemming (it's a long story). But during their conversation, Nancy told this lady that her great (x3) grandfather was Pompey Chase. Mrs. Flemming knew about Pompey Chase - she is originally from Merlin, but is doing research in Essex County (since 1995) for a book. She has proof of 2 people buried at the Matthew Elliot site who were not slaves of Elliot. They are Anne Johnstone (daughter of Pompey Chase) and her husband, a Mr. Tell (who was a servant of Simon Girty). If this is true - then the people buried at the Elliot site were not only slaves (and perhaps, later, servants) of Elliot, but could be other Blacks who lived in close proximity to the Elliot farm.

NOVA SCOTIA, CANADA CEMETERIES

Information on Nova Scotia cemeteries came as a surprise to us, a welcome surprise. Debra Hill writes that many blacks came to Nova Scotia through the Underground Railroad. Hill describes herself as a member of the Black Loyalist Heritage Society in Nova Scotia. A letter was received from Jennifer King regarding the Shelburne County cemeteries. Eight of the cemeteries are listed and brief statements are included for each cemetery.

The Cemeteries of Shelburne County, Nova Scotia

Anglican Cemetery, Churchover
Harbour View Cemetery, Port Saxon
Ingomar Cemetery, Ingomar
Mizpah Cemetery, Birchtown
North East Harbour Cemetery, North East Harbour
Pleasant Plain Cemetery, North West Harbour
Roseway Cemetery, Roseway
St. Paul's United Church Cemetery, Carleton Village

Anglican Church Cemetery
Churchover
Shelburne County, Nova Scotia

Inventory of Grave Markers

Recorded in 1988 by:
Phillip & Deborah Hagar

According to the Anglican Church records, Mrs. George Goulden, west side of Shelburne Harbour, was the first person to be interred in the "new church yard over the harbour". She was George Goulden's first wife, Mary Ann, and the daughter of John & Rosanna (Rapp) Etherington. She was buried 26 July 1842, aged 43 years. There is no stone. - Mrs. Dorothy Freeman

Harbour View Cemetery
Port Saxon (formerly Indian Brook)
Shelburne County, N. S.
Inventory of grave markers

Inventory taken: September 26, 1992
Cataloguers: Barbara Balkam
Emeline Kaufmann
Clyde Stoddart
Patricia Terry

"The property for this cemetery was deeded to the trustees of the Wesleyan Methodist Church in 1863." - Dorothy Freeman

Ingomar Cemetery Ingomar, Shelburne Co., N.S

Inventory of Grave Markers

Inventory Taken: October 24, 1992
Cataloguers: Barbara Balkam
Emeline Kaufmann
Patricia Terry

Compiled For The Shelburne County Genealogical Society by Patricia A. Terry
Mrs. Dorothy Freeman.

Mizpah Cemetery
Birchtown

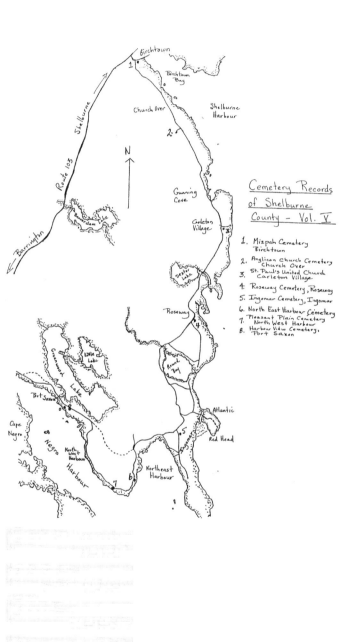

Cemetery Records
of Shelburne
County - Vol. V

1. Mizpah Cemetery, Birchtown
2. Anglican Church Cemetery, Church Over
3. St. Paul's United Church, Carleton Village
4. Roseway Cemetery, Roseway
5. Ingomar Cemetery, Ingomar
6. North East Harbour Cemetery
7. Pleasant Plain Cemetery, North West Harbour
8. Harbour View Cemetery, Port Saxon

Shelburne County, Nova Scotia

Inventory of Grave Markers

Recorded 25 July 1990 By:
Christa Bruce
Mark Scott

"And Mizpah; for he said, the Lord watch between me and thee, when we are absent one from another." - Genesis 31:49

Compiled For The Shelburne County Genealogical Society By Patricia A. Terry

North East Harbour Cemetery
North East Harbour
Shelburne County, N.S.

Inventory of Grave Markers

Recorded October 31 & November 7, 1992 By
Emeline Kaufmann
Mary W. Stoddart
Patricia A. Terry

"North East Harbour Cemetery Was First The King Family Private Burial Ground. In 1822 It Was Deeded To The Trustees Of The Methodist Church." - Mrs. Dorothy Freeman

Pleasant Plain Cemetery
North West Harbour
Shelburne County, N.S.

Inventory of Grave Markers

Recorded September 26, 1992 By
Barbara Balkam
Emeline Kaufmann
Patricia A. Terry

"Land for this cemetery was deeded to the trustees in 1989." - Mrs. Dorothy Freeman

Roseway Cemetery
Roseway
Shelburne County, N.S.

Inventory of Grave Markers

Recorded October 24, 1992 By
Barbara Balkam
Emeline Kaufmann
Patricia A. Terry

Compiled For The Shelburne County Genealogical Society By
Patricia A. Terry

"In 1839, Silas Perry and Alex McKenney deeded this land to the Methodist Trustees for a chapel and burial ground at Roseway. In 1916 an extension was deeded." - Mrs. Dorothy Freeman

St. Paul's United Church Cemetery
Carleton Village
Shelburne County, N.S.

Inventory of Grave Markers

Recorded By
Christa Bruce
Mark Scott

Compiled For The Shelburne County Genealogical Society By
Patricia A. Terry

"The land for the church and burial ground were deeded to the Trustees of the Presbyterian Church in 1895. In 1918 an extension was deeded." - Mrs. Dorothy Freeman

The readers who have family buried in Shelburne, Nova Scotia, please contact the Genealogical Society. Refer to the Appendix; they have clearly listed and classified records.

Elizabeth Cromwell tells an interesting story of her life in Birchtown, Nova Scotia

Elizabeth Cromwell grew up knowing she was the descendant of American slaves.

What she didn't know was that her ancestors were among Canada's first settlers; that her old hometown used to be the largest community of free blacks in North America; that it produced Canada's first black activist and was the scene of Canada's first race riot.

"This wasn"t taught in any school book," Cromwell says.

"It was like we had no history, but we've been here from the beginning, As we discover our own history, then comes the pride."

Cromwell is one of several key people resurrecting the early history of African-Canadians in Nova Scotia. They have found an astonishing treasure of stories, artifacts and archeological sites that chronicle an incredible tale of hardship, perseverance and persecution.

The history stretches across the province, from Birchtown, founded on Nova Scotia's southwest shore by black settlers in 1783, to Africville in Halifax, and up to Cape Breton, where renowned black nationalist Marcus Garvey recruited for his United Negro Improvement Association in the 1920s.

"Our culture goes back to the very beginning of this country," says Cromwell. "We were the first. Our people were the original colonists."

Cromwell traces her Canadian roots to George Stephens who, like thousands of other slaves, was enticed to fight with the British against the American colonists in exchange for his freedom.

When the British lost that war, they agreed to evacuate those who had fought on their side - including the escaped slaves, but there was a hitch. The Americans demanded compensation for the loss of their human property. That ugly fight produced a now priceless document of black history: *The Book of Negroes*, The huge leather-bound tome is a detailed list of the human cargo that sailed on 114 ships out of New York City in 1783; it lists the names, history and descriptions of more than 3,000 former slaves who sailed to Nova Scotia, England and the West Indies.

Few of the promises made by the British were kept, and the former slaves found themselves stranded in winter along the rocky shores of the cold North Atlantic Ocean.

They called their small community "Birchtown", after the general who signed their papers of freedom. The settlement lies about 10 kilometers east of Shelburne, or 250 kilometers southeast of Halifax.

Though many of the former slaves were skilled tradesmen, they had almost no supplies.

Recent archeological digs show they lived in pits in the ground for the first winter. Some found work in nearby Shelburne, where wealthy white Loyalists - those who had fled America and remained loyal to the British monarchy - had begun to build large new homes.

But soon that caused friction with unemployed whites, who complained the black workers were undercutting wages.

In 1785, the friction turned into a riot, with black workers chased out of Shelburne by a mob of former soldiers who followed them to Birchtown, and burned down homes.

That same year, Thomas Peters, a former American slave, sailed to England to complain about how badly black Loyalists had been treated. Peters, a member of the Black Pioneers corps, was approached by a business group that had established a British colony in Sierra Leone, West Africa.

Peters was told that the black Loyalists would receive free land if they were to settle there seven years later. In 1792, 1,196 black Loyalists left Nova Scotia for Sierra Leone, where they founded the capital, Freetown, and formed that country's first government.

"The ones who made it here were the strongest of the strong," says Louise Delisle, who is also descended from Birchtown settlers.

"We need to understand the incredible hardships that they endured, and be proud."

Delisle is one of many people who has helped Cromwell research Birchtown's history. They have put together a museum, a trail, helped sponsor archeological digs, saved the black cemetery from washing into the sea and begun a genealogy centre and gift shop in a former church.

When Irvin Carvery looks at Seaview Park in the shadow of the

Halifax's McKay Bridge, he sees hurts of the past and the promised future.

The plot of ragged grass and old swing sets was once one of Canada's most tightly knit black community collection of clapboard homes known as Africville.

Carvery grew up here, picking berries from the hill behind his home in the summer and hauling wood through the winter that ended when he was thirteen years old. That year he and 83 others were carted away from the community in garbage trucks and homes were destroyed.

The city had ignored Africville, for generations; the neighbourhood had no water or sewer.

In the 1960's, Halifax began to be embarrassed by the eyesore. The city voted to tear it down in the name of urban improvement.

Carvery has launched a $20 million lawsuit against the city on behalf of families who were paid only a few hundred dollars for their waterfront.

Last summer, Heritage Minister, Copps declared Africville an historic site.

Carvery says he and the other descendants of Africville want to turn it into a shrine of African-Canadian history, a place where people from North America can come see black culture and learn about the unique history of black people in that part of the world.

The city recently made an offer to Carvery and he says they are finally in active negotiations regarding reparations for Africville.

African Canadian/American Historic Cemeteries Endangered List:

Matthew Elliott Black slave ccmetery, Lot 5, Conc. 1 (just south of Amherst burg, directly across from the southern tip of Boblo Island). approximately 80 graves

Mount Pleasant Black Baptist Church cemetery, Lot 83, Conc. (1840-1930) approximately 100 graves

Alexander Green, Black pioneer cemetery, Lot 91. Conc 8 (Malden)

John Chavis, Black pioneer cemetery. Lot 13, South Malden Road

Matt Matthews, Black pioneer cemetery. Lot 5. Cont.3, Colchester South

Abandoned but Endangered Cemeteries:

A.M.E. Zion Cemetery (site of present St. Mark's Evangelical Church, 3rd Conc., Colchester - ref Rev. Edsel Smith (519) 738-4645)

Banwell Road Cemetery, fairttlo 143 Rowe Expressway.

B.M.E. Cemetery, Lot 12. Harrow (abandoned church torn down c. 1960) presently "Sanford and Son" Grocery Store

Closed but Maintained:
Fugitive Slave Cemetery (Refugee Home Society, admin. Henry Bibb and Rev. Geo. French. est. 1846) on the site of the John Freeman Walls Museum, Puce. (See previous pages)

Pioneer Cemetery Still in Use:
Central Grove A.M.E. Cemetery. Walker Road. Harrow (north end of town)

Integrated Pioneer Cemeteries:
Rose Hill Cemetery. Amherstburg, Ontario

The Historic St. John's Anglican Cemetery

The oldest date on any tombstone in the church yard is 1793. The community of Sandwich was established prior to the Treaty of Versaille (1783), which defined Canada's southern boundary as the "middle of the Great Lakes as far west as the Lake of the Woods". (See previous page for this cemetery.

Turn to page 599 for the story of Priceville, Ontario. Canada's National Film Board traces the search for tombstones in this racially divided town.

ESCAPED SLAVES' GRAVES SIT UNMARKED IN CANADA

Colin Nickerson of the Boston Globe, wrote about St. Armand Station, Canada saying "North meant freedom, so they followed the 'drinking gourd,' dodging slave catchers and sleeping in woodsheds and basement hidey-holes of the Underground Railroad."

Thousands of slaves in pre-Civil War America fled the plantations of the South for the snow-bound sanctuary of Canada. The runaways were guided by the North Star glimmering at the end of the Little Dipper, the 'drinking gourd' celebrated in black spirituals, just as Canada was sung of as 'Canaan.'

A few settled in the Quebec hamlet of St. Armand-Station, making lives of purpose, if not great prosperity, as hired hands, log hewers and horse drovers. They died there, too. More than a century later, their skeletons lie unmarked, unmourned beneath a frozen pasture.

Now, a U.S. born schoolteacher, Hank Avery, is seeking to consecrate St. Armand-Station's almost-forgotten burial ground for former slaves, one of only a few such sites in Canada. However his attempt has run into a wall of indifference.

"There should be some marker, some fence, something to lend dignity to their memory," said Avery, who is black. The soft-spoken Pennsylvanian came to Quebec, to make a new life after fleeing the military draft during the Vietnam War. "They deserve their place of pride in Canadian history."

Disturbed by rumors that the farm's owner recently excavated sections of the graveyard for dirt to buttress a barn foundation, Avery has mounted a campaign to prevent desecration of a site that he believes should be sacred to the memory of the tiny community of black freemen and escaped slaves that briefly flourished there in the mid-1980s.

Only too typically for Quebec, the controversy generated by Avery's quest has split along linguistic lines, with support for preserving the site coming mainly from the English-descended families of the so-called Eastern Townships region – lying just north of Vermont – while many French-speaking residents shrug off the efforts as Anglo folly.

"Why is he talking about three long-deceased slaves?" demanded farmer Rejean Benolt, who owns the farm where the presumed graveyard is located and is cool to the historical site proposal. "There are no markers, no stones, nothing to suggest it was ever a place important to anyone, just old stories."

Provincial and town officials, meanwhile, seem nonplussed by the situation, each pleading a lack of authority to guard a cemetery that has never been formally designated.

"I don't even know who I'm supposed to call on this," St. Armand-Station Mayor Brent Chamberlin told the Montreal Gazette. "There's nothing in the regulations we can enforce."

Local lore has long held that the farm is the site of a burial ground for blacks who escaped their brutal servitude by way of the Underground Railroad.

"It's part of the community history, people here always recognized the site," said Avery, who teaches third grade in nearby Bedford.

That claim is supported by records. A 1908 publication of the Missisquoi Historical Society refers to the "St. Armand Negro Burying Ground." Other archival records refer to the cemetery as lying on the farm.

The Underground Railroad was the abolitionist-run system of midnight wagon rides, dark forest trails and safe houses that fleeing slaves followed to Canada, which banned the ownership of human beings decades before the United States. Even northern states that outlawed slavery could not prevent escaped slaves from being captured and returned to the South. Detroit was the last major stop before reaching Canada.

Estimates vary widely, but it is reckoned that 10,000 to 60,000 slaves reached sanctuary in Canada from the beginning of the 1800s until the end of the Civil War in 1865. The best-known of them was Josiah Henson, an escaped slave from Maryland who lived out his days in southern Ontario and whose harrowing tale inspired Harriet Beecher Stowe's "Uncle Tom's Cabin."

Many of the country's 800,000 black people descend from those refugees of the Underground Railroad.

The Vermont-Quebec border was one of the important crossing points.

The Eastern Townships region was settled by British Loyalists unwilling to pledge allegiance to the revolutionary American republic. Among the first to start farming near St. Armand-Station was Phillip Luke, a Loyalist whose hatred for slavery was strong enough that he would make annual trips to the South to buy eight slaves at a time, setting them free upon returning to Canada.

These people found work in the area and, according to local accounts, the original black community was enlarged in the 1850s by runaway slaves guided north by the abolitionist conductors of the people smuggling network, which used railroad terminology as a sort of secret code.

For reasons that are unclear, St. Armand-Station's population of blacks dissipated before the turn of this century. Some died; most simply went off to the cities in search of better opportunities. Today fewer than a dozen people of color live in the entire Eastern Townships region. Most, like Avery, are relative newcomers.

For years Avery had heard stories about the black burial ground in St. Armand-Station. But he only became involved in saving the site last fall after rumors started that a section was dug up, uncovering human bones.

The reports are vague, and the site is now covered with snow. Farmer Benoit insists there has been no digging on the site since 1950, when his father unwittingly bulldozed apparent burial mounds, stopping when fragments of skeletons appeared.

"My father reburied everything and forgot about it," farmer Benoit said.

CELEBRITY BURIALS

Author Tod Benoit, in his book *Where are they Buried? How did they Die?* has a remarkable compilation of the final resting places of almost seven hundred famous celebrity graves. We selected a few and enjoyed talking to Mr. Benoit. He is an ardent world traveler as well as a great researcher.

Louis Armstrong
August 4, 1901 – July 6, 1971

Most Baby Boomers remember Louis "Satchmo" Armstrong on variety shows as a smiling older uncle warbling his gravelly voice through "What a Wonderful World" and playing a bit of trumpet afterward. But jazz aficionados remember Louis differently and freely refer to him as a genius. According to Tony Bennett (who ought to know), Armstrong "practically invented jazz singing singlehandedly." Further, out-

CHAPTER FIVE

side jazz circles it's largely unknown that, as a young avant-garde musician, Louis' Hot Five and Hot Seven recordings of the 1920s spurred a musical revolution.

Louis' achievements are all the more remarkable given his early life of extreme poverty in a New Orleans slum. But he somehow turned that adversity into opportunity and, while in the Colored Waifs' Home for Boys after a brush with the law, Louis discovered the cornet and began making music. In Joe Oliver, a cornet king playing the new music called jazz, Louis found a mentor and father figure. Sent to join Oliver's Chicago-based Creole Jazz Band in 1922, Louis shortly thereafter made his first recordings, which have since been called "the Rosetta Stone of Jazz."

Before those recordings, jazz musicians modestly limited their solos, but Louis's were longer and bolder, and he started improvising on the chord structure. With his rhythmic fluidity, he also began playing on and around the beat, heralding the swing style that emerged in the 1930s. Louis also pioneered a new style of singing, imitating the horn with his voice and substituting improvised nonsense syllables for the lyrics. With the passing of the big band era, he formed his All Stars, and they became goodwill ambassadors of jazz throughout the world, helping break down racial barriers wherever they played.

Louis never forgot where he came from and recognized that he was blessed twice, first with a sandpapery, distinctive voice and second with keen trumpet skills. Together, his talents helped him reap the rewards that eluded most of the influential creators of his era. The affinity he felt for his trumpet superseded everything else. As he reflected once, "Anything that'll get in the way of blowing my horn, out it goes. The trumpet comes first, before everything, even my wife."

Louis died in his sleep of natural causes and was buried at Flushing Cemetery in Queens, New York.

At the turn of the century, no one paid much notice to the birth of an illegitimate black baby boy in New Orleans and Louis, never knowing his real birthday, chose to celebrate it as July 4, 1900. A baptismal certificate listing his birth date as August 4, 1901, was finally discovered in 1989, making Louis 69 at his death, not 71, as is generally recorded.

Arthur Ashe
July 10, 1943-February 6, 1993

Arthur Ashe was the first African American man to win tennis' most prestigious tournaments: the U.S. Open and Wimbledon. He first learned to play tennis on a segregated playground, then parlayed that into a twelve-year career that included 33 singles and 18 doubles titles. He later became president of the Association of Tennis Professionals and captain of the Davis Cup team, which won two championships under his direction.

Though the titles and ensuing endorsement contracts made Arthur a millionaire, wealth didn't distract him from the social issues of the day. He became a civil rights activist, fighting for all minorities that were victims of exclusionary practices. He also served as the national campaign chairman for the American Heart Association, edited several books, and contributed generously to African American programs everywhere.

After Arthur disclosed that he had AIDS in 1992, he devoted himself to becoming a role model in the fight against the disease, and began a $5 million fund-raising effort on behalf of his namesake foundation.

At 49 Ashe died of pneumonia, a complication brought on by AIDS, and was buried at Woodland Cemetery in Richmond, Virginia.

Fans of Arthur's will also want to view the statue crafted in his honor that stands on Monument Avenue, the symbolic heart of the city of Richmond and the capital of the Confederacy. As a child, Arthur had not been allowed to play on Richmond's tennis courts because they were segregated. Today, his statue stands tall alongside those of Robert E. Lee and Stonewall Jackson.

Widow of Arthur Ashe Raises Objection to Site for Monument

Jeanne Moutoussamy-Ashe, the widow of the tennis star Arthur Ashe, said in a published article that she opposed the City of Richmond's decision to put Mr. Ashe's statue on Monument Avenue, which now honors only Confederate heroes.

Ms. Moutoussamy-Ashe, a photographer who lives in New York, had remained silent throughout a seven-month debate over race and art that polarized Richmond, where her husband is buried. The statue, now being cast in bronze, was scheduled to be unveiled on July 10, what would have been Mr. Ashe's 53rd birthday. But officials said the statement was certain to reopen the issue.

In an article on the opinion page of The Richmond Times-Dispatch, Ms. Moutoussamy-Ashe wrote, "I am not in agreement with the decision to place the Arthur Ashe monument on Monument Avenue.

"My reasons are not politically driven; nor are they artistically or racially motivated. I have always felt that in all this controversy, the spirit that Arthur gave to Richmond has been overlooked. I am afraid that a statue of Arthur Ashe on Monument Avenue honors Richmond, Virginia, more than it does its son, his legacy and his life's work."

Ms. Moutoussamy-Ashe did not respond to a request for comment today. She wrote that her husband had cooperated with the sculptor for a statue to go in front of an African American Sports Hall of Fame, which Mr. Ashe wanted built in Richmond.

Mr. Ashe, who was once barred from the segregated tennis courts of his hometown, later became known for his global promotion of human rights. He died of AIDS in 1993.

In Richmond, the capital of the Confederacy, many citizens saw a powerful symbol of racial healing in erecting a statue of Mr. Ashe on a boulevard best known for a monument to Robert E. Lee. But others here said it was insulting to Mr. Ashe's memory to put a statue of him on the same street as Confederate memorials. Still others said they wanted to preserve the historic integrity of the avenue.

Thomas N. Chewning, who led the drive to raise money for the Ashe statue, said that if Ms. Moutoussamy-Ashe's view had been known earlier, "it certainly would have put us down a different path."

But Viola O. Baskerville, a member of the City Council said she would urge her colleagues to stick with their decision. "To say that a monument of this significance should be relegated to a sports hall of fame is to put Arthur back in the milieu he transcended," Mrs. Baskerville said.

Florence Ballard
June 30, 1943-February 22, 1976

Stylizing rhythm and blues with a pop flair, the Motown-based Supremes were the number-one American recording group between 1964 and 1967. The vocal trio of Florence Ballard, Diana Ross, and Mary Wilson came from the low-income Brewster housing project in Detroit and rose to international acclaim, enjoying a fantastic rags-to-riches fairy tale. At the height of their fame they sang their blockbuster songs, including "Stop in the Name of Love," to mobs of fans at concert venues worldwide. In those heady days, the girls were featured in fashion magazines, Florence drove a plum-rose Cadillac, and they even had a loaf of bread named after them. The Supremes struck gold.

But in the real world, fairy tales can have unhappy endings, and so it went for Florence, who, in 1967, just as the Supremes reached the peak of their popularity, either quit or was fired from the group, depending upon whose account you believe. Signing away all her rights for only about $100,000, Florence soon lost her home to foreclosure, ballooned to almost 200 pounds, and was living back in the Detroit projects on a $95-per-week stipend from the Aid to Dependent Children program. During that time, she said, "When I go to sleep at night, I have dreams of what it was like when Diana, Mary, and I worked great places like the Copa. Once I had it all. I was

Supreme. Now? Now I have nothing."

One evening in February 1976, two months after reconciling with her husband and moving into his home, Florence became alarmed when her hands and feet began to feel numb. She checked into a hospital that night and, at 32, died the next morning of heart failure. Florence now rests at Detroit Memorial Park in Warren, Michigan.

Cab Calloway
December 25, 1907-November 17, 1994

Involved in show business from an early age, vocalist Cab Calloway worked with a big band, the Missourians, during the 1920s. Although the band consisted of proficient musicians, Cab's flamboyant leadership attracted the most attention; he dressed outlandishly as the eye-catching "man in the zoot suit with the reet pleats," his outfit consisting of a knee-length drape jacket, voluminous trousers, wide-brimmed hat, and a floor-trailing watch chain. Alternately peppering his "singing" with hip phraseology and nonsensical lyrics, including his "hi-de-hi" catch phrase, Cab in a short time became the band's leader. He renamed the act Cab Calloway and his Orchestra, and in 1931 it replaced Duke Ellington's orchestra at the Cotton Club. In that year Cab also recorded "Minnie the Moocher," a song that would remain his theme for his entire life.

With the end of the big band era, Cab reluctantly broke up his orchestra in 1948, but his career didn't end. As far back as 1932 Cab had acted in movies and, once he was free of the band, Cab further promoted himself in that direction, appearing in films such as The Cincinnati Kid and St. Louis Blues. In the 1950s he toured the world with a production of Porgy and Bess as the character Sportin' Life; according to Cab, George Gershwin had modeled the character after him in the first place. In 1980 he reached an entirely new audience when he became known to the college crowd as the "Hi-de-hi-de-hi-de-ho" singer in the movie, The Blues Brothers.

Later in his life, when Cab was asked who his heroes were in the music business, he scoffed, "My heroes are the notes, man. You understand what I'm saying? I love the music. The music is my hero."

Cab suffered a stroke in June 1994 and died five months later at 86. He was cremated and his ashes given to his wife, Nuffie, who keeps them in her room at a Delaware retirement home.

Johnnie Cochran
October 2, 1937-March 30, 2005

Johnnie L. Cochran Jr., whose fierce, flamboyant and electrifyingly effective advocacy in the O. J. Simpson murder trial captivated the country and solidified his image as a master of high-profile criminal defense, died March 30 at his home in Los Angeles. He was 67.

The cause was a brain tumor, said a law partner, Peter J. Neufeld.

Johnnie L. Cochran Jr. was born in Shreveport. Louisiana, on October 2,1937, the great-grandson of a slave, and grew up in a prosperous family.

He was raised In Los Angeles and attended UCLA, supporting himself by selling insurance policies for his father's company. He graduated in 1959 and earned his law degree from Loyola Marymount University in 1963.

He passed the California bar in 1963. then took a job in Los Angeles as a deputy city attorney in the criminal division.

His career was intertwined with celebrities almost from its beginning: Among his early cases was a 1964 effort to prosecute comedian Lenny Bruce on obscenity charges.

In 1965, he entered private practice and soon opened his own firm. Cochran, Atkins & Evans. His current practice, The Cochran Firm, was established in 1981 and has offices in 12 states and the District of Columbia.

Cochran made his name with a series of high profile police brutality and criminal cases in the late 1970s and worked as a Los Angeles County deputy district attorney in the late 1970s and early 1980s.

He negotiated a 1993 settlement in a civil lawsuit against pop star Michael Jackson that accused him of child molestation – a case that has resurfaced in Jackson's current criminal trial on other child molestation charges.

And he represented Reginald Denny, the white truck driver beaten by a black mob at the height of the Los Angeles riots in 1992.

Cochran argued that the city's police department was guilty of discrimination for failing to protect the neighborhood where Denny was assaulted.

In another high – profile case, Cochran represented Abner Louima, the Haitian immigrant sodomized with a broken broomstick by two New York City policemen in the bathroom of a Brooklyn station house in 1997. Settlement was reached for $39 million, and although his 1972 defense of former Black Panther member "Geronimo" Prattt for murder charges wound up in defeat, Cochran's perseverance eventually led to the reversal of that conviction – and his client's release – 25 years later.

Mr. Cochran was already a prominent Los Angeles lawyer in 1994, when Mr. Simpson, the former football star, asked him to join and then lead the lawyers defending him on charges that he had killed his former wife, Nicole Brown Simpson, and a friend of hers, Ronald L. Goldman.

The televised trial riveted the nation for most of 1995 and rocked it that October, when the jury acquitted Mr. Simpson. He was later held responsible for the killings in a civil case, where another jury evaluated much of the same evidence against a more relaxed standard of proof.

Before the Simpson case, Mr. Cochran was best known for bringing police brutality cases on behalf of black clients and for representing celebrities in trouble. Both experiences proved valuable at the Simpson trial.

Drawing on his knowledge of the Los Angeles Police Department gleaned from his days in the Los Angeles city attorney's office, Mr. Cochran focused the Simpson jury's attention on shortcomings in the department's investigation of the killings and on the seeming racism of one of its detectives.

In the trial's aftermath, Mr. Cochran's name became a sort of shorthand, but one that meant different things in different contexts. To some, it stood for legal acumen. To others, a masterly rapport with the jury. To still others, the vexing roles of money and race in the justice system.

Mr. Cochran mostly enjoyed the references to him in films and on late-night television, where he was both admired as a singularly effective trial lawyer and mocked for his smooth style and court rhetoric.

He pleaded guilty to charges of extravagance and flamboyance.

"I like to get paid well and I like to enjoy the rewards of my work," he wrote.

But the money he made, he said, allowed him to work for people he called "the No J's" - "those cases I've taken in which the chances for getting paid are actually pretty slim."

For all the publicity of the Simpson trial, the case that Mr. Cochran always said meant the most to him was that of Elmer Pratt, a leader of the Black Panther Party also known as Geronimo. Mr. Cochran, as mentioned above, represented Mr. Pratt when he was convicted in 1972 of murdering a 27-year-old schoolteacher on a tennis court in Santa Monica, and worked tirelessly to overturn that verdict.

In 1997, Mr. Cochran was part of the team that convinced Judge Everett W. Dickey of Orange County Superior Court to void the conviction and free Mr. Pratt because prosecutors had withheld crucial evidence about a witness.

That same year, Mr. Cochran traded on the fame he achieved in the Simpson trial to form a successful national law firm - The Cochran Firm - devoted mostly to personal injury cases. In "A Lawyer's Life," one of his two autobiographies, Mr. Cochran conceded that he was involved in only a few of the firm's cases and often just tangentially. His name, though, he said, was often "enough to cause the other side to initiate settlement discussions."

"I'm sort of the legal gunslinger," he wrote, "the celebrity lawyer." Mr. Cochran was a steady presence on television after the Simpson trial, serving as the host of programs on Court TV and as a legal commentator on NBC and elsewhere.

His work at Court TV caused him to spend more time in New York, and he became a presence in the city's legal and political circles.

Nat King Cole
March 17, 1919-February 15, 1965

As is the case of many African American musicians, Nat King Cole's early training came through gospel singing at church and hymns learned on a piano. By sixteen, he was up and coming on the Chicago jazz scene known for his versatility on the piano; outside of his father's church, he'd never sung a note. A couple years later, in 1938, Nat landed in Los Angeles and formed the first of the Nat King Cole trios, soon becoming renowned as a swing pianist.

By 1940 the school-boyish Nat had gained confidence in his own singing, and he developed into an outright crooner; in 1944 his trio had their first major hit with "Straighten Up and Fly Right," and, as it received heavy rotation on the radio, Nat began de-emphasizing his piano. By 1950, thanks in part to the success of his landmark recordings of "The Christmas Song" and "Mona Lisa," his smooth vocal style eclipsed his exemplary piano talents, and Nat emerged as one of the day's most celebrated pop artists.

Not everyone was enamored of Nat's success, though, and the ugly issue of race confronted the crooner. A 1954 concert in Birmingham was ended early by a group of Ku Klux Klan members. Later, as Nat mulled the purchase of a beautiful Hollywood home, an uptight community committee moved to block the sale. Telling Nat they didn't want any undesirables in the neighborhood, he famously replied, "If any move in, I'll let you know." Ultimately, restrictive covenants excluding home sales to Jews and Negroes were removed by the courts.

But in 1957, consistent with the civil rights movement that had begun to roil the nation, the issue reached a boiling point when Nat launched his own television program, The Nat King Cole Show on NBC, the first to feature a black host. The show became one of the most popular shows of the time, but not solely for its entertainment value; too, it was a social experiment. Black viewers who were starved for positive television images flocked to the program even as the urbane and elegant Nat was cherished by white viewers. But affiliate Southern stations would not carry the show and, with the deepening racial tensions of the 1950s, it became increasingly difficult to attract corporate sponsors. After Nat outraged some white viewers by touching the arm of a white female guest, the show was cancelled in 1958.

A heavy smoker, Nat's velvet voice and his health deteriorated rapidly in the early 1960s. At 45 he died of lung cancer. At his funeral, Jack Benny offered this epitaph: "Sometimes death is not as tragic as not knowing how to live. This man knew how to live and how to make others glad they were living."

Mr. Cole rests at Forest Lawn Memorial Park in Glendale, California.

Medgar Evers
July 2, 1925-June 12, 1963

Medgar Evers grew up in the Deep South during the Depression, and as soon as he turned eighteen, like many others of that era, promptly joined the Army. In 1944 he found himself on the beaches of Normandy, but little did he know that the biggest battle of his life was yet to be fought.

In 1954, Medgar decided to make a difference in the growing civil rights movement and in a short while was made Mississippi's first NAACP field secretary. The next years found him organizing voter-registration drives and, at times, boycotts in areas where the local populace was most obstinate. During the early 1960s the increased tempo of desegregation activities in the South created high and constant tensions, and the situation routinely reached the breaking point.

One hot night in 1963, President Kennedy made a broadcast on national television describing a bill he was sending to Congress that later became the Civil Rights Act of 1964. A few hours later, just after midnight, while stepping out of his Oldsmobile with an armload of "Jim Crow Must Go" tee shirts, Medgar was felled by a shotgun blast fired by an assailant who had lurked in the shadows outside his home. Fifteen minutes later, Medgar died at a local hospital.

At 37 he was buried with full military honors at Arlington National Cemetery in Arlington, Virginia.

Ella Fitzgerald
April 25, 1918-June 16, 1996

Sliding effortlessly from bebop to ballad and employing endlessly inventive vocal improvisations over three full octaves, Ella Fitzgerald thrilled audiences on her way to becoming the preeminent jazz singer of her generation.

A 1938, swing version of the classic nursery rhyme "A-Tisket, A-Tasket" became her first hit recording and made her a national star but, by the forties, Ella had already moved to "scat" singing, a form based on the complex and spontaneous instrumental style of Dizzy Gillespie's band. The war years were spent with various road shows and, in 1955, signing with the Verve record label, she recorded a series of "songbook" albums, each devoted to the work of a particular composer. These recordings are generally regarded as her best work.

In the sixties, Ella attempted to broaden her range into pop recordings, releasing a country album and a record of Christmas music. She returned to jazz in the seventies, but this era marked the decline of her beautiful voice and of her health. She experienced eyesight problems and other ailments, complicated by the diabetes that would require the amputation of her lower legs in 1992.

By the end of her career, Ella had recorded over 2,000 songs, sold some 40 million albums, and won 13 Grammy Awards.

Ella died of complications from diabetes at 79 and is buried at Inglewood Park Cemetery in Inglewood, California.

Marvin Gaye
April 2, 1939-April 1, 1984

Marvin Gaye was a charter member of that generation of soul artists that sky-rocketed to fame under the Motown label, and his songs, unique blends of soul music and old-time gospel, cut a wide swath from torrid sexual abandon to impassioned social rectitude.

Gaye had grown up in Washington D.C., the son of an iron-fisted Pentecostal minister, Marvin Gay, Sr. (For show business, Marvin, Jr. added an "e" to his surname.) While he was still quite young it became obvious to any-one within earshot that Marvin, Sr.'s son could really sing and the boy became a church fixture, leading the congregation through hymns between his father's sermons. Eventually, the protracted religious discourses and his father's inflexibility induced an animosity that worsened through Marvin's teens. Still, though Marvin's lifestyle later drifted light-years away from the strictures of Pentecostalism, he was always quick to credit his father for instilling in him the faith he felt was central to his success.

At eighteen, Marvin enlisted in the Air Force but, by mutual agreement, was discharged honorably before his duty was up. Next, he played with a few different vocal groups, performances that led to a solo Motown recording contract. In 1964, Marvin hit real pay dirt: a duet with Mary Wells on "My Guy" was the smash that opened the floodgates. For the remainder of the decade, both Marvin and Motown Records cashed in.

After a string of hits, including "Can I Get a Witness?" and "How Sweet It Is to be Loved by You," Marvin released 1971's What's Going On?, an album filled with outspoken social commentary that surprised fans who had come to expect danceable love songs. Still, the album, a Motown milestone, demonstrated that its popular artists were not mere dance-steppers.

Later in the 1970s, Marvin struggled with substance abuse, his marriage disintegrated, and he fell deeply into debt. Marvin fled his demons rather than face them, but after a three-year, self-imposed European exile, he seemed to have a new vitality and went back to the studio. His 1982 release Midnight Love, a modern quilt of electronic sounds woven through an oblique reggae beat, was hailed as a masterful comeback. Marvin won two Grammys for his efforts and the singles "Let's Get It On" and "Sexual Healing" became radio standards.

Though Marvin's professional life seemed to be back on track, his personal life was a runaway train; the IRS dogged him for back taxes, he succumbed to cocaine addiction, romantic relationships imploded, and he was becoming ridiculously paranoid. After a tempestuous tour following the Midnight Love album, Marvin retreated to the Los Angeles home that he'd bought for his parents. But Marvin and his father had never addressed their 25-year-old animosities, and now, living together but apart (Marvin spent his days alone in his room), their conflicted relationship worsened.

On April 1, 1984, after an argument and an altercation concerning Marvin, Sr.'s inability to locate a letter from an insurance agency, the string finally broke. Without saying a word, Marvin, Sr. entered his son's room and shot him while he sat on his bed. Marvin, Jr. slumped to the floor, his father fired again, and his wife Alberta screamed to the heavens for her son. Marvin, Sr. then went outside, threw the gun onto the front lawn, and waited on the porch for the police. Later that afternoon, on the day before his 45th birthday, Marvin Gaye, Jr. was pronounced dead.

After a service at which Stevie Wonder sang, Smokey Robinson spoke, and 10,000 people passed by his open casket, Marvin was cremated and his ashes scattered in the Pacific Ocean.

Marvin Gay, Sr. was arrested and stood trial for his son's death, and Alberta promptly divorced him. At trial, photographs of Marvin, Sr.'s body demonstrated that he'd been abused by his son and, after a no-contest plea of voluntary manslaughter Marvin, Sr. was sentenced to five years' probation. Alberta died in 1987 of bone cancer. Marvin, Sr. died of a stroke in 1998.

Alex Haley
August 11, 1921-February 10, 1992

While serving with the Coast Guard during the Second World War, Alex Haley, a voracious reader, ran out of things to read, which prompted him to start writing. Alex toiled over his short stories for several years, suffering hundreds of rejections until one was finally accepted by a magazine in 1947. By 1952, the service had taken notice of their budding author and created for Alex the new rating of chief journalist, and he began writing for the United

States Coast Guard's public relations office. In 1959, after twenty years of military service, Alex retired from the Coast Guard and launched a new career as a freelance writer.

Alex wrote for Reader's Digest and then moved on to Playboy, where he initiated the magazine's trademark in-depth interview feature. One of the personalities he interviewed was Malcolm X, a meeting that inspired Alex's first book, 1965's *The Autobiography of Malcolm X*.

His hundreds of intriguing conversations with Malcolm prompted Alex to search out his own genealogy; an endeavor that proved to be an exhaustive, eleven-year odyssey. As Alex searched further and further back in time, he eventually landed in the village of Juffure in Gambia, West Africa, where a native oral historian, a griot, recounted to Alex seven generations of Mandinka tribal history. In the griot's account, Alex's early ancestor, sixteen-year-old Kunta Kinte, was wrested from the forest while searching for wood to make a drum, then sold into slavery.

Alex painstakingly chronicled his ancestors' passage from slavery to freedom and, in 1976, his acclaimed book, *Roots: The Saga of an American Family*, jolted America's conscience with its powerful affirmation of black history and shattering view of slavery. *Roots* became a phenomenon. The book became a number-one national bestseller. The twelve-hour television miniseries broke ratings records. Lesson plans based on *Roots* were used in schools, and a new interest in African American genealogy was stimulated. Alex was awarded a special Pulitzer Prize, received honorary degrees, was lauded with a resolution by the U.S. Senate, and labeled a "folk hero" by Time magazine. *Roots* was indeed a cultural milestone, bringing the issues of slavery and racism to the forefront of American consciousness. It was groundbreaking and monumental but, unfortunately, it was also fiction.

In 1977, Harold Courlander filed a suit charging that *Roots* plagiarized his novel, *The African*. In fact the history of Kunta Kinte closely resembled that of a character named Hwesuhunu as chronicled in Courlander's work, and several passages in *Roots* were copied almost verbatim from *The African*. After a threat of perjury from a trial judge, Alex settled out of court for $650,000.

And there were even more unsettling discoveries. Subsequent investigation of tapes in Alex's own archives revealed that Kunta Kinte was a historical imposter invented with the full cooperation of Gambian government officials. From a review of Alex's private papers, virtually every genealogical claim in Alex's story has been shown to be false. Even his attempt to recreate the Middle Passage experience of enslaved Africans by sleeping on a "rough board between bales of raw rubber in the hold" of a transatlantic ship is fundamentally inaccurate; he sailed the Red Star from Dakar to Florida in 1973, but never stayed in the hold, according to the ship's first mate, Frank Ewers. "I had the keys to the hold and Haley never went down there at night. He would have died from the cocoa fumes."

In 1980, Alex wrote a television series called Palmerstown, USA. In 1988, two books were published posthumously. They were, *A Different Kind of Christmas*, and *Queen: The Story of an American Family*. Unfortunately, none of these works had the impact of *Roots*. On its own merits, *Roots* is an astounding piece of culturally significant fiction, and if Alex had released it as such, with appropriate bibliographic footnotes, his reputation would be untarnished and permanent. As it is, his place in literary history stands under a shadow.

At 70, Alex died of a heart attack and was buried at his boyhood home in Henning, Tennessee. (See chapter three)

Aaliyah Haughton
January 15, 1979-August 25, 2001

In her short life, Aaliyah Haughton, known simply as Aaliyah, lived a modern fairy tale of stardom. The sultry and ethereal-voiced R&B singer hit the music scene young. At just eleven years, she performed on Star Search and with soul legend Gladys Knight. By age fourteen Aaliyah had earned a recording contract. The next year her debut album went platinum. During her senior year in high school, Aaliyah released a second hit album and was nominated for an Academy Award for her performance of the song "Journey to the Past" from the soundtrack of the animated movie Anastasia.

Movie deals and acting roles came next. In quick succession Aaliyah costarred in Romeo Must Die, garnered a starring role in the supernatural adventure film Queen of the Damned and won coveted roles in two sequels to The Matrix.

There should have been many more chapters in this story, but it ended abruptly instead. While in the Bahamas shooting a music video, Aaliyah and her entourage were onboard a small charter airplane that crashed immediately after takeoff, killing all nine people aboard. It was later learned that the pilot did not have clearance to fly that particular airplane and, just twelve days earlier, had been in court on cocaine charges.

At age 21, Aaliyah was buried at Ferncliffe Mausoleum in Hartsdale, New York.

Billie Holiday
April 7, 1915-July 17, 1959

Billie Holiday was born in the Baltimore ghetto and at age six, when perhaps she should've been in school, she was instead working at Alice Dean's brothel, running errands and scrubbing floors for a living. At ten, she was raped by a neighbor and for that "offense" was sent to a home for wayward girls. By thirteen Billie had surfaced in Harlem and was working as a part-time prostitute.

Fortunately, at around sixteen, it was discovered that she was a bit of a jazz singer, and Billie went from selling her physical talents to her musical ones. She became a fixture of the nightclub scene and in 1932, Columbia talent scout John Hammond (who years later discovered both Bob Dylan and Bruce Springsteen) heard Billie's wailings and arranged for her to record a few titles with Benny Goodman's orchestra.

After recording with Goodman and touring with a number of other popular orchestras over the next few years, Billie had elevated her technique and, despite never having received any technical training, her delicately wavering voice made her the outstanding jazz singer of her day. Billie came to be known as Lady Day, and between 1933 and 1944, she recorded over 200 "sides," though, egregiously, she never received royalties for any of them.

From 1944 to 1950, Billie recorded with Decca and, with trademark white gardenias fastened in her hair, she turned second-rate love songs into jazz classics. During the mid-1940s, though her demon was knocking at the door, Billie was at an artistic peak. "Singing songs like the 'The Man I Love' or 'Porgy' is no more work than sitting down and eating Chinese roast duck, and I love roast duck," she wrote in a 1956 autobiography.

The demon that Billie was dueling was of a familiar variety. She was addicted to heroin and spent much of 1947 in a federal women's prison in West Virginia for heroin possession. Furthermore, for years after her release, she was refused a New York cabaret license, which she needed in order to sing at the popular clubs that were the fundamental venues of her career.

By 1959, Billie was a physical wreck. She collapsed during a Greenwich Village performance after just two songs and was admitted to a city hospital in Harlem, suffering from cirrhosis and heart trouble. In those sad last days, she was arrested again for heroin possession, on her gurney, after a nurse said she found a foil package of the white powder near her bed. At 44, Billie's lungs became congested and her heart gave out. When she was removed from the bed, fifteen $50 bills were found taped to one of her legs, an advance for some autobiographical articles.

Wearing her favorite pink lace stage gown and pink gloves, Billie was buried at St. Raymond's Cemetery in the Bronx, New York.

Prophet Jones
November 24, 1907-August 12, 1971

When James Francis Marion Jones was almost two years old he reportedly told his mother that his daddy would come home bloody. That evening his father, a railroad brakeman, staggered home, bleeding from the scalp where a hobo whom he had ejected from a boxcar had hit him with a chunk of coal.

This prophesy began the long, flamboyant career of Detroit's Rev. James F. (Prophet) Jones, who at the height of his popularity claimed to have six million followers nationally.

Jones was born November 24, 1907, in Birmingham, Alabama, to the railroad brakeman and a school teacher.

Already recognized as a prophet, at the age of six he joined and began preaching sermons to a Birmingham sect known as Triumph the Church and Kingdom of God in Church, similar in character to the one he later founded in Detroit. At 11 he quit school to devote full time to preaching.

In 1938, The Triumph sect sent the 21-year-old Jones to Detroit as a missionary where enthusiastic converts soon pressed expensive gifts upon him. The gifts, his superiors ruled, were rightfully the property of the church. Rather than give them up, Jones broke away to launch his own sect.

Prophet Jones founded the Church of Universal Triumph, the Dominion of God Inc. in 1938 in Detroit. Originally headquartered in the old Oriole Theater at 8450 Linwood, the church later moved above the Fine Arts Theater at 2940 Woodward. He blessed his inner circle with royal and noble titles, such as "Sir," "Prince" and "Princess," "Lord" and "Lady" and other majestic appellations. His mother who died in 1951 was known as Grace Rev. Lady Catherine Jones. He called his flock "Citizens." At one time, Jones claimed he had six million followers nationwide spread among 35 "thankful centers," or local churches. Detroit's membership was about 1,500.

Jones reached his peak as a religious leader in the 1940s and late '50s, and lived like a millionaire. He resided in an 18th century-style French castle at 75 Arden Park, in Detroit. The three-story, 54-room graystone chateau had been built in 1917 by Edmund A. Vier, a General Motors Corp. executive, at a cost of $100,000.

The interior of the home boasted hand-carved woodwork, gold-painted ceilings, ornate brocade drapes and wall-to-wall carpeting with pile as deep as an English lawn. Furnished with a $7,000 grand piano, $8,000 worth of silver plate, a stained glass window installed at a cost of $1,200 and rooms of expensive furniture, it awed visitors.

The Prophet received visitors in a small paneled study, dominated by a life-size portrait of himself in a white robe. The room was stifling because a gas fire burned in the fireplace 24 hours a day. Jones explained to visitors that God had told him never to let it go out. Permanently arranged in front of the fireplace were dozens of children's toys meant to symbolize the lack of toys in Jones own impoverished boyhood.

Although Jones lived like a millionaire, he would often say "I am only rich in wisdom and the knowledge of God." During his heyday, he had 12

servants, five Cadillacs, each with its own chauffeur, a wardrobe of 400 suits, a white mink coat, jewelry, and thousands of dollars worth of perfumes.

Prophet Jones held five services a week in Detroit's old Oriole Theater, which cost $300,000 to redecorate. It included a $5,000 crimson and gold throne supposedly patterned after King Solomon's. Fitted in the canopy arching overhead, was a telephone "in case anyone should want to call during service." The temple also provided 2,000 plush seats and luxurious carpeting.

Prophet Jones converted the Oriole Theater at Linwood and Virginia Park into his church.

Once Jones took the floor to preach, he held it for five or six hours. "I stand longer than any other preacher," he boasted. Part of his service he delivered in a chanting, rhythmic "unknown tongue" peppered with phrases like "cosmic illuminability" and "the lubritorium of lubrimentality." The services gradually reached a pitch of shouting, stamping, and holy-rolling frenzy.

Prophet Jones wore an ankle-length, red-velvet coat with white silk lining. Underneath a robe of red crepe was aglitter with sequins. His graying locks were neatly arranged under a gem-encrusted white beret.

Jones claimed to be the embodiment of the Savior. Many blacks and some whites believed fervently in his divinity. They expressed their adoration by lavishing him with costly gifts: a five-carat, $10,000 topaz ring, a $6,000 diamond bracelet watch, a $17,000 bracelet with 812 diamonds. A $13,500 mink coat was given to him in 1953 by two Chicago school teachers, who credited Jones with curing their sick mother.

When he traveled to New York in 1954 he rode in a Cadillac, carried a gold-handled cane and was accompanied by four valets, four bodyguards, three secretaries, a cook, a dietitian, a housekeeper, a hairdresser, three musicians and 60 singers.

No one knew what the prophet's actual earnings were. He regularly filed income tax returns claiming income of less than $5,000 yearly. His sect was chartered under state law as a nonprofit corporation and the money taken in was presumed to be spent on organizational expenses only, making it tax exempt.

The prophet's popularity diminished in 1956 after he was accused of gross indecency. Although he was acquitted in Detroit's Recorder's Court, his influence waned, and he moved to Chicago, commuting between the two cities.

A stroke in October 1970, robbed Jones of his speech and ability to walk. He died August 12, 1971, of a heart attack at the home of a friend on LaSalle Boulevard in Detroit.

Approximately 15,000 people paid their last respects, and more than

2,000 attended a three- hour service in the Adlai Stevenson Building Auditorium on Grand River. Twenty ministers came from 36 states and the West Indies to take part in the services. Detroit's black community leaders also attended.

The Rev. John Smettler, who was once an altar boy for Jones, was among many who spoke at the service. He ended with Jones' well-known phrase: "All is well, All is well, All is well."

The prophet was buried in his silver-embroidered robe in a bronze coffin at Elmwood cemetery in Detroit.

Florence Joyner
December 21, 1959-September 21, 1998

While growing up in the Watts ghetto of Los Angeles, Florence Joyner took up running through a local youth foundation. She later attended UCLA on a track scholarship and, the year after graduation, earned a Silver Medal in the 200-meter event at the 1984 Olympic Games. After the Olympics, Flo worked as a bank service representative during the day and as a hair stylist at night and, at one point, added almost 60 pounds to her previously superbly athletic physique.

But by 1987, in a resolve to return to competition and qualify for the 1988 Games, Flo began training anew with her husband, Al Joyner, and her sister-in-law, Jackie Joyner-Kersee, who had each already won their own gold medals. By the time of the Olympic Trials, Flo's comeback was on track and she shaved an astonishing 2.7 seconds from the women's 100-meter dash, a record that stands today.

At the games in Seoul, Flo's comeback was complete. Flashy and confident, she stunned the world's track community by claiming three gold medals for the 100-, 200-, and 400-meter races, as well as a silver medal for the 1600-meter relay. During that summer of spectacular performances, Flo (or Flo-Jo, as she came to be known) also teased audiences by showing off her perfectly toned physique in signature one-legged racing outfits with low-cut tops. She made a further fashion statement with her lengthy and elaborately painted fingernails Not surprisingly, on the heels of her Olympic knockout performance, rumors swirled that Flo had been taking performance-enhancing substances. She always denied the accusations and never failed a drug test. She soon announced her retirement and lived comfortably on her endorsements of athletic gear and fingernail products. Later, Flo established the Florence Griffith Youth Foundation, a nonprofit program for disadvantaged youth.

On a September morning in 1998, Al Joyner awoke to find Flo unresponsive and not breathing. She had died during the night. A preliminary investigation suggested that she suffered some kind of cardiac problem, and the public's immediate assumption was that Flo had died of a heart attack instigated by the excessive use of steroids. However, an autopsy revealed that Flo had died of "positional asphyxia due to epileptiform seizure" caused by a brain abnormality known as "cavernous angoima." In layman's terms, a deviation in her brain had caused an epileptic seizure, though not of the common convulsing variety, and Flo had simply suffocated in her pillow. The Orange County coroner added that he knew of no connection between that condition and steroid use.

But the story wasn't over. Another of Flo's endorsements was for milk and she had appeared in print advertisements wearing a "milk moustache" in a familiar Milk Council campaign. There is in milk a particular protein called casein that can produce a violent histological reaction in some people, especially in African Americans who happen to be more commonly lactose allergic. There is now a small movement afoot, initiated by folks who are adamant that humans have no business drinking cows' milk in the first place. They suggest that Flo's death was triggered by an allergic reaction to a dairy product, but that the information is being suppressed for fear of damaging the dairy industry.

At 38, Flo was buried at El Toro Memorial Park in Lake Forest, California.

Martin Luther King, Jr.
January 15, 1929-April 4, 1968

After receiving his doctorate in theology from Boston University, Martin Luther King, Jr. moved to Montgomery, Alabama, in 1955, where he was to be a preacher at a Baptist church. Having grown up in Atlanta he was no stranger to Southern prejudice, but the scale of racial bigotry in Montgomery was so outrageous that Martin's ambitions were refocused, and he dedicated his life to amending those inequities and presenting his race with a fair chance at the American Dream.

By refusing to give up her seat on the bus to a white person, Rosa Parks was the catalyst for a boycott of Montgomery's city buses, organized by King and others, which ended only after the United States Supreme Court ruled that segregation on public transportation is legally and socially unacceptable. Building on that success, achieved through nonviolence, Martin founded the Southern Christian Leadership Conference in 1957 and became a figure with a national platform. The Civil Rights Movement had begun.

In the years following, Martin organized many similar nonviolent protests and the movement reached its zenith when the Civil Rights Act of 1964 was passed. The broad-reaching legislation guaranteed equal rights in all areas of the public domain, and a civil rights commission would ensure that these laws were enforced. Though Martin and his thousands of followers had not struggled in vain, the victory had come at a cost. They had endured high pressure fire hoses, midnight cross burnings, and backwoods lynchings. But Martin had remained peaceful throughout, and in biblical cadence assured his followers that their fight could be victorious if they did not resort to bloodshed.

At 39, Martin was killed in Memphis, Tennessee. While he stood on the balcony of the Lorraine Motel, a single bullet was fired at him from the bathroom of a flophouse across the parking lot. A fugitive from a Missouri prison, James Earl Ray, was staying in the flophouse and a rifle and a pair of binoculars marked with his fingerprints were found in a bag near there. Arrested in London two months later, Ray never stood trial, but instead pleaded guilty in order to avoid the death penalty. Ballistics tests were never able to prove, or disprove, that the bullet had come from Ray's rifle and, largely on that basis, Ray tried to recant his guilty plea and repeatedly petitioned the court for a trial. However, no court ever recognized his request and, in 1998, he died of hepatitis at 70 and was cremated.

In a magnificent crypt atop a reflecting pool, Martin lies at his own Martin Luther King Jr. National Historic Site, established in Atlanta in 1970.

Joe Louis
May 13, 1914-April 12, 1981

In the opinion of many, Joe Louis, the plain, unobtrusive legendary Brown Bomber, was the best heavyweight fighter of all time. He held the world championship title for twelve years, defending it an amazing 25 times, including during a period of time beginning in December 1940 known as the "Bum of the Month" campaign, when he met challengers at the rate of one per month.

Many years after his career was over, Joe found himself in the public eye again when the IRS dogged him for more than a million dollars past due, which they eventually forgave as Joe was penniless and his earning days over. Despite all his money woes, Joe never considered himself broke. As his wife Martha described, "Joe is rich with friends. If he said he needed a dollar, a million people would send him a dollar and he'd be a millionaire."

At 66, just hours after attending a heavyweight championship fight at Caesar's Palace, Joe died of cardiac arrest and was buried at Arlington National Cemetery in Arlington, Virginia.

Jesse Owens
September 12, 1913-March 31, 1980

During the 1936 Olympic Games, Jesse Owens achieved the finest one-day showing in track history by winning an unprecedented four gold medals. What made his accomplishments even more memorable was that they unfolded directly in front of Adolf Hitler, in his own Nazi Germany capital, where it was expected that the Games would be a forum for his supposed

Aryan supremacy. Instead, a black athlete named Jesse ruined Hitler's day by affirming that it was again only individual excellence, rather than race or national origin, that distinguishes one from another.

Upon his return to the States from that tremendous performance, Jesse was showered with accolades. But in those days athletes were not offered lucrative endorsement contracts, and Jesse needed to support his young family. Taking a position as a playground director in Cleveland, Jesse took his first step toward a lifetime of working with underprivileged children, and for the remainder of his life, he was tirelessly and continuously involved in the promotion of youth guidance activities. In 1976, Jesse was recognized for his efforts with our nation's Medal of Freedom award, the highest civilian honor.

Seventy years ago, the detrimental effects of smoking weren't as well-known, and certainly not as well-publicized, as they are today. Many professional athletes smoked, and some even appeared in print ads advocating smoking because they had been led to believe that it helped open the lungs. Jesse was one of those misinformed athletes but, by the time the dangers of tobacco were widely publicized in the 1960s, it was too late for Jesse; he was hopelessly hooked on cigarettes.

Jesse died of lung cancer at 66 and was buried at Oak Woods Cemetery in Chicago, Illinois.

Rosa Louise Parks
February 4, 1913-October 24, 2005

In 1955, Rosa Parks' quiet act of defiance changed the course of history. Fifty years later, this former seamstress who was arrested for refusing to give up her seat on a Montgomery, Alabama, bus to a white man, thus inspiring Rev. Martin Luther King, Jr. and others to initiate a 381-day bus strike, has made history, once, again, in death.

Parks, who died October 24 at the age of 92 was the first woman and second African American (U.S. Capitol police officer Jacob J. Chestnut in 1998 was the other) to lie in state at the Capitol Rotunda, an honor until that day set aside only for presidents and war heroes.

Her body arrived at the Capitol Sunday, October 30, and eight military pall-bearers carried her casket into the Rotunda, placing it on a platform draped in black. A choir then sang "The Battle Hymn of the Republic."

Hundreds of people lined up on Constitution Avenue to watch the motorcade enter the Capitol. By 9:30 p.m., the line was already one mile long. All people in line by midnight were allowed to view the body.

Thousands of people came to pay their respects, including President George W. Bush and his wife, Laura, who placed wreaths at the casket.

U.S. Rep. John Conyers of Detroit who employed Parks on his congressional staff for 20 years (she retired in 1988), said that this tribute was much more than a civil rights victory. "It's an American victory," he stated.

Before her body arrived in Washington, she was flown to Montgomery, where she was honored at St. Paul A.M.E. Church, the church she once attended. With hundreds of people showing up for the ceremony, the church was forced to open a separate wing for the overflow. Still more mourners were lined up outside the church and stayed throughout the entire service, which ran longer than its anticipated two hours.

Secretary of State Condoleezza Rice, herself an Alabama native, spoke at the ceremony. "I can honestly say that without Mrs. Parks, I probably would not be standing here today as Secretary of State," she said.

On Wednesday, Nov. 2, Parks' body was buried in Detroit. The president ordered all U.S. flags to be flown at half-staff over all public buildings.

O'Neil Swanson Jr., of Detroit's Swanson Funeral Home, told the Detroit Free Press he was honored when Parks chose him to handle her funeral arrangements – 25 years ago. He told reporters, "She is like Mother Teresa, someone revered the world over." He also explained that much planning went into Parks' funeral, coordinating the various locations as well as the large number of dignitaries who came to the ceremonies.

Swanson's classic, white 1940 LaSalle and horse-drawn hearse were used to transport Parks' body between multiple Detroit locations: a viewing at the Charles H. Wright Museum of African American History, the service at the Greater Grace Temple and, finally, Woodlawn Cemetery, where Parks' husband, mother and brother are buried.

Among Parks' wishes for her funeral was that ordinary people be allowed to attend. Standing beside celebrities and dignitaries, they came in droves.

Richard Pryor

December 1, 1940 -December 10, 2005

Richard Pryor, whose blunt, blue and brilliant comedic confrontations confidently tackled what many stand-up comics before him deemed too shocking to broach, died early Saturday. He was 65. Pryor suffered a heart attack at his home in the San Fernando Valley section of Los Angeles early Saturday morning. He was born on December 1, 2005, in Peoria, Illinois.

The comedian's tremendous body of work, a political movement in itself, was steeped in race, class and social commentary, and encompassed the stage, screen, records and television. He won five Grammys and an Emmy and was an Academy nominee for his role in "Lady Sings the Blues" in 1972.

At one point the highest-paid black performer in the entertainment industry, the highly lauded but misfortune-dogged comedian inadvertently became a de facto role model—a lone wolf figure to whom many an up-and-coming comic from Eddie Murphy and Chris Rock to Robin Williams and Richard Belzer have paid homage. Pryor kicked stand-up humor into a brand new realm.

"Richard Pryor is the groundbreaker," comedian Keenen Ivory Wayans once said. For most of us he was the inspiration to get into comedy and also showed us that you can be black and have a black voice and be successful."

Pryor had a history both bizarre and grim: self-immolation (1980), a heart attack (1990) and marathon drug and alcohol use (that he finally kicked in the 1990s). Yet Pryor somehow — often- times miraculously, it seemed — continued steady on the prowl, even after being diagnosed with multiple sclerosis in 1986, a disease that robbed him of his trademark physicality.

Verbally potent and physically eloquent, Pryor worked as an actor and writer as well as a stand-up comic throughout the '70s and into the '80s. He won Grammys for his socially, irreverent concert albums and in 1973, he walked away with a writing Emmy for a Lily Tomlin television special.

Pryor starred in major feature films — from "Lady Sings the Blues" and the semiautobiographical writing, starring and directing turn in "Jo Jo Dancer, Your Life is Calling," to the less memorable "The Toy" and "Superman III." He also co-starred with comedian Gene Wilder in the highly popular buddy films "Silver Streak" and "Stir Crazy."

But it was his concert films, particularly "Richard Pryor — Live in Concert" (1979) — that many critics considered to be his best work.

Called genius by some, self-destructive madman by others, Pryor, throughout the tumult of a zigzagging career, remained an inclement force of nature.

"He was actually one of the rare people of that era who was a product of the chitlin' circuit and the white, liberal, coffee shop thing," said journalist and cultural critic Nelson George. "Where Bill Cosby immediately made it into the crossover realm ... Pryor was a product of both." Commenting on his battle with addiction, Pryor told the Washington Post in 1999: "The drugs didn't make me funny. God made me funny. The drugs kept me up in my imagination. But I felt ... pathetic afterward. Drugs messed me up."

Pryor was married six times. In addition to Lee and Rain, his survivors include sons Richard, Steven and Franklin, and daughters Renee, Elizabeth and Kelsey.

Jackie Robinson
January 31, 1919-October 24, 1972

On April 15, 1947, Jackie Robinson, grandson of a slave, crossed the white chalk line at Ebbets Field to play first base for the Brooklyn Dodgers and broke Major League Baseball's rigidly enforced color barrier. It's true that if not he, then some other black player would have integrated the national pastime eventually, but it was Jackie who did it, and because he did it so incredibly well, he became a near-mythic figure.

After a four-sport college career at UCLA and a stint as the top player in the Negro League, Jackie was asked by Branch Rickey, general manager of the Dodgers, to play for one of their farm teams. At first Jackie was disbelieving, not even interested, but Branch persisted and Jackie signed on. Many owners, sportswriters and fans were against the integration, claiming that it would destroy Major League Baseball, but Branch ignored his detractors, advanced Jackie through the ranks, and added him to the team's Major League roster. The Brooklyn Dodgers instantly became the favorite team of African Americans nationwide.

It's now been more than 50 springs since that day when Jackie first walked onto Ebbets Field and today it's difficult to appreciate the full weight of the event; it would be eight years before Rosa Parks would refuse to move to the back of a Montgomery bus and no one had any idea who Martin Luther King, Jr. was.

While black fans huddled around radios and crowded together in the bleachers to delight in Jackie's achievement, Jackie himself suffered lonely indignities; pitchers took pleasure in picking him off, base runners tried to spike him, fans mocked him, and he was subjected to a steady stream of racial insults and hate mail. But Jackie let his playing do the talking. He was named Rookie of the Year and just two seasons later won the Most Valuable Player award. Renowned for his daring steals of home, Jackie came to be one of the sport's most exciting players, and baseball fans both black and white filled ballparks to see him in action. The Dodgers set new attendance records, he led them to the World Series six times, and by 1950 he was the highest paid player on the team.

He retired in 1957 and during his induction into the Baseball Hall of Fame five years later, Jackie asked Branch Rickey to stand with him on stage as he accepted the honor; time hadn't eroded his appreciation for the opportunity that Branch had afforded him and all others of his race.

For all of his strength and athletic prowess, Jackie's health deteriorated at a relatively young age and, nine days after throwing out the ball to open the second game of the 1972 World Series, he succumbed to complications from diabetes at 53.

Jackie was buried at Cypress Hills Cemetery in Brooklyn, New York. His epitaph reads: A man's life is not important except in the impact it has on other lives.

Luther Bojangles Robinson

1878-November 25, 1949

Luther (Bojangles) Robinson was born in 1878 to Maxwell, a machine-shop worker and Virginia Robinson a choir singer in Richmond Virginia. After the death of his parents. Robinson and his siblings were raised by their grandmother.

He was christened Luther, a name he did not like, so he suggested to his younger brother Bill that they should exchange names. When Bill object-ed, Luther applied his fists. and the exchange was made! The former Bill later adopted the name Percy and became a well-known drummer.

As a child Robinson studied the "clog" and the "buck and wing," African American variations of the Irish gig. At the age of six he began danc-ing for a living, appearing as a "hoofer," or song-and-dance man, in local beer gardens. Several years later, in Washington, D.C., Robinson toured with Mayme Remington's troupe. At age of 12, he joined a traveling company in "The South Before the War". Robinson joined with George Cooper in 1905 and the two worked as a vaudeville team.

In Chicago, and in 1908, Robinson met Marty Forkins, who became his lifelong manager. Under Forkins' tutelage Robinson matured and began working as a solo act in nightclubs, increasing his earnings to an estimated $3500 per week.

During his career, Robinson set a world's record of 8.2 seconds for the 75-yard backward dash!

Robinson developed complicated and rhythmic dances, including his signature staircase dance he taught Shirley Temple on screen in the movie The Little Colonel. He claimed the "stair dance" was developed on the spur of the moment when he was being honored by the King of England as he danced up the staircase to meet the King. He also appeared with Temple in The Littlest Rebel, Rebecca of Sunnybrook Farm, and Just Around the Corner. In 1937, Robinson played opposite singer Lena Horne in "One Mile From Heaven."

In 1939, Robinson danced from Columbus Circle to 44th Street in New York City in celebration of his 61st birthday.

After his first marriage to Fannie Clay failed, Robinson married Elaine Plaines on January 21,1944 in Columbus, Ohio.

Robinson died of chronic heart condition at Columbia Presbyterian

Medical Center in New York City on November 25,1949. His body lay In state at an armory in Harlem; schools were closed. Thousands of people lined the streets waiting for a glimpse of his bier. Funeral services were held at the Abyssinian Baptist Church and he was buried at the Cemetery of the Evergreens in New York City.

Wilma Rudolph
June 23, 1940-November 12, 1994

With the cards stacked against her from birth, Wilma Rudolph was an unlikely Olympic hero. Besides being born with polio and wearing a steel leg brace until she was eleven, she was also stricken with double pneumonia and scarlet fever.

At fourteen, though, after years of intensive therapy began to affect her legs positively, she began participating in track meets and, incredibly, only two years later, at just sixteen, Wilma Rudolph was named to the 1956 Olympic team. That year, she failed to qualify for the 200-meter event but did run on the bronze-winning relay team. Four years later, at the 1960 Games in Rome, Wilma shocked the world by becoming the first American woman to win three gold medals at a single Olympics.

After her Olympics career ended, Wilma graduated from Tennessee State University and held a succession of positions as teacher, coach, and community service leader. In 1977, her autobiography was published, and it later became a television movie. Her story has served as an inspiration to handicapped youths ever since.

At 54, Wilma died of brain cancer and was buried at Foston Memorial Gardens in Clarksville, Tennessee.

Sarah Vaughn
March 27, 1924-April 3, 1990

As the daughter of two musicians, Sassy Sarah Vaughan was classically trained and thus tended to treat her voice more as an instrument than as a vehicle for lyrics. Negotiating wide leaps within her full-bodied contralto range and making fluid alterations of timbre from a bell-like clarity to a bluesy growl, she set the improvisational world of jazz on its head and carved for herself a secure role in its history.

Through the 1940s, Sarah recorded with many of the jazz greats of the day, including Dizzy Gillespie and Miles Davis, after which record companies clamored for her rights. She subsequently enjoyed her own recording contracts with numerous labels throughout the remainder of her life. In 1989 she received the Grammy Lifetime Achievement Award and was inducted into the Jazz Hall of Fame in 1990.

At 66, Sarah died of lung cancer and was buried at Glendale Cemetery in Bloomfield, New Jersey.

Muddy Waters

April 4, 1915-April 30, 1983

McKinley Morganfield was born to a Mississippi Delta share-cropping family and, as the legend goes, he earned his moniker as a small child for always playing in the mud. But by thirteen Muddy had taken up guitar and developed an interest in blues music.

During a 1941 visit to the Delta region in search of artists to record for the Library of Congress folk-song archives, Alan Lomax found Muddy who, by then, had developed his own jagged bottleneck guitar-playing style. Prompted by Lomax, Muddy moved north to Chicago, where he soon went electric because, "couldn't nobody hear you with an acoustic." That provided the boost that lifted him above his contemporaries; Muddy's earthy, traditional vocals layered over an urgently amplified sound touched off the modern Chicago-blues movement. Into the 1950s, Muddy refined his artistry in releases such as "Hoochie Coochie Man" and the anthemic "Got My Mojo Working," and his style ultimately shaped the development of rock and roll music.

As the 1950s gave way to the '60s, blues of the sort that Muddy performed so definitively became less and less relevant to black listeners, who increasingly involved themselves with soul music and its offshoots. But no matter - by this time, Muddy had been taken up by a new audience, anyway: the young, white middle class that had been born of the folk music revival. The taverns and back halls in which Muddy had performed in the previous decade gave way to college auditoriums, jazz clubs, and festival stages where he was widely accepted by the rock community and accorded the respectful adulation given a founding figure. In the last decade of his life, Muddy made three of his best-selling albums, Hard Again, I'm Ready, and King Bee, and he frequently performed with such acts as Eric Clapton and the Rolling Stones, who regarded him as their mentor.

Muddy died in his sleep at 68 and was buried at Restvale Cemetery in Worth, Illinois.

Flip Wilson

December 8, 1933-November 25, 1998

One of eighteen children born to a poor New Jersey household, Clerow "Flip" Wilson lied about his age and joined the Air Force at sixteen. With a lively sense of humor, he excelled in the service and it was his fellow servicemen who branded him "Flip," for his "flipped-out" personality. After leaving the Air Force at 21, Flip worked as a bellhop and moonlighted as a stand-up comedian. In 1965 he was invited to appear on The Tonight Show, and after that exposure, his star rose meteorically. Within a few years he had his own television show, The Flip Wilson Show.

The variety comedy show received only a tepid response at first, but wide-eyed Flip quickly drove the show to the top of the ratings with his keen wit and a collection of stock characters to which he brought comedic life with his hysterical body fluidity: Geraldine Jones was the sassy and swinging liberate who "don't take no stuff." There was the lecherous and slightly less-than-honest Reverend LeRoy of the Church of What's Happening, and Sonny the White House janitor was the "wisest man in Washington."

In 1974, after four award-winning seasons, the show's time was up and, strangely enough, so was Flip's. Though he'd exhibited that he could draw audiences, his career immediately lost its momentum and, except for an occasional guest spot, Flip vanished from show business.

At 64, Flip died after surgery to remove a malignant tumor on his liver. He was cremated and his ashes given to his family.

Malcolm X and Betty Shabazz
May 19, 1925-February 21, 1965

Malcolm X's father was an outspoken supporter of black leaders long before "civil rights" became a buzzword. As a result, the family was harassed by vigilante groups and Malcolm's father eventually ended up on streetcar tracks with a crushed skull and a body nearly severed in half, though the death was ruled accidental.

Malcolm was sent to prison for burglary in 1946, and it was there that he converted to the Black Muslim faith, the Nation of Islam. By the time of his 1952 parole, he wholeheartedly embraced the faith's beliefs and tirelessly championed its basic argument that evil is an inherent characteristic of the white man's world. He believed that in order to flourish blacks had to completely separate themselves from white civilization. Malcolm was soon ordained a minister, and in 1956 he met his future wife, Betty, who had also taken the last name "X," as many Nation of Islam followers do – it represents an African family name that can never be known.

Throughout the 1950s and into the early 1960s, Malcolm developed a brilliant platform style and, with bitter eloquence, took the Nation of Islam from an insignificant splinter group to an organization that boasted thousands of official members and an untold number of sympathizers. By far the Nation of Islam's most effective and prominent preacher, Malcolm was in almost constant demand on college campuses, where he derided the civil-rights movement and rejected integration and racial equality, calling instead for black separatism and the taking up of arms against whites. This message was the opposite of the nonviolent approach that activists such as Dr. Martin Luther King, Jr., preached and, as a result of this militant stance, many whites viewed Malcolm with fear and contempt, while many blacks distanced themselves from his tirades.

As Malcolm became increasingly famous, he provoked tension and jealousy among the Nation of Islam leaders. Its founder, Elijah Muhammad, sought to rid himself of the formidable threat to his own power. After Malcolm described John F. Kennedy's assassination as a "case of chickens coming home to roost," Muhammad suspended his protégé from the faith.

In 1964, Malcolm followed a pilgrimage to Mecca with a prolonged period of study in the Middle East, where he was impressed by the sight of people of all races coming together in the name of Islam. He returned to the United States a changed man, proclaimed himself a convert to orthodox Islam, adopted a new name, El-Hajj Malik ElShabazz, and fostered a new philosophy known as Black Consciousness encouraging blacks to share their racial and cultural heritage.

Malcolm no longer accepted that white people were evil, and he became critical of the now-rival Nation of Islam, condemning its ideas as counterproductive; it was economics, not color, that kept blacks from succeeding, the new Malcolm insisted. Further, Malcolm raised questions about Nation of Islam financial irregularities, and denounced Elijah Muhammad as a fake and an immoral philanderer. As the two sides traded accusations, the conflict escalated into outright violence and death threats were recorded.

While preparing for an address at Harlem's Audubon Ballroom in February 1965, Malcolm X was ambushed and died after being shot more than a dozen times. Though his three assassins had ties to the Nation of Islam, they insisted someone else had paid them. Nonetheless, they were convicted of the murder and sentenced to life in prison.

After her husband's death, Betty Shabazz earned a doctorate in education and traveled widely to speak on civil rights and racial tolerance. In 1994 she spoke publicly about a long-held suspicion that Louis Farrakhan, the current leader of the Nation of Islam, had been behind the assassination of her husband, and a year later, her daughter Qubilah was charged with trying to hire a hit man to kill Farrakhan. Qubilah avoided prosecution by agreeing to accept responsibility for her conduct and completing treatment for alcohol and psychiatric problems, while Betty reconciled with Farrakhan at a fund-raiser for her daughter's defense.

In June 1997, Betty died after being severely burned in a fire started by her twelve-year-old grandson (Qubilah's son), reportedly set because he was unhappy that he had been sent to live with her.

Malcolm X and Betty are buried side by side at Ferncliffe Cemetery in Hartsdale, New York.

GENEALOGY FOR THE BEGINNER

I'M GONNA WALK TO DE GRAVEYARD

'HIND MA FRIEND, MISS CORA LEE

GONNA WALK TO DE GRAVEYARD

'HIND MY DEAR FRIEND CORA LEE

CAUSE WHEN I'M DEAD SOME

BODY'LL HAVE TO WALK BEHIND ME.

—LANGSTON HUGHES

Recently, a prominent Southerner was heard to remark, "If you don't give a whit about the past, how can you plan for the future?" In a way, he was paraphrasing those words written by Edmund Burke almost two hundred years ago: "People will not look forward to posterity who never look backward to their ancestors."

With this thought in mind, Evelyn M. Frazier writes in *A Guide for Amateur Genealogists* that an avid interest in ancestry is not always the "ancestor worship" that some would assume. More people in the United States than ever before are compiling family histories, or genealogies, as they are called by people specializing in this type of work.

Once you begin your own research into your family background,

CHAPTER SIX

313

you too enter the field of the genealogist. Just as a writer must compile a multitude of facts about a certain period of time in researching a historical novel, the genealogist must be well-informed on all phases of life relating to the period he or she is researching. In uncovering family histories, you, as researcher, must look beyond mere dates and statistics. A creditable history of your family, if properly and creatively compiled, will be interesting reading as well as a *true* history.

For this process, cemetery records and tombstone markers are a primary source of information; they often yield interesting and reliable information. However, much more must be done before embarking upon a cemetery search. Those tracing the lives of African Americans are encouraged to determine what records—either at home or in repositories such as libraries, state or church archives, or historical societies—may be available for genealogical research in the regions where their ancestors once lived. Information also appears in records a family historian would normally expect: personal family records, like Bibles, letters, diaries, and photographs; census, church, court, military, naturalization, and vital records; passenger-ship lists; newspapers; and numerous other sources, both primary and secondary (like transcriptions or indexes of original records). City directories, social security files, and school and hospital records also act as excellent resources. The pages that follow discuss these and other records, the types of information that they contain, their location, and their strengths and limitations as they apply to African Americans. Also included is a brief survey of the types of charts and record keeping systems used by genealogists in their research, and a few peripheral charts to help you assimilate information for your own history-seeking process.

Charting and Record Keeping

Probably the most important part of any type of research is developing an efficient way to organize information. This is particularly true for genealogical research. Without a system for organizing information in place at the start of the project, as more data is uncovered it becomes increasingly difficult to locate each particular piece. A variety of methods for taking notes and organizing information exist; the key is to find one that works well for you.

Keeping good notes involves several factors. As simple as it may sound, a good researcher should be able to read his or her own handwriting later, when the notes may not be as fresh in the mind as when they were taken. Select the type and size of paper, note cards, or notebooks that will be most convenient for each particular type of note-taking. Notebooks, for example, can contain many notes and are easily accessible, particularly if there is a lot of information to be recorded at one place. Whenever possible, documents and other information should be copied verbatim, exactly as they appear in the original source, except when lengthy legal documents, such as deeds, would be more easily recorded and later understood as a brief summary or abstract.

The source containing the information and the location wherein the information was found should be completely cited. The name of the repository (such as the county courthouse), the source (name or title, volume and page numbers, copyright date), and the results (whether or not information was found, how reliable the data is) should be noted. For example, "Mobile County Courthouse, Mobile, Alabama, Recorder of Deeds office, Deed Book 1, page 10, January 12, 1850," should be included in your notes. You should be as specific as possible when identifying sources, primary or secondary. When citing information from a book, the author's name, title of the book, place of publication, publisher, publication date, and page should be listed. If nothing on the person or topic being researched was located in a specific source, you should still note that the book was examined to avoid examining it again later. Consult a style manual for more details on how to cite sources: Richard S. Lackey's *Cite Your Sources: A Manual for Documenting Family Histories and Genealogical Records* and *The Chicago Manual of Style* are among those available.

You may use a number of different charts to organize your research notes. Basic forms, such as a family group sheet, pedigree or ancestor chart, research log, and correspondence log are important tools that may be purchased from genealogical societies, the Church of Jesus Christ of Latter-day Saints (LDS) Family History Centers, or Everton Publishers in Utah.

You should complete a family group sheet with all the documented evidence on a particular family. The sheet may contain spaces for some or all of the following data: father's name; mother's name (including maiden name); dates and places for births, baptisms, marriages, deaths, and burials; occupations; religion; military service; names of other spouses. Information on children should include date and place of birth, marriage, death, and name of spouse. Each fact on the family sheet should be individually referenced by number to its source in the researcher's file. You, as the compiler, should be identified by name, address, and date. Appended to the group sheet should be a chronological summary of everything found to date on every person in raw note form, not as a narrative summary.

For example, if the husband of the person you're researching has been located in several census records, indicate the birthplace from each record on the group sheet, and use a number to indicate each specific source, such as "The federal census, population schedule, Cole County, Missouri, page 43." On a separate sheet, record the complete citation of the data with notes from the sources. This would include the names, dates, and other data found in the census, for example, on each family member. The complete citation would include the census year, schedule, county, page, dwelling and household numbers, and line numbers.

Pedigree or ancestor charts contain basic genealogical data: names; dates of birth and marriage for the person being researched; and similar data, along with dates of death, for the research subject's parents, grandparents, great-grandparents, and so on. These charts can provide a quick overview of one's family. Numbering individuals on these should refer researchers to the correct family group sheet and vice versa. For example, if Joe Smith is person 16 on pedigree chart 4, you would find his family group sheet numbered 4–16.

Other useful charts include a research calendar or log and a correspondence record. The former contains spaces for the ancestor's name; date of the research; location and/or call number of the source; description of the source, such as census or will book; time period searched, such as 1850–1900; and comments (names searched, purpose of each search, results, etc.).

A correspondence record may contain your ancestor's name, addressee, address, date sent, purpose of the letter, date replied, and results of the correspondence.

Before You Begin

"Who am I?" is a question most people ask at some point in their life. To find the answer you must be prepared to work hard, digging in dusty archives as an archaeologist might delve into the darkness of a newly discovered tomb. But the starting point is you. Unless you build a firm foundation with the facts surrounding your immediate past, the structure built of the lives of those you are researching will be weak. As you begin to record facts about yourself, plan a course of action that establishes a pattern you can easily follow for receiving and recording new information. A form like the example included at the end of this chapter can help you with this process. Your first form, about yourself, will help you shape the beginning of your research and, ultimately, your family tree if you choose to create one. The forms about your ancestors and other family members, which were adapted from Rosemary A. Chorzempa's *My Family Tree Workbook, Genealogy for Beginners*, can be studied and completed with information that you might already have at hand.

As a next step, approach your closest relative and ask for information on him or her, as well as other persons known to your relative who could be helpful. Make telephone calls, visit relatives, write letters, and practice your interviewing skills, using a tape recorder at times, if appropriate. Remember to remind the person you are interviewing to check Bibles, diaries, and files of old records and papers.

Even before you begin to use the resources outlined in this chapter, you should consider the possibility of using a computer to help with your search. There are numerous publications and computer programs that can aid in recording and structuring data. One in particular is *Family Treemaker* by Banner Blue Software Inc. Even if you choose not to use a computer, you can and will have fun playing detective, delving into nooks and crannies and pursuing all the possible leads that open before you.

However, before elaborating on the variety of primary sources available for investigation, you should be aware of certain caveats, which, if ignored, could extend the time you spend on research unnecessarily. They involve dates, note taking, and letter writing.

DATES

Be certain that you pay *close* attention to all dates you encounter. Upon close examination of dates in statements of fact, inconsistencies are often discovered. Does the date of the child's birth correspond with the age of the mother? Is the date of death recorded that of the actual death, or the date of the funeral or placing of a memorial? Were the months correctly transferred into roman numerals? Of course, these inconsistencies can only be discovered after you have gathered considerable information. But even in the early stages of research, it is easy to reverse numbers—and lengthen someone's life by nine years by transcribing a death date of "1878" as "1887"—or habitually record a Revolutionary War–era birth date as "*1957*" rather than "1757."

NOTE TAKING

There is no set rule on the type of paper to use; some prefer index cards, others notebooks. Whatever your chosen medium, be sure to record: (1) the topic; (2) the source of information (books, etc.), along with inclusive page numbers; (3) the city and institution where you found the source; and (4) the date you took the notes. Set aside separate cards or pages for each ancestor before transferring the information to your charts.

LETTER WRITING

During your research, you will often find it necessary to write letters to people you believe will be a source of needed information. Here are some suggestions:

- Make your request as clear as possible. Let him or her know the record you want, the *complete* name of the person who you are interested in, and the birth and death dates, if you have them.

- Keep your letter as short as possible. If you are asking for birth and death records, spell it out quickly and don't bury your purpose for writing in chatty prose.

- Enclose a self-addressed, stamped, business-size envelope with your request, so the person can respond quickly.

- If it seems appropriate, enclose a small amount of money and offer to pay for any additional expenses encountered.

- Enclose your phone number and ask that the person call collect if he or she has any questions.

- If you have access to a fax machine, include the number to which he or she can fax questions or responses to your request.

- Be sure to extend your thanks at the time; sending an additional thank you after the information is received is sometimes also appropriate.

Now you are ready to explore the primary sources of information.

Sources of Information

Searching for clues to your past begins at home, building basic genealogical skills by reviewing your own family records and interviewing members of your immediate family. To facilitate the search, you should examine family Bibles, letters, diaries, photographs, scrapbooks, legal documents such as deeds or wills, military discharges, tax receipts, birth or death certificates, obituaries, and any other personal or legal documents you can find at home that may contain information about the family. Family Bibles sometimes contain valuable data concerning marriages, births, and deaths—information that may not have been recorded in civil or church records. Personal letters may also contain clues to further research. Photographs, which may be inscribed with the names of those pictured, a date when the picture was taken, or the name and location of the photographer, provide direct glimpses into the past. Even with just the name and location of the photographer—usually obtainable from a city telephone directory—information may be ascertained regarding the approximate date of the picture. Clothes, buildings, or people in the picture might provide clues concerning the date of the photograph. Identifying the type of military dress worn by someone in the picture could help you locate the service records of that individual. A tax receipt might provide a street address, a clue for further research in deed records or city directories. The latter source may list that person's occupation, or other relatives who resided at the same address. Wills and estate settlements may contain the names and addresses of other family members.

Any record that contains information about the family, however minor it might seem, should not be overlooked as a potential clue to the question, "Who am I?" After you have extracted all the possible data from the people and things in your home, and organized all your notes, it is time to take your search to other locations.

A note of caution: Before using any published source, check through any introduction wherein the author may describe limitations to the work, criteria for inclusion, location of the records, or problems, such as legibility, that might undermine the integrity of the original records.

CENSUS RECORDS

There is perhaps no other source used more frequently by genealogists than census records. Beginning in 1790, and in every tenth year since, the federal government has taken a census, a count of the nation's population along geographic, demographic, and numerous other divisions. You should immediately note that federal census schedules less than seventy-two years old are restricted and are not made public. And the amount of information recorded in the census has changed over the years; earlier records are not as detailed as later ones, but they all are important sources for those tracing the ancestry of any ethnicity. Although pre-1850 censuses do not contain the names of every free member of the household in any racial category, they can at least confirm that a family resided at a certain place at a certain time and can reveal the age and sex composition of the household. Census records should be read carefully, as the data contained therein may not be accurate and may conflict with data from other sources.

Federal censuses from 1790 to 1840 contain only the names of the heads of households and are not "every name" censuses. Members of the household—white, nonwhite, slave, and free—were enumerated in age brackets by sex, with the age categories revised through the years. Unlike later censuses, information such as relationships, birthplaces, or other personal data, was not listed. The 1790–1810 censuses listed free nonwhites as "all other [free] persons" and did not specifically mention free people of color. The 1820–1840 record provided a separate listing for free people of color. For example, the Mobile, Alabama, household of Richard Field, a free man of color, contained two people, according to the 1830 U.S. census: a free woman of color between thirty-six and fifty-five years old, and Field, between fifty-five and one hundred years old. The household of John A. Collins in the same city, as outlined in the 1840 census, contained three free males of color, one between thirty-six and fifty-five years old, one between ten and twenty-four, and the third under ten years. It also contained five free women of color, one between thirty-six and fifty-five years old, one between twenty-four and thirty-six, and three under ten. One female slave aged between ten and twenty-four also resided with the Collins family. The household of John McDonald, a white male, contained two male slaves, two female slaves, and a free woman of color.

For all U.S. censuses between 1790 and 1849, it is important to note that the "other free" or "free persons of color" categories do not distinguish between individuals of African ancestry and those of Native American descent. No assumptions about ethnicity can be made from this data without evidence from other records.

Help with Your Family Tree

Here are nine quick-start ideas for researching your family tree. Keep your mind open to the information you hear and where you hear it. Try to cross-reference material whenever possible. Be creative in your research. You are sure to learn some surprising and interesting facts about your family.

Relatives. Interview relations both close and distant. Ask to see scrapbooks, Bibles, and photo albums. Ask permission for copies of pictures, etc., that you would like to include in your own album.

Public libraries—genealogy and local history departments. Libraries have a variety of reference documents (maps, newspapers, directories, etc.) available, and can often help with other sources to contact for additional assistance. Some even have genealogy sections.

continued on next page

A major change occurred with the 1850 census. For the first time, the population schedule listed the names of each free member, white and nonwhite, of the household. In addition, the enumerator was instructed to record each person's age, sex, color (white, black, or mulatto), profession or occupation of males over the age of fifteen, value of real estate owned, place of birth (state, territory, or county), whether married within the year, whether attending school within the year, whether able to read and write (if over twenty years of age), and whether deaf and dumb, blind, insane, idiotic, pauper, or a convict. For example, the same John Collins listed in the 1840 census was identified in 1850 as a fifty-year-old mulatto carpenter who resided with four other mulattos: Isabella, fifty; Virginia, seventeen; Emma, sixteen; and John, fifteen. Each member of the family was born in Alabama.

One additional column of information was added to the 1860 federal census: the value of personal property owned by the family. The household of the same Collins family that appeared in the 1840 and 1850 censuses included the same individuals, but the assessed value of personal property was added. As stated earlier, inaccuracies in censuses are not uncommon, and the entry of John A. Collins provides an excellent example. From the 1850 to the 1860 census, Collins did not age: both censuses listed him as fifty years. His wife aged seven years in that decade, Virginia nine, and John only five years.

The 1860 census is important, as it was the last federal census conducted prior to the Civil War. As such it can provide clues for nonwhites, who have traced their ancestry at least as far back as the 1870 census, as to whether a particular ancestor was a free black or slave prior to or during the war. This information can be uncovered by searching for ancestor surnames in the 1860 census within the same general area where they resided in 1870. One should also consider searching the 1860 census for the white neighbors so listed in 1870. Comparisons can also be made between 1870 census data and sources such as slave schedules, estate records, and bills of slave sales.

Beginning in 1870, population schedules of the federal census began to list the names of all nonwhites. Of particular interest to the researcher would be the place of birth for each person: state, U.S. territory, or foreign country. The additional information recorded for each person basically repeated that contained in the previous census: age, sex, color, occupation, values of personal and real estate, whether parents were of foreign birth, whether born or married within the year, and citizenship status for males twenty-one years of age or older. Following the same Collins family, the 1870 census indicated that John A. Collins was a seventy-one-year-old carpenter, Isabella was a sixty-year-old housewife, and that the household now contained Clara, twenty-one years old, and John, one year old. All were mulattos born in Alabama.

While conducting your research, you should note that none of the federal censuses considered up to this point state any relationship between members of a household. You may hypothesize that Isabella was the wife of John A. Collins; that Clara was their daughter; and that young John was Clara's son; but you must seek evidence supporting the hypothesis elsewhere.

The 1880 census provided even greater detail on family members. It was the first federal census to specifically state the relationship of each person to the head of the household. Also shown are marital status (single, married, widowed, or divorced), whether a person was sick or disabled, and the birthplace for each individual as well as his or her parents.

Thus, if the census recorded the names of a family consisting of a father, mother, their children, and grandparents, it may be possible to trace that family to another area, or perhaps to the previous census in the same state. Tracing the migration of a family would be possible if, for example, the children were born in a different state from their 1880 residence. If the entire family was born in the same state where they resided in 1880, then that state's 1870 census could be checked. For example, John Collins continued to reside in Mobile. He lived with Isabella, whom we now know to be his wife, and John A. Collins Jr., his grandson. Each was a mulatto born in Alabama, and each person's parents were born in Alabama. The identification of the grandson, John, supports the hypothesis drawn from the 1870 census suggesting that Clara of 1870 should be sought as the mother of the child John of 1880. Thus, the 1880 census contains valuable clues that previous censuses do not.

continued from previous page

State bureaus of vital statistics. You can often obtain copies of birth and death certificates for a small fee. You'll find addresses for contacting the proper state bureau at the library.

Church records. Call first and explain what you are doing. Church records are private, but the pastor will often help if you are polite. Church records are often more accurate and informative than government records.

Cemetery records. If the records books have been carefully kept, the cemetery office can provide a wealth of information, especially if the graves do not have markers.

Federal census records. Every decade since 1790, a census has been undertaken, and it can provide much information. Many libraries have census records on microfilm (records up to the early 1900s are open to the public; those dating from the present to seventy-two years previous are closed to protect the privacy of those still living).

continued on next page

continued from previous page

County courthouses. You can do a search for vital records, such as land and naturalization records, by calling and arranging a visit to the county courthouse.

Historical and genealogical societies. Many localities have groups that collect and preserve information about their area's history. They will often sponsor lectures and workshops, and may have research materials available to help the amateur genealogist.

Church of Jesus Christ of Latter-day Saints (Mormon) library. The Mormon Church is very much involved in genealogy and the preservation of records. Their records are available on microfilm at some libraries, or you can arrange, for the cost of postage, for particular reels to be lent from the church to your branch library. For information, contact the Genealogy Department, Church of Jesus Christ of Latter-day Saints, 50 East North Temple Street, Salt Lake City, UT 84150.

Do not overlook the special schedule of so-called dependent, delinquent, and defective classes from the 1880 census. Many nonwhites may be found in them. People from prisons, jails, mental hospitals, or orphanages, for example, were enumerated like others in the 1880 population schedule, but because they were inmates of public institutions they were removed from the family unit and often from the counties—or even states—in which their families lived. The supplemental schedules may contain the person's home residence (city/town, county, and state), as well as other relevant data that varied from class to class. The schedule for homeless children included, for instance, whether the child was orphaned or abandoned and whether he or she was born in the institution where residing at the time of the census. For instance, in Florida the "insane" schedule shows that Leonard Basset, a nonwhite resident of Jacksonville, was afflicted at age twenty-eight, that he was sight and hearing impaired, and that he was a patient of an institution. Dolores Hull, a resident of a colored asylum, appears in the homeless children schedule as a resident of St. Augustine, Florida.

Most of the 1890 federal census was destroyed by a fire in the Commerce Department building in 1921. The National Archives has prepared an index to the surviving schedules, available on two rolls of microfilm (National Archives microcopy No. M496). Partial listings exist for areas in Alabama, the District of Columbia, Georgia, Illinois, Minnesota, New Jersey, New York, North Carolina, Ohio, South Dakota, and Texas.

The 1890 special federal census of Union veterans, as well as widows of Union veterans, of the Civil War was one of two censuses that contained information about military personnel; the other was the 1840 census that listed pensioners for Revolutionary War service. Information provided in the 1890 special return may include the enumeration district, house and family number from schedule one of the same census, name, rank, company, regiment or vessel, dates of enlistment and discharge, length of service, post office address, disability incurred, and other remarks. For example, William Wiggens was a private in Company C of the United States Colored Troops who served from November 1863 to March 26, 1866. His address and length of service are also listed. With this information, the researcher could check

Civil War service and pension records. According to *The Researcher's Guide to American Genealogy* by Val D. Greenwood, the 1890 special censuses from "those fourteen states and territories alphabetically from 'A' through 'Kansas' and into part of `Kentucky' have been lost."

Several changes occurred with the 1900 census. The following items were included: dates of birth (year and month); number of years married; for mothers, the number of children born and number living; for immigrants, the year of arrival in the United States, number of years in the United States, and whether naturalized; whether one's house was owned or rented; and whether the house was mortgaged. The census form also contained other information. Some of this new information can be especially useful to the researcher since it may provide the only existing record of the number of children born to a slave mother, and whether those children were still living when the census was taken.

Data in the 1910 census are similar to that of 1900. For example, location; relationship to the head of the family; personal description (sex, color, age, marital status, and, if a mother, number of children, and number yet living); place of birth; place of birth of parents; year of immigration; whether naturalized; occupation; literacy; whether home was owned or rented and, if owned, whether mortgaged; whether a survivor of Union or Confederate army or navy; and other data. Unlike the previous census, the 1910 census did not provide the month and year of birth.

The 1920 census contains much of the same data as the 1910 census. Information on the 1920 form included address; name; relationship to head of household; whether home was owned or rented; personal description (sex, color or race, age); marital status; year of immigration; whether naturalized; year of naturalization; literacy; place of birth for both resident and parents; occupation; and other data.

Censuses for 1900–1920 are valuable to the researcher as one of the first sources of information usually checked outside the home. They are useful in verifying information gathered from family documents found in the home, other written documents, and oral histories. If the researcher has located family members in the 1920 enumeration, for example, a possible next step would be to trace the family backward through the censuses and other appropriate records.

In addition to the federal census, additional governmental agencies have required their own censuses. These include special enumerations taken by the federal government—such as the military censuses discussed above—and those taken by territories, states, counties, and cities. For example, some Missouri state censuses, which are incomplete, are available at the Missouri State Archives. Selected city and county of St. Louis censuses were taken in the antebellum period and are available at the Missouri Historical Society in St. Louis. Thus, thorough researchers should inquire about the availability of non-federal censuses and how they may be obtained in the area in which he or she is conducting research.

African Americans trying to trace their enslaved ancestors need to first identify the slave-owner family. Freed slaves did not always take the name of former owners. According to *Ancestry's Guide to Research: Case Studies in American Genealogy:*

> Some slaves took surnames before the Civil War ended, while others waited until they began establishing themselves as free citizens. Many slaves took the surname of their last owner or their father who might have been a white slave owner or overseer, a deceased slave, or a slave sold to another owner several years prior to the Emancipation. Hundreds of slave families took the name of a prominent American, a local political figure, or the given name of the father of the family. It wasn't uncommon for freed slaves to be known by several surnames, making a final choice years after the Emancipation.

Slave schedules are a valuable source for the African American researcher attempting to bridge the gap between slavery and freedom. Compiled in 1850 and 1860, they typically contain the name of the owner and list the age, sex, and color of each slave, though not the name (although some exceptions exist). As noted in the article "To My Daughter and the Heirs of Her Body," by Curtis G. Brasfield, from the *National Genealogical Society Quarterly,* "When researchers identify a potential master through other sources, they can compare the age, sex, and color of each tallied slave against the data given for freedmen on later censuses; this process may strengthen or eliminate the possibility of a connection." While by itself this source of information can be inconclusive, by comparing such data with the information in deed books containing bills of sale, owner's records, etc., connections may be strengthened. Some free people of color owned slaves, and sources providing information on these people should not be overlooked by researchers looking for African Americans who were freed before 1865. Although not a typical slave owner for either race, a South Carolina free man of color in 1860 owned sixty-three slaves. In Alabama, a free nonwhite owned six slaves aged between one and twenty-eight years.

What if your pre–Civil War ancestors were enslaved and cannot be located easily by assuming that they took their former owners' surname? It may be necessary to check records on possible white families in the neighborhood where the black family was known to reside after Emancipation. This would entail examining antebellum documents, such as wills and bills of sale, and comparing data found in those records with the information contained in pre-war sources. Thus, when examining census records, you should attempt to identify slave owners' neighbors, whose records may provide sought-after answers to your questions.

In addition to the population and slave schedules, agricultural schedules of the federal census, 1850–1880, are available. These schedules provide data on farm size and value, number and type of livestock, livestock value, amount of crops produced, and other information. Though agricultural producers were not identified by race, and owning land was not a requisite to be listed, these schedules can provide more detail on ancestors already discovered elsewhere. In 1860, for example, Zeno Chastang Sr., one of the more prosperous free Negro farm owners in Mobile County, Alabama, owned eighty improved acres, 1,230 unimproved acres, and produced, among other items, twelve hundred bushels of corn. The value of his farm was $3,900.

Mortality schedules of the federal census are another valuable source for genealogists. These records cover the years 1850–1880 and contain the names of persons who died in the twelve months preceding the date of the census. Obviously, there are limitations to these schedules. For instance, they listed deaths for only every tenth year, and they were not complete. According to researchers, "It is estimated that in the mortality schedules for 1850, 1860, and 1870 only 60 percent of the actual deaths within those twelve-month periods were reported—that means that less than 8 percent of the actual deaths for this thirty-one year period are in the mortality schedules."

The 1850 and 1860 forms contained the same data for each person: name; age; sex; color; whether slave or free; marital status; place of birth; month of death; occupation; disease or cause of death; and number of days ill. Data in the 1870 schedule include the number of the family as given in the second column of schedule one (population); name; age; sex; color; whether parents of foreign birth; month of death; occupation; and cause of death. Data in the 1880 schedule include the number of the family as given in column two of schedule one (population); name; age; sex; color; marital status; place of birth; place of birth of the person's parents; occupation; month of death; disease or cause of death; length of residence in the county; and other data.

Several examples illustrate the value of this source. In March 1850 Tom Smith, a fifty-five-year-old free black born in Virginia, died in Dallas County, Alabama, of rheumatism. Harriet Smith, a forty-four-year-old free mulatto born in Georgia, died in the same county in June of unknown causes. In St. Louis, Joseph Dooley, a free black laborer born in Africa, died in June 1849 from cholera. In Howard County, Missouri, several slaves born in Kentucky were listed consecutively; each died in the same month from the same disease—cholera. Information in this source may not have been recorded in other records, especially for slaves. Obviously, for the researcher especially interested in tracing family medical history, these records have a special significance.

An example from the 1880 schedule provides greater clues. For example, if one checks the St. Louis schedule for the surname Washington, several entries are discovered in enumeration district 145. Betty and George L. Washington, two black children born in Missouri, whose father was born in Virginia and mother in Missouri, died in the same month and from the same disease. By examining the population schedule with the same enumeration district and knowing the family number from the mortality schedule, the researcher can locate the children's family. George L. Washington, his wife Hester, and their daughter Mollie are enumerated and information on them can now be extracted, such as the birthplaces of both the elder George and his wife.

You can obtain census records in several ways. Microfilm copies of agricultural, mortality, population, and slave schedules are available at many public, university, and genealogical libraries, as well as historical societies. If a local library does not have the needed census records, the interlibrary loan department may be able to order them from another library or rental program. For a nominal charge, you may also order films through the LDS Family History Library system. In addition, you can rent various microfilms, including census records, from the National Archives Microfilm Rental Program or the American Genealogical Lending Library. For a fee, these organizations lend microfilms and send them directly to individual researchers.

Printed indexes are generally available for pre-1880 censuses, as well as some indexes to the 1890 special federal census of Union veterans and widows of Union veterans. Information in most of these indexes is divided by state and listed alphabetically by surname. A special index, called the Soundex, is available for the 1880, 1900, and 1920 censuses. The key to the Soundex system lies in its name: According to researchers, census records "were alphabetically coded and filed by state under a system where all names sounding alike, regardless of spelling differences or errors (if they began with the same letter of the alphabet), would be interfiled."

The Soundex is comprised of index cards listing volume, enumeration district, sheet or page number, and line number, that direct the researcher to specific census records. Soundex cards also contain the name of the head of the household; that person's color, sex, age, birthplace, city and county of residence; and the names of all members of the household, their relationship to the head of household, ages, and birthplaces. The index to the 1910 census, called the Miracode, is similar to the Soundex but has indexed only twenty-one states.

Both the Soundex and Miracode indexes use complex coding systems, and both are limited in their ability to provide complete information. If you cannot locate a family, check variant spellings of the surname. Use your imagination with regard to the way an enumerator recorded a name; it was recorded as the enumerator heard it, and regional dialects of the period may have affected how the recorder spelled the name.

In the antebellum period, if a white man was the head of a free Negro family, his children may have been listed in censuses (and other records) under the name of either their white father or nonwhite mother. For example, in the 1840 population schedule for the city of Mobile, Mobile County,

Alabama, the household of Polite Collins, a free woman of color, included several other free Negroes and an adult white male. Ten years later, Collins resided with several nonwhites and four children assumed to be white because their race was left blank. All children went by the surname Collins. However, in 1860 Polite Collins resided with Roswell Swan, a white man, and several of their children who were identified as mulattos and who went by the surname Swan. (In other records, Swan acknowledged that he had children by this free woman of color.)

According to researcher Gary B. Mills, in addition to the problem of identifying offspring of an interracial union, "any assumption of ethnicity on the basis of census data from a single year (or any other single document) may err. Determining the ethnic identity of any family labeled *free people of color* (or *f.p.c.*) on any record invariably requires exhaustive research in the widest-possible variety of resources." For example, a twentieth-century white governor of Alabama, Braxton Bragg Comer, "appears as a child on the 1860 Federal Census, Population Schedule, of Barbour County, whereupon he and his entire family . . . were clearly identified as *black,*" Mills notes. Lawrence Brue appears as white in the 1860 federal census, but in previous censuses and in other records he appears as a free person of color. In 1860, in census records for Natchitoches Parish, Louisiana, the ethnicity of seventy-six of the 1,614 families was misidentified.

Although such inaccuracies in census records are frustrating to novice genealogists, some enumerators recorded more specific data than their instructions required. They sometimes included detailed information concerning places of birth, marriage, or other subjects for both whites and non-whites. For example, an apparently free black couple residing in Arkansas informed an enumerator of their exact year of marriage. A free woman of color in the 1860 census for St. Louis, Missouri, ward 2, page 802, indicated that she had been "freed by Benjamin Soulard," and that she was "married to slave John Harris." In addition, the name of John's owner and the couple's birthplace, St. Louis, were listed. A free woman of color, born in New Orleans, was "on visit" in St. Louis in the same area. In another instance, a female slave was listed last in the household of a white man who had hired her. Not only was her given name recorded but also the complete name of her owner. The value of such information cannot be overlooked as such "errors" provide clues for additional research.

Viewed as a whole, census records contain a variety of detailed information. Generally, each successive census includes more detailed information than its predecessor. As a researcher, you should follow an individual through the complete schedules of all censuses, from birth to death, and extract additional information about the area wherein that person resided. Although censuses contain errors, they are particularly valuable genealogical sources that you can rely on with a reasonable amount of caution.

Maps Can Help Unearth Clues

Early maps often indicated locations of families, as well as geographic locations. You can find such maps, including the *Mill's Atlas* and *Ruddock's Map,* in most county libraries, as well as in state archives. However, just because a person's name is indicated, this does not necessarily mean that person was living at the date of publication, since the material may have been compiled some years previously.

In Fairfax, Virginia, a staff librarian named Brian A. Conley has spent years tracking down long-forgotten cemeteries, from well-known church sites to abandoned family burial grounds. Once tipped off about a possible location (he works with historians, residents, and archaeologists), he plots the approximate location on aerial and topographic maps, and then travels to that location to start his search. He has thus far recorded over three hundred cemeteries.

Conley's tips include looking for tall, mature trees, knowing that trees near grave sites were usually left standing even when the surrounding land was cleared; and looking for flowers that don't grow naturally in the area but were planted over graves. He uses a three-and-a-half-foot steel pole with a T-shaped top to feel down into the earth. Even centuries after a burial, the earth remains loosely packed. The pole slides effortlessly into the ground when it hits the right spot.

Conley documents the locations he has found and marks them on county zoning and tax maps, hoping they will be safe from future destruction. He says, "These cemeteries are a part of cultural heritage. Nobody can divorce themselves from their own past."

CHURCH RECORDS

Religion has traditionally played an important role in the lives of African Americans, and the activities of various denominations are documented in both sacramental registers and business minutes. Most major denominations accepted both free nonwhites and slaves. In the antebellum era, for example, Roman Catholic and Protestant churches contained both white and nonwhite members. Many predominantly black churches were also in operation, each with their own set of records. Whenever separate registers for the races were kept, researchers are urged to check both, as some nonwhites appear in the "white" registers.

Sacramental registers provide a wealth of information, including baptisms (which may list birth data), marriages, and burials (which may list death data). Information from these registers may not be available in any other source, especially in the periods before the 1850 census and before the recording of such vital records became mandatory. Registers may also contain the dates of birth and death for a child who lived between census years. You should note that some owners freed their bondsmen or slaves at baptismal ceremonies. As was the case for free people, the names of slaves, approximate ages (sometimes exact dates), and often mother's name were recorded.

Baptismal records also may contain a variety of other information: names of parents (when known), dates when parents (white or black) acknowledged paternity (if unacknowledged at birth), dates of birth and baptism, names of sponsors (who were often related to the individual being baptized), and, in the case of slaves, the name of the owner. For instance, baptisms of the children (and slaves) of a free nonwhite couple appear in the "colored" register ("Baptisma Nigrorum, 1806–1828") of the Parish of the Immaculate Conception located in the Mobile Church Archives, the Catholic

Center, Mobile, Alabama (entries 251, 352). The researcher should note all information, even if it appears irrelevant at the time.

Marriage records may contain the names of the bride and groom, date of marriage, witnesses, place of origin, ages, and names of slave owners. In some instances, priests or ministers may have recorded other information pertinent to the marriage, including the fact that a couple had applied for a civil license or even that a man had previously changed his name. In Alabama, the marriage of Zeno Chastang and Maria Teresa Bernoudy, both free people of color, appeared on page 108 in the "white" register of the Parish of the Immaculate Conception, "Marriage Records Book 1, 1726–1832." John Baker married Marie Denise (of French-African descent) on October 25, 1820, at Natchitoches, Louisiana. The Spanish priest identified the groom as aged thirty-two, a native of Broneston, Virginia, and the son of John Baker, a man of color, and Nancy, a white woman. The bride was fourteen and a half years old, and the daughter of Marianne Baden, a free Negro, according to Elizabeth Shown Mills, in *Natchitoches Church Marriages, 1818–1850: Translated Abstracts from the Registers of St. Francois des Natchitoches, Louisiana*. When slaves Charles and Marie were married at the Cathedral of St. Louis, Missouri, the priest also recorded the names of their owners in the "Register of Marriages, 1840–1849." This register is now held in the Basilica of St. Louis, the King, the Old Cathedral, St. Louis.

In the absence of civil death records, church burial records are especially important. Data in Catholic registers may include dates of death and burial, place of origin, age, and names of the deceased's parents. Again, all information in a source should be skimmed. In one case, when a priest recorded several slave burials, he only identified the owner, a free man of color, by his given name ("Burials for Coloured People," Parish of the Immaculate Conception, Mobile Church Archives). A different priest, however, recorded the same man's complete name. In the same volume, John Martin, a free man of color, native of Virginia and approximately twenty-seven years old, received the benefit of a Catholic burial, as did a nonwhite woman who was a native of St. Domingo (entries 2, 19). On November 18, 1805, in New Orleans, Carlos Brule, son of Carlos Brule, "captain of the mulatto militia of this city," according to Earl C. Woods in volume 8 of the *Archdiocese of New Orleans Sacramental Records*, and Maria Constanza Gaillard, age six, were buried.

Protestant church records in the form of either minutes or registers also contain valuable information. Some Episcopal registers (baptismal, marriage, burial, and confirmation) contain data concerning African Americans similar to that found in Catholic records, including origins or former residences. Ministers did not always identify free nonwhites as such; they may appear as colored, and not necessarily as free colored or free persons of color.

Several examples illustrate this type of data. A minister of the Church of the Good Shepherd in Mobile, Alabama, recorded the baptism of William A. Saxon, "free" son of Armstead and Mary Saxon, in the Parish Register baptisms dated July 15, 1855 (volume 2). The Second Presbyterian Church, Mobile, received John Burton and wife Mary Ann, free people of color, as members, according to the "Session Book," Volume 1, 1842–1855. They previously had been members of the Presbyterian church in Demopolis, Alabama. This same book, located at the Central Presbyterian Church Archives in Mobile, also states that "Francis Godfrey a coloured (sic) servant, having been examined as to her experimental knowledge of religion, was unanimously received to the communion and fellowship of this church." In 1835, the First Baptist Church of Christ (with records located at the First Baptist Church Archives in Mobile) "received into the fellowship as a member of the church coloured brother William Jones belonging to J. G. S. Walker, upon a letter of dismission from the Baptist Church in Augusta, Georgia" ("Minutes, 1835–1848"). On October 5, 1845, in the Second Baptist Church "Minutes" (1845–1875) located in the same archives, it is stated that, "at the waters edge a free woman of colour Sally Chamberlain, presented herself for membership when upon her Christian experience she was received for baptism." On May 16, 1847, the same church licensed four nonwhites (Charles Leavens, Tom Knight, Guiford Ward, and Cupid Redwood) to preach in its African branch. "Being of good character, orderly and consistent in their conduct," they were "licensed to preach or exhort according and in conformity with the laws of Alabama."

Church records may be located in many different places. You should first determine if the church or parish is still in operation: if so, a phone call or letter may be a first step toward the examination of the records. If the church has been closed, a church or archdiocesan archive may house the records. Sometimes, however, other churches may acquire the records of a closed church. Libraries, historical societies, and state archives hold church records, either originals or microfilm copies. The Family History Library in Salt Lake City has microfilmed many church records, which may be borrowed through Family History Centers around the country. Other records have been published, although those researchers finding information in published (secondary) sources are urged to examine the original records.

In addition to possible difficulties in locating a specific church's records, you may encounter other obstacles when using these sources. Not all identify nonwhites as such, especially records kept during the antebellum period. All records are not accessible to the public; each parish or church has its own guidelines concerning the use of its holdings. Records may have been kept in a language other than English. Not all records have been indexed. Finally, unlike public facilities that house government records and are open during regular hours, church archives may be open for limited periods of time.

COURT RECORDS

Many types of court and legislative records may be used to trace the lives of African Americans, including civil and criminal records, probate documents, deed or general record books, and acts of state legislatures. Different courts operate throughout the United States on both federal and state levels, including circuit, chancery, probate, city, land, (state) supreme, county, and mayor's, and each generates its own records. To begin studying these records, first examine city directories (usually available in local libraries) to ascertain which courts operate in a particular area. Court records may consist of loose paper files or record, minute, and docket books; examine all the different types. Some items of interest that might otherwise be missed may be located by reading the books page by page, often necessary if indexes are not available. As with other records, nonwhites may not have been identified as such.

Court records are usually located in county courthouses. However, some may be found in other repositories, such as city, state, or university archives or historical societies. Many have been microfilmed.

Throughout history, African Americans' legal rights varied considerably. "Free Negroes in the South (like most of their Northern counterparts) did not enjoy all rights of citizenship; the court systems represented one area in which these abridgments are most noticeable," states Gary B. Mills, author of *The Forgotten People*. For example, most free nonwhites in the North and South were not allowed to testify in court against whites. "They were, in fact, prohibited from even instituting a suit against a white in most states before the Civil War," Mills states. There were, of course, exceptions to this. Free people of color were involved in a variety of lawsuits against whites and others of their class, and a variety of illegal acts were ascribed to African Americans. Nonwhites were able to purchase and sell real and personal property. Also, divorce proceedings involving African Americans may be found among civil records.

Several examples illustrate the value of these records. In 1850, Peter Bolling appeared in a Mobile County, Alabama, circuit court and indicated that, in 1837, he had been a slave of Thomas Batte, a resident of Dayton, Marengo County, Alabama (University of South Alabama Archives, Mobile). In 1830, George Mulhollen, a free man of color, brought suit in Adams County, Mississippi, alleging that he had been born free in Easton, Pennsylvania, in 1798 or 1799, and that he was being illegally held in slavery by a white named Robert McCullough. The defendant demanded that Mulhollen present proof of his freedom. Despite the fact that Mulhollen could only offer his testimony, a jury of twelve whites granted him his freedom (Record of Judgment, May 1830–May 1831). In another case, Sarah, a free woman of color, indicated that she had been claimed as a slave by Louisa Higgins of Mobile County. Sarah stated that she was approximately twenty-one years old, was born in Montgomery County, Alabama, that she had been held by Higgins but that she was not claimed by her as a slave until 1853, that her mother was also a free-born woman, and that she had a child. A witness for Sarah indicated that he knew Sarah's mother, Delphi, when they were in Upson County, Georgia, about 1829 or 1830, that a Negro slave named John was Delphi's husband, and that "in the neighborhood where she lived in

Georgia, it was generally reputed and believed that she (Delphi) was the daughter of a white woman, by a black man. I have heard the same report in the neighborhood where she lived in this state." This information was culled from the "Final Record Book, 1852–1856," of the Mobile County, Alabama, Circuit Court (University of South Alabama Archives) and the "Loose Paper File Collection," Mobile County (same archives, Circuit Court Case 27493). Finally, according to records at the University of South Alabama Archives, the court ordered a free man of color to contribute to the "support and education of the bastard child" of a free woman of color since he was "the reputed father" ("Circuit Court Minutes, 1856–1858," Mobile County, Alabama).

Abstracts of files from superior court records that deal with slaves and free people of color have been published by Helen T. Catterall. But, as in other records, in court cases not all free people of color are identified as such. After you have located a case, you should also read the published state court records, available at law libraries, which contain greater details. In fact, you must check the state records to determine the county from which the case was appealed. Catterall lists the name of the case, the source (published state court records), the date, and an abstract of the case. For example, in *Stikes, Administrator* v. *Swanson*, 44 Ala. 633, June 1870, 44 represents the volume number, and 633 the page on which the case appears in *Reports of Cases Argued and Determined in the Supreme Court of Alabama, During the January and June Terms, 1870*. Legal librarians can help you find the volumes wherein the citation exists. Note that only appellate cases are recorded in casebooks.

These court records may contain genealogical data. In one Louisiana case, several nonwhites sued for their freedom. The names of a slave mother and her master, her two children, and several grandchildren are provided. Case records reveal that Cassius Swanson was formerly a slave in Florida where he was emancipated, and that he later moved to Mobile and had at least three sons by two slave mothers; his date of death is also recorded. Antebellum cases may contain data about the post-war lives of nonwhites. In *Donovan* v. *Pitcher et al.*, 53 Ala. 411, Dec. 1875, for example, William Pitcher was a man of color "who had been a slave, permitted by his master to go at large, retain and dispose of his earnings, to acquire property, make contracts, and in all respects to conduct himself as a free man." During the 1850s, Pitcher left Alabama on two different occasions and went to Ohio, where he eventually died. His wife, born a slave in North Carolina and the daughter of a free man of color who purchased her and brought her to Alabama, also went to Ohio to live with her husband.

Criminal Records

Don't overlook criminal records as a source for genealogical information. Some dockets may contain names, offenses, judgments, and other useful data. In Daviess County, Indiana, Charles Brown was arrested for grand larceny (for allegedly stealing a coat worth $7.00), convicted, fined $10.00, and sentenced to three years in the state prison, after which he would be disenfranchised for five years. Before the Civil War, one free woman of color was arrested for failure to post bond. The record provided data on her background: "It appears from the evidence in the case that the defendant is descended from a white woman, [and] she is discharged not being subject to the free Negro laws" (Daviess County, Indiana, "Circuit Court Book D"; City of Mobile, Alabama, City of Mobile Municipal Archives, "Guard House Docket, 1862–1863").

Other criminal records, such as those of the mayor's court, list names of the defendants and the alleged crimes (such as assault or disorderly conduct). Interesting information available in such records includes facts regarding a jury finding a nonwhite guilty of grand larceny and ordering him to be sent to the state penitentiary. Newspapers also contain information concerning criminal and civil cases.

Probate Court Records

Records of the probate court are among the most important to the beginning genealogist. They include wills, court minutes, administrator account books, loose paper files that may contain all transactions of an estate record, guardianships, and other miscellaneous books of the court. Indexes to individual books, estates, or perhaps a general index covering all records of the court are usually available. One such computerized index (Mobile County, Alabama) contains all references to a person's estate as recorded in the various court documents. Thus, instead of having to check the indexes to each court book, you would only have to check one index. Most county courts, however, do not have one general index, so you may have to examine several relevant indexes.

Wills contain a wealth of information; often they mention relationships. In 1805, for instance, Abraham Jones, a farmer in Anson County, North Carolina, manumitted (released from slavery) his wife Lydia and their seven children whom he named in his will. He also carefully detailed how his estate was to be divided (North Carolina State Archives). In another instance, Romeo Andry indicated that he was the "son of the late Simon Andry by a free woman of color named Jane or Jeanne" (Mobile County Courthouse, Alabama, "Will Book 3"). In a will filed in 1866 another nonwhite indicated that he had purchased land from his brother, and that he owned land jointly with his sister. He also named his father and son-in-law, and left property to his children. The names of each relative were provided. In St. Louis, a free woman of color not only identified her grandson but also mentioned his age. Although she indicated that she had purchased him, she did not state his owner. However, a witness to the signing of the will had the same surname as the woman's grandson, suggesting some connection between the two.

Wills can also document previous relationships and former residences. In 1857 one free man of color made several bequests. In addition to identifying his wife by her maiden name, he made special bequests to his sons born from a previous union. The mother of those children was also named. Similarly Regis Bernoudy, "a free man of color of the city of Mobile" (Mobile

County Courthouse, Alabama, "Will Book 1"), left property to his three daughters, children of a free woman of color who predeceased him. He also left lots in Mobile and Pensacola. A free woman of color indicated the name of her father and his previous residence in a nearby county where she owned land. Cyrus Evans, a free man of color, acknowledged that his son was "born in the bonds of slavery and purchased by me for a fair consideration from Oregin Sibley of Baldwin County" (Mobile County Courthouse, Alabama, "Will Book 2"). Finally, in St. Louis, Elmira Hawken stated that she was the former slave of Mrs. Victoire Labadie. Hawken also identified her two children, who had a different surname. She also mentioned a man who previously had conveyed to her several lots in the city of St. Louis; his surname was the same as that of her children (St. Louis County, Missouri, Probate Court, "Will Book E," Civil Courts Building).

African Americans tracing their enslaved ancestors are urged to check probate records of both whites and nonwhites. If former slaves did not take the name of a former master, researchers are encouraged to check the records of whites (or other nonwhites) who resided in the same neighborhood as their ancestors in 1870.

Wills also may contain the names and ages of slaves. Among the slaves Zeno Chastang bequeathed to his wife were Margaret and her two children Tom and Frank (Mobile County Courthouse, Alabama, "Will Book 3"). Probate minute books also contain the names and ages of slaves and the names of those who inherited them.

Probate and deed records may also contain references to slave sales, manumissions, and free papers which may list previous residences or other relatives. (Free people of color often carried proof that they were free, and these documents were recorded in the courts. Newspapers sometimes published these lists.) George Rootes of the town of Fairfax, Culpeper County, Virginia, freed his "wife Sarah and her three children, Ellen, Sarah Ann, and James . . . all of whom I have lately purchased for the purpose of carrying with me to the state of Ohio whither I am about to move" ("Deed Book 20," 1830). A public notary residing in the city of New York certified that a black twenty-one-year-old seaman was a free person. The papers showed that he was born in Scoduc, Rensselaer County, New York.

Deed Books

Deed, conveyance, or general record books usually contain the buying and selling of real property between two or more people, and not between individuals and the government. Indexes, direct and indirect or grantor and grantee, are normally available; the amount of information they contain varies from county to county. For example, one commonly encountered printed index contains the name of the grantor, grantee, type of instrument (such as deed or power of attorney), date recorded, book name and number, page number, and description of the property. Nonwhites were not identified as such in the index. Thus, if whites and nonwhites with the same names purchased real property, data from other sources such as tax records may be needed to determine if a particular deed is relevant to the researcher. An index published by Oscar W. Collet, 1804–1854, for St. Louis County, Missouri, lists the grantor, grantee, book and page numbers, and some genealogical information. Researchers are urged to copy all information from such indexes and then seek out the original documents for additional detail.

The types of data in deed books varies considerably. In addition to references to real property sales, including slave sales, deed books may contain information on free papers, manumissions, deeds of gift or partition (and possibly a list of heirs), or leases. They may also contain records of slaves who purchased their own freedom. Even the most mundane books can provide information on prior residences, family cemeteries, or occupations.

Among the most common types of instruments recorded in these deed books were land sales. Nonwhites sold and purchased land from whites and other nonwhites. Deeds may contain names of the buyer and seller, date of the transaction, description or location of the property, references to previous sales of the same property, or some genealogical data such as the names of a spouse or children. For example, Magdalene, a free woman of color and widow of Etienne Fuselier, sold to her son Pierre S. Fuselier land in St. Landry Parish, Louisiana (St. Landry Parish Courthouse, Opelousas, Louisiana, "Conveyance Book E," April 15, 1820). In Greenville County, South Carolina, Samuel Taylor, a free Negro who had been emancipated by Arthur Taylor in 1806, bought 131 acres in 1812 and ninety acres in 1813. Five years later he sold two acres to the Baptist Society of Columbia, South Carolina ("Deed Book I"; "Deed Book K"). In 1852 William Dugger purchased a lot in the city of Mobile, Mobile County, Alabama, on the north side of St. Louis Street between Lawrence and Cedar Streets. The deed did not indicate that he was a free man of color, but tax and census records did ("Deed Book 4," new series; City of Mobile, Alabama, "Tax Book, 1856," ward 7, City of Mobile Municipal Archives; "1850 Population Schedule").

Slave sales and manumissions may also be found in deed books. Slave bills of sale cite the name of buyer and seller, counties of residence, date of sale, and the market value of the slave. Often the name, age, gender, and color of the slave is also listed. According to "Conveyance Book F-1," in St. Landry Parish, Louisiana, a free woman of color sold a male slave named Nicholas, aged about thirty-six years, to her daughter. A court approved Robert Taylor's request to manumit his slave Milly, a mulatto who was about forty-five years old, "for and in consideration of the long and faithful conduct and services." Jack, a free Negro and previously the slave of Charles Comeau, freed Letty who "lived with him many years as a wife" (St. Landry Parish, "Conveyance Book A").

Other valuable genealogical information may be contained in deed records. In 1854 for example, a nonwhite mentioned that part of his land contained a family cemetery. He also indicated that his father, who was not identified as such, was buried in said cemetery. In another deed record, the possible origin of a free woman of color was documented when a record indicated that, when a resident of Pensacola, Florida, she had purchased land in Alabama.

State Legislative Acts and Petitions

Two other important record groups are state legislative acts and petitions. Most state legislatures in the South ruled upon manumission attempts made by white or free Negro slave owners. Researchers should check house and senate journals for "unsuccessful attempts at manumission," according to Gary B. Mills in *Tracing Free People of Color*. The researcher may have to search these records page by page. In 1827 the Alabama legislature approved an act to emancipate Cyrus, slave of the free woman of color, China Evans, of Baldwin County (Acts Passed at the Ninth Annual Session of the General Assembly of the State of Alabama 1828). In 1836 the North Carolina legislature emancipated "Henry Howard, Fanny Howard and John Howard, children and slaves of Miles Howard, of Halifax County (Laws of the State of North Carolina, 1837)." Although some legislative acts required the freed person to leave the state, many continued to reside there in contravention of the law.

Thus, a variety of court records contain valuable genealogical information. Civil, criminal, probate, and deed records, as well as legislative acts and petitions, document the activities of nonwhites (and whites). African Americans seeking information concerning manumissions, land and slave sales, estate records, free papers, divorces, and patterns of migration are urged to examine these records. Although they have limitations—including the fact that many do not identify ethnicity—the records may serve as valuable primary or secondary sources, enabling researchers to flesh out the facts already obtained from other sources or provide clues as to how the investigation into the lives of their ancestors should proceed.

VITAL RECORDS

In a genealogical context, vital records refer to records of births, marriages, and deaths. Kept even prior to statewide requirements for the filing of such records, local and family records such as church registers and Bibles help fill the void for researchers. Not until the early twentieth century were national requirements passed for the filing of such records. Some cities and states, particularly in the South and in New England, did maintain them prior to 1900, but not all were complete. Laws for maintaining vital records varied. And, for slaves, the laws were more loosely applied, according to one author. For instance, slave marriages were seldom registered or legally recognized.

Vital records are maintained by city, county, or state government offices, such as health departments for birth and death certificates, and county courthouses or city halls for marriage records. Usually for a fee, clerks will check their files for a particular record over a specific time period, such as a five-year span. Some indexes and records have been published and may be available in public or genealogical libraries; many have been microfilmed and may be obtained from LDS Family History Centers. While some newspapers also listed births, marriages, and deaths, these records remain selective at best.

Birth Records

The content and availability of birth records vary, depending upon the time period. For example:

Virginia began to register births and deaths in 1853. Birth records contain the gender but not the names of the baby or the parents. The slave owner's name, however, was listed. For slave records, the name of the plantation may be listed as well as the area in which the child was born. These county registries have been microfilmed and are available at the LDS Family History Library.

Records from Fayette County, Pennsylvania, include a register of Negro births from 1788 to 1826. It shows the slave owner's name, birth dates, and names of the child and parents.

An act of the New York legislature providing for the gradual abolition of slavery stipulated that any child born of a slave after July 4, 1799, should be "deemed and adjudged to be born free," according to researcher Marcia J. Eisenberg in "Birth Registrations of Children of Slaves" in the *Journal of the Afro-American Historical and Genealogical Society*. Records from the town of Bath, Steuben County, New York (located in the New York State Archives in Albany), indicate that the elder Presley Thornton's slave Lucinda gave birth to Mima, born March 15, 1806.

New Jersey has birth records, which sometimes designate race, dating from June 1848 to 1878.

In Missouri, records created mainly during the 1880s and early 1890s may contain the name of the child and parents, race, date and place of birth, nationality, occupation of father, maiden name of mother, and ages and residence of parents. A standard certificate may contain the date and place of birth (county, city, name of hospital); child's name; mother's place of residence; whether mother was married; data on parents (name, race, birthplace, age, occupation); and physician's name.

Marriage Records

Data in marriage records also vary. The names of the bride and groom, dates of the license and marriage, whether the license was returned and signed by the person who performed the ceremony (a justice of the peace or clergy member), and location of the wedding may be cited. If two slaves who had resided as husband and wife before the Civil War were legally married after 1865 and if they had children before the legalization of their marriage, the document may contain information on those children. If the clergy member's name was provided, but not the name of the church with which the cleric was affiliated, other sources, such as city directories, may provide this information. Church records can then be located to provide further details. Marriage records do not necessarily identify nonwhites as such, although some records were classified by race.

Indexes to marriage records, some of which have been published, are available. They may contain the names of the bride, groom, or both, and volume and page numbers of the marriage books wherein the record is located. Some indexes may contain separate sections for the races, and nonwhite entries may be located after the white ones (as was the case in antebellum St. Louis County, Missouri). Other indexes may signify nonwhite marriages by the letter *C*, to indicate that the marriage involved a "colored" couple. Still others did not identify individuals by race. Indexes before the Civil War may also contain references to slaves and free people of color.

The following examples obtained from city or county civil records illustrate the variety of data that exists. When Jane Deveraux married Arthur Donnelly in Hancock County, Georgia, in 1819 the record did not cite either party as nonwhite, although other records created throughout their lives refer to them as free people of color ("Marriages: February 1819," Ordinary's office). According to "Marriage Records," St. Louis County, Missouri, St. Louis City Hall, Joseph Labaddie, a free mulatto, and Mary Anne Price, whose ethnic background was not recorded, were married by a priest, as were two slaves at a different time (volume 1). Another record indicated that two "colored persons" were married by an assistant minister, but it did not mention whether they were slave or free. According to "Colored Marriages," Jefferson County Missouri, a microfilm located at the St. Louis County Public Library, Richard and Sarah E. Collier were married in Jefferson County, Missouri, in 1869 and the names of their six children were also recorded. In the same county, John Posten married Josephine Becket, and the minister certified that Posten had an eleven-year-old daughter named Lucy. Frank Marshall and Louisa Reno, both "colored" persons, were married in that same county at the residence of Archie Reno. Similarly, in Natchitoches Parish, Louisiana, when Marie Eloise Jones married Auguste Delphine on February 8, 1876, the civil record of the marriage did not state whether both parties and all three witnesses were former slaves or free people of color ("Marriage Book 5").

Death Records

Death records, like marriage records, may contain a wide range of information. Depending upon the year, they may provide any or all of the following: dates of birth and death, age, sex, race, cause of death, place of birth, names and birthplaces of parents, places of death and burial, whether slave or free, occupation, marital status, residence, and name and address of undertaker. If death records are not available, coroners' or sextons' records may be of some use. As is true for other records, information in death records may not be accurate, and researchers are encouraged to compare and verify information in other sources.

Several examples illustrate the value of this material. Published records from Rhode Island contain references to slaves and free Negroes. In 1847, the St. Louis coroner reported that Sarah, a slave aged eight years and two months, "came to her death by violence inflicted on her person while in the employment of Edwin Tanner" (St. Louis County, Missouri, "Coroner's Record of Inquests, 1838–1848," volume 1, entry 84, Missouri Historical Society). Mary Walker, who was identified as a free woman of color, was forty years old when she died on August 18, 1864, in Mobile. The record indicated that she was born in Alabama, that the cause of death was consumption, that she was buried in the New Grave Yard (Mobile), and that her color was "dark." (Mobile, Alabama, "Death Certificates," reel 56, entry 834, August 18, 1864).

The LDS Family History Centers have the United States Social Security Death Index in their extensive CD-ROM collection. It contains information on people who died as early as 1937, but the emphasis is on deaths reported to the Social Security Administration since 1962. Researchers may find birth and death dates (month and year only for death dates through 1987; after that, the day of death is also listed), last place of residence, Social Security number and the state of issuance, state of residence at death, and where death benefit was sent. The index does not contain data about the person's family or birthplace. In addition, the researcher can contact the Social Security Administration directly.

Some areas may have laws that restrict access to vital records. In St. Louis, for example, the general public does not have access to the index of birth and death records; professional researchers may check the index to the latter, but not the former. Family historians, however, may obtain copies of records once they prove their relationship to the person whose records are being sought.

MILITARY RECORDS

African Americans have served in U.S. military units since the colonial period, and numerous records document the contributions made by these troops. These resources are available at the National Archives, state archives, historical societies, and libraries. Many have been filmed and are available through one of the commercial lending programs. The contents of the records may vary depending on the time period during which the person served his country.

Revolutionary War
Several sources dealing with the Revolutionary War contain information relevant to genealogists tracing their African American ancestry. A

review of Military Service Records (National Archives Trust Fund Board) lists several sets of records in the National Archives. One of them is the *General Index to Compiled Military Service Records of Revolutionary War Soldiers.* Each index card in this file contains a serviceman's name and unit and possibly his rank, profession, or office. Compiled service records are also available; many such records and indexes have been microfilmed. Other groups of records are the *Revolutionary War Pension and Bounty Land Warrant Application Files,* and *Selected Records from Revolutionary War Pension and Bounty Land Warrant Application Files.* Applications may list an individual's former rank, unit, age or birth date, residence, birthplace, and the names and ages of his wife and children. Applications from a widow who sought pension or land warrants may provide her age, maiden name, place of residence, date and place of her marriage, date and place of her husband's death, or a copy of a marriage record. Another useful source is the National Genealogical Society's *Index of Revolutionary War Pension Applications in the National Archives.* The listings provide access to the pension and bounty land application records. "A simple check of entries, however, tells one that many more servicemen recorded in this source were black men than are so designated," advises genealogist Marcia J. Eisenberg in "Finding Your Revolutionary War Ancestor and His Family," from the *Journal of the Afro-American Historical and Genealogical Society.* Some nonwhites who participated in the war are listed in Debra L. Newman's *List of Black Servicemen Compiled from the War Department Collection of Revolutionary War Records.*

Records of the Continental and Confederation Congresses also provide information on nonwhites who served during the Revolutionary War. Lists of former slaves taken by the British when they evacuated New York in 1783 were created so that the American government could pay reparations to former owners. These "inspection rolls" may show the slave's name, sex, age, and physical description; the former owner's name and residence; and additional remarks. The records are held at the National Archives on roll 7 of *Miscellaneous Papers of the Continental Congress, 1774–1789,* [M332], and roll 66 of *Papers of the Continental Congress, 1774–1779,* [M247]. These records are available on microfilm through the National Archives or the American Genealogical Lending Library.

Civil War

During the Civil War, African Americans served in the Union army, navy, and marines. They also contributed to the Confederate cause. African Americans served in regiments of U.S. Colored Troops; the *Index to Compiled Service Records of Volunteer Union Soldiers Who Served with United States Colored Troops,* a group of records in the National Archives available on microfilm at various libraries, contains an alphabetical listing of their names. Index cards provide a soldier's name, rank, and the name of the unit in which he served. For various reasons, the names of volunteer Union soldiers may not appear in the index: the serviceman may have been in a state-level unit, served under a different name, or used a variation of his name; or his record may have been lost or destroyed.

After locating an ancestor in the index, you may check the compiled military records at the National Archives. These papers provide the unit in which a soldier served, his physical description (age, height, complexion, color of eyes and hair), place of birth, occupation, enlistment data (date, place, term), and other remarks. For example, Murray Egins (or Higgins or Eggins) was a twenty-three-year-old farmer in Company G of the 7th U.S. Colored Infantry, Maryland, with black complexion, black eyes, and curly hair, and was born in Calvert, Maryland. Among his papers were a deed of manumission and evidence of title that indicated how and when his last owner had acquired him (Civil War, Record Group 94).

Other Civil War materials for tracing nonwhites are housed at the National Archives. They include a group of records titled *Compiled Records Showing Service in Volunteer Union Organizations,* which provides historical data concerning volunteer organizations. There is also *Tabular Analysis of the Records of the U.S. Colored Troops and Their Predecessor Units in the National Archives of the United States* (Joseph B. Ross), Special List 33, which contains data on regimental records, correspondence, orders, descriptive books, and morning reports; and "Colored Troops Division Records," which include fifty-four volumes of lists of nonwhite volunteers who enlisted in Missouri in 1864. Indexes are available for the lists, showing each person's name, age, physical description, place of birth, occupation, and date of enlistment. Also, in some instances, masters' names for former slaves may be given. Some of these records have been microfilmed and are available at or through the National Archives (Record Group 94).

You may also find valuable information on African Americans in Civil War pension files. An index, which has been microfilmed and made available at various libraries, contains references primarily to Civil War service. Index cards contain the veteran's name, rank, unit, and term of service, names of dependents, filing date and place (state), and application and certificate num-

Creative Projects for the Amateur Genealogist

Once you've started gathering data about your family, there are many things you can do with that information. You can build a more elaborate family tree, or write the history of your family. Here are a few ideas to get you started.

Autobiography. Write about your life in relation to your family. Ask others in your family to write one (or perhaps they already have).

Family photo album. Collect photos from other family members, making copies and returning the originals. Always label the photos with as much information as you know: who is in it, what is the event, the date, etc. Start a family photo album.

Family scrapbook. Collect newspaper articles about members of your family (weddings, awards, obituaries, favorite things), and start a family scrapbook. This could also be incorporated into the family photo album.

Ancestral country scrapbook. Collect information about your ancestors' countries of origin and compile a scrapbook.

continued on next page

continued from previous page

Gravestone rubbings or photographs. Tape a large piece of strong paper to the gravestone and rub black crayon over the surface. You will get an image of the raised design, many of which are quite beautiful. Or, start a collection of photographs of your family gravestones.

Autograph album. Start an album and ask your relatives to write a few lines and sign their name. This could also be incorporated into the photo album.

Photos of old homes. Take pictures of homes your family has lived in, and ask relatives to come along and tell you any stories. Include photos of schools and places of worship members of your family have attended.

Pen pal. Ask family members if there are relatives or friends living in the "old country," and write to them. This is especially fun for children or relatives that are about the same age.

Newspapers from the day you were born. At the library you can look up newspapers from the day you were born. If it is possible, photocopy the headline and any other sections you find interesting, and include them in your scrapbook or album.

bers. Information in one such file contained a serviceman's death certificate (which listed a birth date); county of birth; dates of enlistment and discharge; name under which he enlisted; marriage data; and names and birth dates of children. Documents indicated that his first wife died, that he remarried, and that his widow applied for a pension. Her file also contains valuable genealogical information. Another file showed the maiden name of the pensioner's wife, date and place of his marriage, and the names and birth dates of his eleven children.

Four other Civil War collections at the National Archives deserve mention. They comprise part of the holdings of the Adjutant General's Office in Record Group Ninety-four. The "Records of Slave Claims Commissions, 1864–1866," includes claims registers of slave owners seeking reimbursement for slaves who served in the U.S. army in some capacity. Registers for Delaware, Kentucky, Maryland, Missouri, Tennessee, and West Virginia are extant. Data include the date, owner's name, and the former slave's name and address. Proceedings of some commissions are also provided. The "Register of Claims of United States Colored Troops, 1864–1867," comprises three volumes and contains claims by slave owners from Kentucky, Maryland, and Tennessee. The register includes the name and residence of claimant, name and date of enlistment of slave, organization of the individual, and amount of owner's claim. The files are arranged by state, and then alphabetically by owner's name. Third, "Registers of Officers of United States Colored Troops, 1863–1865," comprises six volumes and indicates the officer's name, rank, birthplace, place of appointment, and remarks. This collection is "arranged by arm of service, thereunder by regiment, and thereunder by officers' name entered according to rank" according to Lucille H. Pendell and Elizabeth Bethel in *Preliminary Inventory of the Records of the Adjutant General's Office*. And "Descriptive Lists of Colored Volunteers, 1864," consisting of fifty-four volumes, records nonwhite volunteers from Missouri. The record lists the volunteer's name, age, eye and hair color, complexion, height, birthplace, occupation, date of enlistment, and (if a former slave) owner's name. The numerous volumes are indexed and arranged chronologically.

Similar records that detail the work of nonwhites during the war are located in at least one other repository. After the Union army took control of Nashville in 1862, fugitive slaves sought protection and basic necessities; the Army responded by impressing them for service on the railroad. Impressment rolls, which offer the slave's name, age, and height, and the slave owner's name and residence, are located in the Tennessee State Library and Archives. Nearly ninety percent of the slave surnames were the same as their owners, suggesting, perhaps, that military personnel may have chosen the surnames.

If an ancestor appears in U.S. Army records, the researcher should not assume that he was a free Negro before the Civil War. A number of enslaved blacks also joined the Union army. Arlene Eakle and Johni Cerny state in *The Source: A Guidebook of American Genealogy,* "Whenever a black citizen disappears from the records of an area in which he previously appeared, the possibility that he was a slave prior to that time should be considered."

Slaves and free Negroes also served in the Confederate military. Records of their involvement are located in the War Department Collection of Confederate Records, Record Group 109, at the National Archives: "Record of Details [unit assignments] of Free Negroes, Camp of Instruction at Richmond, 1864," records the date of detail, name of Negro, to whom detailed, date detail expired, and remarks. Entries are arranged chronologically. The "Register of Free Negroes Enrolled and Assigned, Virginia, 1864–1865," includes the Negro's name; age; color of eyes, hair, and complexion; height; birthplace; occupation; date and place of enlistment; by whom enlisted; assignment and date of assignment; and remarks. Entries are arranged alphabetically by name. The "Register of Slaves Impressed, 1864–1865," cites the slave's name, date of impressment, description, market value, and owner's name. References, which seem to include only those in Mississippi, are listed by county, and an index appears in the beginning of the volume.

The names of slaves also appear in Confederate payroll records. "Slave Payrolls, 1861–1865," contains information about slaves who worked on military defenses and includes length and place of service, slave owner's name, and slave's name and occupation. The "Index to Slave and Other Payrolls, 1861–1865," lists the name of owner and individual who signed the payrolls.

Other records at the National Archives generated in the aftermath of the Civil War include those of various claims commissions. The French and American Claims Commission and the Mixed Commission of British and American Claims were created to help French and British citizens in the United States regain property lost at the hands of the Union army. The government handled similar claims through the Southern Claims Commission from residents of the former Confederate states who professed to have been loyal to the Union. The files contain testimony from whites and nonwhites, including slaves and free people of color. According to Gary B. Mills, "Indeed, the claimants before the Southern commission included not only free

Negroes but also the quasi-free and slaves whose masters allowed them to accumulate property."

One example from the Southern commission illustrates the type of information you may find in the files. Details in one claim indicated that one man was born a slave, worked as a barber, and borrowed $2,500 to purchase his freedom. Because he married a slave who was not for sale, he bought another slave woman, lived with her during the Civil War, and later legally married her. The file contains other information about the man, his family, and the witnesses who testified on behalf of his family.

The names of claimants appearing before these commissions have been indexed, but only two of the indexes—the Southern and British—have been published in Donna Rachel Mills's *Civil War Claims;* and Gary B. Mills's *Southern Loyalists in the Civil War.* An unpublished index to the French commission (Record Group 76) is available at the National Archives. Even if an ancestor did not file a claim, it is possible that he or she testified on behalf of a relative or friend. So searching for the names of any of his or her acquaintances in the indexes may lead to information on your ancestor.

After 1865 African Americans served in the regular army. Several units were organized, and published works detail their involvement. Among these are William H. Leckie's *The Buffalo Soldiers,* Arlen L. Fowler's *The Black Infantry in the West,* and Marvin Fletcher's *The Black Soldier and Officer in the United States Army.* Frank N. Shubert's *On the Trail of the Buffalo Soldier* contains biographical data on thousands of nonwhites, including dates and places of birth, and military service.

World War I

World War I Selective Service records are available at the National Archives, Southeast Region, in Atlanta. This facility has more than twenty-four million World War I registration cards filed by state and draft boards. To access a particular file, you'll need the full name and city and/or county at time of registration. A home street address or other specific location (such as ward) is required for certain cities, such as Chicago or Los Angeles; if necessary, you can often glean this information from city directories. The records contain the serviceman's date and place of birth, age, race, and father's birthplace.

Other World War I records may be located in various repositories, including state archives or historical societies. Examples include:

The Missouri State Archives, which has some certificate-of-war service documents containing the serviceman's name, residence, place and date of induction, place of birth, age or date of birth, the organization in which he served (with dates of assignments), and other related information.

The Missouri Historical Society, which has several records from the State of Missouri Adjutant General's Office containing genealogical information. The records, however, are not complete.

Selective Service System records at the National Archives, Central Plains Region in Kansas City, Missouri, which contain lists of men ordered to report to local boards for induction, and docket books of the local boards in Iowa, Kansas, Missouri, and Nebraska. Some of the records may show the county of residence, address, marital status, number of dependents, citizenship, and remarks pertaining to discharge or alien status.

Other Military Records

Other twentieth-century military records may be located at the National Personnel Records Center in St. Louis. For example, certain records for army, air force, navy, and coast guard officers and enlisted personnel can be found here. However, a fire destroyed many records in 1973, and access may be limited. Records such as the "Separation and Qualification Record" and the "Enlisted Record and Report of Separation Honorable Discharge" may provide Social Security number; permanent mailing address; dates of birth, entry into active service, and separation; military and civilian occupational history; military and civilian education; physical description; decorations and citations; place of separation; race; and marital and citizenship status.

LDS Family History Centers have two military indexes available on CD-ROM that show American military personnel who died in Korea or Vietnam (Southeast Asia) from 1950 to 1975. The indexes may contain dates of birth and death, place of enlistment, country of death, and race. They do not contain information about the person's family or birthplace.

CEMETERY RECORDS

Chicago resident, University professor and renowned genealogist, Tony Burroughs, has written over four hundred pages of a Beginners' Guide to tracing the African American family tree (see bibliography). He tells of some of the experiences he had while researching his own family records.

Burroughs states that cemeteries as sources for genealogical information are often overlooked by beginning genealogists. The cemetery is the final resting place for our ancestors. It is next venue we should visit after interviewing relatives and researching family papers. Many people have not been to the cemetery since their relatives passed away. Some people visit the cemetery on Memorial Day, Veterans Day, or on the birthdays of their deceased spouses or parents. Some people are even afraid to go into cemeteries. However, once you start visiting cemeteries for genealogical research, you'll find that many of them are very beautiful and serene places. And they can be an excellent place to learn of ancestors you never knew about. That's what happened to me.

After talking with my parents and grandmother about the family's history and seeing all the photographs and family documents, I was fired up! I

ELEGY: FOR HARRIET TUBMAN
AND FREDERICK DOUGLASS

I LAY DOWN IN MY GRAVE

AND WATCH MY CHILDREN

GROW

PROUD BLOOMS

ABOVE THE WEEDS OF DEATH.

THEIR PETALS WAVE

AND STILL NOBODY

KNOWS THE SOFT BLACK

DIRT THAT IS MY WINDING

SHEET. THE WORMS, MY FRIENDS,

YET TUNNEL HOLES IN

BONES AND THROUGH THOSE

APERTURES I SEE THE RAIN.

THE SUNFELT WARMTH

NOW JABS

WITHIN MY SPACE AND

BRINGS ME ROOTS OF MY

CHILDREN BORN.

THEIR SEEDS MUST FALL

AND PRESS BENEATH

THIS EARTH,

AND FIND ME WHERE I

WAIT. MY ONLY NEED TO

FERTILIZE THEIR BIRTH.

I LAY DOWN IN MY GRAVE

AND WATCH MY CHILDREN

GROW.

—MAYA ANGELOU

was eager to visit Oakridge Cemetery, where my grandfather is buried. I was not living in Chicago in 1971 when he died, so I had no idea what the cemetery was like.

It was a long drive to Hillside, Illinois, a suburb west of Chicago. I arrived at the office and gave the clerk the names of my grandfather and his parents, who were buried there. She pulled out a large ledger and showed me the list of names entered for two different lots my family owned. Each had a diagram of the graves and indicated which ones had gravestones. She then gave me a map to show where the grave site was located and how I'd recognize the section when I got there. I then drove along the winding road inside the cemetery and located it near the rear of the cemetery, close to the fence.

I saw the flat two-toned gray headstone for my grandfather, which merely stated "Asa M. Burroughs 1894-1971." I thought about his life and what I remembered about him when I was a kid, in addition to the things I had learned about his legal career from his funeral program. Close to his stone was one for my grandmother's mother, "Minnie Rice 1875-1949." I was only a baby when she died, and Grandma mentioned her only briefly.

Having learned we had two family lots from cemetery deeds and correspondence saved by my grandfather, I sought out the second lot, which was closer to the road, only a few steps away. I was quite surprised to see a large granite stone, pinkish in color, about three feet high, great-grandfather and another great-grandmother, Morris and Mary Jane Lillie Burroughs. It read "Burroughs" at the top, and on the face "Father: Morris 1864-1903" and "Mother: Mary J. L. 1870-1914." I realized the words "father" and "mother" had come from my grandfather, who bought the stone.

These were two ancestors I had never known and had learned about only through genealogical research. After researching their lives and seeing photographs of them, I was emotional being at their grave site, knowing their remains were a few feet underground. It was as if I had made another connection and we were communicating. I thought about the challenges they'd overcome and thought they were probably thanking me for uncovering their past and telling their descendants (and the public) about them.

After paying homage to my ancestors, I drove back to the office and asked the clerk for a copy of the record in the large ledger. At first she balked at photocopying the pages because of the unwieldy size. I looked at it and showed her how the book could be turned and the posts taken out in order to make it easier to photocopy. She realized it would take only a couple of minutes. She smiled and said it was no problem. When she returned, I examined the record more closely. This time I saw the listing for my grandfather's brother, Robert Burroughs. I realized he did not have a headstone. But I noticed there were other names, also without markers, I did not recognize-Malchias Williams, age twenty-two, interred June 1905; Georgia Martin, age thirty-four, interred June 15, 1905; Martha Williams, age forty-seven, interred June 15, 1905; and Bertha Lewis, age fifteen months, interred January 26, 1911.

I asked the clerk about them, and she said there was no relationship listed or other information . So there was no way of telling who they were.

I drove home wondering who these people were. I showed the list to my father; he said he didn't have a clue as to who they were. He told me to ask my grandmother. I then showed the list to her and said she had no idea who they were. Naturally, I was perplexed. I wanted to know who all these individuals were who were buried in our family cemetery lot, and I was determined to find out. I went on a mission. It wasn't until I did more genealogical research that I began to unravel the mystery and identify the individuals.

I began getting death certificates and census records, which I'll cover later. Slowly I began to identify the names on the list. I found out Martha Williams was Mary Jane Lillie (Williams) Burroughs's mother. She was my grandfather's grandmother and my great-great-grandmother! I was stunned. Malchias Williams was Mary's brother, my grandfather's uncle. Georgia Martin was Mrs. Georgia (Williams) Martin, Mary's sister and my grandfather's aunt. These were Mary's relatives-my ancestors. They all died before my father was born, even before my grandmother met my grandfather. And my grandfather did not leave a record of them in his little book. His grandmother died when he was only seven years old, and his aunt and uncle died when he was six years old. He had very little memory of them, if any, and there was no oral history to bring their names down to other family members. Here they were, buried in the family cemetery lot, right where they were supposed to be, and none of their descendants knew who they were. It was a very sad feeling. (Incidentally, I still don't know who Bertha Lewis is, but I'm on her trail.)

So you need to visit each cemetery where your ancestors are buried. Request copies of all the cemetery's records. I also suggest taking older relatives to the family cemetery and doing another interview in the cemetery. Reminiscing about the people buried in the cemetery and looking over the area will stimulate old memories. Have your tape recorder with you so you can record these spontaneous stories.

I also thought about the three people who were interred on the same day, June 15, 1905. I had figured they had died in an accident or from an epidemic. Several ancestors died of tuberculosis, which is highly contagious. It was the leading cause of death at the turn of the century. However, after I began receiving death certificates, I realized they did not all die on the same day. That's why you have to be very careful with cemetery records. They record the date of interment, not the date of death.

The date of interment versus the date of death cannot be taken lightly. They can be far apart. In northern cities that get severe winter weather, grave diggers could not penetrate ground. Bodies were stored in receiving vaults until the spring thaw. So the severity of weather sometimes determined when the remains were put into the ground. With modern technology that problem no longer exists, and most receiving vaults have been destroyed.

Coffin plates were placed on the front of caskets so grave diggers could identify them. Once the remains were interred, the coffin plate was given to the family. I had one of these for years before my friend Helen Sclair explained what it was. Everyone calls Helen "The Cemetery Lady" because she researches only cemeteries. She's not a genealogist. The coffin plate was silver metal with ribbed border and had the following inscription:

Morris Burroughs
Died Dec. 15, 1903
Aged 39 years

I found out my ancestors had been reinterred in Oakridge Cemetery on June 15, 1905, from Forest Home Cemetery in Forest Park, closer to Chicago. After analyzing the dates of death and interment and Mary's cemetery deeds, I figured out what had happened. After Mary's husband, Morris, died in 1903, she bought a cemetery lot in the newer Oakridge Cemetery, farther out from the city. After burying her husband, she had her other relatives disinterred from Forest Home Cemetery and reinterred in the newer Oakridge Cemetery so the family would all be together. Forest Home Cemetery opened in 1873, and it may have been difficult to get a cemetery lot for all the family members. Even though Oakridge was a little farther from the city, it was only four years old in 1905 and undoubtedly had more space. Price and competition between the two cemeteries may also have played a role in the change.

I then went to Forest Home Cemetery and checked for records of the original interments. When I got copies of their records, I realized Georgia

Martin was actually Mrs. Georgia Martin, Mary's sister. So be very careful in analyzing records in the cemetery.

Records and Tombstone Inscriptions

The information offered by cemetery records and tombstone inscriptions varies, and many records have since been published. Whenever possible, however, you are encouraged to examine the original registers or visit the cemetery to verify the information provided in these sources. In addition, locating the correct section and lot in the cemetery (a task that may present some difficulties, even in large cemeteries where maps are available) may introduce you to other ancestors.

If the stone is no longer readable, however, or if it has been destroyed, published accounts can help fill the void. Published cemetery and tombstone inscriptions may be found in libraries, state archives, and historical societies. Cemeteries or churches sometimes retain their own records. If a cemetery or church no longer exists or is small, records may be housed at nearby libraries, genealogical or historical societies, or at a particular denomination's archives. These sources of information are particularly important for time periods preceding the nationwide requirements for filing of death records. In St. Louis, for example, the books of several smaller Catholic cemeteries have been consolidated and are held in two different places.

Some years ago, members of the Church of the Latter-day Saints went about the country collecting cemetery records, which are now available at their archives in Salt Lake City, Utah. These are accessible to historical and genealogical groups, and to any individual seeking information. In *How to Trace Your Family Tree,* the American Genealogical Research Institute staff provide the following useful information:

> [When treating] gravestones as a source of genealogical data . . . we are dealing with what a researcher calls primary, original, or raw material. For the time being we can forget about libraries, records, and files, and take a trip outdoors to do research. Cemeteries are, in fact, storehouses of genealogical and historical information and for generations have created a genealogical pastime. They are particularly valuable sources of information when municipal death records or church burial records have been destroyed.

> While some people may hesitate at the thought of visiting a graveyard, its value to genealogists cannot be ignored and it certainly need not be an unpleasant experience. Graves are marked so than an individual, in his or her death, can be remembered by the living; a visit to a cemetery can activate this remembrance. It is interesting to note that several cities across the nation are planning to make several large cemeteries into park areas, not in disrespect to the dead, but in mutual respect for the

deceased, for the land, and for the living.

Many old, private cemeteries have been neglected because families of the deceased have moved to other parts of the country. But in early America, when people were less mobile and one family lived in the same locale for several generations, whole families were buried together, often on their own land. This fact is particularly valuable to the genealogist who, in searching for records of one particular ancestor, may discover the gravestones of other related individuals. The first step in approaching this type of research is to determine the approximate death date and place of your subject. Most local historical societies will then be able to tell you which cemeteries were in use at that time. Note should be taken to check cemeteries of neighboring towns as well, since the boundary lines have probably altered somewhat from the original survey lines. You might eliminate some choices by starting with a cemetery affiliated with the religious denomination of your subject.

When you visit a cemetery, go equipped to tackle the weathering effects of time on a gravestone. In other words, stones may need to be cleared of moss and underbrush before they can be read. If you plan to photograph a headstone, bring chalk to trace over the lettering so that it will show up clearly in your picture. If you wish to make a rubbing of the stone, for the best results bring wrapping paper and either a marking crayon or a soft lead pencil.

Headstones can be difficult to read, usually because of the effects of age or because of the style in which the inscriptions were made. If read incorrectly, confusion will abound, so special effort should be made to be as accurate as possible. Always copy the stone exactly as it is written—letter for letter, word for word—including all punctuation. These precautions should be taken to narrow or eliminate the margin for error. If parts of the inscription are illegible, indicate this on your transcript.

Gravestones of the late 1700s were hand chiseled in roman letters on a dark slate. While this lettering was easy to read, the stones were easily split and weathered. In the early 1800s a harder, grayish-blue slate was used, but the change to a very difficult to read italic script has rendered many of these stones illegible. In the 1840s hard marble was used and in the later 1800s granite was employed. More recent gravestones have sandblasted inscriptions, which survive the longest by far.

The basic information provided on a gravestone—death date and approximate age—has been consistently retained through the years, but stated or worded differently, so that it can at times lead to confusion. The age statement is not always exact: "died in her seventeenth year." If you are not given or cannot figure out the exact age of your subject, it is almost always possible to approximate that age. Occasionally, you may discover a stone that gives not only the year, month, and day of your subject's death, but also the hour. In the case of a child, the gravestone usually mentions the names of the child's parents (and the child's grave is usually situated close to the parents' graves). In the case of a married woman, her husband's name is generally given.

In studying headstones, always view them in association with surrounding gravestones and never assume too much from one marker; chances for error enter if the stone is difficult to read and if the original marker has at one time been replaced by a newer one. In addition, because of the expense involved in having a stone inscribed and erected, occasionally blatant errors in the inscription are left unaltered. You should also search the sexton's records. These files often indicate who purchased the lot, who pays for its upkeep, and who currently owns the lot. These files also have complete records of all burials in the cemetery and the locations of all graves. Records of now defunct cemeteries are usually held by a local historical society.

While the typical gravestone reveals few personal characteristics of your subject beyond their age, date of death, and possibly the name of a relative, frequently you will find short or even lengthy inscriptions which provide a clue to their personality. A visit to a cemetery can help you to verify facts you already have, or present new ones. And in judging the simplicity or the splendor of the stone, you often gain an insight into the lives of an entire family.

Consulting a combination of resources can offer the researcher an interesting range of data: place of birth, birth and death dates, age, whether free or slave, race, spouse's name, marital status, cause of death, parents' names, or occupation. In addition, legal descriptions (section, township, range) providing the location of a rural cemetery may be included. If the cemetery is no longer in operation or cannot be readily found, cemetery records may still be extant which describe the location where it once stood.

These records may be organized in several ways. Published accounts may be arranged chronologically and/or alphabetically. Others may list names alphabetically and then by section/lot numbers. For example, if a name is located in an alphabetical list, and section/lot reports are available, you should check those reports for further details. The section/lot accounts indicate who else was buried in the same lot with the ancestor. Thus, additional family members may be located. Other documents may be arranged by section and lot only. In such instances, one should check an index to locate all individuals with the same surname as the one being researched.

As with any other source, cemetery and tombstone materials have their shortcomings. Race may not be noted. Information on tombstones may not be accurate, meaning you'll have to compare the information you find with that of other sources. In *Amite County, Mississippi, African American Cemeteries,* author Marva F. Peavy cautions users of one published account that "names were copied as found. Many spellings of names in current usage have evolved over the years from different spellings in one or more steps. The index should be checked for these."

Examples of the types of data found—as well as the problems associated with cemetery records and inscriptions—demonstrate their value:

Published cemetery records for Amite County, Mississippi, provide the location (legal description) of one rural cemetery, list the names alphabetically, and copy dates as they appear on the stone. For example, records of the nonwhite Big Antioch Cemetery in Amite County indicate that four individuals with the surname Butler were buried there between 1957 and 1975. Names were listed alphabetically and do not appear in any section/lot format. Thus, researchers would not know the names of other individuals who were buried in the same area as their ancestors, according to Peavy.

In St. Louis, sexton's records of the period 1862–1863 were used to reconstruct the names of burials at the City Cemetery. These documents distinguished between slave and free nonwhites. For example, the free man of color, Israel Dyson, born in North Carolina, was fifty-five years old when he died in May 1863. John Alfred, a slave, died in the fall of 1862; his age was not listed according to the St. Louis Genealogical Society's *Old Cemeteries, St. Louis County, Mo.*

Registers for Oakland Cemetery in St. Paul, Minnesota, show names, burial dates, location in the cemetery, place of birth, and date and cause of death. Sharon Bruckner, project coordinator for *Oakland Cemetery Records, Volume 2* notes, for instance, that the records indicate that Amanda Wilkinson was a free woman, that she was "colored," that she was born in Missouri, that she was eighteen when she died on March 29, 1868, and that the cause of death was consumption. Minerva Lewis, "formerly a slave," was from Alabama and died in 1868.

In South Carolina, the inscription on the stone of William Ellison, a socially prominent, free man of color who was buried in the family cemetery, included the phrase "In God we trust," according to *Black Masters: A Free Family of Color in the Old South* by Michael P. Johnson and James L. Roark.

In Mobile, the tombstone inscription for Constance Hugon indicated that she was born in New Orleans and died on October 16, 1845. Her race was not identified, but other sources indicated that she was a free woman of color. Church records, however, list a different date of death, according to Col. and Mrs. Soren Nelson in "Burials for Colored People, 1828–1877," from the Church of Mobile, Alabama Archives, The Catholic Center.

NEWSPAPER ADS AND COLUMNS

Newspapers are a useful source for genealogical research. Births, marriages, deaths, legal notices (probate court proceedings, civil or criminal court cases, etc.), runaway slave notices, advertisements for businesses or lost relatives, tax lists, city or state laws, manumissions, and registrations of free people of color are some examples of the type of information that has appeared in newspapers over the years. If public records have been destroyed or lost, researching newspaper archives may be the only means available to retrieve this information. And newspapers from the relevant period and region are an excellent way to learn about affairs in the community where one's ancestors resided, as well as national events of the time.

Finding newspapers of past centuries may be a difficult task. However, directories, guides, or county histories may indicate where they are housed. The Library of Congress publication *Newspapers in Microform* contains names of newspapers arranged by state and thereunder by town or city, their location, and dates available. Another source is K. G. Saur's *Microfilms in Print*. After you identify pertinent papers, you may be able to order microfilmed copies through the interlibrary loan department of a public or university library. *American Newspapers, 1821–1936: A Union List of Files Available in the United States and Canada* by Winifred Gregory, which lists titles and repositories of extant papers, and Clarence S. Brigham's *History and Bibliography of American Newspapers, 1690–1820*, are other sources you can find in the reference departments of public or university libraries. In addition, some published abstracts specialize in certain types of information gleaned from newspapers, such as marriage or death notices.

Runaway Slave Notices

Runaway slave notices contain a variety of information. The advertisements may mention the slave's name, age, physical description, residence, former owner, and any unusual characteristics that could be useful in identifying the slave, such as the type of work the slave performed. Slave owners placed notices in newspapers circulating in the geographic areas in which they lived or, if necessary, places to which they thought their slaves may have run. Sheriffs also published accounts that indicated when a nonwhite had been committed to jail as a runaway slave. In some cases these nonwhites claimed to be free.

Some examples illustrate the nature of runaway slave notices: In Illinois, a "Negro man, who calls his name Jack," reported that he belonged to Duncan Steward who was "of or near New Orleans," writes Helen Cox Tregillis in *River Roads to Freedom: Fugitive Slave Notices and Sheriff Notices Found in Illinois Sources*. In 1810 James Norris offered a reward for the return of his bondsman James, aged thirty-five years, who had run away from Smith County, Tennessee. The slave was "African by birth," and his wife was named Rachael, according to Sherida K. Eddleman's *Genealogical Abstracts from Tennessee Newspapers*. In 1781, two Negroes, Paris and Anthony, fled from their master in Charleston. Their owner indicated that they had been seen in the town of Savannah, Georgia, where they hired themselves out and passed for free. The advertisements also provided physical descriptions of each man, according to *Runaway Slave Advertisements: A Documentary History from the 1730s to 1790* by Lathan A. Windley. In Albemarle County, Virginia, Philip Thurmond Sr., feared that his slave Ben, formerly owned by George Thomas of Hanover County, had either returned to that county or boarded a vessel. Lovick Jones of North Carolina advertised that his slave Sam, previously owned by Henry Chew, "may attempt to get to Virginia or Maryland, as he has Sisters and Brothers there." Jones also described Sam and the clothes he wore when he left, writes Windley. Cyrus, a slave belonging to John Lloyd of present-day Connecticut, ran away in 1761. Lloyd described the slave and the clothes he took with him, and reported that Cyrus was a butcher who spoke English and some French, according to researchers Billy G. Smith and Richard Wojtowicz in *Blacks Who Stole Themselves: Advertisements in the Pennsylvania Gazette*.

Registrations of Free People of Color

Registrations of free people of color were sometimes published in newspapers. The lists may show the individual's name, age, height, racial composition, place of birth, and length of residence in the area. Pre-1850 lists are especially important as they may contain the type of information that would not appear in census records before 1850 for persons of any race. In 1819, for instance, John Coleman, a thirty-five-year-old carpenter from Virginia who resided in Augusta, Georgia, had been in the state for six years, writes Chris Nordmann in the article "Georgia Registrations of Free People of Color" published in the *National Genealogical Society Quarterly*. In 1830, John Williams, a forty-three-year-old mulatto born in Virginia, was a thirteen-year resident of Mobile (*Mobile Commercial Register*, May 15, 1830).

Legal Notices

Take time to glance through the many columns of legal notices that appear in newspapers. Legal newspapers are also available which carry similar information. These columns may contain data pertaining to land sales, probate, divorce proceedings; tax lists; names of property holders (with descriptions and locations of the property) who did not pay their taxes; or other legal items. One note: Editors did not always identify people by race.

In 1830 the names of a free Negro's estate executors appeared in one notice that also listed the man's date of death. Letters of administration for the estate of another free nonwhite were granted by the judge of the probate court although the notice did not contain any other genealogical information. The executors representing the estate of another free man of color notified the public that his real property would be sold. The location of the property was listed.

Advertisements

Nonwhites placed advertisements to help locate displaced family members or even missing or stolen property. Advertisements in *The Colored Tennessean,* a newspaper run by African Americans that was published for only two years (1865–1867), may show the missing person's name and location of a former master, last known residence, age, or other relevant information. For instance, in 1865 Levy Done of Nashville was looking for his mother, Kissy Done, whom he last saw in 1862. Samuel Dove of Utica, New York, wanted to locate his mother, three sisters, and a brother. George Dove, their former owner, resided in Rockingham County, Shenandoah Valley, Virginia. Samuel Williams of Nashville desired to find his mother, Sylvia Williams. Their former owner was James Maxwell, a resident of Augusta, Georgia. Previous to Maxwell, Sylvia had been the property of a Dr. DeGarr. As noted by Sandra G. Craighead in "Abstracts from *The Colored Tennessean,* 1865–1867: Want Ads for Lost Relatives," in the *Journal of the Afro-American Historical and Genealogical Society,* the notice also indicated that Henry Williams, father of Samuel, resided in Liberia. In Mobile, a free nonwhite offered a reward not only for the return of his mule but also for the apprehension of the thief.

Advertising one's business was another way African Americans used local newspapers. In South Carolina, a prominent free man of color began to advertise his cotton gin firm in 1817 and most likely continued to do so until the outbreak of the Civil War. However, none of the notices ever mentioned his racial background.

Lists of Letters

Newspapers published lists of letters left in the post office. Among the names appearing in such lists in Mobile papers were nonwhites who were sometimes identified as such. In the *Mobile Commercial Register,* for instance, one list contained the name Addison Lewis, "colored man." Under the heading "French Letters" appeared Zenon Chastang, although his ethnic background was not given (October 3, 1826). Several issues carried the name of Registe Bernody, another free nonwhite (April 7, 1823; January 6, 1826; June 3, 1829; March 5, 1830). These two men are probably the same two men (with variations in the spelling of their names) discussed earlier in "Court Records."

Vital Listings

Lists of marriages, births, and deaths were also published by the press. For older newspapers, a page-by-page search is recommended as these lists may appear in any part of the paper. After a certain time, editors generally placed the notices in the same location or section. Searching for obituaries by examining the column heading may be misleading unless the complete article is read. The amount of data in an obituary or death notice may vary. Look for an obituary, for example, several days or even weeks after the date of death. Society columns may also contain information on births, deaths, weddings, and the like.

Examples illustrate the type of information that has appeared in the press. In 1858 an Illinois newspaper reported that a marriage license had been issued to the "colored" couple Charley Weathers and Van King. On July 24, 1841, Sophia, daughter of John Thomas of Sumter County, Alabama, married J. D. Pollard of Mobile, both free people of color (*Mobile Daily Register and Patriot*, August 1841). In 1850 Henry Brooks and Catherine Stassbury, both "colored," were married by Edmond Douglass at St. Michael Street Church (*Mobile Daily Advertiser*, August 8, 1850). "Grandma Coleman," who died in Macomb, Illinois, was buried in the city cemetery of Macon, Missouri, where her son James Coleman resided, according to Phyllis E. Mears in *Macon County, Missouri: Obituaries*. Mears also notes that Mrs. Nellie Houston, believed to be over one hundred years old, died at her home in Macon where she was a member of the Colored Baptist Church. She was survived by several children, including Babe Houston of Macon. A Mobile editor reported the death of Pierre Chastang, a former slave who was "so remarkable a man in many respects, that a brief sketch of his life, will, we are sure, interest many of our readers, and, perhaps, have a beneficial influence upon his own caste" (*Alabama Planter*, August 8, 1848). The notice listed the names of his former owners as well as his accomplishments. "No person in this community, white or black," the editor opined, "was ever more highly esteemed and respected, and no one in his sphere has been a more conspicuous, honest, benevolent and upright man."

Crimes

Crimes committed by and against nonwhites also received the attention of local newspapers. In Maryland a mulatto named Roger was executed for "breaking open the store of James Weems, senior," notes Karen Mauer Green in *The Maryland Gazette, 1727–1761, Genealogical and Historical Abstracts*. Ursin August, a free man of color in St. Landry Parish, Louisiana, was sentenced to two years for stealing hogs (*Opeloussa Courier*, December 12, 1857). In Mobile, the court released a white woman who allegedly struck a free woman of color, and the mayor fined a white man for abusing a free nonwhite woman.

PASSENGER SHIP LISTS

Several types of records document the arrival of passengers at American ports. Those which might be useful for African American study include customs passenger lists and immigration passenger lists, many of which are available at the National Archives. The records are either original lists, copies, abstracts, or transcripts. Many of the records have been microfilmed and are available through commercial lending programs or at large public libraries housing a genealogical collection.

There are limitations to the files. The majority of passenger-arrival records cover the period between 1820 and 1945, and those before 1819 are mainly cargo manifests or baggage lists that also offer passengers' names. Most of the registers pertain to Atlantic or Gulf ports, and the National Archives does not have lists for every possible port where an individual may have disembarked. As with any other record, the handwriting may be difficult to read.

Indexes to many of the passenger lists are available. Such indexes may contain the name of the passenger, age, nationality, last permanent residence, destination, port of entry, name of vessel, date, occupation, sex, and other relevant genealogical information. The indexes, however, are not complete and transcription errors are possible. To facilitate the search, some naturalization records, especially those of the twentieth century, may show the name of the port, the date of arrival, and the ship's name.

Customs passenger documents may be in the form of original lists, copies and abstracts, or transcripts from the U.S. Department of State. Original registers are available for only a few ports, and some have been microfilmed. The lists generally cover the period from 1820 to 1902. These papers were prepared aboard ship, and they may show, for example, the name of the vessel, master, port of embarkation and arrival, and the passenger's name, occupation, age, and country of origin. Passengers may have included immigrants, U.S. citizens, or tourists. Copies and abstracts of original lists date from 1820 to 1905 and were made by the customs collectors. Copies and abstracts contain information similar to that found in the original lists. Transcripts from the State Department were evidently compiled from copies or abstracts sent to them by customs collectors. Some of the same categories of information found in the other forms also appear in the transcripts.

The National Archives has microfilm copies of immigration passenger lists that begin in 1883 for the port of Philadelphia. The records of the remaining thirty-five U.S. ports of call date to the 1940s.

By 1893, federal forms may have included the names of master, vessel, and ports of arrival and embarkation; and the passenger's name, age, occupation, marital status, last residence, and nationality. If the individual was joining a family member already in the U.S., that relative's name and address would be listed, as well as his or her relationship to the individual. From 1903–1907, several revisions were made to the form, including the designation of one's race. The records contain names of immigrants, visitors, and American citizens coming home from abroad. The documents are arranged by port and therein chronologically. Microfilmed card-indexes are available for some of them. There is a restriction period of fifty years before the indexes and records of a specific year are available for inspection by the general public.

A few examples illustrate the content of index records and passenger lists. One index card from the *Index to New Orleans Passenger Lists* (Series T618, Roll 4, 1900–1952) shows that John Brown, whose race was marked as African, arrived in that port in 1913. His birthplace (Kingston, Jamaica), last permanent residence (Celon, Panama), age (nineteen years), and destination (New Orleans) was recorded. He was to join Mary Brown in New Orleans, but their relationship was not explained. John's height and hair and eye colors were also listed. In 1920, according to the same index, another John Brown arrived in New Orleans. His age (twenty-seven years), occupation (marine fireman), race (African, black), nationality (Barbados, British West Indies), last permanent residence (Bridgetown, Barbados), destination (New Orleans), complexion (black), and color of hair and eyes (black, brown) were shown on the card. On September 23, 1900, several nonwhites arrived at the port of New York from Barbados on board the ship *Hevelius,* including Joseph Dummett, a blacksmith, who was going to join his brother. His age (twenty-five years), marital status (single), final destination (New York), brother's name (William Dummett), and address (1455 Broadway) were also listed. This was the first time that Joseph had been in the United States. Other details are provided (*List of Alien Immigrants, Passenger and Crew Lists of Vessels Arriving at New York, New York, 1897–1942,* Series T715, Roll 150).

It would appear that for the majority of researchers tracing the lives of African Americans (especially those transported as slaves), passenger lists would not be as useful as other standard genealogical records, such as censuses. At the turn of this century relatively few blacks in the United States could claim that one or both parents were of foreign birth.

NATURALIZATION RECORDS

Naturalization occurs when one is allowed to become a citizen of a country. With the passage of the Fourteenth Amendment in 1868, black Americans legally secured rights of citizenship. As late as 1910, relatively few African Americans were foreign born, and thus, few at that time could have been naturalized. In that year, about one half of one percent of the total African American population in the United States was foreign born. The total black population for the same year was about 9.8 million, so only about forty thousand people were born outside the United States. Seventy percent of that number resided in the North, about 25 percent in the South. Thus, even in 1910 relatively few nonwhites would have been naturalized (or probably could have appeared in passenger lists). Unless a researcher of African American ancestry had good reason to believe that a family member was foreign born and still living in 1868, time might be better spent checking other sources. However, these records do contain some references to nonwhites.

The naturalization process has undergone several changes. Before 1906, an individual could be naturalized in any court of record. Naturalization papers have been filed in local, county, state, and federal courts; historical societies; state archives; even the National Archives. It is wise to check with the courts or archives in the area where an ancestors resided. Some of these records have been microfilmed and are available through the Family History Library in Salt Lake City. Others have been published by various compilers. In 1906 Congress established the Bureau of Immigration and Naturalization to help regulate the naturalization process; in 1933 its name was changed to the Immigration and Naturalization Service. Thus, records created since 1906 may be located in federal courthouses, the National Archives, or its own regional archives.

Naturalization records may consist of declarations of intention or intent and petitions as well as records of naturalization. Intent papers show that an applicant renounced allegiance to a foreign government and intended to become a U.S. citizen. Prior to 1906, these intent files may show the date, and the applicant's name, country of origin, and residence. The amount of information varies by location. After 1906 the form provided more details, offering the applicant's name, date and place of birth, occupation, residence, marital status, names and birthplaces of children, and ports of embarkation and arrival. In some instances, as in St. Louis, the Works Progress Administration prepared a card-file index to records that appeared in various St. Louis courts prior to 1906. In other locations, the researcher should check indexes that may appear at the front or back of court books.

In addition to the declaration of intent, people applying for citizenship filed a petition of naturalization. Before 1906 petitions may contain a person's name, occupation, residence, dates of birth and arrival in the United States, and port of entry. After 1906, an individual's name, occupation, date and place of birth, marital status; names and birthplaces of children; ports of embarkation and arrival; and other information was most likely noted. Naturalization depositions are statements by witnesses who supported an applicant's petition. The files show the applicant's length of residence in a certain place, and other information pertinent to the case.

Documents showing the granting of citizenship are records of naturalization and oaths of allegiance. Court minute books contain many early naturalizations. Certificates were used later and are arranged chronologically in bound volumes that have surname indexes.

In 1868, for example, ten nonwhites filed declarations of intention to become naturalized citizens. In addition to listing their place of origin, Africa, the records also listed their ages and length of residence in the United States. Among those who expressed their desire to become naturalized were Cudjo Lewis and Ossa Kibbe, both twenty-one years of age and both ten-year residents of the United States. Eight of the ten had arrived in 1858 aboard the slave ship *Clotilde,* and later resided near Mobile (Mobile, Alabama Circuit Court Records, "City Court Minute Book, No. 8, 1868–1871," University of South Alabama Archives; King and Barlow 1986).

Searching for an ancestor's homeland is not an easy task. Locating a document that identifies the place of origin is something that researchers of all races hope to accomplish. Naturalization records can provide that information. To facilitate the search, other sources, such as the census, can be used to determine whether an ancestor was naturalized. When and where an ancestor arrived in the country may help determine the location of naturalization.

OTHER TYPES OF RECORDS

Numerous other sources may contain information on African Americans. These include, but are not limited to, records of private organizations, orphanages and asylums, banks, and schools; voter lists; city directories; local histories; employment and Social Security records; *Who's Who* publications; oral histories; hospital registers; tax lists; and coroner's inquests. In some instances, these files may be used to trace people who may have been in an area for a limited time and may not be located in censuses. Also, in the absence of 1890 census records, some other records from 1890 to 1900 may help locate individuals.

Some of these records may be indexed. Others are simply lists of names (with associated data) arranged alphabetically or chronologically. Not all sources identify individuals by race. These documents may be located in archives, libraries, historical societies, museums, government buildings, or in the agencies that generated them. Some organizations or institutions may have been exclusively for nonwhites, and city directories may help determine during what particular period of time they were operating.

Hospital Records

Some hospital records are available to the public; others are confidential. Among those that you might have access to are registers that may show a patient's name, age, race, place of birth, marital status, occupation, date of admission, diagnosis, place of residence, length of residence in the city, and date of death. For instance, according to the "Register of Patients, City Hospital #1, Female Hospital, St. Louis, Missouri, April 1, 1886–March 31, 1983," register numbers 1638 and 1642, Code Y 3240, Cabinet T, Drawer 6, Row 5 at the City of St. Louis Archival Library, St. Louis City Hall, on January 17, 1893, Julia Porter, a twenty-four-year-old nonwhite servant from Mississippi, was admitted to the Female Hospital in St. Louis suffering from phthisis pulmonalis. She was married and had been in the city for only one year. She died two days later. Porter resided at 1545 South 2nd Street. City directories could be searched for the name of her husband, and newspapers could be searched for an obituary. On January 19, 1893, Matty Williams, a forty-four-year-old African American "washwoman" from Mississippi, was admitted to the same hospital. She was a widow, had been in the city for three years, and was treated for malaria and released on February 11, 1893. A different register ("Index to Patients' Registers and Register, 1927–1929 and Mortuary Records, Female Hospital, 1900–1912, St. Louis Hospital #1" Code Y 3270, Cabinet T, Drawer 7, Row 2) from the same institution contained death records that provided the deceased's name, date of death, date and place of birth, cause of death, date and place of burial, and the birthplace of both parents. In Mobile, Alabama, "Hospital Reports, 1843" show that "Cheeseman," a free nonwhite, was a forty-five-year-old shoemaker. The document also provided a clue as to his economic status in the community: His name appeared under the heading "list of paupers or vagrants" (City of Mobile Municipal Archives, Box 5, Envelope 7, Folder 4, Documents).

School Records

School records document the educational activities of African Americans. School board minutes may describe the administrative affairs of nonwhite schools and mention specific individuals associated with the schools. Such was the case in Mobile with the school established for Creoles of color. In St. Louis County, an enumeration was taken in 1876 for whites and nonwhites; it showed names and ages, with each race in a separate section. For instance, William, John, Gibson, Joseph, and Nelson Taylor, ranging in age from eight to nineteen, and Jane, Mary, Eliza, and Annie Switzler, ranging in age from seven to sixteen, were recorded, as noted in *School Enumeration Records for Sub-District No. 2, Township No. 45, Range No. 7 East, County of St. Louis, and State of Missouri,* by Oliver Adams. From September 1928, to June 1932, Harold Washington, African American and former mayor of Chicago, attended St. Benedict the Moor School in Milwaukee, Wisconsin. St. Benedict's records provided his address, date of birth, general health, and parents' names and address. The Milwaukee school also showed that he had previously attended a public school in Chicago, according to Curtis G. Brasfield in *The Ancestry of Mayor Harold Washington.* Yearbooks and alumni directories are other possible sources of information.

Biographical Sources

Biographical sources contain genealogical information. Biographical directories for African Americans began in 1915 with *Who's Who of the Colored Race,* by Frank Lincoln Mather. Names are listed alphabetically. Sample entries: William C. Chance, born on November 14, 1880, in Martin County, North Carolina, the son of William V. Chance, was reared by his grandparents, Bryant and Pennie Chance. The names of the schools that he attended are also listed. On May 28, 1914, he married Evelyn Darlin Payton of Washington, North Carolina. The next year Chance was president of Parmele Industrial Institute in Parmele, North Carolina. His political and religious affiliations are also shown. *Who's Who among African Americans,* by Shirelle Phelps, provides similar information. You may also want to consult *Black Biographical Dictionaries, 1790–1950; Black Biography, 1790–1950,* by Randall K. Burkett, Nancy Hall Burkett, and Henry Louis Gates; *Black Biographical Sources: An Annotated Bibliography* by Barbara L. Bell; *Who's Who in Colored America; Biography and Genealogy Master Index* by Barbara McNeil; and *Black Women in America: An Historical Encyclopedia* by Darlene Clark Hine.

Employment Records

Employment records can also be useful to novice historians. The records of the Social Security Administration, which began in 1934, are restricted, but applications for Social Security account numbers may show the person's address, date and place of birth; parents' names; employer's name and address when the applicant applied for the number; and signature. To obtain a copy of application form SS-5, you must provide proof of death (death certificate) and a Social Security number. A Social Security Death Index is available on CD-ROM through the LDS Family History Library, as well as at many local Social Security offices. The index gives basic data including name, place and date of death, and Social Security number. Several different types of railroad employee records, such as those of the Railroad Retirement Board (the Board, located in Chicago, houses records of anyone who received a pension from a railroad) and those maintained by the particular railroads, contain genealogical information. Some of the latter documents may be located in museums or historical societies, including those of the Brotherhood of Sleeping Car Porters, which are housed at the Chicago Historical Society. Before the Civil War some free nonwhites found employment in maritime trade and navigation while others apprenticed themselves to learn trades, such as blacksmithing. County court records often contain apprenticeship contracts.

Civic, Social, and Fraternal Organizations

Such organizations were formed by free nonwhites, especially in the South. In Charleston, for example, the Brown Fellowship Society, which was restricted to mulattos, limited its membership to fifty. The Humane Brotherhood was formed by free black men, and membership was limited to thirty-five. Both clubs assisted their own members, who, for example, were too ill to work or could not afford to pay funeral and burial expenses. In Mobile, Creoles of color operated a fire company. Their activities were documented in club minutes, the local press, and city government records.

Orphanages

Orphanages were established to help orphaned or abandoned children and were run by state and local governments, religious organizations, or private groups. Officials may have recorded the name of the child, age at the time of commitment, dates of commitment and release, reason for the commitment, disposition of the child after being released, and miscellaneous remarks. Locating the records may present a problem, but you may check historical societies, archives, or agencies that currently operate such institutions. Perhaps, as in St. Louis, writes Peggy Greenwood in "Beyond the Orphanage" from the *Saint Louis Genealogical Society Quarterly,* someone has eased the task and published an account in a local genealogical journal that provides the location of the records. City directories usually list names of orphanages or asylums.

In St. Louis, for example, on August 3, 1854, Thomas Jefferson, "colored," age fourteen years, was committed to the House of Refuge for incorrigibility. He was released the same day and sent to the city workhouse. On September 28, 1855, William Johnson, also "colored," age thirteen years, entered the same institution, but for a different reason: larceny. Johnson was released a week later, on October 4, and also transferred to the city work-house. The journal did not indicate whether they were free or slaves. In 1888 the St. Louis Colored Orphan's Home was organized to help orphaned and neglected black children. In 1946, it was renamed the Annie Malone Children's Home. At least one other asylum served St. Louis's African American community. Other communities had similar homes for nonwhites.

City or County Directories

Local directories are another valuable source of information, especially for the period around 1890 when most federal census records are not available. The books, located in libraries or historical societies, provide the names of individuals, organizations, institutions, churches, or cemeteries. The directories also contain advertisements and useful information concerning the community. Check all possible variations in the spelling of a name to find an ancestor. It is best to search directories for several years beyond the last located entry, as names sometimes were not listed every year. Information may include the person's name, address, race, occupation, employer's name, and marital status. A list of abbreviations is usually included at the front of the book, which should help you interpret the data. Inclusion of nonwhites in city directories was often erratic. Property owners or boarders with a trade were more likely to be included. The higher up the socioeconomic ladder an African American was, the more likely it was that he or she would appear in a directory.

City directories may be used in conjunction with other sources. For instance, if census indexes are not available, or if, as in the case of the 1880 Soundex, not all families were entered, data in city directories may help locate the appropriate household in census records. Locate the address in a directory closest to the census year and then determine the ward number for that address. Some books provide maps with ward boundaries, while others include street directories that help pinpoint the ward number. If you have ascertained the ward number, you can then check census records for the same ward. City directories may be used to determine an approximate year of death. For example, a man's name may have been located in one year, but the following year his wife's name may include the designation *widow*. These volumes are also helpful in determining the location of church records. For instance, civil marriage records may provide the name of the clergy member but not the name of the church. City directories may show the names of the clergy member and the church where the ceremony was performed. You can then check church records for further details.

Several examples illustrate the type of information the directories provide: In St. Joseph, Missouri, in 1898, Louis Ellsworth, a barber, resided at 1702 Howard; Robert Ellis worked at the Columbia Foundry and Machine Company; and Mary Emery, a "domestic," lived at 1020 Charles, according to the *1898 Directory of St. Joseph*. In Quincy, Illinois, John J. Gunn, a cook who worked at Ellis Restaurant, resided with his family at 711 North Ninth;

and Mrs. Anna Steele, widow of Samuel Steele, resided with her family at 818 North Eighth. The individuals in St. Joseph and Quincy were identified as "colored," as noted in *Stone's Quincy, Illinois City Directory* from 1898. In Mobile, free Negro barbers advertised their services. Elam Page, a barber, informed readers that he was a "hair cutter, wig dresser, hair curler & shaver." In addition, he offered for sale numerous items, including "soaps of various kinds, razors, and razor straps," says the *Mobile Directory of Strangers' Guide* from 1839. The guide also features a full page advertisement: George McBride indicated that he could accommodate his customers "all hours, day or night, either at his shop or their private residences."

Voting Rolls

Voting rolls should not be ignored. In Louisiana free people of color did vote "when politically expedient," and in North Carolina and Tennessee they were allowed to vote until the 1830s, notes author Gary B. Mills. Efforts to disfranchise nonwhites after the Civil War have been well documented and need not be mentioned here. Some canceled voter affidavits are available and may show, for instance, the individual's name, race, address, occupation, and date of birth. In 1938, Robert James Johnson, a colored laborer born on September 3, 1907, resided in St. Louis on LaBaume Street (City of St. Louis, Missouri, "Cancelled Voter Affidavit Cards," Code DA 424-425, Cabinet X, Drawer 5, Row 4, St. Louis City Hall Archives).

Tax Rolls

Tax rolls are another valuable resource. They may be used for a variety of purposes, such as a substitute for census records. To interpret the information you find, examine laws that govern tax rates. For example, in the antebellum period the rate for a poll tax on free people of color was sometimes twice that of whites. If you have not been able to determine the race or status of the person you're researching, a higher tax rate may suggest the person's racial status.

Tax lists may be arranged alphabetically and may show an individual's name and property location, amount of tax, or value of real estate. The rolls may also provide the number and value of slaves or tax on other personal property. For instance, Virginia records that began in 1782 provide names of white and free nonwhite heads of households over twenty-one years of age, the numbers of slaves over and under sixteen years, and other data. Some early Virginia personal property tax lists (1782–1786) include a slave's first name, age by category, and the person who was to pay the tax.

Oral History

Oral history provides invaluable information. Stories are often handed down from generation to generation, and the family historian tries to confirm these traditions through genealogical sources.

A few of the published oral histories or bibliographies of autobiographies that are available in public or university libraries demonstrate the value of this method of research. Among those that may be consulted are George P. Rawick's *The American Slave;* Belinda Hurmence's *Before Freedom;* Robert S. Starobin's *Blacks in Bondage;* Charles L. Perdue, Thomas E. Barden, and Robert K. Phillops' *Weevils in the Wheat;* Russell C. Brignano's *Black Americans in Autobiography;* and John W. Blassingame's *Slave Testimony.*

SECONDARY SOURCES

Printed secondary sources usually refer to newspapers, periodicals, books, microfilm, and newsletters. They are important for several different reasons. First, they direct you to actual records that can then be examined for accuracy and details. Also, by checking published accounts of records someone else has already discovered, you may save endless hours duplicating the research. In some cases, original records may no longer exist. Finally, you may not have access to original records or be able to travel to the repositories where the records are housed. One of the fundamental weaknesses of secondary sources is that they sometimes contain errors.

The library is one of the better sources of information, with its broad collections of books, magazines, newspapers, and pamphlets. Larger libraries often have film and record collections. Trained librarians can help you use specific items for research.

A bibliography from the library can provide a general guide to sources for your research. Some guides will, for example, tell you what kinds of military records are available, what types of data they include, and where in the archives they are located. If you're researching a surname, bibliography surname histories can help.

Newspapers

Although we have already discussed newspapers, you should note that a number of historically black newspapers—along with guides to help you locate them—are available. Especially valuable are the following publications: Georgetta Merritt Campbell's *Extant Collections of Early Black Newspapers: A Research Guide to the Black Press;* Neil E. Strache's *Black Periodicals and Newspapers: A Union List of Holdings in Libraries of the University of Wisconsin and the Library of the State Historical Society of Wisconsin;* Frankie Hutton's *The Early Black Press in America, 1827 to 1860;* Donald M. Jacobs's *Antebellum Black Newspapers;* Warren Brown's *Check List of Negro Newspapers in the United States (1827–1946);* and North Carolina Central University's *Newspapers and Periodicals by and about Black People: Southeastern Library Holdings.* One of these guides might mention *The Colored Tennessean* (later *The Tennessean*) which was published from 1865 to 1867 and contains information on slavery and advertisements to help locate displaced persons.

Periodicals

Numerous periodicals can assist you, including historical or genealogical journals, quarterlies, and magazines; the scope can be national, state, or local in orientation. The coverage of each varies, depending on their professional or scholarly status. Some may publish Bible, church, cemetery, county, military, funeral home, school, and organization records; census indexes; newspaper abstracts or indexes; deeds or bills of sale of slaves; cohabitation or impressment records; lists of free nonwhites; or manumission records. Periodicals accept articles dealing with sources, methodology, or family histories. Some periodicals contain a query section where members looking for information on their ancestors solicit help from other researchers. (Sometimes researchers may obtain information from individuals that might not be found in courthouses or archives. In addition, this approach might introduce the researcher to someone working on the same family, who might be willing to share the results of their research.) Recently published books are also reviewed in journals. Indexes to many of these periodicals are available at public, genealogical, or university libraries. Notable among these is Michael B. Clegg and Curt B. Witcher's *PERiodical Source Index* (PERSI).

The *National Genealogical Society Quarterly* has published excellent articles dealing with African American genealogy. Genealogists are encouraged to read them and to apply the same methods used by others in their work. The *Journal of the Afro-American Historical and Genealogical Society* and the *Journal of Negro History* publish materials specifically oriented toward nonwhites. Magazines like *The Genealogical Helper* and *Heritage Quest* cover a wide variety of topics of general interest to family historians. Many more periodicals are aimed at the national, state, or local level.

Newsletters

Newsletters offer current information concerning the affairs of a specific organization and the events of other genealogical or historical groups. Genealogical and historical societies publish newsletters on a regular basis, often monthly or quarterly. They may provide noteworthy information on a member's activities or contributions to the field of genealogy, forthcoming conferences, queries, book reviews, computer programs, repositories, calendars of events, and family reunions. Newsletters may also contain brief articles and lists of library acquisitions.

Books

Historical or genealogical books are valuable sources. The former place ancestors in proper historical perspective and may show how national, state, or local events affected their lives. Some books may serve as guides for those who want to publish a family history or locate abstracts of records. Bibliographies in books help readers locate sources that might otherwise be overlooked.

Books published on a variety of subjects—including indexes to records;

Creating a Family Tree

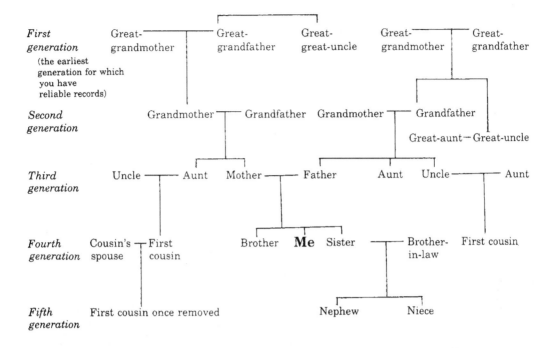

| First generation | Great-grandmother | Great-grandfather | Great-great-uncle | Great-grandmother | Great-grandfather |

First
generation
(the earliest
generation for which
you have
reliable records)

Second
generation
Grandmother — Grandfather   Grandmother — Grandfather

Great-aunt — Great-uncle

Third
generation
Uncle — Aunt   Mother — Father   Aunt   Uncle — Aunt

Fourth
generation
Cousin's — First   Brother   **Me**   Sister — Brother-   First cousin
spouse   cousin   in-law

Fifth
generation
First cousin once removed   Nephew   Niece

censuses; compiled genealogies; archival and library guides, including guides to African American research; church, county, or family histories; directories; biographies; and many more topics—are available in public, genealogical, or university libraries. For instance, you may consult *Bibliography of Sources for Black Family History in the Allen County Public Library Genealogy Department* (available at the Allen County Public Library, Ft. Wayne, Indiana), or the guide to African American genealogical research published by the South Carolina Department of Archives and History in Columbia, South Carolina.

It is clear that secondary accounts play an important role in genealogical research. Identifying relevant books and articles should be one of every researcher's goals. These works may help you locate information about different types of sources or methods of research, or they may contain the one piece of data necessary to complete a family group sheet.

*This **collateral** family tree shows all your relatives—not just your direct ancestors. Each name should be written in full, along with complete birth and death dates.*

REPOSITORIES

Family historians should become familiar with all types of repositories, including those at the local, state, and national level. Among these are university, public, and genealogical libraries; archives; historical or genealogical societies; and museums. The sources they house can be very useful to researchers looking for information on their ancestors. State archives or his-

PEDIGREE CHART

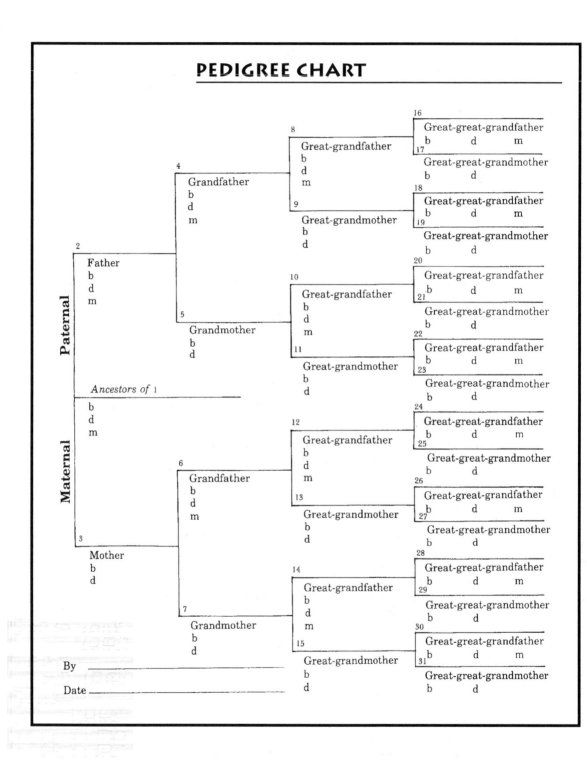

Paternal

2
Father
b
d
m

4
Grandfather
b
d
m

8
Great-grandfather
b
d
m

16
Great-great-grandfather
b   d   m

17
Great-great-grandmother
b   d

18
Great-great-grandfather
b   d   m

9
Great-grandmother
b
d

19
Great-great-grandmother
b   d

5
Grandmother
b
d

10
Great-grandfather
b
d
m

20
Great-great-grandfather
b   d   m

21
Great-great-grandmother
b   d

11
Great-grandmother
b
d

22
Great-great-grandfather
b   d   m

23
Great-great-grandmother
b   d

Ancestors of 1
b
d
m

Maternal

3
Mother
b
d

6
Grandfather
b
d
m

12
Great-grandfather
b
d
m

24
Great-great-grandfather
b   d   m

25
Great-great-grandmother
b   d

13
Great-grandmother
b
d

26
Great-great-grandfather
b   d   m

27
Great-great-grandmother
b   d

7
Grandmother
b
d

14
Great-grandfather
b
d
m

28
Great-great-grandfather
b   d   m

29
Great-great-grandmother
b   d

15
Great-grandmother
b
d

30
Great-great-grandfather
b   d   m

31
Great-great-grandmother
b   d

By _____

Date _____

FAMILY RECORD

[Place photo above]

- ❏ Myself
- ❏ Mother
- ❏ Father
- ❏ Sister
- ❏ Brother
- ❏ Maternal Grandmother
- ❏ Maternal Grandfather
- ❏ Paternal Grandmother
- ❏ Paternal Grandfather
- ❏ Extended relation (aunt, uncle, cousin, niece, nephew, etc.):

FULL NAME
_____

NICKNAME
_____

NAMED AFTER
_____

ADDRESS
_____

SOCIAL SECURITY #
_____

FATHER'S NAME
_____

MOTHER'S NAME
_____

DATE AND PLACE OF BIRTH
_____

DATE AND PLACE OF DEATH
_____

PHYSICAL DESCRIPTION
_____

MARRIED TO
_____

ON (DATE)   AT (PLACE)
_____

NAMES OF CHILDREN
_____
_____
_____

OCCUPATION AND PLACE
OF EMPLOYMENT
_____

HOBBIES AND SPORTS
_____

OTHER INTERESTING FACTS
_____

torical societies may contain records not available in other places; they also have materials common to other libraries. Some city archives house governmental or other records. The city of St. Louis, for example, maintains a microfilm library containing tax rolls, voting and probate records, and other documents that may not be available at other locations. Each facility may contain primary and/or secondary sources, and guides to some of these facilities are available. For instance, Debra L. Newman's *Black History* deals with civilian records in the National Archives, while the catalog *Black Studies* deals with National Archives microfilm records. Card catalogs, many of which are computerized, can be used to access the holdings of various repositories. One can search for specific authors, titles, or subjects. Reference librarians and archivists are available to provide assistance.

When you start your research, find and visit repositories in the geographical region where your ancestors resided, as well as those in the community where the family currently resides. Facilities in both areas may contain local and national sources. Librarians in the genealogy or local history section may be able to direct you to other libraries, archives, or organizations that can provide further help.

Guides showing the location of each department or section in the library are one of the aides that such facilities have to offer. It is important to see what materials are available and how they are arranged in a particular repository. Books and periodicals may be arranged by one or more classification systems. In addition, manuscript collections may be arranged by county agency or organization; and some have inventories. Certain collections have sources that are specific to African Americans. For instance, in the Civil War files of the Dexter P. Tiffany Collection at the Missouri Historical Society in St. Louis are free Negro bonds that often include physical descriptions and occupations.

Ask the right questions when visiting a library or other repository. In a university library, for example, it may be best to ask where the local history section or the microforms department is located. If you were to ask where the genealogy section is located, the response might be that there is none. However, if the question is rephrased as stated above, you may be directed to several sections with useful information. On the other hand, while a good public library may have a separate section devoted to local history and genealogy, they may have another area for such microfilms as censuses, newspapers, or county records. You also should ask whether the library has a special collection dealing with African American history or genealogy. Vertical files in some libraries or historical societies may contain newspaper clippings. These articles might otherwise be overlooked or not located if newspaper indexes are not available. The files may provide information concerning church or family histories, or other topics related to African American history, such as slavery.

Certain repositories have important African American sources. The Mississippi State Archives has an index to the labor contracts entered into by former Mississippi slaves after the Civil War. The original documents are part of the records of the Freedmen's Bureau at the National Archives. The Amistad Research Center on the Tulane University campus in New Orleans, which specializes in the history of African Americans, houses original manu-scripts, letters, family papers, organizational records, photographs, and other materials. The holdings of the Southern Historical Collection at the University of North Carolina at Chapel Hill, and the libraries at Duke University and Louisiana State University, contain many valuable antebellum resources, some of which have been microfilmed; and printed guides provide access to the records that deal with the purchase and sale of slaves, marriage and family life among slaves, and slave genealogies. The Schomburg Center for Research in Black Culture, a branch of the New York Public Library, holds records from African American churches.

Various repositories throughout the country maintain records created by anti-slavery organizations and their activities. Abolition society papers may show places of origin, ages, births, deaths, and marriages. Such docu-ments are located in the Maryland Historical Society, the Chicago Public Library, and the Southern Historical Collection at the University of North Carolina at Chapel Hill.

When beginning genealogical research, you should not expect to find one book that has all the answers concerning your family history, nor should you expect librarians to do the research. Librarians may suggest certain mate-rials but will recommend that the researcher do his or her homework *before* going to the facility and have a general idea of names, places, time periods, and the particular genealogical information he or she desires.

OTHER SOURCES

If you wish to hire a professional genealogist, there are several ways to locate one. You may obtain names from the roster of certified persons issued by the Board for Certification of Genealogists; the list of accredited genealogists offered by the Genealogical Department of the Church of Jesus Christ of Latter-day Saints in Salt Lake City; the directory of the Association of Professional Genealogists; advertisements in genealogical publications; or lists maintained by historical or genealogical societies and libraries with genealogical collections. When contacting a professional in writing, it is best to include a self-addressed, business-size, stamped envelope and a brief overview of what work is needed.

Information on family associations is also available. Consult Elizabeth Bentley's *Directory of Family Associations* or *Everton's Genealogical Helper* mag-azine's annual March/April listing of family associations and family periodi-cal publications.

In short, a wide variety of sources are available to researchers of African American families. Family historians are encouraged to examine all types of documents—primary and secondary—including, but not limited to, census, church, court, vital, military, and cemetery records. Researchers are urged to identify potential records, whether they are located in local, state, or nation-al repositories, and then carefully examine them. Without question, African Americans have a traceable ancestry and the wealth of information that may be uncovered and recorded can be used as the basis of your family tree.

Much of the research gathered from books and archives, talks with close and distant relatives, and the examination of other records can be used as the seeds of a family tree. The family tree, when completed, will provide an at-a-glance look at where relatives, living or dead, are in relationship to you and to each other. The tree shows how you are linked by blood or marriage to each of your relatives. Until this very important step is completed, the question "Who am I?" is not fully answered.

Most of us want to know who our relatives are, and genealogy is interesting, even fascinating. But discovering information about past family members is important and useful for other reasons. In particular, concerning legal matters, a carefully coded family tree can be of the utmost help in regards to the law of inheritance.

In cases where the deceased dies without having made a will or where it is important to determine the line of descent, the search is facilitated if a well-documented family tree is available. There are instances on record, in fact, where persons have attempted to inherit property by masking the truth about their family connections, assertions that a family tree would negate. Also, when persons attempt to falsify their background in order to gain status by claiming to be part of an important family, a family tree can help present the truth.

Don't be discouraged if many of the relationships are not full, but are "half" or "step" relations. For example, when one parent in a family dies or when parents get divorced, a second family may be started. The children of the second family—the half brothers and sisters—can be so designated. Also, in cases where a stepfather or stepmother brings stepbrothers and stepsisters to the family table, make such entries and design your chart so it will be all inclusive.

FAMILY RECORDS AND CHARTS

The "Family Record" form included here will help you gather the information you will need to construct and display your family tree in a graphic, well-organized manner.

The larger family tree illustration, called a *pedigree chart* or *lineal* family tree, records only your direct ascendants. Rosemary A. Chorzempa, who first published these charts in her book *My Family Workbook*, explains that in the chart, you are number 1, your father is number 2, and your mother is number 3. A father is two times his child's number; a wife is one more than her husband. Thus all men are even numbers, and all women are odd numbers.

The smaller illustration, called a *collateral* family tree, shows all your relatives—not just your direct ascendants. Write each name in full, along with complete birth and death dates, and add ancestors as you discover them and new family members as they are born or married into your family.

A family tree is a living thing; it will continue to grow, and you can continue to add information as you discover it.

GENEALOGICAL SOCIETY GIFT IS INDEX OF AREA CEMETERIES

Dan Dulin, editor of Independent Messenger, Emporia, Virginia, writes that the Greensville Genealogical Society last week presented copies of a 135-page alphabetical index of the names on headstones in county and city cemeteries to the Greensville Historical Society and the Riparian Woman's Club.

The Society has indexed 8,694 names from over 300 cemeteries. In addition to the names, the listing includes birth and death dates and any military affiliations.

The presentations were made because members of the organizations are interested in the history of the Greensville and Emporia.

The index joins a host of other information the Society has collected since it organized in 1997.

In addition to the headstone index, other materials available to the public at the Richardson Memorial Library include family histories, old maps, a census index from 1840-1870 for Greensville, index of wills to 1928, a volume of abstracts of wills, alphabetized funeral cards, guardianship records and land patents.

Society members divided the country into two quadrants, according to members Becky Gregory and Jean Pair. Word of mouth has led them and other Society members to old cemeteries, many of which are overgrown, and gathering names from their stones will wait until winter takes care of insects and snakes, they said. One such grave has a stone from the 1700s.

Collecting the information still has sometimes been a challenge. "Having to climb many fences, cutting brush, running from a herd of cattle, sliding down a ditch, and crawling through low hedges" have been part of the task, Pair said. "Contacting poison ivy, ticks, red bugs, and strange dogs" has, too.

"It has been a very rewarding experience," Pair said. "I only wish more people would care for cemeteries on property they rent or own, especially the families of the deceased."

A service that Society members are performing is for the stones on the graves of veterans, many of which are in disrepair. They photograph the stone, record data about the veteran, and give it to the Veterans of Foreign Wars who arrange for a new stone.

"Lots of Civil War ones are really in poor condition," Gregory said.

Including Society members, they said, 80 to 90 people have been involved in the headstone project by giving directions or making lists of cemeteries.

CEMETERY PRESERVATION AND RESTORATION

CHAPTER SEVEN

The customs, tales, stories, and songs of today and times past paint an engaging portrait of the men and women who created them. Besides their value as entertainment, these acts of the imagination hold messages—serious messages—of both despair and hope. For many people who are concerned about the preservation of African American history as a means of understanding themselves and their future as a people, burial grounds mirror many important customs. The genealogist who visits cemeteries and reviews valuable burial records will gain precious insight. Such visits can reveal critical findings, often opening the way to further fruitful investigations. The destruction of burial grounds is a threat to a heritage about which few written records remain, a heritage in danger of being lost. By preserving African American cemeteries, we are

Crispus Attucks and the Boston Massacre

Crispus Attucks, a black man, was the first to give his life at the commencement of the American Revolution. Eighteen years previous to the breaking out of the war, Attucks was held as a slave by Mr. William Brown of Framingham, Massachusetts and from whom he escaped about that time, taking up his residence in Boston. The Boston Massacre, March 5, 1770, may be regarded as the first act in the great drama of the American Revolution. The presence of the British soldiers excited the patriotic indignation of the people. Led by Crispus Attucks, shouting, "The way to get rid of these soldiers is to attack the main guard; strike at the root; this is the nest!" they rushed to King Street and were fired upon by Captain Preston's company. Crispus Attucks was the first to fall; he and Samuel Gray and Jones Caldwell were killed on the spot. Samuel Maverick and Patrick Garr were mortally wounded.

continued on next page

sustaining the memories of the folk ways they represent; the sermons, prayers, and testimonials are expressions of life's hardships, its stresses and strains, and, in the end, its beauty.

People with the greatest stake in the historic preservation of cemeteries are those who use cemetery data for reasons other than remembrance. Cemeteries as fields of history, cultural landscape, religion, folklore, anthropology, and even folk art, show patterns of change over time. Students of these areas seek to understand social status, family and community values, customs, and precedents. Rather than visiting cemeteries to obtain a single fact, such as a date of death, we find historians and others viewing the cemeteries as "communities of the dead."

As we have seen, particularly in the history of the Sea Islands cemeteries, considerable effort is being expended in fighting the elements of both nature and politics to maintain the integrity of black burial grounds. Often a single family member, small families, groups of advocates, or sometimes even entire communities will move forward to prevent a cemetery's destruction, whether by regularly raising funds, evoking community awareness, or designating clean-up days. Hope remains alive; the will to remember the past is ever constant. "Do not forget" has become the traditional chant of the historic cemetery advocate.

Richard E. Meyers, a writer for the *Journal of the Association for Gravestone Studies,* considers "communities of the dead" to be a challenge to the researcher: "Far more than merely elements of space sectioned off and set aside for the burial of the dead, cemeteries are, in effect, open cultural texts, there to be read and appreciated by anyone who takes the time to learn a bit of their special language."

Much can be ascertained from cemetery artifacts regarding the ethnicity and mores of the people who once populated the surrounding region. Church cemeteries, as well as community cemeteries, reflect all types of significant information about those interred there. In most cases, people buried in church cemeteries during the same generation knew each other as family or friends, shared the same religion, and interacted with each other during the course of their daily lives. To a lesser extent, the same is true of the smaller community cemeteries.

Preservation methods and requirements vary in accordance with the cemetery involved. For example, in large cities, which house larger cemeteries, there tends to be an immeasurable amount of broad-based information available, but less communal information. And persons interred in military cemeteries have a wide diversity of backgrounds—different ethnicities, religions, and residences—but share common military experiences.

Some cities and states give cemetery restoration a high priority. The Boston Parks and Recreation Department, for example, hosts an annual "Tour de Graves," a twenty-five-mile bicycle tour of Boston's historic burying grounds. The city has sixteen historic burying grounds; seven date back to the 1600s, three to the 1700s, and six to the 1800s. Several remained active well into the twentieth century. The burying grounds are located in neighborhoods city-wide, and three are sites along the city's historic Freedom Trail.

Proceeds of the Tour de Graves (and the Petit Tour de Graves) go directly toward the restoration and conservation of these sixteen burying grounds. The Boston Parks and Recreation Department's Historic Burying Grounds Initiative is the largest municipal cemetery restoration project in the United States.

Historic cemetery preservation is still an emerging field, stimulated by the urgent need to safeguard irreplaceable cultural resources threatened by imminent loss. The city of Boston's historic burying grounds may very well comprise the largest collection of historic cemeteries owned by any U.S. municipality. The Boston Experience, as it is called, is set forth in the *Manual for Historic Burying Grounds Preservation,* which provides a comprehensive guide for those interested in the subject. As pointed out by the *Manual*'s writers and editors, in addition to containing some basic "how to" information, it is primarily a presentation of the "why tos" of burial-ground preservation. Chapter headings range from "Getting Started" and "Grave Marker Inventory and Analysis" to "Master Plan" and "Implementation."

continued from previous page

Three days after, on the 8th, a public funeral of the martyrs took place. The shops in Boston were closed; and all the bells of Boston and the neighboring towns were rung. It is said that a greater number of persons assembled on this occasion than were ever before gathered on this continent for a similar purpose. The body of Crispus Attucks had been placed in Faneuil Hall, with that of Caldwell, both being strangers in the city. Maverick was buried at his mother's house on Union Street; and Gray at his brother's on Royal Exchange Lane. The four hearses formed a junction in King Street; and from there the procession marched in columns six deep, with a long file of coaches belonging to the most distinguished citizens, to the Middle Burying Ground, where the four victims were deposited in one grave, over which a stone was placed with this inscription:

Long is in Freedom's cause the wise contend,

Dear to your country shall your fame extend;

While to the world the lettered stone shall tell

Where Caldwell, Attucks, Gray, and Maverick fell.

—WILLIAM WELLS BROWN, *The Negro in the American Rebellion*

What directly follows is information from the section "Getting Started." For those who wish to follow through on obtaining an historic designation, we encourage you to contact Boston's Historic Burying Grounds Initiative.

Getting Started

Successful historic burying ground preservation involves becoming aware of the complexity of the issues. The first step in the preservation process requires identifying all foreseeable problems. After several informal meetings to assess the situation, concerned parties should involve the owner of the burying ground or those responsible for its continuing maintenance. Local and state preservation agencies can be called upon for technical assistance. Three important issues to focus on are markers, site features, and management issues.

MARKERS

How old are the markers, tombs, and memorials? Are several kinds of stone or other materials present? What do their conditions appear to be? What significance do they possess in terms of both artistry and social history? Has an inventory or a history of the burying ground been prepared?

SITE FEATURES

What is the character of the setting? Is it simple and rural, with tall unmown grass and informally placed trees; or more formal, with a designed path system, planting plan, and features such as ornamental gates or signs? Is the topography relatively flat or hilly? Are views into, within, or out from the cemetery important features?

Does the cemetery exhibit a unified style characteristic of development over a short period of time, or show features that indicate long-term evolution, perhaps over more than a century? Do accretions over time add to or detract from the character of the site? What are the general conditions of trees, fences, walls, paths, signs, and other site features?

MANAGEMENT ISSUES

Who owns and who maintains the cemetery? What regulatory agencies have jurisdiction over the site, such as a local historical commission or state archaeologist? Are access and security adequate? How many visitors does it receive? Is over-use or under-use a concern? Is increased public awareness or site interpretation needed? Who will pay for preservation activities? Who can supervise or perform them? What about other kinds of support, such as the formation of a friends of the burying ground group?

For purposes of burial ground preservation, the follow- # Preservation Terminology
ing definitions regarding processes apply:

Preservation refers to activities that help perpetuate and care for historic burial sites, including planning, maintenance, documentation, and education.

Conservation refers to mechanical and chemical processes used to treat damaged markers and other cemetery structures.

Restoration may occasionally apply to burial grounds, although it implies significant intervention, which should be avoided whenever possible. When a mausoleum, for example, has deteriorated to the point where a partial rebuilding is required, restoration is appropriate. True restoration includes documentation and research to determine the original appearance of the artifact, its structure, and the treatment required.

Stabilization refers to treatments executed to retain the greatest cultural and structural integrity of the artifact and the site overall, with a minimum of intervention into the historic fabric. In some cases it may approach restoration, although it generally does not include replacement of nonstructural detailing. Most marker repair may be classified as either conservation or stabilization.

In addition to its sections on "Getting Started" in cemetery # A "Shopping List"
preservation and "Preservation Terminology," the Boston
Experience *Manual* sets forth a comprehensive list of interre- # Approach to Planning
lated areas of concern that comprise; a "shopping list"
approach to preservation planning. Such areas include "Marker and Tomb Conservation," "Protective Measures," "Vandalism and Security," "Landscaping and Site Improvements," "Engineering Interpretation," "Maintenance," "Fundraising and Manpower Support," and "Resources of State Historic Preservation Organizations."

As staff members of the Boston Parks Department and Boston Landmarks Commission worked with local preservation agencies and advocacy groups to determine the preservation needs of the city's sixteen historic burying grounds, a comprehensive list of tasks and interrelated areas of concerns began to emerge within the central task of mapping out a philosophy of conservation:

MARKER AND TOMB CONSERVATION

Determine the extent and types of damage; do a grave-marker inventory, including an inventory of specific materials: slate, brownstone, granite, brick, marble, etc. Determine options for recutting and replacing markers; develop a policy to determine which stones will be selected for repair, and the method of restoration and storage for damaged stones and fragments. Make proposals as to how, who, and where methods of maintaining the grounds can be used to reduce further damage.

PROTECTIVE MEASURES

Make up a grave marker inventory. Apply for National Register listing, if appropriate. Determine gravestone rubbing policy and/or prohibition. Find out about access to funding; decide upon a public education and involvement policy. Find out about state and local laws protecting graveyards and grave markers; is it appropriate to adopt a local ordinance to enforce any prohibition of reproduction and/or removal of significant gravestones?

VANDALISM AND SECURITY

Determine any misuse of grounds—vandalism, loitering, occupation by homeless individuals. Look at fencing, lighting, tree canopy, police surveillance, neighbors, abutters. Are there local regulatory signs supervision and enforcement repair policies concerning graffiti, tombs, or overturned or broken stones?

LANDSCAPING AND SITE IMPROVEMENTS

List the site's aesthetic and physical condition, including access and circulation. What about the pruning, feeding, and other care of mature trees; the possible introduction of new trees or seasonal plantings (flowers); the desired length of grass/sod/ground cover; the effects of shade trees on gravestones (i.e., roots, visibility, soiling); or soil erosion and compacting problems? Check for historical accuracy—are landscape elements such as fencing and decorative iron retained and/or restored? Should they be repaired or replaced with the same or other material? Should stone walls be heightened or should they be repaired, repointed, replaced, or made solid? What types of gates, stone steps, gateways, handicapped access, and pathways are used?

What are the current materials? What is best for maintenance, upkeep, longevity, safety, and historical accuracy? What about location: what will cause the least damage to grounds, stones, etc., for a logical circulation pattern? What is the lighting like? Are there special-effects or floodlighting? What is the effect of lighting on adjacent structures? Is it vandalproof? What is the location of fixtures and attachments and what is the cost of electricity? Are benches inside and/or outside and, if so, what is the type and location? Are there trash receptacles? What about signage: what is the appearance, location, and safety factor of any signs or interpretive markers? What about rodent extermination? Is the facility locked or open? And what is the ease of visitation and access to keys?

Determine engineering requirements: what is the deterioration of retaining walls, tomb structures, and drainage or irrigation systems? What about on-site maintenance and safety factors: are there walls along public ways, open tombs, or ground subsidence?

INTERPRETATION

Determine objectives for an informational signage system and its value as a public education or fundraising tool. Is protection of historic markers and plaques provided on-site? Are original gravestones displayed off-site and replaced by on-site reproductions? Should there be brochures? Who provides litter pick-up?

MAINTENANCE

Coordinate trash removal and mowing techniques with landscaping restoration/gravestone conservation. Weigh the efficiency vs. precision of clipping, weeding, or other maintenance methods. Should there be specialized training of maintenance personnel in simple conservation techniques, such as fragment collection or resetting sunken/tilted stones?

FUNDRAISING AND MANPOWER SUPPORT AND RESOURCES

The Massachusetts Historical Commission determined its potential funding sources to be foundations, charitable trusts, descendants, corporate donors, the Boston city budget, and the federal government. Who pays for what? How are funds matched with needs? Is it feasible to phase in projects as funding becomes available, or to use volunteer sources—"friends" groups, youth groups, local civic organizations, et al? Which local businesses/contractors might be willing to donate services or supplies? Is professional project management needed for documentation, fundraising, implementation, or record-keeping?

Preservation Philosophy and Strategy

In addition to using a "shopping list" approach, it is important to develop a preservation philosophy. In order to establish an overall mind-set in regard to restoration, a series of questions needs to be formulated and then answered. Answering such questions will result in a foundation on which to build a preservation philosophy. Some suggested questions are as follows.

- What kinds of information should be collected to formulate a plan for restoration?

- How should this data be standardized?

- Should restoration include recreating now-illegible markers?

- What are the criteria for choosing stones for repair and how many should be chosen?

- Should exceptionally significant stones be reproduced and removed from their original location?

- Can original stones removed from the burying ground be stored or put on exhibit near the site of origin?

- What about reproduction of grave markers for commercial purposes?

- What kinds of information are needed for public education?

- Should the burying ground be restored to one period in time or should it show a historic continuum?

- What additions should be made for visitors to the site, such as benches or interpretive markers?

- Should regulations regarding picnicking, gravestone rubbing, or the presence of dogs be considered?

- Is handicapped access adequate?

- Are current plantings in keeping with the original design?

- Are some maintenance practices harmful to the markers, such as scraping by lawn mowers; removal of graffiti using harsh chemicals, abrasives, or high-pressure wash; or the use of pesticides, herbicides, or fertilizers around gravestones?

These pertinent questions deserve very serious thought; each and every answer is important in the formulation of a comprehensive restoration philosophy and program.

After you've clearly established a preservation philosophy, your next step is to develop a preservation action strategy. In other words, how much work is the individual or group willing to do? Sometimes priorities are obvious due to safety reasons: Open tombs or retaining walls in danger of collapsing require immediate attention. Other priorities must be organized in view of the preservation philosophy.

Creating a Master Plan

Comprehensive planning is essential, though each city and town—and even each burying ground—have needs that vary. The responsible stewardship of Boston's sixteen burying grounds, for instance, required a formal master plan, one that accommodated phased implementation over a number of years and provided the basis for developing annual budgets for capital improvement well into the future.

For preservation of a single burying ground the planning product need not be as formal. However, the process should be equally comprehensive. Every burying ground has a unique and complex set of interrelated issues. Action addressing one problem in an isolated manner has the potential to create a different problem down the road. For example, the use of acid to remove graffiti on marble monuments has resulted in the stone's deterioration to the point that carvings have become damaged; likewise, planting trees in the vicinity of underground brick tombs has caused damage decades later when their expanding root systems have broken through the tomb's masonry walls.

A master plan is long-term. Designed to be future-oriented, it must necessarily allow for flexibility. Priorities change, as can preservation philosophy, technology, and available support. Consequently, the budget limitations that usually necessitate proceeding with historic preservation projects in phases can actually prove beneficial, enabling new techniques—such as those developed through monitored pilot or outdoor laboratory projects on carefully chosen gravestones or masonry tombs—to add to our ability to care and plan for the future.

Grave Marker Inventory and Analysis

A grave marker inventory is a key element in developing any burying ground preservation program. This inventory, in the form of a final report, provides a working document containing accurate data about the number of grave markers, the types of materials used on the site, the historical and artistic significance of such markers, and the conditions of both the grave markers and the burying ground site at project inception.

The challenge of any inventory is to amass a large amount of data within a format that can be adapted for a variety of uses. In Boston, the need for consistency in dealing with sixteen geographically separate sites containing over twelve hundred grave markers was especially important. This resulted in the development of a standardized inventory form containing categories for recording inscriptions and other physical data. To facilitate the use of inventory data in planning for grave-marker conservation, a detailed *conditions assessment* is particularly useful. During the Boston project, for example, the initial inventory form was revised to incorporate specialized conditions terminology developed by the consulting masonry conservator.

An information booklet on preservation written by Lynette Strangstad, a specialist in the preservation of historic burial grounds, also provides in-depth information on all aspects of the subject. The following are excerpts:

> In the last decade, increased public interest and concern for our threatened burial sites has resulted in the development of this new area of historic preservation. Due to the recent nature of this development, relatively little written information is available and locating professionals knowledgeable about the preservation of historic burial sites can be difficult.
>
> The publication of the National Trust for Historic Preservation is designed to meet the need for information that both the general citizenry and professionals may have when considering the preservation of historic burial grounds. Basic knowledge of the field is offered to help organizations and individuals understand the significance of historic burial grounds, identify concerns relevant to their preservation, and recognize methods appropriate to their conservation.
>
> Cemeteries and graveyards, often visited as parks and historic sites, are places to commemorate the dead—whether family member, friend, or historic figure—and to reflect on the past. Visitors often find these sites peaceful and serene settings in which to spend a pleasant afternoon. Historical burial sites offer this, of course, and much more. Such sites yield vast amounts of information regarding our bicultural, historic, artistic, and architectural heritage.

Understanding and Respecting the Site

The first recommended action in any preservaton project is to understand the site. In the preservation of historic burial grounds one must understand the nature of the grounds in relation to the surrounding physical environment and its cultural context. Next—and particularly if the historic significance is not at first apparent—one must search diligently to obtain a broader understanding of the history of the surrounding area. Discoveries of unexpected artifacts, including cultural artifacts, may be of great help in determining the particulars relating to the history of the site. In short, all preservation work should take place with the greatest caution, to assure that no information is lost to future generations of researchers.

The National Trust suggests that only professional archaeologists, sensitive to the requirements of historic burial sites and familiar with the burial customs and practices of ethnic groups, should undertake below-ground archaeological investigation of historic burial sites. Since any soil disturbance will also disturb the landscape surface, including relic plants, all landscape inventories must be completed prior to beginning any archaeological work. Shallow soil samples taken as part of a preservation project—perimeter samplings taken in conjunction with the repair of a wall or fence, for example—may provide valuable information regarding earlier buildings or activity alongside the burial site. Likewise, shallow samplings taken within the burial ground can be used to locate lost burials or identify earlier walkways, walls, monuments, or buildings.

The excavation of burial sites for scientific investigation raises many moral and ethical questions. The conservative viewpoint holds that excavation of burials is acceptable only in cases of inadvertent discovery—human remains found in an otherwise unmarked spot during road construction, for example. Such discovery should result in a respectful move of the remains to a suitable burial location. Most archaeologists, however, feel that such discovery legitimately may be used for scientific inquiry.

Although now less acceptable, it has been common in the past for burials—particularly of paupers or ethnic groups including African Americans and Native Americans—to be unearthed and examined in such an inquiry. But disturbing the burial places of their ancestors is abhorrent to most groups; the African-American tradition that firmly resists disturbing burial grounds in any way survives to this day. Such traditions should always be respected when planning burial ground preservation efforts.

Cultural Context and Physical Setting

Whether in a busy metropolitan area, near a small factory town, next to a tiny white church surrounded by cornfields, or in a neglected and forgotten wood, the burial ground's cultural context and physical setting are important considerations in determining the direction take by preservation efforts. Is the burial ground on a flat, featureless plain? Is it bordered by tall pines or cedars? Or is there a profusion of mature vegetation enclosing the site? Is it a rolling, rambling, romantic setting straight out of a Victorian novel? Or is the setting severe, almost sterile, in its simplicity?

Examining the burial ground within its larger physical context results in a fuller understanding of the site's historical evolution. It enables accurate interpretation of the site, and a more realistic plan of its future use. If the graveyard is bordered by a pine or oak forest, for example, the acid generated by these species of trees has a potentially detrimental effect on marble and limestone markers. On the other hand, such trees could also provide some protection from a road or factory that produces pollutants even more damaging to these stone types. It is as inappropriate to remove the trees as it would be impractical to move the road or the factory, but both must be addressed in any preservation project.

In most cases little can be done to alter properties adjacent to a burial site, although occasionally circumstances may require action. For example, the owner of a contiguous property may dispute a property line. Research and physical investigation can sometimes clarify original boundaries that may have become unclear over the years. This is particularly important when the disputed area contains burials that are now considered to be outside the graveyard.

Changes to adjacent property may affect the burial ground even if no burials are directly threatened. Rerouting a nearby drainage ditch could result in erosion of the soil due to run-off; and constructing a large building nearby could significantly alter the site visually. It is reasonable, appropriate, and, in some cases, essential to address any proposed changes to adjacent real estate by attending planning commission meetings, discussing problems with local government officials, and working with them toward a solution.

Features of the Site

Once the broad context of the site is understood, but before specific preservation planning can begin, it is essential to undertake an evaluation of the burial ground's features, including entrance gates and perimeter walls, ironwork, enclosure gates and fences, masonry plot enclosures, vegetation, roadways and walkways, retaining walls, open spaces, buildings, and the markers themselves. Each feature requires careful study in order to understand its importance within the context of the entire site and to aid in developing a useful, comprehensive, and appropriate preservation plan.

ENTRANCES

The entrance is the visitor's introduction to the graveyard. Be it through elaborately wrought black iron gates or between two large rocks of moss-covered granite, an important statement is made to visitors at the entrance of the site. Except for security or legal reasons, a simple site that has stood for many years without a perimeter fence, walls, or gates should remain so. Wrought iron, cast iron, or early twentieth-century wire fences and gates may surround more elaborate cemeteries. Other sites may have walls of brick, stone, coquina, tabby, or wood. Each of these styles and materials provides significant information regarding the site's historical period, the availability of materials, the representative culture, and local craftsmanship. In addition, the perimeter can determine a guided point of entry, security, boundary definition, and aesthetics.

PLOT ENCLOSURES

Within the burial ground, the variety of fence-types and other plot definitions and enclosures may reflect the sophistication of the site, the era in which it was most active, the availability of materials and craftspeople during different historical periods, individual expression, the relative wealth of those buried at the site, and other historical, artistic, and demographic information.

VEGETATION

Understanding the importance of vegetation to a site is essential to site preservation. A mature tree canopy is often a site's most significant organic feature and the one most important in creating its character. It is also an important historic feature, since in many cases trees were planted as memorials, as part of the original site plan, or even as part of an earlier restoration effort. In all cases, these are sufficient reasons to retain existing trees and mature shrubs. Smaller vegetation, too, such as low-growing shrubs, perennial flowers, and ground covers, can be of historical significance, having often been planted as a memorial. Traditional graveyard plantings include such evergreens as cedars, pines, hollies, and spruce; deciduous trees such as crape myrtles, oaks, and maples; lilacs and old-fashioned shrub roses; and perennial flowers such as irises, lily-of-the-valley, and peonies. Common succulents include hen-and-chicks, live-for-ever, and creeping sedums. In many cases, particularly in graveyards that have been untouched or neglected for considerable periods of time, early varieties of plantlife that still flourish at the site have become rare elsewhere in the local or regional landscape. Sometimes such relic plants serve as the only marker, standing over a grave site as a living tribute to the deceased.

GRAVE MARKERS

As the most obvious feature of any burial ground, grave markers are the objects most commonly earmarked for preservation. Most people recognize the significance of large stone monuments honoring prominent individuals, markers representing well-known historical figures, markers intricately carved by talented artisans, and curiosity pieces to which bits of local folklore or other mystique are attached. However, these are only a few of the markers included in the overall picture. In order to understand the history of any particular site and region, an understanding of the total assemblage of markers is essential. Each marker is another piece of the puzzle. When sufficient pieces are lost, no matter how insignificant each alone might be, the puzzle cannot be completed and the full history of the site and the region is unattainable.

Less understood, but often of even greater importance than stone markers and monuments, are the pioneer markers of early settlers. These, along with other vernacular expressions, were commonly made of wood, shell, stone, or cast concrete as a unique expression to be lovingly placed on a grave site by a family member or other mourner. In preserving a site, no marker is insignificant. Many small pioneer markers, important by virtue of their scarcity and cultural importance, are overlooked, misunderstood, or discarded by well-meaning individuals untrained in recognizing marker types and their significance. The grave goods found in African-American and other ethnic burial grounds are such examples.

TREE AND VEGETATION SURVEY

Together with its accompanying vegetation conditions assessment, the tree and vegetation survey is used in identifying and recording all forms of vegetation within a cemetery. Part of the historical record, it is used for maintenance and management. The survey is conducted by a horticulturist, consulting arborist, landscape historian, or preservation landscape architect familiar with both historic plantings and the preservation of landscaping in historic burial grounds. Sometimes urban foresters or country or university extension services are able to offer needed guidance. It is essential that the professionals chosen for such a survey be familiar with historical vegetation found in burial grounds. Many landscape architects, for example, are more familiar with planning than plantings and with modern hybrids rather than with the earlier varieties sometimes found in old burial grounds, but infrequently grown today. Native wildflowers, grasses, and other vegetation may remain from the pre–settlement terrain, particularly in sparsely populated areas.

The survey is designed to document the location, variety, size, age, and condition of plant species. It outlines general maintenance and recommends treatment for the various plantlife grown on the site. It also recommends removal of invasive, weedy, or scrub vegetation and may contain notes as to the historic character of various plantings. Surveyors should conduct the survey during at least three seasons: spring, summer, and fall. Some plants may be easily overlooked if the survey takes place during only one growing season.

Maintaining and Preserving Burial Sites

According to the National Trust for Historic Preservation, there are a variety of ways to maintain a cemetery. The following is reprinted from their newsletter, *Information:*

GRAVE DEPRESSIONS

Shallow depressions in old burial grounds are often actually grave depressions. While it is advisable to in-fill sink holes or holes left by the removal of diseased trees, grave depressions should be retained. Often they are the only evidence of otherwise unmarked graves. Since no burial may be considered unimportant, information regarding each must be preserved and care taken before altering any aspect of the terrain.

IRONWORK MAINTENANCE

To maintain existing ironwork, sound areas of the metal need to be cleaned and primed. Once iron surfaces are free of oils and grease, salts, dirt, and loose rust deposits, and the surface is allowed to dry, a rust inhibitor may be applied directly to rusted surfaces without sandblasting or extensive sanding. Elimination or reduction of the sanding step is cost-effective, since time is saved. It is also sound as a preservation policy, since as much as possible of the deteriorating iron is retained and re-adhered to the sound surface. The question of whether or not to paint the ironwork, and if painted, what color to use, can be answered through a *paint analysis,* a procedure performed by an expert in the field to determine what colors were applied to structures at the time of their construction. The state historic preservation officer may be of help in finding a professional to assist with paint analysis.

When existing ironwork structures, such as fences, are not complete, a preferred preservation solution is to repair and maintain the remaining work rather than add historically incorrect substitutes.

ROAD AND PATH MAINTENANCE

Roads and paths, particularly in nineteenth-century cemeteries, are often a key feature in the cemetery's landscape design; as such, their preservation and maintenance are essential. Such preservation includes maintaining existing widths and contours, the small triangles or circles often found at path intersections, and the original paving surfaces. Brick gutters should be maintained rather than ignored or eliminated. Introduction of asphalt for the convenience of modern vehicles seriously alters the site and erodes its integrity. To preserve certain existing roadways, traffic can sometimes be limited to pedestrians only. Replacement of original crushed stone or early brick with new brick pavers or other paving materials likewise compromises the site. If brick was the original material, roads or paths should be resurfaced with as much of the original brick as possible and reproduction brick that matches the original in color, size, texture, and strength, intermixed as necessary. When a custom-made brick is required, restoration brick firms have little difficulty in producing good replica brick. Brick and gravel paths and roadways need regular maintenance. Especially important are monitoring and repair or correction of erosion problems.

ADAPTING FOR CURRENT USES

Because tourists and other interested persons are among the most common visitors to burial grounds, minor adaptations to accommodate them, such as benches and trash receptacles, can enhance the burial site as well. In Victorian cemeteries, cast-iron benches and cast-iron or wire trash receptacles might be appropriate at strategic points. In an earlier, simpler burial ground,

Cleaning Burial Markers

When to clean: Determine the nature of soiling agents: lichens, fungi, vines, and other biological growth that can obscure inscriptions. They may promote acidic surface conditions or actually feed on stone material. Carbonaceous deposits may cause gypsum to form.

Who should clean: Cleaning is generally undertaken by conservators prior to stone treatment. Cleaning may be undertaken by maintenance personnel, plot owners, and volunteers following a brief workshop illustrating correct methods and materials.

How to clean: Unstable stones: Leave for a conservator or leave alone. Stable stones in good overall condition: Begin by flooding stone with clean water. Sometimes water alone or water and a soft-bristled brush is enough. If a cleaning agent is desired, use plain household ammonia diluted with water 1:4. Always complete the process by rinsing thoroughly with clean water. Gypsum may be removed with continuous extra-low-pressure water application.

continued on next page

such accommodations are best left outside near the burial ground's entry. Placement and choice of these element requires careful consideration; obviously, an orange plastic industrial drum with "Trash" gaily painted on it in white letters is not a fitting enhancement to any historic burial ground.

URBAN GREEN SPACES

Uses beyond tourist visitation are important and, indeed, probably essential to the survival of many sites. Burial grounds are typically visited by genealogists, history buffs, and people interested in gravestone carvings. In urban areas, cemeteries and early burial grounds provide open areas that offer urbanites the tranquility and respite found in tree-lined, grassy areas. Delightful places for strolling or bird watching, burial sites also serve as minor habitats for wildlife, particularly small creatures such as birds and squirrels. Some nineteenth-century cemeteries also serve as botanical gardens. Such uses are very much in keeping with the original intent of the site and serve today's public admirably as well.

SIGNAGE

Signage is an important aspect of the visitor's overall experience during his time spent at the cemetery grounds. Signs should be uniform throughout and should reflect the style of the era most appropriate to the burial ground. In most cases, simple, clear, unobtrusive signs are best suited to burial sites and, wherever possible, should be limited to the entryway. The use of numerous signs throughout the site, in addition to being disruptive, compromises the site's historical integrity unless signs were similarly placed at a very early date in the site's history. In many cases, a style similar to that used by the National Park Service at its historic sites is most appropriate: effective, simple, and clear.

The content of signs is primarily informative. Sometimes a map at the entryway can effectively direct visitors to points of interest. Historical information is also useful. In addition to providing visitor information, signs can also set forth state regulatory policy. In some cases, a direct statement of what is or is not allowed is appropriate. Often, however, a positive approach which involves visitors and asks them to take a personal interest in the site is more effective. Remind visitors that the site is both historic and sacred ground that deserves care and respect. A note about the fragility of the site may be appropriate as well.

REGULATIONS

Regulations apply primarily to visitors and delineate appropriate behavior, hours of operation, and acceptable maintenance procedures. They are generally site-specific and may vary greatly from one location to the next. Site regulations might open the yard at 8 or 9 a.m., and close at dusk. A notice that trespassers apprehended after such hours will be prosecuted may aid the monitoring efforts of local police and reduce vandalism.

continued from previous page

What to remove by hand: Encroaching vegetation that keeps markers damp (trim historic vegetation; remove scrub vegetation), and vegetation in mortar joints or seams.

What to avoid: Cleaning sugary, cracked, split or otherwise unsound stones with muriatic acid, household bleach, household detergents, pressure cleaning, unidentified chemicals, sandblasting, stone refinishing. letter recutting, paint, sealants, metal implements, and biocides.

What to use: Rubber gloves and goggles, nylon or tampico scrub brush, cleaning solution of plain water or common household ammonia and water diluted 1:4, tongue depressors, cotton swabs, spray bottles, and garden hoses.

NATIONAL TRUST FOR HISTORIC PRESERVATION, *Information*

Gravestone rubbing should be strongly curtailed or eliminated due to the potential long-range damage to markers. Irreparable and significant damage has been done by people who thought themselves both careful and knowledgeable. In addition to the damage caused by pigment residue, most visitors are not able to accurately distinguish between sound stones and unstable ones. Because of the potential damage, rubbing is best avoided altogether.

It is essential to the well-being of the burial site—for legal clarity, for proper site maintenance, and for permanent archival records—that any governmental body with jurisdiction over an active burial ground enforce any existing ordinance or, if necessary, implement a new one, mandating the recording of all new burials within each cemetery under its jurisdiction. The burial record should include, at minimum, the name, location (mapped), and date of the burial. Obviously, no burials should be allowed in otherwise claimed spaces. A permit to bury, issued following proof of ownership of the proposed grave space, should be required at the site before a burial can take place. Such records, appropriately maintained by the city or county and upheld with the mutual cooperation of the governmental body and the burial site administration, bear the force of law. Other regulations appropriate to effective management and care of the site should also be developed.

ADDITIONAL ACTIVITIES

Other current uses, particularly of the larger Victorian sites, include organized activities: tours, holiday and memorial observances, community picnics, fund raisers such as walks or runs, and more. Such activities, when managed by informed, sensitive groups working as custodians of the site, can add much to the overall value of such historic cemeteries as a community resource without adding damage to the site.

Such expanded use of burial grounds is desirable both to the site—well-visited sites are less subject to the destruction caused by vandals and derelicts than are less-visited sites—and to local residents. Activities draw individuals to the site who may not otherwise come to know and appreciate burial grounds. They create a vested interest by individuals in protecting and promoting the site. In addition, they broaden the base of community support needed to speak up, either when inappropriate changes are proposed or when much needed funding is required. In the long term, preservation of historic burial grounds is impossible without the broad-based interest of the community. Carefully managed, hosting activities on the site of early burial grounds can benefit both the historic site and its modern-day visitors.

Cemeteries and graveyards face dramatic pressures - from development, abandonment and decay, nature, and vandalism. They are also very different from other historic resources, since they involve a variety of functions - sacred, artistic, historic and genealogical. The resources present include not only the human remains, but also the sculptures and monuments, as well as the landscape itself, making cemeteries - and their preservation - very complex.

Often there's a feeling by those trying to save a cemetery that work must be immediate. This usually isn't the case and, when preservation efforts are rushed, there is often the potential for very serious - and long-lasting - damage.

The preservation of graveyards and cemeteries involves a wide range of disciplines, including landscape architecture, historic and archival research, conservation, and at times even a structural engineer. In other words, it is unlikely that any one organization can do everything on any cemetery preservation project.

The Chicora Foundation in Columbus, South Carolina has expert advice for restoring or repairing your cemetery. We are including a list of common problems, set forth by Dr. Michael Trinkley, director of the Foundation in his paper on Preservation and Restoration.

Common problems and answers are as follows:

1. We've been told to set our stones in cement to help keep them upright.

Don't do it! Concrete is very inflexible and much harder than most tombstones. There's no "give" and the stones are much more likely to snap off - making your preservation problems far worse and more expensive.

2. A local firm said they could repair all our stones using some kind of adhesive.

Get more information. In fact, require that anyone offering their services provide you with a "treatment proposal" that puts in writing specifically what they intend to do, what materials or chemicals they intend to use, and how they are proposing to treat your stones. Ask questions. Also understand that stone conservation is a very technical, specialized skill. Just because you are a mason, or a monument supplier; doesn't mean you have the expertise-to repair old stone.

3. One firm wants to completely rebuild one of our monuments.

Maybe this is necessary, but maybe not. Sometimes a monument is in such poor condition that you need to start work from the "ground up." But if you replace virtually everything you wind up with a new monument, not the old, historic marker you are trying to save. Do you really want a new monument? Or do you want to respect the original material and try to preserve as much as possible?

4. Someone wants to pressure wash our cemetery stones using some kind of chemical.

This is hardly ever necessary. Harsh cleaning removes both the outer layer of the stone and its patina. This means that the stone soils even faster than before - and it also loses its old, historic look. It's much better to use low pressure, gentle techniques. And examine any chemical very carefully. Sometimes cleaning chemicals - even those meant for stone - can leave stains or cause other problems.

Examples of Treatments

Cleaning Stones - Chicora typically uses low pressure water with detergents intended specifically for stone, such as Triton-X and Vulpex. Where necessary we also use specially formulated biocides to control lichen and other organic growth.

Resetting Stones - Toppled stones can be safely reset to restore their beauty and dignity. Where possible we use resetting techniques similar to those originally used by the artisans, such as lime-based mortars, but can also add pins for additional security.

Stone Repair - Both simple and complex breaks can be repaired using specially formulated epoxies, stainless steel or nylon pins, and other restoration adhesives. These repairs are done to ensure that water movement in the stone is not interrupted and that the repair materials are able to expand and contract without damage to the stone.

Infill of Missing Stone and Recasting of Missing Elements - Sometimes it is necessary to compensate for loss of original stone. We prefer to use Jahn Restoration Mortars and have received the special training to use this material. They are specifically formulated to match the physical properties of the stone being repaired.

Chicora Foundation, Inc.

Dr. Michael Trinkley, director of Chicora Foundation, does an amazing job of surounding himself with great staff, and community persons and attacking gignatic tasks in and around Columbia, down past Beaufort, South Carolina and other adjacent areas and the many Sea Islands. His research includes titles, such as the following:

The Second Phase of Archaeological Survey on Spring Island, Beaufort County, South Carolina: Investigation of Prehistoric and Historic Settlement Patterns on an isolated sea island.

An Archaeological Survey of Longpoint Development, Charleston County, South Carolina: Palmetto Grove Plantation

Monrovia Union Cemetery, Charleston, South Carolina.

The St. John's Burial Association and the Catholic Cemetery at Immaculate Conception, City of Charleston, South Carolina: What Became of the Repose of the Dead (55 pages).

Of course, these are a very few of the many, many Research Projects undertaken by Chicora Foundation...P.O. Box 8664, Columbia, South Carolina, 29202.

BURIAL SOCIETIES, LODGES AND CLUBS

CHAPTER EIGHT

I SING—

FOR FAR TOO MANY WRONGS ARE LEFT UNRIGHTED

AS BLACK FOLKS BEND BEFORE THE SCOURGE OF HATE

AND SEND ENTREATING PRAYERS UP TO ANOTHER,

BEGGING AND PLEADING FOR A KINDER FATE;

WE NEED TO KNOW, AS SAMSON DID OF OLD,

THAT OUR OWN STRENGTH CAN BREAK THE GIANT HOLD

THAT KEEPS US DOWN BENEATH THE FEET OF MEN,

FEARING TO RISK, LEST WE BE HURT AGAIN—

SO I MUST SING.

—RUBY BERKLEY GOODWIN

Burial societies and lodges served as the precursors to modern-day insurance companies for America's black communities, filling the important gaps in security and peace of mind created by racial discrimination. In exchange for a monthly, or in some cases weekly, premium or dues, these organizations guaranteed their members health care in the event of sickness or accident. Members provided support for the disabled and worked together to plant or harvest crops for a fellow member unable to do so. Many of these societies, which also supported schools for black children, became, in fact, the social and religious center of some black communities. But perhaps most importantly, they contracted to guarantee a proper funeral and burial for their dues-paying members. "Without a doubt their major concern was the death benefit; making sure their members received not only a decent but a special burial," says Robert L. Harris, professor of Afro-American History at the African Studies and Research Center at Cornell University.

Burial societies developed in both urban and rural settings, mainly to counter the discriminatory practices that prohibited African Americans from sharing white health facilities. Their importance to the community stems from the belief that the soul of an African American would eventually return to the mother continent—but only if the body was given a proper and respectful send-off. Hence a great deal of attention was given to burials. Elaborate funeral ceremonies, such as the famed funeral parades in New Orleans, complete with trumpeters and singers, were the order of the day.

These institutions almost always had a religious or spiritual flavor. "Many of these societies developed prior to the formal development of black churches and filled a gap in social and religious areas for the black communities," explains Harris. But as the black churches began to grow, they slowly took over many of the functions of the societies and lodges, including burials. Some societies and lodges themselves evolved into local churches.

Melville H. Herskovits was a distinguished professor of anthropology who taught on the faculties of Columbia University, Howard University, and Northwestern University prior to his death in 1963. The author of many articles and books, including *The Myth of the Negro Past,* he was the founder of the first university program of African studies in the United States. In describing the importance of burial insurance and burial societies, Herskovits maintained that the principle that life must have a proper ending as well as a well-protected beginning is the fundamental reason for the importance of the funeral in Negro societies. This results from several causes, the most important being the widespread African belief in the power of one's ancestors to affect the living.

H. W. Odum, writing in his *Social and Mental Traits of the Negro,* published in 1910, recognized the important place accorded to death within the mores of the Negro community:

> It is a great consolation to the Negro to know that he will be buried with proper ceremonies and his grave properly marked. . . . There are few greater events than the burial, and none which brings the community together in a more characteristic attitude. The funeral is a social event, for which the lodge appropriates the necessary expenses.

About the Mississippi community of the 1930s, Hortense Powdermaker notes in *After Freedom:*

> Burial insurance is usually the first to be taken out and the last to be relinquished when times grow hard. It is considered more important by

the very poor than sickness or accident insurance, although the latter
is becoming more important.

The benevolent secret societies of
the Negroes, with their special stress
upon burial ceremonies, may have had a
faintly African origin. Ulrich B. Phillips
states in *American Negro Slavery* that they
were also strongly influenced by white
orders like that of the Masonic Temple.
There may well have been similar lodges
among the enslaved that left behind no
tangible record whatsoever. Those in
which the colored freedman figured,
however, were slightly more affluent,
formal, and conspicuous. Such organizations were as much a recourse for the
enhancement of social prestige within
the black community as they were a network for mutual aid.

The founding chapter of the
Brown Fellowship Society at Charleston
in 1790 (which is described more fully
later in this chapter), with a membership
confined exclusively to mulattos and
quadroons, appears to have prompted
free blacks to found an organization of
their own in emulation. Phillips writes
that, by 1835, there were over thirty-five
such lodges in Baltimore, with memberships ranging between thirty-five and
150 men and women. The tone and purpose of these lodges can be gathered in
part from the constitution and by-laws
of the Brown Fellowship Society or from
the Union Band Society of New Orleans,
founded in 1860 with the motto "Love,
Union, Peace." The Union Band Society's
officers included a president, vice-presi-
dent, secretary, treasurer, marshal, mother, and six male and twelve female
stewards; its dues were fifty cents per month.

Members joining a lodge were pledged to obey its laws, to be humble
to its officers, to keep its secrets, to wear the society's regalia on occasion, and
to live in love and union with fellow members: "to go about once in awhile
and see one another in love."

A Pauper's Burial in Trinidad

A story was often told about an incident that occurred in the Trinidad
village of Toco during the summer of 1939. An extremely poor man,
whose wife and children no longer lived with him, was found lying
dead, on the floor of his shack. Since he had no relatives and belonged
to no insurance society, his burial was left to the officials charged with
the care of paupers. In the tropics, a corpse is ordinarily buried in early
morning or late afternoon. During the day following the man's death,
public works carpenters could be heard hammering on "de box" they
had been hired to make. After they had finished their work, the young
men who had made the crude coffin lay the man's body inside, placed
the box on their shoulders, and, with no concern to form a procession,
walked down the road with it to the cemetery and laid it on the ground
until the grave was dug. Then they lowered it, refilled the hole, and went
on their way. Indignation and pity for the deceased was voiced on every
hand. Expressions of opinion were heard from all members of the village. One minor official said: "It wasn't right to put him in the hole just
like he wasn't human, it wasn't right of the ministers to stay away, and
wasn't right nobody laid him out."

No one was surprised when, one day shortly afterward, some children
who had stopped after school to gather fruit from beneath a tree growing
in front of the pauper's hut, ran with fear as, glancing into the branches,
they "saw" him glowering at them. And the door of his poor hut, blown
open by the wind, remained unshut as folk sedulously avoided what
must be a residence haunted by an angry, dissatisfied, vengeful spirit.

Any member three months' in arrears of dues would be expelled unless, upon his plea of illness or poverty, a subscription could be raised to meet his deficit. It was the duty of all to report illness to the membership; the function of the officer's mother was to delegate members for the nursing. The secretary saw to the washing of the sick member's clothes and paid for such work, as well as the doctor's fee, from the lodge's funds.

The marshal had charge of funerals, and was given the power to commandeer the services of such members as might be required. He could fee the officiating minister not more than $2.50, and draw pay for himself along a similar schedule. Negotiations for the custody of the corpse and the sharing of expenses with any other lodge were provided for in case of the death of a member who had fellowship in more than one organization. A provision was included that when a lodge was given the body of an outsider for burial, it would furnish coffin, hearse, tomb, minister, and marshal at a price of fifty dollars, all told. The stress on matters of death in the by-laws, however, didn't necessarily signify that the lodge was more funereal than festive. A Negro burial was as sociable as an Irish wake.

In an article by St. Clair Drake and Horace R. Clayton called "Urban Burying Leagues," the authors contend that the burial association represented the impact of a southern cultural pattern upon the northern community. In the South, the church "burying leagues" and lodges had, by 1920, been replaced in many areas by associations organized by local undertakers. Each member paid weekly or monthly dues, and the undertaker guaranteed an impressive burial. The founder of a Chicago burial association defended the innovation thusly:

> There was a need for one here in Chicago. You know they are a common thing in the South. Since the Depression, you will find more people in funeral systems than previously carried life insurance. I suppose it's because they had to cash in the policies for what they could and didn't have any protection left.

The largest burial association in Chicago was founded in 1922 by an undertaker with an eye for increased business. At that time, masses of African American migrants to the city were unprotected, except for lodge benefits. Many who had insurance policies had been forced to let them lapse or had cashed them in. While white companies charged exorbitant premiums, northern Negro companies had not yet attained sufficient prestige to inspire confidence in their potential customers. Into the breach stepped the burial association, offering a policy which, while without a "turn-in" or borrowing value, assured the holder of a funeral, required no medical examination, and imposed no age limit. The Depression made burial societies even more popular, since when an insurance policy was turned over to the association in lieu of paying dues, it did not need to be listed as an asset when its owner applied for relief.

Burial societies existed primarily to assure its members that there would be money for their funeral. Granted, there was added social status conferred upon members of burial societies, but the dues that were paid assured these members that they would not be neglected at death. But often, even if the interment was immediate, the funeral ritual was sometimes delayed. Herskovits describes some slaves' manner of honoring the dead:

> One of the big days among our people was when a funeral was held. A person from New Jersey who was not acquainted with our customs, heard it announced that: "Next Sunday two weeks, the funeral of Janet Anderson will be preached." "Well," said the stranger, "how do they know that she will be dead?" The fact was, she was already dead, and had been for some time. But, according to custom—a custom growing out of necessity—the funeral was not held when the person was buried. The relatives, and friends, could not leave their work to attend funerals. Often persons would be buried at night after working hours. If the deceased was a free person, and the immediate family could attend a weekday funeral, there might be others, both friends and relatives who could not attend, hence, the custom became general.

In 1990, the members of the Brown Fellowship Society commemorated their # The Brown Fellowship Society

200th anniversary with a grand celebration. Brown member Herbert A. DeCosta Jr., born in Charleston, South Carolina, and a descendent of Richmond and Benjamin Kinloch, is an architect specializing in reconstructing old mansions. On October 13, 1990, DeCosta, one of Charleston's most prominent residents, delivered an address commemorating the organization's anniversary:

> We are pleased to pay tribute to the resourcefulness of the founders of this group, who organized as a sick and death benefit society, and, we can imagine, enjoyed a measure of camaraderie at the same time. Although, today, we may not understand or agree with all of the rules and regulations of the original society, we must remember that they reflected the pattern of society when the organization was founded.

> We also honor our ancestors who kept the organization alive for two centuries, making changes in its structure as needed to accomplish this feat.

> Nonetheless, it is still admirable, but hard to believe that 200 years ago on November 7th, our forebears gathered together to form a society to help themselves in times of sickness, misfortune, and death. Although they were considered free persons of color, we know that they lived in a world of shadow, constantly fighting to retain the degree of freedom

they enjoyed.

Further, it is hard to believe that 200 years ago there were free persons of color who could read, write, and express themselves in such an articulate manner as so clearly shown in the beautifully handwritten minutes of the Brown Fellowship Society.

It is hard to believe that 200 years ago, while some of our ancestors were trying to free themselves from the shackles of slavery, others owned property and operated successful businesses in the city of Charleston.

Finally, it is also hard to believe that 200 years ago the members of this society were successful and independent enough to meet at 12 o'clock noon and sit down to a meal at 3:00 in the afternoon.

So, today, 200 years later, we the descendants and relatives of these early members, commemorate the founding of this society by meeting at 12 o'clock noon and will sit down to a meal, the Lord willing at 3 o'clock this afternoon. . . . May the accomplishments of our forefathers, in spite of tremendous adversity, be an inspiration for us and for future generations.

Burial societies and lodges were important historically because they provided a major service to the community. Although for all intents and purposes many of these groups no longer exist, some, as in Charleston and on St. Helena Island, are still functioning. In the 1700s persons of color in several states, both southern and northern, were met with great opposition when they sought to bury their loved ones. The reaction to this denial provided the impetus for founding many of these groups. The first and most prominent of such burial societies was Charleston's Brown Fellowship Society.

The society's original cemetery on Charleston's Pitt Street no longer exists, having been lost to commercial development. Several tombstones have been moved, however, to a quiet plot in the city's Magnolia section. Although the society briefly changed its name to the Century Club in 1890 to mark its 100th anniversary, it returned to its original name in the 1940s, the same time that it began accepting women as members.

Robert L. Harris Jr., of Cornell University's African Studies and Research Center, has written about the society. In his essay, "Charleston's Free Afro-American Elite: The Brown Fellowship Society and the Humane Brotherhood," included in the society's 200th anniversary commemorative booklet, the story of the Brown Fellowship Society is fully told.

The Brown Fellowship Society was founded in 1790 by five charter members: James Mitchell, George Bampfield, William Cattel, George Bedon, and Samuel Saltus. These free African Americans belonged to the white St. Philip's Episcopal Church where they worshipped, were baptized, and married, but, unlike the white members of the church, could not be interred in the burial ground.

The society was organized as a voluntary association with the motto "Charity and Benevolence." Between 1790 and 1844 it admitted 131 men to its ranks. During that fifty-four year span, forty-eight of its members died, twenty-five were excluded, and six resigned, leaving an active membership of fifty-two men.

The most prominent case of exclusion from the society occurred in 1817. George Logan, who had joined the Brown Fellowship on October 2, 1800, was expelled when the association discovered and confirmed his collusion in the sale into slavery of a free black man named Robinson. The society labeled Logan's conduct "base and notorious," but granted him a hearing at which he failed to defend his conduct satisfactorily. He was subsequently banished and any claims or benefits for himself or his heirs were nullified. This particular action in reprimanding one of its own demonstrates the organization's concern for the rights of all free African Americans in Charleston in addition to those of its in-group.

Rules and regulations for the Brown Fellowship Society were established on November 1, 1790. The following preamble well describes the frustration and discontent of the society's five originators:

> Whereas we, free brown men, natives of the city of Charleston, in the State of South Carolina, having taken into consideration, the unhappy situation of our fellow creatures, and the distresses of our widows and orphans, for the want of a fund to relieve them in the hour of their distresses, sickness and death; and holding it an essential duty of mankind to contribute all they can towards relieving the wants and miseries, and promoting the welfare and happiness of one another, and observing the method of many other well disposed persons of this State, by entering into particular societies for this purpose, to be effectual, we therefore, whose names are underwritten, do comply with this great duty, have freely and cheerfully entered into a society in Charleston, and State aforesaid, commencing the first of November, 1790, and have voted, agreed and subscribed to the following rules for ordering and conducting the same.

Rules I through XI discuss, in detail, the organizational structure, duties of the officers, payment of dues, voting, and other privileges and procedures. Rule XII, which follows, speaks more specifically of illness and death:

> In case sickness afflicts any member, it shall be the duty of the Stewards, in conformity to the 7th rule, to call on the sick, examine their circumstances, and finding he is in need of assistance from the Society, he shall be entitled to, and allowed a weekly sum of not less than $1.50, by an order from the President, Vice President, or any one presiding in their

absence, to the Treasurer, in order to be given to the sick member by the hands of the Stewards, and if he dies, the Stewards shall attend in like manner, as before mentioned, after which he shall report the case to the President, or presiding officer, who shall order a meeting immediately, and consult on the management of the funeral; and in case the circumstances of such deceased member be low and indigent, that a decent funeral cannot be afforded out of their own estate or effects, the President or presiding officer shall have power and authority to appoint a committee, to regulate things in as frugal a manner as possible, for the funeral, which charges shall be paid off of the Society's funds, in such manner as before stipulated. Every member in Charleston shall attend the funeral, with a Black crepe around the left arm, by invitation from the Secretary; and on neglect (if able) to attend, he shall be fined in a sum not exceeding twenty-five cents, payable at the next meeting, unless a good and sufficient excuse be then made.

It is clear, therefore, that the Brown Fellowship Society was a pioneering effort. Its members paved the way for an important and powerful method of joining together, pooling resources, developing friendships, and easing the burdens that each knew must be faced at death. By studying their rules and regulations and reading their preamble, one can see and even feel the strictness and the seriousness of the procedures. Everything—from their attendance to their dress code to their demeanor—was carefully outlined. Monetary penalties were imposed for violations.

Because of the society's careful attention to record-keeping, persons researching their backgrounds would do well to make use of their records and books. Brown Fellowship's minutes are all written in precise, beautiful, and legible penmanship.

Today the Brown Fellowship Society has evolved into a commemorative organization comprised mostly of descendants of families who belonged during its heyday more than a century ago. With a membership of about twenty people by the mid-1990s, it now meets on an irregular basis, no more than two or three times a year. Dues are no longer charged and the society is no longer involved in the burial business. "The society has evolved from a group that helped people in time of sickness and assisted with burials to a social organization," says current president Herbert DeCosta. "We are certainly not a burial society anymore." He adds, "There is a great tradition that may soon pass and our culture will be worse off for it. This is some of our history that is worth preserving."

Humane Brotherhood

A rival organization to the Brown Fellowship Society, called the Humane Brotherhood, organized in Charleston, South Carolina, in 1843. The Humane Brotherhood had forty-two members consisting exclusively of blacks and mulattos and listed, as was the system at the Brown Fellowship Society, by certain specific data. Members of these two organizations were traced in the 1850 and 1860 federal manuscript census for Charleston, the 1848 city census, city directories, and the 1859 and 1860 city taxpayer rolls. The sources yielded date and age, occupation, value of real estate, slave holdings, place of birth, and complexion. Such information makes possible comparisons between the two associations within Charleston's broader free African American population.

The Humane Brotherhood's preamble explained its purpose as "alleviating the couch of pain, and helping a brother when distressed." It further resolved "That we, free dark men of the City of Charleston, do form ourselves into a compact body for the purpose of alleviating each other in sickness and death." The death benefit to a deceased member's family was twelve dollars for a decent burial—Brown Fellowship provided sixty dollars for widows. Surviving members had to wear a mourning cloth for thirty days. Widows could collect a twelve-dollar annuity, while orphans were to be supported and educated until they were ready to take up a trade under apprenticeship to a Humane Brotherhood craftsman.

The Brown Fellowship Society and the Humane Brotherhood each maintained burial plots on Charleston's Pitt Street, adjoining each other but separated by a fence. Brown's burial plot operation was more extensive; they provided services for subscribers who did not belong to the organization.

According to the commemorative booklet honoring their 200th anniversary celebration, major differences between the two associations, in addition to complexion, wealth, and slaveholding, were age and occupation. Humane Brotherhood members were 12.9 years younger than their Brown counterparts. Their mean age in 1850 was 33.6 years, as opposed to 46.5 years for the Brown Fellowship. On the whole, Humane Brotherhood men were artisans in the employ of others; the fact that most Brown Fellowship men were shopkeepers and small businessmen helps to explain their greater wealth.

Though no one is able to say so with complete certainty, surviving members of other South Carolina societies and lodges believe that the Humane Brotherhood no longer exists.

The Bury League

In *The Book of Negro Folklore,* edited by Langston Hughes and Arna Bontemps, Julie Peterkin describes the Bury League as a cooperative society that grew out of the Negro's sincere desire for an elaborate and respectful funeral. Every neighborhood had a local chapter headed by a "Noble Shepherd," and the members paid a small sum each week to a common fund that provided enough funds for the next funeral. The Noble Shepherd kept the "treasury," a black tin box with a lock and key; once a month, when the treasury was heavy with dues, he took it over the river and emptied it into the hands of the Leader of the Flock, who owned and drove the automobile hearse and provided fine, store-bought coffins and white stones to stand at the head of the graves.

Bury League members, Peterkin explained, are required to attend every burial unless hindered by providence. They all wear white gloves, the women carry white paper flowers, and the Leagues' officers, who carry the banners of the organization, wear large badges.

The Leagues' moderate dues must be paid promptly, and every member must visit the sick and take presents of money or food. To fail in the least of these obligations means expulsion from the league, but nobody fails. The reward for complying is a fine coffin, a journey to the grave in the automobile hearse, and a tombstone.

Before the Bury League was organized, coffins were simple pine boxes made by the plantation carpenter and hearses were farm wagons drawn by mules. Nobody was buried before the sun had "set in the grave" to make it sweet for the last long sleep. The services were long, with much mourning and praying and singing, and fat lightwood torches provided visibility for the burial and the march round and round the grave.

All this has changed with time: The Bury League's membership is now large and the hearse has to travel all over the country. Some roads are rough, the hearse sometimes refuses to run, and it has taken as many as three people to their graves in one day. There no longer the time to wait on the setting sun; people now have to trust in Jesus to make their graves sweet and restful. Times have indeed now changed, but change has been for the better, for poor people used to have a much harder burden to bear when death took those dear to them.

The members of the Bury League are not alone in their attitude toward death. Most people crave a proper burial, and pride often plays a part in making funerals so expensive that families are left with uncomfortable debts. Unscrupulous undertakers of all races have made fortunes out of the feelings surrounding death that attend every human creature.

Peterkin continues her delightful story, combining the frivolity of a spirited imagination with reality. She explains that the Negroes delight in making a good appearance before their fellows, but when death takes one of them, their pride is accompanied with fear that their failure to give the departed a proper burial will result in disaster for the lonely spirit on its way to a final home. This fear is probably a lineal descendant of the old African belief that without proper rites for its protection a soul may be hindered by other spirits from finding its destination and become a pitiful wanderer on the face of the earth. A proper funeral ceremony is believed to be of great help in enabling a soul to find the right road, either to heaven and God, or to hell and Satan. Otherwise, the spirit of the deceased will haunt houses, burial grounds, and lonely roads, thereby frightening the very people it loved best on earth.

As a rule, spirits resemble the bodies they occupied in life. The most unfortunate ones become plat-eyes and change quickly from one shape to another: Now a dog, then a horse, a man without a head, a warm cloud, or a hot smoke that suffocates all living creatures. "Plat-eyes" fear nothing and stop at nothing. Wise people and beasts flee from them, for "a coward never totes broke bones."

People with vivid imaginations are often terrified by apparitions that walk at night when the moon is young. The vicinity of cemeteries is carefully avoided after dark and so are places where people have met with fatal misfortune. Animals have "second sight" and can see spirits, but only people born with cauls over their faces have this keen vision.

One particular story has been handed down from among the members of the Bury League. While it has varied in content through the retelling, the tale's sense of fun heavily salted with superstition remains the same in Peterkin's rendition:

> One Saturday evening a plantation mother who had second sight sent her two small sons on a trustworthy mule to the crossroads store to fetch home the week's supply of groceries. She warned the boys to hurry home before sundown, since a young moon was due to shine and set spirits to walking all over the country. The boys put the paper bags of rice, sugar, white flour and coffee all together in a large crocus sack so that none would be dropped on the way home.
>
> The lonely road ran through thick woods that looked scary, but the mule walked along quietly until the sun dropped and a young moon [shone] in the sky. Then he began to back his ears and switch his tail. Just as they came in sight of the spot where a man had been mysteriously killed years ago, the mule stopped short in his tracks and would not budge. At first the boys thought he was being contrary, so the older one got a stick and frailed his sides, then beat him on the head, but the beast only rolled his eyes and snorted like he smelt something dangerous. They did not know what to make of such carrying on until a warm gust of air passed over their faces and a small white cloud floated across the road right in front of their eyes.
>
> The hair on their heads stood up and pushed off their hats, for the cloud smelled like smoke from burning sulfur. The mule shivered and leaped backward with hoarse hee-haws, and tried his best to talk. The boys fell off his back and the groceries tumbled into the road. They did not tarry to pick up the groceries or hats but scrambled onto the mule's back just as he struck out for home. He had always been too lame and broken-winded to go faster than a walk, but he galloped like a colt until he reached home, then he fell down flat in the yard where he laid all

night gasping for breath.

The mother did what she could to comfort him, then she thanked God on her knees that the poor beast had sense like people and brought her sons home safe instead of letting them be smothered by death by the evil-smelling cloud. It was undoubtedly the spirit of the man who had been secretly killed years ago. His strange end was due to turn him into the most dangerous of all ghostly things, a plat-eye.

The groceries and hats stayed where they fell until the sun shone the next morning, for spirits of all kinds, even plat-eyes and hags, dread sunlight and hide in [the shadows] until first dark comes. The incident furnished the preacher with a subject for his sermon the next Sunday. He explained that if the dead man had been given a proper burial, instead of being hurried into the ground with not even a church deacon to pray over his body, he might have been a harmless "ha'nt" instead of a plat-eye which changes from one ugly thing to another as it strives to harm innocent people.

The moral: The dead are helped by thoughtfulness just as the living are, and the very poorest people must struggle to pay insurance dues to the Bury League, not only for themselves but for every member of their families. This, then, is the message: the payment of dues is important. The power and fright-value of the story is forceful, and it remains an interesting tale. Another story that has been told:

[A] black father came to get the plantation carpenter to make a box for his dead baby. He was pitifully grief-stricken because the child had not been "insured" in the Bury League, and since he lacked money to buy a nice coffin the baby was condemned to be laid away in a simple box of pine boards. As he helped to saw the short lengths and plane them smooth, he sobbed over his "bad mistake" that kept the child from being put away right.

The carpenter tried to console him, for the child was too young to have sinned and was bound to reach heaven; death levels everything and makes a home-made pine box as soft a bed as a Bury League coffin. The father shook his head and sobbed as he explained that he and his wife and every other child in his house were Bury League members. Times were so hard and money so scarce, it pinched him to pay all their dues, but he did it. This baby was so healthy he never thought it would sicken and die. It was his only boy child, too, the flower of his flock, the child he ever loved best. Nobody ever saw a finer little boy child or one so smart for its age.

The mother took more pains with him than any child she ever birthed. Three or four times every day she left her work in the field and went home to suckle him. And now, this failure to provide a proper burial would work the child heavy harm. No common sickness killed him, for he was ailing only one day and night.

Some people thought the mother was to blame because she would not wean him when she started breeding again. Others thought maybe her breast milk was too hot or poisoned with weariness from hoeing grass so long in the sun. That could not be so. The mother was an able woman and never minded sun-hot or hard work when she was carrying a new child. Evil spirits must have killed the little boy child, for they saw how his parents loved him more than the little gal-children. They loved him more than life itself, and now their hearts were pure broken because he was dead and would be buried in a home-made box.

The mother believed some jealous-hearted woman with no child to equal him had put a "black hand" on him. A strong healthy child would not die so quick unless somebody cast a spell on him or a spirit tricked him into leaving this world. It was hard to think anybody could be mean enough to do such a damage to an innocent little baby, but evil spirits are all over the land. They know everything about everybody, and they pleasure themselves with causing sorrow.

The Cemetery As a Spiritual Symbol

As seen across the rural areas that have traditionally supported an African American population, the cemetery is very special. Not only is it the realm of the deceased, but it is also where we find the strongest material demonstration of African-inspired memories. In earlier times, the attitudes and practices manifested by African Americans derived from their belief that the deceased could, in some way, affect the lives of families and friends still living. Because of this, it has always been important to take care in the planning of the funeral and the burial.

Strong feelings about the last rites led to the formation of many of the burial societies. Burial insurance was usually the first to be taken out and the last to be relinquished when times grew hard. It was considered more important by the very poor than sickness and accident insurance.

The book *Afro-American Tradition in Decorative Arts*, a publication of the Cleveland Museum of Art, points out that "a proper funeral must be conducted with decorum and respect. The deceased must be honored and his remains treated with dignity and reverence. To encounter Afro-American graveyard decoration is to witness a physical manifestation of strong religious belief. The cemetery gives us a glimpse of the spiritual force that has ever been the source of hope and inspiration for black America."

Tears leaped out of the father's eyes as he lifted the little pine box and put it on his head to take home. Its small weight was slight for his strength, but his broad shoulders dropped and his feet stumbled along the smooth path as if they bore a heavy burden. The carpenter groaned with pity as the short, narrow box balanced on the father's head made a stark pattern against the sunset sky. Then he set about boiling water to scald the tools that had cut and nailed together the little coffin boards.

This Peterkin story is sad and mournful, but like her next story, it mixes reality with a logical imagination:

The earth from which people spring clings to their feet no matter where they go, and will try to fetch them back home. The Negroes delight in taking journeys, but a dread of being sent home "cold in a box" often keeps them from tarrying long when they go away. When a message came from a town some miles away saying "Diana dead. No insurance. Promised to send her home," everybody cheerfully contributed something to bring Diana's body home "right." The next day a fine hearse and automobiles filled with Diana's friends made a long funeral procession that moved toward the river bridge which marks the town's limit. The elegant vehicles halted at the bridge, where they were met by a pitiful line of wagons and carts drawn by mules and oxen. Diana's body in a fine coffin was taken out of the hearse and put in one rickety wagon. The mourners got out of the automobiles and climbed into broken-down wagons and carts. The humble procession went slowly across the bridge and followed the highway until it reached the narrow winding road which led to the country graveyard where Diana wanted to lie.

These simple people could not afford the hearse and automobiles for the whole journey, but they had done the best they could to give Diana's soul a good start on the way to its eternal home.

When the original graveyard became full another one had to be started, which upset the members of the Bury League terribly. There is a powerful superstition that the first person buried in a graveyard never rests easy. Peterkin again lets the reader enjoy the make-believe aspects of her stories while still providing thought-provoking innuendo. Superstitions here are not trivial beliefs to be disregarded or laughed away; this one involves everybody's peace of mind.

Nobody knows what would have happened if an old woman who was respected by everybody in the community had not come forward and said that she was willing to lie first in the new graveyard. She had thought the matter over. She knew her time on this earth was almost out, for lately, one rainy day she was walking home and her dead husband came and held an umbrella over her. It meant he wanted her to come with him. She would trust the master to take care of her. He knew she had tried to live a good life and would see to it that her last long sleep would not be restless.

[The old woman] had never joined the Bury League or accepted changes that crept into the plantation. Her old baptizing robe, made when she was baptized many years ago, had been put away carefully in her trunk to serve as her shroud. Time had yellowed and weakened the cloth, so it was hardly fit to serve as a pattern, but she bought new white cloth, and asked a "seamster" to make a robe exactly like it. When the shroud was made and pressed with a "laying-out head rag" to match it, she bought a pair of white gloves and new shoes to wear with them. She examined them all carefully, then put them in the trunk to wait. "I'm all ready for de journey now," she said with a gentle smile.

She talked of this journey as if she were going home to live forever, not only with God and Jesus and the angels, but with her father and mother and husband and the children who had gone on before. All her treasures were kept in the trunk where the shroud was laid. She took them out and gave all away except a pretty blue china mug wrapped in a clean white cloth. This was to be kept until a white lad whom she had nursed and tried to teach and train should marry and have a son. The mug had been saved for the little boy child she had hoped to nurse like his father and grandfather before him.

As she unwrapped it her mind went away back into the gentle past, and she told how, forty years ago, when she was a middle-aged woman, a group of Polish people came to the neighborhood to farm. Only one was a woman and she had children, one of whom was a beautiful, red-cheeked blue-eyed girl child. Soon after they came, the girl child sickened and died. The mother mourned in a strange language, but her grief was something any mother could understand. She refused to have the child buried in the white people's graveyard, but laid her away in a shady spot on the edge of the woods near a little waterfall that made music day and night. [Only a] lonesome grave told where the child had so loved to wade in the clear water, and gather pebbles and pick white violets that bloomed along the banks. The poor woman would not believe [it when she discovered that] the stream had stolen the child's spirit although it was plain enough to everybody else.

The child's death made the Polish people unhappy there and they decided to go away. When the mother said good-bye she left the china mug for a keepsake. It had been a parting gift to the little dead girl from an old grandmother in Poland. The old trunk had held it for over forty years, and now it must be kept for the white lad's first boy child or for his first grandboy in case he got only girl children. No girl child must ever own it, for it brought bad luck to one and it might do the same thing again.

Trees and bushes hid the little Polish girl's grave long ago, but sometimes when a thin young moon shows in the west her singing can be heard above the music of the water, and the words of her song are strange, same like those of her mother.

When [her memory of the] story of the cup ended, the old woman slowly wrapped it up again, as she added, "When I first thought on leavin' dis world, one mind told me to stay until Christmas when my white baby will come home from school; but my other mind said I better go spend Christmas in heaven wid my own li'l chillen. Maybe li'l chillen don' grown up in heaven, but my white baby is done tall, like a man. I would like to look in his blue eyes one more time. I ever dream 'bout em same like I dream 'bout de chillen I birthed my own self. I won' forget em when I get up yonder. I'll pray for em same like I pray for em here, Gawd bless em." It was useless to argue with her about staying until her white baby came home. Her mind was made up.

Her last request was, "After I'm laid out do watch my eyes so dey won' crack open an' scare de li'l chillen what comes to look a last look on my face." She refused to eat and drank only enough water to wet her dry lips, but she reached heaven in time for Christmas. Her burial was one of the greatest celebrations the plantation has ever known. She was not a Bury League member, but the Bury League hearse brought her coffin, and the Bury League members marched behind it carrying banners and white paper flowers. The sun set in her grave to make it sweet, and pine torches made light to fill the dirt in. When the low mound of earth was smoothed and the Bury League white paper flowers laid on it, things she prized on earth were put with them: a clock that had not ticked for many years, the cup and saucer she used, a glass lamp filled with kerosene, and a china vase holding fresh blossoms from those growing around her doorstep.

When the funeral sermon was preached, some months later, the church could not hold the congregation. Windows and doors were crowded with people who strained their ears to hear the preacher describe the welcome she received from God and Jesus, her parents and friends, her husband and children, when the angels flew through heaven's gate with her soul. People rocked their bodies from side to side and hummed the tune of "I'm gwine home to die no more" while the preacher told how she walked on golden streets, and flew down the sky on her strong white wings to watch over those she loved on earth.

Funeral sermons are never preached at a burial, but, rather, afterward at church on a following Sunday. The sermon tells with utter frankness whether the deceased is happy in heaven or wretched in hell, or driven by pains far worse than torment to roam through the air, without rest or peace day or night. Peterkin ends her description of the Bury League with a gentle finale, a striking description:

The old graveyard, unused and deserted, waits for Judgment Day on the edge of a hill that drops to the river with a steep fall called "Lover's Leap." Below it lie untamed miles of swamp where the river bends into Devil's Elbow, or swollen by rains, makes a vast yellow lake that uproots and drowns the swamp's undergrowth. Yellow stains high on the trunks of tall trees mark the height of its flood long after it has passed. But no flood can reach the old graveyard.

Spring shows early in the tender, misty green of willows that mark the river channel where strong roots clutch swamp mud and strive to hold the unruly stream to its rightful road. Maples flame scarlet, poplars make bright yellow splashes, wood duck quack gaily, turkey hens call gobblers who deserted them and their children in the fall to gang together all winter like carefree bachelors. Then the old graves sunken with waiting so long for Gabriel to blow his trumpet and clothe old bones with living flesh are sprinkled with blue violets; tangles of yellow jessamine drop golden bells and crab apple thickets send down showers of fragrant pink petals to lie among carved wooden heads of wheat placed on some of the graves long ago. Nobody knows who carved them or why the wood lasts so long, but everybody knows they are symbols of eternal life carved by somebody who believed that some day "The trumpet shall sound and the dead shall be raised incorruptible . . . and this mortal must put on immortality."

Sea Island resident Billie Burn writes about the three secret lodges or orders on Daufuskie Island, South Carolina. They included the Oyster Union Society, the Knights of Pythias "Pity," and the Odd Fellows. The Oyster Union Society was begun in October of 1919 to financially benefit the oyster gatherers and shuckers when they became sick or disabled and couldn't work. The Knights of Pythias was begun in 1916 and ended circa 1934. The Odd Fellows started in 1927 and ended about three years later.

Once these organizations were established, reports Burn, meetings were held once a month in the Maryfield Praise House on the grounds of the First Union African Baptist Church. Dues were one dollar per month. Soon the members bought a vacant two-story building known as the "Hall" and the meetings were held there. The Oyster Society always met downstairs—they had women members who dared not go upstairs where the other orders, who had no female members, tended towards the boisterous.

The members of all the orders would have parties and sell shrimp, crabs, and have oyster roasts—anything to make money to help with the expenses of illness, including medicine, doctor bills, and, should the worst happen, to aid the family should there be a funeral.

The Oyster Society outlasted the other two. With its members gradually dying through the years, there were so few members by 1980 that the society was finally abolished. The treasury money was divided equally among those who were still living; the hall and the land were sold in 1981.

The Knights of the Wise Men Lodge

"The Knights of the Wise Men Lodge," a paper prepared by Laura Hansen for the Sea Island Preservation Project at Penn Center, provides a comprehensive look at this fraternal order, organized in 1870. Provided with financial and farming assistance, lodge members also enjoyed social functions and fellowship in addition to fulfilling their mission to establish a common treasury. Between 1870 and 1930 more than thirty other such benevolent societies were formed on St. Helena Island. Today, only the Knights of the Wise Men Lodge, Ladies Union, and Rome of Victory Society continue to function as burial aid societies. The following is taken from Hansen's treatise:

> During the reconstruction era (1863–1877), burial-aid societies flourished in African American communities and were an essential aspect of [black] life well into the twentieth century. By the 1930s there were some thirty-seven burial societies found in the sea islands alone.
>
> In 1889, the Knights of Wise Men purchased a quarter-acre plot on the old Corner Plantation in St. Helena, for eight dollars. Sometime thereafter they built the first of two structures. The first was a two-story frame building.
>
> At its height in the early 1920s, the Knights of Wise Men Lodge had more than 350 members, representing almost every plantation community on St. Helena Island. Many of the communities had burial aid societies of their own, but the Knights of Wise Men's prominent location at the Corner gave it a special prestige. Located at the intersection of Highway 21 and Lands End Road Drive (historically Church Road, and now known as Martin Luther King Drive) and in close proximity to Penn Center, the Corner Community has been the commercial center of St. Helena since at least the 1860s. Most shopping was done here, and a number of other transactions such as public record keeping and loans and credit activity, took place here as well.
>
> The lodge building is situated at the rear of the Green (now known as the King Park), the traditional gathering place for island-wide celebrations. Around 1940, the wood building burned and was replaced shortly thereafter by a concrete block structure. Members were "taxed" to provide the building fund, and local bricklayers were hired to construct the new hall in similar fashion to the first one. The major design change was to place the stair to the second story on the outside and at the rear of the building to allow members to come and go without intruding on the first floor tenants.
>
> Following the 1940 hurricane, in which many Island buildings were heavily damaged, other societies and lodges used the Knights of Wise Men hall for their meetings while waiting on repairs. Like most burial aid societies, the Knights of Wise Men exemplified the cooperative ideal. Members paid monthly dues for which they were assured a substantial use of their money for their funeral and family. In the early years, this money was usually more than enough to cover burial expenses. Dues were twenty-five cents per month for most of the first

part of the century. In recent years, they have increased to $1.25. The death assessment in the early years was one dollar; today it is four dollars. It was optional for members to purchase stock in the lodge. The lodge's stock certificate is printed on an elaborate and beautifully rendered full-color image of the Biblical Wise Men. At the time of this certificate, circa the 1930s, a share of stock sold for $5. Upon a member's death, his family was paid the full value of his stock. During the past twenty years or so, the Knights of Wise Men have organized excursions to raise funds, primarily for building maintenance, expenses, and taxes. These events included oyster roasts on the Green and bus trips to Myrtle Beach.

Lodge brothers would deliver and administer medicine, and they would take a member to the Savannah hospital by boat if necessary. All the while, they would see that the farm and household chores, like chopping wood and caring for animals, were maintained. All of this was carefully organized. The lodge's plantation committees would make assignments when "one of theirs" was sick. Two at a time, the members would sit with the patient. Each night two more would come to serve. The rotation would move from plantation to plantation and would start over again if the illness continued for that long.

The Knights of Wise Men were leaders in the islanders' eyes. Perhaps the most prominent resident of St. Helena, Dr. Y. W. Bailey, was the lodge's treasurer for many years, until his blindness in the 1950s. A native of St. Helena, Dr. Bailey was the area's first black doctor, and the island's only doctor for much of the twentieth century. He is fondly remembered as a doctor and as an officer of the Knights of Wise Men. Officers often served for many years, as long as they were serving the lodge well in the eyes of the other members. Appointment to membership in this lodge, like most, came through member recommendation. They were the "wise men." While the origin of the lodge's formal name is unknown, one long-time member likens it to the wise men seeking for Jesus Christ, and the stock certificate image would support this.

Ceremony was a fundamental component of the burial aid societies' organization. Their meetings were formal and standardized, as was their role at members' funerals and the annual "turning out." Monthly meetings were held every second Friday at the lodge hall, presided over by the Arckon, or president, who used a gavel to call the meetings to order and to keep order throughout the proceedings (unruly behavior was subject to fine). The room was arranged like a church with the president facing rows of wooden benches; the secretary and treasurer sat to his side, much like deacons in a church. During the 1920s and 1930s there were usually thirty to forty members in attendance. The opening prayer was offered by the chaplain, and was followed by the lodge song, "Blessed Be the Name of the Lord," kept in its own separate book. Business was conducted regarding recruitment, building mainte-nance, etc.; dues were collected (monies were kept in a bank in Beaufort); and reports on sick or distressed members were made by the plantation committees. If new members were being inducted, a secret initiation ritual involving stations was performed. Throughout the meeting a doorkeeper admitted latecomers only if they knew the secret rap. If a death was reported, there was a death assessment, and plans were made for the attendance at the funeral.

The Knights of Wise Men would often meet at their lodge hall prior to a funeral service. In their required dress—black trousers, jacket, tie and shoes, ceremonial hat, and special Lodge badge worn with the black side forward—they would march as a group to the church. There they performed their funeral rites, including songs and a speech on the member's character as a brother in the lodge. At the burial site, the Knights of Wise Men would file by the grave, each dropping a palm leaf or flower onto the coffin. They occasionally acted as pall bearers or helped make the coffin. There was a moment when the Knights of Wise Men would announce to the family the amount of money they would receive from the lodge, and a promise was made that within sixty days, the Knights would deliver that sum. The president and possibly other officers would later call on the family to deliver the money. Attendance at funerals was mandatory, and absence was subject to a fine of up to $5.

The ceremony and ritual was in part imitative of organizations of European origin, such as the Masons and other guilds. The Masons and the Odd Fellows were the oldest black fraternal orders. Organized by free blacks in Boston and New York, respectively, these organizations were chartered directly from Europe after rejection by the American white orders. They thrived in northern cities, and even established lodges in a few Southern ones. Free southern blacks during the antebellum period also organized a number of mutual benefit societies, which were less ritualistic than the orders, and were instead specifically concerned with fulfilling "their obligations to the deceased...and to assure their own avoidance of a pauper's burial or, worse, disposal of their body to a medical school."

The legacy of the sea islands burial aid societies is an intangible system of values—values of individual and community responsibility, cooperative welfare, and dignity in life and death. For the Knights of Wise Men, this legacy is also a collective memory of the hundreds of community leaders who were members through the years, which is embodied in the tangible artifact of its lodge hall. Since 1889 the hall, first the frame building and then the block one, has been a central component of St. Helena life. It stands as quiet testimony to the actions of the Knights of Wise Men and the values they represent. The Knights of Wise Men Lodge has plans to dissolve, as its membership continues to dwindle. The count now is about fifteen to twenty men. They meet only occasionally, at Scott Community Hall. They also own property in the area. Theirs is a wonderful history, a great tradition, that is no longer viable in today's fast paced, unstructured society. The Knights of Wise Men will not be forgotten as they take their place in the annals of history. The hall, however, could continue to function as an active and vital component of community life at the Corner. Its reuse would be a most appropriate example of cultural continuity in the face of inevitable change.

In the northern United States, burial societies and lodges began to lose their role to churches in the decades following the 1830s. Because of slavery and the suppression of many mainstream black churches in the South, however, this same evolution took place at a much slower pace; southern burial societies were still active up until the Civil War. As the year 2000 approaches, the few remaining burial societies and lodges are approaching extinction.

Harry Mack, a current member of both the Knights of the Wise Men Lodge and the Young Men's Social Club—two societies on South Carolina's

The History of Dissolved Lodges

During the early days of burial lodges, several traditions were common to such organizations. During a funeral procession, for example, the society's members walked behind the body of the deceased, which was carried by an oxen cart or mule- or horse-drawn wagon, singing and waving green branches on their way to the graveyard.

The lodges were established for many purposes, such as caring for sick and disabled members; relieving other family members by sitting up all night with a sick member; distributing monetary benefits to cover the costs of burying the deceased; cooking, washing, and cleaning the house; and harvesting any crops in the field during planting season.

Among those lodges since dissolved were **The Women Labor Union**, an all-female labor union established in 1907; **The Blue Mountain Lodge**, whose members were both male and female, which was established in the early 1900s; **Little Supreme**, with both male and female members, established in the early 1900s; **Household of Ruth**, an all-female organization established in the late 1800s; **Oak Tree Lodge**, with both male and female members, established in the 1800s; and **Little Bethlehem**, with both male and female members, established in the late 1800s.

St. Helena Island that now barely function—believes that these organizations now function more like social clubs, places where an aging membership can go to reminisce and keep the traditions of oral history alive. For amateur genealogists seeking to trace a family tree or burial sight, Mack admits that the burial societies of today would probably be of little use.

In the South at least, few written detailed records of such societies and lodges have survived. There is at least one exception. The Brown Fellowship, perhaps the best known of all black burial societies, kept detailed minutes of its meetings through the decades. Those minutes are now housed in the archives of the College of Charleston.

Lodge and society members of St. Helena still pay dues, usually less than three dollars per month, and the clubs still pay out a token burial benefit—usually less than $300—but their role as the black community's life-line, insurance company, and social center has long since passed to others. "There are a few of us holding on to these traditions," says Mack. "But with all the facilities—things like hospitals, schools and everything—we can't get new people to join. They don't need us for much."

"We really don't do burials or funerals any more," Mack continues. "Before, many years ago, people needed our help. Now they don't need so much help. Back in the old days, there were no hospitals, not many doctors. There really was no place to go if you got in distress. Things are way different today."

Ladies Union

By 1995 the Knights of the Wise Men lodge had fewer than forty members, none younger than age sixty. The lodge usually meets once a month. Club dues are one dollar a month. There is a special $2.50 "debt assessment fee" in the event of a member's passing to cover the club's payment of its standard $150 death benefit.

The Ladies Union of St. Helena Island remains active as a burial society; dues are still collected monthly. Their creed and their responsibilities remain similar to those of the Knights of Wise Men, with whom they have maintained a good relationship. It is no longer just a women's union, having partially combined with the Young Men's Social Club many years ago. The purpose of these united groups is to pay dues to cover burial expenses, but these days the dues only partially cover the rising costs of a funeral. Still, the Ladies Union and the Young Men's Social Club are probably the most prosperous of South Carolina's surviving burial societies.

The Ladies Union and the Young Men's Social Club meet at Scott Community Center on St. Helena Island.

Mothers and fathers often enroll their small children in the group and begin to pay their dues. The bookkeeping is done carefully and meticulously. It's estimated that close to two hundred members meet on the first Sunday of every month at their well-kept hall, near the Orange Grove Baptist Church and the Capers Community. When the women have a "turning out"—their term for the club's annual celebration—the men join them, and vice versa. Although men and women meet in the same hall, their activities, except for the turning out, are separate.

Rome of Victory Society

"We still visit the sick and we still give people some-thing when they are buried, but it isn't really much," says club member Harry Mack. The standard burial benefit is $250. He says the club's main efforts and much of its resources are aimed at maintaining the hall, which is used for recreation and rented out for special events. "The young just don't want to join us. They just don't care about tradition."

The Rome of Victory Society at 21 Seaside Road, St. Helena Island, was founded in 1896 by Elizabeth Richardson, a local resident and landowner. The society, originally set up to assist families with burial arrangements and to attend to the sick and needy, boasted more than three hundred members at its peak, but by 1995 membership had dwindled to less than thirty people, all over the age of sixty.

Surviving members are not sure how the organization came about its name. "Elizabeth Richardson named it and I'm not sure anyone today remembers why," said George Austin, a member of the society who was signed up by his mother right after his birth in 1910. "I guess it had to have a name and that name was as good as any other."

Austin said the Rome of Victory Society has had no new members in years and now faces bankruptcy. Dues are $1.50 per month. Members still meet every other month but do little charity work. "We still take care of the sick, but we can't do as much as we used to. There isn't the money or the people," said Austin. The society continues to contribute money toward the burial expenses of members. The standard payout is $150, down from $200 just a few years ago.

Like other burial societies on St. Helena, the Rome of Victory Society owns a lovely building in the Cuffy community that is used for meetings and is rented out occasionally for church services and fund-raising dinners. "This society is dying out and I don't see how it can survive for much longer," said Austin. "Young people are not interested. They are out in the world now. Some don't even care about going to church."

Benevolent Societies, Social Aid and Pleasure Clubs, and Second Line Clubs of New Orleans, Louisiana

These societies and clubs provided health care services for blacks because the mortality rate increased after the Emancipation. "It all started because black people did not have enough money to bury themselves nor could they afford above ground burials. So they started a second burial tax, which they put together like a society and it's called a Benevolent Society." Recalled by Lucille Le'Obia, a tour guard. They were not open to all blacks because they had to have the funds to pay the required fees. Benevolence societies became an essential part of life for both blacks and whites, writes Claude F. Jacobs. There were also societies that helped slaves purchase their freedom, and to campaign against the social class exclusiveness of black Creoles in the city. The criteria for membership for black Creoles include wealth, education, and the ability to speak French.

When New Orleans experienced a plague or a natural disaster, some people would organize a benevolent society to socialize and help aid each other with illness or death. The residents of New Orleans suffered a great loss because of flooding due to hurricanes. In 1833, many people including slaves died from a cholera epidemic, which wiped out a sixth of the population. Yellow fever made its way around the city periodically and many died. In 1878, the last year that yellow fever returned, so many lives were lost that many inhabitants talked about it for years. Henry Walker wrote about one elderly woman who said:

I belonged to this society for over fifty years. I forgot the year it was organized, but I think it was in the sixties before the founding of the Ladies of Seven Sorrows. I joined it in the year of the yellow fever in seventy-eight. I know it was organized a good while before I joined. A lot of these societies were organized to help the people fight the yellow fever.

Some societies were restricted to certain age groups, writes Jacobs, while other groups were just for males or just for females. There were two types of memberships for males. The adult males required regular membership, and their wives and children were "passive members" who received benefits from the society.

There was a benevolent group for women called the Ladies Friends of Faith. To be a part of their society, one had to request to join, pay a dollar application fee, and supply a documentation of their health status. Then someone from the organization would go to the applicant's home and tell the society what they found. Next, the society would vote on the applicant. Any applicant over the age of forty-nine could not be a member. If the applicant's lifestyle was not up to the group's standards then the person would not be considered. From the number of announcements recorded for special meetings and funerals between 1914-1916, there were about one hundred fifty members.

Each Benevolent society had elected officials who were voted into office: president, vice-president, recording and financial secretaries, treasurer, chaplain, and grand marshal. To run for president, the candidate had to be serious about the position and be ready for some major campaigning.

Benevolent societies participate in Jazz Funerals which, as a whole, celebrate a person's life. They are basically funerals with music played by brass bands. They originally played for military funerals and the music was meant to be solemn, dignified and sorrowful. The Masonic members of the band wore military uniforms with Napoleonic hats, and the women wore white dresses. The men carried sabers. Jermaine Devezin, the president of the Steppers, said that the dress code for his club is very relaxed. "We usually get a tailor made suit with some gator shoes. The only thing I really like spending money on is the hat. We spend like a hundred dollars on our hats. Jazz funerals have an African influence as well as an European influence. Both cultures dance and play joyful music at funerals. During the yellow fever epidemic in New Orleans, the band would play sorrowful music on the way to the cemetery, and then play a faster and more joyful music after the funeral."

In 1905, brass bands started segregating. The white bandmasters stopped playing at funerals, and so it happened that they stopped around the time that jazz was being born. The whites stopped performing at funerals because they saw a tradition changing right before their eyes. They experienced a change in the music, people dancing and joining in. Indoor music suddenly became the music for jazz funerals. To them, the dancers were more wild, less restrained, and distasteful. Those people are known as second liners. Second liners included the family of the deceased, the benevolent society, members from other clubs, and random people from the street. There are also second line clubs that second line for events around the city. Anyone can join in; it didn't matter what they had on. People who belonged to a club would wear club colors. This was a tradition reshaped by blacks. Whites were not the only ones who stopped playing in the jazz funerals. Creoles that were strictly Catholic had a problem with the change; it was considered to be a tradition of the Baptist religion.

When clubs were second lining together in the 20th century, it was important that they had unity. There was a certain order in which they paraded. The police lead most of the parades, and they were followed by designated club members who carried the club's banner and sometimes the American flag. The brass band and a group of second liners were next. Sometimes the police followed the brass band if the parade was particularly large. If there were any Mardi Gras Indians, they followed behind the brass band. The hard core second liners and the casual second liners were two groups of second liners. The hard core second liners was the group that follow right after the brass band. The casual second liners included the women, men with children, and older men. There was always a police car at the end of the parade.

A famous social aid and pleasure club that was a benevolent society at one time is The Zulu Social Aid and Pleasure Club. The Zulu Social Aid and Pleasure Club started when a club called "There Never Was and Never Will Be a King Like Me," and it was about the Zulu Tribe. That seems to be the story that everyone tells before giving the history of Zulu. Zulu originally got members from benevolent societies, The Tramps, and other ward based groups. They first marched in Mardi Gras in 1901, but their first appearance as Zulu was in 1909. The King of Zulu at the time was William Story. The club wore old, tore up, raggedy pants with grass skirts, and black painted faces. The King of Zulu wore a lard can as a crown and a "banana stalk" scepter. They first used a float in 1915, and it was decorated with palmetto leaves and moss. Zulu Social Aid and Pleasure Club was incorporated on September 20, 1916.

The Zulu Club did experience some controversy in its day. Zulu was quite unpopular in the 1960's, which was during the height of black awareness. People did not like the fact that Zulu paraded with their faces painted black with grass skirts on. Society thought of it as being demeaning. This controversy led to the decrease of membership to sixteen men. In 1968, Zulu paraded through St. Charles and Canal Street for the first time. During this time, segregation laws separated the blacks and whites, so the blacks had to take the back streets to see Zulu.

One of the most popular throws during carnival time is the coconut, and Zulu started the tradition in 1910. The coconut is also called the "Golden Nugget." Lloyd Lucas was the first to paint the coconut. Zulu faced a number of lawsuits because people were getting injured by thrown coconuts. A coconut bill was passed excluding the coconut from liability for injuries arising from the coconuts handed out from the floats.

New Orleans has such a rich culture, and Benevolent Societies, which are now known as Social Aid and Pleasure Clubs, Jazz Funerals, and Second Line Clubs is just a little taste of New Orleans's rich heritage. New Orleans is a parading kind of town. Think of an occasion, and the city celebrates with a parade. The premise for a New Orleans Jazz Funeral is "you come into this world crying and go out of it singing." (See chapter twelve for New Orleans, Louisiana.)

FUNERAL AND BURIAL CUSTOMS

WE ARE SO FOOLISH ABOUT DEATH. WE WILL NOT LEARN

HOW IT IS WAGES PAID TO THOSE WHO EARN,

HOW IT IS GIFT FOR WHICH ON EARTH WE YEARN

TO BE SET FREE FROM BONDAGE TO THE FLESH;

HOW IT IS WINNING HEAVEN'S ETERNAL GAIN.

HOW IT MEANS FREEDOM EVERMORE FROM PAIN,

HOW IT UNTANGLES EVERY MORTAL MESH

WE FORGET THAT IT MEANS ONLY LIFE—

LIFE WITH ALL JOY, PEACE, REST AND GLORY RIFE,

THE VICTORY WON AND ENDED ALL THE STRIFE.

—AUTHOR UNKNOWN

Social customs and cultural attitudes toward death continue to evolve, even in our more enlightened, less superstitious age. Three significant issues—cultural, environmental, and business concerns— affect the day-to-day and long-term operations of burial grounds in particular. This chapter will examine how each of these concerns influences private, municipal, and national cemeteries.

Cultural concerns have had a significant effect upon burial practices and procedures since the pre–Civil War days. The range of customs and traditions is wide, varying from region to region and

CHAPTER NINE

421

culture to culture. Traditions that have become established have sprung from the local residents' strong ethnic heritage, the result of nature's impact on the surrounding landscape, or reactions to changing attitudes over time. In addition, several traditions were born of practicality; the lack of technical expertise in earlier times left little chance for experimentation and progress in the operation of cemeteries.

Environmental concerns, likewise, have had a significant impact on the entire field of burial ground management, especially in the areas of cemetery properties and procedures. There was little genuine awareness in earlier times of the destructive forces now known to cause decay and deterioration. In time, however, cemeteries have become much more alert to the impact of the environment and have put in operation various methods of defense.

Business concerns have ranged from becoming more financially savvy to, in essence, going into the "death care business." In fact, in some instances small "corner" establishments have grown to become major industries within this modern-day milieu. Many small and independent cemeteries remain intact, however, and have no interest in becoming a part of a mega-company operation.

Municipal cemeteries remain viable alternatives to privately owned cemeteries. There is no sign, however, of a surge in activity to promote these many city-owned cemeteries. Although they are viewed as potentially viable business ventures, such burial grounds encounter many of the same problems as the privately owned cemeteries.

The national cemetery system has plans to expand, however, and several new properties are on the drawing board. In spite of the increased number of cemeteries in the system—from 103 in the 1970s to more than 114 in the 1990s—many of them are now closed for interments because of the lack of space. For some who already have family burial sites, second interments in single graves or cremation of remains may be all that can be accommodated.

As with any other business, today's cemeteries must also offer security. To that end, some have installed high-tech security systems designed to shield the property from unwanted intruders and would-be vandals. While some perpetrators target specific cemeteries or grave sites, most do only random destruction; African American cemeteries, as a whole, have not been targeted as a specific group.

Both municipal and national cemeteries are currently being presented with interesting challenges. Although municipal cemeteries show a slow, steady growth, the national cemetery system has found itself faced with an almost constant need for expansion. Many more families of veterans now select national cemeteries over local burial grounds because of the increased knowledge and understanding of the system and its benefits and provisions.

In the twenty-first century, writes William H. Whyte in *Cemetery Management* magazine, one characteristic of the American marketplace will be diversity. One way the industry can meet this changing marketplace across the United States will be to offer a broader product line, contends Whyte, who also predicts that the area where change will be most dramatic will be cremation. As recently as 1970, most cemeteries did not need to offer specialized inventory for those selecting cremation. However, cemetery managers are urged to continually reexamine such policies and practices and to keep in mind the cemetery's heritage.

Cultural Concerns

Dubbed by journalist Maria Dickerson as the "Culture of Death," people-oriented concerns are important both to those in the cemetery business and those involved in auxiliary services to the industry. Dickerson, writing in the *Detroit News,* finds sharp contrasts between the death rituals of the past and modern-day practices. Death rituals continually evolve and serve as a mirror of societal changes, as a look into the past will illustrate.

Mourning periods of a year, sometimes two, were routine up into the nineteenth century. Death was so frequent among early colonists that it was planned for far in advance. Upon the birth of a child, many families put away a cask of wine to be used for the offspring's wedding or funeral—whichever came first. And the early European custom of giving small mementos of the deceased to mourners was transplanted to the New World, where it quickly took root and grew out of control. Some eighteenth-century families nearly spent themselves into the poorhouse, passing out jewelry, scarves, gloves, books, and other gifts to mourners, while widows were literally eaten out of house and home by ravenous relatives.

PREPARING THE DEAD

The bodies of the deceased were almost always prepared at home, where young children could be exposed to the sobering influence of death. Adolescents served as pallbearers for their peers well into the early part of the twentieth century. Children who died of infectious disease were sometimes held up to the nursery window so playmates could say good-bye.

The old custom of watching over the body of a loved one from death until burial was not only a spiritual vigil but a practical one as well, since the "deceased" weren't always dead. Colonial annals are peppered with anecdotes of comatose "corpses" who revived before they were buried. This vigil was known in many cultures as a "wake," a term that is thought to have derived from a Celtic word meaning "the watching."

Offerings to the Dead

The mode of decoration used in African American graveyards is so different from what is commonly expected in a cemetery that the graveyard may not be recognized for what it is. A report of the Institute of Archeology and Anthropology at the University of South Carolina included the following evaluation: "A man was dispatched to check out the area (Charlestowne Landing) and he returned reporting that there didn't appear to be anything there other than some late nineteenth-century and twentieth-century junk scattered throughout the area."

Writing off the area turned out to be an unwise decision. What the man viewed as "junk" turned out to be an important black graveyard site with a wide variety of offerings. Far from being heaps of garbage, funeral offerings are sanctified testimonies; material messages of the living intended to placate the potential fury of the deceased.

Preserving the bodies of the deceased, whether for sanitation, viewing, or religious purposes, has preoccupied humankind since ancient times. The first American settlers generally buried their dead quickly, thus avoiding the need for preservation. But because relatives sometimes had to travel long distances to attend funerals, early colonists also experimented with several crude methods of embalming, according to the *History of American Funeral Directing*, a seminal work on U.S. death history. Those techniques included disemboweling the corpse and filling the body cavity with charcoal, immersing the body in alcohol, or wrapping the deceased in a cloth soaked with alum. The tidier, simpler principal of refrigeration supplanted these methods once ice could be manufactured with ease. "Cooling boards" and coffins with special ice cavities became the standard until well into the mid-nineteenth century, even as medical pathologists were making great advances in chemical embalming. Then came the Civil War, which changed everything as both North and South had to face death on a massive scale. The process of transporting the bodies of soldiers fallen in battle long distances back to their homes and loved ones spurred the demand for chemical embalming. The battlegrounds of Manassas, Shiloh, Antietam, and Gettysburg were, in effect, the birthplace of modern mortuary science.

The Civil War gave Thomas Holmes, the "Father of American Embalming," the opening he was looking for to introduce safe, sanitary chemical embalming. Unfortunately, Holmes's breakthrough spawned a flurry of fast-buck artists and charlatans. Civil War chronicler Francis Lord once commented that Washington, D.C., was plastered with "ghastly advertisements of embalmers" who flocked to the battlefields distributing handbills like expectant vultures. One shameless entrepreneur erected billboards along the route used by soldiers marching to the front. "When a staff member pointed out their demoralizing influence, General Butler ordered the embalmer to desist from this method of advertising," Lord wrote.

Some seemingly modern twists in death rituals are really just updated versions of age-old customs. The lavish 1988 send-off for reputed cocaine dealer Richard "Maserati Rick" Carter—who was laid out in a casket outfitted with rubber car tires and a chrome Mercedes-Benz front grill—is not unlike the ship burials once reserved for ancient Viking warriors. Death historians note the fact that families today still bury their loved ones with religious objects, jewelry, pictures, tools, and sporting equipment—as humankind has done for millennia. In fact, sending a loved one to his final rest without a personal token is considered unusual.

Mourning periods of a year, or even more, were considered routine into the nineteenth century. Widows were expected to don black clothing, wear somber expressions, and shun all social events. It was both a show of respect for their deceased spouse and an acknowledgment to the community that these unattached women stood somewhere outside the normal social milieu in a patriarchal society.

Americans no longer bury the living along with the dead through such prescribed mourning periods. Still, something has been lost in our rush to dispense with the deceased and "get on with our lives," as the 1990s mantra goes. People who mourn excessively today are sent to grief counseling for their "problem." Employer-paid bereavement leave is a few days at most. The radical shift from one year of mourning to one day in the space of only a century makes a statement on the priorities of America's evolving culture.

While our culture's seeming coldness is partly the result of weathering the loss of family and friends to two world wars within our recent past, the changing nature of the funeral industry has also had its effect. Corporations are busy buying up independent funeral homes, cemeteries, and mausoleums, pursuing the standardized, chain-store approach that has worked in everything from muffler repair to fast food. Can undertaking franchises outlets be far behind?

Some death historians worry that the American funeral could become less solemn if corporate culture and death culture ever become synonymous. "Caring for the dead is *the* most sensitive job," Mr. Huntoon, a mortician from Pontiac, Michigan, believes. "Flipping hamburgers and changing oil filters isn't the same as showing empathy for the family, going the extra mile with personal service. . . . If we ever start treating our dead like toxic waste, Lord help us as a society."

Environmental Concerns

Modern-day concerns have shifted in focus from those of centuries, or even decades, past. Today Americans are becoming more aware of the impact of many years of misuse and abuse of natural resources upon our planet. This misuse has taken its toll on the life and survival of many burial grounds. While a concern over industrial pollution wasn't of great significance in small towns and rural areas, natural weathering, neglect, and the encroachment of hungry land developers have been particularly harmful to the traditional cemeteries of the 1800s and early 1900s. These churchyard and neighborhood burial grounds were especially affected by such "elements" when funds to legally protect or routinely clean and maintain the grounds were not forthcoming. This shortage of funds forced a kind of neglect that could not be remedied. Fortunately, these burial grounds were less likely to suffer the vandalization of more urban areas because the entire community had a distinct relationship with the cemetery.

As cities have started assuming more responsibility for their own cemetery properties, and laws and regulations have been enacted to govern them, the large urban cemeteries have been able to provide various degrees of care, many becoming gardens of beauty. However, it is difficult to control troublesome vandalism by gangs and groups that enjoy this kind of destruction of property. In addition, increased industrial pollution causes "fallout" materials that are harmful to markers and stones.

CHEMICAL POLLUTION OF CEMETERIES

Concerns about the environment now reach even beyond the grave and are troubling the cremation and cemetery business, writes Warren E. Leary in the *New York Times:*

> More than 2 million people die each year in the United States. Those responsible for disposing of the remains say their work is increasingly constrained by federal, state and local laws aimed at protecting air, land and water quality.

> Some environmentalists have questioned the industry's effects upon the living, wondering, for example, if buried bodies might contaminate underground water or if cremation could be a source of toxic air pollutants.

> The American Cemetery Association expressed concern: "As an industry, we are concerned because environmental issues generally are the issues of the 1990s. We don't anticipate any serious environmental problems now, but we follow issues such as reauthorization of the Clean Water Act to see if there are any changes that could affect us."

> Because of concern about underground water pollution, questions have been raised about formaldehyde and other chemicals in embalmed bodies seeping into local water tables.

> In addition, blood and other body fluids removed during embalming, which may contain infectious agents or toxic chemicals used to treat cancer and other diseases, are usually flushed into the regular sewer system.

No one is sure how many cemeteries there are in the nation, but industry estimates put the number between 75,000 and 100,000. These vary in size from small churchyard plots to large military and municipal establishments.

Federal officials have discussed plans to drill in some cemeteries to check water quality, but industry spokesmen said they did not expect any adverse findings.

Most graves are lined with concrete, brick, metal or other materials that should separate caskets from any groundwater in places where it could be a problem. In addition, unpublished findings from test borings done in cemeteries in Canada indicate no groundwater problems.

CEMETERIES AND WATER POLLUTION

The "Washington Report," a recent Canadian report by Stephen Morgan and Robert M. Fells, finds cemeteries don't significantly contribute to water pollution. The Ontario Ministry of the Environment (MOE) published the results of its study, "Cemeteries and Groundwater: An Examination of Potential Contamination of Groundwater by Preservatives Containing Formaldehyde." The MOE's Water Resources Branch conducted a "groundwater renaissance sampling survey" by using six well-sites located downgrade from cemeteries.

Based on a survey of standard burial practices in populated areas of Ontario, it was determined that 90 percent of the human remains in the cemeteries involved in the survey were embalmed and then placed into a casket. "Caskets range from soft to hard woods to steel. Steel caskets are hermetically sealed. The casket may be placed into a concrete vault and sealed with impermeable caulking."

The report is also based upon various calculations, including the following: A quantity of approximately one quart of a two-percent solution of formaldehyde is used in the embalming process; there is a maximum burial density of five hundred bodies per cemetery acre; the six wells tested are located in sandy shallow areas down grade of cemeteries; the wells ranged in depth from 3 to 24 meters (approximately 10 ft. to 79 feet) the burial time ranged from a century to eight years ago; and the distance ranged between 500 and 2,000 meters.

Water samples from the survey sites were analyzed for evidence of formaldehyde, nitrates, and phosphates. The report concluded "that cemeteries are not a significant source of groundwater contamination by formaldehyde. In addition, the calculated loading estimate for formaldehyde and nitrates being released from cemeteries supports a low potential for groundwater contamination."

Harvey Lapin, legal counsel for CANA, writes that the federal Environmental Protection Agency (EPA) is proposing to regulate crematories under the Environmental Protection Laws in an adverse manner. Seven Draft Reports were issued. Crematories are featured in the seven reports. Based on the limited information available, the EPA is proposing that crematories be required to update existing facilities in three stages to house state-of-the-art equipment over the next few years, while also stressing strong combustion and emission controls.

CITIES RUNNING OUT OF BURIAL SPACE

Cemeteries in urban and suburban areas are also experiencing a critical lack of grave space. Burial grounds located in New York and Boston have, for years, warned that the year 2000 will see a complete lack of burial space in these and other cities. Because of increasing land costs and stringent zoning laws, cities cannot continue to set aside large tracts of land for use as cemeteries.

Expected and unexpected solutions to the problem have been voiced. As far back as 1975, D. W. Peabody noted in a *New York Times* article that he thought "the ideal thing would be to bury bodies immediately after death, without embalming them, in places where they could disintegrate naturally, and the elements return to their respective cycles." An architect in New Jersey drew up plans for a cemetery in which coffins and vaults would be eliminated; bodies would be wrapped in shrouds or burial cloths and buried in the earth. The cemetery he envisioned would resemble a park with trees planted as grave markers. "Such a cemetery would never have to expand to make room for more and more concrete burial vaults," he points out. "There would be almost no limit to the number of burials. Human compost, like all other kinds, returns very quickly to life again."

Society's traditional respect for the dead, as well as modern burial practices, would, of course, prevent such pragmatic scenarios from being considered by most tradition-minded people. However, mausoleums are now universally acceptable, as are cremations. But while there is an increasing acceptance of these alternatives, the conventional cemetery remains the prime choice of most Americans. Even though a plot of cemetery land is expensive, as indicated, people are willing to pay the price to be buried in the earth.

ENVIRONMENTAL CHALLENGES AND CREMATION

The problems regarding cremation are slightly different than those of in-ground burials but still of concern to environmentalists. The cremation industry faces its biggest environmental challenge from the passage of state-dictated air quality laws that are tougher than current federal standards. One man heavily involved in interactions between the state congress and the industry is Bob Wise of West Virginia. California and Florida, states with large death and burial industries because of their large, elderly populations, have the strictest laws affecting crematoriums, explained Wise. "I don't see anything in federal environmental law that will be a big problem for the industry," he predicted, "but state laws will be the most stringent."

A statement by Clean Water Action, a Washington-based environmental, non-profit group, reflects Wise's belief:

> Clean Water Action, Greenpeace and other environmental groups raising cautions about emissions from crematorium smokestacks are encouraging tougher monitoring and regulation.

> Greenpeace, for instance, has accused medical officials and federal regulators of not keeping close track of people with plutonium-powered heart pacemakers.

> If people are cremated with those devices, the groups say, dangerous radioactive particles could be released into the air. . . . Also people are worried that crematorium emissions might contain mercury from dental fillings, toxic heavy metals from cancer chemotherapy and other dangerous substances.

> We would encourage states to pass rigorous laws, controlling emissions from crematoriums.

CREMATION AS AN ALTERNATIVE TO BURIAL

Jack Springer, executive director of the Cremation Association of North America (CANA) is familiar with the questions people frequently ask about cremation. Why do people really choose cremation? Answer: "People in this country are dying older. Just a decade ago, 10 percent died over eighty years old; now more than 20 percent of the population dies over eighty. They look at cremation as less expensive," he continues. "They have outlived many of their friends and family. Older people often live far away from where they grew up." Springer believes that cemeteries will become obsolete: Because a casket funeral doesn't hold the same social weight it used to, cremation begins to look simpler and make more sense economically, socially, and ecologically.

This trend is not as evident in African American cemeteries. For example, although several funeral directors in the Metropolitan Detroit area note an increase in families requesting cremation, they maintain that the percentage is minimal. These morticians indicate that a significant number of families with African roots who request cremation after death are also making more frequent visits to their homeland. Included in their wills is often a request to return their ashes to Africa. However, the casket funeral and the ground burial remains far more popular than cremation or the more expensive mausoleum burials.

In her presentation at the seventy-sixth annual CANA convention, Joanne B. Hawkins stated that African Americans have a full-service funeral most of the time. Imbedded in the African American community and reflected in the tradition of Negro spirituals, the focus has always been on the fact that what comes after leaving this earth is superior. Death is an important rite of passage; the funeral rite must contain suitable emotional impact.

Still, some blacks are choosing cremation. African Americans have traditionally sent their loved ones "home" (to where they originally came from) after death. Home could be Louisiana, North Carolina, Georgia, or Montana. There would, of course, be a service wherever the deceased was living at the time of death; then the body would be sent "home" where there would be another service.

Cremation provides a much more efficient and cost-effective manner of sending the person home. Also, in certain cases (as when the cause of death was a disfiguring accident), cremation can be performed with no viewing of the body. A memorial service as elegant and reflective as with a traditional cemetery burial generally follows. (See chapter ten)

The February 1994 edition of *American Cemetery* magazine included an article by M. R. Sandy, called "Cemetery Geology." In it, Sandy states that cemeteries are a veritable treasure-trove to the geologist—that the history of the earth can be told from a cemetery's monuments and features. Studying Woodland Cemetery in Dayton, Ohio, Sandy discovered that headstones, obelisks, and mausoleums crafted from rock quarried in North America, or in far-off places such as Africa, Asia, and Europe could be found at the site.

Paul Laurence Dunbar (1872–1906), acknowledged as the first black writer to receive international acclaim, is buried in Woodland Cemetery. The cemetery was founded in 1841, and has approximately one hundred thousand monuments covering 247 acres. Sandy describes the markers of Wilbur and Orville Wright, world famous for developing and performing the first powered flight in 1903. Dunbar, he says, was a classmate of Orville Wright in Dayton's Central High School's class of 1890. Dunbar's grave marker is glacial erratic, or "field stone," deposited by melting glacial ice at the end of the Ice Age, approximately 17,000–20,000 years ago. The erratic is granitic in composition, with cross-cutting veins. The author explains that this rock was probably eroded from the Canadian Shield and transported by glacial ice.

THE EMBALMING DISPUTE

The effect of embalming fluids on cemetery soil was, and still is, a topic of major dispute. The following article by Melissa Johnson Williams and John

L. Konefes, first printed in *American Cemetery* magazine, discusses the environmental aspects of embalming.

Many past practices have come back as problems, including indiscriminate waste disposal, asbestos use, and persistent pesticide use on land and water. In many cases, the "bad" practice was originally done with good intent: waste disposal as an improvement in visible sanitary conditions and removal of hazards, asbestos as a very good fireproof material, and pesticide use to curb damaging insects and weeds.

Even further back in our history, arsenic embalming began as a sanitary practice, and a practical means to preserve the body until burial or for transport. Considering that the alternative was use of ice, arsenic embalming was a significant improvement. What the embalming practitioners, or undertakers, did not consider were the long-term effects of placing significant amounts of arsenic in concentrated burial areas—cemeteries.

The advent of embalming brought with it a new era in funeral service. Families who once had to bury their loved ones quickly to prevent the spread of disease or before the body started to decompose would now plan funeral services that allowed family members from out of town to attend or to allow the body to be returned home.

Advertisements of this new "process" made a variety of claims— "Bodies embalmed by us never turn black," and "will remove all offensive odors, whiten the body, restore it to a natural sleeplike appearance." The latter was made by Dr. Thomas Holmes, the man considered to be the father of American embalming. He manufactured his own fluid called The Innominata, which proclaimed to be "guaranteed to contain no poison." Nearly 130 years later it would be discovered that his fluid contained a high amount of arsenic.

The search for a formula to preserve the dead human body did not begin in the United States. It is well documented back to early Egypt

Gravestone Group Develops Headstone Database

There are many benefits to computerizing cemetery records. Burial records can be located in seconds on "fields," such as "First name," "Last name," and "Maiden name." A list of Civil War veterans at a given cemetery can be generated in minutes. The location of a gravestone can be found with a simple clacking of a key.

One less obvious benefit is protecting records. It is truly sad when cemetery records have been destroyed in a fire, tornado, or other disaster. This can be avoided by entering records into a computer database and duplicating them on a floppy disk or tape and storing them off site. Genealogists and gravestone researchers have been using computers as a research tool for about a decade. But the exchange of data between researchers has been hampered by a lack of standards for gravestone data bases. The Association for Gravestone Studies (AGS) has been working for about a year to establish a standard database software program for recording gravestone information. . . .

continued on next page

continued from previous page

The AGS database standard springs from a research project that began five years ago. The goal of the project is to log data from every gravestone in Rhode Island. Thirty volunteers have been working on this. During its first 200 years, most of Rhode Island's cemeteries were small farm graveyards. Thus, of 3,200 cemeteries in the state, 3,000 are family cemeteries, with four to twenty burials. More than 2,500 are abandoned and overgrown, in the woods and fields, on private and public land. As of May 1995, 260,000 gravestone inscriptions in 2,663 cemeteries had been recorded and entered into the computer database (used by many genealogists at the Rhode Island Historical Society). The AGS database standard allows for entry of all obvious gravestone data: date of death, age, relationships, and location or cause of death. It also contains information like dimensions (height and width); composition (slate, marble, granite); condition (good, fair, poor); shape of top (round, square, fancy); status (upright, down, broken); carving (skull, angel, urn); and legibility (good, fair, poor). (The AGS database contains code letters for these characteristics and will reject invalid codes.)

continued on next page

and proof of its success still exists today. Throughout medical history the need for such a preservative is also well documented. Modern medicine would not be where it is today without dead human bodies to use for anatomical dissection and exploration.

During the course of the American Civil War, Dr. Thomas Holmes was engaged by the medical department of the Union Army to set up battlefield embalming tents to return home the bodies of Union dead. Because of the large and extensive territory of the Civil War, many were trained to carry on the embalming. Holmes provided the fluid which initially "some protégés of Holmes" contended contained arsenic and zinc chloride. Holmes throughout his lifetime vehemently denied this and wrote extensively against the use of these and other poisonous agents. Holmes never patented his fluid which he contended would then give others his formula. Test results from a 1990 sample of a body embalmed by Holmes indicated arsenic in the remaining tissue at 2.8%, and it was probably the major embalming agent!

Burials during this time period were made primarily on wood coffins that were put directly into the ground of local or church cemeteries. There were few metallic burial vaults or casket cases used and the Fisk Cast Iron Coffin was in limited use around the country. Towards the end of the 19th century, metallic cases were more widely used, particularly in urban areas.

As these wood coffins and metal cases disintegrate or corrode because of exposure to moisture and shifting cemetery ground, what are the possible consequences of twelve pounds of arsenic being absorbed into the soil and surrounding groundwater?

This question had not been raised until nearly 100 years after the widespread and continuing use of arsenic in embalming preparations. With more emphasis being put on environmental hazards and safety this question is now up for consideration.

Arsenic was widely used as an embalming ingredient from about 1880 to 1910. Burials occurred in wooden coffins or metal containers that could degrade in the underground environment. These containers are subject to corrosion, and will eventually deteriorate. Arsenic, a basic element, will not change or degrade, but must remain with the buried body, or move into the environment. As the containers degrade, water moving downward through soils of cemeteries can dissolve arsenic. A logical conclusion is significant potential for groundwater contamination at many locations throughout the U.S. from arsenic-embalmed bodies.

Without an extensive review of public agency or private funeral establishment records, accurate determinations of the number of arsenic-embalmed bodies present in the nation's graveyards is impossible. Even if records were made available, they may not contain sufficient information to verify use of arsenic in certain cases. And the effort to obtain such information would be enormous. To understand the potential impact, let's focus on a hypothetical cemetery in a modest-size town. It is reasonable, for the period 1880 to 1910, to assume that 2,000 people died in that time period. If 50% of those were embalmed with arsenic, using six ounces of fluid per person, then the cemetery contains 380 pounds of arsenic. If the embalmers in the area used more arsenic, such as three pounds per person, then the cemetery would contain over one ton of arsenic. In either case, this is a significant amount of a potent, toxic material to find in the ground at one location.

Arsenic-embalmed bodies can release the toxic metal as rainfall percolates through the soil, into degraded burial containers, and on down to

continued from previous page

A database normally has a "date" field allowing an entry in a format like, 09/15/1852. This can be a problem when the entire date cannot be read, because the database will not accept incomplete or invalid dates. This problem is solved on the AGS database by entering dates in this format: 15 SEP 1852 [if any of the three parts cannot be read, the part or parts can be left out]. (The computer checks to see that the month entered is one of the 12 valid months, and that the sequence of numbers-to-letters-back-to-numbers is in place; it will not permit deviations from this sequence.)

North Burial Ground in Providence has been in continuous use since 1700. It includes 110 acres of slate, marble, sandstone, and granite monuments marking graves of some of the city's earliest and most influential citizens.

In summer, genealogists flock to the cemetery office looking for records, which were not kept until 1848. A computer in the office is now loaded with the above-mentioned software; data on most of the earliest gravestones has been transcribed by volunteers. Before records were computerized, thousands of early gravestone inscriptions were accessible only to those willing to trek through the cemetery. The program being used to store and search at North Burial Ground is an early version of the program to be offered by AGS.

continued on next page

continued from previous page

Another cemetery with computerized records is Rhode Island Veterans Memorial Cemetery, which contracted with my business in 1993 to develop a computer program to store data on veterans buried there. The program stores enlistment place and date, discharge place and date, and war served. It also stores data on future burials and next of kin, with mail-merge options. One feature visitors here especially like is the veteran's memorial card—a map printed by the computer which includes the location of the grave, military record, and birth and death information.

In closing, it is clear genealogists look forward to the day when all cemeteries have records on computer. For some of the dead, the gravestone carries the only written record of their life.

—JOHN E. STERLING, *American Cemetery*

the shallow groundwater table. Such periodic releases of arsenic can occur over many years, and may be accelerated as burial containers degrade.

Based on the knowledge of embalming and burial practices, it is reasonable, from the standpoint of an environmental engineer, to assume that arsenic contaminated remains can have a significant impact on soil and groundwater. Certainly, if hundreds of pounds of arsenic pesticides were thought to be buried at a site, action would be taken to verify and determine the extent of contamination. But with the justifiable sensitivity toward cemeteries and burial sites, little has been done to assess potential impacts on soil and groundwater resources.

Prince Greer

The history of embalming as described by Robert G. Mayer in his book, *Embalming, History, Theory and Practice* actually evolved in three periods: 3200 BC to AD 650; the Period of the Anatomists, AD 650-1861 and the Modern Period, beginning in the year 1861.

At the beginning of the Civil War, as in all previous wars fought by the United States, there was no provision for return of the dead to their homes. In the Seminole Indian Wars (during the 1830s), the Mexican War (1846-1848), and the campaigns against the Indians up to the outbreak of the Civil War, the military dead were buried in the field near where they fell in battle. It was possible for the relatives to have the remains returned to their home for local burial under certain conditions:

1. The next of kin was to request the disinterment and return of the body in a written request to the Quartermaster General.

2. On military authority confirmation that the burial place was known and disinterment could be effected, the family was advised to send a coffin capable of being hermetically sealed to a designated Quartermaster Officer nearest the place of burial.

3. Such Quartermaster Officer would provide a force of men to take the coffin to the grave, disinter the remains and place them in the coffin and seal

it. The coffined remains would then be returned to the place of ultimate reinterment.

During the early days of the Civil War and less frequently as the war dragged on some family members of the deceased personally went to hospitals and battlefields to search for their dead and bring them home for burial. Civil War embalming was carried out with a variety of chemicals and techniques. Arterial embalming was applied when possible. An artery, usually the femoral or carotid, was raised and injected without any venous drainage in most cases. Usually, no cavity treatment was administered. When arterial embalming was believed impossible because of the nature of wounds or decomposition, other means of preparation of the body for transport were resorted to. In some cases the trunk was eviscerated and the cavity filled with sawdust or powdered charcoal or lime. The body was then placed in a coffin completely imbedded in sawdust or similar material. In other cases, the body was coffined as mentioned without evisceration.

The most interesting account of the Civil War embalming surgeons relates the method of the transmission of embalming technique from a medically trained practitioner to an undertaker, who in turn, trained a layman in the skill. Dr. E. C. Lewis was a former U.S. Army surgeon. W. P. Cornelius (1824-1910) was a successful undertaker in Nashville, Tennessee, and Prince Greer was a former orderly, bodyservant, and slave of a Colonel Greer of a Texas cavalry regiment who died in the fighting.

Prince took it upon himself to return the body of his former master to his estate and contacted Dr. W. P. Cornelius, a successful undertaker in Nashville. Dr. Cornelius arranged to have the body of Greer's master shipped back to his Texas home and at same time, Dr. Cornelius found himself in a dilemma for his assistant, a young surgeon who had been trained in the embalming arts by Dr. Thomas Holmes. (Dr. Thomas Holmes who discovered an embalming fluid during the War of the Rebellion had embalmed 4,028 bodies), decided that embalming the dead was a good occupation for him. Prince Greer had remained on the Cornelius's premises and indicated he would do work to secure his room and board. Dr. Cornelius taught Greer the embalming arts and wrote:

"Prince Greer appeared to enjoy embalming so much that he himself became an expert, kept on at work during the balance of the war and was very successful at it. It was but a short time before he could raise quickly as anyone. He was always careful, always of course coming to me in a difficult case. He remained until I quit the business in 1871." Prince Greer was the first documented black embalmer in United States history.

One of the many facets of embalming is the study of structural anatomy. J. Sheridan Mayer in his book, *Restorative Art,* written in 1980, makes some startling observations. To prepare students for the study of embalming, he defines us and them in this manner, Mayer says: without delving deeply into the field of anthropology and its belief in the common ancestry of man; there still exist three distinct races ...white, black and yellow. Each has certain physical characteristics which distinguish it from the other races. In each race, inherited characteristics vary among offspring but, in addition to the individual variations, there frequently occur radical changes which may be inherited by some but not all of the offspring. Add to this the breakdown of racial barriers and differences within each race are to be expected. Nevertheless, certain broad characteristics persist.

White (Caucasoid) Race: a species of man including the light skinned people of Europe, North Africa, Eastern Asia and their descendents in other parts of the world. The dark skinned Hindu of Northern India has all Caucasoid characteristics but the color of his skin.

The "typical" white man has blond, brown, red or black hair; it may be curly or straight. His head is long or rounded and has a high cranial vertex while his forehead is full or dome-like. His nose is long and narrow; his lips are thin. His complexion ranges from a pinkish white to a dark brown. His eyes may be blue, gray or brown.

Black (Negroid) Race: a species of man including the dark skinned people of Africa, Southern India, etc.

The "typical" black man has curly or kinky hair. He has a long, narrow bead with a low cranial vertex. His nose is broad and flat. He has thick, inverted lips, projecting face (pronathism, which may also be found on some Caucasoids), and a recessive chin. His complexion may range from a light tan to a blackish-brown. His eyes are dark.

Yellow (Mongoloid) Race: A species of man including the Mongols, Manchus, Chinese, Japanese, Koreans, Siamese, Tibetans and, to some extent, Alaskans and aboriginal inhabitants of America.

The "typical" yellow man has long, straight black hair, a short, broad head and a high cranial vertex. He has wide cheekbones, a relatively small nose and slanting eyes (which may also be found on some Caucasoids). The distance from his nasal root to the inner corner of the eye is minimal. His complexion ranges from a yellowish-tan to a deep swarthy brown.

Your authors have no clue as to how someone, for example, highly disfigured in an accident, would end up looking, by this "well-trained" embalmer.

The public concept of a cemetery is as a plot of ground set aside for the burial of the dead. But what is a cemetery, in business terms? A cemetery is considered a special-purpose property: a burial park for earth interments, a mausoleum of crypts or vaults, and/or a crematory. The proper valuation of cemeteries, mausoleums, crematoriums, and the like on a balance sheet can serve a variety of purposes, including the determination of leverageable equity. Few cemeterians would say that their property, with whatever services it offers, couldn't use some restoration and revitalization. Roads need repaving. Dead trees need to come down. Headstones need to be realigned. The mausoleums' masonry needs to be repointed. The problem, of course, is money. The expenses to maintain a burial ground through several generations are not insignificant.

Business Concerns

Some cemeteries were mismanaged during the last century, run by people with little or no business acumen and no interest in acquiring any. Some established no perpetual care or endowment funds until states passed laws requiring them to. The legacy of this lack of foresight is the struggling cemetery of the late twentieth century.

In the past, a funeral at a smaller church or neighborhood cemeteries incurred no particular burial costs. Consequently, the founders had no thought of profit making. Only recently have "white" cemeteries in cities like Detroit been receptive to the burial of African Americans. As cemetery grounds in those urban areas were purchased by African Americans in the early twentieth century, these new owners were motivated more by necessity than by the bottom line on a balance sheet.

In those same cities, now occupied anywhere from 60 to 90 percent by African Americans, cemetery owners direct their public relations campaign toward the black market; the bottom line is now, realistically, profit making. In general, most burial grounds are purchased for the purpose of earning income on the sale of grave plots and articles of implementation. Encouraged by the tax-free status of cemetery property and the sometimes low costs of large acreage in agricultural and rural settings, big businesses have been developed.

National Public Radio's *Morning Edition* aired a program entitled "Death Care Business Is Big and Getting Bigger" on December 1, 1993. Much of the discussion was between the reporter and an analyst for the Chicago Corporation Brokerage House, who specializes in "death care," the current preferred term for the funeral and cemetery business.

The analyst reminded listeners that the first baby boomer turns sixty-five in the year 2010, and that demographics, for this industry in particular, become very compelling beyond that. Overlooking the sobering fact that one has to die to be a customer, a look at the trends in the death care industry reveals many similarities to other growth industries. Such potential for profitmaking is something with which institutional investors feel particularly comfortable.

We now spend $8 billion a year burying our dead, cremating them, and memorializing the more than two million Americans who die each year. By the year 2030, one-fifth of our population will be over age sixty-five. While medical advantages have delayed mortality, health care experts don't expect much more good news there. Instead, the good news, certainly profit-wise, can be found in death care. Three large companies heard the good news early on and started buying up funeral homes and cemeteries around the country. The brokerage analyst reported that these companies' stocks increased in value by 40 percent in 1993 alone. While big investors might be hesitant at first, the demographics of the situation remain enticing.

DEATH CARE CORPORATIONS

One of the big three death care corporations described on NPR's *Morning Edition* is Stewart Enterprises, based in New Orleans. A regional representative for Stewart Enterprises travels through Pennsylvania, Virginia, West Virginia, and the Carolinas, looking for possible cemetery properties to buy. One of the company's current holdings is Fort Lincoln, the largest cemetery in the state of Maryland. It is situated on the outskirts of Washington, D.C.

Fort Lincoln has several burial operations. These include a large, hilltop mausoleum and a three-story stone building with a tower, arched openings, stained glass windows, and handsome burial chambers. Many customers, of course, prefer less lavish burials, but even these are not cheap. The average cost of death care at Fort Lincoln in 1995 ran to about $5,700.

The place of business at Fort Lincoln includes a new funeral home—the cemetery was without one until it was purchased by Stewart. Now it boasts what the NPR analyst called a "combo operation," a logical retailing development. Such combinations are based on a superstore concept and adapted to the death care industry. A couple can prearrange their respective funerals, select merchandise for service options, and then literally walk right next door to the cemetery to select a ground plot or mausoleum space.

The NPR reporter stated that such operations are why large companies like Stewart are doing so well. They have the money to advertise extensively, they can afford to buy funeral homes and cemeteries from families who want to get out of the business, and they realize economies by sharing some costs among several facilities. The funeral home at Fort Lincoln Cemetery opened in 1992 and was turning a profit by 1994. It has benefitted from a built-in market; of the hundreds of families using the cemetery every year, a certain percentage will use the funeral home.

Trends in the cemetery industry in the United States have paralleled other industries in the areas of growth and acquisition. In addition to Stewart Enterprises, two other multi-million dollar corporations grew rapidly:

one is SCI (Service Corporation, Inc.). The other, The Loewen Group filed for bankruptcy sometime after African American attorney Willie Gary won a multi-million dollar lawsuit against the Corporation. The new owners are Mikocem, LLC. These corporations also have been purchasing cemeteries and funeral homes throughout the country. Some are also active in related industries, such as casket manufacturing, cremation, and memorialization.

The days of church burial grounds and local funeral director–owned cemeteries are rapidly fading. It has become easier for owners to sell than to maintain expensive properties, fund perpetual care trusts, adhere to increasingly rigorous EPA and OSHA regulations, and operate in an increasingly litigious society. In some cases, families will be the losers in this battle for growth and acquisition. There will be less personalized service; the local undertaker who has served families more than two generations will cease to be available for comfort when the bereaved come calling. This is not to say that large corporations will not be courteous and offer counseling and follow-up care. Large organizations that focus on death, burial, and related services have large, well-trained sales counselors who excel in marketing their products and services. How many of us can say that we don't need what they are offering? Everyone who has passed childhood is a potential target of a good mailing and/or telemarketing campaign. Obviously, such pre-arrangement is smarter, cheaper, and less stressful than contacting death care providers at the time of need.

BURIAL ALTERNATIVES IN FLORIDA: A MODEL FOR THE FUTURE?

Charles Strouse, a staff writer for the *Miami Herald,* wrote in his article "Alternatives to Burials on Increase":

> More and more Dade residents are rejecting traditional burials and taking an alternative approach after death. The number of people in Dade County who opt for cremation, a sea grave, or who donate their bodies to science has been rising consistently during the past few years, according to the Dade County medical examiner's office.

Saying the increase in burial alternatives is reflective of nationwide trends, Strouse cited such reasons for the increase as rising costs for burials, a decrease in available land, greater acceptance of cremation, and a more mobile society whose families don't necessarily have special, meaningful places in which to bury their members. Commenting on the local and nationwide trend, Strouse continued:

In Dade, the cremation rate is 20 percent, or one in every five deaths. Both state and county records confirm the number is rising. The nationwide rate is 17 percent, and that has nearly doubled since 1980.

But Dade's rate is lower than in the rest of Florida, where about one in three bodies are cremated. Experts say blacks and Hispanics, who make up the bulk of Dade's population, have traditionally shunned cremation.

"There was a time when it was unheard of for anyone with a Hispanic name or for an American black to ask for cremation," said Joseph Davis, Dade's medical examiner for thirty-five years. "But now I'm seeing more and more of them."

The Norfolk, Virginia cemetery exemplifies the municipal cemetery system and tradition in the United States. Like Oak Ridge Cemetery in Springfield, Illinois, the final resting place of President Abraham Lincoln, the Norfolk cemetery is an old and historic site. Although one of the country's oldest municipal cemeteries, it still shares the same plight as others of its type. Some of these are large, some small, some operate efficiently, others are struggling, yet each of these city-run burial grounds faces similar difficulties as they move towards the next century.

Norfolk established its first city cemetery on fourteen acres just north of the city boundary. Today, it owns and operates eight cemeteries totaling 350 acres. The initial venture, started in 1825, was born of necessity, as no private cemeteries provided this service. These early burials were provided at a minimum cost with no thought of maintenance of the grounds. As Norfolk's population expanded, area were set aside for wealthier families; likewise "Strangers and Paupers" sections were designated for the underprivileged.

Today, municipal cemeteries and private cemeteries find themselves competitors. City cemeteries, offering services at prices below break-even levels—the city absorbs the losses—are not only unfair competition for private cemeteries, but are a bargain for a few paid for by every resident taxpayer. In the past few years, however, municipal budgets have become strained, and cemeteries such as Norfolk have begun facing the same concerns over funding cemetery operations and the future provision of services and maintenance as their private cemetery counterparts.

The shift from providing a community service to running a viable business necessitates an almost paradigmatic change of philosophy. The cost of operating cemeteries like Norfolk has far outpaced income, and the cemetery operators realize that changes must be made. To remain competitive after raising prices, the cemetery operators must become sensitive to the needs and wishes of the public in developing new programs and services. To this end, they have begun offering such things as marker sales, flowers, and marker cleaning; the long range plan is to develop a care fund. Cemetery administration is being empowered to fine-tune prices and the product/service mix as necessary to compete with the private sector. Norfolk has a difficult task ahead in its move from a municipal service to a business.

FUNDING OF MUNICIPAL CEMETERIES

LuAnn Johnson writes in *American Cemetery* magazine that common perceptions about municipal cemeteries are two-fold. First is the attitude of the community itself, which views such cemeteries as a public service, giving little thought to their operation. Secondly, people closer to the problem, such as cemeterians and those involved in community affairs, recognize these cemeteries as a drain on tax dollars that are seldom managed as a business. Private cemeteries see public-owned cemeteries as unfair competition.

Most municipal cemeteries are funded through tax dollars, putting them in competition with other city departments for their revenue. Small city-owned cemeteries may not have full staff, while larger municipal cemeteries often lack resources and knowledge to perform efficiently. In some instances, the cemetery manager is a municipal employee who lacks the specialized expertise to operate a cemetery.

Most all the problems common to municipal cemeteries stem from inadequate or nonexistent care funds. If such care funds can be established with the cooperation of city officials, the cemeteries will eventually become self-supporting. It is in the best interest of all in the community, especially taxpayers, to cease viewing municipal cemeteries as public services and view them as viable business ventures.

Municipal cemeteries should be able to charge a rate for goods and services comparable to those in the private sector; likewise, they should provide the same well-cared for and attractive grounds as private cemeteries. Also, their personnel must keep abreast of legislation and regulations affecting cemeteries, and need to become aware of what the American Cemetery Association (ACA) and their state associations can offer. The American Municipal Cemetery Council, a suborganization of the ACA, is also an excellent resource for its members and those who request assistance. Funds should be provided for membership in these organizations.

National Cemeteries

The U.S. Department of Veterans Affairs manages 114 cemeteries, and either the Department of the Interior or the U.S. Army runs fourteen other national cemeteries. The National Cemetery System began in an effort to cope with the many casualties caused by the Battle of Bull Run in 1861. When the battle ended, it was obvious that space would be needed to lay out graveyards. The first national cemeteries were set up for Union soldiers in Alexandria, Virginia; Philadelphia, Pennsylvania; New Albany, Indiana; Fort Leavenworth, Kansas; and Sharpeburg, Maryland, the site of the Battle of Antietam, where 4,476 Union soldiers were killed in one day's slaughter.

By 1863, there were eight more cemeteries, including one on the site of the Battle of Gettysburg; in 1864 Arlington National Cemetery was established for those dying in hospitals surrounding Washington, D.C. Of the nearly 360,000 Union soldiers killed in the Civil War, only 101,736 graves were registered in national cemeteries. However, by June 1866, 87,664 additional remains had been discovered on various battlefields, buried where they had fallen; they were reinterred at forty-one national cemeteries. By 1870 there were almost three hundred thousand Union soldiers buried in seventy-three national cemeteries.

By an act of Congress in 1872, burial rights in national cemeteries were granted to "all soldiers and sailors of the United States who may die in destitute circumstances." In March 1873, the act extended burial rights to all honorably discharged veterans of the Civil War and provided one million dollars for headstones—in white marble or granite—to mark each grave at each national cemetery. San Francisco National Cemetery was laid out in 1884, and was the first national cemetery on the west coast. By the end of the 19th century, soldiers killed in the Spanish-American War and the Philippine insurrection were frequently brought to Arlington or San Francisco National Cemetery.

By 1920, "All soldiers, sailors, or Marines dying in the service of the United States . . . or who served or hereafter shall have served during any war in which the United States has been . . . engaged, and, with the consent of the Secretary of War, any citizen of the United States who served in the army or navy of any government at war with Germany or Austria during the World War and who died in such service or after honorable discharge therefrom, may be buried in any national cemetery free of charge."

In 1929, more cemeteries were planned and in October 1943 a bill was introduced in Congress requiring at least one national cemetery in each state. After much debate in Congress and protests from the private cemetery sector, the bill died. In 1948 Congress again extended national cemetery burial privilege eligibility, this time to wives, husbands, widows, widowers, and dependent children of eligible veterans and some reserve officers. In 1960, because of lack of space for expansion, Congress replaced its policy of separate grave sites for family members to one grave site per family.

During the Vietnam War era, President Johnson asked the Department of Veterans Affairs (VA) to improve all veterans' programs, including the National Cemetery System; in 1973 the National Cemeteries Act was the beginning of a new era for America's national cemeteries. The law required that all but two of the cemeteries—Arlington and Soldiers Home—be transferred from Army control to that of the VA, which also assumed responsibility for providing headstones and markers.

A plan was submitted to Congress in January 1974, calling for the establishment of one regional cemetery in each of ten standard federal regions. The first four regional cemeteries were established in Texas, Missouri, Colorado, and Oregon. In the years following, the requirements of the regional cemetery concept were fulfilled.

Slowly, the Department of Veterans Affairs, purchased land, suitable for national cemeteries throughout the country. Plans for southeastern Michigan's long-awaited veterans cemetery were started and delayed during 2002 and 2003. Contracts were finally awarded late in 2004 with a possibility of completion of the cemetery sometime in 2005.

Michigan's present veterans cemetery, the Fort Custer in Battle Creek and scattered private cemeteries, were the only options in the meantime.

The new cemetery, named Great Lakes National cemetery, in Holly Township includes five hundred acres and serves metro Detroit's thousands of veterans, their spouses and dependent children, who can be buried there at no cost.

After considerable delay during the years 2002-2003, the Great Lakes National Cemetery came closer to reality slowly. In 2004, more than a thousand people attended a groundbreaking ceremony.

Secretary of Veterans Affairs, Anthony J. Principi gave the keynote address during the groundbreaking, which included a military flyover.

Principi heads the federal government's second largest department with a multimillion-dollar budget for health care and benefits for the nation's 25 million veterans.

Any veteran with an honorable discharge from service can be buried at government expense in a national cemetery, along with his spouse and immediate dependents.

About 20,000 veterans in Michigan die each year, according to the Department of Veteran Affairs

The first burials were set for Great Lakes Cemetery, which will be operated by the federal government. In 2005 there were still delays. About 6,200 sites were finally available in 2006. The Great Lakes Cemetery will have room for about 127,000 gravesites, when completed.

Kathleen Gray writes about the first look at the cemetery. The rolling hills and flame-orange trees surrounding Fagan Lake in Holly Township held a special place in the hearts of the 200 people who gathered there for a first look.

For Anthony Principi, secretary of the U.S. Department of Veterans Affairs, the new home for the Great Lakes National Cemetery is a "magnificent setting sanctified by the service of veterans who will rest here. "

"This is the place where children and grandchildren will walk among the silent markers and reflect that freedom is not free," he said during the official groundbreaking ceremony for the firsf of 11 national veterans cemeteries that will be built in the next five years.

Veterans, especially those from World War II, are dying at a rate of about 650,000 a year, said U.S. Sen. Carl Levin, a Democrat from Detroit.

The new cemetery is long overdue, said Rick Anderson, its director. It will serve a region that includes all of metro Detroit and Flint, which is home to about 480,000 veterans who would otherwise have to travel to Ft. Custer National Cemetery near Battle Creek to reach the closest national cemetery.

The 544-acre cemetery has all the accoutrements of a national shrine: an avenue of flags with 64 of the stars and stripes flying at the entrance; a military honor guard complete with a 21-gun salute for every burial, and a shelter overlooking Fagan Lake, where services are conducted.

At national cemeteries, burial is free for veterans, their spouses and dependent minor children, saving a family the estimated $2,000 cost for a plot in a private cemetery. In 2005 there were still delays.

For more details on Veterans Cemeteries and what to be cautious about when seeking a cemetery, see Chapter 13

Kathleen Gray, Detroit Free Press staff writer regularly reported on the problems and frustrations associated with the Great Lake National Cemetery. She wrote: The delay is causing a backup of caskets and cremated remains at Michigan funeral homes which are holding on to the remains of veterans and their family members until they can be buried at the cemetery. The Sharp Funeral Home in Fenton is storing the remains of 170 people destined for the new cemetery.

Gray writes about numerous complaints from families..

The construction delays at Michigan's long-awaited new veterans cemetery have left them frustrated and the remains are waiting on a funeral home shelf.

The Great Lakes National Cemetery in northern Oakland Csounty's Holly Township was to open Memorial Day, but contractors told federal officials that a wet winter delayed their progress. The cemetery's web site now says that burials will begin late this year.

Roger Sharp, owner of the Sharp Funeral Home, said many of the families he's dealing with are upset.

"We've called everyone and assured them that as soon as they are able to dig a grave, we'll have them in there.'

The lure of a National Cemetery is obvious; the pomp and circumstance associated with military burials, the reverence for veterans and the free plots for any honorably discharged veteran, a spouse and any dependent, minor children.

Rick Anderson, director of the cemetery, said the site is sacred and needs to be done right. Neither he nor VA could say what work remains.

"Once those burial sites are turned over to us, they constitute a national shrine," he said. "It may take a little longer, but it has to be done right."

The cemetery is to be developed in five phases with the last phase tentatively scheduled for completion by 2034.

The first phase will have space for 5,000 graves and, when completed, should handle needs for at least 75 years, said Anderson. An estimated 480,000 eligible veterans live within 75 miles of the new cemetery.

Michigan has one other Veterans cemetery, the Ft. Custer National Cemetery near Battle Creek.

In light of the unfavorable publicity about the Great Lakes National Cemetery, Richard A. Wannemacher, Jr. responded to some of the critics. Mr. Wannemacher, acting Undersecretary for Memorial Affairs in Washington, D.C. replied by stating "I know there are families wanting to bury their hallowed dead. We can assure them that we are preparing a national shrine to honor veterans with a final resting place and lasting memorials that commemorate their service to our nation. We have planned a shrine worthy of their endeavors and their service.

Following the announcement, Kathleen Gray, announced the opening in Holly Township on October 17, 2005. Construction is to continue as the cemetery is completed in five phases but phase one is completed and burials began.

THE MARKER BUSINESS

The Veterans Administration was put in charge of the Government Headstone and Marker Program. From the first congressional directive in 1873, which stated that a permanent marker should be provided for every grave in a national cemetery, more than five million headstones have been provided.

In fiscal 1992 alone, the Office of Memorial Programs within the Veterans Administration delivered nearly 303,000 headstones and markers. Of these, 24 percent were placed on graves in national cemeteries, 71 percent were delivered to private cemeteries, 3 percent to state veterans' cemeteries, and 2 percent to other federally operated cemeteries.

Currently twenty-five memorial companies supply headstones and markers to the government. Eleven manufacture granite markers, two make bronze memorials, five make flat marble markers, six manufacture upright marble markers, and one makes bronze niche covers. Contracts are awarded on a state-by-state basis for terms of one year with two one-year renewal options.

Many people have voiced continued concern and confusion over the issue of the veteran's marker benefit. In answering a letter to the editor of *American Cemetery,* the magazine notes that:

> There are no charges for national cemetery services provided to veterans and certain other eligible family members. These services include burial space, whether in-ground, full-length, or cremation or columbarium niches, together with perpetual care and the provision and installation of a variety of headstones, markers, and niche covers or plaques.

> Of course, these services depend on availability of burial space and the type of headstones or markers used in the particular national cemetery.

> The law, Title 38 U.S. Code, directs the Veterans Administration to provide government headstones or markers at the expense of the United States for the unmarked graves of any individual buried in national, [military] post, and state owned veterans cemeteries.

> The same law authorizes furnishing government headstones or markers in private cemeteries for veterans, but excludes the surviving spouse. The VA is not authorized to pay the cost of installing a veteran's headstone or marker in a private cemetery.

> When a non-veteran spouse predeceases the veteran and burial in a national cemetery is chosen, a government head stone or marker is provided and installed. When the veteran dies and is buried in the same grave site, the headstone or flat stone marker is destroyed and replaced with a new one.

We have found over the years that because of our high volume and lower costs for markers, this is generally the most economical way to provide the second inscription. Bronze markers and columbarium niche plaques are returned to the manufacturer for credit to the government after the new marker with both inscriptions is installed. When a non-veteran spouse predeceases the veteran and burial in a private cemetery is chosen, the VA is not authorized to provide a headstone or marker. When the veteran dies and is buried in the same grave site, the VA is authorized to provide a headstone or marker. Placement and installation is at the discretion and cost of the cemetery and next-of-kin. The change suggested by Mr. Goldblatt—that is, provision of a VA marker or headstone for the non-veteran spouse buried in a private cemetery—would require Congress to change the law governing the headstone and marker program.

It becomes apparent that the funeral and burial business is by no means static. Significant changes in each of its facets—cultural, environmental, and business concerns, municipal cemeteries, national cemeteries, and the marker business—have had a direct effect on the whole. Historic and rural cemeteries retain an important place in the development of the industry, but it is the large, urban cemetery that reflects, to a greater extent, the many changes wrought throughout the years. While all cemeteries find themselves knowledgeable about such cultural and political changes occurring within our evolving society, it is the growning concern over environmental issues that weighs most heavily on the continued existence of the traditional burial ground.

MORE CUSTOMS AND WHAT'S NEW AND WHAT'S DIFFERENT

CHAPTER TEN

There are many options for disposing of a deceased person, but they center upon two alternatives, burial and cremation. When taken alone, the cost of either form of disposition is minimal. It is the costs of the attendant services and merchandise that increase the total expense of a funeral.

Burial is the most common method in America for disposing of human remains. However, cremation is gaining in popularity. In-ground burial is still the most common, but "above-ground" interment in mausoleums is on the rise. It is not difficult to trace back four or five generations to the European ancestors who settled in North America to understand why in-ground burial came to be the choice. It was quick, effective, and it could be accomplished anywhere. In-ground burial also suited the customs of Africa. A grave could be marked for memorialization.

A relatively recent trend is above-ground interment. In our society the wealthy have sometimes built their own small buildings within cemeteries to house their families after death. In older cemeteries they can be easily found with the family names inscribed. They were generally built solidly of large stones and mortar with closed niches in the side for the caskets to be placed. The entrances were guarded by locked bronze doors and/or gates. It is a simple matter to unlock the door and place a new casket in a vacant niche. Now this concept is available to the general public via large, group mausoleums.

It doesn't take a financial genius to figure out that a cemetery running out of grave space can make more money by putting 2,800 caskets in a building covering as much ground as is required to bury 800 caskets. The cemetery can sell the above-ground space for far more money than a below-ground grave and there is virtually no cost to open the mausoleum space for the casket. The expense to the cemetery is the cost of the building and the advertising necessary to sell it. The advertising would have the consumer believe that grave space is limited and that there are many advantages to the above-ground burial. Quoting from the brochure from a local cemetery, "Entombment in an above-ground mausoleum provides your loved one with a final resting place free from the unfriendly elements of the earth."

BOOMERS GO OVERBOARD IN PERSONALIZING DEATH

Kalya Cengel of the Louisville, Kentucky Courier-Journal writes that adding a personal touch to death is catching on.

At least that's what College of Charleston sociology professor George Dickinson thinks. The South Carolina professor says the trend is driven by baby boomers who don't seem to like to stick with tradition.

"I think methods that a few decades ago were thought very bizarre are now very appealing to people," says Dickinson, who has written textbooks and anthologies on death and dying.

Methods that include blasting remains into space and putting them in paintings, lockets and birdbaths. Other afterlife options include turning the deceased into man-made diamonds and artificial reefs.

The latter has proved popular with environmentalists–the reefs closely mimic natural reef formations–fishermen, members of the Navy, scuba divers and people who live or vacation by water, says Eternal Reefs spokeswoman Amanda Leesburg.

Headquartered in Atlanta, Eternal Reefs mixes cremains (ashes remaining after cremation) with environmentally safe concrete to make reef balls, which are then dropped into the ocean off the shores of Florida, New Jersey, South Carolina, Texas and Maryland.

Since 1998, when the first memorial reefs were cast, almost 300 people have become reefs, says Leesburg. Thousands more have signed up to undergo the process eventually, she says. Now all they have to do is die.

Then there is the crowning jewel. Irene Bodkin wanted to hold onto her mother, Rose Daniels, so she had her cremains made into a diamond. "I wanted something near me," says Bodkin, a cancer-registry coordinator in South Bend, Indiana.

Bodkin 55, had the remains turned into a diamond by LifeGem, a Chicago-area company that came up with the idea of using carbon from cremains to make diamonds.

Bodkin had her mother made into a canary yellow, tear-shaped stone last year.

Bodkin had the stone set into a ring, which she wears daily. She likes looking at it so much, and taking part of her mother with her, she has asked her daughter, Elizabeth Bodkin, to do the same with her.

Diamonds and sea pearls aren't for everyone. That's why there are bird-baths, wind chimes and sundials–all made with cremains. Or if you want to at least acknowledge tradition, there are ways to turn funerals into "Celebration of Life" services, says Bob Jesch funeral director of D.O. McComb & Sons Funeral Homes in Fort Wayne, Ind. "We are finding they (customers) want something other than what Grandma and Grandpa did," says Jesch. This can mean bringing a golf cart or Harley-Davidson into the chapel – the company has done both.

For Batesville Casket Co., it has meant offering caskets with gardening, music and cooking themes represented by embroidery on the inside and decorations on the outside. The Indiana-based casket maker, one of the largest in the world, also offers suggestions on how funeral directors can turn funerals into theme events by adding details such as saxophones.

AFTER THE CREMATION, A UNIVERSE OF CHOICES

Barry Rehfeld of the New York Times writes more in detail about the trends.

Next month, a rocket is scheduled to lift off from Vandenberg Air Force

Base in California with 125 "passengers" on board, destines to orbit Earth for many years. Hundreds of family members and friends from around the world will watch the voyage of those passengers—actually part of the cremated remains of their loved ones, including a movie producer, a married couple and three teenagers.

In death as in life, traditions are crumbling, and independent-minded baby boomers are shopping for cremations with final destinations of all kinds for themselves, their parents and even their pets.

Cremation, now the choice of 28 percent of Americans, has been gaining on traditional burial for three decades.

The low cost – less than $1,000, according to consumer groups – has been cited as the primary reason for the shift. But simplicity isn't the hallmark of all cremations.

Ashes are being packed into fireworks, incorporated into artificial reefs, floated in balloons, painted in portraits or compressed into synthetic diamonds. That isn't all; ashes are also being sunk on putting greens or embedded into duck decoys, shotgun shells and basketballs.

"It's about everything being customized," said Charles Chafer, chief executive of Space Services Inc., the Houston company that arranges the rocket rides. "You're getting what you want. The people we serve have always loved space."

Mr. Chafer's method remains exclusive, if for no other reason than spaceflights don't follow a regular schedule; he has been able to arrange just four launches since 1997. The last in 2001 for the ashes of 50 people, became the first not to fulfill the mission of orbiting the Earth; the rocket fell into the Indian Ocean.

Even so, 46 of the 50 from that flight will be represented on the next rocket – Mr. Chafer reserves some ashes for a second flight, if needed.

This trip has been in the making for three years, and a delay would not be unexpected. The venture combines public and private interests. The $6 million Falcon I rocket is financed by Elon Musk, co-founder of Pay-Pal. He contracted with the federal government to carry one of its telecommunications satellites into space; Space Services paid to have the ashes included in the rocket.

Space Services charges $5,300 to load seven grams of ashes into a lipstick-shaped container that will be placed on the rocket. (An alternative is $995 for one gram, in a smaller container.)

Earlier flights carried the remains of Timothy Leary and Gene

Roddenberry, the "Star Trek" creator.

Alice Beach, a retired school psychologist in Palo Alto, California, had a different kind of farewell in mind when she was dying of cancer two years ago. In the months before her death at the age of 83, she told her niece that she wanted "to go out with a bang" in a fireworks display she saw advertised on the Internet. After her death, her niece, Laura Beach, paid a company, Angels Flight of Castaic, California, $3,500 to produce the show.

On a clear night last August, the niece and about 20 friends and relatives went to Dockweller State Beach, beneath the takeoff path from Los Angeles International Airport. Drinking champagne and listening on their Ipods to Marlene Dietrich singing "Falling in Love Again," they watched more than a dozen fireworks shells containing the cremated remains explode over the water.

"We were very pleased," Laura Beach said, "She had done a lot of interesting things, and this was a celebration of her life."

Joanie West, 66, of Crystal River, Florida, and her husband, Clyde, 72 operate a business, the Eternal Ascent Society, that uses high-altitude balloons to scatter remains. It releases biodegradable balloons, five feet in diameter, filled with helium and containing the ashes of humans, pets or both. The balloons float to an altitude of around 30,000 feet, where they freeze and burst, scattering their contents.

The Wests have recently begun franchising their business. "For less that $20,000 you can get a turnkey operation," Ms. West said. Five franchises have opened for business in the last couple of years.

Eternal Reefs, based in Decatur, Georgia, mixes ashes with concrete to create artificial reefs that are placed in the sea. Prices range from $495 for pet remains to $4,995 for human remains, depending on the size of the concrete casts. This year, the company will mold reefs and place them in eight offshore sites, from New Jersey to Texas; it plans to add sites off the Pacific Coast next year. The company places the reefs only in sites approved by federal, state and local governments.

And a Chicago company, LifeGem, will compress a bit of the carbon from remains into a diamond. A ring with a yellow diamond goes from $2,500 for a quarter carat to $14,000 for just under one carat.

Some consumers have ideas of their own and are willing to pay whatever it takes to carry them through. Mike Baty, an executive at Stewart Enterprises, based in Jefferson, Louisiana, which owns funeral homes, cemeteries and crematoriums, handled one such cremation and ceremony. It involved a racehorse, the ashes of its owner and a splash of Wild Turkey.

452

As Mr. Baty tells it, family and friends met at the late owner's stable, where food and drink were served in a tent, and one of his thoroughbreds was brought out by a stable hand. The owner's ashes were then piled on the horse's back.

Next, two shots of Wild Turkey–his favorite drink and the name of the bird he liked to hunt–were poured over the remains by another employee. Finally, the horse was given a whack and, trailing a cloud of ashes, ran off into the pasture.

Mr. Baty provided the cremation as well as the tent, chairs, tables, help with catering and a keepsake book. It didn't amount, in dollars, to the cost of a traditional funeral, but the income for Stewart which Mr. Baty put at $3,000 to $4,000 was more than what the company would have received just for cremation.

Such new options could help the financial picture of the funeral industry in general.

"Cremations are less profitable than funerals," which average $6,500 excluding cemetery costs, said Stephen Prothero, a Boston University professor who is the author of book on cremation, "Purified by Fire." "But they're finding out they can make money from them with new things, and they're adjusting."

At Catawba Memorial Park, a Stewart site in Hickory, North Carolina, that is near a golf course where a P.G.A. senior golf tournament is held, Mr. Baty's colleague Chuck Gallagher built a putting green last summer that will house human ashes when it opens this spring.

The green was built over two large ossuaries, or containers that can hold the ashes of many people. Visitors can pour the remains of their loved ones down one of the two putting-green holes that lead to the ossuaries.

And a visitor can choose to sink a few putts without fear of losing the ball, because the hole at the bottom of the cup is too small for it to pass through.

Around the green will be individual plots for remains and family columbariums in the shape of bronze golf bags. Prices for the plots are higher in the rows closest to the green.

Barry Laney, 54, a computer salesman and a golfer with a handicap of 8, saw the green while attending a funeral and has already paid for a place in the front row.

"I just thought it was a good idea." He said, "I have two adult children, and they play golf , too, so I figured this would give them something to do when they visit. They could putt and talk to me, I told my friends. They're interested, I hope so. I don't want to be alone."

CREMATION

Cremation offers an inexpensive alternative to in-ground or above-ground burial. It literally is the applying of extreme heat to the body to effect first, partial dehydration then burning. Cremation takes place in "retorts" which are the actual sealed chambers in which the process takes place.

Crematoriums have varying rules regarding how the deceased is to be delivered to them. Most have never dealt with a crematory that did not require that the body be in a container of *some type*. Cardboard is allowed as is "flakeboard" at some crematories. But this is likely to change as environmental laws become more strict. Since the gases from the process are vented to the outside, clean burning is becoming a concern. With the extreme heat, the compounds in glues used in fabricating burial containers are a concern to environmentalists. A rigid container must be purchased. These were available to the families for under $100. Don't ask the funeral directors who work for you to handle bodies that were not embalmed or in a proper container, regardless of what the crematory allowed. The cost of the actual cremation, with no other fees, can be as little as $130 or less.

Most people think of cremated remains as "ashes." Because of the high heat, the container (or casket) in which the body is placed has burned off, with one exception: the metal fastenings and handles do not burn. What the crematory is left with is some bone fragments and the metal fittings of the casket. What is commonly referred to as "ashes" is actually ground-up bone fragments with any other foreign matter removed. For an average adult, the remains fill a box about 12 inches by 4 inches. These processed remains are then returned to the family or the funeral director in inexpensive containers made of cardboard or plastic.

Many things can be done to memorialize the remains. They can be buried, scattered, or placed in urns for above-ground display. Many families have chosen to memorialize their loved ones by leaving them on funeral director's shelves for years! That is understandable, since cremation is regarded as a finality, if survivors do not feel the need to memorialize the cremated remains, the ashes are often forgotten. Cemeteries offer gardens for placement or scattering as do some churches. As far as law in New Jersey is concerned, cremation is final disposition. Within the bounds of environmental law, cremated remains can be scattered. In some states this can be done over public land or over private property. For instance, scattering cremated remains at sea is by far the easiest and least expensive way to bury at sea. You must travel beyond a designated mileage limit, the container must be opened so that the "ashes" dissipate, and a record must be filed as to the fact that cremated remains were disposed of in that manner. One can place cremation urns in a casket or bury them in a grave next to a casket. They can also be placed in a cemetery mausoleum. As a practical matter "ashes" are sterile and nonpolluting.

The consumer should look at cremation for what it is: an inexpensive alternative to burial. The services leading up to the act itself can be exactly the same as would take place before a burial, if the family's religious and philosophical beliefs can entertain the concept.

The cost nationwide for an "immediate cremation" varies. We define an immediate cremation as the direct disposal of, a deceased human being without any attendant services. It should be viewed as the most cost effective way to dispose of a decedent. To some people, services without the body present are sufficient for their needs.

An alternative, sometimes sought, is burial of a casket at sea. This is a difficult and complicated procedure. Veterans of the service can be aided in doing this by the Navy, which will actually take a casket to sea for burial as part of its duties. There are very stringent requirements as to the preparation of the casket and places of interment. For our purposes here, suffice it to say that it can be done.

In learning the options of burial or cremation, you as the consumer have a better idea as to how the costs of these methods of final disposition can vary. It should have become obvious at this point that you must rely on the funeral director or the cemetery salesperson to present your options to you.

MAUSOLEUMS GET LIVELIER

Ray A. Smith, writing for the Wall Street Journal in September 2003, calls the building of mausoleums, as a tomb home. He says:

> Many Americans over the past few years have upgraded where they live. Now, some are raising the standards of where they want to spend eternity. Cemetery owners, driven in part by baby boomers who are planning their parents' burials or preplanning their own, are plotting high-end mausoleums that contain amenities like waterfalls, interactive technology, elaborate chapels, gazebos and even cafés. Some tout computer chips that contain photos, bios and in some cases the voice of the deceased.

> Mausoleums, which date back to the time of the Pharaohs, are free-standing buildings used for the entombment of human remains. Inside, stacks of crypts containing caskets line the walls, many of them marked with the name of the deceased. Funeral-industry representatives say larger, so-called community mausoleums, as well as cremation burials, have increas-

ingly become a popular alternative for people who don't like the idea of in-ground burials.

But while the older mausoleums tended to be somber and foreboding, the most recent ones are a lot more welcoming, decorative and high-tech. Forest Lawn Memorial Parks and Mortuaries in Glendale, California, is planning a three-story community mausoleum complex in Renaissance style. It will feature a 2,700-crypt mausoleum; a statuary garden; a 800-seat auditorium for religious services lectures and films; a café serving coffee and light sandwiches; a space for exhibitions by local artists; and a museum displaying a permanent exhibit of artwork owned by the cemetery. The crypt area will feature technology that lets visitors press buttons on hand-held devices to retrieve photos, history and even a recorded message from the deceased via computer chips affixed to individual crypts.

In New York, Green-Wood Cemetery in Brooklyn is constructing a five-story, $16 million, 2,500-crypt mausoleum that will look "more like an office tower you might see in Manhattan," says Lou Bortolin a Portland, Oregon-based Milne Construction Co., the developer. It is expected to be completed soon, and will feature a saw tooth glass roof and two 20-foot skylights to bring in natural light, as well as two four-story waterfalls that flow into reflecting pools.

While no one tracks the construction of mausoleums nationally, Tribute Cos, a Delafield, Wisconsin, company that provides design and building services to cemeteries, says above-ground burials now account for up to 30% of all burial work it does, up from 5% to 10% just a year ago. The Prairie Home Cemetery in Waukesha, Wisconsin, says sales of above-ground burial plots have nearly tripled over the past three years.

Cemeteries began building more community mausoleums, which are more space-efficient than ground plots, partly in an effort to preserve burial space, since some have been running out of land. Even with the frills, people in the cemetery industry say mausoleum burials are often a few thousand dollars cheaper than traditional burials, which require an outer burial container to enclose the casket in the ground, a headstone, gravedigging, fees for opening and closing the grave and maintenance.

The popularity of upscale crypts is a boon for the death industry, which is a pretty stagnant business. The number of deaths per year is growing but not by much. Meantime, profits have been hurt by rising costs.

TAKING CREMATION TO THE MALL

If you're in Indianapolis, you don't have to go to a funeral home or cemetery to check out cremation options - just go to the mall.

Summer 2004, Flanner & Buchanan Funeral Centers & Crematory started renting information kiosks from Simon Malls at their Castleton and Greenwood malls. The company wanted a creative way to showcase the numerous service and product options available to people who choose cremation.

The kiosks are unstaffed and brochures with reply cards were not added until the middle of August. Even so, as of the beginning of September, company Vice President Bruce Buchanan said 15-20 phone calls, three preneed sales and four cemetery placements for cremated remains had resulted from the kiosk campaign.

The company had no problem getting the mall's management to approve the idea. Buchanan said

When approached by Flanner and Buchanan staff, mall management had that initial reaction that anyone would have of "this is an unusual topic," he said, but they quickly agreed that cremation is a topic many people are interested in, it's an important topic and there aren't a lot of places people can go for information.

In the end, Buchanan said, "instead of us having to sell the idea, they came right back to us and said it was a great idea. They really embraced it."

Flanner &. Buchanan operates both funeral homes and cemeteries, so why a display focusing on cremation? "Cremation is the fastest growing service choice in the country." Buchanan said. The company installed the first crematory in the state in the early 1900s and has been a leader in cremation services ever since. "This is just an extension of something we already provide, and have for generations."

He hopes the kiosk will spark discussions among family members "about what they want for themselves when they die," Buchanan said.

In planning what to place in the limited space available, Flanner & Buchanan wanted to "get across some sense of the value of a service - which is hard to do in a display like that, because it's a concept." Buchanan said, "We didn't want this to be overly product-oriented, but that's kind of the outcome, because the products help make up the kiosk."

Even so, in addition to the urns and other vessels for holding cremated remains, remember that cremation is not an alternative to a funeral or other service.

"We have pictures of a memorial service," Buchanan said, "and we show cremation gardens, some of the beautiful places in our cemeteries."

What we're finding is that people need permission to do some of the things they would like to do but are afraid to bring up because they're afraid they're going into a very traditional environment with a set way of doing things. We want them to know what some of their options are.

It's so hard to get information out, and there's so much misinformation about cremation. And there's a whole romantic myth that's built up around scattering.

"I try to tell people that one of the values of a cemetery is it provides tangible proof that someone in your past or someone you loved actually lived."

A computer that shows people the company's family legacies life tributes is also part of the kiosk. Using the touch screen technology people can look up their loved ones' profiles or simply see how the system works to record and preserve the life story of the deceased.

"We've had four individuals call us to make a placement of previously cremated remains in one of our cemeteries, which we think is spectacular.

The local media had just begun to take notice of the kiosk, Buchanan said at the beginning of September. "I would be surprised if we don't get more coverage."

Though they were concerned that the display would create more questions than answers, they decided not to staff the kiosks. An informational kiosk is less expensive than a selling kiosk, for one thing. For another, "often when you have someone standing there, it repels people," Buchanan said. "We wanted to let people walk up and look things over."

SOME FIND ETERNAL REST AT COSTCO

A cemetery management publication reports that it is quite possible that in the near future, shoppers will be getting even more than what they bargained for at Costco, one of the country's major wholesale clubs.

Don Baldwin of the Associated Press, writing on the same subject states that at a Costco on Chicago's north side, shoppers checking out the new casket kiosk seemed to like the idea that the same store where they buy so many things for this life was branching into the afterlife. "A casket at Costco, yeah, I think it's pretty bizarre," said Inga Barton, 53. She wondered about buying a casket with only a kiosk and small samples of the caskets' material to look over, saying, "When you go casket shopping, you want to see the whole thing." That didn't trouble John Neuhaus. "I want the adjustable bed and mattress for my neck," he joked pointing to one of the featured highlighted at the kiosk. "After all" he said, "It says eternal rest."

Others liked the idea of being able to shop for the casket long before a loved one's death. Too often, that is a time when the survivors are distressed, under time constraints and are at the mercy of funeral homes.

The retail discount store, that sells food, toiletries and other items in bulk, is now test marketing caskets at two of their Chicago area locations. Although casket sales at Costco are still in the test marketing stage, plans are to go national. The 18-gauge steel caskets, which will retail for $799 are being offered in six colors, including purple and blue. Costco also said that the caskets can be delivered within 48 hours. And, according to Busch, this product is being sold "with a lot of sensitivity," and will offer Costco members a good deal, which may save consumers $600-$800 for comparable, but not identical products at a typical funeral home.

Funeral directors are divided on their opinions about whether or not Costco's venture will last. Some believe it will go the way of many of the casket stores. That is to say, the business will not last. After all, especially in the Chicago area, cremation is becoming much more popular and none of the caskets sold by Costco can be used in the Illinois crematories. David Walkinshaw, spokesman for the National Funeral Directors Association, told CNN that he doesn't think Costco's casket market will impact the funeral home business too harshly.

Third party suppliers have been around for a while now. Costco sells caskets at $800, but many funeral homes offer caskets for much less than that amount. "I don't think this will change the landscape of the market."

Walkinshaw also said that in moments of death, people are looking for peace of mind and comfort, and don't want to be running around to different stores. "With a funeral home, they can be guaranteed that the condition and delivery of the casket will meet their requirements. With retail stores, those issues are no longer the funeral director's problem."

George Lemke, executive director of the Casket & Funeral Supply Association, said, "My immediate reaction is that we are dealing with another third party supplier. I think the final answer is going to be totally dependent on the volume of sales that this generates. We won't know that until Costco decides to take it national or fold the tent."

Lemke has done the math and doesn't see where the Costco venture will result in big numbers.

"If Costco has 40 million members nationally, let's say 5 percent of those are over age 65 and if 10 percent of those people die in a year, what kind of numbers are we looking at as potential buyers – and that's nation wide not in Chicago?" he asked. "I think those numbers tend to get fairly small fairly fast."

Lemke noted that Costco has very little invested in the casket program. "The kiosk is provided by Universal Casket Company who also provides the delivery," he said, "then you have Preferred Funeral Choices that supposedly will help the consumer find a funeral director who will offer them additional savings. How far this all goes, how much Preferred Funeral Choices makes on funeral homes that enroll in the program, how much they make in terms of commission on the services in unknown."

In the State of Illinois in October-December 2003, there were 23,209 deaths. Of those deaths, Lemke estimates that probably half were taken in the Chicago metropolitan area (11,604) and half down state. Subtract roughly a 20 percent of cremation rate (9,284), which puts the number of burials in the Chicago Metropolitan area at just over 9,000. "If Costco has 100,000 members in Chicago, I don't see big numbers," Lemke said.

If they have 100,000 members in Chicago, Lemke said there is a statistical potential for 1,000 deaths in that group per year. Subtract 20 percent for cremation. "How many of those 800 are willing to purchase a casket from Costco?" Lemke asked.

And, according to the CNN poll, less than one-third of respondents said they would consider purchasing a casket from Costco, so that reduces the universe to a potential 536 per year in the test area, or 134 per quarter. Divided by two, each test store may sell a maximum of 67 caskets.

"It's not going to hurt anybody and it is not going to make Costco rich," Lemke said.

He added, "There is no easy answer, but I feel absolutely certain that funeral directors will find a way to compete with this relatively successfully. They are not going to rollover and play dead."

Other funeral directors are more worried about Costco stealing business from the funeral home due to the fact that many people in today's society have forgotten the need for a funeral at all.

FUNERAL HELP IS A CLICK AWAY

Bob Mims of Salt Lake Tribune writes:

Sure you can buy a car, order flowers, download music, purchase videos, fill prescriptions, and even order pizza and grocery deliveries via the Internet.

But when a loved one passes away, would you log on to FuneralDepot.com, Online~Funeral.com or CasketXpress.com to Caskets-to-Go.com to send her on the way to the hereafter?

Those are real Web sites and real choices - for a growing number of Americans who don't find the concept of clicking for bargain coffins and funeral services at all bizarre in today's cyber-technology mad society.

Dean Mafliocca, president of FuneralDepot.com - "Where Overpaying Is Not Dignified" - makes no apologies for his 5-year-old site. He offers around 150 brand name caskets online, arrangements for funerals, cremations, markers and monuments, all with low price guarantees.

Through a network of nearly 50 funeral homes. Mafliocca boasts quick service anywhere in the country. He declined to identify his partners, though, noting his offering of 25 percent to 75 percent savings has made FuneralDepot.com enemies among the more traditional members of the industry.

"They are not thrilled at all," Mafliocca said. "We even have one of the largest casket companies in the world dragging us through the courts right now."

That would be the Batesville (Ind.) Casket Co., at odds with Mafliocca for selling its caskets online- purportedly a violation of the company's long-time policy of selling direct to licensed funeral homes.

"People have counted on the funeral home to help them make the best decisions, and quite often those decision are also in the best interest of the funeral homes," he said. "Then the Internet came along."

Salt Lake City's Larkin Mortuary is well aware of that, but tries to find what it sees as a dignified marriage of technology and a reputation for trust built over 120 years. The family-run business relies on references to survive - yet it is not ignorant of the Web's marketing appeal.

But Kyle Cherrington one of the firm's directors and resident computer expert, says he has taken care not to cross the line between utility and commercialism in designing http://www.LarkinMortuary.com. The site is both sensitive and well crafted, featuring an open musical interlude culminating in a field of pink tulips. There is a gallery of casket photos, and options to view online obituaries, send email condolences or order flowers delivered.

"There is no shopping cart, we aren't selling anything online, Cherrington stressed. "It exists to be educational, to help people make an informed decision. Then we can talk and work out the details together.

PartingWishes.com doesn't sell caskets, but it does promote itself as a one-stop shop for end-of-life products and services. Customers can establish online memorials, plan their own funerals, write a will or power-of-attorney, and even create, edit and securely store last messages to family and friends.

The site was co-founded four years by Tim Hewson. Today, PartingWishes.com handles 40,000 visitors monthly and has more than 15,000 clients. That, Hewson maintains, is ample evidence that a generation of cyber savvy Americans is willing to use the Internet for even the most somber of human transactions.

Online-Funeral.com offers a particularly high tech take: Internet broadcasts of funerals as they happen. And if you miss the requiem, you can purchase CD-ROMs with the ceremony movie and memorial photos, testimonials and digitized condolences included–or log on to your loved one's memorial web site to view the stored video.

Mafliocca denies his services in any way dehumanize the grieving process. Rather, he is merely using 21st century know-how to help distant mourners connect to the dearly departed.

TRI STATE CEMETERY FRAUD

Because this was such an unusual situation, the authors are presenting the story about Ray Brent Marsh of Rome, Georgia. Marsh was accused of and later found guilty of scattering over three hundred bodies around his property in Rome, Georgia.

The decaying bodies, discovered in 2002, were a shock to the authorities and the community who had no knowledge of the heinous crime being committed.

The bodies were given to Marsh, operator of the Tri-State Crematory by families for cremation. But apparently he (Marsh) had no real concern about his decision to "stash" the bodies instead.

Special Agent Cole Seal of the Georgia Bureau of investigation was so stunned by the scene when he first arrived that he could barely describe it. "I see dead people," he told reporters. "I see a whole bunch of them. I also smell dead people, and that is not good".

Tri-State was largely unregulated under Georgia law since the company generally did not deal directly with customers. This isolation from direct interaction may have been a big reason why the dumping was not noticed sooner. Funeral directors only became suspicious in the last year when Marsh began offering a new list of services.

Marsh allegedly told one mortician; "We can bury her, burn her or ... dump her decaying corpse somewhere on my property."

Georgia chief medical examiner Kris Sperry told us that even given the state and nature of the situation, the fact that the victims were already dead does little to mitigate the crime, "Plus, it would be a bit of a shock if she wasn't quite dead."

Marsh told authorities that his ailing company lacked the necessary funds to fix the incinerator and that stashing the bodies was just a way to save money. However, one fact remains that continues to stump investigators: according to experts, it takes more time and money to not cremate people than it would to go ahead and cremate them.

Recent reports have indicated that at least one of the discarded corpses was found In Marsh's own house. Marsh told friends that he was keenly interested in interior decorating, antiques mostly.

"I've been thinking of starting a themepark," Marsh told investigators. "Kind of like Bush Gardens but with hundreds of rotting corpses."

Marsh, 28 years of age, was formally charged in March 2002. Authorities in Georgia had found 339 discarded bodies in the Tri-State grounds. Of those, 109 were identified. He was charged with 174 counts of fraud for allegedly taking money for cremations he did not perform and for giving loved ones faked remains. Marsh's parents and his sister were arrested on charges of making false statements on a death certificate.

An $80 million settlement was finally reached in 2004. Families of those who had relatives scored a victory but more litigation is expected over the insurance policy that may or may not fix the Georgia facility. Will the Marsh family or the widow of the crematory founder be covered and able to receive their share of the insurance?

INSURANCE FIRMS PAY IN BIAS SUITS

Jeff Donn of the Associated Press writes that African Americans are routinely charged more than whites for burial coverage. For a century, it was standard practice at many American insurance companies. When it came to burial insurance, African Americans were charged more than whites for the same coverage.

The policies were small, paying out just enough for a modest funeral, but millions of them were sold, many to poor African American families in the South.

Now, the industry is being called to account for the years of discrepancies between what African Americans paid versus what whites paid for insurance.

Insurance regulators In many states have filed complaints. Lawyers representing African American families have brought class-action suits. And companies with policies sold by scores of insurers, unwilling to defend what is now viewed by society as indefensible racial discrimination, are settling out of court.

Between 2000 and 2004, sixteen major cases were settled, according to interviews with insurers, state regulators, and lawyers for policyholders.

Those cases covered 14.8 million policies sold by 90 insurance companies between 1900 and the 1980s.

Together, the settlements require the companies to pay more than $556 million–most of it in restitution to policyholders or their survivors, but some of it in fines, legal costs, and charitable contributions.

The two biggest settlements: American General Life and Accident Insurance Co. of Nashville, Tennessee agreed in 2000 to pay $250 million in a case involving 9.1 million policies. Metropolitan Life Insurance Co. of New York agreed in 2002 to pay $157 million for 1.9 million policies.

In one of the most recent cases, Mutual Savings Life Insurance Co.. of Decatur, Alabama agreed in June to a settlement valued at $11.6 million, according to federal court papers. Now, a final judge must approve the settlement in order for it to be in effect.

More cases are still being adjudicated, but they involve relatively small numbers of policies.

The settlements don't threaten the stability of the life-insurance industry, which has resources to cover $25 trillion work of policies.

As of 2002, more than 21 million old burial policies worth $16 billion remained in force, according to rating firm AM Best Co. But by the 1980s, the small policies had become unprofitable and few new ones were being sold. "We believe in our heart of hearts that this practice is a thing of the past," says Jose Montemayor, a Texas regulator who chaired a committee on this type of insurance for the National Association of Insurance Commissioners.

Jack Dolan, spokesman for the American Council of Life Insurers, a trade group, said the insurance industry settlements are best understood "in the context of America's complex history of race relations."

Burial insurance, also known as industrial insurance, was originally developed in Britain for sale to factory workers. Introduced in America in 1875, it spread nationwide, taking especially a stronghold in African-American neighborhoods in the Southeast.

Bessie Jones, 75, a retired domestic worker in Sarasota, Florida, says she bought a policy because, "I had no money to bury myself." Eventually, she said, she bought at least a dozen more for her children and grandchildren.

Instead of consolidating muitiple policies into a single one at a better rate, African American customers are encouraged to keep buying individual ones, po1icyholder lawyers say.

That racial bias built into these policies was long an open secret in the insurance industry. Insurance forms asked the applicant's race, and routinely charged more than whites for the same coverage, the insurance industry now publicly acknowledges.

Typically, it was one-third more, according to lawyers representing policyholders.

FUNERAL TRAFFIC: MENACE OR NOT?

Tom Greenwood writes: "I recently received an interesting e-mail from reader Carol Paquette who had a couple of comments about funeral processions.

"I wonder if you've ever done a piece on funeral processions. I personally think they should be banned. I've seen some containing over 100 cars. It's not a matter of inconvenience to others, it's a menace.

"I think It would make much more sense to simply leave the funeral home and travel to the cemetery, driving as you would normally to any destination. Considering the tremendous congestion on the roads today, the procession seems a bit outdated and very dangerous. Should funeral processions be prohibited? What do you and others think?"

Well, first of all, let's look at the laws pertaining to funeral processions. In most cases, funeral processions have to meet specific criteria when they're on the road, including:

- All vehicles in a funeral procession are supposed to have their lights on or be marked with funeral flags.

- Vehicles in a procession are to follow the preceding vehicle as closely as is practical and safe.

- A funeral procession approaching an intersection with a red light is supposed to stop, just like normal traffic. However, if the light turns red while the procession is traveling through the intersection, opposing traffic has to wait until the entire procession passes through the intersection before pulling forward.

- Pedestrians and drivers not part of a funeral procession are not to drive between, obstruct, or hinder a procession being led by a funeral lead vehicle or funeral escort vehicle.

- Funeral processions are supposed to yield the right of way to any approaching emergency vehicle giving an audible end/or visual signal.

- Funeral processions are to yield the right of way when so directed by a police officer.

So much for the ground rules. I suppose funeral processions are a pain to some people who are always in a hurry, but to tell you the truth, I don't see that many of them. As for being a menace to other drivers, I can't recall any accidents involving funeral processions.

Although I know there must be crash stories out there that involve funeral processions. I've come across more accidents involving EMS, police and fire trucks than caravans of mourners headed to a cemetery.

So I guess my personal answer is that I don't think funeral processions should be banned. The idea of everyone trying to arrive at the cemetery via separate route seems OK on the face of it, but what about out-of-towners or those who don't know their way around a map or might not find the final resting place without the procession?

To me, funeral processions are, at best, a minor inconvenience compared to the real problems out there; tailgaters, speeders, cell phone phonies and super-aggressive drivers who think they own the road.

BILL WOULD CUT FUNERAL AIRFARES

John Hughes writes that the U.S. Senate voted to require airlines to offer the lowest available fare to people flying to family funerals, after a lawmaker said the trips cost too much.

Studies show bereavement fares bought on short notice are as much as $400 higher than trips purchased in advance, said U.S. Senator John Breaux, D-La., who wrote the legislation.

A Breaux staff member paid "an extremely high price" to attend her grandmother's funeral in Lafayette, Louisiana, and brought the problem to his attention, he said.

The Senate added the proposal Tuesday to legislation that would create a national intelligence director. The Senate last week voted to restrict carriers including AMR Corp.'s American Airlines and UAL Corp.'s United Airlines on setting charges for tickets issued by an airline that fails.

Passengers complain that bereavement fares are high though "the marketplace is supposed to solve these issues," said David Stempler, president of the Air Travelers Association consumer group. "This is getting a toe in the door in terms of managing the pricing of the airlines, which we think is a bad thing."

On October 1, the Senate approved language in the intelligence bill that extends a law forcing carriers to honor tickets of failed rivals for a fee of no more than $25 each way. Neither provision is included in House version of the legislation. The Senate could pass the intelligence bill this week.

Breaux's proposal requires carriers "to the greatest extent practicable" to make the lowest fare available on a bereavement flight.

CREMATED REMAINS POSE AIRPORT PROBLEM

Cremated human remains may not seem like a national security threat, but officials at Sky Harbor International Airport in Phoenix say passengers carrying urns have become a sensitive hassle at checkpoints.

The problem: x-rays can't penetrate some urns, and screeners with the Transportation Security Administration are not allowed to open the urns.

Metallic containers often fail the X-ray test, causing a bottleneck at the checkpoint and more grief for a passenger who already carries a burden of sorrow.

"It's definitely an emotional issue," noted Catherine Burnett, a security agency liaison with commercial airlines at Sky Harbor. "Aunt Bertha is a part of their lives, and the air carriers are still having challenges with it."

Nobody knows exactly how many loved ones are carried through airport terminals, but agency officials say Southwest Airlines alone, for example, gets the remains of 60 bodies a day in Terminal 4 at the Phoenix airport. A typical urn contains about seven pounds of bone dust and crushed fragments.

Officials say the mix-up is a convergence of two major trends: tighter airport security and more human cremations.

Cremations in North America have tripled in the past three decades. In Arizona alone, more than 42,000 people die each year. The Cremation Association of North America reports that 57 percent of the Arizona corpses are incinerated.

Joe Livingston, funeral director at Hansen Mortuary in Phoenix, said people want to carry a loved one's ashes onboard to make sure they reach that final destination safely. "It's one thing to lose your underwear," he said. "It's another thing to loose an urn."

SENATE PROPOSAL FOR
PRISON BUILT CASKETS

Jun Yang of Capitol News Service in Lansing, Mich states that Bacarella Funeral Home in Monroe spends about $10,000 out of its own pocket to provide free burial services for indigent people every year.

But it would be able to save part of those costs if a bill passes to allow state prisoners to build caskets for funeral homes that offer indigent burial services.

"That'll be a great idea" owner Bill Bacarella said, "That'll make us save a lot of money."

The state now pays part of the expenses of indigent burials - a maximum of $603 for funeral homes, $200 for a cemetery plot or cremation, and $144 for vaults, which totals $947. Relatives and friends can pay up to $2,600 more for the burials.

The value of the assets and estates that decedents and responsible relatives hold can't exceed the maximum state payment to qualify for indigent burial services, according to the Family Independence Agency (FIA).

Bacarella said an indigent burial costs about $4,000 on average, and participating funeral homes absorb the amount that the state payment and family contribution don't cover. He added the price of a casket alone often exceeds the state payment.

"You've got to have a casket, a vault and staff for a burial. There's a lot to it, Bacarella said.

He said his funeral home handles about six indigent burials per year, and about half of the families contribute to the costs of burials.

Sen. Patricia Birkholz, R-Saugatuck Township, said her bill would help funeral homes handle the expenses. Sen. Beverly Hammerstrom, R-Temperance, is a co-sponsor.

"Funeral homes subsidize the costs for indigent burials, but the state doesn't reimburse them for the costs," Birkholz said.

She added there are enough resources in prisons such as carpentry classes to make her plan work.

Prisoners already are widely engaged in manufacturing wooden products, so there will be no additional financial burden on the state's part, said Leo Lalonde, the public information administrator for the Department of Corrections.

Beverly Neal, recording secretary of the Michigan Funeral Directors Association, said the bill is in an infant state and it's hard to measure how much money it would save funeral homes until the association has more discussions with Birkholz.

"The bill has come into our radar very recently. It's still being reviewed," said Neal, a director for Harrison & Neal Funeral Home in Belleville. According to the FIA, there were about 6,800 indigent burials, costing the state $5.5 million in 2004.

Bacarella said funeral homes should provide indigent burials as part of the community service, but the state needs to provide more support.

What they do is put the burden of the expense on funeral homes, he said.

Doug Rupp, who owns Rupp Funeral Home in Monroe, said even though indigent burials don't take place often, the costs still can be burdensome.

"The state doesn't provide much of assistance for folks who can't afford burials," he said. "Anything that can help them is good."

NATION IS HIT BY EULOGY OVERLOAD

Jeffrey Zaslow of the *Wall Street Journal* writes:
Like most funeral directors in America, Thomas Lynch of Milford has been hearing more and more eulogies lately. Many eulogists have delivered beautiful, heartfelt tributes. And then there are the others.

"They talk too much," he says. "They bring up inappropriate things. They're more into performance than remembrance." And they can't be stopped. "It's like karaoke. Once you open the microphone, people are going to step up to it."

At funeral homes and houses of worship, eulogists are now grabbing microphones in unprecedented numbers. Some mourners believe that if they don't speak up, their loved ones won't get a proper sendoff. With people now moving around so much, their clergy-men often don't really know them. More crucially, baby boomers now burying their parents are often more vocal and empowered than previous generations.

Before 1980, fewer than 10 percent of funerals included a eulogy by someone other than a clergyman, says Robert Vandenbergh, past president of the National Funeral Directors Association. By 1990, the percentage had risen to about 25 percent, he says. "Now, it's in excess of 50 percent." Other funeral directors say that the new popularity of the eulogy has almost doubled the average length of a funeral service, from 20 or 25 minutes in the 1980s to 35 or 40 minutes today.

But as more people buy eulogies off the Internet or confuse a eulogy with an off-color best-man's wedding speech, funeral directors are working harder to maintain decorum. They're teaching mourners basic eulogy-giving techniques: write it out, keep it short, avoid controversy, resist sobbing, and focus on the deceased, not yourself.

In Southfield, funeral director David Techner watched one eulogist speak at length about a deceased gambler's favorite bookie. Another man gave a eulogy mentioning his late father's daily habit of squeezing favorite parts of his wife's anatomy. "The point was his father loved his mother," says Techner, "but there are other ways he could have said that."

Religious leaders are looking for ways to make eulogies more appropriate and to give verbose eulogists the hook. (A minister's consoling hand on a eulogist's shoulder really means, "Enough.") Earlier this year, Roman Catholic Archbishop John J. Myers of Newark, N.J., caused a furor by decreeing that eulogies don't belong at a funeral mass.

Understandably, many mourners argue that eulogies are the most meaningful part of a service. In 2002 at an Episcopal church in Colorado Springs, Colo., Katie McNerney gave a eulogy for her fiancé, Scott Billingsley, who died suddenly of a heart ailment at age 31. She spoke movingly about his strong faith, his loyalty to friends, and his job as legislative director for a congressman. She also talked about his impersonations of George W. Bush and Marlon Brando. Since her eulogy, she says, "people have told me they were able to find some peace knowing he led such a full life."

Lynch calls eulogies "the first draft of remembrance," and he's heard many good ones at the 7,000 funerals he's overseen. Still, he's not sure all the words are necessary. "Sometimes," he says, "the best eulogy is a moment of silence."

NATIONAL FUNERAL DIRECTORS AND MORTICIANS ASSOCIATION

NFD&MA is a membership association of professional funeral directors and morticians and embalmers, whose members and members-at-large also belong to state associations of funeral directors, morticians and embalmers dedicated to promoting the common professional and business interests of its members.

The objectives of the Association are as follows:

(a) to foster research, conduct workshops and seminars, investigate funeral practices, develop and maintain standards of conduct designed to improve the business condition of its members and to maintain high standards of service for the benefit of the public.

FUNERAL HOMES AND DIRECTORS

CHAPTER ELEVEN

(b) to provide a continuing program of service and to develop and disseminate information beneficial to members and the public at large.

(c) to represent the common professional and business interests of its members before various federal, state and local legislative, administrative and judicial bodies, subject to the limitations of Section 501(c) of the Internal Revenue Code of 1954 or the corresponding provision of any future United States Revenue Code.

(d) to engage in any other activities consistent with the enumerated purposes and objectives of this Association; provided that such related activities are not inconsistent with the Code of Laws of the District of Columbia or Section 501(c) of the Internal revenue Code of 1954 or the corresponding provisions of any future United States Internal Revenue Law.

NFD&MA was organized under the name of the Independent National Funeral Directors Association in 1924 under the leadership of R.R. Reed. It was organized by a group of licensed funeral directors seeking to maintain professional standards for the benefit of the public and their own business community. The funeral directors had been meeting with the National Business League, but there was a feeling that the funeral directors were not able to develop their full potential in the Business League because it was made up of general business groups.

The first official president of the National Association was G. William Saffell, Jr. of Shalbyville, K.Y. In 1926 the name of the Association was changed to the Progressive National Funeral Directors Association. In 1940, a merger of the National Colored Undertakers Association, and those members still a part of the Independent National Funeral Directors Association, took place to become the National Negro Funeral Directors Association.

Because of the NFD&MA, African American funeral directors have had vast involvement with many historical events.

During the 1800s and the Yellow Fever epidemic, the Free African Society furnished volunteers to assist the stricken whites. These activities included gathering the human remains and carrying them away.

In 1978, African American funeral directors traveled to Dover Air Force Base in Delaware to recover victims of the Rev. Jim Jones Mass Casualty from Guyana. Many of these victims were transported to African American funeral homes to be buried by loved ones. NFD&MA member and past national treasurer, Andrew W. Nix, Jr., owner of the Nix Funeral Service, in Philadelphia, Pennsylvania had the government contract and was in charge of handling the human remains from this tragedy. There were 913 bodies, including those of Jim Jones and his family.

The NFD&MA's State Association and The Georgia Funeral Service Practitioners assisted during the mass flooding in Albany, Georgia in 1994 where more than 400 caskets were displaced from cemeteries throughout Albany.

In April of 1995, the NFD&MA's State Association, the State Embalmers and Funeral Directors Association of Oklahoma, coordinated their efforts with officials after the Oklahoma City bombing that killed 168 people.

Danny L. Percell, Sr.

Under the direction of John McGuire, the lead Disaster Coordinator for Washington, DC, funeral directors traveled to Dover Air Force Base to receive the victims of the Croatian air crash. With the group was Commerce Secretary Ron Brown and other members of his party.

The NFD&MA has a number of organizations in its association. There are some members of the NFD&MA who are also members of Epsilon Nu Delta Mortuary Fraternity, Inc. founded in 1944 in Chicago. The National Ladies Auxiliary was founded in 1952. The Birdies and the 100 Black Women in funeral service was founded in 1993. The NFD&MA is comprised of chapters throughout the United States, Caribbean and South Africa.

Some of the officers and past officers of the organization are Danny L. Percell, Sr., Percell & Sons Funeral Home in Elizabethtown, Kentucky; David Boone, Sr., Boones' Funeral Service in Chicago, Illinois; Howard C. Burton, McKenzies' Funeral Home in Tuskegee, Alabama; Hall Davis, IV, Hall Mortuary Inc. in Port Allen, Louisiana; Richard A. Lewis, Sr., Lewis & Wright Funeral Home in Nashville, Tennessee; Althea B. Pringle, Enterprise Funeral Home in Meridian, Mississippi and Wayne F. Sparrow, Sparrow Funeral Home in Orange, Texas. Sharon L. Seay is the Executive Director of this notable and influential Association, based in Decatur, Georgia.

The October 2005 issue of the International Cemetery & Funeral magazine writes about the active group – **The 100 Black Women of Funeral Service, Inc.**

Region covered: The United States and the Caribbean and we have one member from South Africa, a former scholarship recipient from Cincinnati College, states the founder.

Approximate membership: 400

Contacts: Elleanor C. Starks, CFSP, Founder and Executive Director, P.O. Box 2652, Orlando, FL 32802, 407.595.9277.

Doretha F. Hector, CFSP-CPS, president and CEO; EL Phillips Funeral Home. 1721-27 N. Monroe St., Baltimore, MD 21217, 410.523.4918;

Issues/topics of concern, states Starks:

- Founded in 1993, we are a premier leadership organization for minority women who have chosen a funeral service career. We have an active affiliate of the National Funeral Directors & Morticians Associations Inc. and give out annual leadership awards to funeral service professionals at the NFD&MA Inc. convention.

- Annual awards include Woman of the Year, Traditional Funeral Home of the Year, Nontraditional Funeral Home of the Year, President's Award of Excellence, Pyramid of Success Award in Funeral Service, Minority Entrepreneur of the Year and Funeral Service Student of the year.

- Our goals include sisterhood, scholarship, professionalism, service, leadership, networking and mentoring.

- We want to make a difference for funeral service students! We offer a student membership and provide scholarships twice a year to deserving and needy mortuary students. Their membership is for at least a two-year period; we match students with mentors if they do not currently have one.

Our goal is to ensure students' success in college and at the professional level by helping them pass the national conference exam and get internships to develop relationships with funeral directors in the states where they attended school and plan to practice. We found that many students not associated with funeral service family cannot get internships and eventually leave the profession because their lack of experience hinders their job search.

We are striving to have a working relationship with mortuary school directors and instructors.

FUNERAL HOMES

Two of the Directories read by the authors when they chose to add some older, family-owned funeral homes to the book, were the Purple Directory and the Redbook. The Purple Directory, published by Shugars of Detroit, Michigan has a complete listing of African American Funeral Homes throughout the United States with pertinent data included.

The Redbook is sub-titled the National Directory of Morticians and Buyers Guide.

Choosing funeral homes to include was one of the authors' most difficult decisions. We were proud to learn about the many family-owned funeral homes that exist coast to coast and were organized prior to 1900s.

Limited in space, we were forced to narrow our choices. Thanks to the assistance received from several funeral directors in suggesting some of the businesses.

Detroit area funeral homes are listed in the Appendix. Two responded with wonderful dated photographs. Karla Cole, director of the Cole Home for Funerals, responded with a photograph that we have enjoyed even though some of the Morticians have not been identified. James Fritz of Fritz Funeral Home allowed us to interview him and a photograph of the McFall Brothers Funeral Home and hearse was donated by Ted Talbert of WDIV Television.

Roger Husband of Swanson Funeral Home gave us some interesting history, particularly of the embalming practices of years gone by. Husband is a funeral director/mortician and also a Professor/Lecturer at Wayne State University School of Mortuary Science.

Roger Husband

Updated photograph of George B. McFall Funeral Home located at 457 Palmer in Detroit.

Pictured left to right are Paul Edwards, funeral home attendant, George B. McFall, owner.

Mr. McFall closed his business in the 1950s and joined McFall Brothers Funeral Home on

Dexter Avenue. Photo courtesy of Ted Talbert, Detroit's WDIV, Channel 4.

This photo, the property of
Karla Cole of the James H.
Cole Home for Funerals in
Detroit, Michigan shows the
Wolverine Funeral Directors
Association on November
12, 1929. Identified in the
front row are Mr. Riley,
E.M. Mason. Mack Haney,
Ben McFall, James McFall
and Mr. Willis. In the back
row are Fred Anderson,
James Cole,
Charles C. Diggs, Sr.,
Mr. Chambers, A. G. Wright,
Mr. Cook. Some are
unidentified.

SCARBOROUGH AND HARGETT FUNERAL HOME, INC.
Durham, North Carolina

Joseph Croome (J.C.) Hargett was born in 1858 and died in 1900. John Clarence (J.C.) Scarborough was born in 1872 and passed away in 1972.

In 1888, Hargett and Scarborough went into partnership in Kinston, North Carolina.

Scarborough, Sr., Scarborough, Jr., Scarborough III, and the Hargett family have an amazing story. J.C. Scarborough, Sr. received his Funeral Directors and Embalmers License on June 6, 1906, making him the first "colored" man in North Carolina to become a licensed funeral practitioner. Scarborough, Sr. also established the first licensed day care in the state of North Carolina, Daisy E. Scarborough Nursery School, in 1938. He was the founder of the Funeral Directors and Morticians Association of North Carolina which was originally the Colored Undertakers & Embalmers Association. Scarborough, Sr. was one of the organizers of the One O'clock Luncheon Club of the Durham business and professional chain. He also was a charter member of Doric Lodge #28, Free and Accepted Masons and was given the title of "The Dean of Black Business" in Durham, North Carolina.

J.C. Scarborough, Sr. and J.C. Hargett have left the present owners and managers of the business that bears their name a precious legacy symbolized in the motto, "A Dignified Service in a Sympathetic Way."

More than a motto, the phrase is a way of life for the company. It originated with an experience involving the late J.C. Scarborough, Sr. in Kinston, his birthplace, late in the last century.

The energetic young Scarborough was the son of Mrs. Fannie Harrison, who predicted her son would someday do great things for his people. At the time, however, the youth worked for a black grocer named Wiley Lowery.

As Mr. Scarborough related the story years later, at the time of Lowery's death there was only one funeral service in Kinston. It was operated by a white man. The undertaker used a horse-drawn hearse for whites and a horse and wagon for blacks.

Lowery's prominence and the appeal of his friends for a dignified funeral with the horse drawn hearse failed to move the white funeral director. He refused to change his policy for Lowery. What he did, however, was to direct young J.C. Scarborough's attention to the disparity in racial treatment and to motivate the young man to enter the undertaking business to correct the inequity.

By that time young Scarborough's path had crossed that of J.C. Hargett, another enterprising black businessman of Kinston. Hargett was well aware of that phase of Mr. Scarborough's reputation which he used to describe so colorfully as having run "errands at age 3 and clerked at age 7."

Taking the promising young man under his experienced wing, Hargett first sent him to Kittrell College, later helped him get a United States rural mail route, going so far as to supply the horse and buggy that the job required.

It was during this period that Mr. Scarborough and Mr. Hargett's daughter, Miss Daisy E. Hargett, were married. Two children, who became active in the managerial end of the business, John Clarence Scarborough, Jr., and Mrs. Ernestine Scarborough Bynum (June 27, 1911-June 12, 1996), came from this union.

Hargett's desire to see the young couple prosper led him to help his son-in-law realize his dream of establishing a funeral home for black people. Thus, early in the present century with Hargett capital and encouragement, young J.C. Scarborough opened an establishment on Queen Street in Kinston. It was given the trade name the firm uses today, Scarborough and Hargett.

The practice of embalming was spreading during the period and it became necessary for young Scarborough to meet the competition. Again, with Hargett's assistance, he ventured out — this time to the Renouard Training School for Embalmers in New York City. The year was 1903. Mr. Scarborough was the only black member of the class of 27 students.

After completing the Renouard course he considered locating in Asheville. However, Alec Moore, an agent for North Carolina Mutual Life Insurance Company, persuaded him to come to Durham, in 1906.

After several moves in 1925 the company moved to 522 E. Pettigrew Street for a 40-year stand. Then, under the influence of urban renewal, Scarborough and Hargett took up temporary quarters at 919 Fayetteville Street for nearly five years.

In a personal way the decade of the 1920s brought some changes into Mr. Scarborough's life. After many years of happiness and pioneering in business with her husband, the first Mrs. Scarborough passed. And, in March, 1926, Mr. Scarborough married the former Miss Clydie Fulwood, a humanitarian-minded teacher who shared fully her husband's dedication to public service.

One daughter, Mrs. Edythe Stanford was born to Clydie Quinn Fulwood Scarborough during Mr. Scarborough's last marriage. There was one son, J.C. Scarborough, Jr. and another daughter, Ernestine Scarborough Bynum and two grandsons, J.C.Scarborough,III and Peter Stanford.

The Scarborough and Hargett business has enjoyed several open house celebrations throughout the years. On April 21, 1974, approximately 2,000 people attended a service for the Memorial Chapels and Gardens. The mayors of Durham and Raleigh were in attendance as were numerous representatives from businesses, banking, federal government officials and funeral directors. The eighty-six years of doing business were saluted.

On Sunday, June 26, 1988, the 100th founding anniversary re-dedication service was held with even greater acknowledgement from the community. On July 5, 2006, J.C. Scarborough Sr. was posthumously honored and named by the North Carolina State Senate and the House of Representatives as the first licensed African American funeral diretcor in the State of North Carolina.

Because of its uniqueness, the facility was described in detail from the exterior to the spacious interior. The authors regret not being able to include the several pages of descriptions. In summary the property is unbelievably special. The exterior has four fountains around the building, the interior has a fountain in the lobby and the walls, lighting and furniture are magnificent. There is a garden atrium and the main chapel seats about 300.

The leadership of the Scarborough and Hargett Funeral Home for many years and the current president is J.C. Scarborough, III. He was born in Durham, North Carolina on September 12, 1937 and is the son of J.C. Scarborough, Jr. and Hattie Bell Strong Scarborough.

He is a member of Epsilon Nu Delta Mortuary Fraternity, Kappa Alpha Psi Fraternity, Mason Doric Lodge #128, Durham Consistory #218, Shrine Zafa #176, Alpha Tau Boule, and Sigma Pi Phi. He has been a member of St. Joseph's AME Church for approximately 40 years. He is a member of seven boards and a former member of six other boards and other organizations.

Mrs. Ernestine Scarborough Bynum was one of the proprietors of Scarborough & Hargett Funeral Home, Inc., and was treasurer of the organization. She was a licensed funeral service director and enjoyed the distinction of being North Carolina's first black female embalmer. She was responsible for planning, supervising and directing the complete business management functions of the funeral home.

Mrs. Bynum, determined and authorized, usually through subordinates, handled all purchases of equipment, furnishings and repairs. She was responsible for decisions, salary levels, employment terms of all staff including independent contractors, part-time staff and interns. She initiated internal personnel activities to meet objectives for staff training, equal pay, equal opportunity and managed on-going personnel activities.

In this capacity, Mrs. Bynum brought to the position the possession of a valid license as a funeral service director issued by the North Carolina State Board of Mortuary Science. She was called upon to possess extensive knowledge of the principles and practices of mortuary science, business or public administration, thorough knowledge of budgeting and accounting principles and practices and the ability to plan and direct the work of others.

In 1950, Mrs. Bynum became the first black female licensed embalmer in North Carolina. When she was a young child she was assigned some small duties by her father around the funeral home. So, she grew up in the funeral home atmosphere.

Her leadership has been evident in many organizations and she served on numerous boards.

Mrs. Bynum, as evidenced through long hours and determination to apply all of her extensive skills, gave the very best of herself through mortuary service.

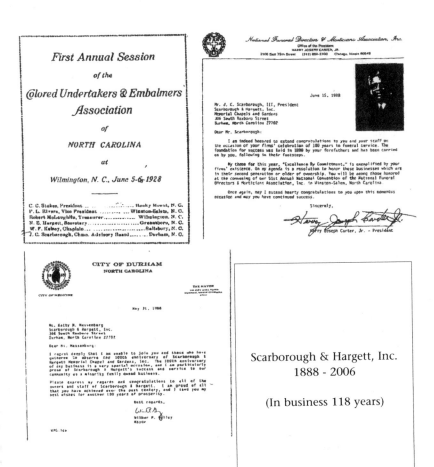

Scarborough & Hargett, Inc.
1888 - 2006

(In business 118 years)

MANIGAULT-HURLEY FUNERAL HOME
Columbia, South Carolina

After more than sixty years, what was first called Manigault-Gaten-Williams Funeral Home, and now Manigault-Hurley Funeral Home is still one of Columbia's leading funeral homes.

The businesss was founded in March 1923 by the late William and Mrs. Annie Rivers Manigault at 714 Main Street. In January 1959, they moved to 2229 Two Notch Road.

In addition to operating their funeral business at 714 Main Street, the Manigaults also owned and operated a successful casket manufacturing business, the Congaree Casket Company, at the same location. This business employed more Blacks than any other business in South Carolina at that time. Many, now prominent, Columbians worked there making caskets.

The Manigault's son Walter, who established a funeral home business in Georgetown, passed away in 1967. Their only daughter, Anna May, who married the late Anthony S. Hurley of Eatontown, N. J., had one son, Anthony Manigault Hurley, who is now the president and general manager of Manigault-Hurley Funeral Home. He is the third generation to operate the business.

Mrs. Anna May Manigault Hurley passed away on April 15, 1976. After her father's death, she had entered the famous Renouard Training School for Embalmers in New York City. After completing a very successful course study there, she returned to South Carolina and became one of the first, if not the first, females to be licensed by the state as an embalmer.

When they moved to their present location, they added the name Hurley because Mr. Hurley, who had graduated several years earlier from the Cincinnati College of Embalming had joined the firm as vice president and manager. Since this time, he has become the president and has added to his funeral home operations a beautiful ten acre cemetery, Woodlawn Memorial Gardens, located on Highway 555 (Farrow Road) about eight miles north of Columbia.

After serving the families of Columbia and surrounding areas for more than sixty-three years, the Manigault-Hurley Funeral Home continues its tradition of offering the same high calibre service to the families they serve, according to Mr. Hurley, with every detail of a funeral service receiving the utmost attention. Their staff of licensed embalmers and funeral directors have many combined years of experience and dedication.

Mr. Hurley is assisted by his wife, the former Alice Lewis Wyche of Charlotte, N. C., a retired coordinator of School Social Work Services from Richland County School District One. She is also a licensed funeral director.

The Hurleys are the parents of three children: Dr. Brian W. Hurley, who is affiliated with the Mayo Clinic Hospital in Phoenix, AZ; Kelly L. Hurley, a Phi Beta Kappa and magna cum laude graduate, who is currently employed by the Medical College of the University of South Carolina as Director of Development; Michelle Hurley Johnson, attorney for the Richland County Department of Social Services, Columbia, SC. Brian is a licensed funeral director and Michelle is a licensed funeral director and embalmer.

Michelle M. Hurley tells us about the family and some interesting tales:

Having been in business for four generations we have witnessed many communal traditions, family traditions and rites of passage. African-American, funeral parlors were born out of the necessity to honor our African customs by adhering to proper burial practices. These customs were not always practiced during slavery because white slave owners often would not allow slaves the time to properly bury the dead. Many times slaves were buried without their families being present or without even giving notice to the family that the person had died. However, the burial ritual among the Africans was so vital to the slaves that many variations of their rituals have survived many generations and are still practiced in some form today.

In the late 1800's and 1900's, Blacks capitalized on the business opportunities that arose out of the white funeral parlor owners not exactly refusing to bury blacks, but having their black neighbors do the work for them. Eventually Black owned funeral parlors began to open up all across the south and Columbia was no exception. During the nineteen twenties, we were one of four Black owned funeral parlors operating in Columbia.

In South Carolina, there are many burial traditions among the African-American Commmunities. We view dying not as the last horizon, but as a "Going Home" to a place where there is no more hardship, grief, or disappointment, but where we walk the streets of gold in a land where God has promised man we would be eternally happy and free. Death is seen as a passage to everlasting life. There is a story I hear at many funerals that relates to dying as the way to eternal life: Every day on a city bus the bus driver stops at a cemetery and this old lady gets off and walks through the cemetery. One day a man asks the bus driver, why does the old lady get off at the cemetery everyday? What could she possibly be doing in that cemetery? The bus driver pulls the bus up a few feet and asks the man if he sees the chimney on the over side of the cemetery. He continues by saying that the old lady has to walk through the cemetery to get home.

Having lived next door to our funeral home all my life and having been blessed with looking like "Your father spit you out", I have been well acclimated in this business. I remember riding on the hearse on a funeral service before I could even walk. As I grew older, my jobs began to change.

At one point, I was the keeper of the smelling salts. When I was little,

William & Annie Rivers Manigault
Founders

Mr. & Mrs. Anthony Manigault Hurley
Managers amd Directors

SINCE 1923
Manigault-Hurley
FUNERAL HOME, INC.
3229 TWO NOTCH ROAD   COLUMBIA, S.C. 2
Phone: 803/254-0639

Four
Generations
Of
Service

Anna May Manigault Hurley
In Memoriam
Pioneer Female Mortician

Michelle Manigault Johnson, Esq.
Our Fourth Generation

people would more often than now "get the Holy Ghost" and fall out during funerals. My job was to run up to the people and stick the salts under their noses. I had to jump back quickly though, because those were some powerful salts and the people would jump up and I would get pushed in the chaos.

I have also witnessed, and heard about many funeral customs in the Black community, many of which grew out of superstitions and fear of the dead. For example, I recall my father telling me that my grandmother and great-grandmother would bury stillborn and newborn babies face down. Doing so, would ensure that the next child born would not die. Also, passing a child over the open casket and/or grave would ensure that the child would not be afraid of the dead persons spirit. Sometimes people would bury babies underneath the home so that the spirit of the baby would not roam around looking for its familiar home or parents.

Often times, all the clocks in the house would be stopped at the hour of death. This custom, it was believed, was to stop the dead spirit from spending more time on earth. Sometimes mirrors would be turned toward the walls. I have heard people say this was done because it was believed dead spirits could be seen in mirrors. Also, I have seen people put all kinds of earthly materials inside caskets. Things that the person will need on his journey to Heaven, like bottles of water, or bottles of liquor, food, stuffed animals, their favorite records, coins and dollar bills.

Many customs are steadily changing. Wakes originally evolved during the time of Jesus. When Jesus died, he arose on the third day. The reason we know this is because during those times there was no such thing as modern medicine; therefore, people would keep watch over the dead person, making frequent visits to the sepulchre for three days, hoping there would be some signs of life. After three days, the person was buried. I recall hearing about wakes, where the deceased person would be returned home and the family and friends would sit up all night with the body. During the short twenty six years I have lived on this earth wakes have changed tremendously. At one time a wake meant the family would come to the funeral home and sit for three to four hours while friends would console the family. A minister would deliver a short eulogy, there would be choir members, an organist and a few remarks made. Eventually the wake has become "the family hour". Usually there is no eulogy given, no remarks made, no choir members to sing and no organist to play. The family comes to the funeral home for an hour or so to greet friends.

Another custom that is still practiced today, and that undoubtedly originated from the fear of the dead, is the wearing of mourning clothes. Fearing the return of the dead spirit, people first wore dark clothing as disguises, so that the spirit would not recognize its family members, and therefore, would not be able to haunt them. Originally mourning clothes were worn for a long period of time after the death of a loved one. However, these days, such clothing is usually worn the day of the funeral, and is done so out of respect for the dead.

Since I have been home working in our funeral home, I have looked through old funeral records and have realized that looking through funeral files is the perfect way for people to research their family trees. We have records that often identify birth places, names of relatives, old addresses, phone numbers, burial places, maiden names, etc... Sometimes, after cross referencing, I will be able to find records of entire families. I have been amazed and mesmerized by the gold mine of history the funeral home has in records that date back almost 100 years.

I am blessed to have been born into a family of Funeral Directors. I have learned that there is nothing more important than knowing one's history. I find complete joy when I sit down and talk with a person, someone who knew my grandparents, or great-grandparents or who lived through segregation or who has a knowledge beyond anything I could ever learn in school. There is so much to be said and so much to be heard. Each family has a story to tell about their own piece of land where their history lies.

We, at Manigault-Hurley Funeral Home will continue our tradition of helping and caring for bereaved families. Our experience in funeral service spans four generations. I am proud to be a part of this history.

N. J. FORD & SONS FUNERAL HOME

Memphis, Tennessee

Lewis C. Ford and Ophelia Edna Geeter Ford, who were born shortly after slavery in the United States, had a child, NEWTON JACKSON (N. J.) FORD, who was born on June 13, 1914 in Memphis, Tennessee. His paternal grandparents, Newton F. Ford and Lonnie Ford were prominent in the community. Newton F. Ford, for whom he was named, was a Squire (Shelby County Commissioner now) of Shelby County in the 1890's. Ford Road School and Ford Road were named in his honor. He also gave land to the A.M.E. Zion Churches and, subsequently, Ford's Chapel A.M.E. Zion Church was also named in his honor. His maternal grandparents were Jackson Geeter and Mrs. Geeter for whom Geeter School and Geeter Road were named.

Newton Jackson Ford

1914-1986

Newton Jackson (N. J.) Ford attended school in Shelby County, Tennessee graduating from Manassas High School. He was employed for a short time as the keeper/trainer of the famous Peabody Ducks at the Peabody Hotel in Memphis, TN, where he met his wife of 53 years, Vera Davis Ford. N. J., a mortician and licensed funeral director and, Vera, a licensed funeral director, were Blessed to have 15 children, 12 children that survived them at the time of his death. Their involvement in community and public affairs inspired their children to also pursue political careers as well as Funeral Service. Consequently, Harold E. Ford was elected to the Tennessee State Legislature in 1970, and to the U. S. House of Representatives for the Ninth District of Tennessee in 1974 for 22 years, until 1996 when his eldest son, Congressman Harold Ford, Jr., the current Congressman, won election. John N. Ford was elected to the Memphis City Council in 1972 until 1980, and in 1974 to the Tennessee State Senate to date. Emmitt H. Ford was elected to the Tennessee State Legislature in 1974. Dr. James W. Ford, also an ophthalmologist and Pastor of Fellowship Church of God in Christ, was elected to the Memphis City Council in 1979 and to the Shelby County Commission in 1994, until his death in 2001. Joseph S. Ford, President and CEO of the Funeral Home, was elected to the Memphis City Council in 1994, and to the Shelby County Commission in 2002, to present. Edmund H. Ford was elected to the Memphis City Council in 1999 to present. Other siblings working in the business include Ophelia E. Ford, CFSP, and Joyce F. Miller. Melvin D. Ford lives in St. Louis, Lewis G. Ford lives in Pasadena, Vera Ford lives in Detroit, and Barbara Ford Branch lives in New York.

Lewis Ford established Ford Funeral Home in 1932, and died six months later. N. J. was not of age, legally, to carry on the business. His mother, Ophelia Edna Geeter Ford, did not like running the business and petitioned the Probate Court to have his minor handicap removed to carry on the business and prevailed. In the meantime, as recorded on a live taped interview dated October, 1977, N. J. indicates that a Mr. Whitney and Mr. Marshall approached his mother to become her partners. They became partners for less than two months and N. J. decided that he wanted to be in charge himself. He named the business the N. J. Ford Funeral Parlor. Many years later, he changed the name to N. J. Ford & Sons Funeral Parlor, in recognition of his sons' interest in the business.

N. J. further explains that in 1933, and over the years it was rough, because he had only handled a few cases. However, by 1936 business had increased to 50 cases that year, by 1977 volume had increased to 366, and the business got better every year. He tells how the ambulance service business and public relations with the community helped to make ends meet. Today, approximately 800 cases a year are served.

Throughout the years the funeral home was housed in seven other locations before the current location that N. J. designed himself in downtown Memphis at 12 Newton J. Ford Memorial Parkway. The number 12 was available at that time, consequently he chose 12 South Parkway West, symbolically representative of each of his children. He added 14 windows to the main chapel of the Funeral Home, representative of his 12 children and he and Vera. Additionally, the Funeral Home has buried numerous greats as *Roots'* Alex Haley, Blues entertainer Albert King, assisted with Detroit's Martha Jean (the Queen) Steinburg, Atlanta Life Insurance Company's Lieutenant Lee, Chancellor Floyd Peete, Honorable Judge Luke Moore, Songwriter and Rhythm and Blues Artist Homer Banks, to name a few.

The outreach program includes Adult Vacation Bible School, booklets about families then and now and information on clothes and fashion.

When the name N.J. Ford is brought up, people immediately think of the Ford family. This is easily understandable for this man lived for his family. He and his wife of fifty three years, Mrs. Vera Davis Ford, were blessed with fifteen children, twelve of whom survived him at his passing in 1986.

As mentioned, Newton Jackson Ford was born in Shelby County on June 13, 1914. His parents were Lewis and Ophelia Geeter Ford. He was named for both his grandfathers, Newton Ford who served on the county commission in the 1890s and Jackson Geeter who served in the United States Army during the Civil War. Geeter School, located at Horn Lake Road and Shelby Drive was named after the Geeter family.

Mr. Ford attended elementary school in Shelby County and graduated from Manassas High School. After graduation, he was employed for a short time as a busboy and keeper of the legendary ducks at the Peabody Hotel. It was during his employment at the Peabody that Mr. Ford met and married his wife.

As mentioned, while only eighteen years of age, Mr. Ford established N.J. Ford Funeral Home which he later renamed N.J. Ford and Sons Funeral Parlor, in recognition of his sons' interest in the business.

His involvement in community and public affairs inspired his sons to pursue political careers. Harold E. Ford was elected United States Congressman in 1974; John Newton Ford was elected to the Memphis City Council in 1972, to the State Senate in 1974 and to the General Sessions Clerk's Office in 1992; Emmit H. Ford was elected to the State Legislature in 1974 and Dr. James W. Ford to the Memphis City Council in 1980.

Congressman Harold Ford describes his father as "a champion, one who knew how to live with pain and move right ahead and offered strength to his family".

Senator John Ford said his father was an inspiration and "he worked all of his life to insure that all of his children were educated".

For more than twenty years, Mr. Ford was a member of the Southwest District Chickasaw Council of the Boy Scouts of America. He was a former president of the Bluff City Funeral Directors Association, a former chairman of the Tennessee State Funeral Directors and Morticians Association and a former assistant executive secretary of the National Funeral Directors and Morticians Association.

Mr. Ford held a life membership in the National Association for the Advancement of Colored People and was the recipient of numerous awards and honors from local and national institutions and organizations.

FRITZ FUNERAL HOME

Detroit, Michigan

James B. Fritz tells the story of Fritz Funeral Home and his late father, M. Kelly Fritz.

In the early years of the twenties, Mr. Samuel W. Franklin established a funeral home in Detroit. Franklin later moved his firm to 217 East Garfield Street between Brush & John R. Street in Detroit.

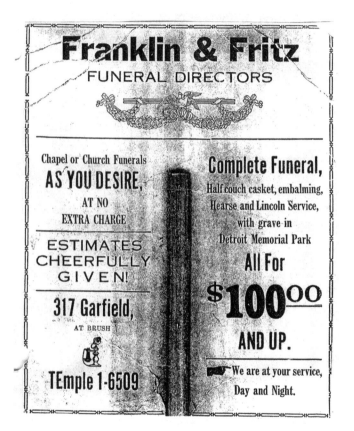

During this time, M. Kelly Fritz, my father was in Philadelphia, Pennsylvania attending the very prejudiced Eckels College of Mortuary Science, finally receiving his degree. The College had a fine reputation but was lacking greatly in civil rights skills and upon my father's graduation in 1925, he and the other few students of color could not even attend the graduation party sponsored by the school.

My father then moved to Washington, Pennsylvania where he worked at the George Washington Hotel as a waiter and bus boy to save money to return to Detroit, Michigan where he had moved from Uniontown, Alabama where he spent his early years. It was in Washington, Pennsylvania where my father met my late mother, Miss Dorothy Christina Brady who had lived there for many years. After approximately two years my father and mother married and in 1927, I, James B. Fritz was born.

In approximately 1930, my parents moved to Detroit and my dad worked at the Detroit Athletic Club waiting tables and trying to save more money to attempt to get in the funeral services business.

In 1933 or soon after, my father met Samuel Franklin and he was allowed to work and train under Mr. Franklin at his funeral home. In 1935, they formed an alliance and renamed the funeral home as the Franklin & Fritz Funeral Home. It was located at the corner of 329 Garfield Street at Brush Street and they had a fine reputation for many years and the business reasonably prospered.

Unfortunately, Mr. Samuel Franklin died in 1937 and my father then changed the name of the funeral home to the Fritz Funeral Home where he worked and established a business with a very good reputation in the city.

Looking back on those years, I can remember being in a group of my father's friends at the businessmen's favorite gathering place, the St. Antoine YMCA. We attended many lunches and met many of Detroit's well-known and productive citizens of the era. I remember meeting people with names like Dr. J. J. McClendon, Dr. Robert Greenidge, Ramon Scruggs, Dr. Haley Bell, Dr. Harmon, Dr. Guy Saulsberry, Dr. Postles, and many others too numerous to remember. Also I cannot forget names like John Dancy of the Urban League, and so many others.

In 1949, my father purchased the present funeral home at 246 East Ferry Street and we have been at this location for all these many years. This business has been a forerunner in Detroit for many years and in 1961, I, James B. Fritz joined the business where I have now completed 50 years of service. Fortunately, my late father who died in May 1995, lived to see my daughter, Christina become our third generation in funeral services in 1994. We have attempted to continue the same quality services started by my father to this present day.

As I have said, we continually try to maintain the classic services and the reputation started and founded by my beloved dad.

Author's note: In June 2006, James B. Fritz and his wife Mary, closed their funeral home and sold the building to a near-by educational institution. We want to congratulate the family for the many years of dedicated service in the Detroit area. Fritz Funeral Home will be missed. However, we wish the family many wonderful years of retirement.

INDIANAPOLIS, INDIANA

Black funeral homes in Indianapolis

Many African American funeral homes have been recognized for their tradition of serving families in Indianapolis and for lending a gentle, comforting hand during times of need. In years past, funeral directors and their businesses were among the major sources of economic pride.

Staff writer, Brandon A. Perry of The Indianapolis Recorder writes about the outstanding black-owned funeral homes in Indianapolis, but he also deals with the questions of shifts in clientele and, to some, the matter of competition. As in many large cities, white-owned funeral homes and large conglomerates are vying for African American clients as never before.

Willis Mortuary

Willis Mortuary, formed in 1890, is the oldest surviving black funeral home in Indianapolis. Formed by Missouri native Cassius Clay Willis, the establishment later became one of several flourishing African American business ventures located on or near Indiana Avenue. Upon Cassius Willis's death in 1920, his son Herbert Willis became owner and steered the company through good and tough times. Although the mortuary is no longer in the Willis family, current owners have emphasized that they would like to continue the Willis legacy of providing "services within the means of all."

People's Funeral Home

The second oldest funeral business in Indianapolis, **People's Funeral Home** was established not far from Willis Mortuary at 536 N. West St. in 1919. The company, recently celebrating its 85th year, was incorporated by attorney Harry Dunn and his wife Lula, who had originally used the name People's Burial Co.

After her husband's death, Lula Dunn undertook sole responsibility and it is widely believed she was the first African American woman to be licensed as a mortician in the state of Indiana. In 1939, however management was turned over to her brother, B.J. Jackson.

People's Funeral Home gained a significant amount of social and cultural importance over the years as many local funeral directors enjoyed apprenticeships at the company before starting out on their own. In 1979 Robert M. Hayes, current owner, purchased People's and moved the business to its current facility at 5252 E. 38th St.

Robert Hayes takes tremendous pride in the legacy of the 85-year-old business. He lives by its reputation and maintains that the staff, throughout the decades, has worked hard and continues to be very honest with people in every way by treating them fair.

"We have never had a funeral over $10,000 at the company since I have been in the business here," Hayes said. "We just don't charge unreasonable amounts and I always say to people that it isn't necessary to spend a whole lot of money on the right funeral. A family can have a proper, decent funeral within an affordable perimeter without sacrificing quality".

Hayes also noted that People's has a large dining area on the second floor of his building. After moving People's into the former insurance company facility, Hayes decided to keep the casket room downstairs to make space for a cafeteria where families can congregate and enjoy meals after returning from graveside services. He declared that People's was the first funeral home in Indianapolis to offer such accommodations and his innovation is now being copied by larger companies.

Craig Funeral Home

Coming in at No. 3 on the list of Indianapolis' surviving historic black mortuaries is **Craig Funeral Home**, located at 3447 N. College Ave. Brothers William L. and Joseph Craig opened their original facility in January 1936 at 102 S. Senate Ave., in an effort to service the growing African American neighborhoods on the near Southside.

Craig Funeral Home has the distinction of being the only funeral business in the city to be relocated twice due to highway construction, first from their Senate Avenue building, then had to move out of the subsequent location on Capitol Avenue.

Finally, in 1974 Craig bought its current building from the Patton Funeral Home. That same year William Craig died and his son, William Jr., assumed leadership along with his late mother, Julia (Joseph had moved to California). William Craig Jr. operates the business along with his brother James and sister, Ellen Craig Johnson.

Willis Mortuary, Peoples Funeral Home and Craig Funeral Home are three of the older funeral homes in Indianapolis. However the list of several other funeral homes with distinct family ties though not historic, were brought to the authors' attention.

In 1948 Dr. William Weir Stuart, a dentist and his wife May were looking for a building that could house a mortuary business that had just been formed by their sons Charles E.Q. and Joseph Stuart. The family purchased Flanner House's original facility at 812 N. West St. and **Stuart Mortuary** was officially incorporated in 1951.

Mara Stuart, daughter of Charles Stuart and a current director for the family enterprise, described her father and uncle as progressives who introduced many innovations in funeral service during the 1950s.

"My father always said that he and his brother were the first Black funeral directors to carpet the chapel," she said. "Our former facility was refurbished with ornate tiling and was among the few to have central air conditioning."

Stuart Mortuary has long since abandoned the use of standard hearses in favor of white Cadillac flower cars, which are recognized instantly by passersby. After moving to their current building at 2201 N. Illinois St. in 1979, the Stuarts also became the first funeral directors, black or white, to employ the use of six door presidential limousines.

Mara Stuart said the company has found itself in a major era of transition following the deaths of Joseph and Charles Stuart in 1999 and 2002, respectively.

Stuart Mortuary at 2201 N. Illinois St. has placed an emphasis on maintaining a high standard of services for over 50 years.

"My father always said that we have to be able to sleep at night," said Mara Stuart. "So therefore we have always prided ourselves on the merchandise we offer to the families. The quality of our services speaks for itself. From a personal perspective this is a calling for us, not just a means to make money. We are very blessed to have a staff of funeral directors who have a heart for serving, regardless of the long hours and emotional trauma that is often associated with this business."

Lillard Boatright opened his funeral home just a block south of the Stuart building in 1951. Despite its status as one of the most popular Black mortuaries in the city, **Boatright Funeral Home** was sold shortly before its founder's death in 1998. His son, Marvin L. Boatright, currently operates his own facility at 2701 N. California St.

Marvin L. Boatright said his family has always prided themselves on going beyond the call of duty to ensure that families are more than satisfied with the service they receive.

During the 1995 funeral of Rev. Arthur Johnson, former pastor of Friendship Baptist Church, Boatright said he was able to arrange for 800 chairs, a 40 by 80 foot tent at the church, a special-order horse drawn carriage and 10 large-screen televisions for visitors in a matter of days. During another service, he said, the funeral home saved a family money by going down to Mississippi to pick up a 400 pound accident victim instead of insisting on the family using an airline, which would have led to huge cargo costs.

In addition many families have placed faith in Boatright because of his company's reputation of restoring a life-like appearance to relatives who have died in unusual circumstances such as shootings and car accidents. This enables a family to actually see a victim for one last time.

"Many will tell you that there have been a number of families who thought the casket could not be opened because of what may have caused the death," Boatright said. "But through talent and God-given skill I have created a name for myself individually as a good embalmer and restorative artist. My father always said if you are doing everything right in the back room, then the family will be pleased up front in the chapel."

Boatright recently moved his family's business back to its original facility at 2163 N. Illinois St.

Boatright speaks clearly to the issue of black families and black funeral homes. He recalls the variety of ways used since the very beginning: "When we talk about decent advertising let's mention the parishioners sitting in their church on a hot day keeping themselves cool by using fans with pictures of a black funeral home on the back of them," he stated. "What about Aunt Sally's wedding and all the extra chairs that were used from one of our chapels? And don't forget the fact that even recently young couples were borrowing limousines from Black funeral homes during a time of year when there aren't enough to go around for everyone who's having a prom".

Joseph W. Summers, a graduate of the former Indiana College of Mortuary Science, opened **Summers Funeral Chapel** near the corner of 34th Street and Keystone Avenue in 1962. In addition to his reputation as a shrewd businessman, Summers was also viewed as someone who cared deeply about his community. After serving as deputy Marion County coroner, he was elected to the Indiana House of Representatives in 1976.

Upon his death from cancer in 1991, Summers was succeeded as operator of the chapel by his daughters Natalie Summers-Henson and Vanessa Summers, who was also elected to his seat in the Indiana House.

Also, in 1962 Richard Williams established Williams Funeral Home at 2451 Andrew J. Brown Ave. before purchasing a second building on West Street. In 1992 Nathan L. Bluitt, Jr. whose father still operates a funeral home in Kokomo, purchased the business from Williams and renamed it **Williams & Bluitt Funeral Home**.

Many industry insiders agree that Bluitt's reputation for commitment to customer service led to a rapid expansion of the enterprise. Within a few years the chapel was refurbished, and Williams & Bluitt replaced their older hearses and limousines with a shiny, new fleet of black cadillacs.

Although Richard Williams died in 1999, Bluitt said he will always keep his name on the company.

"We have decided to keep his name connected to the funeral home as a sign of respect and dedication to all the hard work he put into developing this business," Bluitt said.

Williams and Bluitt Funeral Home, a thriving black business, has been reaching out to Hispanic families, conducted a massive refurbishment of its chapel and has, in addition to their already impressive fleet of cars, ordered a new flower car to better serve and offer more variety to families.

Oscar Grundy, a licensed mortician, spent many years working for Mark Batties after the latter purchased Patton Funeral Home in 1946. When the Batties family moved Patton Funeral Home from 2357 Dr. Martin Luther King St. in 1972, Grundy stayed behind and formed **Grundy Memorial Chapel** two years later.

One funeral home that is known for its warmth is **Lavenia's Home for Funerals** at 5811 E. 38th St., created in 1987 by Lavenia C. Jacobs. She is the widow of Rev. Plummer D. Jacobs, who along with his brother Cary, founded Jacobs Brothers Funeral Home in the early 1930s. Not long after Rev. Jacobs died in 1980, Jacobs Brothers Funeral Home closed its doors, and Lavenia Jacobs saw the need to branch out on her own.

In 2002, Lavenia's Home for Funerals, and Summers Funeral Chapel merged with Emanuel Smith to create the full-service Lavenia, Smith & Summers Home for Funerals.

Lavenia, Smith and Summers Home for Funerals, still at 5811 E. 38th St., has gained acclaim for their dove release program at graveside services. The most popular version takes place after the committal during which three doves, representing the Holy Trinity are released into the sky, circling the grave once. A final dove representing the spirit of the departed person joins the previous three in flight, circling the grave three times before flying into the heavens.

"The dove release program has been a tremendous blessing that the Lord has inspired us to do," said Emanuel C. Smith of Lavenia, Smith and Summers. "It's just beautiful and really adds closure to the service."

In addition, the funeral home offers scholarships for students, offers a Bible to each family it serves and has a fleet of gold Lincoln funeral cars that remain unique in Indianapolis. During the 2004 Indiana Black Expo,

Lavenia, Smith and Summers hosted a booth that offered helpful information about funeral pre-planning arrangements.

Local families have also been keeping their eyes on two relatively new additions to the funeral service industry in Indianapolis, **Ellis Mortuary** and Mahogany Funeral Parlor.

Ellis Mortuary is located at 1503 Columbia Ave. inside a facility once owned by the legendary King and King Funeral Home, which went out of business during the 1980s. Darryl Ellis, who arrived on the scene in 2000, has an establishment that puts what many see as cosmetic gimmicks aside in an effort to maintain a linear focus on properly serving families in their time of need.

"We strive to do one thing extremely well – providing superior, premium service for those who place their trust in us," Ellis said. "Our goal is to serve families the way they want and need to be served."

Jeffery Perkins, who opened **Mahogany Funeral Parlor** in 2003 after 12 years of working for other funeral homes, hopes to attract families looking for a special, unique experience as they bid their final farewell to loved ones. Some clients who have visited the 98-year-old building at 2215W. 16th St. have remarked that attending a service at Mahogany is like stepping back in time to a classic funeral from the 1940s or '50s, hence the fact that it is called a funeral parlor instead of a funeral home.

Perkins said some people might call his style old fashioned, but he wants to ensure that family members have all the time and personalization they need to completely celebrate a life, instead of trying to be extremely efficient and ushering a family out of the parlor.

"With us there is no such thing as a standard funeral, and we believe each service must be as unique as the person it honors," Perkins stated. "With this type of parlor we are able to give much more attention to detail."

Crown Hill Cemetery And Funeral Home

Several of the Indianapolis funeral home directors have expressed their opinions regarding the African American clientele that select the white-owned cemetery-funeral home combinations. (This is not legal in some states, including Michigan.) Crown Hill Funeral Home with Crown Hill Cemetery, and Flanner and Buchanan Mortuary chain, with cemeteries at Washington Park North and Washington Park East have gradually begun to service greater numbers of African Americans because they reportedly have the advantage of operating the funeral home on cemetery grounds.

Keith Norwalk, president and CEO of Crown Hill Cemetery, admits that Crown Hill Funeral Home attracts approximately fifty percent of black families in the local industry, but added that the impact has been across the board, affecting traditional white-owned funeral homes in the city also.

"It's not the African American funeral homes any more than it is those who serve other parts of the city," said Norwalk "The Crown Hill Funeral Home was built ten years ago with the mission of providing expanded and convenient services for families," Norwalk said.

"When you have a family who can take care of both their funeral and cemetery arrangements simultaneously, particularly at the time of need, the convenience is measurable. I think what we're seeing is that families are recognizing that convenience."

Norwalk added that because Crown Hill Funeral Home is nonprofit, revenue generated by Crown Hill Funeral Home goes to the perpetual care of the cemetery, which is attractive to clients who already have relatives buried there.

"I really think it's a service issue. Our mission is to serve the families of Crown Hill. We do look at families who have a heritage, and we believe it's in their best interest that a variety of services are available at one location for them. Families end up making the best decision that fits their needs," he said.

Leon D. Smith, an Indianapolis man who held services two weeks ago for his wife Henrietta, said race was not a factor in selecting Crown Hill Funeral Home for the service, "Crown Hill is close to us and all of my relatives are buried over there. Our family just thought it would be a good move," Smith said. "They did an excellent job and I never thought anything about them being white owned."

Ethel Mae Hood, on the other hand, is symbolic of families who have remained true to certain black funeral homes for several years and plan to continue doing so. When her husband Harry died in March at the age of 74, Hood had him taken straight to Stuart Mortuary.

"Our family has been doing business with the Stuarts since they buried my father back in 1956," she said. "Other members of our family have been laid to rest by them since that time and they place a strong emphasis on quality. When I say we're friends for life, that's what I mean."

Critics of the management at black funeral homes have often said that these professionals must do a better job of advertising and marketing in the community if they want a bigger piece of the industry pie.

In September 2005, the Detroit Free Press ran a long story on Crown Hill with a detailed map and a photograph of the gigantic and impressive 34th Street Gate. Jenny Montgomery writes that this is the third largest non-government cemetery in the nation.

Today, Crown Hill is home to more than 100 species of trees. About 25 miles of road and 4,000 trees lie within Crown Hill, which, at 555 acres, is one of the largest cemeteries in the country.

The grounds feature a Gothic Chapel built in the late 1800s and a burial plot including the remains of more than 1,600 Confederate soldiers who died in Indianapolis as prisoners of war. Their names are inscribed on 10 bronze plaques that make up a monument to those fallen.

Among the 190,000 people buried at Crown Hill are Rev. Mozel Sanders, a civil rights and community leader, 1924-1988 and actor James Baskett, best known for his role of Uncle Remus in Disney's Song of the South.

CHURCHMAN FUNERAL HOME
Newark, New Jersey

To my family, families we have served in the last 100 years, and other friends:

I am extremely proud of our high standard of ethics and professionalism that have been passed by my grandfather and father to me as the third generation of funeral directors in my family. I have been licensed now for 50 years as the result of the encouragement of my mother and father.

My respect and pride reached unlimited levels when both my son James E. Churchman III and daughter Edith C. Churchman became licensed funeral directors hence the fourth generation of Churchmans in the funeral service profession.

Much of the success of our family goes to the never failing love, support and willingness to always be there when needed by my wife, E. Corinne Churchman.

I am extremely indebted to the families we have served for their faith and loyalty that in their time of need allow us to serve them.

One of my granddaughters informed me that she would be a fifth generation funeral director. So, at this time, I have a promise from one out of seven of my grandchildren with a hope and wish for more to follow in our footsteps.

I thank my family, colleagues, neighbors and staff for their help and assistance for the past generation of service. We look forward to many more years of serving God by serving human kind.

James E. Churchman, Jr.

For the past 100 years, there has been a member of the Churchman family actively involved in the funeral service profession in the greater Essex County area of New Jersey. The story of the Churchman family is both complex and simple. It is a story of determination, vision and a desire for betterment.

It all began in 1863 with the birth of James E. Churchman in Loudon County, Virginia. James, the son of Thomas and Isabella Churchman decided to move to New Jersey in the waning days of the 19th century to further his goals of establishing his own business and having a positive impact on the lives of men and women of color. James was a business man, minister, poet, author and social activist. In 1916 he authored the pamphlet "Welcome My Colored Brother," a work devoted to telling newly arrived immigrants from the south how to deport themselves in public in their new Northern home state. Rev. Churchman's social activism included an arrest for demonstration during the screening of Birth of a Nation which he deemed deroga-

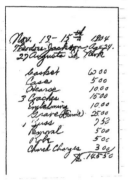

100th Anniversary Celebration

James E. Churchman, Jr.
Funeral Home
345-13th Avenue
Newark, NJ 07103
(973) 242-8454

1899   1999

tory. He later went on to pastor St. Luke AME Church when it was located on Baldwin Street in Newark, and heated by a pot belly stove. However, Rev. Churchman's greatest accomplishment and legacy, which spanned 100 years was the establishment of his funeral home in 1899 at 3 Baldwin Street Orange, NJ. A sign in the window proudly proclaimed, "James E. Churchman & Co., Undertakers," and Rev. Churchman became, as far as is known, the first of his race to actively practice funeral service in Essex County. Indeed Rev. Churchman was the first African American to own a hearse and coaches during the time of horse drawn livery. In 1917, Rev. Churchman died. Before his death, he had conducted business in Orange, Morristown, Newark and Plainfield New Jersey as well as Washington, DC.

Upon his death, a temporary license for funeral home operation was given to his widow Minnie. She carried on the activities of the funeral home until the licensing of her son J. E. Churchman Sr. in 1918. Mr. Churchman's first location was 23 Centre Street in Orange. He later expanded and had establishments in Newark and other New Jersey locations. His last business location was at 132 Clinton Avenue in Newark. Upon his retirement from active business in 1980, he moved his offices to his son's establishment where he continued to conduct funerals until his death in 1983. J .E. Churchman was a veteran of World War I, and a dedicated Masonic Brother. The James E. Churchman Shrine Club of East Orange New Jersey was named in his honor. Mr. Churchman Sr., was a charter member of the Independent Funeral Directors Association, a fore-runner of today's National Funeral Directors and Morticians Asoociation.

Having grown up in the funeral profession, James E. Churchman Jr. decided to enter the profession after serving in the US Navy during World War II. James received his license in 1949. He at first worked with his father, until receiving a vision to open a separate facility of his own in Newark. With the help and dedication of his wife Corinne, they operated a business at 397 Bergen Street Newark for 20 years until purchasing an expanded facility in 1971 at 345-13th Ave. in Newark.

In 1976, James E. Churchman and Edith Churchman both received their licenses as funeral directors and embalmers from the state of New Jersey. becoming the fourth generation in their family to have such licensure, and becoming the only 4th generation family owned and operated African American funeral home in Essex County.

And so ends the beginning chapters of a story of an African American family, whose forefather saw a need to serve, and passed on this legacy of care, devotion, and vision to generations to come. We continue to uphold the rich legacy of Rev. James B. Churchman, not only in our desire to aid families in their time of need, but by our quest to stay abreast of the latest in technology and regulation of the profession, membership in civic, fraternal and funeral service organizations, and the sure and certain knowledge that this outstanding story of American history has many chapters yet to be written.

A. A. RAYNER & SONS
Chicago, Illinois

Mr. Ahmed A. Rayner, Sr. was born in 1893 in Calvert, Texas. He graduated from Prairie View A & M University in Prairie View, Texas in 1911. Following his graduation from Prairie View, he migrated to Chicago, Illinois. He eventually became a graduate of both Worsham College of Mortuary Science (in 1914) as well as a graduate of John Marshall Law School (in 1934). While in Chicago, he started working for Jackson Funeral Home. After leaving Jackson Funeral Home, he began a career as the Livery manager for Metropolitan Funeral Home, which was affiliated with the Chicago Metropolitan Mutual Life Assurance Company. A.A. Rayner, Sr. eventually resigned from the "Met" in 1947 to begin his own company.

In 1947, A.A. Rayner & Sons Funeral Home was established at 4141 South Cottage Grove Avenue. Joining A.A. Rayner were his children: A.A. "Sammy" Rayner Jr., Anne Rayner, Susie J. Rayner, and John B. Rayner. A.A. Rayner, Sr. was also joined in business by his brother, Loris M. Rayner. Business was successful, and expansion soon became necessary. Additional locations were established at 3660 West Roosevelt Road in Chicago, managed by Loris M. (Hortense) Rayner and nephew Ivan E. Rayner, II; 1317 Emerson Street in Evanston, managed by John B. (Narvel) Rayner; and 318 East 71st Street in Chicago, managed by A.A. Sammy (Alice) Rayner. A.A. Rayner, Sr. managed the funeral home at 4141 South Cottage Grove Avenue with his daughter Anne (Charles) Childs.

In 1955, a distraught, grieving young mother by the name of Mamie E. Till contacted A.A. Rayner, Sr. to conduct funeral services for her young son who had been viciously tortured and murdered and dumped into a Mississippi river. She wanted the whole world to witness man's inhumanity to man. Her young son was Emmett Till. Her courageous actions were instrumental in catapulting the nation into the Civil Rights Movement.

In the 1960s and 1970s, A.A. "Sammy" Rayner, Jr.'s peaceful involvement in the Civil Rights Movement and its struggles helped to galvanize the community. Through his political actions and aspirations, many changes were realized for the poor, underprivileged, uneducated, and the financially and socially forgotten. A.A. Rayner, Jr. was a decorated United States Air Force bomber pilot, and one of the original members of the Tuskegee Airmen. Throughout his professional and political career, his dedication and service to the city and to the members of his community were very rewarding. He was humbly elected to the City of Chicago council in 1967 as Alderman of the 6th Ward.

In 1971, the funeral home at 3660 West Roosevelt Road was sold, and a new funeral home was established at 5911 West Madison Street in Chicago. Shortly after the passing of John B. Rayner in 1974, the funeral home at 1317

Emerson in Evanston was sold. Currently, the home at 5911 West Madison Street is managed by John B. Rayner's daughter, Janelle B. Strong, as well as his son, John B. Rayner Jr., and Susie's daughter Tonee Ann Spurlin. They are members of the family's third generation.

In the 1980's, the funeral home located at 4141 South Cottage Grove was leveled and the funeral home located at 318 East 71st Street was converted into the main facility. Coincidentally, 71st Street is now known as "Emmett Till Road."

In 1987, family members of the Honorable Harold L. Washington contacted A.A. Rayner, Jr. to conduct funeral services for their beloved brother. Mr. Washington was the first African-American Mayor of the City of Chicago, the United States Congressman for the 1st Congressional District, an Illinois State Senator, and an Illinois State Representative.

A.A. Rayner, Sr. passed away in 1989. A.A. Rayner, Jr. passed away in 1990. Susie J. Spurlin passed away in 1995. Anne Rayner Childs passed away in 1997.

In 1997, A.A. Rayner & Sons celebrated their 50th Anniversary. The family marked the anniversary with an extensive renovation of the 318 East 71st Street funeral home. This funeral home is managed by other members of the family's third generation, including Pamela C. Rayner; Charles S. Childs, Jr.; Enna Sue Aikens, A.A. Rayner III, Donna L. Rayner, Nancy L. Martin, Ivan E. Rayner II, and Attorney Cheryl B. Rayner. The family's fourth generation continues to provide service and is committed to the communities in which we serve, with the addition of Zachary J. Triplett, Chloe E. Rayner and A.A. Rayner IV.

Our history, states the family, is blessed and rooted in Chicago's history with each and every family we've served and continue to serve. We are honored to have been able to serve our community, and we consider it a privilege and an important responsibility to offer our very best. A.A. Rayner & Sons leadership and commitment to affordable, ethical and professional service will continue for generations to come.

Rayner & Sons also offers cremation, a process of preparing the body for final disposition that is as old as history itself, and as modern as today. Contrary to popular belief, cremation need not replace the funeral traditions that have become so important to so many families. Cremation memorialization assures that you can preserve the comforting values of funeral traditions as well as provide a fitting tribute to honor a life that was well lived.

Cremation is simply another form of final disposition, just like burial. The means of final disposition is a personal choice, and one that should meet your needs and wishes. Any options you select should meet your wishes, desires, and traditions. We hope that you will take all the time you need to consider the choices and options available to you, ask questions, and depend on us to assist you in any way possible.

We offer several options for cremation, including:

- Direct Cremation

- Direct Cremation followed by Memorial Service

- Funeral Service followed by Cremation

For information on these options or if you have any questions regarding our services, please feel free to contact us at one of our two locations, and one of our professional funeral directors can help you choose or customize the correct services for your family.

SMITH AND SMITH FUNERAL HOME
Lexington, Kentucky

The Smith Family Funeral Home has a very unique heritage in that it has served Lexington and surrounding communities since 1881. It began at 509 East Chestnut Street, Nicolasville, Kentucky. John W. Smith, who succeeded his father in 1914 and continued until 1939 when his sons, John W. Smith, Jr. and Morton Smith, Jr. joined him in the funeral business. Also in 1939, John W. Smith bought a half interest in the Jackson Funeral Home in Danville, Kentucky and the name of the firm was changed to its present day name of Smith-Jackson Funeral Home. In 1945, he purchased the other half of the business but retained the name of the firm which was, by then well known. Several years later, J. W. or Jay (as he was called) bought the Edward W. Jackson Funeral Home in Lexington, Kentucky. The funeral home operated under the Jackson name until 1956 when the partnership of John W. Smith and Horace R. Smith was formed. The name was changed to Smith and Smith Funeral Home. J. W. owned and operated four firms at one time, the other being Smith Funeral Home in Frankfort, Kentucky.

J. W. Smith was married to Evelyn Truitt of Atlanta and they have two sons, Norman B. Smith and Michael M. Smith.

The Smith-Jackson Funeral Home at 106 W. Walnut Street in Danville was destroyed by fire. Mr. Smith then purchased the old "Woodcock House" at 4446 Bate Street, one of the old historical homes of Danville which was designated by the Kentucky Heritage Commission as "Crutchfield Homes". Mr. Smith completely remodeled the home into the present modern quarters of Smith-Jackson Funeral Home.

The steady volume of growth of business is a silent testimony to the high quality of service given at both funeral homes. The partnership of Michael Smith and Horace R. Smith continues to serve the Lexington community as Smith & Smith Funeral Home and Michael Smith operating Smith-Jackson Funeral Home.

They offer a complete service, which includes Family Consultation before and after a need, Funeral Services for all Faiths, Pre-Arrangement and Cremation.

The motto is "Service Measured Not By Gold, But By The Golden Rule."

BYNES-ROYALL FUNERAL HOME, INC.
Savannah, Georgia

The Bynes-Royall Funeral Home , located at 204 West Hall Street, was founded by Major William H. Royall in 1878, at 22 1/2 Whitaker Street, as a firm dealing in coffins, caskets and cooling boards. The technique of vascular injection embalming had not been invented and the method of preserving the human remains for funeral services consisted of placing the body on a wooden board which was approximately 24 inches wide and seven feet long. A three hundred pound block of ice was then placed into a tin receptacle and the board on which the body was placed was put on top of the slab of ice. A curtain was drawn around the board and a heavy drape placed over the body extended to the floor. This set up was called a cooling board and that is the origin of the terminology in the prayers of our elders when they said: "Lord I thank thee for permitting me to rise this morning and that my bed was not my 'Cooling Board'."

Mr. Royall conducted his business as a master cooling board operator from 1878 until 1888 when he moved his operation to a new location at 315 South Broad Street, now known as Oglethorpe Avenue. The water fountain in front of the Savannah Civic Center now stands on the spot. Here on Oglethorpe, two carriages and a hearse, all horsedrawn, were added to the rolling stock and a six-horse stable was erected. A business, the Mutual Aid Society was also formed.

In 1905, following the death of Major Royall at the age of 58, a young letter carrier employed by the United States Post Office, named Lachland McIntosh Pollard, bought the Royall Funeral Home business from the Royall family and with his brother-in-law, Walter S. Scott, who spearheaded the Mutual Burial Society, merged their two businesses into an already existing Johnson and Fields Funeral Service, founded in 1900, and moved the combined to 327 Jefferson Street as the new home of Royall Undertaking Company. Mr. Pollard became the manager of the company. The business remained at this location until the end of World War I.

In 1919, the company once again moved to a building known as the Globe Theatre at 501 West Broad Street and remained there until 1963. However, the company had already changed hands in 1955. Major Frank H. Bynes, a Savannah born military officer, who had studied and trained himself in this line of work, had purchased it in 1955. He moved the business to a historic building at 204 West Hall Street in 1963. The present building once housed President Woodrow Wilson and the family of his first wife, the late Ann Axson Wilson.

Perhaps most people do not know that Bynes-Royall Funeral Home is the oldest black business establishment in continous operation in the City of Savannah. The Savannah Tribune, the black weekly newspaper, founded in 1875, was discontinued in 1960 and reorganized in 1974. Prior to 1920, there were no professional schools for the training of black morticians. Many of the prominent black funeral establishments throughout the State of Georgia were founded by embalmers who received their training and mortuary license as apprentices at Royall Funeral Home - such names as S. G. Sellers, Founder of Sellers Brothers Funeral Home in Atlanta; Paul G. Steele, Founder of Steele Funeral Home in Savannah; Frank Hutchins, Founder of Hutchins Funeral Home of Macon; Sidney A. Jones, Founder of Sidney A. Jones Funeral Home of Savannah; Sandy D. Allen, Founder of Allen Mortuary of Columbia, South Carolina; Andrew Monroe, Founder of Monroe Funeral Directors of Savannah; Robert L. Byrd, Founder of Byrd & Hall Funeral Home of Brunswick; Ossie H. Williams, Founder of Williams & Williams Funeral Home of Savannah and T. H. Bynes, Founder of Bynes Mortuary of Bainbridge. Each one of these businessmen was a former employee or apprentice in embalming at Royall Funeral Home between 1910 and 1960. Mr. Earl Ashton of 520 East Anderson Street, a retired letter-carrier, received his embalming license at Royall Funeral Home in 1916.

Major Frank H. Bynes who bought this oldest black business and moved it to its present location, is one of the outstanding leaders in both black and white communities. Bynes-Royall Funeral Home is the oldest funeral home business in the State of Georgia. Frank, born in Savannah, attended Savannah State College and Atlanta Mortuary College. He joined the army in 1940 as a private and rose to be a major. He made the highest grades in the mortuary college.

Frank Bynes is a Deacon of St. John Baptist Church, member of Prince Hall Masons, a Shriner, member of First District Georgia Funeral Practitioners Association, member of National Funeral Directors & Morticians Association, member of Mutual Benevolent Society and N.A.A.C.P.

Mrs. Frenchye Bynes, his wife and Secretary-Treasurer of the business, was born in Jackson, Mississippi. She attended Jackson State College and graduated from the Henderson Business College of Memphis, Tennessee. She met Frank in Jackson in 1941 and they were married in 1942. She is a Deaconess of St. John Baptist Church, Treasurer and Board member of Wesley Community Center, Secretary of the First District Georgia Funeral Practitioners Association, member of the Board of Directors of National Funeral Directors & Morticians Association, member of the Wolverines, member of Lebedoze, member of the Grasshoppers Bridge Club and Nu Epsilon Mortuary Fraternity.

Bynes-Royall Funeral Home is celebrating its 127th anniversary in 2006. Royall opened the funeral home in 1879 and the Bynes family joined the business in 1955.

The Bynes have five children, 13 grandchildren and 4 great grandchildren. The youngest son, Raleigh D. Bynes graduated from Gupton- Jones Mortuary College in Atlanta.

Mrs. Olga Musgrow, the daughter, graduated Cum Laude from Savannah State College with a B.S. Degree in Business Administration.

Frank H. Bynes, Jr. graduated from Meharry Medical College in Nashville, Tennessee. He is an emergency room physician.

Frenchye, 18, graduated from Savannah State College in business law.

Lisa, the youngest, is a pharmaceutical sales representative.

Alfred Mullice presently manages the Funeral Home.

ANGELUS FUNERAL HOME

Los Angeles, California

Angelus Funeral Home history is one which has its roots firmly entrenched within the Black Community of Los Angeles. Originally established in 1922, the company was incorporated in 1925 when nineteen individuals pooled their resources to buy the business.

The early years were difficult, and for the first four years, the organization failed to show a profit. Unimpressed with their return, and with the depression looming, the number of stockholders dwindled to just three, who would form the nucleus of the firm. It was their diverse backgrounds that would enable Angelus to establish itself within the roots of the community.

The Group was led by an ambitious and enterprising custodian L. G. Robinson (who would later become head of L. A. County's building service employees), and by Lorenzo Bowdoin (a postal worker) and John L. Hill (a railroad porter). Bowdoin and Robinson were part of the original group of investors, while Hill acquired his interest in the company in 1929. These three became the steering force behind the company during its first 20 years.

None of the three owners was involved in the day-to-day functions of the firm as they continued to pursue their original vocations. With the company running in the red, it was decided that a hands-on approach was needed to protect their investment. Drawing upon his lengthy experience in personal service while with the railroad, Hill assumed the position of general manager. Within three months he had turned the company around and began to show a profit.

Under his management the firm prospered, and Hill became an equal partner with Robinson and Bowdoin. Within a few years it became apparent that the facility on East Jefferson would not be able to accommodate the rate of growth the company was achieving. Hill commissioned the renowned architect, Paul R. Williams, to design and build a new facility at the same site in 1934. It was completed where it still stands at 1030 E. Jefferson Blvd.

In 1936, Angelus became the first Black business in Los Angeles to sponsor, on a sustained basis, a commercial radio program. Presenting religious services from the Peoples Independent Church of Christ, Angelus afforded many shut-ins the opportunity to hear the services they had been unable to attend. This began a precedent which Angelus has continued to follow to this day. In 1979 Angelus sponsored 21 different church services every Sunday on KJLH-FM Radio.

The management and control of the company was left in the hands of Robinson and Bowdoin when Hill died suddenly in 1942. Utilizing the experience gained while working at Angelus during high school and college, John L. Hill, Jr. assumed a management role upon his return from military service.

Following Robinson's retirement in 1949, Hill was selected to become the Company's president. He became the sole owner within a few years when he acquired the balance of the Company's stock.

Under his guidance the firm prospered. Once again, the demand for the company's services outstripped the facility. Faced with the problem of expansion and maintaining the level of service, four branch locations were opened over the next few years. However, it became apparent that the quality of service could not be maintained when equipment and personnel were spread too thin. The decision to consolidate operations in one large facility was made. In 1964, property for the current location at 39th and Crenshaw was purchased. Once again Paul Williams was called upon to design a new building.

It took three years before Angelus could comply with the detailed zoning and planning requirements, as well as resolve neighborhood concerns; construction finally began. And a year later, in 1968, the project was finished. At the time, it was one of the largest independently-owned mortuaries in the country. The Williams-designed facility has received acclaim from many sources including the "Los Angeles Beautiful Award" in 1969. After 45 years at the helm of Angelus, Hill stepped down as the firm's president. Keeping with family tradition, John L. Hill, III was named the company's new president in 1991. Like his father, he also worked part-time at Angelus when in high school, and has been with the company since ending his military service in 1968. With more than 25 years of experience, he was prepared to tackle the responsibilities of the organization's leadership.

Continuing with the philosophy of his father, and his grandfather before him, John L. Hill, III has recognized the need to maintain the Company's commitment to the people it serves. He has continued to support the many charities and civic events which have made Angelus an acknowledged leader in neighborhood involvement. Not only is the history of Angelus embedded in the community, but its future as well.

MARCH FUNERAL HOMES
Baltimore, Maryland
Richmond, Virginia

March Funeral Homes is reported to be one of the largest minority funeral service companies in the United States. In 1992, the March Family acquired ownership of the cemetery, King Memorial Park, and then expanded to 154 acres making it one of the largest Black owned cemeteries in the country. Unlike Michigan, Maryland allows funeral homes to also own cemeteries.

Back in 1957, William C. and Julia Roberta March challenged themselves to become entrepreneurs. William's desire to support his family and educate his children was his greatest motive and inspiration. The pursuit of a funeral business actually stemmed from a friend. William considered the funeral business as one that might supply financial security for his family,

On January 2, 1957, William opened a three story row home on the corner of East North and Cecil Avenues to accommodate the business and to shelter his family. Being new in the business, the income was not enough to support his family, so William maintained his full-time job at the U.S. Post Office. He worked one part of the day for financial remuneration and worked another part of the day preparing himself for the success he desired. His wife, Roberta, assisted him with his duties as a Funeral Director and she later acquired a license to practice Funeral Directing in the State of Maryland. It then became a true partnership that acquired a reputation of being a concerned and caring couple providing professional funeral services at the most reasonable price in Baltimore.

The initial financing of the firm came from small personal loan companies such as HouseHold Finance. These monies were primarily used to renovate the row home and for the necessary equipment needed for operation.

The first year, William did no more than two funerals and the second year, four. By 1965, they were conducting over 200 funerals per year. Much of the growth they attribute to reasonable prices and professional conduct in service. William and Julia Roberta became known as the "funeral directors with a heart". Their reputation for helping families bury loved ones when they had little money for such needs spread throughout Baltimore. Their belief was that providing funeral service was not just a profession, but a ministry and that all God's children deserved a dignified burial.

The first sizeable loan was from the Small Business Administration in 1967 for $515,000, which allowed the purchase and renovation of the next-door row house in order to enlarge the facility. March Funeral Home was on its way to be the largest African American owned funeral service company in the country.

In 1973, in partnership with three other funeral directors, William C. March founded King Memorial Park, a 50-acre cemetery in Baltimore County catering to the African American community. Here, William C. March ventured into something he believed was needed for the people of Baltimore. This project too required much of his time to maintain and manage.

The business grew steadily until 1975; the business grossed $800,000 and serviced over 1000 families. Believing in his dream and without the financial support, William acted on his faith and pre-paid an architect $60,000 and acquired a lot for construction, one block away from the pioneering business on North Avenue. The plans were made to construct a million dollar facility that would occupy an entire city block. Major loans were then sought. In their misfortune, they received many regrets regardless of excellent credit and income. This type of investment for banks was not customary or traditional for a funeral service business.

Finally, the opportunity came when the Small Business Administration, Advance Federal Savings & Loan Assn and Ideal Savings and Loan Assn provided loans that totaled $845.000. In 1978, the one million dollar facility was opened. It served 2000 families the first year. Within four years, March Funeral Homes had a clientele of 2400 families per year. The facility was constructed and designed with a modern atmosphere that later became a trendsetter for the rest of the funeral industry. It dissimulated the public's typical idea of a funeral home as being one of gloom and sadness. The William C. March Funeral Home is among the largest single funeral operations in the United States.

In 1982, plans were then devised to expand to another facility. the second project, a 2 million dollar project erected in West Baltimore. It also, replicated the modem, high-style, comfortable atmosphere that appealed to the public's eye.

In 1984, Marcorp Ltd..(a holding company) was established as a vehicle to expand into other related services. Marcorp Ltd. became the parent company of six independent companies: William C. March Funeral Home, March Funeral Home West, Monetary Development Group Inc., an insurance division, Family Florist Inc., Maryland Service & Leasing Inc., livery service. and King Memorial Park Cemetery. The staff now consists of 150 people and has a total gross of $8 million.

Much of the growth and development can be attributed to the support and contributions of William & Roberta Marsh and their four children who continue their legacy. However, their success they contribute to God's mercy and to obedience to their ministry of serving others. Remarkably, all four of their children sought their own personal careers and then returned to the family business to make their individual contributions.

In August of 2003, the March Family expanded its territory of funeral service to the Richmond, Virginia area. The March Family celebrated the Grand Opening of the Laburnum Chapel in Richmond, Virginia in May 2004, where they continue to provide the highest standards of care and quality products in funeral service as they have to the community of Baltimore.

NEW BEDFORD, MASSACHUETTS
FUNERAL HOMES

William D. Harris (1897-1932) started his funeral business at 360 Kemptom Street in New Bedford in 1914. He was a graduate of Virginia Union University and learned his business at the Renouard School for Embalmers in New York. He operated as a mortician for eighteen years. He preceded Burgo, Santos and Onley funeral homes.

The Burgo Funeral Home, Inc. (formerly the Santos and Burgo Funeral Home) is a long-standing institution in the Cape Verdean community. The business was established in 1933 by Joaquim Santos and Jimmy Burgo. In the early years, since many "old folks" said, "When I die, I want to be buried from my home," Burgo's almost always conducted wakes and funerals from the home of the deceased. In June 1982, under the ownership of Jack Pina and his late son George Pina, the Burgo Funeral Home hosted an open house at the newly renovated establishment at 8 Wing Street, now owned by Jack Pina.

Charley Dudley Onley (1898-1991) owned and operated a funeral home at 147 Smith Street for some 45 years. Mr. Onley and his business were "community institutions." Born in New Bedford, he was a graduate of the New England Institute of Anatomy and Embalming. He started out by working with the funeral business of Santos and Burgo, and at first his 147 Smith Street residence was a branch of the **Santos and Burgo** Funeral Home. His training, initially, for the ministry undoubtedly contributed to how he handled bereaved families over the years; he was a graduate of the New England School of Theology and also studied religion at Gordon College and was an ordained minister, licensed to preach. Charles Dudley Onley, by virtue of his profession, kept meticulous records of the many New Bedford Black families that he served and so contributed to New Bedford's Black family genealogy and Black family history during his senior years.

Randall B. Pollard, Grand Historian of Prince Hall Grand Lodge of Massachuetts is a resident of New Bedford was a close friend of Charles Dudley Onley. Pollard led us to the book written by our friend, Robert C. Hayden, author, professor and researcher who lives and works in the area and is a highly recognized scholar of African American history including the Underground Railroad and the New Bedford History. His book *African Americans and Cape Verdean Americans in New Bedford* is among his many publications.

The New Bedford Historical Society is an important link to the community and has strong roots in the area. The Society is a non-profit organization dedicated to celebrating and documenting the history, legacy and presence of African Americans, Cape Verdeans, Native Americans and West Indians who contributed to the development of the city of New Bedford, a great whaling town that was a stop on the Underground Railroad. The town was a destination for many fugitives from slavery including Frederick and Anna Douglass, who lived here for five years and began their family. It was a destination for Henry Box Brown and William Wells Brown, who sent his daughters here to live in relative safety. The town was also the home of many of the African Americans who fought for the Union Army as members of the Fifty-fourth Regiment, including Sergeant Wiliam Carney, the first African American to receive the Congressional Medal of Honor.

New Orleans, Louisiana

Cemeteries, Funeral Homes and
Hurricane Katrina

Cemeteries

In New Orleans, one can't escape the dead for long. It's possible not to include a burial site on a tour of the city, but if you miss the cemeteries, you bypass the very essence of New Orleans- the "live life now" attitude that might not be so prevalent if the specter of death wasn't so ominously, yet some- how comfortingly, present. Visitors might not see a cemetery—but only if they don't stray as far as Rampart Street, the lakeside boundary, from which the imposing walls and sky-reaching society tombs of St. Louis cemetery No. 1 are clearly visible.

In what other American city would a museum, in this case Cabildo on Jackson Square, devote an entire room of exhibits to disease, death, mourning, cemeteries, and hospitals?

CHAPTER TWELVE

Such was the savage immediacy of death and its cohorts in the Crescent City, which for much of the antebellum period had the highest death rate of any American city. This is from the remarkable writings of Anne Rice whose stories and research are contained in *Haunted City* by Joy Dickinson, *An Unauthorized Guide to the Magical, Magnificent New Orleans* of Anne Rice. Death, she writes, was such a preoccupation for antebellum New Orleanians that the newspapers actually printed helpful advice on topics such as "How to Tell Whether a Person Is Dead or Alive." The method: "Apply the flame of a candle to the tip of one of the great toes of the supposed corpse, and a blister will immediately arise. If the vitality is gone, this will be full of air, and will burst with some noise if the flame be applied to it a few seconds longer. Though very few are actually buried alive, many more may be abandoned as dead while life is still in them, and then die from being handled and exposed as corpses are. The test, therefore, should be applied as soon as life is supposed to be extinct, and before an undertaker is called in."

From an airplane or the elevation of the freeway, it's easy to understand how the cemeteries got their nickname: cities of the dead. The whitewashed vaults, often topped with angels, lambs, or other statuary, mixed with the lushness of the Louisiana landscape, combine to create a picturesque miniature mirror of an eighteenth, or nineteenth century village.

St. Louis No.1 (1789), New Orleans

Even the most jaded tour guides whisper when they take groups through St. Louis Cemetery No.1, located at 400 Basin Street between Conti and St. Louis, just one block from the lakeside edge of the French Quarter. No matter how sunlit the day, St. Louis No.1 exudes a nearly palpable air of the sacred and the immortal, of dark emotions and fleeting, furtive shadows. If a guide or visitor says something funny, the ensuing laughter echoes uneasily, almost obscenely, off the walls of cracked, weathered tombs, some with their tops broken open, others sporting resilient tropical weeds flourishing along the sides and out of fractures in the masonry.

Established by royal decree in August 1789, St. Louis No.1 is the oldest existing cemetery in New Orleans and the Mississippi River Valley and is still used today, though fairly infrequently. Cemeteries in New Orleans are either city, or church owned; St. Louis No.1 is owned and administered by the Catholic Archdiocese of New Orleans. One of the earliest decipherable epitaphs is that of one Nannette F. de Bailly, dated September 24, 1800.

Homer Plessy, who fought for racial desegregation in the landmark Supreme Court case Plessy vs. Ferguson, died in 1925 at age sixty-three and is buried in St. Louis No.1. Plessy's loss in the 1896 case led to an other half century of court sanctioned, legalized segregation.

St. Louis No. 1 is also the final respite for "voodoo queen" Marie Laveau, whose crypt bears hundreds of rusty-colored chalk Xs. Marking an X on Marie's tomb supposedly ensures believers that their wishes will be granted (no word on success rates). Visitors also leave little gifts to Marie–beans, Mardi Gras beads, candles, bones that may or may not have belonged to animals (believe what you wish!). The tomb of Marie Laveau was restored in 1983 by the New Orleans Archdiocesan Cemeteries organization. A plaque marking the crypt reads: "Marie Laveau. This Greek Revival tomb is the reputed burial place of this notorious 'voodoo queen.' A mystic cult, voodooism, of African origin, was brought to [sic] city from Santo Domingo and flourished in [sic] 19th century. Marie Laveau was the most widely known of many practitioners of the cult." Only in New Orleans, one suspects, would the Catholic Church erect a marker pointing out the burial site of voodoo royalty.

St. Louis Cemetry #1

Marie's life would have been fascinating even without her involvement in voodoo-she was a free woman of color, born either in New Orleans or Saint Domingue (Haiti) around 1794, possibly to a white father and black mother. In 1819, Marie married Jacques Paris, a free black man, in a Roman Catholic ceremony officiated by the beloved Père Antoine. In 1826, Paris died, and Marie took up with another free black, Christophe Glapion. Her daughter, called Marie Junior, was born in 1827 to uncertain paternity. In any case, the elder Marie's relationship with Glapion was never legitimized by the Catholic Church, but Marie had borne fifteen children by the time she died in 1881.

The security guard stands ready to lock the gates of St. Louis Cemetery. Visitors are told not to go in near closing hour without knowing exactly where the entrance is at all times; it's amazingly easy to get disoriented and one wouldn't want to get locked in.

Marie, a hairdresser by trade, began practicing voodoo in the same year her husband died, and remained active in the hybrid cult-religion until her old age. A March 1869 New Orleans Times account describes a voodoo ritual involving both blacks and whites:

The rites having been commenced, an elderly turbaned female dressed

in yellow and red (Marie Laveau), ascended a sort of dais and chanted a wild sort of fetish song, to which the others kept up an accompaniment with their voices and with a drum-like beat of their hands and feet. At the same time, they commenced to move in a circle while gradually increasing the time.

As the motion increased in intensity the flowers and other ornaments disappeared from their hair, and their dresses were torn open, and each one conducted herself like a bacchante. . . . In the midst of the Saturnalia of witches, the pythoness of this extraordinary dance and revel was a young girl. . . . In this awful state of nudity she continued her ever- increasing frantic movements until reason itself abandoned its earthly tenement. In a convulsive fit she finally fell, foaming at the

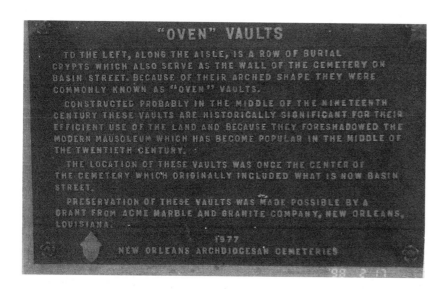

mouth like one possessed, and it was only then that the mad carnival found a pause.

Some suspect, fear, or hope (depending on one's outlook) that Marie has never really left New Orleans; that her ghost, along with that of her daughter, haunts the area around the "voodoo crypt" at St. Louis Cemetery No.1.

Most of the earliest inscriptions have long since disappeared from the tombs of St. Louis No.1, victims of time, neglect, and the persistently inhospitable climate. One early engraving, copied by a Daily Picayune reporter on All Saints' Day 1903, reads: "Ci git un malheureuse qui Jut victim de son imprudence. Vers une larme sur sa tombe, et un 'De Profundis' s'il vout plait, pour son arne. Il n'avait que 27 ans, 1798." Translation: "Here lies a poor unfortunate who was a victim of his own imprudence. Drop a tear on his tomb and say, if you please, the psalm 'Out of the depths I have cried unto Thee, 0 Lord,' for his soul. He was only 27 years old, 1798."

Today, the paths of St. Louis No. 1 are treacherous and overgrown, sometimes ending in abrupt dead-end alleys. The first families to use the cemetery simply wandered in, found an open spot at random, and erected their tombs with little regard for tidiness or symmetry. The result is a twisting, eerie maze that can quickly turn from charming to terrifying. Don't go in near closing hour without knowing exactly where the entrance is at all times; it's amazingly easy to get disoriented, and I wouldn't want to get locked in. Many of the families whose ancestors are buried here have moved away or died out, leaving no one to tend the graves. Nowhere in New Orleans are decay and desolation so evident as at St. Louis No. 1.

The cemetery now occupies roughly one large city block; it once extended at least one more block closer to the river (nearly to Rampart), and several additional blocks on either side of its current walls. Supposedly, as the original cemetery was eaten up by development and streets cut through its borders, all displaced remains were exhumed and reinterred within the current walls. Tour guides will tell you, though, that it's highly likely that the folks living all around St. Louis No. 1 are resting just a few feet or so above those in a far more permanent sleep.

At the front of the cemetery, to the left of the entry gates on Basin street, are the famous wall vaults, or "oven" tombs (so nicknamed for their resemblance to the ovens used for baking bread). These community tombs, for those with no family or society tomb (tombs purchased by benevolent societies and organizations, and maintained for their members) , were put to use repeatedly. Remains from previous burials were simply pushed to the back of the extra long chambers to make room for new occupants. Some of the lower oven tombs at St. Louis No.1 have sunk so deeply into the ground that it is now impossible to open them; their occupants, at least, can rest easy that they will not be disturbed to make way for new tenants.

At the rear of the cemetery was a section for Protestant burials; within it was a tiny parcel set aside for blacks. The Protestant section blocked an extension of Tremé Street, so many of these remains were moved in the 1830s to the new Girod Street Cemetery. What remains now of the Protestant area of St. Louis No.1 is a forsaken, depressing strip of land that even the tours don't bother with. Girod Street Cemetery, in the American sector across Canal Street from the Vieux Carré, also fell victim to "progress" and was closed in 1957. Part of the Louisiana Superdome now sits on part of the site; one is tempted to speculate on the effect this has had on the New Orleans Saints' record in the National Football League.

Many tombs feature marble slabs on the front, bearing simple inscriptions (usually limited to the name of the deceased, with accompanying birth and death dates). The slabs were bolted into place for easy removal when another family burial was required. Ever practical, New Orleanians "recycle" their family tombs over and over; some bear witness to ten, fifteen, even twenty or more burials in one two-vault tomb. The methodology is simple and efficient: New burials are placed in the upper chamber. When another person dies, the decaying casket is removed from the upper chamber, and what's left of the human remains are placed in the lower chamber. Law prevents opening a tomb less than one year and one day from the previous entombment, in the interest of disease prevention.

On October 9 in 1929, Ernest Morial was born. Morial was an African-American politician.

He was born the youngest of six children in Louisiana. He was nicknamed Dutch. The Morial family were devout Catholics. His education began at St. Louis Catholic School. He later attended Xavier Prep. Morial graduated from Xavier University, a historically Black Catholic college, in 1951. At the, time, he was attending Xavier, (the only historically Black Catholic College in the country at the time); he became president of Alpha Phi Alpha Fraternity Inc., the first Black Greek Fraternity.

Morial was Mayor of New Orleans (1978-1986), a lawyer, and a Judge in the Fourth Circuit Court of Appeal, and Juvenile Court, Orleans Parish. He was also the first African-American assistant U. S. attorney and the first elected to the Louisiana legislature since Reconstruction. Ernest Morial died on Dec. 24, 1989.

HOLT CEMETERY, NEW ORLEANS

An article written in American Cemetery Magazine by Ryan M. Seidemann and Ericka L. Seidemann gives us an excellent view of one of the African American cemeteries in New Orleans. It is owned by the City of New Orleans and sometimes referred to by locals as a "Potters Field". The authors give a detailed story of this

Tomb of New Orleans Mayor 1978-1986 Ernest Morial

unusual cemetery and its great history. They call it "Where art, junk, nature and death blur."

Near Mid-City, New Orleans, just down the street from Metairie Cemetery and many other cemeteries, lies Holt Cemetery: a low-lying parcel of land strewn with handmade grave markers. The fact that all of these cemeteries line City Park Avenue is where the similarities between Holt and the others end. Holt is unlike most New Orleans cemeteries. It reflects homemade personal expression and is created with objects of necessity, more so than the extravagant architecture typical of other New Orleans cemeteries.

Holt cemetery was first mentioned in city records in 1879, most likely named for Joseph Holt, a physician at Charity Hospital. Holt was founded as an indigent cemetery; its remoteness and ease of transporting the indigent dead through back roads rather than through the center of town. Although Holt was originally mainly black Protestant, there were many people of European descent buried there between 1876 and 1879. It may have been used as an "overflow" cemetery during this time. Despite its more than century-long history, today none of the 19th century markers are visible.

Holt Cemetery, as mentioned, is often referred to by locals as a "Potter's Field." The cost for interment is about the cost of digging a grave. If a grave remains in a state of disarray or abandonment for some time, it may be allocated by the city for another burial.

Holt is characterized by its personal, expressive graves that are often accompanied by decorative, handmade markers and "offerings." Even when a military stone has been placed on a grave, a handmade marker or personal decorations usually accompany it. If a marker with multiple names is on a grave including a military stone, the name on the military stone will also be added to the family marker, presumably intending to include this person with the rest of the family. The cemetery is, generally, poorly maintained; however, some of the graves are kept in decent condition by relatives. Additionally, grounds maintenance and upkeep is provided by volunteers from Hope for Holt and Save Our Cemeteries. Because the graves are available for "re-use" after a period of neglect, multiple headstones often accompany one grave, or many names, sometimes unrelated, appear on one headstone. This "re-use" seems to contribute to the maintenance problem at Holt.

Many of the graves in Holt cemetery express some Christian affinity, though it is often difficult to distinguish between Catholic and Protestant graves. Some Catholic images, such as the crucifix and statues of the Virgin Mary are seen, however. There is no segregation of religion, and some graves have no religious decoration at all. Religious expression is often accompanied by personal items of expression. Catholicism is so integrated into south Louisiana culture that many Catholic images may be a reflection of local tradition rather than religious affiliation. This is especially true with some items, such as Mardi Gras beads left on graves. Mardi Gras coincides with a

Christian holiday, though most everyone in southern Louisiana participates in it regardless of what religion they practice. Most of the religious symbols on the graves at Holt are a kind of "religious generic," not really representing a particular denomination.

The grave markers at Holt are constructed from a variety of materials, mostly those found locally that are easy to acquire, such as wood, stone, fencing, carpet and PVC pipe. Even a purchased, engraved stone often will be decorated and personalized, or a blank stone will be painted or carved by hand. Landscaping and gardening materials are heavily used, either to mark the grave boundary or to decorate the grave itself. Other works of necessity are also seen in Holt's markers: bricks, metal, cinder blocks and tile. One unusual aspect of the graves at Holt is the use of carpet or Astroturf to cover the grave. This decoration seems to be used to make the grave look "pretty," almost like a bed.

Boundary markers seem especially important at Holt. As seen historically and as we have seen around South Louisiana, Anglo graveyards are typically grouped by enclosures around family plots, while traditionally African-American graveyards have delineations around individual graves. Many graves appear to be "claimed" by such a boundary. Such overt boundary markers, in most cases, are likely to ensure that the families comply with the maintenance provisions required to retain a burial location.

Another unique feature of Holt is the virtual absence of fraternal or benevolent organizations so common in other cemeteries, such as the Freemasons and the Woodsmen of the World. We have only observed one marker with a Masonic symbol, and no Woodsmen of the World markers were observed. Indeed, this one Masonic symbol appears to be hand-scratched or pressed into the cement marker.

Some studies suggest that the materials used on African American graves symbolically incorporate religious beliefs from African cultures such as the Yoruba. The use of items related to water, such as shells, piping and even glass beads, may symbolize the afterlife and the world of the dead, a realm closely associated with water, according to some African religions. The use of such materials at Holt, however, does not seem to support such an interpretation. One must consider the fact that Holt is a mainly indigent cemetery and the graves are decorated with items that are readily available. There may be some African influence in the grave decorations and borders found at Holt, and certainly in the ever-changing and often flamboyant veneration of the dead, but these graves reflect such a myriad of cultural traditions and individualization that one must question profound and certainly overt African ties.

Another observation that lends credence to the notion that the Holt graves do not incorporate any deep African symbolism is the fact that many objects typically found on African graves used to represent the afterlife, such

An example of both the flamboyant veneration of the dead, through colors not typical of standard cemeteries, and of a wooden boundary marker or "box" around the grave.

as broken crockery and shells, are absent at Holt. We have not observed any broken crockery at all and only two graves were associated with shells. However, in the absence of the shell so common at other African-American cemeteries, river cobbles or gravel are evident in several grave markers at Holt. It is possible that this use of river cobbles or large gravel is a recoding of the West African use of water-related implements in the commemoration of the dead, where attractive shell material is not readily available. It could be, too, that this is purely decorative. Instead of the expected African symbolism, one finds flowers, Christian symbols, and sentimental decoration, like hearts and doves, painted on the grave markers.

The presence of such seemingly bizarre symbolism and the dominant ethnicity of the cemetery leads many people to think that some burials are associated with the practice of Voodoo. However, this is not the case. The most suspect plots, owned by a man named Arthur Smith, appear to be an almost ritualistic arrangement of junk, complete with an eerie-looking plastic owl that gazes intently at passers-by. One of the plots holds members of his family; the other is what he calls his "chapel." This plot does not seem to contain the remains of anyone; at least, no one known to Smith. Rather, the plot and the decorations thereon represent a memorial to all of those interred at Holt. It is not known whether this is a collection of Smith's belongings or items that he has assembled from around the cemetery.

Surprisingly, Holt cemetery is also the final resting place of several local celebrities. One example of this is the grave of Jessie Hill. Quite well known locally, Hill had one national hit song in 1958, "Ooh Poo Pah Doo." This song and the man are memorialized on an expressive wooden marker. How is it that a local celebrity came to be buried in the indigent cemetery? Hill suffered from financial problems in his later life and a benefit concert was held by his friends to cover the costs of his funeral. However, Holt cemetery has become somewhat of a beacon for the African-American community in New Orleans. Indeed, although it is known and operated as an indigent cemetery, the tradition of being buried in Holt has led to the continued interment of nonindigent members of the New Orleans African-American community there in order to remain close to family. So, it is possible, though we will never know for sure, that Jessie Hill would have elected to be buried in Holt cemetery even if money had not been an issue.

Another notable celebrity marker is that of coronet player Buddy Bolden. This stone is not actually the original stone associated with Bolden's grave. He is not even buried at this location. Rather, it is a cenotaph for the man considered by many to be the father of jazz.

Bolden's story is equally as sad as that of Jessie Hill. Bolden, born in New Orleans in 1877, rose to local fame as a coronetist and band leader performing ragtime and protojazz in the city between about 1895 and 1906. He suffered from alcoholism as his fame increased. The alcoholism exacerbated what has been diagnosed as a likely manic depressive/paranoid schizophrenic condition, leading to his musical downfall at the height of his popularity in 1906. Following numerous drunken fights, he was committed to the Louisiana State Psychiatric Hospital in Jackson, La. Bolden lived out the remaining 24 years of his life in a semi-coherent, but progressively deteriorating state at the asylum and died there at the age of 54 in 1931. Rather than burying Buddy Bolden in the adjacent cemetery in Jackson, his sister, Cora, had his body returned to New Orleans. All that Cora could afford was some space in Holt Cemetery, where Buddy was buried in plot C-623 in a pine box, with no fanfare. Both because she could not afford the upkeep of the plot and because the plots were renumbered with the original records being lost, it is unclear where Bolden's remains lay today. Indeed, when Bolden's biography was published in the 1970s, the

Overview of Holt Cemetery

author, Donald Marquis, speculated that at least eight or nine people had been buried on top of Bolden since 1931.

The only African American cemeteries that we have found in the course of our research that stylistically resemble Holt in any way are limited to the area around New Orleans Carrollton Cemetery in New Orleans and Belle Grove Cemetery in Kenner (a suburb of New Orleans). However even these cemeteries are not as expressive or active as Holt. Additionally, some of the similarities at Carrollton are due in part, to the influence of Holt's artisan, Arthur Smith, who also maintains an equally interesting grave at Carrollton.

Unfortunately, as best we can tell, there are no stylistic trends to report from Holt, save one: individualism. Each family member of loved ones buried in Holt Cemetery communes with the past in their own way. There is an absence of conformity in the cemetery unlike any we are aware of, even any other predominantly African American Cemetery. In this place, described by a local reporter as an area where, "boundaries separating art, junk, nature, and death blur," every marker is a study unto itself. Unlike in many high-styled cemeteries, the markers at Holt cannot be categorized. Sure, the markers can be grouped by construction material or by some other arbitrary means, but the range of individual expression on them cannot be reduced to any set of standards.

Holt cemetery is indeed a unique place. It is unique in its ephemerality. The temporary nature of most of the markers flows for a constant evolution of the cemetery, unlike the semi-permanent nature of most marble-clad cemeteries in New Orleans. It is also unique in its divergence from other African-American cemeteries. There is no broken pottery, there are few shells,

and few overt expressions of a truly African heritage. Indeed, Holt represents a unique cultural melting pot in grand American style, one that likely could not, and to our knowledge does not, exist outside of the New Orleans area. The cemetery is a direct reflection of the colorful city in which it is situated. Virtually every religion is represented in a nonsegregated nature. The icons that New Orleans is so well known for, Mardi Gras and jazz, flow through the cemetery. Holt is a living cemetery, a dynamic expression of constantly changing culture.

Cemeteries in the Civil War regions of the South are especially distinctive for their rich history. Those in larger cities often have facilities for care and maintenance, while most smaller cemeteries are cared for by the families of the deceased. Large facilities in cities like Atlanta, Georgia, as well as select smaller cemeteries, have adequate funding. But, in general, there are very few exceptions to the continual struggle against time and the encroachment of "progress."

Several cemeteries with unique, fascinating, and sometimes quite troubled histories exist. Among them is Geer Cemetery in Durham, North Carolina, where focused, loving effort was expended towards making it a showcase property, a goal that was not achieved. And Mount Ararat, in Nashville, Tennessee, with its great heritage, showed a promising beginning but a sad ending—until its rescue. (See chapter three)

There are fewer African American–owned cemeteries in the North than in the South; most burial grounds of the Northeast are integrated. Throughout this historic region stories of struggle and hope abound. Helen

Y. Davis, a Boston funeral director, tells of a cemetery in nearby Nantucket that was traditionally a black cemetery, but which is now overseen by the Nantucket County office. Lucille Barbour, a licensed mortician in New Jersey, explains that burials are not permitted in Atlantic City because it is actually an island. The nearest cemetery on the "mainland" is seven miles away in Pleasantville, and it is not black-owned. "Many years ago," she writes, "there was a black-owned cemetery called Lincoln Memorial Park, located in Mays Landing, New Jersey, about fifteen miles from Atlantic City. Mr. Rice, the owner, died, and the cemetery was sold to whites."

Burial grounds located in the less temperate regions like the Northeast and northern Midwest face additional maintenance problems. The ability to keep driveways and paths clear for processions in wintertime, and to open and close graves during freezing weather, takes on added dimensions of difficulty. Even during the warmer months, groundskeeping must also be more aggressive. Unlike the heavily wooded Sea Island cemeteries, which have little or no grass, lawn upkeep becomes a regular chore in other locations. Cemeteries that adhere to the "memorial park plan" forbid upright markers on the graves; maintenance is somewhat easier when markers are flush with the ground.

There are also few exclusively black cemeteries in the Middle and Far West. Most cemeteries are not owned by African Americans and most are reportedly integrated. The cemeteries of the central states have special histories and traditions, as do those of the South. In general, however, they are owned and managed by boards of directors. However, the board of Detroit Memorial Park Cemetery is still comprised of "family"; most members are related to the founders of 1925. In the West, California has several black-owned cemeteries, including Angeles Abbey Memorial Park, which was owned by the late cemeterian Jean Sanders.

Canada, too, has some quaint "family style" burial grounds, a reflection of the major role that she played in the lives and struggles of those escaping bondage prior to the Civil War. Canadian cemeteries like the Fugitive Slave Cemetery in Puce, Ontario, and the North Buxton Cemetery serve primarily family and extended family. See the Hurricane Katrina section for more information on Holt Cemetery in New Orleans.

Funeral Homes
BOISSIERE-LABAT FUNERAL HOME
New Orleans, Louisiana

New Orleans is a city that loves its traditions. For generations, trades and skills have been passed from parent to child. The "family owned" funeral service was the first industry to develop. The industry was born in the New Orleans of the 1800s. The fires were fueled by the rising demands created by a swelling population, and partially by high mortality rates resulting from plagues, climate, and other hardships. While many of our traditions have fallen by the wayside over the generations, the family-owned funeral service is still a mainstay within the community.

For 133 years, the Labat family has buried our dead and comforted those left behind. In fact, there has been a member of the Labat family providing undertaking services in New Orleans since 1871 when Alcide Labat and Joseph Ray established Ray & Labat Mortuary. According to a 1946 article from the Clarion Herald, theirs was "New Orleans oldest undertaking establishment". Four generations later, Emile J. Labat, III carries on the family vocation at Family Funeral Services.

In his office on Claiborne Avenue, seated behind his desk, Emile J. Labat, III is surrounded by family history. The walls are covered with photographs and plaques. From Alcide Labat's involvement in the Plessy vs. Ferguson supreme court case in the 1890s, to Emile Labat's service as chairman of the Community Chest (the forerunner of the United Way) along with his help in organizing and serving as one-time chief of the New Orleans Area Boy Scouts, to Emile Labat, Jr's help in organizing pro sports in the Crescent City long before The New Orleans Saints came to town. The family certainly has a proud past and a rich legacy much deeper than just the "family trade".

Although Emile III is managing partner, the day-to-day responsibilities of the business are split between Emile and Renard Boissiere a member of another prominent family of the New Orleans funeral scene.

The entire funeral industry has gone through a tremendous metamorphosis. For generations the funeral business was based on long-term relationships with families. Intense competition involving major corporations with deep pockets have bought out most family owned businesses. Moreover, with their ties to major manufacturers, have created, what some may call a stronghold on the industry.

At one point in history funeral homes didn't advertise or directly solicit business. Today, everyone is forced to, and large conglomerates have replaced many of the small, family-owned funeral services. Pricing wars associated with this increased competition is responsible for the demise of many of the city's once family-owned funeral homes. As competition from major market players increased, mortuaries became more price sensitive. They kept their prices low to be competitive. The problem was the prices were so low they couldn't make profits sufficient to reinvest in the business–to upgrade the facilities, equipment, or technology. Some of the only ones to survive were the ones with ties to insurance companies. And to these arrangements, it was the insurance companies that were profitable. The funeral homes merely serviced the insurance companies. The insurance companies would issue policies with low cash value. This, in effect, locked the consumer into using the insurance companies' funeral home. In some cases, this practice continues today. These stock insurance companies have been doing business for a long time; their services weren't available to all folks, largely because of economics. Those who could afford coverage purchased the minimum.

Intensive market competition was the impetus that has formed Family Funeral Services.

While many of New Orleans' family-owned funeral services have been either bought up by large corporations or gone by the wayside, Family Funeral Services remains viable, because of a commitment to service. Emile Ill's methodical, analytical approach to business coupled with Renard's charismatic charm and unstoppable humor play a large part in the companies' continuing success.

"When I first started managing the business, I came in and valued the cost of everything," says Emile III. "Since then, we have restructured the companies' prices to reflect true costs. Additionally, the emphasis is on service instead of pricey caskets."

"Our goal is to provide the family with a complete turn-key system. That way, family members don't get bogged down in the details. Besides, folks have the opportunity to choose a better quality casket rather than a cheaply made casket with an expensive price tag. Our system of service takes care of even the most minute detail, right down to the Heirloom Bibles given to all at-need family members who purchase pre-arrangements." And, since both Emile III, and Renard agree that their job doesn't stop, after the funeral service, the company recently organized a Family Service Counselors to help families cope with their loss. According to Emile III, the result has been more customer support services such as our Financial Planning Seminars and Free Estate Planning Guide and equally as important, a larger selection of quality caskets at very competitive rates.

In keeping with the spirit forged by Alcide Labat more than a century ago, Family Funeral Services maintains a strong commitment to community service. The companies' service activities run the gambit from its paid apprenticeship program to its Church Memorial Fund. The company maintains a strong relationship with the New Orleans Embalmers Association which provides a scholarship program intended to assist deserving high school and college students in New Orleans who are entering into the Death Care Industry.

The authors are sad to announce that these two funeral homes on Claiborne Avenue are completely destroyed. They became water-logged from Hurricane Katrina and their interiors are so bad, both homes have to be torn down. Late in November 2005, we talked to Errol Demasiliere, a funeral director at Boissiere-Labat who said the entire area is devastated, everything is grey - no green foliage and it looks as though an atomic bomb has exploded in the neighborhood.

He indicated that Boissiere-Labat's six limousines are a total loss. Their clientele has moved to other states and the few African Americans living in dryer suburbs are using white funeral homes. From his perspective, few if any of the hundreds of blacks will return to New Orleans. Because the fast food restaurants are in need of workers, some persons are driving long distances each day from Baton Rouge, Louisiana and even from Mississippi to work at a quite high wage at these businesses and some have jobs in the French Quarters which is doing good business. Many residents express hope that by the end of 2006, some recovery will be visible. Fortunately, Boisssiere-Labat has funeral establishments in other locations.

RHODES FUNERAL HOME

New Orleans, Louuisiana

The Rhodes name has been associated with quality and service throughout the New Orleans community and is currently celebrating 116 years of continuous service.

Duplain W. Rhodes, Jr. was born on September 13, 1899 to Carolyn Toups and Duplain Rhodes, Sr. He was the third child born after his sisters, Florence Rhodes Jordan and Flavia Rhodes Brent. Baptized at St. Peter AME Church as a child, his early spiritual growth was fostered by the African Methodist Episcopal Church. Mr. Rhodes explained that, "my father owned land in Thibodaux following the civil war. He settled in uptown New Orleans in the latter part of the 1800s and made his living hauling whatever people had to haul around New Orleans. At the time there were no Black funeral homes, so often Blacks ended up being prepared in the stable where horses were kept. My father decided to go into the funeral business to provide burial services for Negro New Orleanians. He establishes his first funeral home on Valence street in uptown New Orleans.

The Rhodes Undertaking Company progressed steadily as a result of hard work, careful planning, and forward thinking. Mr. Rhodes, Jr. pointed out that, "around 1917, my father saw the advantage of automobiles. In spite of his pride of having some of the finest horses. In fact my father was the first Black person in New Orleans to own an automobile."

The only son and namesake of his father, Rhodes, Jr., was destined to carry on a legacy of funeral service and community commitment. While the Rhodes Undertaking Company was establishing itself as a quality burial service for Black New Orleans, Mr. Rhodes, Jr., was still a young boy. He attended McDonough No. 6 School, which at the time was located near Magazine

Street and Napoleon Avenue. After graduation, he attended the Straight University on Canal Street and then the newly founded Xavier University on Magazine Street. He was one of the first graduates and credited Sister Francis, and the sisters of the Blessed Sacrament, as having a substantial influence on his life. She was responsible for getting Mr. Rhodes admitted to Creighton University in Nebraska as one of their first Black students, but after a brief stay at Creighton, Mr. Rhodes decided to go back to New Orleans and take up the profession of his father.

After consolidating forces with his father, Mr. Rhodes expanded the Rhodes Funeral Home services in 1928 by developing a close relationship with Enterprise Benevolent Association to provide a means for people to pay for burial services.

The funeral home business also experiences growth during those years. In the early 40s, Mr. Rhodes moved the funeral home to a new location, 2616 Claiborne Avenue. He later acquired the entire Negro business of the St. Louis Industrial Life Insurance and Sick Benefit Association, also the National Service Insurance Company, the St. John Berchman Life Company, and the Prompt Succor Life Insurance Company.

He moved from the South Claiborne site in the early 50s and opened Rhodes Funeral Home, located on North Claiborne (the present location of the Rhodes primary downtown funeral home). He also began to open branches of the Rhodes Funeral Homes, starting with the westbank Funeral Home on Virgil Street. He then bought the old Tivoli Theater and remodeled it to become the uptown location of Rhodes Funeral Home. Next, Mr. Rhodes acquired a funeral home in Baton Rouge and bought the Rhodes Good citizen Funeral Home on Martin Luther King Boulevard in New Orleans.

In the tradition of his father who went to automobiles service when the other funeral homes were using horses and wagons, Duplain Rhodes, Jr. always looked for ways to stay ahead of the competition. Aside from continually expanding his services, Mr. Rhodes broke tradition in the early 60s when he bought an entire fleet of white limousines for his funeral service. He was ridiculed by his fellow funeral directors who said that no one would want to use his cars for their burial services. Not only did he continue to get the lion's share of the Black funerals, but by going white, he was able to capitalize on the weddings and special events that the more affluent Black middle class could afford by the 1960s.

While Mr. Rhodes is well known for his business acumen, he worked behind the scenes throughout his life in the interest of social justice. He proudly pointed out the fact that the National Funeral Directors Association, of which he served as president, was one of the first Black organizations to provide financial resources to Dr. Martin Luther King, Jr. in his civil rights efforts. Mr. Rhodes also provided financial resources to the NAACP and many other organizations and individuals who were active in the human rights struggle. He was a standard bearer and a shining example for Black businessmen in the City of New Orleans.

Duplain W. Rhodes, Jr., Doris Millaud Rhodes, his wife and business partner, Edith Rhodes-Gomes, his daughter and Rev. Halley Rhodes Harris have departed this life. However, they leave the fourth, fifth and sixth generations, Sandra Rhodes-Duncan, D. Joan Rhodes, Kathleen Rhodes-Astorga, Stephanie Rhodes-Navarre, Duplain W. Rhodes, III, their grandchildren and their great-grandchildren, along with the employees of the family business to continue the legacy of entrepreneurship and a tradition of trust. As mentioned on page 532, this site was seriously damaged by Katrina. However the other funeral homes owned by Rhodes were able to continue in business. Page 551 mentions the business across the Mississippi River in Gretna.

HURRICANE KATRINA - NEW ORLEANS

Hurricane Katrina came ashore on August 29, 2005 with a wash of violence and anger. Early reports spoke not of funeral homes and not of cemeteries but of collecting bodies. On September 9, 2005 the Detroit News wrote about the makeshift mortuary task of counting the dead. The arduous task, they stated, was hampered by the lack of proper records for many of the poor victims. The wire services story:

Doctors, fish-and-game officials and even tour-boat operators arrived in the Big Easy from all over the United States this week to help rescue survivors of the great New Orleans flood.

What they found were precious few residents left to rescue and an ugly task in the strange, calm setting, searching for the dead.

"Everyone in the city of New Orleans is now in the process of changing direction and the process of collecting bodies," said Col John Fortunato of the Jefferson Parish Sheriff's Department.

Dozens of bodies are being pulled out of the murky water; they are busy being brought to a makeshift mortuary at what is essentially a boat ramp on Interstate 10.

The bodies are being flown by helicopters to a federal disaster mortuary in St. Gabriel state prison near Baton Rouge. There, fingerprints, dental impressions and DNA will be taken in hopes that names can be affixed to the dead.

No one knows how many bodies there are; Mayor Ray Nagin said it could be as many as 10,000 in New Orleans alone. Several have been spotted floating around areas where, until now, rescue workers have been concentrating on removing the living.

"I think there are going to be numerous bodies, but we'll have to wait," said Joe Bradshaw, spokesman for the Kentucky EMS tactical rescue squad.

Among the challenges recovering the bodies: How do you establish the victims' names, especially when many of them were so poor they probably did not even have dental records? And how do you return the dead to their relatives when no one knows where the family members are living?

At two collection sites federal mortuary teams collect any information that may help identify a body, including the coordinates of where each corpse was found. They also have collected whatever personal effects were on the bodies, in hopes that something — say, a hairbrush — might be used later to identify the victims.

At the temporary morgue set up in nearby St. Gabriel, the bodies are photographed, and forensic workers hope to use dental X-rays, fingerprints and DNA to identify them.

Edward J. Defort, reporting for *American Cemetery* writes that, as the news arrived that the breached levees that gave way during the devastation of Hurricane Katrma have been repaired and the waters have been receding from the city, the task of collecting, counting and processing the bodies continues. That task is expected to last months.

Television news stories have aired photographs of dead bodies floating in waters that were once streets. Cemeteries, including those historic final resting places in New Orleans, had casketed bodies unearthed by the storm, concerning health officials.

The majority of New Orleans' historic cemeteries have been compromised causing the bodies to become unearthed and float alongside the victims of the hurricane, according to Dr. Frank Minyard, Orleans parish coroner. He said this situation will cause a unique challenge. "They'll have 100-year-old skeletons to try and identify along with the hurricane victims," he said.

Also on September 9, the *Wall Street Journal* wrote that the City that made an art of funerals now just makes do. Steven Gray and Evan Perez, write that services are relocated, kin are scarce and the dead are still turning up. Looking back, they state that a solemn parade of uniformed officials and horses typically marks the funeral of a New Orleans police officer.

But the funeral Wednesday of Sgt. Paul Accardo fell far short of that: No horses. No parade. Not a single uniformed member of the New Orleans police department in attendance. The flooding of New Orleans meant that Sgt. Accardo, a New Orleans police spokesman who shot himself to death Saturday, was eulogized 75 miles away, in Baton Rouge. Nor did the body then proceed to the New Orleans cemetery where Sgt. Accardo wanted to be buried. Some family members and friends wore T-shirts to the funeral because their Sunday clothes were ruined in the flood.

"This isn't his city," said Cpl. Don Kelly, police spokesman in Baton Rouge.

Few cities bury their dead in the high style of New Orleans, where funerals can last a week, feature jazz bands as well as parades and draw bigger crowds than weddings do. But those traditions are, for the time being, yet another casualty of Hurricane Katrina. The same flood that ended so many lives in New Orleans shut down most of the city's institutions of death—its funeral homes, churches and cemeteries. It also scattered the crowds that make New Orleans funerals so extraordinary.

For thousands of survivors, this loss could complicate the effort to accept the death of a loved one. "It means the end of the world to these people if they can't bury their dead in the traditional manner," says Larry Moore, general manager of the Rabenhorst Funeral Home in Baton Rouge.

Yesterday, a woman, her daughter and son-in-law held a short funeral service for the woman's husband, a 59-year-old man who died in the aftermath of the storm. Unable to reach family members displaced in the evacuation of New Orleans, the three sat alone sobbing in a small chapel at Mothe Funeral Home in suburban Harvey, as Boyd Mothe, a funeral-home official read the 23rd Psalm. Mr. Mothe, who described the service, wouldn't identify members of the family by name.

They had held the hastily arranged service to beat the local government's order that residents leave by the end of the day.

The woman had returned to Jefferson Parish on Monday, only to find her husband dead in their home, where he had stayed behind while the others headed to Houston as the storm approached. It's likely he died of asphyxiation from the exhaust of his electric generator. "She started to cry as she was telling me she didn't want to have to cremate him because of the condition of the body," says Mr. Mothe, whose family-run company runs 13 funeral homes in the region, several of which are still flooded.

In the end cremation wasn't necessary, and the body was interred before noon at Westlawn Memorial Park and Mausoleum

Among the biggest adherents of the New Orleans funeral tradition are those most affected by Hurricane Katrina: impoverished blacks whose burial processions often feature parades and jazz bands. Some scholars have traced these so-called jazz funerals back to Africa. Duke University professor Karla F.C. Holloway says slaves brought to America burial processions involving call-and-response chants and musicians beating drums and tambourine-like instruments to help the dead on their way to heaven.

"The slaves in New Orleans would always accompany the dead to the burial site with rejoicing, because the rejoice was a release into a different kind of spiritual world, an ancestral world, which mixed with the Christian idea of being released into heaven," says Dr. Holloway.

In recent years, the tradition took a turn, when street gangs adopted the ritual to bury their murdered members. Then, the tradition gained a hip-hop quality. One of the biggest jazz funerals in recent years was for James "Soulja Slim" Tapp, an up-and-coming rapper who was fatally shot on his mother's front lawn. Soulja Slim's jazz funeral in 2003 sent thousands into the city's streets.

So deeply connected are music and death in New Orleans that the Web site of the Orleans Parish Coroner features the sound of its chief, Frank Minyard, playing the jazz trumpet.

But Katrina began wrecking that tradition even before making landfall. Death notices published in the days before the hurricane arrived struck tentative notes. "The service for Jennie is contingent on the current storm conditions," read the obituary for 63-year-old Jennie Marie Latino, who was scheduled to be buried on the morning Katrina hit New Orleans.

Now, the dead in New Orleans include some corpses that were already lying in funeral homes before the storm hit. Some funeral homes are under water, says Gene Walters, executive director of the Louisiana Funeral Directors Association.

Some funeral homes evacuated their dead. The Mothe chain moved about 10 bodies to the Jefferson Parish Forensics Center, a new facility with plenty of refrigeration capacity. The center is now storing nearly 200 bodies of people who failed to survive the aftermath of the storm.

Tradition in New Orleans calls for open caskets. But the bodies still lying in the flooded wreckage of New Orleans won't be viewable.

Once rescue workers turn their attention from the living to the dead, corpses will be brought to a refrigerated warehouse put up after the hurricane by federal officials outside New Orleans. But already, coroners' offices across Louisiana are filling up with the dead from New Orleans, most of them people who failed to survive the evacuation. "We had four buses pull into town with DOA's among the evacuees," says Sherri Basco of the Rapides Parish Coroner's Office, a nearly four-hour drive from New Orleans.

Several coroners' offices are fielding double their usual number of fatalities, says Randolph Williams, president of the Louisiana Coroners' Association.

Funeral directors around New Orleans are receiving calls from coroners' offices far and wide, reporting the deaths of evacuees who had wished to be buried in New Orleans. But Mr. Walters of the state funeral directors' association says those wishes are going unfulfilled because of the flooded condition of New Orleans cemeteries which are above ground. They were designed that way because the city is largely below sea level. "We're recommending that these people be entombed in holding crypts, until the dead can be returned to New Orleans, he says.

Holding crypts and refrigeration could preserve not only the dead but also the tradition of New Orleans funerals, but not now. And not with the sheer number of Katrina victims.

In an average year, Louisiana buries 44,000 bodies.

A September 11 *New York Times* article by Sheila Dewan tells of what is called unusually daunting challenges. She writes:

Faced with the loss of dental records, the rapid decomposition of bodies in this hot coastal environmental and the vast destruction of personal possessions, public health officials face a difficult, if not insurmountable, task in identifying many of the countless dead from Hurricane Katrina.

In fact, experts say, many of the advances in forensic science, developed in, the aftermath,exactly four years ago, of the nation's last calamitous loss of life are likely to be of little help in the circumstances of this storm, leaving many officials worrying over how many of the dead will remain nameless, and for how long.

"We're in a whole new realm of experience here," said Ricardo Zuniga, a spokesman for the Federal Emergency Management Agency's (FEMA) mortuary team. "People expect quick answers based on the paradigm they're used to. But this is not TV."

Some of the problems existed well before the storm plowed ashore. Louisiana and Mississippi are among the states with the lowest percentage of residents going to the dentist, for example, making it harder for officials to use that extremely reliable form of identification.

The storm itself caused plenty of problems as well, from the destruction of dental and medical records that did exist to the wide dispersal of family members who could provide DNA samples, photographs or basic information.

The task has been made more difficult by what some have criticized as a slow retrieval effort, with bodies in easily accessible, and visible locations remaining there for days. Coroners have said that even the bodies of people they knew personally were unrecognizable by the time they were collected.

"The ability to capture useful information from that body diminishes week to week," said Terry M. Edwards, the commander of the morgue operations in St. Gabriel, La., run by the Disaster Mortuary Operations Response Team, a division of Federal Emergency Manangentment Agency (FEMA).

Workers from the Kenyon Worldwide Emergency Services, a company contracted to retrieve bodies, reached Louisiana at the beginning of September but then awaited instructions from FEMA for several days, said Bill Berry, a spokesman for the company.

"I don't know how fast things could have gone, but it's going well now," Mr. Berry said Saturday, adding that in the three days that the crews had been working at full strength they had recovered every body whose location had been provided by search and rescue teams.

In response to questions about the rate of recovery, Mr. Zuniga said that resources had first been directed toward rescuing the living and were only now being refocused on collecting the dead.

The slow pace of retrieval partly explains the relatively slow death toll so far. As of Sunday, the number of confirmed deaths stood at 214 in Mississippi and 197 in Louisiana, although officials say it will be far higher when the final count is made.

Last week emergency management officials said that the final number in New Orleans would be well below a predication by the Mayor, C. Ray Nagin, that as many as 10,000 could have perished. But the news is not all good — FEMA is on the brink of setting up a second morgue in St. Gabriel, Mr. Zuniga said. The state is also looking for a place to bury even temporarily those remains not immediately identified.

Bob Johannessen, the chief spokesman for the Louisiana Department of Health and Hospitals, said a toll-free number had been set up for families to call if they had relatives feared dead. "It's a place for the process to start, to work through the grief of beginning the long road for possible identification," he said, adding that if bodies were buried and later identified, they would be exhumed and returned to families.

After the September 11 terrorist attacks, the problems confronting forensic scientists had to do primarily with the condition of the remains, which were desiccated or pulverized by fire or falling buildings, making it difficult to extract testable DNA. In other words, the challenge lay in collecting post-mortem information — body parts and fragments. Of the 2,749 people missing, 1,594 were identified by the office of the chief medical examiner in New York, or 58 percent.

Working with commercial laboratories, the medical examiner's office developed ways to test smaller and more degraded pieces of DNA than commonly used before.

With Hurricane Katrina, such methods will not be necessary in most cases because the bodies are intact. Far more formidable is the problem of collecting antemortem data — the dental records, photographs, fingerprints and DNA that will be compared to the bodies themselves. After September 11, families were asked to bring in toothbrushes or other personal items that bore the DNA of the deceased. Hurricane Katrina has destroyed or contaminated many of those items, making it necessary to take cheek swabs from blood relatives to get a DNA sample. The more family members; and the closer the relation, the more reliable the tests will be.

In Mississippi, the forensic dentists on the federal mortuary team have already identified dental offices on the coast that are still open and begun calling them to explain what they will be looking for, said Warren Tewes, a member of the team.

Edna Hall, who manages her grandson's dental office in Gulfport, Mississippi, said she had gotten a call from a FEMA dentist explaining that they would be asking for records and that the federal health privacy law did not apply. Ms. Hall said that although the office had lost its roof, X-rays kept inside filing cabinets were mostly dry and intact. But, she said, she knew of at least two other dentist's offices that had been destroyed.

That is not to say that the condition of bodies that have been submerged in water or trapped in hot attics for days will not compromise identification efforts. While cold water can slow decomposition, warm water accelerates it, experts say. After rigor mortis comes bloat and putrefaction, which can deteriorate some forms of DNA, making it necessary to use less exacting test methods. The next stage of decomposition in which soft tissue liquefies, happens more rapidly in water. .

After a week or more, bodies in water lose their skin and with it any fingerprints, tattoos or other distinct marks, said Lawrence Kobilinsky , a professor of forensic science at the John Jay College of Criminal Justice in New York. The environmental conditions of the Katrina floodwaters will only make the problem worse, Dr. Kobilinsky said, estimating that 20 percent of the bodies may never be identified.

"You, have incredibly large amounts of microorganism's in the water and reptiles, snakes, fish, that are all going to accelerate the decomposition rate," he said.

Still, in Mississippi, 46 of 161 bodies from the coastal counties have already been identified at the FEMA morgue.

In Louisiana, the bodies that have been identified, said Mr. Johanessen, were primarily hospital or nursing home patients whose identities were printed on bracelets or were otherwise easy to determine.

Coffin settled between the limbs of a tree.

In other cases, however, officials said that knowing the address where a body was found or finding a driver's license might not be sufficient to make an identification.

In Louisiana, the FEMA morgue is not making identifications or performing autopsies, both of which are the responsibility of the parish coroners, Mr. Johanessen said. The morgue is taking fingerprints, dental X-rays and photographs of bodies, as well as collecting any personal items found with them, to be used for later identification. Mr. Edwards, the morgue commander, declined to talk about the conditions of the bodies that had reached the morgue, which can handle 140 bodies a day.

The state's crime laboratories have taken charge of DNA identifications, said Ray Wickenheiser, the director of the Acadiana Crime Lab in New Iberia, La. He said a flow chart had been devised, beginning with the simplest means of visual identifications and going up through fingerprints, dental X-rays and pacemaker serial numbers to the most rarefied forms of DNA matching. "By the time we're done, we're going to try every possible means to identify them," Mr. Wickenheiser said.

"The big challenge is going to be getting those samples to compare," he said. "When the next of kin have been so widely dispersed, to try to now bring those people together, get the samples together from the next of kin, even find out who's missing — the tasks are going to be monumental."

Jan Kiernan, writing for the November issue of American Cemetery, includes the photograph of a coffin settled between the limbs of a huge tree. The article is entitled "Survivor Cemeteries".

"Survivor Cemeteries"

Kiernan writes: New Orleans, famous for rowdy Mardi Gras celebrations and sultry jazz, is also defined by its cemeteries, their beauty of which is equal parts historic and haunting and unique, made all the more so in the days after Hurricane Katrina battled its way across the city. That said, the uniqueness of these cemeteries – their above-ground tombs in particular – may in fact have protected them from an even worse fate.

The above-ground tombs of New Orleans, which appear as rows and rows of tiny houses, helped coin one of the city's high water tables, which will force airtight caskets buried any deeper than a few feet to unearth themselves and literally float. Early settlers of New Orleans tried various solutions, such as drilling holes in the caskets or lodging boulders on top of the gravesite. Yet, none of these was successful, leading to the famous, above-ground tombs of New Orleans which have been endlessly toured and photographed.

But the tours, for now, have stopped and the photographs have shifted from marble statue shots and lush landscapes to mausoleums ripped at the seams and rust-colored water lines striped across crypts. Hurricane Katrina hit New Orleans hard and individuals involved in all aspects of the cemetery industry have been scrambling to help in any way they can.

Much of Kiernan's story refers to cemeteries and funeral homes owned by Stewart Enterprises, a large conglomerate that owns five cemeteries and three funeral homes in New Orleans.

We, primarily, are writing about the privately owned African American funeral homes with long family ties, and about the church owned or city owned cemeteries.

St. Louis No. One, featured in our story, is said in November 2005, to have fared "pretty well" and was under water, but not destroyed.

Holt Cemetry, also one of our special cemeteries, established in the 1800s as a potter's field, did not fare quite as well, probably due to economics; most of the bodies are interred in the ground.

The cemetery records at Holt Cemetery were spotty at best, even before the hurricane, and some of the stones were already chipped and broken.

It is estimated by the city of New Orleans that it may take months for a careful evaluation and tours will probably not resume until spring of 2006.

The question of **Restoration** is major to the funeral directors, the cemetery owners, and to the families of the deceased.

David A. Yearsley, president of Ensure-a-Seal in Export, Pennsylvania, a company that manufactures a casket protection product for entombment, has offered his expertise to FEMA as well as to cemeterians hit by the hurricane, although he has not yet been asked to assess the damage.

Several of Yearsley's New Orleans' clients have contacted him, though, concerning temporary storage of casketed remains for an indefinite period of time in their cemeteries. "One cemeterian is going to take the casketed remains and seal them and then place the sealed unit in a burial vault," said Yearsley. "This burial vault will remain above ground until the New Orleans cemeteries are again operational."

Yearsley's expertise in on-site mausoleum and crypt chamber inspection and cleaning as well as casket removals and re-entombment place him in a unique position to advise those cemeterians who were the hardest hit, particularly those with damaged mausoleums, about what to expect in the coming months.

"It is my observation that the primary goal of everyone involved is the initial recovery of bodies and existing caskets," said Yearsley. "They will remove the bodies and casketed remains to a secure location, make an initial determination of the condition of the remains, identify the remains if possible and contact the next of kin."

The identification process is what will take time, according to Yearsley, as there are certain to be remains with no identification at all. With family members now scattered across the country and medical records, in some cases, lost, identification will be a tedious and time- consuming task.

Also, "the remains are going to be in various stages of decomposition, resulting in the additional task of identification and storage for a long period of time," added Yearsley.

Yearsley explained that several community mausoleums in the area were damaged in the storm's surge. The water, which in some cases completely removed the granite and marble crypt fronts of the mausoleums as high as five stories, also broke and removed plastic shutters that were caulked in place.

From that damage, "caskets were easily removed from the existing concrete crypt chambers as the water receded," added Yearsley.

In cases where the mausoleums were damaged, the immediate tasks, according to Yearsley, must include the following:

- determine how many caskets are missing;

- determine if any structural damage was caused to the mausoleum;

- examine the occupied crypt chambers to determine if any water damage exists;

- control any existing caskets; and clean the open crypt chambers.

After these immediate needs are taken care of, the cemeterian will need to purchase new plastic shutters and granite or marble crypt fronts to replace the lost ones. In addition, the crypt fronts will require a personalized bronze crypt front or bronze lettering, and the existing crypt front hardware will have to be inspected for any damage.

Finally, the cemeterian must find a way "to control the conditions that exist with the final disposition of the remains." And, perhaps most importantly, the cemetery must be able to assure families that their loved ones' casketed remains are clean and dry.

Of course, said Yearsley, "a major concern is the enormous cost that will be attached to this catastrophic event." But he also believes that "in the weeks and months ahead, everyone in the memorialization industry will strive to provide a professional and dignified approach for the final disposition of the remains of the victims of Hurricane Katrina."

Yearsley is right. According to Joe Budzinski, internal chief operating officer for the International Cemetery and Funeral Association (ICFA), many of the association's members have come forward offering assistance to the cemeteries that were damaged.

"We are in contact with various individuals and organizations in the affected areas," said Budzinski. "Because so many of the affected areas are still uninhabitable, the various government, military and recovery organizations are going to be managing the situation for the time being."

Incidentally, Hurricane Katrina forced (ICFA) International Cemetery Funeral Association to reschedule its annual convention, scheduled for March 15-17 in New Orleans, for March 13-16, 2006 at the Venetian Resort & Casino in Las Vegas.

In the meantime, ICFA has been encouraging its members to give to charitable organizations that have "taken on such a massive task in caring for and relocating the victims from Louisiana, as well as helping to rebuild homes and provide food and shelter throughout Mississippi," added Budzinski.

Eventually, though, restoration specialists will be in demand. FEMA has circulated one call for 15-20 volunteer preservationists to work as part of the organization's "environmental and historic preservation cadre of reservists." According to FEMA, "this is on-call employment, but due to Hurricane Katrina, there are immediate needs for these specialists."

Pennsylvania historian Frank G. Matero is likely to travel to New Orleans with a specific mission in mind. Matero, who chairs the department of historic preservation at the University of Pennsylvania, spent a lot of time with his graduate students on the Dead Space Project, a two-phase documentation and conservation project which focused on New Orleans cemetery, St. Louis Cemetery No. 1. Matero and his students comprehensively mapped and surveyed the cemetery in order to create practical conservation guidelines for its continued care and maintenance.

Digital technology, which was central to this project, assisted in the study by allowing the group to link archival maps, images and text with the field survey information, thus building a robust database. In addition, they used Geographic Information System (GIS) mapping to provide descriptive and analytical tools to guide the conservation efforts.

Matero's work is especially meaningful after Hurricane Katrina. "Right now we have the best before data on all physical aspects of the tombs and landscape for St. Louis No.1," said Matero. "We want to return to assess conditions and especially to verify that our work was successful."

Although he does not yet know the extent of the damage to this cemetery, he said that any unstable tombs could "fill with water and explode or collapse, spilling the contents."

Fortunately for St. Louis No.1, "emergency repairs were made to most 'at risk' tombs several years ago as part of our Save America's Treasures Grant."

As far as the future of St. Louis No.1 and the other cemeteries hit by the storm, Matero said the restoration process will include reassessment, water release from tombs, drainage and the shoring of unstable walls and elements, all of which will cost money and take time.

Matero also worries about vandalism which, he said, "was rampant before the flood and I suspect more will occur now, especially theft of iron-work and stone sculpture."

Whether they are historians, preservationists, members of the community, associations or even cemeterians not directly affected by the storm, thousands in and around the industry have, indeed, been affected.

Bruce Weber, writing for the New York Times, gives a heart-wrenching view of Holt Cemetery

Holt Cemetery, one of the poorest and most poorly tended burial grounds in New Orleans, was submerged in floodwater after Hurricane Katrina ravaged the city on August 29, 2005. Afterward, its markers were left askew, its grasses browned and lifeless.

But it may never have been a sadder place than it was on Tuesday, All Saints' Day, when Roman Catholics here traditionally visit the graves of loved ones and honor the dead.

Last year on this day, Holt was "packed, packed," said Karin Legohn, as she weeded the plot where her grandmother lay. But this morning the only mourners in sight were Ms. Legohn and her mother, Leverne O. McWilliams, who left a red flower in a slender vase in front of her mother's tilted stone.

"I never miss putting a flower in the vase," Ms. Mc Williams said quietly.

Holt is where many of the city's poor black citizens bury their dead, and its emptiness was one more reminder that the storm disproportionately displaced more of the city's poor than the rich. People were not at the cemetery, said Ms. Legohn, because they were no longer in New Orleans.

"This place doesn't look so bad," said Ms. Legohn, who left after Hurricane Katrina for Decatur, Alabama, and returned to look in on her mother, whose neighborhood did not flood, and to go to the cemetery. "I lost everything so it looks a lot better than my house."

At other Catholic cemeteries, where burials have only just resumed, visitors were plentiful, but even there the usual crowds were thinned, and their fellow mourners actively missed by those who were there.

At Greenwood Cemetery, where stones had toppled and water lines were visible on many rows of crypts, Kay Marie Miller, with her husband, her mother, daughter and granddaughter — four generations — paid homage to an infant daughter who died in 1976.

"It's sad to see the tombstones knocked over, and sad that not very many people are here," Ms. Miller said.

All Saints' Day thus played out in much the way its secular twin, Halloween had done the day before, with a hunger for the famIliar ritual but a tinge of urgency and desperation. With schools still closed and children in exile, trick-or-treaters were harder to find on Monday.

Uptown, on State Street, where children usually traipse in great gangs from brightly decorated house to brightly decorated house, the celebration was muted.

"Halloween is a big part of living on this block," said Isaac Ryan, a lawyer who was leading his 5 year old daughter Claire, who was dressed as a snow princess, on a trick-or-treating mission. "It's known in the city. There used to be busloads of kids dropped off here. We'd like it to get back to nomal as soon as possibble."

Even in the French Quarter, although the annual costume parade gamely strove for noisy normalcy, it caused only a flicker of its customary chaos. Some revelers marked the occasion by wrapping themselves in blue plastic FEMA tarps or wearing black and white tie-dyed pajamas to represent mold or enclosing their torsos in white cardboard boxes, embodying refrigerators, the city's momentary icon of detritus. But it did not quite add up to letting the good times roll.

"There's a lot of grief in this city now, so the question people always ask about New Orleans is even more pertinent," said Martha Ward, a writer and professor of anthropology and urban studies at the University of New Orleans. "Are they just throwing a party? Or are they celebrating life against the inevitability of suffering?"

Indeed, the confluence of these two holidays, Halloween and All Saints' Day, is always keenly felt here, because more than any other American city, New Orleans is a place where spiritual and secular rituals are plentifully entwined, as much a part of the strange-bedfellows Creole culture as andouille sausage and crawfish in the same soup bowl.

Catholic fervor coexists in New Orleans with the mysticism of voodoo in an atmosphere of neighborly tolerance, where ancestors are revered and revelry and mourning are often one.

That is one reason jazz funeral processions – one on Saturday, a mock funeral for the victims of Katrina, and one on Tuesday, an annual ceremony to honor the dead – bracketed the two holidays.

"It's a very spiritual place," said Sallie Ann Glassman, a voodoo priestess who leads a Day of the Dead ceremony every November 1 in the temple behind her house in the Bywater neighborhood."

"It's our baseline," she said. "We're not a financially driven, or financiially successful city. But we're rich in the spirit here."

That the floods after Hurricane Katrina left bodies floating in the street and the city still with unburied dead was an image that escaped few people during All Saints' Day and Halloween and made this year's observances especially poignant.

"All Saints' Day is especially important this year because of the lives lost in the storm," said Duplain W. Rhodes Ill, whose family business of funeral homes, founded by his grandfather, dates back to 1884.

His main mortuary was lost to flooding, but a second funeral home, across the Mississippi River in Gretna, was the host of All Saints' Day that preceded Saturday's jazz funeral for the storm victims.

"A thousand people dead!" he said. "A large number not identified yet! It's very, very frustrating for the families we've spoken to."

When a city cannot bury its dead, "the thin veneer of civilization is off," said Ms. Ward, the anthropology professor who is also the author of "Voodoo Queen," a biography of Marie Levaux, the leading voodoo priestess of 19th century New Orleans.

"Halloween is usually a kind of theater for us, in which the dead come back and mingle with the living" she said. "It's an occasion where we're playing at horror, but it can't be any scarier than what we've just gone through."

Msgr. Andrew Taormina,who celebrated All Saints' Day Mass at the Metairie Funeral Home, spoke about the dead as a reason for rebuilding the city.

"People have been asking, 'Should, we come back here?'" he said. "But this is where our people are buried, This is where we visit to show them honor. When I perform funerals, I tell people, 'A little bit of every one of you is in the coffin with that person.' And this time of year, at All Saints' Day and even Halloween, it's even clearer that we're going to lose something very, very precious here if we don't try to come back. So we've got to try."

St. Louis One, the city's oldest burial ground, is famous in New Orleans, but like many other places here, famous and not, it was left disheveled by the storm. Marie Levaux is buried there. So is Homer Plessy, whose failed Supreme Court challenge, in 1896, Plessy v. Ferguson, ushered in the era of "separate but equal" statutes that defined the Jim Crow South.

Eleanor Bellas, who was there today, is not famous. She had come to see her husband, Christy T. Bellas Jr., who died a year ago, at 52.

"I usually like coming on All Saints' Day because it's the only time of year you see fresh flowers," she said. "This year you don't see anything. It's sad." She kissed her fingertips and touched them to her husband's crypt.

"You should never forget the dead," she said. "A lot of people do. I don't."

Going the Distance with Katrina's Dead, Thomas Lynch writing for the American Cemetery:

Among her many cruelties is the one by which Katrina has widened the gulf and blurred the borders between the living and the dead. There are so many gone, missing and adrift, disappeared or unidentified or unaccounted for, swept away from the people and homeplaces that knew them and named them and called them their own. Lost forever or for the time being. And "good" news in New Orleans this September is like the good, god-awful news in New York four Septembers ago, or in the world washed away last St. Stephens Day – that we have recovered what "remains" – something, anything – that what was lost has been found; that we have got them back to let them go again.

These sad duties are unique to our species – this searching and watching, this waiting and waking, this going the distance with our dead. Other things that live and die do not seem to bother. But we do. Wherever our spirits go, or don't, ours is a species that has learned to deal with death (the idea of the thing) by dealing with the dead (the thing itself) in all the flesh and frailty of our human condition. Drowned or damaged, disfigured or decomposed, we process grief by "processing" the objects of our grief, the bodies of the dead, from one station to the next in this most difficult pilgrimage. We bear mortality by bearing mortals – the living and the dead — to the brink of a changed reality: Heaven or Blessed Memory or Whatever Is Next. We commit and commend them into the nothingness or somethingness, into the presence of God or God's absence. Whatever afterlife there is or isn't, human beings have marked their ceasing to be by going the distance with their dead – to the fire or the grave, the holy tree or deep sea, whatever sacred place we consign them to. We've been doing this for forty thousand years; before we learned farming or alphabets, we learned funerals. Before we built levees or governments, we built tombs and pyres. Our kind cares for their dead: not because it matters to those who have died, but because it matters to those who survive them.

The bodies of the newly dead afloat in New Orleans are neither debris nor remnant, nor are they entirely icon or essence. They are, rather, changelings, incubates, hatchlings of a new reality that bore their names and dates, their image and likeness as surely in the eyes and ears of their people as word of their birth did in the ears of our parents and their parents. It is wise to treat such new things tenderly, carefully, with honor.

God bless the heroes who are saving lives in those sodden parishes.

And the heroes – God bless them, God help them too – who serve the living by caring for the dead.

This essay was broadcast on National Public Radio's "All Things Considered"

FEDERAL TRADE COMMISSION RULES

CHAPTER THIRTEEN

"Goin' Home"

Goin' home, goin' home, I'm a-goin' home;
Quiet like, some still day, I'm jes' goin' home.

It's not far, jes' close by, Through an open door;
Work all done, care laid by, Gwine to fear no more.

Mother's there 'spectin' me, Father's waitin' too;
Lots o' folks gathered there, All the friends I knew.
All the friends I knew.

(Home, home, I'm goin' home!)

Nothin' lost, all's, gain, No more fret nor pain.
No more stumblin' on the way,
No more longin' for the day,
Gwine to roam no more!

Mornin' star lights the way. Res'less dream all done;
Shadows gone, break o' day, Real life jes' begun.

Dere's, no break, ain't no end, Jes' a-liv-in' on,
Wide awake, with smile, Goin' on and on.

Goin' home, goin', I'm jes' goin' home;
It's not far, jes' close by, Through an open door.
I'm jes' goin' home.
Goin' home.

When a loved one dies, grieving family members and friends often are confronted with dozens of decisions about the funeral - all of which must be made quickly and often under great emotional duress. What kind of funeral should it be? What funeral provider should you use? Should you bury or cremate the body, or donate it to science? What are you legally required to buy? What other arrangements should you plan? And, as callous as it many sound, how much is it all going to cost.

Pre-Need

To help relieve their families of some of these decisions, an increasing number of people are planning their own funerals, designating their funeral preferences, and sometimes even paying for them in advance. They see funeral planning as an extension of will and estate planning.

Planning

Thinking ahead can help you make informed and thoughtful decisions about funeral arrangements. It allows you to choose the specific items you want and need and compare the prices offered by several funeral providers. It also spares your survivors the stress of making these decisions under the pressure of time and strong emotions.

You can make arrangements directly with a funeral establishment or through a funeral planning or memorial society - a nonprofit organization that provides information about funerals and disposition but doesn't offer funeral services. If you choose to contact such a group, recognize that while some funeral homes may include the word "society" in their names, they are not nonprofit organizations.

One other important consideration when planning a funeral pre-need is where the remains will be buried, entombed or scattered. In the short time between the death and burial of a loved one, many family members fmd themselves rushing to buy a cemetery plot or grave - often without careful thought or a personal visit to the site. That's why it's in the family's best interest to buy cemetery plots before you need them.

You may wish to make decisions about your arrangements in advance, but not pay for them in advance. Keep in mind that over time, prices may go up and businesses may close or change ownership. However, in some areas with increased competition, prices may go down overtime. It's a good idea to review and revise your decisions every few years, and to make sure your family is aware of your wishes.

It's a good idea to review and revise your decisions every few years.

Put your preferences in writing, give copies to family members and your attorney, and keep a copy in a handy place. Don't designate your preferences in your will, because a will often is not found or read until after the funeral. And avoid putting the only copy of your preferences in a safe deposit box. That's because your family may have to make arrangements on a weekend or holiday. before the box can be opened.

Prepaying

Millions of Americans have entered into contracts to prearrange their funerals and prepay some or all of the expenses involved. Laws of individual states govern the prepayment of funeral goods and services; various states have laws to help ensure these advance payments are available to funeral products and services when they are needed. But protections vary widely from state to state, some state laws offer little or no effective protection. Some state laws require the funeral home or cemetery to place a percentage of the prepayment in a state-regulated trust or to purchase a life insurance policy with the death benefits assigned to the funeral home or cemetery.

If you're thinking about prepaying for funeral goods and services, it's important to consider these issues before putting down any money:

What are you are paying for? Are you buying only merchandise, like a casket and vault, or are you purchasing funeral services as well?

What happens to the money you've prepaid? States have different requirements for funds paid for prearranged funeral services.

What happens to the interest income on money that is prepaid and put into a trust account?

Are you protected if the firm you dealt with goes out of business?

Can you cancel the contract and get a full refund if you change your mind?

What happens if you move to a different area or die while away from home? Some prepaid funeral plans can be transferred, but often at an added cost.

Be sure to tell your family about the plans you've made; let them know where the documents are filed.

If your family isn't aware that you've made plans, your wishes may not be carried out. And if family members don't know that you've prepaid the funeral costs, they could end up paying for the same arrangements. You may wish to consult an attorney on the best way to ensure that your wishes are followed.

The Funeral Rule

Most funeral providers are professionals who strive to serve their clients' needs and best interests. But some aren't. They may take advantage of their clients through inflated prices, overcharges, double charges or unnecessary services. Fortunately there's a federal law that makes it easier for you to choose only those goods and services you want or need and to pay only for those you select, whether you are making arrangements pre-need or at need.

The Funeral Rule, enforced by The Federal Trade Commission, requires funeral directors to give you itemized prices in person and, if you ask, over the phone. The Rule also requires funeral directors to give you other information about their goods and services. For example, if you ask about funeral arrangements in person, the funeral home must give you a written price list to keep that shows the goods and services the home offers. If you want to buy a casket or outer burial container, the funeral provider must show you descriptions of the available selections and the prices before actually showing you the caskets.

Many funeral providers offer various "packages" of commonly selected goods and services that make up a funeral. But when you arrange for a funeral, you have the right to buy individual goods and services. That is, you do not have to accept a package that may include items you do not want.

According to the Funeral Rule:

You have the right to choose the funeral goods and services you want (some exceptions).

The funeral provider must state this right in writing on the general price list.

If state or local law requires you to buy any particular item, the funeral provider must disclose it on the price list, with a reference to the specific law.

The funeral provider may not refuse, or charge a fee, to handle a casket you bought elsewhere.

A funeral provider that offers cremations must make alternative containers available.

What kind of funeral do you want?

Every family is different, and not everyone wants the same type of funeral. Funeral practices are influenced by religious and cultural traditions, costs and personal preferences. These factors help determine whether the funeral will be elaborate or simple, public or private, religious or secular, and where it will be held. They also influence whether the body will be present at the funeral, if there will be a viewing or visitation, and if so, whether the casket will be open or closed, and whether the remains will be buried or cremated.

Among the choices you'll need to make are whether you want one of these basic type of funerals, or something in between.

"Traditional," full-service funeral
This type of funeral, often referred to by funeral providers as a "traditional" funeral usually includes a viewing or visitation and formal funeral service, use of a hearse to transport the body to the funeral site and cemetery, and burial, entombment or cremation of the remains. It is generally the most

expensive type of funeral. In addition to the funeral home's basic services fee, costs often include embalming and dressing the body; rental of the funeral home for the viewing or service; and use of vehicles to transport the family if they don't use their own. The costs of a casket, cemetery plot or crypt and other funeral goods and services also must be factored in.

Every family is different and not everyone wants the same type of funeral.

Direct Burial

The body is buried shortly after death, usually in a simple container. No viewing or visitation is involved~ so no embalming is necessary. A memorial service may be held at the graveside or later. Direct burial usually costs less than the "traditional," full-service funeral. Costs include the funeral home's basic services fee, as well as transportation and care of the body, the purchase of a casket or burial container and a cemetery plot or crypt. If the family chooses to be at the cemetery for the burial, the funeral home often charges an additional fee for a graveside service.

Direct cremation

The body is cremated shortly after death, without embalming. The cremated remains are placed in an urn or other container. No viewing or visitation is involved, although a memorial service may be held, with or without the cremated remains present. The remains can be kept in the home, buried or placed in a crypt or niche in a cemetery, or buried or scattered in a favorite spot. Direct cremation usually costs less than the "traditional," full-service funeral. Costs include the funeral home's basic services fee, as well as transportation and care of the body. A crematory fee may be included or, if the funeral home does not own the crematory, the fee may be added on. There also will be a charge for an urn or other container. The cost of a cemetery plot or crypt is included only if the remains are buried or entombed.

Funeral providers who offer direct cremations also must offer to provide an alternative container that can be used in place of a casket.

Choosing A Funeral Provider

Many people don't realize that they are not legally required to use a funeral home to plan and conduct a funeral. However, because they have little experience with the many details and legal requirements involved and may be emotionally distraught when it's time to make the plans, many people find the services of a professional funeral home to be a comfort.

Consumers often select a funeral home or cemetery because it's close to home, has served the family in the past, or has been recommended by someone they trust. But people who limit their search to just one funeral home may risk paying more than necessary for the funeral or narrowing their choice of goods and services.

Comparison shopping need not be difficult, especially if it's done before the need for a funeral arises. If you visit a funeral home in person, the funeral provider is required by law to give you a general price list itemizing the cost of the items and services the home offers. If the general price list does not include specific prices of caskets or outer burial containers, the law requires the funeral director to show you the price lists for those items before showing you the items.

Sometimes it's more convenient and less stressful to "price shop" funeral homes by telephone. The Funeral Rule requires funeral directors to provide price information over the phone to any caller who asks for it. In addition, many funeral homes are happy to mail you their price lists, although that is not required by law.

When comparing prices, be sure to consider the total cost of all items together, in addition to the costs of single items. Every funeral home should have price lists that include all the items essential for the different types bf arrangements it offers. Many funeral homes offer package funerals that may cost less than purchasing individual items or services. Offering package funerals is permitted by law, as long as an itemized price list also is provided. But only by using the price lists can you accurately compare total costs.

In addition, there's a growing trend toward consolidation in the funeral home industry, and many neighborhood funeral homes are thought to be locally owned when in fact, they're owned by a national corporation. If this issue is important to you, you may want to ask if the funeral home is locally owned.

Funeral Costs
Funeral costs include:

1. Basic services fee for the funeral director and staff

The Funeral Rule allows funeral providers to charge a basic services fee that customers cannot decline to pay. The basic services fee includes services that are common to all funerals, regardless of the specific arrangement. These include funeral planning, securing the necessary permits and copies of death certificates, preparing the notices, sheltering the remains, and coordinating the arrangements with the cemetery, crematory or other third parties. The fee does not include charges for optional services or merchandise.

2. Charges for other services and merchandise

These are costs for optional goods and services such as transporting the remains; embalming and other preparation; use of the funeral home for the viewing, ceremony or memorial service; use of equipment and staff for a graveside service; use of a hearse or limousine; a casket, outer burial container or alternate container; and cremation or interment.

3. Cash advances

These are fees charged by the funeral home for goods and services it buys from outside vendors on your behalf, including flowers, obituary notices, pallbearers, officiating clergy, and organists and soloists. Some funeral providers charge you their cost for the items they buy on your behalf. Others add a service fee to their cost. The Funeral Rule requires those who charge an extra fee to disclose that fact in writing, although it doesn't require them to specify the amount of their markup. The Rule also requires funeral providers to tell you if there are refunds, discounts or rebates from the supplier on any cash advance item.

Calculating The Actual Cost
The funeral provider must give you an itemized statement of the total cost of the funeral goods and services you have selected when you are making the arrangements. If the funeral provider doesn't know the cost of the cash advance items at the time, he or she is required to give you a written "good faith estimate." This statement also must disclose any legal, cemetery or crematory requirements that you purchase any specific funeral goods or services.

The Funeral Rule does not require any specific format for this information. Funeral providers may include it in any document they give you at the end of your discussion about funeral arrangements.

SERVICES AND PRODUCTS

Embalming
Many funeral homes require embalming if you're planning a viewing or visitation. But embalming generally is not necessary or legally required if the body is buried or cremated shortly after death. Eliminating this service can save you hundreds of dollars. Under the Funeral Rule, a funeral provider:

may not provide embalming services without permission.

may not falsely state that embalming is required bylaw.

must disclose in writing that embalming is not required by law, except in certain special cases.

may not charge a fee for unauthorized embalming unless embalming is required by state law.

must disclose in writing that you usually have the right to choose a disposition, such as direct cremation or immediate burial, that does not require embalming if you do not want this service.

must disclose in writing that some funeral arrangements, such as a funeral with viewing, may make embalming a practical necessity and, if so, a required purchase.

CASKETS

For a "traditional," full-service funeral:

A casket often is the single most expensive item you'll buy if you plan a "traditional," full-service funeral. Caskets vary widely in style and price and are sold primarily for their visual appeal. Typically, they're constructed of metal, wood, fiberboard, fiberglass or plastic. Although an average casket costs slightly more than $2,000, some mahogany, bronze or copper caskets sell for as much as $10,000.

When you visit a funeral home or showroom to shop for a casket, the Funeral Rule requires the funeral director to show you a list of caskets the company sells, with descriptions and prices, before showing you the caskets. Industry studies show that the average casket shopper buys one of the first three models shown, generally the middle-priced of the three. So it's in the seller's best interest to start out by showing you higher-end models. If you haven't seen some of the lower-priced models on the price list, ask to see them - but don't be surprised if they're not prominently displayed, or not on display at all.

Traditionally, caskets have been sold only by funeral homes. But with increasing frequency, showrooms and web sites operated by "third-party" dealers are selling caskets. You can buy a casket from one of these dealers and have it shipped directly to the funeral home. The Funeral Rule requires funeral homes to agree to use a casket you bought elsewhere, and doesn't allow them to charge you a fee for using it.

No matter where or when you're buying a casket, it's important to remember that its purpose is to provide a dignified way to move the body before burial or cremation. No casket, regardless of its qualities or cost, will preserve a body forever. Metal caskets frequently are described as "gasketed," "protective" or "sealer" caskets. These terms mean that the casket has a rubber gasket or some other feature that is designed to delay the penetration of water into the casket and prevent rust. The Funeral Rule forbids claims that these features help preserve the remains indefinitely because they don't. They just add to the cost of the casket.

Most metal caskets are made from rolled steel of varying gauges - the lower the gauge, the thicker the steel. Some metal caskets come with a warranty for longevity. Wooden caskets generally are not gasketed and don't have a warranty for longevity. They can be hardwood like mahogany, walnut, cherry or oak. or softwood like pine. Pine caskets are a less expensive option, but funeral homes rarely display them. Manufacturers of both wooden and metal caskets usually warrant workmanship and materials.

For cremation:

Many families that opt to have their loved ones cremated rent a casket from the funeral home for the visitation and funeral, eliminating the cost of buying a casket. If you opt for visitation and cremation, ask about the rental option. For those who choose a direct cremation without a viewing or other ceremony where the body is present, the funeral provider must offer an inexpensive unfinished wood box or alternative container, a non-metal enclosure - pressboard, cardboard or canvas - that is cremated with the body.

Under the Funeral Rule, funeral directors who offer direct cremations:

may not tell you that state or local law requires a casket for direct cremations, because none do;

must disclose in writing your right to buy an unfinished wood box or an alternative container for a direct cremation; and

must make an unfinished wood box or other alternative container available for direct cremations.

Burial Vaults or Grave Liners

Burial vaults or grave liners, also known as burial containers, are commonly used in "traditional," full-service funerals. The vault or liner is placed in the ground before burial, and the casket is lowered into it at burial. The purpose is to prevent the ground from caving in as the casket deteriorates over time. A grave liner is made of reinforced concrete and will satisfy any cemetery requirement. Grave liners cover only the top and sides of the casket. A burial vault is more substantial and expensive than a grave liner. It surrounds the casket in concrete or another material and may be sold with a warranty of protective strength.

State laws do not require a vault or liner, and funeral providers may not tell you otherwise. However, keep in mind that many cemeteries require some type of outer burial container to prevent the grave from sinking in the future. Neither grave liners nor burial vaults are designed to prevent the eventual decomposition of human remains. It is illegal for funeral providers to claim that a vault will keep water, dirt or other debris from penetrating into the casket if that's not true.

Before showing you any outer burial containers, a funeral provider is required to give you a list of prices and descriptions. It may be less expensive to buy an outer burial container from a third-party dealer than from a funeral home or cemetery. Compare prices from several sources before you select a model.

Preservative Processes and Products

As far back as the ancient Egyptians, people have used oils, herbs and special body preparations to help preserve the bodies of their dead. Yet, no process or products have been devised to preserve a body in the grave indefinitely. The Funeral Rule prohibits funeral providers from telling you that it can be done. For example, funeral providers may not claim that either embalming or a particular type of casket will preserve the body of the deceased for an unlimited time.

Cemetery Sites

When you are purchasing a cemetery plot, consider the location of the cemetery and whether it meets the requirements of your family's religion. Other considerations include what, if any, restrictions the cemetery places on burial vaults purchased elsewhere, the type of monuments or memorials it allows, and whether flowers or other remembrances may be placed on graves.

Cost is another consideration. Cemetery plots can be expensive, especially in metropolitan areas. Most, but not all, cemeteries require you to purchase a grave liner, which will cost several hundred dollars. Note that there are charges - usually hundreds of dollars - to open a grave for interment and additional charges to fill it in. Perpetual care on a cemetery plot sometimes is included in the purchase price, but it's important to clarify that point before you buy the site or service. If it's not included, look for a separate endowment care fee for maintenance and groundskeeping.

If you plan to bury your loved one's cremated remains in a mausoleum or columbarium, you can expect to purchase a crypt and pay opening and closing fees, as well as charges for endowment care and other services. The FTC's Funeral Rule does not cover cemeteries and mausoleums unless they sell both funeral goods and funeral services, so be cautious in making your purchase to ensure that you receive all pertinent price and other information, and that you're being dealt with fairly.

GLOSSARY OF TERMS

Courtesy of the California Department of Consumer Affairs, Cemetery and Funeral Bureau

Alternative Container

An unfinished wood box or other non-metal receptacle without ornamentation, often made of fiberboard, pressed wood or composition materials, and generally lower in cost than caskets.

Casket/Coffin

A box or chest for burying remains.

Cemetery Property
A grave, crypt or niche,

Cemetery Services
Opening and closing graves, crypts or niches; setting grave liners and vaults; setting markers; and long-term maintenance of cemetery grounds and facilities.

Columbarium
A structure with niches (small spaces) for placing cremated remains in urns or other approved containers. It may be outdoors or part of a mausoleum.

Cremation
Exposing remains and the container encasing them to extreme heat and flame and processing the resulting bone fragments to a uniform size and consistency.

Crypt
A space in a mausoleum or other building to hold cremated or whole remains.

Disposition
The placement of cremated or whole remains in their final resting place.

Endowment Care Fund
Money collected from cemetery property purchasers and placed in trust for the maintenance and upkeep of the cemetery.

Entombment
Burial in a mausoleum.

Funeral Ceremony
A service commemorating the deceased, with the body present.

Funeral Services
Services provided by a funeral director and staff, which may include consulting with the family on funeral planning; transportation, shelter, refrigeration and embalming of remains; preparing and filing notices; obtaining authorizations and permits; and coordinating with the cemetery, crematory or other third parties.

Funeral Planning Society
See Memorial Society.

Grave
A space in the ground in a cemetery for the burial of remains.

Grave Liner or Outer Container
A concrete cover that fits over a casket in a grave. Some liners cover tops and sides of the casket. Others, referred to as vaults, completely enclose the casket. Grave liners minimize ground settling.

Graveside Service
A service to commemorate the deceased held at the cemetery before burial.

Interment
Burial in the ground, inurnment or entombment.

Inurnment
The placing of cremated remains in an urn.

Mausoleum
A building in which remains are buried or entombed.

Memorial Service
A ceremony commemorating the deceased, without the body present.

Memorial Society
An organization that provides information about funerals and disposition~ but is not part of the state-regulated funeral industry.

Niche
A space in a columbarium, mausoleum or niche wall to hold an urn.

Urn
A container to hold cremated remains. It can be placed in a columbarium or mausoleum, or buried in the ground.

Vault
A grave liner that completely encloses a casket.

APPENDIX

Small Cemeteries throughout the USA

Detroit area African American Funeral Homes

Past Detroit Mayors buried at Elmwood Cemetery

Canadian Historians

Mortuary Science Schools in the USA

African Burial Ground - Memorial Design,
New York City

Those Who Prepare The Ground

Buried History of Rural Town's Black Pioneers

Officer Funeral Homes-Illinois and Missouri

Photographs of Funeral Directors, 1947 & 1951

SMALL CEMETERIES THROUGHOUT THE USA

Alabama

Bullock County
County Line AME Zion
Church Cemetery

Butler County
Bennett Cemetery
May Cemetery
St. Luke Cemetery
Pressley Cemetery
Springhill Cemetery
Stamps Cemetery
Chambers County
Finley Cemetery

Colbert County
St. Paul's Baptist Church Cemetery
Covington County
Good Hope Cemetery
Henry County
Balkum Baptist Church Cemetery
Little Rocky Mount Freewill Baptist
Church Cemetery

Houston County
St. Stephens AME Church Cemetery

Jefferson County
New Grace Hill Cemetery & Zion
Memorial Gardens

Lamar County
Wells Family Cemetery

Lowndes County
David Gordon Cemetery
Mi. Moriah Baptist
Church Cemetery
Rudolph Hill Cemetery

Macon County
Tuskegee Cemetery

Marengo County
Antioch Baptist Church Cemetery
Ayers Cemetery
Clover Hill Cemetery
Coleman Cemetery
First Baptist Church
Cemetery of Linden
First Missionary
Baptist Church Cemetery
Glovers Primitive Baptist Church
Cemetery
Hosea Cemetery
Howell Cemetery
Jackson Cemetery
Living Church Cemetery
Lovely Baptist Church Cemetery
Magnolia Church Cemetery
Millers Chapel Cemetery
Mount Mariah Baptist Church
Cemetery
Mount Zion Cemetery
New Hope Church Cemetery

Old Union Cemetery

Paradise Church Cemetery

Pine Grove Baptist Church Cemetery

Rivers Cemetery

Shady Union Baptist Cemetery

Sidney Chapel AME Zion Church Cemetery

Small Memorial Cemetery (AMEZ Church)

St. James Church Cemetery

St. Luke Church Cemetery

St. Paul Church Cemetery

St. Paul Baptist Church Cemetery

St. Wisdom Cemetery

Stephens Cemetery

Union Baptist Church Cemetery

Mobile County Bailey Cemetery

Prichard Memorial Gardens

Whistler Citizens Cemetery

Monroe County

Antioch Missionary Baptist Church Cemetery

Randolph County

Bethel East Cemetery

Canaan Baptist Church Cemetery

Galilee Primitive Baptist Church Cemetery

McBurnett Cemetery

Oak Ridge United Methodist Church Cemetery

Pleasant Grove Cemetery

Rockdale Cemetery

Union Hill Cemetery

Tuscaloosa County

Brookwood Cemetery

Fairview Cemetery

Mt. Zion Holiness Church Cemetery

Old Prewitt Slave Cemetery

Washington County

Friendship Missionary Baptist Church Cemetery

St. Union Missionary Baptist Church Cemetery

Wilcox County

Antioch Baptist Church Cemetery

Arkadelphia Baptist Church Cemetery

Bear Creek AME Church Cemetery

Bethel AME Church Cemetery

Bethel Church Cemetery

Boiling Spring Baptist Church Cemetery

Brazeal AME Church Cemetery

Dulaney AME Church Cemetery

First Baptist Church Cemetery

Harris Hill Cemetery

Little Rock AME Church Cemetery

Little Zion #1 Baptist
Church Cemetery

Macedonia Baptist
Church Cemetery

McConnico Cemetery

Mt. Olive AME Church Cemetery

Mt. Pleasant Church Cemetery

Mt. Zion Church Cemetery

Old Zion Missionary Baptist
Church Cemetery

Old Snow Hill Cemetery

Payne Chapel - Johnson Cemetery

Rosemary Church Cemetery

St. Francis Church Cemetery

St. John's Baptist Church Cemetery

St. Paul Church Cemetery

St. Paul's Lutheran
Church Cemetery

Arkansas

Calhoun County
Pleasant Grove Cemetery

Drew County
Bethel Cemetery Lacey Cemetery

Howard County
Hickory Grove

Nevada County
De Ann Cemetery

Forest Hill Cemetery

Sweet Home Cemetery

Mt. Vernon Cemetery

Snell Cemetery

White Church
(Waters Chapel) Cemetery

Ouachita County
Cedar Grove Cemetery

Eternal Rest Cemetery

Good Hope Cemetery

Mt. Olive Cemetery

Phillips County Bean Cemetery

Hampton Springs Cemetery

Scott Bond Family Plot

Saxon Cemetery

Spring lake Memorial Cemetery

Dixon Cemetery

Odd Fellows Cemetery

Sebastian County
Cherokee African American
Cemetery Union County

Lott Burgy Cemetery

California

Siskiyoa County
Mt. Shaska Baptist
Church Cemetery

District of Columbia

Female Union Bond Cemetery

Old Methodist Burying Ground

Mt. Zion Cemetery

Florida

Alachua County
Grass Lawn Cemetery

Mt. Pleasant Cemetery

Sand Hill Cemetery

Bay County
Gainer Cemetery

Bay County
Redwood Cemetery

Brevard County
Hilltop Cemetery
(Cocoa Black Cemetery)

Broward County
Blountstown Colored Cemetery

Hallandale Cemetery

Memorial Colored Cemetery

Pompano Colored Cemetery

Woodlawn Colored Cemetery

Calhoun County
Gray's Creek Colored Cemetery
Scotland Colored Cemetery

Dade County
Evegreen Memorial Park Cemetery
Lincoln Memorial Cemetery

Desoto County

Oakridge Cemetery County
Shamrock Colored Cemetery

Duval County
Phillips Cemetery
(Craig Swamp Cemetery)
St. Nicholas Cemetery

Escambia County
Roberts - Noble Cemetery
(Gull Point Cemetery)
St. Joseph's Cemetery
Whitmire Cemetery

Flagler County
St. Joe Colored Cemetery

Gadsden County
Greenboro Community Cemetery
Hopewell AME Church Cemetery
Oak Grove Cemetery
St. James Missionary
Baptist Cemetery
St. James P.B. Church Cemetery
St. Mary Missionary Baptist
Church Cemetery
Springfield A.M.E. Church
Turner Cemetery
Unnamed African
American Cemetery

Gulf County
Williamsburg Cemetery

Hamilton County
Bethel Colored Cemetery
Burnham Colored Cemetery
Geiger Colored Cemetery
Hamilton Colored Cemetery

Harrison Colored Cemetery
Jennings Bluff Colored Cemetery
Mt. Pleasant Colored Cemetery
New Hope Colored Cemetery
Sasseryland Colored Cemetery
West Lake Cemetery
White Springs Colored Cemetery

Hardee County
Baptist Colored Cemetery

Jackson County
Alford Cemetery
Antioch AME Church Cemetery
Baker Cemetery
Bascom Assembly of God
Bellamy Cemetery
Bethel Missionary Baptist
Church Cemetery
Brooks Cemetery
Buckhorn Cemetery
Compass Lake Cemetery
Danzy Cemetery (near Round Lake)
Ealy Cemetery
Ebenezer Cemetery
Evergreen Cemetery
Freeman Cemetery
Friendship Cemetery
Gainer Cemetery
Galilee Baptist Church Cemetery
Gray Cemetery
Haywood (Haynes Belleview)
Cemetery
Hinson Cemetery
Holyneck Cemetery
Macedonia Cemetery
McChapel A.M.E. Church Cemetery
Mack's Chapel Cemetery
Magnolia A.M.E. Church Cemetery
Mt Ararat Church and Cemetery
Marvin Chapel Cemetery
McChapel (Mack's Chapel)
Cemetery Methodist Cemetery

Mt Calvary Holiness Cemetery

Church of Christ Cemetery

Mt Cello M. B. Church Cemetery

Mt Olive Cemetery

Mt. Sinai Cemetery

Mt Zion Cemetery

New Hope Missionary Baptist
Church Cemetery

Orange Hill Cemetery

Pelt #2 African American Cemetery

Pleasant Hill Baptist
Church Cemetery

Pope Chapel AME Cemetery

Popular Spring Cemetery

Pugh Cemetery

Riverside Cemetery
African- American Section

Robinson- Cemetery

Roulhac Cemetery

Saint Mary's Cemetery

Saint Paul Cemetery

Saint Peter Cemetery

Shiloh Cemetery

Sims #2 Cemetery

Spears Plantation Cemetery

Smith Cemetery

Snow Hill Cemetery

Snelling Cemetery

Springfield Cemetery

St. John M. B. Church Cemetery

Union Hill Church Cemetery

Wynn Cemetery

Rocky Creek Cemetery

Liberty County
Bethel Church Cemetery

St. Stephens Church Cemetery
(Watson Cemetery)

Marion County
Sim's Cemetery aka Slave Cemetery

Polk County
Tiger Flowers Cemetery

Seminole County
Stewart Memorial Grounds

Suwanne County
Suwanne County Cemetery

Saint James Cemetery

Georgia
Chatham County
Cherokee Hill Cemetery

East Savannah Cemetery

Evergreen Cemetery

Lake Mayers Cemetery

Land Grove Cemetery

Laurel Grove Cemetery

Lincoln Memorial Cemetery

Laurel Grove South Cemetery

New Guinea Cemetery

Oak Grove Cemetery

Sandfly Cemetery

Wood Grove Cemetery

Woodville Cemetery

Zion White Bluff Cemetery

Coffee County Upton Cemetery

Decatur County
Bethel AME Cemetery

Fleatown Cemetery

Garden of Peace Cemetery

Mount Olive AME Cemetery

Sherman Cemetery

DeKalb County
Albert-McGuire Family Cemetery

Doraville Cemetery

Mason Baptist Cemetery

Mt. Pleasant Baptist Cemetery

Mt. Zion AME Church Cemetery

Poplar Springs Baptist
Church Cemetery

St. Paul Baptist Church Cemetery

Early County
Ebenezer Missionary Baptist
Church Cemetery

Evergreen AME Cemetery

Friendshp Missionary Baptist
Church Cemetery

Good Hope AME Church Cemetery

Green Cemetery

Jerusalem AME Church Cemetery

Matt Gilbert Cemetery

Midway Missionary Baptist
Church Cemetery

Mt Zion Cemetery

New Prospect AME Cemetery

Oak Grove AME Church Cemetery

Old Town Cemetery

Shiloh Cemetery

St. Maryland Missionary
Baptist Church

St. Mary's Church Cemetery

St. Paul AME Church

Wesley Chapel CME
Church Cemetery

Fulton County
Historic Oakland Cemetery

South view Cemetery

Grady County Cairo Cemetery

Jonas Lobe Cemetery

Henry County
Antioch Baptist Church Cemetery

Cleveland Chapel AME Cemetery

Mt. Bethel Baptist
Church Cemetery

Mt. Carmel Baptist
Church Cemetery

Mt. Vernon Baptist
Church Cemetery

O'Neal AME Church Cemetery

Providence Primitive Baptist
Church Site Cemetery

Rock Spring Baptist
Church Cemetery
(McDonough Pentacostal)

Rocky Mount Baptist
Church Cemetery

Zion Baptist Cemetery

Jefferson County
Bethlehem AME Church Cemetery

Sand Valley AME Church Cemetery

Spread Chapel AME
Church Cemetery

Stone Springfield AME
Church Cemetery

Jenkins County
Bethlehem Church Cemetery

Jenkins County

Brinson Rock Baptist
Church Cemetery

Carswell Grove Cemetery

Gordon Grove Cemetery

Fountain Springs Baptist
Church Cemetery

Johnson Chapel Cemetery

Jones Place Cemetery

Jones Temple Cemetery

Kelsey Baptist Church Cemetery

Lane Grove Cemetery

McCoy Church Cemetery

Old Fountain Springs Cemetery

W.A. Law's Place Cemetery

Mcintosh County

Belleville Cemetery

Butler Cemetery

Ebenaza Cemetery

Hudson Cemetery

Hutchinson 'Cemetery

Mitchell County
Camilla Cemetery

Newton County Oxford
African American Cemetery

Pike County
Baptist Church Cemetery

Fuller Chapel Methodist Cemetery

Roberts Chapel Church Cemetery

Richmond County
Cedar Grove

Mt. Olive Memorial Park

Southview Cemetery

Summerville Cemetery

Walker Memorial Park

Sumter County

Antioch Missionary Baptist
Church Cemetery

Bethel Primitive Baptist
Church Cemetery

Cameron Family Cemetery

Cobb Cemetery

Daniel Cemetery

Dowdell Cemetery

Felder Cemetery

Foster Cemetery

Freeman Hill Cemetery

Ginning Cemetery

Greater Cedar Spring
Baptist Church Cemetery

Hawkins Cemetery

Hill Cemetery

L.S. Cooper Memorial Gardens

Maxwell Cemetery

Mitchell Grove Baptist
Church Cemetery

Mt. Creek AME Church Cemetery

Mt. Salem Baptist Church Cemetery

Telfair County
Old Coloured Folks Cemetery

Thomas County
Old Magnolia Cemetery

Upson County
Cedar Grove Cemetery

Old Mill Cemetery

Illinois

Cook County
Burr Oak Cemetery

Pope County

Miller Grove Cemetery

Wabash County

Negro Cemetery, Bellmont Precinct

Indiana

Clark County
Black & White Cemetery
(Weir Cemetery)

Briar Hill Cemetery

Henry County
Trails Grove Cemetery

Marion County
Sutherland Park Cemetery

Morgan County
Crockett Cemetery

Orange County
Lick Creek Settlement

Kansas

Graham County

Nicodemus County
Mount Olivet Cemetery

Samuels Cemetery

Shawnee County
Auburn Cemetery

Bethel Cemetery

Yale County
Yale Cemetery

Kentucky

Carroll County
Sanders Cemetery

Fayette County
African Cemetery #2

Greenwood (Co-Haven) Cemetery

Floyd County

**Peaceful Gardens Garrard
County**
Buckeye Negro Cemetery

Ohio County
Colored Cemetery at
Bethel Pulaski County

Mt. Olive Cemetery

Stanford-Pike Cemetery

Louisiana

Caddo Parish

Ebenezer Negro Baptist
Church Cemetery

Calcasieu Parish Chloe Cemetery

High Mount Cemetery

West Fork Cemetery

Cameron Parish

Ebenizer (LeBlanc) Cemetery

St. Martin dePores Cemetery

St. Rose of Lima Cemetery

Concordia Parish

Dunbart Plantation Cemetery

Ferriday Cemetery

Minorca Cemetery

Iberia Parish

Mt. Zion #2 Baptist
Church Cemetery

Jefferson Parish

Mt. Olivet Cemetery

Livingston Parish

Black Graves at Frost

Morehouse Parish

Cherry Hill #2 MBC Cemetery NEW

Green Grove Missionary
Baptist Church Cemetery

St. Joseph AME Church Cemetery

St. Luke Missionary Baptist
Church Cemetery

St. Mark Missionary Baptist
Church Cemetery

Natchitoches Parish

Allen Baptist
African-American Cemetery

Allen Methodist
African-American Cemetery

Choctaw Island Baptist Church
Cemetery

Robeline Cemetery

Shady Grove Cemetery

North Caddo Parish

Negro Cemetery on Raines Lease

Rapides Parish

Holly Oak Cemetery

NEW Richland Parish

St. Deed Cemetery

St. Helena Parish

Jackson Chapel Independent A.M.E.
Cemetery

St. Martin Parish

Union Baptist Church Cemetery

Tangipahoa Parish
Barnett Cemetery

Chubby Bottom Cemetery

409 East Thomas
St. Black Cemetery

Hands of Jesus Christian
Center Cemetery

Macedonia Landmark Missionary
Baptist Church Cemetery

Mt. Bethel Baptist
Church Cemetery

Mt. Pleasant Baptist
Church Cemetery

Mt. Zion Baptist Church Cemetery

New Star Baptist Church Cemetery

Pleasant Valley Missionary Baptist
Church Cemetery

Ponchatoula African American
(Baptist) Cemetery

Ponchatoula African American
(Methodist) Cemetery

St. James A.M.E. No.2 Cemetery

St. John Temple Cemetery

Warren Cemetery

Union Parish

Springhill Cemetery

West Feliciana Parish

Rosedown Baptist Church Cemetery

Winn Parish

James Chapel

(Pennywell) Cemetery

Old Morning Star Church Cemetery

New Morning Star Cemetery

Maryland

Dorchester County

Bucktown Cemetery

Fork Neck (Pinder) Cemetery

Graveyard across from
Stanley Institute

Mt. Pleasant UM Church Burial Site

Old Hughes Mission Church Burial
Site Silent City Cemetery

Union Chapel Cemetery

Montgomery County

Good Hope Church Cemetery

Somerset County

Centennial United Methodist
Church Cemetery

Samuel Wesley United Methodist
Church Cemetery

Mississippi

Carroll County

Bethel Methodist Church Cemetery

Forrest County

Pineridge Cemetery

Hattiesburg Riverview Cemetery

Scott Street Cemetery

Shady Grove Missionary Baptist
Church Cemetery

Monroe County Blair Cemetery

Sullivan Cemetery

Simpson County Camper Cemetery

James Chapel Cemetery

Mt. Zion Colored Cemetery

New Zion MB Church Cemetery

Pilgrim's Rest Cemetery

Rose Hill Cemetery

Springhill Cemetery

Unidentified Cemetery

Stone County

Fairley Cemetery

Tallahatchie County

Blue Cane M.B. Church Cemetery

Brooklyn Church Cemetery

Colbert Hill Cemetery

Eagle Plantation Cemetery

Elijah Chapel Cemetery

Good Hope Church Cemetery

Hitt Chapel Church Cemetery

Jerusalem M.B. Church Cemetery

Johnson Church Cemetery

Jordan Hill Cemetery

Little Hubbard
M.B. Church Cemetery

Mount Calvary Baptist
Church Cemetery

Mount Calvary M.B.
Church Cemetery

Mt. Zion Cemetery

Newton M.B. Church Cemetery

Olvis (Oliver Grove M.B. Church)
Cemetery

Oxberry Cemetery

Persimmon Grove
M.B. Church Cemetery

Pleasant Grove Church Cemetery

Providence Cemetery

St. Clare M.B. Church Cemetery

Saint John M.B. Church Cemetery

St. John Church Cemetery

St. Luke M.B. Church Cemetery

St. Mark M.B. Church Cemetery

St. Mark's M.B. Church Cemetery

Swamp Grove M.B.
Church Cemetery

Taylor Chapel CME
Church Cemetery

Tillatoba Cemetery

Whitehead M.B. Church Cemetery

Missouri

St. Louis County
Bellefonte Cemetery

Jefferson Barracks and
National Cemetery

Moses Dickson Cemetery

New Cold Water Burying Ground

St. Charles Borromeo
Church Cemetery

New Jersey

Burlington County
Harmony Cemetery for Negroes

Johnson Cemetery

Camden County
Johnson Cemetery

Somerset County
Lamington Cemetery

New York

Cayuga County
Fort Hill Cemetery

Clinton County
Hudson-Mohawk River Cemeteries

Essex County
John Brown Cemetery

Nassau County
Young's Cemetery
(Calvary A.M.E. Church Cemetery)

New York County
African Burial Ground

Rockland County
Mount Moor Cemetery

Tompkins County
Speed's Farm Slave Burial Ground

North Carolina

Bertie County
First Baptist Church
Cemetery (Colored)

First Baptist Church of
Colerain Cemetery

Hoggard's Cemetery aka
Cherry's Cemetery

Holley African American Cemetery

Holloman African American
Family Cemetery

Saint Elmo Baptist
Church Cemetery

Sessoms Family Cemetery

Burke County
Mission AME Church Cemetery

Cabarrus County
Holly Grove Primitive Baptist
Church Cemetery NEW

Cleveland County
Brook's Chapel Methodist Cemetery

Green Bethel Church Cemetery

Durham County Geer Cemetery

Edgecombe County
Mercer Farm Cemetery

Gaston County
Long Creek Presbyterian Cemetery

Harnett County
Clark & McGregor Cemetery

Hertford County
Mount Sinai Cemetery

Hertford County
Oak Grove Methodist Cemetery

Mecklenburg County
Alexander Slave Cemetery

McCoy Slave Cemetery

Mount Olive Presbyterian
Church Cemetery

Neely Slave Cemetery

Nash County
Bascoe Hinnant Cemetery

Sandy Fork Missionary
Baptist Cemetery

Stokes Family Cemetery

Northhampton County

First Baptist Church Cemetery

Old Nebo Baptist Cemetery

Pitt County

Brown Chapel Holiness
Church Cemetery

Burney Church Cemetery

Butler-Wynne Cemetery

Clemons Cemetery

Crandell Cemetery

Crandol Cemetery

Ebron Cemetery

Fleming-Brown Cemetery

Forbes Cemetery

Hopkins Cemetery

Holy Temple Holiness
Church Cemetery

Jackson Cemetery

John J. Tyson Cemetery

Langley-Hopkins Cemetery

Live Oak Cemetery

Mitchell Mortuary Cemetery

Morris-Robbins Cemetery

Newsome Cemetery

Rebovia Cemetery

Rountree Cemetery

Saint Peter MB Church Cemetery

Shirley Cemetery

Smith Cemetery

Sweet Hope FWB Church Cemetery

Turnage-Jones Cemetery

Yankee Hall Slave Cemetery

White-Chapman Cemetery

White Oak MB Church Cemetery

Wimberley Cemetery

Zion Chapel Baptist
Church Cemetery

Polk County

Union Grove Baptist Cemetery

Rutherford County

Buck Shoals Baptist Cemetery

Cedar Grove Cemetery

Crews Cemetery

Doggett Grove Cemetery

Duffey-Twitty Cemetery

Gold Hill Cemetery

Haynes Grove Cemetery

Hopewell AME Zion Cemetery

Jerusalem Baptist Cemetery

Johnson Cemetery

Matthew Chapel AME
Zion Cemetery

Mt. Nebo Baptist Cemetery

Mt. Pleasant CME
Church Cemetery

New Hope Cemetery

New Salem Church Cemetery

New Zion Baptist Cemetery

Piney Ridge CME Cemetery

St. John's Missionary
Baptist Cemetery

St. Paul AME Zion Cemetery

Union Hill AME Zion Cemetery

Webb Baptist Cemetery

Well's Springs United Methodist
Cemetery

White Oak Springs
Baptist Cemetery

Whiteside Cemetery

Stanly County

Kendalls Cemetery

Wake County I Banks Cemetery

Banks Family Burial Location

(Blacks in the) City Cemetery,
Raleigh

Cary 1st United Church of
Christ Cemetery

Holly Springs United Church of
Christ Cemetery

Jeridan Cemetery

Jones, Turner, Booker, Adams,
Stewart Cemetery

McKoy Cemetery

New Poplar Springs UCC Cemetery

New Providence Baptist
Church Cemetery

Old Poplar Springs Cemetery

Pleasant Hill Church Cemetery

St. Mary's Free Will Baptist
Church Cemetery

St. Peter's Church Cemetery

Thomas Banks Cemetery

Turner Evans Cemetery

OHIO

Gallia County
Morgan Bethel Cemetery
(USCT Veterans)

New Hope Cemetery
(USCT Veterans)

Pine Street Cemetery
(USCT Veterans)

Viney Cemetery (USCT Veterans)

Greene County
Cherry Grove Cemetery
(USCT Veterans)

Lawrence County
Mt. Pisgah Cemetery

Logan County
Day Cemetery

Lorain County
Westwood Cemetery

Meigs County
Gomer Cemetery

Pike County
Jackson Cemetery

Straight Creek Cemetery

Ross County
Greenlawn Cemetery
(USCT Veterans)

OKLAHOMA

Atoka County
Greenhill Negro Cemetery

Macedonia Negro Cemetery

Stringtown Colored Cemetery

Murray County
Five Mile Cemetery

James Cemetery

Oak Ridge Cemetery

Muskogee County
Four Mile Branch Baptist
Church Cemetery

Wagoner County Jackson Cemetery

Jackson Grove Cemetery

Pennsylvania

Chester County
Calvary Cemetery

Chester Morris County
Morris Cemetery

Dauphin County
New Negro Cemetery

Old Negro Cemetery

Delaware County Eden Cemetery

Fayette County
Thomas Cemetery

Montgomery County Merion
Memorial Park

Rhode Island

Newport County
"God's Little Acre" common
Burial Ground

South Carolina

Abbeville County
Lakeview Cemetery

AKA Thompson Cemetery

Beaufort County
Adams Street Baptist
Church Cemetery

Amelia White Cemetery

Beaufort National Cemetery

Bloody Point Cemetery

Braddock Port
(Harbortown) Cemetery

Brick Baptist Church Cemetery

Coffin Point Cemetery

Cooper River Cemetery

Corner (Major) Cemetery

Cuffy Cemetery

Ebenezer Baptist Church Cemetery

Faith Memorial Baptist
Church Cemetery

Elliot Cemetery

Fripp Cemetery

Gerhard Spieler and Lay Down
Body Haig's Port Cemetery

Jenkins Island Cemetery

Joe Pope Cemetery

Lawton Cemetery

Mayfield Cemetery

New Hope Christian
Church Cemetery

Orange Grove Baptist
Church Cemetery

Pilgram Cemetery

Pineview Cemetery

Red House Cemetery

Saint Joseph Baptist
Church Cemetery

Simmons Memorial Gardens

Sixteen Gate Cemetery

Spanish Wells Cemetery

Talbot Cemetery

Union Cemetery

Webb Track Cemetery

Charleston County

Brown Fellowship Society Cemetery

Brotherly Cemetery

Friendly Union Cemetery

Old Bethel United Methodist
Church Cemetery

Unity and Friendship Cemetery

Cherokee County

Island Creek Baptist Cemetery

Clarendon County

Bennett Cemetery

Biggers A.M.E. Church

Brown Cemetery

Pinwood Brown Chapel U.M.E

Butler Cemetery

Calvary Baptist Church & Zion Hill

Chapel A.M.E. Church

Cypress Fork Free Will

Delaine Cemetery

DuRant Cemetery

Elizabeth Baptist Church

Elizabeth Cemetery

Friendship A.M.E.

Gum Springs Baptist

Harmony Elizabeth

Hickory Grove Baptist Church

Laurel Hill Baptist Church

Liberty Hill A.M.E. Church

Manning Cemetery

Melina Presbyterian Church

Mt Chapel Baptist Church

Mt Nebo Missionary Baptist Church

Mt. Pleasant AME

Mt Sanai AFW, Bloomville

Mt Zero Baptist Missionary Church

Mt Zion A. M. E. Church

Muldrow Cemetery

New Hope A.M.E.

Providence A. M. E. Cemetery

Reeseville A.M.E.,Church
and Cemetery

Rock Hill Baptist Church

Society Hill A.M.E.

Spring Grove Cemetery. &
St Peters A.M.E.

St James A.M.E. Church

St Lukes Church

St Marks A.M.E. Church

St Marks Baptist Church

St Matthews & Spring Hill
A.M.E. Church

Taw Caw Baptist Church

Union Cypress A.M.E. Church

William Chapel Baptist Church

Zion Hill, Milford Plantation, aka Bloom Hill

Charleston County
Randolph Cemetery

Razing the Dead

Dillon County

McClellan I Mason
Family Cemetery

Dorchester County

Boone Hill United Methodist
Church Cemetery

Camel Hill United Methodist
Church Cemetery

Murray United Methodist
Church Cemetery

Edgefield County
Carey Hill Cemetery

Poplar Springs Cemetery

Shady Grove Cemetery

Fairfield County
Camp Welfare Cemetery

Laurens County
Bethel Hall Missionary Baptist
Church Cemetery

Horry County
Bethlehem Church Cemetery

Horry County I Freemont Baptist
Church Cemetery

Greater St. James AME
Church Cemetery

McNeil Chapel Cemetery

Mt. Calvary No.1 MB
Church Cemetery

Mount Vernon Baptist
Church Yard Cemetery

Montgomery Cemetery

Old Chesterfield Cemetery

Popular Cemetery

St. Paul Missionary Baptist

Church Cemetery

Marion County I Smith Cemetery - African American side

Richland County
Colored Asylum Cemetery
(SC State Hospital)

Spartanburg County
Gaffney Chapel Cemetery

Sumter County
Allen Chapel A.M.E.

Antioch A.M.E. Church
and Cemetery

Barfield Cemetery

Bethel A.M.E.

Bethesda Baptist Church

Beulah A.M.E.

Bradford Cemetery

Cane Savannah Cemetery

Congruity Pres. U. S. A.

Ebenezer United Pres.

Ellison Family Burial Ground

Fourth Cross Roads

Francis Cemetery

Goodhope UM Church

Good Will Pres.

Grant Hill Baptist

Haynesworth/Smith Cemetery

High Hills A.M.E.

High Hills Baptist

Hopewell Baptist Joshua
Lane Family Burial Ground

Mt Bethel Baptist Church

Mt Pisgah A.M.E.

Mulberry Baptist

New Bethel

Old St Luke's Cemetery

Orangehill A.M.E.

Orangehill RUME

Rafting Creek Baptist

St Augustine Epis.

St John's Baptist

St Lukes's AME
St Mark's Cemetery
St. Michael's
St Paul's A.M.E.
St. Paul's Church
St. Phillip's U.M.E.
Spring Grove Cemetery
(used by St. Peter's)
Tiverton Missionary Baptist
Union Baptist
Walker's Cemetery
Wayman Chapel A.M.E.
Willow Grove A.M.E. Church

Tennessee

Anderson County
Mt. Sinai Baptist Church Cemetery

Chester County
Hamlett Cemetery

Davidson County
Edgeville Benevolent Cemetery
Greenwood Cemetery and
Mount Ararat
Nashville City Cemetery

Decatur County
Decaturville Negro Cemetery

Gibson County
Carnes Cemetery

Greene County
New Hope Colored Graveyard
Pruitt Hill Cemetery

Madison County
Cerro Gardo M.B. Church Cemetery
Riverside Cemetery

Lauderdale County
Alex Haley State Historic Site
and Museum
Bethlehem Cemetery
Canfield Cemetery
Shelby County Zion Cemetery

Wayne County

Lizard Glade
(Lizard Lake) Cemetery

Texas

Bell County
Grave of Ead White,
Old Stockton Cemetery

Bastrop County
McShan Memorial
Garden Cemetery
Pleasant Hill Baptist
Church Cemetery

Crosby County
Mt. Zion Cemetery

Fannin County
Oakhill Cemetery
Annex St. Mark's Cemetery
Union Cemetery
Gonzales County Ellis Cemetery
Elm Slough Cemetery
Foster Negro Cemetery
Harwood Negro Cemetery
Hodge Negro Cemetery
McKeller Negro Cemetery
McVea Cemetery
Monthalia Negro Cemetery
Mt. Enon Cemetery
(Demit, Jones Cemetery)
Princeville Negro Cemetery
Smith Black Cemetery

Grayson County
White Rock Negro Cemetery

Harris County
College Park Cemetery
Kohrville/Pilgrim Branch Cemetery
Olivewood Cemetery
Henderson County
Barker Cemetery

Madison County
Southside Cemetery

Navarro County

Woodland Cemetery

Polk County
Grace Hill Cemetery
New Hope Cemetery
St. Andrews Cemetery
Victory Place Cemetery
Washington Cemetery

Sabine County
Dennis Cemetery
William Gasby Cemetery

San Jacinto County
Lone Star Cemetery
Smith County
Center Cemetery
Goodman Cemetery
Harris Creek Memorial Cemetery
High Cemetery
Kay Cemetery
Mt. Olive Cemetery
Mt. Zion Cemetery
New Home Cemetery
Piney Grove Cemetery
Pinkston Cemetery
Pleasant Grove Cemetery
Shady Grove Cemetery
Siloam Cemetery
St. Violet Cemetery
Warren Chapel Cemetery
Waters Bluff Cemetery

Travis County
Texas State Cemetery

Virginia
Bedford County
Thomas Slave Chapel and Cemetery

Buckingham County
Stanton Family Cemetery

Dinwiddie County
Dinwiddie Memorial Park Cemetery

Fauquier County

Peoples Cemetery
Blandford Cemetery
Little Church Cemetery
East View (Witherson Memorial)

Henrico County
Evergreen Cemetery

Page County
Bundy Cemetery
Dougans Cemetery
Jeffries Cemetery
Marshall Cemetery
Mason Cemetery
Mt. Carmel Baptist
Church Cemetery
Prince William County
Bates Family Cemetery
Harden's Hill Cemetery
Mount Calvary Baptist
Church Cemetery
Mount Zion Baptist Church
Cemetery

Russell County
Ray/Whited Cemetery

Sussex County
Chapel Hill Baptist Church
Cemetery (aka Jefferson Family
Cemetery, Powell Cemetery)
Hassidiah Baptist Church Cemetery
Alexandria I Freedmen's Cemetery

Washington
Black Miners Cemetery

West Virginia
Cabell County
Bethel (Crossroads) Cemetery

DETROIT AREA AFRICAN AMERICAN FUNERAL HOMES

Andrew Funeral Home

Andrews/Hardy Funeral Home

Barksdale Funeral Home

Cantrell Funeral Home

Caver Funeral Home

Chenault Funeral Home

Chapel Of Chimes Funeral Home

Cole Home For Funerals

Ellis Memorial Funeral Home

Fields Funeral Home

Fritz Funeral Home

Gates Of Heaven Funeral Home

Haley Funeral Home

Heavenly Gates Funeral Home

House Of Johnson Funeral Home

Hutchinson Funeral Home

Jeter Memorial Funeral Home

McFall Brothers Funeral Home

Moon Funeral Home*

C. W. Morris/J. W. Henry Funeral Home

Ramsey Funeral Home

Murdock Funeral Home

Paradise Funeral Home

Peace Chapel Funeral Home

Penn Funeral Home

Perry Funeral Home

Pope Funeral Home

Pye Funeral Home

Stinson Funeral Home

Swanson Funeral Home

Thompson Funeral Home

Trinity Chapel Funeral Home

Wilson-Akins Funeral Home

*Flint, Michigan

PAST MAYORS OF DETROIT

Thirty of Detroit's mayors are interred in Elmwood Cemetery. The chronological listing includes the place of burial by lot and section, their primary occupation and noteworthy events during their administration as Mayor of Detroit. Detroit was incorporated as a town on January 18, 1802.

LOT/SEC. NAME OCCUPATION - EVENTS

4 - B **Solomon S. Sibley** (Circa 1806) An attorney who was the first mayor appointed by the Territorial Governor. US. Congress gives authorization to plat the new town in 1806.

September 13, 1806 Detroit was incorporated as a city.

The 1810 population of Detroit was 1,650.

73-A **Elijah Brush, Col.** (Circa 1813) Large land owner, attorney and farmer. Military Commander of Detroit who signed the capitulation of Michigan during the War of 1812. Detroit was recaptured by the American troops on September 29, 1813. On October 29, 1813 Lewis Cass was appointed Military and Civil Governor of the Michigan Territory by General Harrison.

L12-A **John R. Williams** (1824-25, 1830 and 1844-47) Retail merchant and Realtor, Military Commander of Detroit. First elected mayor of the city. The Detroit Common Council was created in 1825. The Temperance Society was created in 1830.

102-A **Jonathan Kearsley** (1826, 1829) Military professional and civil servant. Detroit reached a population of 2,000 in 1829. A typing machine or "Typographer" was patented by William A. Burt in 1829.

47-F **John Biddle** (1827-28) President of the Michigan Central Railroad. In 1827, City Council ordinance required sidewalks (usually of wood plank, cement not used until about 1900). Historical Society organized 1828.

The 1830 population of Detroit was 2,222.

101-B **Dr. Marshall Chapin** (1831,1833) Physician and Druggist. First regular mail from the East Coast began in 1831. The first shoe manufactory was established in the city in 1833.

130-A **Levi Cook** (1832,1835-36) Banker. The first Detroit cholera epidemic breaks out in 1832. Stephens T. Mason was first inaugurated as governor on Nov. 3, 1835.

4-B **Charles C. Trowbridge** (1834) Banker and railroad owner. The city's first real estate tax is voted in 1834. Detroit's population is 4,968. Trowbridge, one of the, founders of Elmwood Cemetery, was defeated in the 1837 election for Michigan Governor.

2.l-B **DeGarmo Jones** (1839) Building contractor and banker. Michigan Central Railroad opened Detroit to Ann Arbor. February 1839, the Detroit Boat Club was organized; it is the oldest river club in the U.S.

The 1840 population of Detroit was 9,192.

10-G **Dr. Zina Pitcher** (1840-4f,1843) Physician and surgeon. Founder of the University of Michigan Medical School. Dr. Pitcher was known as the "Father" of the Detroit Public School System. U.S. Congress appropriates $50,000 in 1841 to construct Fort Wayne. Tobacco manufacturing begins. Detroit will become a leading tobacco-processing center.

5-L **Dr. Douglas Houghton** (1842) Doctor, scientist, geologist and explorer. He was the first to explore and define Michigan's mineral resources. In his honor a county, township, lake, city, a school of mines and a Detroit school are named. The Detroit Board of Education was created in 1842.

102-B **Frederick Buhl** (1848) Fur trader, merchant and banker. First telegraph dispatch was received from New York in 1848. The first bathtub in Detroit was installed. Michigan Central Depot at Michigan and Third St. opened. On May 9 the area bounded by the river, Bates, Brush and Jefferson was destroyed by fire.

57 - B **Charles D. Howard** (1849) Banker and railroad builder. Mariners Church was dedicated. The first Michigan State fair was held in Detroit in the area of Woodward, Columbia and Vernor.

The 1850 population of Detroit was 21,019 (21st largest city in U.S.).

28-L **John Ladue** (1850) Leather and wool merchant. The 2nd Presbyterian and 1st Methodist Episcopal churches were dedicated. Temple Beth El was organized.

49-B **Zachariah Chandler** (1851) Dry goods merchant. One of Michigan's wealthiest men. Detroit Gaslight Co. begins operation. Lt. Ulysses S. Grant in charge of military barracks in Detroit.

73-S **John H. Harmon** (1852-53) Publisher and oil refiner. Detroit's first YMCA organized in 1852. Board of Water Commissioners established to manage the city's water supply.

96-A **Oliver M. Hyde** (1854, 1856-57) Hardware and foundry owner (first Republican mayor). Detroit House of Corrections was opened and Recorders Court established in 1857.

11 - L **John Patton** (1858-59) Carriage manufacturer and civil servant. First high school session (23 boys enrolled) in 1859. John Brown and Frederick Douglas meet at the home of William Webb. Dr. Herman Kiefer hired as city physician.

The 1860 population of Detroit was 45,619 (19th largest city in U.S.).

110 - A **Christian H. Buhl** (1860-61) Industrialist. Michigan organizes for the Civil War: May 2, 1861 the 1st Michigan infantry mustered into service. Girls first attend Detroit High School (85 pupils).

8 - 1 **William C, Duncan** (1862-63) Banker and brewer. Continued involvement in the Civil War. Detroit-Canadian border is heavily patrolled.

22-L **Kirkland Barker** (1864-65) Tobacco merchant. Harper Hospital opens. First mail delivered to homes by carrier. First Detroit Public Library opened.

127 - A **William W. Wheaton** (1868-72) Drug and grocery wholesaler. Black children first admitted to Detroit Public Schools in 1871.

The 1870 population of Detroit was 79,577 (18th largest city in U.S.).

7 - L **Hugh Moffat** (1872-76) Architect. Fred Sanders confectioners first opens and serves the first ice cream soda. The first passenger elevator installed in 1875.

17 - J **Alexander Lewis** (1876-77) Insurance executive and grain merchant. Detroit Public Library building dedicated in 1877. First telephone installed.

The 1880 population of Detroit was 116,340 (17th largest city in U.S.).

192-A **Ralph Phillips** (1883) Attorney and an organizer of Goebel Brewery. Zoological Garden opened on Belle Isle. First use of incandescent light in Detroit at the Metcalf Dry Good Store.

3-K **Stephen B.Grummond** (1884-86) Marine industrialist. Pensions established for firemen's widows. First electric street car.

The 1890 population of Detroit was 205,876 (15th largest city in U.S.)

30-F **William C. Maybury** (1896-1905) Attorney-politician. Detroit celebrates its bicentennial in 1901. Belle Isle Aquarium opened in 1904. The first automobiles were built and driven in the city in 1896.

The 1900 population of Detroit was 304,132 (13tb largest city in U.S.).

136 - A **George C. Codd** (1905-06) Civil servant, Detroit Sheriff 1871-75, Postmaster 1879-86. Detroit's economic emphasis shifts from lumber to the automobile.

The 1920 population of Detroit was 993,678 (4th largest city in U.S.).

9 - A 2nd **John C. Lodge** (1922-23, 1928-30) Newspaperman. In 1929, the Ambassador Bridge opened, and in 1930, the Detroit-Windsor vehicular tunnel was opened to traffic. In 1930, the Detroit Traffic Court began operation.

The 1930 population of Detroit was 1,568,662 (4th largest city in U.S.).

The 1970 population of Detroit was 1,514,063 (4th largest city in U.S.).

32-HZ DL **Coleman A. Young** (1973-93) Union organizer, State Senator, civil servant. The Renaissance Center and Hart Plaza completed. New plants are built for General Motors and Chrysler Corporation.

The 1990 population of Detroit was 1,027,974 (7th largest city in U.S.).

CANADIAN HISTORIANS

Nancy Allen
270 Sunset Ave Windsor
ON N9B 3A7
519-258- t 649
jallen@mnsi.net
(Chase Family film)

Agnes Ellsworth RR 2
Moidstone ON NOR 1 KO
519-727-5368
Iswrth@jet2.net
(History of Puce and Baptist Church)

Leslie McCurdy
943 Eismere Ave
Windsor ON N9 A 2A8
519-256-8564
ll.mccurdy@sympatico.ca
519-256-5657 (Fax)
(Feminist Theatre -plays UGRR figures)

Mark McPherson
24140 East River Road
Grosse Ile MI 48138
734-671-5424 Idbrys@ili.het
(Author - Looking for Lisette)

Nancy Morand
Heritage Planner
City of Windsor
519-255-6770 ext 4449
nmorand@city.windsor.on.co

Pat Moxley
27 Sunset.
P.O. Box 307
Tilbury ON NOP 2L0
519-682-2217
(Hurst Family descendant - extensive obit. research - very well organized)

Ken Turner
25 Prospect St
Kingsville ON
N9Y 1 M6
519-733-8123
ken.turner@syrnpatico.co

(Pres.- Essex County Historical Cemeteries
Society) research Black pioneer graves

Dr. Bryan Walls
519-727-4866
bryanugrt@dol.com
Look up website For John Freeman Walls Historical Site & UGRR Museum
{Bryan is Past Pres of Ont Hist Society}

Resource Centres:

H.E.I.R.S. (Harrow Early Immigrant Research Society)
243 McAfee St.
P.O. Box 53
519-738-3700
Harrow ON N0R 1GO

Marsh Collection Society
235-A Dalhousie St
Amherstburg ON
519-736-9191
call for an appointment historical books, papers, photos, genealogy

University of Windsor
Archives (Dr. Brian Owens) (Leddy Library-lower)
401 Sunset Ave
Windsor ON N9B 3P4
519-253-3000 ext 3184
M-F 1:30-4 p.m. or/appt
Historical Department (Dr. Larry Kulisek)

Windsor Municipal Archives - see Nancy Morand
WPL (Main Branch)
850 Ouellette Ave
Windsor ON N9 A 4MP

Compiled by Andrea Moore 03.01.04

MORTUARY SCIENCE SCHOOLS

Amarillo College
Mortuary Science Program
Jason Altieri, Director PO Box 447
Amarillo, TX79178-0001 (806) 356-
3631
Fax: (806) 354-6096
Email: altieri-jC@actx.edu
www.actx.edul-mortuary/

**American Academy McAllister
Institute of Funeral Service**
Meg Dunn, President
619 W 54th Street
New York, NY 10019
(212) 757-1190
Fax: (212) 765-5923
Email: info@a-a-m-i.org www.a-a-m-
i.org

**Arapahoe Community College
Mortuary Science Program**
Martha Gaidies, Dept Chair
5900 S Sante Fe Dr
Littleton, CO 80160
(303) 797-5954 Email:martha.gai-
dies@arapahoe.edu
www.arapahoe.edu

**Arkansas State University
Mountain Home**
Funeral Service Program
Ron Schofield, Director
1600 S College St
Mountain Home, AR 72653
(870) 508-6100
Email: rschofield@asumh.edu
www.asumh.edu

Bishop State Community College
William Thompson,
Program Director
1365 Dr MLK Ave
Mobile, AL 36603-5898
(251) 405-4439
Fax: (251) 405-4427

Email: wthompson@bishop.edu
www.bishop.edu

**Briarwood College Mortuary
Science**
Bernard J Laskowski,
Program Director
2279 Mount Vernon Rd
Southington, CT 06489
(860) 628-4751
(800) 952-2444
Fax: (860) 628-6444
Email: laskowskib@briarwood.edu
www.briarwood.edu

Carl Sandburg College
Mortuary Science Program
Tim Krause, Coordinator
2400 Tom L Wilson Blvd
Galesburg, IL 61401
(309)341-0831
Fax: (309) 34[-[040
Email: tkrause@Sandburg.edu
www.sandburg.edu

**Cincinnati College of
Mortuary Science**
Dr Dan Flory, President
645 WNorth Bend Rd
Cincinnati, OH 45224-1462
(888) 377-8433 (513) 761-2020
Fax: (513) 761-3333
Email: dflory@ccms.edu
www.ccms.edu

**Commonwealth Institute of
Funeral Service**
Todd W Van Beck, President
415 Barren Springs Dr
Houston, TX 77090
(281) 873-0262
Fax: (281) 873-5232
Email: tvanbeck@yahoo.com

Community College of Baltimore County Catonsville Campus, Mortuary Science Dept.
Joyce Torchinsky, Chairperson
800 S Rolling Rd
Baltimore, MD 21228
(410) 455-6950
(410) 455-4262
Fax: (410) 719-6547
www.ccbcmd.edu

Cypress College Mortuary Science Dept.
Glenn A Bower, Program Director
9200 Valley View St
Cypress, CA 90630
(714) 484-7278
Fax:(714)484-7417
Email: mortsci@earthlink.net
www.cypresscollege.edu/divisions

Dallas Institute of Funeral Services
James M Shoemake, President
3909 Buckner Blvd
Dallas, TX 75227
(800) 235-5444
(214) 388-5466
Fax: (214) 388-0316
Email: difs@dallasinstitute.edu
www.dallasinstitute.edu

Delgado Community College Dept. of Funeral Service Education
Malcolm L. Gibson
City Park Campus Allied Health
615 City Park Ave
New Orleans, LA 70119-4399
(504) 483-4014
Fax: (504) 483-4609
Email: mgibso@dcc.edu
www.dcc.edu

East Mississippi Community College Funeral Service Technology
Don Webb, Director

PO Box 158
Scooba, MS 39358
(662) 476-5100
Fax: (662) 476-5086
Email: odickerson@eastms.edu
www.emcc.cc.ms.us

Fayetteville Technical Community College Dept. of Funeral Service Education
Michael Landon, Chairperson
PO Box 35236
Fayetteville, NC 28303
(910) 678-8301
Fax: (910) 484-6600
Email: landonm@faytechcc.edu
www.faytechcc.edu

Fine Mortuary College, LLC
Louis Misantone PhD, President & Manager
150 Kerry Place
Norwood, MA 02062
(781) 461-9080
Fax: (781) 461-8787
Email: Iynlou@tiac.net
www.fine.ne.com

Gupton-Jones College of Funeral Service
Patty Hutcheson, President
5141 Snapfinger Woods Pr
Decatur, GA 30035-4022
(800) 848-5352
(770) 593-2257
Fax: (770) 593-1891
Email: gjcfs@mindspring.com
www.gupton-jones.edu

Holmes Community College Funeral Services Technology
Tommy Garrett, Director
412 W Ridgeland Ave
Ridgeland, MS 39157
(601) 605-3300
Fax: (601) 605-3410
Email: tgarrett@holmescc.edu
www.holmescc.edu

Hudson Valley Community
College/Mortuary Science Dept
Elaine P Reinhard
80 Vandenburgh Ave
Troy, NY 12180
(518) 629-7113
Fax: (518) 629-8025
Email:reinhela@hvcc.edu

Jefferson State Community
College Funeral Service
Education Program
William Counce, Program
Coordinator
2601 Carson Rd
Birmingham, AL 35215
(205) 856-7844
Fax: (205) 856-7804
Email:
wcounce@jeffstateonline.com
www.jeffstateonline.com

John A.Gupton College
B. Steven Spann
1616 Church St
Nashville, TN 37203
(615) 327-3927
Fax: (615) 321-4518
Email: spann@guptoncollege.com

John Tyler Community College
Funeral Service Program
Rick Sikon, Department Head
13101 Jefferson Davis Hgwy
Chester, VA 23831
(804) 706-5113
Fax: (804) 796-4237
Email: rsikon@jtcc.edu
www.jtcc.edu

Kansas City Kansas Community
College, Mortuary Science Dept.
7250 State Ave
Kansas City, KS 66112
(913)288-7607
Fax: (913) 288-7677
Email: wwright@toto.net

Malcolm X College.
Dept. of Mortuary Science
Alta Williams, Director
1900 W Van Buren St
Chicago, IL 60612
(312) 850-7214
Fax: (312) 850-7453
Email: alwilliams@Ccc.edu
www.malcolmx.ccc.edu

Mercer County Community
College Funeral Service
Curriculum
Robert C. Smith III, Director
1200 Old Trenton Rd
Trenton, NJ 08550
(609) 586-4800
Fax: (609) 586-5602
Email: smithr@mccc.edu
www.mccc.edu

Miami-Dade College
W. L. Philbrick School of
Funeral Service
Ralph Covert, Chairperson
11380 N W 27th Ave Miami, FL
33167
(305) 237-1245
Fax: (305) 237-8195
Email: rcovert@mdcc.edu

Mid-America Funeral College
John R. Braboy, President
3111 Hamburg Pike
Jeffersonville, IN 47130
(812) 288-8878
(800) 221-6158
Fax: (812) 288-5942
Email: macfs@mindspring.com
www.mid-america.edu

Milwaukee Area Technical
College (West Campus)
James Augustine, Coordinator
W Allis, WI
(414) 456-5319
(414) 456-5500
Fax: (414) 456-5360

email: augustij@matc.edu
www.matc.edu

Mississippi Gulf Coast Community
Colege/Funeral Service Technology
Gaston W. Garrett, Director
PO Box 548
Perkinston, MS 39573
(601) 528-8909
Fax: (601) 528-8422
Email: gaston.garrett@mgccc.edu
www.mgccc.edu

Mount Royal College
Karen McCarthy
2204 2nd St SW
Calgary, MS
Alberta Canada T2S 1S5
(403) 503-4887
Email: fde@mtroyal.ca
www.mtroyal.Ca/fde

Mount Hood Community College
Dept. of Funeral Service Education
Doug Ferrin, Director
26000 S E Stark St
Gresham, OR 97030
(503) 491-6941
Email: malcolmw@mhcc.edu

Nassau Community College
Mortuary Science Dept.
John M. Lieblang, Chairman
357 East Road
Garden City, NY 11530-6793
(516) 572-7277
Fax: (516) 572-0626
Email: lieblaj@sunynassau.edu
www.ncc.edu

New England Institute at Mount
Ida College
Jacquelyn Taylor, Executive Director
777 Dedham St
Newton Centre, MA 02459
(617) 928-4714
Fax: (617) 928-4713
Email: jstaylor@mountida.edu

www.mountida.edu

Northampton Community College
Dept. of Funeral Service Education
John Lunfford, Director
3835 Green Pond Rd
Bethlehem, PA 18017
(610) 861-5388
Fax: (610) 861-4581
Email: jlunsford@northampton.edu

Northwest Mississippi Community
College
Funeral Servlie Technology Prog
Larry Anderson
DeSoto Center
5197 WE Ross Parkway
Southaven, MS 38671
(601)280-6137
Fax: (601) 280-6161
Email: landerson@northwestms.edu
www.northwestms.edu

Ogeechee Technical College
Michael Burrell, Dean of Funeral
Service Program
One Joe Kennedy Blvd
Statesboro, GA 30458
(800)646-1316
(912) 681-5500
Email: mburrell@ogeecheetech.edu
www.ogeechee.tec.ga.us

Pittsburgh Institute of Mortuary
Science
Eugene C. Ogrodnik CFSP, President
& CEO
5808 Baum Blvd
Pittsburgh, PA 15206
(412) 362-8500
Fax: (412) 362-1684
Email: pims5808@aol.com
www.p-i-m-s.com

San Antonio College
Mortuary Science Program
Dr Francisco E Solis NTCI24
1300 San Pedro Ave

San Antonio, TX 78212-4299
(210) 733-2905
Fax: (210) 733-2907
Email: fsolis@accd.edu
www.accd.edu/sac/mortuary/home.htm

**Simmons Institute of Funeral
Service Inc**
Maurice C. Wightman,
President/CEO
1828 S Ave
Syracuse, NY 13207
(315) 475-5142
Fax: (315) 475-3817
Email: mcwightman20@aol.com
www.simmonsinstitute.com

**Southern Illinois University
Mortuary Science Funeral
Service Program**
Cydney Griffith, Program Director
ASA-Mail Code 6615
Carbondale, IL 62901-6615
(618) 453-7214
Fax: (618) 453-7020
Email: cgriffit@siu.edu

**St. Louis Community College
at Forest Park,
Dept. of Funeral Service
Education**
Steven B. Koosmann, Director
5600 Oakland Ave
St Louis, MO 63110
(314) 644-9327
Fax: (314) 644-9752
Email: skoosmann@Stlcc.edu
www.stlcc.edu/fp/funerals

**St Olaf College
Dept. of Sociology**
Dr Michael Leming
1520 St Olaf Ave
Northfield, MN 55057
(507) 646-2222
Email: leming@stolaf.edu
www.stolaf.edu

**St. Petersburg College
Funeral Service Program**
Kevin L Davis, Director
PO Box 13489
St. Petersburg, FL 33733
(727) 341-3781
Fax: (727) 341-3770
Email: davisk@spcollege.edu
www.spcollege.edu/hec/funeral

**State University of New York
College of Technology at Canton**
Barry Walsch
Mortuary Science Program
Canton, NY 13617
(315) 386-7193
(315)386-7110
Fax: (315) 386-7959
Entail: walsch@canton.edu
www.canton.edu

**University of Arkansas
Community College at Hope**
Karen Davis, Director
Funeral Service Program
PO Box 140
Hope, AR 71702-0140
(870) 722-8206
Fax: (870) 777-5957
Email: kdavis@uacch.edu
www.uacch.edu

**University of Central Oklahoma
Dept. of Funeral Service
Education**
Kenneth Curl
100 N University Dr
Edmond, OK 73034-5209
(405)974-5192
Fax: (405) 974-3848
Email: kcurl@ucok.edu
www.ucok.edu/funeral

University of District of Columbia
Mortuary Science Dept.
Courtney Terry, Chair, MB4407
4200 Connecticut Ave NW
Washington, DC 20008
(202) 274-5858
Email: cteny@Udc.edu

University of Minnesota
Program of Mortuary Science
Michael LuBrant, Director,
MMC 740
420 Delaware S E
Minneapolis, MN 55455
(612) 624-6464
Fax: (612) 626-4163
Email: mortsci@urnn.edu
www.med.urnn.edu/mortsci

Vincennes University
Funeral Service Education
Program
John Alsobrooks, Chairman,
1002 N First St
Vincennes, IN 47591
(812) 888-5469
Fax: (812) 888-4550
Email: jalsobro@indian.vinu.edu
www.vinu.edu

Wayne State University
Dept. of Fundamental &
Applied Sciences
Peter D. Frade PhD, Chairperson,
Mortuary Science Program
5439Woodward Ave.
Detroit, MI 48202
(313) 577-2050
Fax: (313) 577-4456
Email: pfrade@Wayne.edu
www.cphs.wayne.edu\mortsci\index.htm

Worsham College of Mortuary
Science
Stephanie J. Kann, President,
495 Northgate Pkwy
Wheeling, IL 60090-2646
(847)808-8444
Fax: (847) 808-8493
Email: soulfillet@aol.com
www.worshamcollege.com

AFRICAN BURIAL GROUND MEMORIAL DESIGN

Alicia Young, writing for *Crisis* magazine: Nearly 15 years after its discovery, an 18th-century African cemetery in lower Manhattan will be memorialized in a stunning permanent structure.

The African Burial Ground Memorial was designed by Rodney Leon, a 36-year-old architect and New York City native. Leon submitted the winning design, beating out 61 others, in a competition organized by the United States General Services Administration (GSA) and the National Park Service. Leon, president and co-founder of AARRIS Architects, PC, was named the winner on April 29, 2005.

"Clearly, Rodney Leon's work will prove a fitting and lasting testament to the legacy of the African Americans who helped build New York City and this nation," said Maria Burks of the National Park Service in a statement.

The African Burial ground consists of the remains of more than 20,000 free and enslaved African Americans. Archaeological experts believe that the cemetery—estimated to have been about half the size of a football field—was used between 1710 and 1790.

It was discovered during excavations for a federal office building in 1991. The following year, after much public outcry calling for the land to be recognized as sacred, Congress earmarked $3 million and directed the GSA to develop a plan to protect the human remains. The National Park Service declared the site a historic landmark in 1993.

The African Burial Ground Memorial will be located near New York's City Hall and will consist of two major physical elements: the Ancestral Chamber and the Libation Court.

The Ancestral Chamber includes a "wall of memory" and the "Door of Return," which was named as the counterpoint to the "Door of No Return" that refers to the trans-atlantic slave port on Goree Island in Senegal.

Inscribed on the wall of the Libation court is the phrase, "For all those who are lost/For all those who are stolen/For all those who are left behind/For all those who are not forgotten." The court also features reflecting pools to signify purification, renewal and a conduit for return to the place of origin.

A Brooklyn resident, Leon is a graduate of the Pratt Institute's School of Architecture. The African Burial Ground is the first memorial designed by Leon, who hopes that in viewing the memorial, people will get an understanding of the importance of the site as well as the sacrifices and contributions of those buried there.

"We hope that people leave with something specific that they can pass on perpetually so that the African Burial Ground is no longer an anonymous place where anonymous people are interred," Leon says.

The African Burial Ground Project announced in June 2006, that the four-volume Archaeology Final Report, prepared by Howard University, is complete. The multi-authored chapters contain answers to the many questions asked through the years since the grounds were uncovered. Using excavation and laboratory records, the scientists have reconstructed the social and physical landscape of the graves and of the cemetery. The amazing story of the slaves that were buried there is a history lesson in itself.

Those Who Prepare The Ground

Corey Kilgannon writing for the *New York Times,* states that to become a gravedigger at Green-Wood Cemetery in Brooklyn, you have to pass the traditional test of digging a standard single grave – 3 by 8 feet, and 5 feet down – in less than four hours.

"Some guys will say right then and there, 'I quit, this isn't for me,'" said George Barreto, 54, the foreman of Green-Wood's gravediggers.

The key, he said during a visit on Friday, is to start slow and begin your dirt pile far from the hole, so there is room nearby to put the last shovelfuls when fatigue sets in and you're deep in your first grave.

"I don't need a ruler to measure the depth," he said, pointing to a short gravedigger on his crew. "I just take him by the collar and stick him down there. If I can't see him, that's five feet."

The other men on the crew laughed and piled into their truck, a big, green box truck with an open back that takes them from plot to plot. Inside, there are soil and shovels on the floor and the men sit police-wagon style as the truck lurches and bounces along the curving cemetery roads.

Once, Green-Wood had scores of gravediggers and 50 new graves a day. Space is running short, though, and cremations are on the rise, so there are only a handful a day at Green-Wood now, and most are dug by a single man operating the levers of a backhoe. Graves are hand-dug if they are on a slope or wedged between headstones or trees, or if the coffin is for a small child.

Families often buy a plot with a plan to add a second or third coffin months, years or decades later. Most of those graves are dug nine feet deep to accommodate three stacked coffins.

"See, this grave is full now," Frank Bernardini said Friday morning, standing over a grave he was about to fill in. "You could put cremated remains on top, or a baby's casket, but the health laws say you have to have something like three or four feet of dirt on top."

With firm, dry soil, a good gravedigger can turn out a neat, steep rectangular grave, said Mr. Bernardini, a backhoe operator on the gravedigging squad.

"You can dig a nine-footer in about 20 minutes if there are no cave-ins," Mr. Bernardini said. If the soil is rocky and loose or moist, he added, the sides keep caving in and have to be shored up.

Like most of the gravediggers at Green-Wood, Mr. Bernardini, 42, who has worked there for 20 years, started by mowing grass. Since then, he said, he has dug tens of thousands of final resting places.

"I've put away a lot of people," Mr. Bernardini said. "The saddest ones have definitely been the children. Digging a kid's grave, that's the worst. I've definitely shed tears. Also with the 9/11 victims we buried."

Green-Wood's diggers belong to Teamsters Local 966. The job pays around $45,000 with full benefits, and advancement is possible, in mausoleum and crematory work.

"It's not just digging and lifting," said Felix Hernandez, another gravedigger. "You have to be strong to handle the death and grief."

The gravediggers begin their day preparing grave sites for the flurry of burial ceremonies that usually come by late morning. The afternoon is mostly spent filling in graves after burials and digging new ones for the next morning.

They arrive at new plots, staked out by a superintendent, and lay down plywood sheets to put the dirt on. The backhoe pulls out big buckets of dirt and the gravedigger crew trims stray roots and otherwise makes the site neater. A support frame is set over the hole, to hold the coffin during the ceremony.

A Green-Wood foreman, James Loiacono, 33, pointed out the crematorium as he drove the gravediggers in the truck on Friday morning.

He stopped at an open grave and soon a hearse pulled up, leading a long line of cars. Four gravediggers opened the hearse's back door, slid out the coffin and walked it to the grave to place it on the platform over the hole. The mourners, in dark, formal clothing, gathered around the grave, and the gravediggers, in their soiled green uniforms, receded to watch and chat amid gravestones. Down the road, Mr. Bernardini idled his backhoe.

"Families don't like to see the machine," he said. "They know it's burying their loved one for good."

Afterward, the diggers lowered the coffin into the ground.

Film Digs for Buried History

Deneen L. Brown of the Washington Post writing from Priceville, Ontario states that some say only the dead in this town can speak the truth about how a virtually all-black settlement in Canada turned virtually all-white. But then some of the living won't let them.

For years, the history of this rural settlement in southern Ontario was wrapped in a spooky silence. Photographs disappeared. Gravesites were plowed over, and tombstones from the black cemetery were stolen, hidden in stone piles, used as home plates in baseball games and as steppingstones in a wet basement.

It was as if the town was trying to erase the existence of black pioneers who settled in the early 1800s and also hide the fact that some of the whites that came here later married some of the blacks. They wanted to hide the fact that many generations later, some white people still living in this town may not be white at all. Just a drop is what they used to say.

"There is a lot in history people don't know about", said Howard Sheffield, whose black ancestors lived in Priceville, about 100 miles northwest of Toronto. "The white people wanted to cover that history up because it relates back to them. They are black people that are passing for white. Some of those whites drove the rest of the blacks out".

Eventually the only trace that black people had ever been in Priceville, working the land and building homes and a school, was the cemetery. Then in the 1930s, a white farmer named Billy Reid bought the land, plowed over the cemetery and planted tomatoes.

That is what they say became of the history of black people in this part of Ontario. It was plowed over, buried and hushed up. But some of it survived, as when adults would whisper secrets, unaware that children were listening.

Now, black Canadians-who make up about 1 percent of the country's 31 million people are trying to put the broken tombstone back together, pick up the pieces of their ancestry and fill in the spaces that were left in the history books. Books, plays and documentaries about the black experience in Canada have recently been released as a new generation of African Canadians comes of age and attempts to tell a history it was not taught in school.

"It was a shameful spot in the history of the community", said Jennifer Holness, director of *Speakers for the Dead*, a film distributed by Canada's National Film Board that traces the search for tombstones in a divided town. "Shameful they eradicated the gravestones, which indicates how blacks were treated, that blacks were forced off the land and white settlers took their land. There were some intermarriages they thought of as shameful.

James Walker, author of *History of Blacks In Canada, A Study Guide for Teachers and Students*, said the first black person to have lived in Canada was a young black boy who came to the country as a slave in 1628 and was sold in Quebec.

From the 1600s to early 1800s, "there was never a time when blacks were not held as slaves in Canada. Slavery is thus a very real part of our history, yet the fact that slavery ever existed here has been one of our best-kept secrets".

White Loyalist escaping the American Revolution brought many blacks as slaves to Canada. Freed blacks came as Loyalist themselves, and many of them fought with the British in the War of 1812.

Holness and filmmaker David Sutherland have pursued the story of Priceville because, they said, they wanted to tell the story of blacks in Canada who were not recent immigrants but who arrived here more than seven generations ago.

"Ultimately, what we wanted to do is expose these ridiculous ideas about race", Holness said. "We wanted to say, "You are so ridiculous that you are going to discriminate against me because of the color of my skin and you know what? You might be related to me".

Sutherland said that in Priceville the filmmaker often ran into people who were reluctant to talk. "The underlying thing up there is you are who your grandparents are", Sutherland said. "We found some people who didn't want to stir up trouble".

"I thought, trouble?" What does that mean? The idea of black ancestry, is that supposed to be trouble, "As a black person I don't see how that is trouble, but if more names were discovered, that might unsettle some people."

OFFICER FUNERAL HOMES

OFFICER FUNERAL HOMES are family-owned and operated with locations in East St. Louis, Illinois and St. Louis, Missouri. We proudly celebrate over 80 years of service to the community, spanning three generations of licensed funeral directors and embalmers. Through the years, the women and men of our family have shared equally in the responsibilities of operating a successful, community-centered business and in preparing the next generation with the commitment to continue the family tradition.

Officer Funeral Home was founded in 1918 by visionaries, Annette Harris Officer and William E. Officer, Jr. Their son, the late Marion E. Officer, Sr. and his wife, Myrtle B. Officer, succeeded his parents as President and Vice-President of the firm in 1954. Their children, M. Bernadette Officer and Carl E. Officer are active members of the firm and officers in the corporations. Myrtle B. Officer became CEO of the corporation in 1989.

Officer Funeral Home, P.C., located in East St. Louis, Illinois was one of the first establishments in southern Illinois. It was designed and built as a funeral home in 1929. This facility was remodeled several times through the years to keep pace with our commitment to excellence. Fire severely damaged the building in December of 1986. It was rebuilt on the original site in 1988.

The second location, Officer Funeral Home, Inc., was acquired in 1984 with the purchase of the former Ellis Funeral Home in St. Louis, Missouri. This expansion affords us the opportunity to serve a greater segment of the metropolitan community.

The late Marion E. Officer, Sr. and his wife, Myrtle B. Officer, succeeded his parents as President and Vice-President of the firm in 1954. A dynamic business duo, they elevated funeral service to a higher standard.

Their children, M. Bernadette Officer, Carl E. Officer and Marion B. Officer, Jr., became active members of the firm and officers in the corporations. Myrtle B. Officer became CEO of the corporation in 1989 after the death of her husband.

Mrs. Myrtle B. Officer continued the family tradtion over the next fifteen years introducing to her clientele, industry innovations such as memorial video tributes in 1989 and the launching of our Web site with online memorials in 1999. She was the first in her geographic region to offer custom casket interiors and custom register books. Mrs. O., as she was affectionately called, entered into eternal rest, April 23, 2004.

Mrs. Officer's daughter, M. Bernadette Officer became CEO and President and her son, Carl B. Officer was named Vice-President in 2004. Representing the third generation, this sister and brother team are devoted to honoring the work of their grandparents and parents by keeping the family tradition of providing the very best funeral service.

In October 2004, we proudly added a third location, Officer Funeral Home - St. Clair Chapel in Fairview Heights, Illinois. We continue to expand to better serve our growing clientele.

Through the years, we have supported the community by; opening our doors as a meeting place for numerous organizations; providing sponsorship of athletic, educational, civic, and religous programs; and providing a place of worship for area churches when their buildings were destroyed by fire or were otherwise displaced.

Work Staff

M. Bernadette Officer, CEO and President of the Officer Funeral Homes, is a funeral director and embalmer licensed in Illinois and Missouri. She overseas the day-to-day operations of the corporations.

Bernadette is a graduate of Fisk University in Nashville, TN with a B.A. in Psychology. She also earned a M.A. in Education from George Washington University in Washington, D.C., and a degree in Mortuary Science from the Worsham College of Mortuary Science in Wheeling, Illinois.

Bernadette holds membership in the St. Clair County Funeral Directors Association, the Missouri Funeral Directors Association, the International Order of the Golden Rule (past board member), and the International Cemetery and Funeral Association. Her civic and social involvement includes: Diamond Life membership in Delta Sigma Theta Sorority, Inc., Life membership in the NAACP, The Links, Inc., the Smart Set and the Sunday Jams. As a devoted member of the St. Luke A.M.E Church, her spiritual goal is to deepen her relationship with God. Professionally, she is dedicated to continuing to provide excellence in funeral service.

Carl E. Officer is Vice President of the Officer Funeral Homes. He was the first African American cadet to graduate from the Mormion Military Academy in Aurora, Illinois. He earned a B.S. in Political Science at the former Western College, now Miami University in Oxford, Ohio. Carl is also a graduate of the John F. Kennedy School of Government at Harvard University, Cambridge, Massachusetts. He received a degree in Mortuary Science from Southern Illinois University in Carbondale, Illinois and is a licensed funeral director and embalmer in Illinois and Missouri.

In 1979, Carl became the youngest mayor in the country when he won the office in his hometown of East St. Louis, Illinois. He served as mayor until 1991. After a twelve year hiatus, Carl was re-elected as mayor and returned to office in May 2003. Mr. Officer was ordained as an elder in the A.M.E. Church in 2001.

He holds membership in the Illinois Funeral Directors Association, St. Clair County Funeral Directors Association, National Funeral Directors Association, International Order of the Golden Rule, Kappa Alpha Psi Fraternity, and is a 33rd degree Mason. Carl received a commission as Second Lieutenant in the Illinois National Guard. He is the father of one daughter. Carl is a proud "Keeper of the Family Tradition," and along with his sister, forms a dedicated team representing the third generation in funeral service.

National Negro Funeral

Directors 1951,

Cincinnati, Ohio

Courtesy of McFall Brothers Funeral Directors.

Courtesy of McFall Brothers Funeral Directors.

National Negro Funeral

Directors 1947,

Cleveland, Ohio

BIBLIOGRAPHY

Abrahams, Roger D., ed. *Afro-American Folklore: Stories from Black Traditions in the New World*. New York: Parthenon Books, 1985.

The African American Presence in New York State: Four Regional History Surveys. Albany: New York African American Institute, State Univ. of New York, 1989.

American Cemetery. "Costco's Chicago and Casket Kiosk Conjures Controversy", October 2004.

American Cemetery. "Eighty Million Settlement Reached in Tri-State Civil Suit", October 2004.

American Cemetery. FCS Worldwide Publishers, April 2005.

American Cemetery. "Going the Distance with Katrina by Thomas Lynch - Essay first broadcast on National Public Radio - All Things Considered. November 2005.

American Cemetery. "Katrina Survivor Cemeteries" by Jen Kiernan, November 2005.

American Cemetery. "Oakland Cemetery - A Window in Georgia's History" by Alexander Kathryn Mosea, September 2005.

American Cemetery. "Restoration", David A. Yiersley (& Kiernan), November 2005.

American Cemetery Management (January 1994).

American Genealogical Research Institute. *How to Trace Your Family Tree*. New York: Doubleday, 1973.

Angelou, Maya. *Maya Angelou: Poems*. New York: Bantam, 1986.

Association of African Museums. Lecture, Dallas, Texas, September 1991.

Atlanta Historical Bulletin 20, no. 2. (summer 1976).

Athens Banner Herald, "Georgia Cemeteries", March 8, 2004.

Austin, Liz. "For Area Man, Green Cemetery Plots Thicken", Associated Press, Houston, Texas, 2004.

Baldwin, Don. "Some Find Eternal Rest at Costco", Associated Press. 2004

Bancroft, Frederic. *Slave Trading in the Old South*. Maryland: J. A. Furst Co., 1931.

Basler, Barbara. "Green Graveyards, A National Way to Go", *AAARP Bulletin*, July-August 2004, New York.

Bates, Angela. "New Promise for Nicodemus." *National Parks* (July/August 1992).

Batson, Roberts. "Carnival 2003 New Orleans Style: Zulus Have Rich History, Traditions", Times Picayune, 2003, pp. 1, 15.

Beaman, Alden G. "Rhode Island Black Genealogy: Inscriptions from the Negro Section of the Common Burial Ground, Newport." *Rhode Island Genealogical Register* 8, no. 2 (October 1985).

Beaufort Gazette: 1991.

Bennett, Lerone, Jr. *Before the Mayflower.* Chicago: Johnson Publications, 1966.

Benoit, Tod. *Where Are They Buried? How Did They Die?* Leventhal Publishers, New York. 2003

Berry, Jason. "Good Grief, New Orleans Jazz Funerals", Louisiana Cultural Vistas. 2001- 2002.

Blockson, Charles L. *African American State Historical Markers (Philadelphia Guide).* Philadelphia: The Charles L. Blockson Afro-American Collection/William Penn Foundation, 1992.

The Boston Experience: A Manual for Historic Burying Grounds Preservation, 2nd Edition. Boston: Boston Parks & Recreation Department, 1989.

Botsch, Robert E., and others. *African Americans and the Palmetto State.* Columbia: South Carolina Department of Education, 1994.

Brown, Cynthia Stokes. *Ready from Within: Septima Clark & the Civil Rights Movement.* California: Wild Trees Press, 1986.

Brown, William Wells. *The Negro in the American Rebellion: His Heroism and His Fidelity.* New York: Citadel Press, n.d.

Buchanan, Bruce. "Taking Cremation to the Malls", Intenational Cemetery & Funeral Management, Fall 2004.

Bucy, Carole Standord and Carol Farrar Kaplan. The National City Cemetery, Nashville City Cemetery Association. Inc., Tennessee 2000.

Burn, Billie. *An Island Named Daufuskie.* Spartanburg, South Carolina: Reprint Company Publishers, 1991.

Burroughs, Tony. *Black Roots*, Simon & Schuster,lnc., (Fireside), New York, 2001.

Byers, Paula K., ed. *African American Genealogical Sourcebook.* Detroit: Gale Research, 1995.

Bynes, Frank. Interview, Savannah, Georgia, August 1991.

Cantor, George. *Historic Black Landmarks: A Travelers Guide.* Detroit: Visible Ink Press, 1991.

Carawan, Guy, and Candie Carawan. *Ain't You Got a Right to the Tree of Life?* New York: Simon & Schuster, 1966, 1989.

"Cemetery Management," *American Cemetery Association* 54, no. 2 (February 1994).

Cengel, Katya. *Boomers Go Overboard In Personalizing Death,* Courier Journal, Louisville, Kentucky, December 3, 2004.

"Changing Philosophies: Is the Municipal Cemetery to Be a Community Service or Business?: City of Norfolk Cemeteries." *American Cemetery* (December 1991).

Chorzempa, Rosemary. *My Family Tree Workbook: Genealogy for Beginners.* New York: Dover, 1982.

Cohen, Hennig. "Burial of the Drowned among the Gullah Negros." *Southern Folklore Quarterly* 22 (1958).

Consumer Reports. Funerals: Consumers' Last Rights. New York: Norton/*Consumer Reports,* 1977.

Cooley, Rossa B. *School Acres.* Westport, Connecticut: Negro Universities Press, 1930.

Cooper, Desiree. "Beneath the Floorboards of the House", Detroit Free Press, 2003.

Cremation Chronicles 1, no. 1 (1991).

Cunningham, Montrose. *Public Information Office.* Dallas: State Department of Highway and Public Transportation, 1994.

Curry, Major General Jerry P. *The Crisis* 92, no. 1 (January 1985): 28.

Daise, Ronald. *Reminiscences of Sea Island Heritage.* Orangeburg, South Carolina: Sandlapper Publishing, 1986.

"Dallas Project Restores Forgotten Freedmens Cemetery." *American Cemetery* (January 1991).

Deas-Moore, Vennie. "Treading on Sacred Grounds." *National Historic Trust and Preservation Society Information Series* 76 (1993).

"Death Care Business Is Big and Getting Bigger." *Morning Edition* (radio broadcast). National Public Radio, December 1, 1993.

DeCosta Herbert, and others. *History of the Brown Fellowship Society and the Human Brotherhood.* Charleston: Brown Fellowship Society, 1990.

Detroit Free Press: October 12, 1993.

Detroit News: July 29, 1990; July 1993; May 14, 1995.

Defort, Edward J. American Cemetery. " As the Water Level Falls, Katrina's Body Count Rises," October 2005.

Dewan, Sheila. "Jazz Serving as Counterpoint to New Orleans Coroners Task," New York Times, Monday, October 17, 2005.

Dickerman, G. S. "A Glimpse of Charleston History." *The Southern Workman* 36, no. 1 (January 1907).

Dickinson, Joy. *Haunted City,* (An Unauthorized Guide to the Magical, Magnificient New Orleans of Anne Rice) Kensington Publishing Corporation, New York Third Edition, 2004.

Donn, Jeff. Associated Press."Insurance Firms Pay in Bias Suits:", Detroit News, September 2004

Dunbar, Paul Laurence. *The Complete Poems of Paul Laurence Dunbar.* New York: Dodd Mead, 1952.

Ellsberry, Daniel. "The City of Savannah's Four Cemeteries: Cemetery Management." *American Cemetery Association* 51, no. 12 (December 1991).

Emanuel, James, and Theodore L. Gross. *Dark Symphony: Negro Literature in America*. New York: Macmillan, 1968.

Estell, Kenneth. *African America: Portrait of a People*. Detroit: Visible Ink Press, 1994.

Family Tree Maker: User's Tutorial and Reference Manual. Freemont, California: Banner Blue Software, Inc., 1993.

Federal Trade Commission. "Funerals: A Consumer Guide".

"Final Resting Places of Famous Blacks." *Ebony* (February 1979).

Fordham, Monroe, ed. *The African American Presence in New State History*. Albany: New York African American Institute, State Univ. of New York, 1989.

Frazier, Evelyn McD. *A Guide for Amateur Genealogists*. Jacksonville, Florida: Florentine Press, 1974.

Fuchs, Marek. "A Crab-Shaped Coffin", Funeral Museum, New York Times, Houston, Texas, January 24, 2004.

"Geographica." *National Geographic* (February 1993).

George, Carol V. R. *American Visions* 12 (1986).

Godolphin, Vincent. "The Henrietta Marie." *About ... Time* (August 1993).

Gray, Kathleen. "Vets Take in National Cemetery Site", Detroit Free Press, October 2004.

Gray, Kathleen. "Grief Persists for Veterans' Families,", Detroit Free Press, 2005.

Gray, Kathleen. "U.S. Tries Cemetery Builder,", Detroit Free Press, September 15 2005.

Gray, Stevens and Evan Perez. "A City that made an Art of Funerals", Wall Street Journal, Vol CCXLVL, No. 49, New York, September 2005.

Greene, Robert Ewell. *Swamp Angels: A Biographical Study of the 54th Massachusetts Regiment*. N.p.: 1990.

Greenwood, Tom. "Funeral Traffic: Menace or Not?, Detroit Free Press, September 29, 2004.

Guillot, Craig. "Cemeteries in New Orleans", Detroit Free Press, October 2004.

Guines, Kevin, and Beth Parkhurst. *African Americans in Newport, 1660-1960: A Report to the Rhode Island Black Heritage Society*. Providence, Rhode Island: Black Heritage Society, 1992.

Guthrie, Patricia. *Catching Sense: The Meaning of Plantation Membership among Blacks on St. Helena, S.C.* New York: Univ. of Rochester, 1977.

Hamilton, Virginia Van de Veer. *Alabama*. New York: Norton, 1977.

Hampton, Henry, and Steve Fayer. *Voices of Freedom*. New York: Bantam, 1990.

Hanson, Laura, *A History of the Knights of the Wise Men Lodge*. St. Helena, South Carolina: Sea Island Preservation Project of Penn Center, 1995.

Harrison, Henry. *Negro Voices*. New York: Poetry Publisher, 1938.

Hawkins, Joanne B. "You Always Go Home Again." *American Cemetery* (November 1994).

Herskovits, Melvin. *The Myth of the Negro Past.* Boston: Beacon Press, 1958.

Historic Oakland Committee, Inc. *Join Historic Oakland—Your Gateway to Oakland.* Atlanta, Georgia: Historic Oakland Committee, 1991.

Holloway, Joseph E., ed. *Africanisms in American Culture.* Bloomington and Indianapolis: Indiana Univ. Press, 1990.

Holt, Rackham. *George Washington Carver: An American Biography.* New York: Dudley Doran, 1943.

Hughes, Langston, and Arna Bontemps, eds. *The Book of Negro Folklore.* New York: Dodd Mead, 1959.

Illinois Generations: A Guide to African American Heritage. Chicago: *Chicago Sun Times*/Performance Media, 1993.

International Cemetery & Funeral Management, published by ICFM Assn, "Hurricane Katrina", October 2005

International Cemetery & Funeral Management. "The 100 Black Women of Funeral Service, Inc". published by the International Cemetery & Funeral Association, Sterling, Virginia, November 2005.

Island Packet: December 1994.

Jacobs, Claude F. "Benevolent Societies of New Orleans Blacks During the Late Nineteenth and Early Twentieth Centuries". Louisiana Historical Association. Wayne State University, 1985, pp. 21-33.

Jankowick, William, Ph.D., "Black Social Aid and Pleasure Clubs: Marching Associations in New Orleans", pp. 51-57.

Jet Magazine, "Lawsuit Settled in Georgia Crematory Fraud Case, March 4, 2004 and February 2005

Johnson, LuAnn. "Municipal Cemeteries: A Change in Perception." *American Cemetery* (December 1991).

Jones, James H. *Bad Blood.* New York: The Free Press, 1981.

Kelsoe, Joe. *Black Civil War Casualties.* Nashville, Tennessee: N.p., 1991.

Korotin, Gayle. "The People's Advocate." *Christic Institute, South* 12, no. 2, (March/April 1991).

Lapin, Harvey I. *The Cremationist of North America* 27, no. 4 (1991).

Law, Marsha. "*A Gift From His Fans,*" Detroit Free Press, May, 2003.

Law, W. W. Interviews, Savannah, Georgia, 1991.

Leff, Lisa. "California Cemetery Offers Green Burials", Detroit News, June 24, 2004.

Leland, Elizabeth. *The Vanishing Coast.* Winston-Salem: John F. Blair, 1992.

Litwack, Leon F. *North of Slavery: The Negro in the Free States, 1790-1860.* Chicago: Phoenix Books, 1961.

Loose, Cindy. "Bishops Empty Tomb", Washington Post, January 2, 1996.

Loving, Susan. *International Cemetery & Funeral Management,* "Food To Die For" and "History Lives in Cemetery", December 2004.

Martindale, Mike. "United States Cemetery Takes Shape", Detroit News, October 13, 2004.

Maynard, Joan, and Gwen Cottman. *Weeksville Then & Now.* Weeksville: Society for the Preservation of Weeksville & Bedford Stuyvesant History, 1983.

Mayer, Robert G. *Embalming — History, Theory and Practice,* Second Edition, Simon & Schuster, N.Y. 1990

Mayer, J. Sheridan. *Restoration Art,* Professional Training Schools, Inc. Publishers Dallas, Texas, 1980

Meriweather, Louise. *The Freedom Ship of Robert Smalls.* Englewood Cliffs, New Jersey: Prentice Hall, 1971.

Meyer, Richard E., ed. *Markers XII.* Worcester, Massachusetts: *Journal of the Association for Gravestone Studios,* 1995.

Mims, Bob. "Funeral Help is a Click Away", Salt Lake City Tribute, August 2004.

Montgomery, Jenny, "Writers, Gangsters, Investors in Repose," Associated Press, September 25, 2005

Morgan, Stephen L., and Robert M. Fells. "Washington Report." *American Cemetery Association* (August 1992).

Mosca. Alexandra K., "Oakland Cemetery", Atlanta, Georgia, American Cemetery, FCS Worldwide Publishers, Vol 77, No 9, September 2005.

Mosca. Alexandra K., *Grave Understandings*, New Horizon Press. Far Hills, New Jersey, 2003.

Moseley, Robert L., ed. *Greenwood Cemetery—100th Anniversary Celebration* (pamphlet). N.p: Greenwood Cemetery, 1988.

Murphy, Beatrice M., ed. *Negro Voices: An Anthology of Contemporary Verse.* Brooklyn, New York: Polygon Press, 1938.

Nash, Gary, and others. *The American People: Creating a Nation and a Society.* New York: Harper & Row, 1996.

"National Cemeteries Date to Battle of Bull Run." *American Cemetery* (August 1994).

National Funeral Directors & Morticians Association, History, Website, March 2005.

National Public Radio. "St. Louis Light Rail System Displaces Black Cemetery," Weekend Edition, June, 1993.

Newport Daily News: August 19, 1994.

New York African Burial Ground Project, Update Newsletter, Spring-Summer 2003, Vol 3, Issue 7.

New York Times, *"A Death That Wasn't."*. Ingleside, North Carolina, February 13, 2005.

New York Times: October 29, 1984; August 13, 1990; July 28, 1991; September 3, 1991; October 10, 1991; December 1991; May 23, 1993; November 11, 1993; February 10, 1994; April 2, 1995.

New York Times - National, *"In New Orleans, Fewer Visitors."*, by Bruce Weber. November 1, 2005.

Nichols, Elaine, ed. *The Last Miles of the Way, 1890 to Present: African American Homegoing Tradition.* Charleston: South Carolina State Museum, 1989.

Nickerson, Colin. "Escaped Slaves Graves Sit Unmarked in Canada", The Boston Globe, February 1977.

Nordmann, Chris. "Basic Genealogical Research Methods and Their Application to African Americans." *African American Genealogical Sourcebook.* Detroit: Gale Research, 1995.

North Buxton's 64th Annual Homecoming & Labour Day Celebration. Brochure printed by North Buxton Centennial Community Club, September 3, 1988.

———— "Nowhere to Lay Down My Weary Head." *National Geographic* (December 1987).

Oppenheimer-Dean, Andrea. Article in *Historic Preservation* (January/February 1995): 29.

Pearson, Elizabeth Ware, ed. *Letters from Port Royal, 1862-1868,* New York: Arno Press, 1969.

Perry, Charlotte Bronte. *The Long Road.* Windsor, Ontario: Summer Printing, 1967.

Phillips, Ulrich Bonnell. *American Negro Slavery.* Baton Rouge: Louisiana State Univ. Press, 1918.

Pine, Vanderlyn R. *Caretaker of the Dead-The American Funeral Director*, Irvington Publishers. Inc., New York, 1975.

Plain Dealer: October 9, 1993.

Powdermaker, Hortense. *After Freedom.* New York: N.p., 1939.

Pransky, Judith. "Looking at History along the Main Line." *Main Line Times* (November 26, 1992).

Preserving Black Heritage for Future Generations. New Orleans: Mount Olive Cemetery, n.d.

Putnam, John J. Article in *National Geographic* 164, no. 6 (December 1983).

Quarles, Benjamin. *The Negro in the Making of America.* New York, Macmillan, 1964.

Redd, Rev. A. C. List of Africanisms in African-American funerary practices.

Rehfeld, Barry. "After the Cremation, A Universe of Choices." *New York Times,* February 20, 2005.

Reid, David, ed. *Sex, Death and God in L.A.* New York: Parthenon, 1992.

Rensberger, Boyce. "Remains Classified as African Americans", Washington Post. Roach, Mary. *Stiff,* W.W. Norton & Co.. New York. 2003.

Riverside Cemetery Inscriptions, 1830-1975. Jackson: Mid-west Tennessee Genealogical Society, 1975.

Robbins, Arlie C. *Legacy to Buxton.* Ontario: Ideal Printing, 1983.

Roediger, David R. "And Die in Dixie: Funerals, Death and Heaven in the Slave Community, 1700-1865." *Massachusetts Review* 22 (1981): 163-83.

Rose, Willie Lee. *Rehearsal for Reconstruction: The Port Royal Experiment.* Oxford: Oxford Univ. Press, 1964.

Rosengarten, Theodore. *Tombee: Portrait of a Cotton Planter.* New York: Quill/Morrow, 1986.

Rowson, Denise, and others. *Reclaiming Yesterday: The Geer Cemetery Project.* Durham, North Carolina: Durham Service Corps., 1992.

Sance, Melvin M., Jr., and others. *The Texians and the Texans.* San Antonio: Univ. of Texas Institute, Institute of Texan Cultures at San Antonio, 1975.

Savannah Morning News: December 31, 1992.

Scarups, Harriet Jackson. "Learning from Ancestor Bones." *American Visions* (February/March 1994).

Seidmann, Ryan M. and Ericka Seidmann. "Where Art and Death Blur,". Holt Cemetery, New Orleans, Louisiana.

Sheumaker, Helen. "The Gravemakers of Nicodemus Kansas as a Test of Black Town Isolation." Master's thesis, Univ. of Kansas, 1988.

Shugar's Purple Directory. National Listing of African American Funeral Homes, 2002-2003, 5th edition, Detroit, Michigan.

Simmons, Zena. "Detroit's Flamboyant Prophet Jones", www.detnews.com/history/prophet/prophet.htm.

Smith, Janet. "Rocking the Boat." *Hilton Head Island Monthly* (February 1991).

Strangstad, Lynette. "Preservation of Historic Burial Grounds." *National Historic Trust and Preservation Society Information Series* 76 (1993).

Summerville, James. *Educating Black Doctors: A History of Meharry Medical College.* Univ. of Alabama Press, 1983.

Sun Sentinel (Fort Lauderdale): December 20, 1992; December 30, 1992.

Taubman, Lara. "Chasing Ghosts Through the Future and Into the Past", The American Cemetery, Vol. 68, November 1996.

Tavining, Mary A., and Keith E. Baird, eds. *Sea Island Roots: African Presence in the Carolinas and Georgia.* N.p.: African World Press, 1991.

Tennessean (Nashville): December 16, 1990: February 9, 1992.

The Redbook. National Directory of Morticians Publishers, 67 Edition, Chagrin Falls, Ohio, 44022.

The State (Columbia, South Carolina): May 22, 1992.

Thompson, Sharyn. *Florida's Historic Cemeteries.* Tallahassee: Historic Tallahassee Preservation Board, 1989.

To Walk the Whole Journey: African American Cultural Resource in South Carolina. South Carolina Department of Parks, Recreation and Tourism/South Carolina State Museum, 1991.

Turner, Ken, Essex County & Historical Cemeteries Preservation Society, Harrow Cemetery Article, 2004.

Ulack, John Michael. *The Afro-American Tradition in Decorative Arts.* Cleveland: Cleveland Museum of Art, 1978.

Venator, Rolayne, and Paul B. Williams. *South Atlanta—A Short Developmental History.* N.p.: N.d.

Walker, Alice. *In Search of Your Mother's Gardens.* New York: Harcourt, 1984.

Walker, Harry J. "Negro Benevolent Societies in New Orleans: A Study of Their Structure, Function and Membership", Fisk University, 1936, p. 22.

Wallis, Charles L., ed. *Words of Life.* New York: Harper & Row, 1966.

Washington, Cheryl. "Grave Situations", Mobil, Alabama Report. February 28, 1998.

Washington Post: July 27, 1991; April 29, 1993; May 17, 1993; March 1994; April 30, 1995; May 1995.

Wells, Ida B. *Crusade for Justice,* edited by Alfreda M. Duster. Chicago: Univ. of Chicago Press, 1970.

White, John. "Veiled Testimony: Negro Spirituals and the Slave Experience." *Journal of American Studies* 17 (1983).

————"Whatever Happened to the Slave Family in the Old South?" *Journal of American Studies* 17 (1983).

Whyte, William H. "The 21st-Century Cemetery." *Cemetery Management* (May 1994).

Williams, Karl. United Memorial Gardens History, 2004.

Williams, Melissa Johnson, and John L. Konefis. "Environmental Concerns of Older Burial Sites." *American Cemetery* (February 1992).

Wilson, G. A. "The Religion of the American Negro Slave: The Attitude toward Life and Death." *Journal of Negro History* 8 (1923): 41-71.

Wilson, Jane Bromley. *The Very First Baltimorians,* White Mane Publishing Co., Inc.

Wilson, Samuel G., and Leonard V. Huber. *The St. Louis Cemeteries of New Orleans.* New Orleans: St. Louis Cathedral, 1993.

Wright, Roberta Hughes and Wilbur B. Hughes, III, *Lay Down Body, Living History In African American Cemeteries,* First edition, Visible Ink Press, Inc. Detroit, Michigan, 1996.

Wright, Roberta Hughes *Detroit Memorial Park Cemetery: The Evolution of an African American Corporation.* Southfield, Michigan: Charro Book Co., 1993 and 2001.

Wright, Roberta Hughes. *Penn Center, St. Helena Island and the Proclamation of Emancipation,* Charro Books, 1995.

Wright, Roberta Hughes. *An Island's Treasure, Penn Center of the Sea Islands,* 1997

Wright, John A. *St. Louis—Black Heritage Trail*. N.p.: Ferguson-Florisant School District, 1990.

Wynn, Linda T. "The Boyhood Home of Alex Haley." *Courier* 24, no. 2 (February 1986).

Yang, Jun. "Prisoners Would Build Caskets," Capital News Service, Lansing, Michigan, *Michigan Citizen*, February 27-March 5, 2005.

Young, Gregory. *The High Cost of Dying*, Prometheus Books. Buffalo, New York. 1994.

INDEX

A

A. A. Rayner & Sons   501
Adams Street Baptist Church
        Cemetery 135
African Canadian Cemeteries
        264
African American Cemeteries of
        Petersburg 237
Africanisms   21
Amelia White Cemetery   93-95
American Cemetery Magazine
        xxixxii
Andrews, William 224-225
Angeles Abbey Memorial Park
        163, 241-242
Angelou, Maya   346
Angelus Funeral Home   508
Angelus Rosedale Cemetery
        243
Appendix   566, 568, 570,
        572, 574, 576, 578, 580, 582,
        584, 586, 588, 590, 592, 594,
        596, 598
Arbutus Memorial Park   257-259
Arkansas Cemeteries   249
Armstrong, Louis 285
Ashe, Arthur   286-287
Atlanta, Georgia 163-165, 210, 228
Attucks, Crispus 375-376
Augusta, Georgia 170

B

Baby "Snookems" 63
Badger, Dr. Roderick D.   168
Ballard, Florence 288

Baltimore, Maryland   257-258,
        260
Bass, DDS, C. Robert   224-225
Bass, Robert Bell 224-225
Beaufort 73, 76, 81, 93, 107-113,
        115, 118-120, 122-123, 130,
        134
Beaufort Gazette 115, 119
Beaufort National Cemetery
        108, 110-111, 113
Bellefontaine Cemetery   211
Bennett, Julius xxvii
Bethel A.M.E. Church Cemetery
        173
Bethlehem Cemetery   191, 193
Bias Suits   463
Big Sixteen   37-38
Birmingham, Alabama   199
Black funeral homes in Indianapolis
        491
Black Miners Cemetery   45-46
Blake, Lee   xxvi
Blakey, Dr. Michael L.   xv, 9
Blockson, Charles L.   91
Bloody Point Cemetery   79
Boatright Funeral Home   493
Boissiere-Labat funeral home
        530
Booker T. Washington Memorial
        Park   226
Boyd, Dr. Robert Fulton   185-186,
        188
Boyd, Reverend R. H.   188
Braddock Point Cemetery 95-97
Brick Baptist Church Cemetery
        128, 130-131

Brotherly Cemetery   143
Brown Fellowship Society Cemetery
    142-143
Brown, Cora   228
Bruce, Blanche K. 245
Burgess, Albert   228
Burgess, Amos   228
Burial Customs   421, 423, 425,
    427, 429, 431, 433, 435, 437,
    439, 441, 443, 445, 447
Burial Societies   394-400, 402,
    404, 406, 408, 410-412, 414-
    418, 420
Burn, Billie   76, 89
Burr Oak Cemetery   216-218
Burroughs, Tony 345
Byars, Juan   92, 95-96, 101
Bynes, Major Frank H. 150, 155, 506
Bynes, Mrs. Frenchye   507
Bynes, Raleigh D. 507
Bynes-Royall Funeral Home, Inc.
    505

C

Cairo Cemetery   172
Calloway, Cab   289
Camp Welfare Cemetery   74, 147,
    149
Campbell, Emory 122, 129
Canfield Cemetery   193
Carver, George Washington
    199, 201
Caskets 557, 559, 561-563
Cedar Grove   170-171, 235
Celebrity burials 285, 287, 289,
    291, 293, 295, 297, 299, 301,
    303, 305, 307, 309, 311
Cemeteries Endangered   281
Cemetery Preservation   374,
    376, 378, 380, 382, 384, 386,
    388, 391-392
Cemetery Records 314, 321, 345,
    348-349, 351-352, 372
Census Records   315, 319, 321,
    324, 326-327, 335, 347, 354,
    360, 363-364
Charleston   73, 109-112, 121,
    125, 137, 140-143, 149, 154
Charleston, South Carolina
    73, 112, 121, 140, 149, 154

Charting and Record Keeping
    314
Chase, Reverend Supply   228
Chemical Pollution   426
Cherokee Hill Cemetery, GA
    156
Chicago, Illinois 212, 216
Chicora xxvi, 159, 391-392
Church Records   318, 321, 328-
    330, 338, 352, 363
Churchman Funeral Home 499
Churchman, Edith   500
Churchman, James E.   499-500
Citizen's Cemetery   118
Clark, Septima   143
Clarke, Lewis   18
Clubs of New Orleans, Louisiana
    417
Cochran, Johnnie   289
Coffin Point Cemetery   136, 139
Cole, Karla   475-476
Cole, Nat King   292
College Park Cemetery   255
Columbia   73-74, 144-147
Combs, Mary   168
Common Burial Ground   193, 234
Cook, Lomax B.   228
Cooper River Cemetery   80-83,
    85
Copeland, John   18, 20
Corner (Major) Cemetery 134
Court Records   330-333, 336,
    355, 359, 362
Cox, Benjamin F. 188
Craig Funeral Home   492
Cream of Wheat Man   65-68
Creating a Family Tree   366
Creel, Margaret Washington
    25
Cremation   422-423, 426,
    428-430, 439-440, 446, 448,
    450-460, 462, 467-468
Cremation to The Mall   456
Cromwell, Elizabeth   278-279
Crown Hill Cemetery And Funeral
    Home   496
Cuffy Cemetery 134-135
Cypress Hills Cemetery   13

D

Dade, Malcolm   xxvi

Daufuskie Island 73, 75, 79-81, 87, 95-96, 102
Deas-Moore, Vennie 74
Death Care Corporations 438
Death That Wasn't 69
DeBaptiste, George 228
DeFrance, Marie 19
DesVerney, Anthony K. 153-154
Detroit Memorial Park Association 203, 219-220, 225
Detroit Memorial Park Cemetery 219, 529
Detroit Memorial Park Directors 222
Detroit Memorial Park West 219, 222
Detroit, Michigan 219
DeVeaux, John H. 153-154
Dines, George xxvi
Dixie 39-40
Dixon Cemetery 251-252
Dobbins, Lee Howard 19
Dunbar, George 224-225
Durham 163, 179-181

E

Early One Morning 31
East Savannah 157
Eden Cemetery 231-232
Elliott Cemetery 105-106
Elmwood Cemetery 227-228, 230, 235
Embalming Dispute 430
Escaped Slaves' Graves 282
Eternal Rest at Cosco 458
Eugenia Cemetery 151-152
Evergreen Cemetery 236, 242
Evergreen Cemetery, GA 155
Evergreen Memorial Park Cemetery 198
Evers, Medgar 293

F

Faith Memorial Baptist Church Cemetery 134
Family Record 369, 372
Federal trade commission rules 554, 556, 558, 560, 562, 564
Female Union Band Cemetery 244, 247

Ferguson, Dr. Joseph 228
Ferguson, Howard Chaka 9
Ferguson, William 228
54th Massachusetts Regiment 112
55th Massachusetts Regiment 111
Finch, William 168
Fish Haul Plantation 92-93
Fitzgerald, Ella 293
Fleatown Cemetery 174
Ford, Newton Jackson 485-486
Fort Lauderdale, Florida 195
Fort Sherman 92-93
Fort Walker 93
Forten, Charlotte 122, 127, 129
Forth, Elizabeth Denison 228
Fred Hart Williams Genealogical Society 225
Free Frank McWorter Burial Site 218
Freedman's Village 42-44
Friendly Union Society 143
Fripp Cemetery 86-87
Fritz Funeral Home 475, 488-490
Fritz, Christina J. 489
Fritz, James B. 488-490
Fugitive Slave Cemetery 270-271, 282
Funeral airfares 466
Funeral Costs 556, 559
Funeral Help 460
Funeral Traffic 465

G

Gaines, Bishop Wesley J. 168
Gaye, Marvin 294-295
Geer Cemetery 163, 179-181
Genealogy for the Beginner 313, 315, 317, 319, 321, 323, 325, 327, 329, 331, 333, 335, 337, 339, 341, 343, 345, 347, 349, 351, 353, 355, 357, 359, 361, 363, 365, 367, 369, 371, 373
Ghosts and Jazz 60
Gideonites 136
GLOSSARY OF TERMS 563
Gospel Pilgrim Cemetery 177-178
Gracelawn Cemetery 219, 222

Grant, Doris   92-95, 99
Grave Marker Inventory   376,
    379, 382
Graves, Antoine   168
Great Lakes National cemetery
    443-445
Green Graveyards 55, 59
Green, Shields   19-20
Greenwood (Co-Haven) Cemetery
    194
Greenwood Cemetery   184-189,
    194-195
Greer, Prince   434-435
Grundy Memorial Chapel 495
Gullah Negroes   137
Guthrie, Dr. Patricia   122

H

Haig's Point Cemetery   87
Haley, Alex   190-193, 295
Harris, Georgia   168
Harrow Cemetery 274
Hattiesburg, Mississippi   204
Haughton, Aaliyah   297
Hayes-Williams, Joyce   47
Hector, Doretha F.   474
Hill, III, John L.   509
Hilton Head Island   73, 76,
    80, 90-95, 98, 102, 106, 110,
    126, 140
Historic St. John's Anglican
    Cemetery   271, 282
Holiday, Billie   297
Holmes, Lula   124
Holmes, Dr. Thomas   431, 435
Holt Cemetery   523-524, 526-527,
    529, 546, 549
Houston, Texas   255
Hudson-Mohawk River Cemeteries
    240
Hughes, III, Wilbur Brandon
    i, xxx
Humane Brotherhood   399,
    401-402
Hurricane Katrina - New Orleans
    537
Husband, Roger   475
Hutchins, Dougherty   169

I

Indianapolis, Indiana   212, 491

Insurance firms   463

J

Jackson Cemetery 272, 274
Jackson, Maynard 169
Jackson, Tennessee   190
James H. Cole Home for Funerals
    476
Jefferson Barracks 211
Jenkins Island Cemetery   103
Joe Pope Cemetery   105
Johnson, Dr. Charles Spurgeon
    189
Johnson, James Weldon   2, 23
Jonas Lobe Cemetery   175-176
Jones, Prophet   298-300
Joyner, Florence   301
Jumping the Broom   32-33

K

Kansas State   213, 215
Kellogg, Mary   20
Kemble, Frances Anne   26-27
Killens, Camille   xxvi, 172
King Sr., Reverend Martin Luther
    164, 167
King, Jr., Martin Luther   302, 307
Kinson, Sarah "Margu"   20

L

Ladies Union   411, 415-416
Lake Mayers   157
Lambert, William 229
Langford, Dawn   xxvi
Langston, John Mercer   18, 20,
    246
Laura Towne   128-130
Laurel Grove Cemetery   151-155
Laurel Grove South   157
Laveau, Marie   517, 520
Lavenia, Smith and Summers Home
    for Funerals 495
Lavenia's Home for Funerals
    495
Lawton Cemetery 106-107
Law, W.W.   153
Leary, Lewis Sheridan   20
Leon, Rodney   10, appendix
Lincoln Cemetery 202-203, 235

Lincoln Memorial Cemetery
155, 197
Lincoln Memorial Cemetery, GA
155
Looby, Z. Alexander   188
Los Angeles, California   241
Louis, Joe   303
Low Bottom   73, 139-141
Low Bottom Cemetery   139-141
Lynchburg   236, 239

M

Malcolm X   296, 311-312
Manigault-Hurley Funeral Home
481, 484
Manijan, Moses J.   xxvi
March Funeral Homes   510
March Family   510, 512
March, Julia Roberta   510
March, William C.   511-512
Martin Luther King Drive   123, 131
Maryfield Cemetery   89
Mays, Benjamin E.   166
McCoy, Elijah   224-225
McFall Funeral Home, George B.
475
Mercy Cemetery   118
Merion Memorial Park   232
Metropolitan Memorial Gardens
226
Military Records   339, 341, 345,
365
Miller Grove Cemetery   217-218
Missouri 176, 209-212, 218, 245
Mitchelville   92-93
Mobile, Alabama 202
Monroe, Andrew 153-154
Montgomery, Ransom   169
Morial, Ernest   522-523
Morris Cemetery   231
Morris, Frank   268
Morris-Hatter Cemetery   267-268
Mosca, Alexandra K.   xxxi
Moses Dickson Cemetery   210
Mount Auburn Cemetery   259-260,
262
Mount Moor Cemetery   12
Mount Olivet Cemetery   207-208,
214

Mount Pleasant Cemetery
Association 13
Mount Vernon Memorial Park
226-227
Mt. Gillin Cemetery   215-216
Mt. Olive A.M.E. Church Cemetery
173
Mt. Pisgah AME Church Cemetery
177
Mt. Zion A.M.E. Church and
Cemetery   174
Mt. Zion Cemetery   244, 247
Mullice, Alfred   507
Municipal Cemeteries   422,
440-441, 447
Munneryln Slave Cemetery
174
Museum of Hilton Head Island
92-93, 95

N

N. J. Ford & Sons Funeral Home
485
Napier, J. C.   189
Nashville   163, 183-189
Nashville City Cemetery   186
Nashville, Tennessee   163, 183
National Cemeteries   421-422,
441-444, 446-447
National Funeral Directors and
Morticians Association
471, 487
Naturalization Records   322,
357-359
New Cold Water Burying Ground
211
New Grace Hill Cemetery 200
New Guinea Cemetery   16-17
New Hope Christian Church
Cemetery   108, 116, 119-120
New Orleans   204, 206-209, 212
New Orleans, Louisiana   515, 530
New York, New York   240
Newport, Rhode Island   233-234
Nichols, Elaine   xxiii, 145
Nicodemus Cemetery   214
Nicodemus, Kansas   203, 213
North Buxton Cemetery   265-266
Nova Scotia, Canada Cemeteries
275

O

Oak Grove Cemetery, GA   156
Oak Hill Cemetery–Pontiac   263
Oakland Cemetery   167-168, 228
Odd Fellows Cemetery   254-255
Officer Funeral Home   601
Old Bethel United Methodist Church Cemetery   143
Old City Cemetery   186, 236, 239
Old Methodist Burying Ground   244
Old Quarters Cemetery   4-5
On-Line Cemeteries   51
102nd U.S. Colored Infantry   229
Ontario, Canada   264
Orange Grove Baptist Church Cemetery   131-132
Orindatus S. B. Wall   20
"oven" tombs   522
Owens, Jesse   303

P

Paradise A.M.E. Church Cemetery   177
Paradise Memorial Park   243
Parks, Rosa Louise   304
Passenger Ship Lists   356
Pelham, Benjamin and Robert   229
Penn Center   109, 122-124, 126, 128-129, 131, 134
People's Funeral Home   491
Percell, Sr., Danny L.   473
Pilgrim Cemetery 109, 116-117, 119-120
Pine View Cemetery   175-176
Pine, Vanderlyn R.   xxx
Pinefield Cemetery   98
Pineridge Cemetery–Hattiesburg   204
Plessy, Homer   516, 551
Port William, Kansas   215
Porter, James   153-154
Portsmouth, Virginia   234
Praise Houses   123-126
Preparing the Dead   423
Preservation Terminology   378
Prince, Bryan   267

Prison Built Caskets   468
Pryor, Richard   305-306
Public Cemetery   186, 199

Q

Quarles, Reverend Frank   169

R

Randolph Cemetery   74, 144-146
Randolph, Curtis 229
Rawls, Allen   224-225
Rawls, Winona   224
Records and Tombstone Inscriptions   349
Red House Cemetery   117, 119-120
Redd, Reverend A. C.   21
Reed, William B.   189
Restorative Art   435
Rhodes Funeral Home   534-535
Rhodes, III, Duplain W.   536
Richards, Fannie 229
Richards, John D. 229
Riverside Cemetery   190
Riverview Cemetery   205
Roach, Mary   xxxi
Roberta, Julia   510-511
Robinson, Jackie 307
Robinson, James 229
Robinson, Luther Bojangles   308
Rosedown Baptist Church Cemetery   206
Rucker, Henry A. 169
Rudolph, Wilma 309
Runaway Slave Notices   353

S

Samuels Cemetery   215
San Marco-Blanco Cemetery   256
Sandfly   157
Savannah   73, 76-78, 83, 87, 89, 102, 109-110, 121, 137, 149-157
Saxon Cemetery   251, 253
Scott Street Cemetery   205
Scott, John H.   20
Sea Islands   72-73, 75, 77, 79,

81, 83, 85, 87, 89-91, 93, 95,
97, 99, 101, 103, 105, 107,
109, 111, 113, 115, 117, 119,
121, 123, 125-127, 129, 131,
133, 135, 137, 139, 141, 143-
145, 147, 149, 151, 153, 155,
157, 159, 161
Sea Pines Plantation   92-93,
    95-96, 106
Seay, Sharon L.   473
Shabazz, Betty   311-312
Shady Grove Missionary Baptist
    Church Cemetery   205
Simmons Memorial Gardens
    91, 101-102
Simms, James M. 153
Sites, Superstitions and Stories
    1
Sixteen Gate Cemetery   108-109,
    114-115
Skrobarcek, James A.   64
Slater, Dr. Thomas H.   169
Slave Cemeteries in the Americas
    4
Small Town Stories   40
Smith, Barbara K. Hughes iii, xxx,
    99
Smith and Smith Funeral Home
    504
Smith, Larry M.   xxvi
Southview Cemetery   164-166,
    171
Spanish Wells Cemetery   101
Spieler, Gerhard   115, 119
Springfield A.M.E. Church
    Cemetery   172
Springlake Memorial Cemetery
    251, 253
St. Armand Station, Canada
    282
St. Charles Borromeo Church
    Cemetery   212
St. Francisville, Louisiana 206
St. Helena Island 73, 121-126, 128,
    130, 133, 136, 140
St. Joseph Baptist Church Cemetery
    133
St. Louis No.1   516, 521-522, 548
St. Louis, Missouri   209
St. Paul Church Cemetery 175
St. Paul Primitive Baptist Church

Cemetery   173
Starks, Elleanor C.   473
Stone, Charles   229
Stoney-Baynard Ruins   93
Straker, D. Augustus   229
Stranger's Cemetery   118
Stuart Mortuary 493, 497
Summers Funeral Chapel 494-495
Summerville Cemetery   170-171
Sutherland Park Cemetery 212
Swanson Funeral Home   475

T

Talbert, Ted   475
Talbot Cemetery 99-100
Tate Sr., James   169
Taubman, Lara   xviiixxi
Texas 191, 230, 255-258
The 100 Black Women of Funeral
    Service, Inc.473
The African Burial Ground
    Unearthed 5
The African Cemetery #2   195
The American Genealogical
    Research Institute   xxii
The Bishop's Empty Tomb 49
The Book of Negro Folklore
    22, 37
The Brown Fellowship Society
    396, 398-402
The Bury League 402-405, 407, 409
The Freedman's Cemetery 14, 16
The Friendly Union Cemetery
    143
The Henrietta Marie   3-4
The Negroes Burying Ground
    5-6
The North American Black
    Historical Museum and
    Cultural Centre   268
The Penn School of St. Helena
    126
The Smith-Jackson Funeral Home
    504
The Unusual   47
The Wrong Man in the Coffin
    36
Thompson, Augustus   169
Three Neglected Cemeteries
    118

Till, Emmett   217
Tombee: Portrait of a Cotton
     Planter   121
Township of Sandwich East
     Cemetery   265
Tri State Cemetery Fraud   462
Trinkley, Dr. Michael   xxvi,
     160, 391-393
Tsadik, Tibebu   225
Turner, Ken   274, 275, 588
Tuskegee Cemetery   201
Tuskegee Study   201

U

Union Cemetery 103-104, 143
United Memorial Gardens 226-227

V

Vaughn, Sarah   309
Vital Records   314, 322, 328,
     336, 339
Voices in the Graveyard   30
voodoo queen   517

W

Walker Memorial Park   171
Walls, Dr. Bryan 269, 270, 273
     589
Walls Historic Museum   269
Ware, Ivan   xxvi
Washington Park Cemetery
     212
Washington, D.C. 244, 247
Washington, D.C. Cemeteries
     244
Washington, Dinah   217
Waters, Muddy 310
Webb Tract Cemetery   90
Webb, William 229
Weeksville   12-13
Wellington-Oberlin   17-18,
     20
West Sr., Dr. Harold D.   189
Westlawn Cemetery   226
Westwood Cemetery   17-18
Whimsical Coffins   53
White, Frank L. 66
Whitfield, Cassandra   xxvi
Whitney Young Jr.   194

Williams & Bluitt Funeral Home
     494
Williams King, Alberta   164, 167
Willis Mortuary 491-492
Wilson Financial Group, Inc.
     xxvii
Wilson, Flip   310
Winnsboro   73-74, 147
Wood Grove   157
Wood, Reverend Joseph A. 169
Woodland and Evergreen
     Cemeteries 235
Woodlawn Cemetery   196,
     244-245, 247-249
Woods, Sergeant Brent   44
Woodville Cemetery, GA   156
Wright, Dr. Charles   94, 96,
     129
Wright, Lorenzo C.   229
Wright, Roberta V. Hughes i, xxx

Y

Young, Gregory W.   xxx

Z

Zion Cemetery   194, 244, 247
Zion Memorial Gardens   200
Zion White Bluff 157

OTHER BOOKS

1976	Reflections, a book of poems
1991	The Birth of the Montgomery Bus Boycott
1991	An Annotated Bibliography, Books of the South Carolina & Georgia Sea Islands
1992	A Tribute to Charlotte Forten, 1837-1914
1993	Detroit Memorial Park Cemetery-The Evolution of an African American Corporation
1995	Penn Center, Inc & The Emancipation Proclamation
1996	Lay Down Body, Living History in African American Cemeteries
1997	An Island's Treasure, St. Helena Island & Penn Center
1999	The Wright Man, Biography of Charles H. Wright, M.D.
2000	The Ring of Genealogy at the Charles H. Wright Museum of African American History
2001	Detroit Memorial Park Association (Revision)
2002	The Wiregrass Warrior, Professor Abner Jackson of Dothan, Alabama
2002	Reflections, An Autobiography
2003	This Beneath The Sky, a Novel (Unpublished)
2006	Rosa Parks, The Birth of the Montgomery Bus Boycott (Revised)
2007	The Death Care Industry, African American Cemeteries & Funeral Homes